THERAPEUTIC RECREATION

AN INTRODUCTION

SECOND EDITION

Edited by

DAVID R. AUSTIN

Indiana University, Bloomington

MICHAEL E. CRAWFORD

University of Missouri, Columbia

ALLYN AND BACON

Boston London Toronto Sydney Tokyo Singapore

This book is dedicated
to our students,
past and present.

Senior Series Editor: Suzy Spivey
Vice President and Publisher: Susan Badger
Editorial Assistant: Lisa Davidson
Executive Marketing Manager: Anne Harvey
Editorial-Production Administrator: Donna Simons
Editorial-Production Service: Shepherd, Inc.
Composition and Prepress Buyer: Linda Cox
Manufacturing Buyer: Aloka Rathnam
Cover Administrator: Suzanne Harbison

Library of Congress Cataloging-in-Publication Data

Austin, David R., 1941–
Therapeutic recreation : an introduction / David R. Austin, Michael E. Crawford. — 2nd ed.
p. cm.
Includes bibliographical references and index.
ISBN 0–13–110736–4
1. Recreation therapy. I. Crawford, Michael E. II. Title.
RM736.7.A96 1996
615.8'5153—dc20 95–50756
CIP

Printed in the United States of America

10 9 8 7 6 5 4 3 2 00 99 98 97 96

CONTENTS

SECTION TWO
SPECIAL AREAS OF PRACTICE

Preface

There has been a revolution in the literature of therapeutic recreation. The first revolution took place with the "first generation" of therapeutic recreation textbooks that were published in the 1970s. These initial works offered direction to an emerging profession and fed the hunger of students and practitioners for information on which to base therapeutic recreation practice. A second revolution is now under way. We continue to witness unprecedented numbers of additions to the therapeutic recreation literature. These publications give testimony to a growing depth and breadth in the body of knowledge in the field of therapeutic recreation.

Our goal in preparing the second edition was to respond to the latest trends and developments in therapeutic recreation practice and provide the most complete, accurate and up-to-date information available. In order to accomplish this goal, we once again called upon several leading therapeutic recreation authors to join us in the writing of *Therapeutic Recreation: An Introduction,* Second Edition. Each of these authors brings his or her expertise to the task of providing the most current information available in his or her particular area of specialization.

NEW TO THIS EDITION

All of the chapters have been thoroughly updated to reflect the most recent research and literature in therapeutic recreation practice. The following list highlights the most significant changes in this new edition.

- A new chapter on Acquired Immunodeficiency Syndrome (AIDS) provides essential information on the social and political significance of therapeutic recreation services.
- The Neuromuscular chapter has been significantly revised to reflect the tremendous growth in applied research over the last five years, including coverage of Parkinson's Disease.
- The Americans with Disabilities Act and its impact on therapeutic recreation practice is now covered.
- The concluding chapter on Trends and Issues has been thoroughly updated to include the latest statistics and information on the future direction of the field.

ORGANIZATION

Chapters in Section One of the book present the nature, purpose, history, and processes of therapeutic recreation. Section Two covers special areas of therapeutic recreation practice. Taken as a whole, these chapters illustrate the richness and diversity of therapeutic recreation. Each chapter is written by an expert on the topic of his or her chapter. To facilitate learning and ensure completeness in approach, all of the chapters in Section Two follow a common outline and use the four-phase therapeutic recreation process. Each chapter presents current practices and procedures in that particular area of therapeutic recreation followed by a brief case study that portrays the actual application of the TR process. This is followed by a section on the trends and issues in that particular area. The chapters in Section Three cover specialized areas of professional activity and trends and issues in therapeutic recreation.

All of the chapters begin with special objectives for the reader and end with a chapter summary, reading comprehension questions, learning activities, and a complete listing of references. Readers who are teaching college and university courses in therapeutic recreation should find the objectives, questions, and learning activities useful in course planning and in the evaluation of student progress. Students and practitioners should be able to use the objectives, reading comprehension questions, and learning activities to understand better the material presented.

A number of people have contributed in many different ways to this book. Our continued thanks to Joe Heider and Ted Bolen of Prentice Hall for their encouragement and assistance in conceptualizing and bringing to fruition the first edition. In a similar light we wish publicly to acknowledge and thank Suzy Spivey, senior editor for health, physical education, and recreation with Allyn and Bacon, and her most able editorial assistant, Lisa Davidson, for their work and dedication in bringing the second edition to press. In addition, our appreciation goes to reviewers M. Gary Thompson, Southwest Missouri State University, and Monica Lepore, West Chester University. Finally, to our co-authors and colleagues who have joined us by providing chapters in their areas of specialization, we must offer particular and heartfelt thanks. Their contributions make this second edition a truly unique work, one that we hope will advance the art and science of therapeutic recreation practice for years to come.

David R. Austin
Michael E. Crawford

CONTRIBUTORS

David R. Austin is professor of recreation in the Department of Recreation and Park Administration at Indiana University, Bloomington. Prior to gaining his master's degree at Indiana University, Austin was a recreation therapist with the Indiana Department of Mental Health. He has held faculty positions at the University of Illinois and the University of North Texas. His Ph.D. was completed at the University of Illinois. He is a Certified Therapeutic Recreation Specialist.

Orazi (Ori) Caroleo is Executive Assistant at Gay Men's Health Crisis (GMHC), New York City. He was Coordinator of Recreation, Assistant/Associate Director for Client Services and Director of Technical Assistance at GMHC. Caroleo serves as Co-Chairperson of the World Leisure and Recreation Association's AIDS/SIDA Task Force. He received his M.A. from New York University, where he is currently a doctoral candidate. He is a Certified Therapeutic Recreation Specialist.

Andrew Chasanoff is director of recreation at Children's Specialized Hospital in New Jersey. He was a therapist at the Rusk Institute of Rehabilitation Medicine and at Blythdale Children's Hospital. Chasanoff received his B.S. from the State University of New York College at Cortland and his M.A. from New York University.

Michael E. Crawford is associate professor and coordinator of the therapeutic recreation program at the University of Missouri, Columbia. Prior to becoming an academic, he worked as a practitioner in therapeutic recreation with a wide variety of clients, including individuals with mental retardation, drug and alcohol dependencies, and forensic mental health needs. He has an extensive background in safety and design of play environments for children with disabilities. His doctorate is from Indiana University.

John Dattilo is a professor in the Department of Recreation and Leisure Studies at the University of Georgia. He is a Certified Therapeutic Recreation Specialist who has experience in providing services to people with various disabilities and in documenting the efficacy of interventions through data-based research.

Jerry Dickason is professor of recreation and leisure studies at Montclair State University in Upper Montclair, New Jersey. He was a recreation therapist at Evansville State Hospital in Indiana, a recreation leader for the American Red Cross in Vietnam, the chief of activity services at Coney Island Hospital, and a research scientist at New York University, where he completed his Ph.D. and served on the faculty.

Maurice K. Fahnestock has worked for the past fifteen years with children and adults with disabilities and their families in community, park and recreation, school, community education, group home, and institutional settings. As a Certified Therapeutic Recreation Specialist, he is currently a doctoral student and graduate research assistant at the University of Minnesota.

Lodene Goodwin is a certified rehabilitation counselor. Her present position is with the South Carolina Department of Vocational Rehabilitation, where she has worked for over 20 years. Goodwin completed her B.S. at Presbyterian College. She holds her master's degree in counseling and guidance from Clemson University.

Arnold H. Grossman is a professor in the Program in Recreation and Leisure Studies, New York University School of Education. In addition to his faculty appointment, Grossman serves as Project Director of the NYU AIDS/SIDA Mental Hygiene Project and Co-Principal Investigator of the NYU HIV/AIDS Mental Health Training Center. He is also Founder and Chairperson of the World Leisure and Recreation Association's AIDS/SIDA Task Force. His M.S.W. and Ph.D. were completed at New York University.

Barbara A. Hawkins is an associate professor in the Department of Recreation and Park Administration at Indiana University. In addition to her faculty appointment, she serves as a reference faculty to the IU Institute for the Study of Developmental Disabilities. She specializes in lifespan development, developmental disabilities, and leisure behavior.

Mark R. James currently is working as administrator in the private sector. Formerly he was employed in the Department of Psychiatry at Elizabeth General Medical Center, Elizabeth, New Jersey. He completed his master's degree in therapeutic recreation at Indiana University. Previously, James was project coordinator for a state grant project providing therapy services to clients with seizure disorders.

Judy Sottile Kinney has worked in therapeutic recreation as a clinician for over ten years. Although she has had experience in many service settings, her main interest and level of experience lies in psychiatry, particularly with treatment of eating disorders. Sottile holds an M.S. degree from Southern Illinois University, Carbondale, and a Ph.D. from Temple University.

W. B. (Terry) Kinney is on the faculty of the Department of Recreation and Leisure Studies at Temple University in Philadelphia. Kinney has extensive experience in the field of psychiatry and mental health and has written widely in this area. He holds his master's from the University of Illinois and his Ph.D. from New York University.

Robin Kunstler is associate professor and coordinator of the Leisure Sciences program at Lehman College of the City University of New York. She has practitioner experience working with nursing home residents and with individuals who have psychiatric illnesses. Kunstler holds an M.S. degree from Northeastern University and an Re.D. from Indiana University. Her research interests include social problems, curriculum development, and leisure counseling.

Miriam Lahey is associate professor in Leisure Sciences and Chair of the Core Curriculum at Lehman College of the City University of New York. Based on her clinical experience in cognitive rehabilitation with elderly nursing home residents she has developed research projects in home care programs with diverse client groups. She earned her doctoral degree at Columbia University.

Gail Levine, CTRS, is professor and director of the Program in Sports, Fitness and Therapeutic Recreation at Kingsborough Community College. She has extensive experience as a clinician with developmentally disabled children, teens, and adults with psychiatric disorders (inpatient and day treatment). Levene holds her Ph.D. from New York University.

Gail McCall is associate professor in the Department of Recreation, Parks, and Tourism at the University of Florida. She has held the position of Chief Probation Officer for Morgan Superior Court in Indiana. She has served as the President, Vice-President, Secretary, Chairman of the Board of Directors, and Board member of the National Correctional Recreation Association.

Francis A. McGuire is the Centennial Professor in the Department of Parks, Recreation and Tourism Management at Clemson University and a Fellow in the Strom Thurmond Institute of Government and Public Affairs. He holds a doctorate in leisure studies from the University of Illinois and is a Certified Therapeutic Recreation Specialist.

Valerie L. McGhee is project manager of Personal Actions to Health in Wichita, Kansas. Ms. McGhee holds a master's degree in public administration from the University of Missouri at Kansas City. McGhee's research and scholarly interests lie in the field of gerontology.

Stuart J. Schleien is a professor and division head in Recreation, Park, and Leisure Studies, with a joint appointment in Special Education Programs, at the University of Minnesota. As a Certified Therapeutic Recreation Specialist, Schleien's research and scholarly interests involve the inclusion of persons with developmental disabilities in community leisure environments.

Michael L. Teague is professor in the Department of Sport, Health, Leisure, and Physical Studies at the University of Iowa. He holds a doctorate in health, physical education, and recreation from the University of Northern Colorado. Teague's research and scholarly interests lie principally in the field of gerontology.

Judith E. Voelkl, Ph.D., CTRS, is the associate director for Education/Evaluation in the Geriatric Research, Education and Clinical Center, Ann Arbor VA Medical Center and the Geriatrics Center, University of Michigan. Voelkl received her Ph.D. from Pennsylvania State University. Her research interests pertain to the leisure experiences of older adults residing in long-term care facilities.

Jane Young, CTRS, is a Ph.D. candidate at Clemson University in Parks, Recreation and Tourism Management, with an emphasis in Therapeutic Recreation. Her dissertation research topic is Lifestyle Change after Myocardial Infarction.

CHAPTER 1

INTRODUCTION AND OVERVIEW

DAVID R. AUSTIN

OBJECTIVES

- Conceptualize therapeutic recreation as a field.
- Understand the relationship of therapeutic recreation to a high level of wellness.
- Understand the relationship of therapeutic recreation to the stabilizing and actualizing tendencies.
- Reduce therapeutic recreation to a series of tenets.
- Identify kindred professions.
- Assess yourself in terms of competencies needed in therapeutic recreation.
- Know the plan for this book.

There are a number of health-related professions. Therapeutic recreation is one of these. Several health-related professions are listed, along with their areas of expertise, in Table 1.1. Each profession has a particular body of knowledge upon which to draw in providing services. It is this body of knowledge that makes the profession unique. In fact, experts (e.g., Schlein & Kommers, 1972; Wilensky, 1964) have long agreed that in order to claim the title of "profession," an occupational group must have a defined area of expertise. What is the area of expertise that therapeutic recreation (TR) claims? What makes TR unique? The editors of this book believe that therapeutic recreation involves the knowledge of leisure and recreation as these phenomena relate to achieving optimal health and the highest possible quality of life.

KNOWLEDGE OF LEISURE AND RECREATION AS A BASIS FOR PROFESSIONAL PRACTICE

Inevitably, textbook authors have emphasized leisure and recreation in attempting to define the still relatively new and emerging profession of therapeutic recreation. One of the earliest conceptualizations of therapeutic recreation (referred to as recreational therapy) contained a definition of recreation within it. Davis (1936) wrote:

> *Recreational therapy may be defined as any free, voluntary and expressive activity; motor, sensory or mental, vitalized by the expressive play spirit, sustained by deep-rooted pleasurable attitudes and evoked by wholesome emotional release (p. xi).*

More modern textbook authors have continued the tradition of including leisure and

TABLE 1.1 Health-Related Professions

Profession	Expertise
Nurse	Caring for persons
Occupational therapist	Purposeful activity
Physician	Illness, disease
Psychologist	Human behavior
Social worker	Support systems

recreation within their definitions of TR. Examples follow:

Therapeutic recreation is a process through which purposeful efforts are directed toward achieving or maximizing desired concomitant effects of a recreation experience (Frye & Peters, 1972, p. 44).

[Therapeutic recreation is] a process wherein recreation experiences are used to bring about a change in the behavior of those individuals with special needs or problems (O'Morrow & Reynolds, 1980, p. 123).

[Therapeutic recreation is] purposeful intervention designed to improve the client's quality of life through recreation and leisure (Iso-Ahola, 1980, p. 323).

[Therapeutic recreation] is the provision of purposeful intervention designed to help clients grow and to assist them to prevent or relieve problems through recreation and leisure (Austin, 1982, p. 60).

Therapeutic recreation refers to the specialized application of recreation for the specific purpose of intervening in and changing some physical, emotional, or social behavior to promote the growth and development of the individual. Therapeutic recreation may be viewed as a process of systematic use of recreation activities and experiences to achieve specific objectives (Carter, Van Andel, & Robb, 1985, pp. 15, 16).

The unique function of therapeutic recreation is to assist the client, sick or well, in the performance of those leisure activities and experiences contributing to health or its recovery, including general recreation participation (O'Morrow & Reynolds, 1989, p. 114).

The term "therapeutic recreation service" describes health-care and human-service programs and experiences that are specifically designed to meet play, recreation, and leisure needs of individuals who must contend with significant mentally or physically disabling conditions (Kraus & Shank, 1992, p. 3).

All of the definitions of therapeutic recreation presented share reference to recreation/leisure activities and experiences. Other common themes found in the definitions are (1) the purposeful nature of the use of recreation/leisure as an intervention, and (2) the personal enhancement of the client as a result of the intervention. In short, these definitions point to the purposeful use of recreation/leisure activities and experiences as a means of producing positive benefits for recipients of TR services. It follows that therapeutic recreation practice demands that TR specialists have a high level of knowledge of recreation and leisure as phenomena, as well as expertise in using recreation/leisure activities to restore health and foster growth.

Leisure and Recreation

Students in college and university departments of recreation and leisure studies are asked time and again to define the terms *leisure* and *recreation.* The purpose of the discussion within this textbook is not to cover old ground for those who have undergone the exercise of conceptualizing the meanings of leisure and recreation. Rather, the purpose here is briefly to discuss these terms as they form a basis for understanding therapeutic recreation.

Leisure. Although many views of leisure exist (Murphy, 1987), authors (e.g., Iso-Ahola, 1980; Neulinger, 1980; Smith & Theberge, 1987) commonly refer to the factors of "perceived freedom" and "intrinsic motivation" as central defining properties of leisure. Perceived freedom is typically viewed as a person's ability to exercise choice, or self-determination, over his or her own behavior. There exists an absence of external constraints. Intrinsic motivation is conceptualized as energizing behaviors that are internally (psychologically) rewarding. Intrinsically motivated behaviors are those engaged in for their own sake rather than as a means to an extrinsic reward.

Iso-Ahola (1984) has described intrinsic rewards in leisure as follows:

> *The intrinsic rewards that the individual pursues through leisure participation can be divided into personal and interpersonal. The personal rewards include, in addition to self-determination, feelings of competence or mastery, challenge, learning, exploration, efforts, and relaxation. In other words, the individual participates in those leisure activities at which he/she is good, that are challenging and allow him/her to use and develop personal talent and skills. The learning of new activities and things, acquisition of new skills, expenditure of effort, and exploration are all intrinsic rewards that a person can achieve when participating in leisure activities for their own sake. On the other hand, the seeking of interpersonal rewards means that in one form or the other, social interaction is the main intrinsic reward to be achieved (pp. 110, 111).*

Further, Iso-Ahola (1984) has argued convincingly that in addition to allowing people to seek intrinsic rewards, leisure participation provides escape from everyday personal and interpersonal environments. People can temporarily set aside problems and difficulties while taking part in leisure. Research by Iso-Ahola (with Allen, 1982) found that escape from personal environments (everyday routines and responsibilities) and interpersonal environments (other people) was seen by participants as a benefit of leisure. Other researchers have presented similar findings, although they have used different terms in reporting their results. Tinsley and Johnson (1984) reported a psychological benefit of leisure to be "expressive compensation," which they described as occurrences different from the everyday. Kabanoff (1982) identified "escape from routine" as a need met through leisure participation.

Benefits of Leisure. Tinsley and Johnson (1984), using cluster analysis as a technique, found seven psychological benefits of leisure. In addition to expressive compensation, they listed intellectual stimulation, catharsis, hedonistic companionship, secure solitude, moderate security, and expressive aestheticism. Kabanoff (1982) identified 11 needs commonly met through leisure. Besides escape from routine, these were autonomy, relaxation, family activity, interaction with others, stimulation, skill development and utilization, esteem, challenge/competition, leadership/social power, and health.

It is clear that leisure provides opportunity for people to do things voluntarily for any number of reasons of their own choosing, including to be with others, to seek security, to receive stimulation, or to relax. Leisure offers freedom of choice to satisfy any number of intrinsically derived needs.

Self-Determination and Intrinsic Motivation. The concepts of self-determination and intrinsic motivation, so central to leisure, deserve further consideration.

An idea deeply rooted in our Western culture is that we, as human beings, strive for control over ourselves and our environment (Grzelak, 1985; Pender, 1987). Our degree of social adjustment is related to the discrepancy that exists between our perceived and desired control (Grzelak, 1985).

Research (e.g., Langer & Rodin, 1976; Overmier & Seligman, 1967; Seligman & Maier, 1967) has found that a feeling of lack of control over adversive life situations produces a sense of helplessness. This, in turn, leads to the development of apathy and withdrawal that, in extreme cases, may ultimately end in death owing to perceived uncontrollability over a stressful environment (Gatchel, 1980). In light of this, it is unfortunate that much of what transpires in modern health care leads to feelings of helplessness. Pender (1987) has exclaimed that too often interactions with health care professionals foster feelings of helplessness in clients because of condescending behavior, paternalistic approaches, and the mystification of health care processes.

Fortunately, therapeutic recreation represents the antithesis of the controlling environment often imposed on the individual who has health problems. Rather than being repressive, therapeutic recreation provides a variety of opportunities for clients to escape the normal routines of the health facility in order to engage in intrinsically rewarding activities that produce feelings of self-determination, competence, and enjoyment.

Intrinsic Motivation. "Intrinsic motivation," according to Deci and Ryan (1985), "is based in people's needs to be competent and self-determining" (p. 58). Intrinsic motivation is inextricably tied to perceived competence in situations where competence is salient, a primary goal of taking part in an activity. The more competent a person perceives himself or herself to be at a given activity, the more intrinsically motivated he or she will be toward that activity, provided the activity is ego involving (Sansone, 1986). Self-determination plays a role as well. In order for the person to experience intrinsic motivation due to competence, he or she must feel a sense of perceived self-determination in terms of the outcome. In short, positive feedback for self-determined outcomes leads to enhanced intrinsic motivation (Deci & Ryan, 1985).

Relationship of Self-Determination and Intrinsic Motivation. Deci and Ryan (1985) have specified that a close relationship exists between self-determination and intrinsic motivation. They state:

> *When people are intrinsically motivated, they experience interest and enjoyment, they feel competent and self-determining, they perceive the locus of causality for their behavior to be internal, and in some instances they experience flow. The antithesis of interest and flow is pressure and tension (p. 34).*

Connected to self-determination and intrinsic motivation is the basic human tendency toward development or the fulfillment of one's potential. Renowned psychologists Piaget and Rogers both postulated this propensity, which Rogers termed the *actualizing tendency* (Deci & Ryan, 1985). The actualizing tendency is directed toward stimulation of the organism in order to promote change, growth, and maturation within the individual. Pender (1987) has described the actualizing process of the actualizing tendency in this way:

> *Human beings are unique in exhibiting a distinct psychological form of the actualizing tendency, which is expressed as the need to experience all facets of self and the world about them. The actualizing tendency is not directed at tension reduction but at positive experiences of tension increase. A state of increased positive tension is often experienced as challenge. Increased tension when serving the actualizing tendency does not result in anxiety or distress but is perceived as a positive state that facilitates performance and growth.*
>
> *The actualizing tendency is proposed as the driving force toward increased levels of well-being. Individuals and families are motivated to engage in health-promoting behaviors when they are aware of their own capacity for growth and their inherent and learned potentialities (p. 9).*

Intrinsic motivation is seen as the energy basis or the energizer of this tendency for growth and development, according to Deci and Ryan (1985). Intrinsic motivation itself rests on the organism's innate need for competence and self-determination. These needs, in turn, motivate us to seek and to conquer optimal challenges that stretch our abilities but are within our capacities. When we are able to achieve success, we experience feelings of competence and autonomy, along with accompanying emotions of enjoyment and excitement (Deci & Ryan, 1985).

In summary, it is clear that the two concepts of self-determination and intrinsic motivation are closely intertwined. People have a basic need to be in control of their environment so that they can exercise choices in their behavior and make autonomous decisions. Intrinsic motivation is based on self-determined behavior that results in perceiving oneself as being competent. Receiving positive feedback during a challenging activity of the person's choice leads to increased interest in the activity (i.e., greater intrinsic motivation for the activity).

Leisure, Self-Determination, and Intrinsic Motivation. Leisure would seem to offer one of the best opportunities for people to experience self-determination because it offers a chance for individuals to be in control. The potential for control often does not occur in work or other situations where external pressure exists. Leisure also provides occasions for achieving feelings of mastery or competence as challenging activities are conquered and positive feedback is received. These occurrences bring about increases in intrinsic motivation for the activity.

Recreation. Recreation has been viewed as activities or experiences occurring within leisure (Kraus, 1971). Recreation has also been perceived to be constructive, meeting socially accepted goals of the participant (Neulinger, 1980). Further, action and activity have been associated with recreation (Smith & Theberge, 1987). Finally, recreation has been linked with being restorative, offering refreshment or re-creation for the participant (Kelly, 1982). It is this ability to restore or refresh both mind and body that perhaps is the property that the average person most attaches to recreation.

If recreation is defined as being restorative or re-creative, the use of the term therapeutic, in combination with *recreation,* may appear to be redundant. If all recreation is restorative, is not then all recreation therapeutic? Perhaps a better term to describe therapeutic recreation would be *clinical recreation* because of the employment of the purposeful intervention element that promotes treatment and rehabilitative outcomes and helps define the profession.

The use of the terms *clinical* and *recreation* in combination may initially seem incongruous because of the connotation of disease and sickness associated with the term *clinical,* and the positive cognitions and emotions evoked by the word *recreation.* Clinical outcomes are serious, whereas recreation is fun. Nevertheless, the two terms *clinical* and *recreation* may be perceived to belong together. Restoration is a goal of both clinical practice and recreation. In clinical programs the object is health restoration, whereas recreation is considered to be a natural restorative phenomenon. Today the terms *clinical recreation* and *recreation therapy* or *recreational therapy* have come into common usage in order to interpret the field as one that employs recreation as a planned clinical intervention directed toward health restoration.

Recreation/Leisure and Therapeutic Recreation

Therapeutic recreation specialists need to have a highly developed understanding of the dynamics of recreation and leisure as they apply to practice within their profession. It is necessary to understand recreation as activity that has restorative properties, and leisure as a phenomenon that provides the individual with perceived control and the opportunity to meet intrinsically motivated needs. We will return to these concepts later in the chapter.

HEALTH

For many years the phrase *absence of disease* was synonymous with health. If you felt "okay" and your doctor did not diagnose you as having medical symptoms, you were perceived to be "healthy."

Over the years other definitions of health have evolved. These definitions stipulate a difference between the absence of symptoms of illness or abnormalities and vigorous health. The most cited definition is the one published by the World Health Organization (WHO) in 1947. The WHO defined health as "a state of complete physical, mental, and social well-being, not merely the absence of disease or informity."

The WHO definition has been criticized by many as being abstract, vague, simplistic, and unsuitable for scientific interpretation (Edelman & Mandle, 1986). It is difficult to deduce from the WHO definition specific criteria by which a state of health may be recognized, and the WHO definition does not recognize the phases of health people experience during their life spans (Pender, 1987).

The WHO definition does, however, offer three concepts essential to the formulation of a positive conceptualization of health (Edelman & Mandel, 1986; Pender, 1987):

1. It displays a concern for the individual as a total system rather than as merely the sum of various parts.
2. It places health in the context of both internal and external environments.
3. It relates health to fulfillment, to creative living.

Good health is a primary requisite to a high *quality of life.* The multifaceted phenomenon of quality of life includes physical, psychological, social, occupational, and leisure functioning, as well as a sense of well being (Followfield, 1990; Jacoby, 1990). To address the total impact of a disease, disorder, or disability, health care personnel with concern for quality of life take a holistic approach that looks beyond primary symptoms. For example, while reduction in the frequency of seizures may be an initial goal in the treatment of a person with epilepsy, quality of life factors such as psychosocial functioning and client satisfaction will also be of concern (Baker, 1990).

Humanistic Perspective. In the 1950s, humanistic psychology came into existence as a "third force" in opposition to Freud's psychoanalytic approach and the behavioristic approach of Watson and Skinner. This humanistic perspective recognized the uniqueness of human beings to be self-directed, to make wise choices, and to develop themselves or realize their human potentials. Humanistic psychologists proclaimed "that striving and growing are essential to human life and health" (Lindberg, Hunter, & Kruszewski, 1983, p. 70).

In general, those who embrace the humanistic perspective:

1. Take a holistic view of the person.
2. Believe that both children and adults are capable of change.
3. See people as being in dynamic interaction with the environment, not just reacting to the external world.
4. View people as healthy who strive for personal satisfaction yet go beyond their own needs to understand and care about others (Austin, 1991, p. 121).

Halbert Dunn's classic definition of health grew out of the influence of the humanistic perspective. Dunn (1961) coined the term *high-level wellness,* which he defined as "An integrated method of functioning which is oriented toward maximizing the potential of which the individual is capable, within the environment where he (or she) is functioning" (p. 4).

Dunn's definition of health is centered on the wholeness of the individual and each person's actualizing tendency, which serves as a propelling human force to move each human being toward the fulfillment of his or her potential. Further, Dunn's notion not only implies an absence of physical illness but positive psychological and environmental wellness as well. Mental and social well-being join the physical well-being of the total person in forming Dunn's concept of optimal health or high-level wellness (Austin, 1991).

Holistic medicine, as proposed by those who have championed high-level wellness, treats the person rather than the disease. Holistic medicine's concern lies with the "whole person" and with permitting individuals to assume self-responsibility for their own health (Austin, 1991). Ardell (1977) has identified the ultimate aim of "well medicine" (in contrast to the "traditional medicine" normally practiced by the medical community) to be that of moving individuals toward self-actualization. Whereas illness is the sole concern of traditional medicine, well medicine deals with wellness or health promotion.

Therapeutic Recreation: Illness and Wellness

Austin (1991) has compared therapeutic recreation with the concepts expressed by Dunn (1961) and Ardell (1977) on high-level wellness. There are striking similarities, as he indicates:

> *Therapeutic recreation, like traditional medical practice, has long dealt with the problems of illness. Unlike traditional medicine, however, therapeutic recreation has not dealt exclusively with illness. Therapeutic recreation has historically promoted the goal of self-actualization, or the facilitation of the fullest possible growth and development of the client. Therefore therapeutic recreation may be conceived to be much like traditional, medically oriented, allied health professions in its concern for preventing and alleviating illness. At the same time, therapeutic recreation specialists join both other leisure service professionals and physicians practicing "well medicine" in their desire to bring about the self-actualization of their clients (p. 125).*

Therapeutic recreation specialists must, by necessity, take on a variety of functions, as dictated by the needs of their clients. The TR specialist initially may join other members of the treatment team in helping the client to alleviate illness. Later, the TR specialist may help the client develop leisure and social skills as a part of a growth-enhancing rehabilitation program. Still later, leisure counseling may be provided by the TR specialist to assist the client in order to assure a favorable environment during community reintegration.

Motivational Forces: The Stabilizing and Actualizing Tendencies. Therapeutic recreation specialists therefore help clients to strive for both health protection (illness aspects) and health promotion (wellness aspects). Major human motivational forces underlie these two aspects. These are the stabilizing tendency and the actualizing tendency (Pender, 1987).

The *stabilizing tendency* is directed toward maintaining the "steady state" of the organism. It is the motivational tendency moving us to counter excess stress (i.e., distress) in order to maintain our levels of health. When faced with excessive stress we engage in adaptive behaviors in order to regain our sense of equilibrium. We attempt either to remove ourselves from the stress or to minimize the effects of the stressor on us.

The stabilizing tendency is responsible for our adapting so as to keep the level of stress in a manageable range in order to protect us from possible biophysical or psychosocial harm. It should be mentioned that potentially harmful stressors may result from internal as well as external stimuli. Negative forms of tension can come from either within us or from our surroundings. It is the stabilizing tendency that is the motivational force behind health protection (Pender, 1987).

The *actualizing tendency* is the growth-enhancement force discussed earlier in the chapter, when we consider self-determination, intrinsic motivation, and high-level wellness. It is this actualizing tendency that is the motivational force behind the achievement of optimal health.

Definitions of Health Considering Both Stability and Actualization

Nursing theorist Imogene King (1971) has offered a definition of health that emphasizes both stability and actualization. King has defined health as follows:

> *[Health is] a dynamic state in the life cycle of an organism which implies continuous adaptation to stress in the internal and external environment through optimum use of one's resources to achieve maximum potential for daily living (p. 24).*

Pender (1987), who, like King, is a nurse, has also provided a definition of health that similarly reflects both the stabilizing and actualizing tendencies. Pender has defined health in the following way:

> *Health is the actualization of inherent and acquired human potential through goal directed behavior, competent self-care, satisfying relationships with*

others while adjustments are made as needed to maintain structural integrity and harmony with the environment (p. 27).

From her definition, Pender (1987) has derived 14 criteria for evaluating an individual's state of health. Pender's criteria offer an appropriate conclusion of this section, because they manifest the most positive aspects of the complex phenomena of health. The criteria are these:

1. Exhibits personal growth and positive change over time.
2. Identifies long-term and short-term goals that guide behavior.
3. Prioritizes identified goals.
4. Exhibits awareness of alternative behavioral options to accomplish goals.
5. Perceives optimum health as a primary life purpose.
6. Engages in interpersonal relationships that are satisfying and fulfilling.
7. Actively seeks new experiences that expand knowledge or increase competencies for personal care.
8. Displays a high tolerance for new and unusual situations or experiences.
9. Derives satisfaction from the experience of daily living.
10. Expends more energy in acting on the environment than in reacting to it.
11. Recognizes barriers to growth and deals constructively in removing or ameliorating them.
12. Uses self-monitoring and feedback from others to determine personal and social effectiveness.
13. Maintains conditions of internal stability compatible with continuing existence.
14. Anticipates internal and external threats to stability and takes preventive actions (p. 27).

HEALTH, ACTIVITY, RECREATION, LEISURE, AND THERAPEUTIC RECREATION

Health is a complex concept that encompasses coping adaptively, as well as growing and becoming. When persons are healthy they can cope with life's stressors. Those who enjoy optimal health are free to develop themselves to the fullest. Barriers to actualization do not exist, so such persons are free to pursue personal growth and development. Health makes actualization possible.

Because of the natural progression from health protection to health promotion, Flynn (1980) has suggested that illness can be positive. The occurrence of a health problem can serve as an occasion for the client to take control over his or her life and to learn how to strive toward optimal health. An example would be an individual who has a health problem (e.g., cardiac or mental health problem) because of stress. Dealing with this problem forces this person to seek the help of a health care professional. As a result of treatment, the client may not only overcome the original health concern but may learn to lead a different life-style that promotes reduced tension and increased enjoyment. By learning how to deal with stress and to take part in healthy activities that provide for growth and enjoyment (e.g., walking and swimming), the person not only is able to conquer his or her initial health problem but rises to a new level of health that might not have been experienced had the presenting problem not happened.

Therapeutic recreation specialists contribute to health by helping persons fulfill their needs for stability and actualization until they are able to assume responsibility for themselves. This is accomplished through client participation in prescriptive activities, recreation, and leisure.

Prescriptive Activity

When individuals first encounter illness, they often become self-absorbed, withdraw from their usual life activities, and experience a loss of control over their lives (Flynn, 1980). For these persons, activity becomes a necessary prerequisite to health restoration. They must begin actively to engage in life in order to overcome feelings of helplessness and depression and begin to establish control over the situation. They need to become energized so that they are not passive victims of their circumstances but can take action to restore their health. Wadeson (1980), an art therapist, has described the effect of engaging in art activity. She has written:

> *I don't know how to explain this observation, but I have experienced the change in energy level in myself over and over again . . . as I have become "activated" in art activity. It may be simply a matter of physical movement, but I doubt it, since often the physical activity is not that much greater than talking. I am more inclined to believe that it is a release of creative energy and a more direct participation in experience than in talking (p. 15).*

Recreation

Recreation involves activity as one component, but recreation is more than activity. As previously discussed, recreation produces restorative results. Through recreation people restore themselves. They regain their equilibrium so they can once again resume their quest for actualization.

Leisure

Leisure may be seen as a means to self-actualization. Through leisure experiences challenges are met. These leisure experiences feature self-determination, intrinsic motivation, and mastery and competence—experiences that lead people toward feelings of self-efficacy, empowerment, pleasure, and enjoyment. A unique virtue of recreation and leisure is that they are components of life free from constraint. People are in control while experiencing recreation and leisure. There are perhaps no other parts of our lives where we, as human beings, are allowed more self-determination. During recreation and leisure we can "be ourselves." We can "let our hair down." We are allowed to be human with all our imperfections and frailties. The caring, accepting attitude the therapeutic recreation specialist assumes in creating a free and nonthreatening recreation/ leisure environment allows for positive interpersonal relationships as well as for opportunities for accomplishment. Austin (1991) has asked, "In what better atmosphere than that achieved in recreation and leisure could growth be fostered and problems met?" (p. 122).

Therapeutic Recreation

Therapeutic recreation is a means, first, to restore oneself or regain stability or equilibrium following a threat to health (health protection), and second, to develop oneself through leisure as a means to self-actualization (health promotion). Additionally, therapeutic recreation may be seen as a means of preventing health problems, although the preventive function of TR has only recently begun to develop.

Therapeutic recreation has the primary goals of restoring health and helping people learn how to use their leisure in optimizing their potentials, in order to enjoy as high a quality of life as possible. TR provides for the *stabilizing* tendency by helping individuals to restore health, and the *actualizing* tendency by enabling persons to use leisure as a means to personal growth.

A Continuum

As illustrated in Figure 1.1, prescriptive activities, recreation, and leisure are avenues through which therapeutic recreation clients achieve health and wellness. As clients move toward optimal health, they exercise greater and greater choice, while the role of the therapeutic recreation specialist continually decreases. Clients ideally move to the point that they experience optimal health in a favorable environment. In this state of optimal health, or wellness, they are free to be self-directed and to pursue self-actualization.

Clients may enter the continuum at any point that is appropriate for their needs. Along the continuum are three broad areas. The first area is one where the stability tendency is paramount. At the extreme, the client is experiencing poor health in an unfavorable environment. Here the TR specialist helps activate the client. The client's role is relatively passive as the TR specialist provides direction and structure for the intervention.

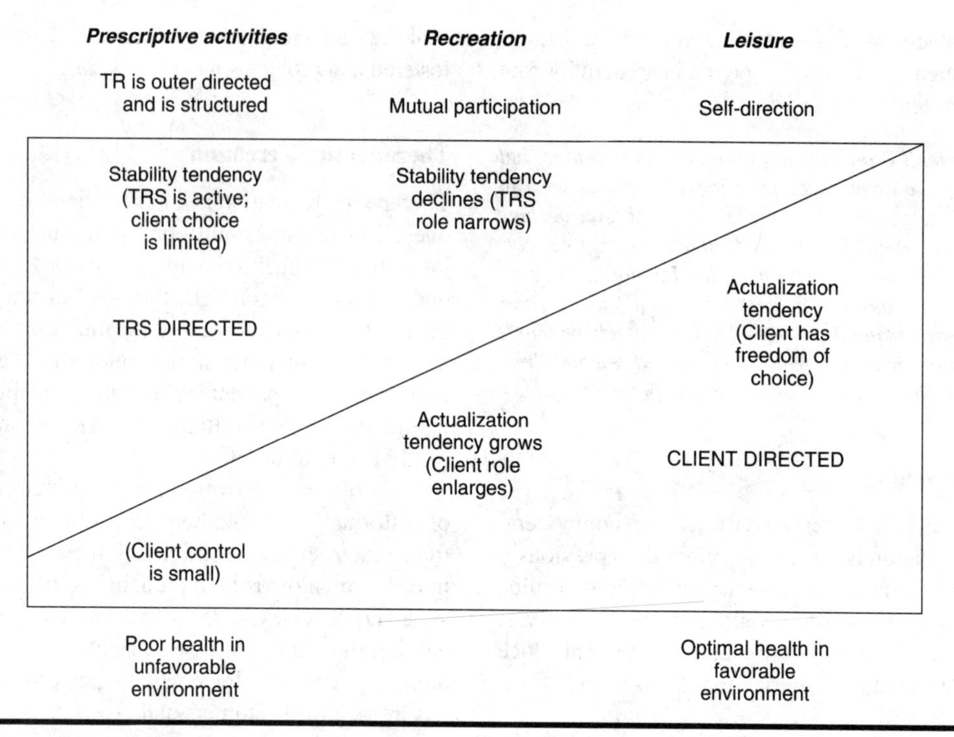

FIGURE 1.1 TR Continuum

Source: The above continuum was modeled after continuum presented by Ball (1970), Fink (1976), and Frye & Petters (1972).

The next area along the continuum represents mutual participation on the parts of the client and TR specialist. Here the actualizing tendency begins to emerge as the stabilizing tendency declines. Recreation participation leads to health restoration.

In the third area the actualizing tendency enlarges as the client's health improves and he or she moves toward self-determination. The role of the TR specialist is to assist the client, who ultimately assumes primary responsibility for his or her own health.

THERAPEUTIC RECREATION AND SPECIAL RECREATION

Therapeutic recreation has been presented in this chapter as a purposeful intervention to help clients achieve as high a level of health as possible in order to achieve as high a quality of life as can be attained. You, the reader, may be asking yourself, "Does therapeutic recreation always involve purposeful intervention? Isn't therapeutic recreation simply providing recreation services for people who are disabled?"

Austin (1987) has indicated that therapeutic recreation has been defined in the literature in two ways. He has stated:

> *It is clear that two types of services operate today under the banner of therapeutic recreation. The focus of one is broad and includes the provision of recreation services for persons with disabilities who require some special accommodation in order to participate. This service has been termed "special recreation" (Kennedy, Austin, & Smith, 1987). The focus of the second is treatment and rehabilitation. It uses recreation for health enhancement, rehabilitation, and independent functioning (p. 156).*

More and more, however, contemporary authors (e.g., Austin, 1987; Bullock, 1987; Kennedy, Austin, & Smith, 1991) present therapeutic recreation and special recreation as two special entities. These writers tend to argue that the mere provision of recreation services for members of special population groups (generally termed *special recreation*) does not constitute a therapeutic approach because it does not involve purposeful intervention aimed at accomplishing specific treatment or rehabilitation objectives.

A well-known figure in the provision of recreation for persons with disabilities has been Charles Bullock of the University of North Carolina. Bullock (1987) has written:

> *Recreation and special populations, or special recreation, must be distinguished from therapeutic recreation. Therapeutic recreation is the purposive use of recreation by qualified professionals to promote independent functioning and to enhance optimal health and well-being in persons with illnesses and/or disabling conditions.*
>
> *Therapeutic recreation is not any and all recreation services for persons who are disabled. Merely being disabled does not qualify a person to receive "therapeutic" recreation services. The person who is disabled may receive therapeutic recreation services or he or she may simply receive recreation services. The determination is made on the basis of need and mandate for treatment rather than on disability. To call recreation services "therapeutic" because they involve a person or group of persons with a disability is doing a disservice to the person who is being served. To deny a person recreation services because of disability opposes the original philosophy of modern recreation services, which began as a social movement concerned with the needs of all persons (p. 203).*

It appears that some of the confusion with therapeutic recreation and special recreation rests in the broad application of the term special recreation. It has been used to describe both making special accommodations (e.g., adaptations of equipment and modification of activities) and the general provision of recreation services for persons with disabilities.

Perhaps the emergence of the term *inclusive recreation* (Smith, Austin, & Kennedy, in press) will help to clarify the distinction between special recreation services and the general provision of opportunities for recreation expression for persons with disabilities. Smith, Austin, and Kennedy (in press) have defined inclusive recreation as "a phrase used to capture the full acceptance and integration of persons with disabilities into the recreation mainstream. It reflects free and equal access to recreation participation by persons with disabilities." Thus the term special recreation may be reserved to describe special or adapted activities, such as the Special Olympics or Wheelchair sports, while the term inclusive recreation may be used more broadly in order to reflect equal and joint participation of persons with and without disabilities.

The editors of this book take the position that the term *therapeutic recreation* should be reserved for purposeful interventions using prescribed activities and recreation or leisure experiences. The term *inclusive recreation* should be employed to describe the general provision of access to recreation opportunities by persons with disabilities, which is now the law of the land in the United States following the passage of Public Law 101-336, The Americans with Disabilities Act (ADA). ADA allows full and equal access by persons with disabilities to any public accommodation, whether governmental or private. Therefore, this act covers not only public park and recreation facilities but includes private recreation facilities such as restaurants, bars, theaters, stadiums, museums, libraries, parks, zoos, and golf courses (Smith, Austin, & Kennedy, in press).

The provision of *special recreation* requiring selective adaptive equipment or some other special accommodation could be used by therapeutic recreation professionals or general recreation professionals, depending on the purpose it serves. If the accommodation is designed as a part of a purposeful intervention, it would be provided by a TR professional. If the accommodation is simply to provide full and equal access to recreation opportunity, it could be made by a general recreator. It is likely that general recreation professionals, lacking experience making accommodations, will consult with therapeutic recreation personnel who have background in this area.

TENETS BASIC TO THERAPEUTIC RECREATION PRACTICE

To function as promoters of health, therapeutic recreation specialists rest their practice on a belief system. The following statements provide basic tenets for therapeutic recreation practice as perceived by the editors. They are intended to further interpret the TR continuum and the purpose of therapeutic recreation (as opposed to special recreation). The beliefs listed are discussed in more detail in Chapter 3, where the therapeutic recreation process is presented. The tenets are as follows:

1. Illness (poor health) and wellness (optimal health) are dimensions of health that may be perceived to be on a continuum.
2. The higher the state of self-actualization, the more optimal is the state of health of the individual.
3. Problems in health produce needs that may be fulfilled through interactions between clients and therapeutic recreation specialists. The stability tendency motivates clients toward need fulfillment leading to health protection.
4. The actualization tendency motivates clients toward health promotion. Therapeutic recreation specialists engage in mutual participation with clients motivated by the actualization tendency, but move toward giving more and more control to clients as they become healthier.
5. Prescriptive activities initially may be used as energizing forces to engage clients with the environment. Therapeutic recreation specialists exercise the greatest amount of control at this stage, but attempt to move clients toward achieving greater health and control.
6. Client participation in recreation activities is restorative and leads to health protection. Therapeutic recreation specialists work cooperatively with clients, assisting them to move toward self-directed leisure experiences that are health enhancing.
7. Optimal health (wellness) is achieved through participation in leisure experiences that feature self-determination and competency and lead to feelings of self-efficacy, empowerment, interest, and enjoyment.
8. The basic goal of therapeutic recreation is the achievement of the highest possible level of health in clients. Illness can be a growth-producing experience for individuals who participate in therapeutic recreation.
9. The goal of therapeutic recreation (i.e., health) is achieved through purposeful intervention using the therapeutic recreation process (i.e., assessment, planning, implementation, and evaluation).
10. The client-therapist relationship is a critical element in the therapeutic recreation process. The essential role of TR specialists is that of a catalyst who works in partnership with clients in order to help them be as self-directed as possible.
11. Therapeutic recreation specialists model healthy behavior and attitudes while helping clients develop personal competence and intrinsic motivation for participating in healthful activities.
12. Therapeutic recreation specialists focus on clients' abilities and intact strengths.
13. Therapeutic recreation is action- or experience-oriented, but the emphasis of therapeutic recreation is always on the client as a person and not on the activity.
14. Therapeutic recreation is concerned with both treatment/rehabilitation and education/reeducation. Therapeutic outcomes emphasize enhanced functioning and the here-and-now.
15. Typical outcomes of therapeutic recreation interventions include increasing personal awareness, increasing interpersonal or social skills, developing leisure skills, decreasing stress, improving physical fitness and functioning, developing feelings of positive self-regard, self-efficacy, perceived control, pleasure, and enjoyment.
16. Therapeutic recreation specialists have a knowledge of demands inherent in specific activities. Activity analysis is employed in order to gain insights into the demands activities make on clients in order to ensure the careful selection of appropriate activities.
17. Purposeful, goal-directed behavior is an important characteristic of therapeutic recreation. Being purposeful means having a plan, which

implies choice making on the part of clients. When choice is involved, clients perceive their actions to be self-determined, leading them to feelings of competence.

18. Recreation and leisure activities offer diversion or escape from personal problems and the routine of health care facilities.
19. Therapeutic recreation specialists assess causes of both client problems and client strengths. From identified problems client needs are determined. Intervention strategies are based on client strengths.
20. All client behavior is meaningful. It is motivated by personal needs and goals that can be understood only from each client's frame of reference within the context in which it transpires.
21. Every client possesses intrinsic worth and the potential for change.
22. Every client functions as a holistic being who acts on and reacts to the environment as a whole person.
23. All clients have common, basic human needs ranging from physical and safety needs to self-actualization. It is the higher-level social needs, esteem needs, and actualization needs that are the primary concerns of therapeutic recreation.

KINDRED PROFESSIONS

Therapeutic recreation specialists do not work in isolation from other health care professionals. In fact, the use of interdisciplinary teams composed of personnel from various specializations has become widespread. The establishment of interdisciplinary teams is largely based on the notion that clients are so complex that no single profession, by itself, can be expected to be able to offer adequate health care (Howe-Murphy & Charboneau, 1987; O'Morrow, 1980). Team membership will vary as a function of the type of setting in which services are being delivered (e.g., center for physical medicine and rehabilitation or psychiatric care) and as a function of the specific problems of the client (Howe-Murphy & Charboneau, 1987).

Types of Health Care Professionals

A variety of health care professionals have been described in the therapeutic recreation literature (e.g., Avedon, 1974; Kraus, 1983; O'Morrow & Reynolds, 1989). Although no attempt is made here to discuss all possible kindred professions, major professions are covered. These include medical doctors, nurses, psychologists, social workers, play therapists, and vocational rehabilitation counselors, as well as various activity or rehabilitation therapy professions.

Medical Doctors. Medical doctors (M.D.'s) use surgery, drugs, and other methods of medical care to prevent and alleviate disease. There are over 30 different specializations of medical doctors (O'Morrow & Reynolds, 1989). Examples of these are psychiatrists (who specialize in mental and emotional disorders), pediatricians (who specialize in the care and treatment of children), and neurologists (who deal with diseases of the nervous system).

Nurses. Registered nurses (R.N.'s) have responsibility for giving nursing care to patients, carrying out physicians' orders, and supervising other nursing personnel such as licensed practical nurses (L.P.N.'s), nurses aides, orderlies, and attendants.

Psychologists. Psychologists usually hold Ph.D. or Psy.D. degrees in psychology. They engage in psychological testing, diagnosis, counseling, and other therapies.

Social Workers. Social workers use case work and group work methods to assist clients and their families in making social adjustments and in dealing with social systems. They prepare the social histories of newly admitted clients and are often the primary professionals to assist clients with community reintegration.

Play Therapists. Play therapy is a form of psychotherapy that uses play activities and toys with children to permit the expression of, and working through, emotional conflicts. Symbolic play is seen as a means for the child to surface problems so that they can be dealt with.

Vocational Rehabilitation Counselors. Vocational rehabilitation counselors (often referred to as "voc rehab" counselors) are concerned with work or career counseling of clients in treatment and rehabilitation programs. They assess client vocational interests and potentials and attempt to find appropriate training or placements to meet clients' abilities.

Physical Therapists. Physical therapists (P.T.'s) are concerned with restoration of physical function and prevention of disability following disease, injury, or loss of body part. They apply therapeutic exercise and functional training procedures in physical rehabilitation.

Occupational Therapists. Occupational therapists use purposeful activities with persons with limitations due to physical injury, illness, psychosocial disorders, developmental or learning disabilities, economic and cultural differences, or aging processes in order to increase independent functioning, maintain health, and prevent disability (Punwar, 1994, p. 4).

Music Therapists. Music therapists (M.T.'s) use music as a medium to reach and involve clients in treatment. Musical therapy is found primarily in psychiatric treatment programs rather than in centers for physical medicine and rehabilitation.

Art Therapists. Art therapists use art as a medium to promote self-awareness, nonverbal expression, and human interaction. Art therapy is used with both physical and psychiatric rehabilitation, although it is most widely used within psychiatric treatment.

Dance Therapists. Dance therapists use movement as a medium to work with clients. It is a nonverbal means of expression employed with both individuals and groups. Although not found exclusively in psychiatric treatment programs, it is most commonly used with people experiencing problems in mental health.

Activity Therapy and Rehabilitation Therapy Services. The terms *activity therapy* and *rehabilitation therapy* are regularly used as umbrella terms for administrative purpose in order to encompass several of the action-oriented therapies. In addition to therapeutic recreation, activity therapy and rehabilitation therapy departments are comprised of occupational therapy, music therapy, dance therapy, and art therapy. Sometimes vocational rehabilitation counseling is also located within an activity therapy or rehabilitation therapy department.

RANGE AND SCOPE OF THERAPEUTIC RECREATION SERVICES

Where does therapeutic recreation take place? Whom does therapeutic recreation serve? What types of programs are conducted by therapeutic recreation specialists? What professional organizations exist to stimulate quality therapeutic recreation?

Settings for Therapeutic Recreation

At one time, practically all therapeutic recreation took place within hospitals and institutions. This is no longer true. Today therapeutic recreation is found in a variety of settings. Austin (1987) has described the situation as follows:

> *While therapeutic recreation was once exclusively concerned with providing services to persons who were institutionalized, it is no longer limited to any specific type of setting. TR takes place in a wide variety of agencies, including general hospitals, psychiatric hospitals, nursing homes, rehabilitation centers, residential schools for students with disabilities, correctional facilities, outdoor recreation/camping centers, mental-health centers and other community-based health and human service agencies, and park-and-recreation departments (p. 155).*

Clients Serviced in Therapeutic Recreation

A therapeutic recreation client can be any person who desires to restore his or her health (engage in health protection) or to enhance his or her level of health (pursue health promotion). Persons participating in mental health programs have traditionally been therapeutic recreation's largest client group. Three other major TR client groups have been persons who are mentally retarded, physically disabled, or aged. Other types of individuals who have benefited from therapeutic recreation are those who are socially deviant or experience social disorder in their families, abuse alcohol or other chemical substances, have cognitive impairments (e.g., head injuries), are autistic, experience convulsive disorders, have multiple disabilities, are hospitalized children, are undergoing correctional rehabilitation, have experienced burns, have cardiac conditions, or have AIDS.

Types of Therapeutic Recreation Programs

There exist a vast array of formats for therapeutic recreation programs. These include clubs; classes; special interest groups; informal recreation opportunities; special events; leagues, tournaments, and contests; large-group activities such as dances; outdoor pursuits such as adventure/challenge activities; and individual and group leisure counseling sessions (Austin, 1987, 1991; Avedon, 1974).

Professional Organizations for Therapeutic Recreation

Two professional membership societies for therapeutic recreation professionals exist in the United States today. The largest of these, with over 3,900 members, is the American Therapeutic Recreation Association (ATRA) (Evans, 1995). ATRA was formed in 1984 by a group of clinically oriented therapeutic recreation professionals who wanted to place greater focus on clinical therapeutic recreation intervention strategies.

The second professional membership society is the National Therapeutic Recreation Society (NTRS), a branch of the National Recreation and Park Association. NTRS was founded in 1966 to represent a broad-based constituency having both therapeutic recreation and special recreation concerns.

COMPETENCIES NEEDED BY THERAPEUTIC RECREATION SPECIALISTS

Few would argue with the contention that the competencies needed by therapeutic recreation specialists are different from those required of park and recreation professionals who serve in park districts, municipal and county park and recreation departments, state parks, youth serving agencies, and similar leisure service delivery systems. Certainly, both therapeutic recreation specialists and professionals from the general field of parks and recreation need solid liberal arts preparation. The liberal learning dimension of professional preparation programs offers the depth and breadth of education needed for individuals to be contributing citizens of the world and provides a context for professional practice, together with a greater appreciation for the diversity of persons and environments that will be encountered in professional roles. Both those in therapeutic recreation and those in parks and recreation need understandings of the phenomena of recreation and leisure. But the therapeutic recreation professional is different from the general park and recreation professional in that the TR specialist must possess additional competencies that are specific to the practice of therapeutic recreation.

A study by Card and Rodriguez (1987) found what these researchers described as "assessment" and "leisure education" to be the primary areas of competency needed for TR specialists in clinical settings in Missouri. The choice of the term *assessment* by Card and Rodriguez is misleading, however, because this competency area included many clinical skills other than doing client assessment. A better title for this group of competencies would appear to be *treatment* because of the nature of tasks listed under the heading. These tasks included implementing treatment plans, helping clients learn to deal with problems, providing socially stimulating activities, making necessary adaptations to accommodate clients in programs, aiding clients to develop individual programs, assisting clients to examine attitudes, and developing client relationships to further treatment aims.

If the term *treatment* is accepted to describe more clearly this primary area of competency, then the two paramount areas of TR competency identified by Card and Rodriguez may be described as *treatment* and *leisure education.* This terminology is in accord with the perception of therapeutic recreation as dealing with assisting clients with health protection (i.e., treatment) and helping clients to learn to use leisure for health promotion (i.e., leisure education).

In addition to the work of Card and Rodriguez, several sources have identified competencies needed for therapeutic recreation practice (e.g., Austin, 1994; Brasile, 1992; Council on Accreditation, 1986; Kelley, Robb, Wook, & Halberg, 1974; National Council on Therapeutic Recreation Certification, 1988; Stumbo, 1986). These sources are the primary basis for the listing of competencies for therapeutic recreation specialists that follows. As you review this listing, think about your own preparations for doing therapeutic recreation. Are you personally gaining the competencies necessary for practice in therapeutic recreation?

Areas of competency that you as an emerging TR specialist need to evaluate include:

- theories/understandings of play, recreation, and leisure
- human development throughout the life span
- anatomy and physiology
- basic assumptions about human nature
- etiology, course, and prognosis of various diagnostic categories
- disease sequelae
- effects of stress on individuals
- perception of clients as "whole persons," not just as individuals possessing symptoms
- effects of major drugs
- health and safety information for working with clients
- medical and psychiatric terminology
- principles of rehabilitation
- concepts of health and wellness
- attitudes toward illness and disability
- self as a therapeutic agent
- leadership of various recreation/leisure activities (e.g., arts and crafts, camping, games, sports)
- theory and technique of group leadership
- community leisure resources for client involvement
- activity analysis procedures
- careful selection of activities to meet treatment aims
- interpersonal relationship skills
- interview skills
- leisure counseling theory and technique
- client assessment
- treatment goals formulation
- stating behavioral objectives
- treatment/rehabilitation planning
- theory and application of treatment/rehabilitation approaches (e.g., client-centered approach)
- learning/teaching principles
- behavior management techniques
- evaluation of intervention outcomes
- client records and documentation (e.g., charting on clients)
- referral procedures
- assistive techniques and adaptive devices for specific illnesses and disabilities
- ethical and professional standards of practice
- legal aspects of therapeutic recreation
- procedures for mainstreaming and integration
- giving and receiving clinical supervision
- role and function of health care systems
- role of TR as a component of health care
- role and function of interdisciplinary treatment teams
- role and function of kindred professionals
- current professional issues and trends (e.g., accreditation, credentialing)
- historical foundations of therapeutic recreation as they influence the philosophy of practice

It is expected that your self-assessment of the competency areas will reveal that although you having started to gain rudimentary skills and knowledge, you are still in the beginning phases of development as a therapeutic recreation specialist.

This is normal, so you should not feel discouraged if you do not yet possess the competencies required for TR clinical practice.

It is important to note here that no matter which professional practice skills are learned and applied, growth-promoting relationships are at the heart of therapeutic recreation (Austin, 1991). Flynn (1980) has emphasized the significant impact the personality of the practitioner may have on the client. She has urged health care professionals to assess themselves and to consider developing further the qualities that have been identified as important to the helper-client relationship. These characteristics are listed in Table 1.2. You may wish to review these characteristics in order to conduct your own self-assessment.

PLAN FOR THE BOOK

We have attempted to make you, the reader, the focal point of this book. The book is organized with objectives at the beginning of each chapter so you will know explicitly what you should gain from your reading. Other aids to help your learning are the reading comprehension questions and suggested learning activities found at the end of each chapter.

Chapters in Section One of the book present the nature, purpose, history, and processes of therapeutic recreation. Section Two covers special areas of therapeutic recreation practice. Taken as a whole, these chapters illustrate the richness and diversity of therapeutic recreation.

We are extremely fortunate to have some of the most highly regarded authorities in therapeutic recreation as authors of the chapters in Section Two. Each of these individuals is an expert on the topic of his or her chapter.

To facilitate your learning and ensure completeness in approach, all the authors in Section Two followed a common outline. For example, in each chapter you will learn about current practices and procedures in that particular area of therapeutic recreation, and you will review a brief case study that portrays the actual application of the practices and procedures.

The chapters in Section Three cover specialized areas of professional activity and trends and issues in therapeutic recreation. These chapters, like the others, begin with objectives so you will know what to look for. They will also provide you with a means to assess your learning. It may be helpful for you to scan the objectives at the beginnings of several chapters before proceeding further.

TABLE 1.2 Characteristics Important in Helping Relationships

Sense of humor	Competence
Self-respect	Generosity
Congruence	Self-confidence
Presence	Graciousness
Acceptance	Sense of personal integrity
Balance of body/mind/spirit	Simplicity
Ability to meet with emphatic understanding	Intelligence
Ability to express unconditional regard	Common sense
Ability to experience the other as a person	Genuineness
Ability to listen	Ability to communicate
	Sense of purpose

Source: From a listing in Flynn (1980, p. 20).

SUMMARY

The purpose of this chapter was to provide you with an introduction to therapeutic recreation and to offer an overview of its components. Definitions of therapeutic recreation were presented, followed by an analysis of common elements found in the definitions. Leisure, recreation, self-determination, and intrinsic motivation were granted particular attention.

The relationship of therapeutic recreation to health and wellness was discussed, together with the tendencies for stability and actualization. This discussion culminated in the presentation of the TR continuum. Following a description of the continuum, therapeutic recreation was further defined first by contrasting it with inclusive and special recreation, and second, by providing basic tenets that guide therapeutic practice.

Remaining segments of the chapter offered information on kindred professionals, the range and scope of therapeutic recreation services, and competencies needed by therapeutic recreation specialists. The chapter ended with a brief orientation to the plan of the book.

READING COMPREHENSION QUESTIONS

1. What is the defined area of expertise for TR specialists?
2. Which of the definitions of TR do you like the most?
3. What are common themes found in definitions of TR?
4. Do you agree that perceived freedom and intrinsic motivation are the factors that define leisure?
5. Describe intrinsic rewards found in leisure.
6. Does leisure offer escape? If so, do you see any relationship to therapeutic recreation?
7. What is meant by helplessness?
8. What is the relationship between competence, self-determination, and intrinsic motivation?
9. What properties are found in recreation?
10. Is the use of the terms *clinical* and *recreation* in combination incongruous?
11. How may the WHO definition of health be criticized?
12. What positive dimensions are offered in the WHO definition?
13. Briefly describe the humanistic perspective.
14. What is high-level wellness?
15. Does TR embrace the concepts of holistic health?
16. Explain the stabilizing and actualizing tendencies.
17. What is the relationship of the stabilizing and actualizing tendencies to health?
18. Do you agree with Pender's criteria for health?
19. Can illness ever be positive?
20. What are the goals of therapeutic recreation?
21. Can you explain the TR continuum?
22. Do you agree that therapeutic recreation and special recreation are separate entities?
23. Review the basic tenets of therapeutic recreation. Do you understand each? Do you agree with each?
24. Can you describe interdisciplinary teams? Can you tell why they are widely used?
25. What are the kindred professions?
26. What are the meanings of the terms *activity therapy* and *rehabilitation therapy?*
27. In what types of settings does TR take place?
28. Does a person have to be disabled to be a TR client?
29. Who are types of clients traditionally served by TR?
30. List types of program structures for TR.
31. Name the therapeutic recreation professional organizations.
32. Do you agree with the list of competency areas?
33. How do you assess yourself in terms of moving toward becoming a competent therapeutic recreation specialist?
34. Do you understand the plan of the book?

SUGGESTED LEARNING ACTIVITIES

1. Conduct brief interviews with three or more health professionals from areas such as medicine, nursing, clinical psychology, occupational therapy, or social work. Ask each what he or she feels is the defined area of expertise for TR specialist. Bring your interview notes to class so you may share your findings with other students.
2. Interview 10 to 15 college or university students to find out if they perceive leisure participation to provide escape from everyday personal and interpersonal environments. Write a 2- to 4-page paper on your findings.
3. In a small group, with other students in your class, discuss the concepts of self-determination and intrinsic motivation. Share information about personal experiences that have provided you with opportunities to experience self-determination and intrinsic motivation.
4. Interview several faculty members or fellow students, asking them to define health in their own words. Bring your results to class to compare your findings with those of classmates and the definitions of health found in the chapter.
5. Prepare a 2- to 4-page paper on the relationship between therapeutic recreation and inclusive recreation. Conclude the paper by stating your own position regarding the relationship.
6. Review the tenets of therapeutic recreation presented in the chapter. Pick the five you consider to be most important. Bring your list to class so your instructor can tabulate those you and your classmates have chosen. Discuss the findings in class, assessing the level of agreement.
7. As a class, visit several agencies that have extensive TR services. Later, in class, discuss the types of services provided and the types of clients served.
8. Examine the list of competencies needed for practice in TR found in the chapter. Then, in class, discuss these questions: Do you agree with the list of competencies? Does your curriculum offer the opportunity to gain competencies needed for practice in therapeutic recreation?
9. Review the characteristics in Table 1.2 in order to conduct your own self-assessment. Prepare a 2- to 4-page paper describing your findings and conclusions from your self-assessment.

REFERENCES

Ardell, B. (1977). *High-level wellness: An alternative to doctors, drugs, and disease.* Emmaus, PA: Rodale Press.

Austin, D. R. (1982). *Therapeutic recreation: Processes and techniques.* New York: John Wiley & Sons.

Austin, D. R. (1991). *Therapeutic recreation: Processes and techniques* (2nd ed.). Champaign, IL: Sagamore Publishing.

Austin, D. R. (1987). Therapeutic recreation. In A. Graefe & S. Parker (Eds.), *Recreation and Leisure: An introductory handbook* (pp. 155–157). State College, PA: Venture Publishing.

Austin, D. R. (1994). *Therapeutic recreation education: A call for reform.* Manuscript submitted for publication.

Avedon, E. M. (1974). *Therapeutic recreation service: An applied behavioral science approach.* Englewood Cliffs, NJ: Prentice Hall.

Baker, G. (1990). Chairman's introduction. *Quality of life and quality of care in epilepsy* (pp. 61, 62). Great Britain: Royal Society of Medicine.

Ball, E. L. (1970). The meaning of therapeutic recreation. *Therapeutic Recreation Journal, 4* (1), 17, 18.

Brasile, F. M. (1992). Professional preparation: Reported needs for a profession in transition. *Annual in Therapeutic Recreation, 3,* 58–71.

Bullock, C. C. (1987). Recreation and special populations. In A. Graefe & S. Parker (Eds.), *Recreation and leisure: An introductory handbook* (pp. 203–207). State College, PA: Venture Publishing.

Card, J. A., & Rodriguez, C. (1987). Job task analysis of therapeutic recreation professionals: Implications for educators. *Journal of Expanding Horizons in Therapeutic Recreation, 2,* 33–41.

Carter, M. J., Van Andel, G. E., & Robb, G. M. (1985). *Therapeutic recreation: A practical approach.* St. Louis: Times Mirror/Mosby.

Council on Accreditation. (1986). *Standards and evaluation criteria for recreation, park resources and leisure services baccalaureate program.* Alexandria, VA: National Recreation and Park Association.

Davis, J. E. (1936). *Principles and practices of recreational therapy.* New York: A. S. Barnes.

Deci, E. L., & Ryan, R. M. (1985). *Intrinsic motivation and self-determination in human behavior.* New York: Plenum Press.

Dunn, H. L. (1961). *High level wellness.* Arlington, VA: R. W. Beatty.

Edelman D., & Mandle, C. L. (1986). *Health promotion throughout the lifespan.* St. Louis: C. V. Mosby.

Evans, K. (1995). ATRA Office, personal communication.

Fallowfield, L. (1990). *The quality of life: The missing measurement in health care.* London: Souvenir Press.

Fink, D. (1976). Holistic health: Implications for health planning. *American Journal of Health Planning, 1,* 17–21.

Flynn, P. A. R. (1980). *Holistic health: The art and science of care.* Bowie, MA: Robert J. Brady.

Frye, V., & Peters, M. (1972). *Therapeutic recreation: Its theory, philosophy, and practice.* Harrisburg, PA: Stackpole Books.

Gatchel, R. J. (1980). Perceived control: A review and evaluation of therapeutic implications. In A. Baum & J. E. Singer (Eds.), *Advances in environmental psychology: Vol. 2. Applications of personal control* (pp. 1–22). Hillsdale, NJ: Lawrence Erlbaum Associates.

Grzelak, J. L. (1985). Desire for control: Cognitive, emotional and behavioral consequences. In F. L. Denmark (Ed.), *Social/ecological psychology and the psychology of women.* New York: Elsevier Science Publishing.

Howe-Murphy, R., & Charboneau, B. G. (1987). *Therapeutic recreation intervention: An ecological perspective.* Englewood Cliffs, NJ: Prentice Hall.

Iso-Ahola, S. E. (1980). *The social psychology of leisure and recreation.* Dubuque, IA: William C. Brown Company.

Iso-Ahola, S. E. (1984). Social psychological foundations of leisure and resultant implications for leisure counseling. In E. T. Dowd (Ed.), *Leisure counseling: Concepts and applications.* Springfield, IL: Charles C. Thomas.

Iso-Ahola, S. E. (1982). The dynamics of leisure motivation: The effects of outcome on leisure needs. *Research Quarterly of Exercise and Sports, 53,* 141–149.

Jacoby, A. (1990). Chairman's introduction. *Quality of life and quality of care in epilepsy* (pp. 61, 62). Great Britain: Royal Society of Medicine.

Kabanoff, B. (1982). Occupational and sex differences in leisure needs and leisure satisfaction. *Journal of Occupational Behavior, 3,* 233–245.

Kelley, J. R. (1982). *Leisure: An introduction.* Englewood Cliffs, NJ: Prentice Hall.

Kelley, J. R., et al. (1974). *Therapeutic recreation education: Developing a competency-based entry-level curriculum.* Urbana, IL: Illinois Community College Project, Office of Recreation and Park Resources, University of Illinois.

Kennedy, D. W., Smith, R. W., & Austin, D. R. (1991). *Special recreation: Opportunities for persons with disabilities* (2nd ed.). Dubuque, IA: Wm. C. Brown Publishers.

King, I. M. (1971). *Toward a theory of nursing.* New York: John Wiley & Sons.

Kraus, R. (1971). *Recreation and leisure in modern society.* New York: Appleton-Century-Crofts.

Kraus, R. (1983). *Therapeutic recreation service: Principles and procedures* (3rd ed.). Philadelphia: Saunders College Publishing.

Kraus, R., & Shank, J. (1992). *Therapeutic recreation service: Principles and practices* (4th ed.). Dubuque, IA: Wm. C. Brown Publishers.

Langer, E. J., & Rodin, J. (1976). The effects of choice and enhanced personal responsibility for the aged: A field experiment in an institutional setting. *Journal of Personality and Social Psychology, 34,* 191–198.

Lindberg, J., Hunter, M., & Kruszewski, A. (1983). *Introduction to person-centered nursing.* Philadelphia: J. B. Lippincott.

Murphy, J. (1987). Concepts of leisure. In A. Graefe & S. Parker (Eds.), *Recreation and leisure: An introductory handbook* (pp. 11–17). State College, PA: Venture Publishing.

National Council on Therapeutic Recreation Certification with Educational Testing Service. (1988). *Report on the national job analysis project.* Spring Valley, NY: The National Council for Therapeutic Recreation Certification.

Neulinger, J. (1980). Introduction. In S. E. Iso-Ahola (Ed.), *Social psychological perspectives on leisure and recreation* (pp. 5–18). Springfield, IL: Charles C. Thomas.

O'Morrow, G. S., & Reynolds, R. P. (1980). *Therapeutic recreation: A helping profession* (2nd ed.). Englewood Cliffs, NJ: Prentice Hall.

O'Morrow, G. S., & Reynolds, R. P. (1989). *Therapeutic recreation: A helping profession* (3rd ed.). Englewood Cliffs, NJ: Prentice Hall.

Overmier, J. B., & Seligman, M. E. P. (1967). Effects of inescapable shock upon subsequent escape and avoidance responding. *Journal of Comparative and Physiological Psychology, 63,* 28–33.

Pender, N. J. (1987). *Health promotion in nursing practice* (2nd ed.). Norwalk, CT: Appleton-Century-Crofts.

Punwar, A. J. (1994). *Occupational therapy: Principles and practice* (2nd ed.). Baltimore: Williams & Wilkins.

Sasone, C. (1986). A question of competence: The effect of competence and task feedback on intrinsic interest. *Journal of Personality and Social Psychology, 51,* 918–931.

Schlein, E. H., & Kommers, D. W. (1972). *Professional education.* New York: McGraw-Hill.

Seligman, M. E. P., & Maier, S. F. (1967). Failure to escape traumatic shock. *Journal of Experimental Psychology, 74,* 1–9.

Smith, D. H., & Theberge, N. (1987). *Why people recreate.* Champaign, IL: Life Enhancement Publications.

Smith, R. W., Austin, D. R., & Kennedy, D. W. (in press). *Recreation opportunities for persons with disabilities: Special and inclusive recreation* (3rd ed.). Dubuque, IA: Wm. C. Brown Publishers.

Stumbo, N. J. (1986). A definition of entry-level knowledge for therapeutic recreation practice. *Therapeutic Recreation Journal, 20*(4), 15–30.

Tinsley, H. E., & Johnson, T. L. (1984). A preliminary taxonomy of leisure activities. *Journal of Leisure Research, 16,* 234–244.

Wadeson, H. (1980). *Art psychotherapy.* New York: John Wiley & Sons.

Wilensky, H. L. (1964). The professionalization of everyone? *The American Journal of Sociology, 70,* 137–158.

World Health Organization. (1947). Constitution of the World Health Organization. *Chronicles of WHO, 1,* 1, 2.

CHAPTER 2

ORGANIZATION AND FORMATION OF THE PROFESSION

MICHAEL E. CRAWFORD

OBJECTIVES

- Be able to describe the evolution of the National Therapeutic Recreation Society (NTRS).
- Be able to describe the development of the American Therapeutic Recreation Association (ATRA).
- Identify important historical events which have shaped the NTRS philosophy.
- Differentiate between the historical hospital recreation and recreation therapy movements.
- Name major enabling legislation bills which have played a major role in supporting the TR movement.
- Identify early precursors to modern day services made by ancient cultures.
- Know early leaders of the treatment-with-care era of human services.
- Understand the relationship of initiatives made by modern political and medical leaders to therapeutic recreation practice.
- Identify the six basic characteristics of a profession.
- Define the term "service motive."
- Describe the relationship between therapeutic recreation's service motive and history of organizational development.
- Know the phases of development for the scientific basis of therapeutic recreation.
- Identify important historical events in curriculum development in therapeutic recreation.
- Describe the issues surrounding the development of the National Council for Therapeutic Recreation Certification (NCTRC) and certification of TR personnel.
- Know assumptions upon which a code of ethics for a profession is based.

This chapter will explore the historical development of therapeutic recreation. Today's modern practice standards reflect a diversity of philosophies that have exerted influence on the field's development over a long period of time. In fact, some have referred to the "philosophy dilemma" of therapeutic recreation as the major stumbling block in the development of the profession (Meyer, 1980). Certainly a great deal of the profession's efforts in the 1970s and 80s were devoted to the resolution of differences regarding a single well articulated national philosophy. Further, the emergence of the American Therapeutic Recreation Association (ATRA) in the mid 1980s and its eclipsing of the National Therapeutic Recreation Society (NTRS) membership figures in the 1990s attest to the contemporary relevance of theoretical conflict among practitioners.

Related to the philosophical dilemma has been a rather circular history of professional organizations dedicated to providing therapeutic recreation. In this chapter we will learn how in some ways the professional organizations representing TR have come full circle, beginning first as separate organizations with conflicting philosophies, developing alliances and ultimately merging into NTRS, and then finally, once again driven by conflicting philosophical and professional agendas, dividing into separate organizations.

Prior to looking closely at this contemporary history of therapeutic recreation (the majority of which has taken place in the later part of the 1900s) a brief review of ancient and historical precedents is in order. Within this review we will see how the development of TR, like the development of other human services and adjunctive therapies, has been integrally linked to the attitudes societies have taken in general toward special populations.

HISTORICAL ROOTS

Cultural anthropologists have discovered that most ancient civilizations held beliefs and practices that relate in some way to the modern day approach for activities to be a part of a therapeutic regimen. Although somewhat varied (Greek culture is a notable exception) most of these ancient cultural rituals and practices were tied in some way to religious beliefs. Table 2.1 provides a brief chronology of some of the more prominent historical markers.

Unfortunately many of these ancient practices in providing more humane care and treatment for the sick and disabled were lost to post-twentieth century Europe. In fact many of the more brutal forms of treatment emanated from European practices and some of the more prevalent stereotypes and dehumanizing labels in existence today can be traced to this period of time. For example, individuals with mental problems were frequently locked away in asylums for lunatics, many kept in darkened cells for fear that stimulation or diversion of any kind would create aggressive or insubordinate behaviors. Similarly, many people with epilepsy were labeled as "possessed by the devil," their seizures taken as evidence of demonic possession, and many were summarily burned at the stake as witches or warlocks. Also, we find the mentally retarded and otherwise congenitally disabled persons treated at best as court jesters or fools, and at worst warehoused in segregated institutions.[1]

[1]There was a brief period of time in the United States that a more humane philosophy existed for the mentally retarded. The "happy home" movement was basically fueled by religious leaders who sought to create humane sanctuaries for the mentally retarded. Unfortunately this philosophy of protecting the retarded from society lasted only a few decades. Later in a wave of hysteria in which large numbers of the retarded were rounded up and institutionalized the "happy home"concept was slurred to "funny farm" as society sought to protect itself from the retarded. A detailed historical accounting of the eugenic scare that triggered the end of the happy home era may be found in Wolfensburger's work (1972) on the normalization movement.

TABLE 2.1 Ancient Precedents for Activity Therapy

Egyptian Culture

Priests established temples to treat the sick.

Legal codes with penalties for medical malpractice existed.

Treatment of the ill included dances, concerts and symbolic worship.

Greek Culture

Hippocrates, the father of modern medicine, established oath detailing responsibilities of medical profession, also introduced the case study method as an approach to practice, more importantly made medicine a nonreligious art.

Temples for the sick included libraries, stadiums, theaters, and sanatoriums.

Treatment of mental disorders included music in conjunction with gymnastics and dancing.

Roman Culture

Physicians prescribed games that afforded relaxation to the body and mind.

Heralded the virtues of diet and exercise as a tonic for the body

Circus and spectator activities used as preventative measures for social deviancy

Established the hospital system, infirmaries for the army at physician homes as "nursing homes," forerunners of modern day health care systems

Chinese Culture

Activity used to divert patient's attention from severe primary treatments

Deep breathing and exercise techniques developed for sedentary older persons (Tai Chi)

Source: Many concepts from Table 2.1 paraphrased from Avedon, 1982, p. 12–17, and O'Morrow & Reynolds, 1985, p. 83–115.

Reynolds and O'Morrow's analysis of the Middle Ages in which all science and classical learning passed into the church's keeping (a period lasting over eight centuries) provides an excellent synopsis:

> *Hippocrates had freed treatment and care from religion and superstition, and had taught men that illness and disability were not sent by the gods as punishment, but rather natural phenomena to be studied. Under the church rule, the view of the supernatural origin of disease was revived, partly the result of the fact that to be a physician one first had to be ordained a priest. Very little progress was made in theory and research during the Middle Ages . . . (Reynolds & O'Morrow, 1985, p. 89).*

Not until the early 1800s did the beginnings of institutionalization with treatment (referred to at times as the so-called moral treatment approach, which was actually a philosophical return to the same practices developed by the Greeks and Romans) occur as a counter-movement. Even so, the early leaders of this movement were viewed largely as being out of the mainstream of social thought. A few of the more prominent leaders are featured in Table 2.2.

The early attempts at institutional reform which advocated care and treatment fostered the beginning of the modern era of care. From the early examples set forth by Itard, Rush, and the like, refinements in institutional care took hold. We will learn in the next section that as refinements in societal methods took place (resulting in more humane institutions) the primacy of a variety of therapeutic modalities including professional

TABLE 2.2 Early Leaders of the Treatment with Care Era

Who	When	What
Phillippe Pinel (French Physician)	1700s	Recreational activity in the form of exercise used to treat the mentally ill
Jean Itard (French Physician)	1700s	Training techniques for the mentally retarded utilizing games and sport
John Morgan (American Physician)	1751	Credited with establishing the first medical school in America
Dr. Benjamin Rush (American Physician)	1810	Advocated therapeutic values of recreation for mental health patients
Florence Nightingale (British Nurse)	1873	Recreation huts to combat side effects of soldiering as well as re-design of hospital environments to include color, music, and pets.

Source: Many concepts in Table 2.2 paraphrased from Carter, Van Andel, & Robb, 1985, p. 35–50, and Reynolds & O'Morrow, 1985, p. 119.

recreation services began to develop momentum. This development however was not without both pragmatic and philosophic pitfalls and stumbling blocks.

THE BEGINNING OF MODERN THERAPEUTIC RECREATION SERVICES

The sudden influx of traumatic amputations and similar severe injuries to American society as a result of participation in both world wars served as a national trigger stimulus for improvement in the nation's hospital and institutional care treatment modalities. As services for returning veterans were expanded, a societal "halo" or carryover effect in attitudes and sympathies toward special populations other than the physically challenged slowly began to emerge (emphasis should be placed on the word *slowly* however). Along the way there were a number of important leaders, some professional, some political, who helped to champion this cause. Additionally, there were also a number of landmark legislative bills which provided both direction and funding for the modernization of human and health rehabilitation services. We will review these parallel histories briefly in order to build a chronology and a greater context than a discussion specific to the development of the therapeutic recreation profession will fit into. In Table 2.3 a brief synopsis of modern-day leaders and their contributions to the "treatment with care" movement is provided.

Collectively, these individuals (and others like them) were responsible for the expansion of recreation programs both within clinical and/or custodial and community-based settings. Sometimes this support was a deliberate act of advocacy (as in the case of Haun and Menninger and Rusk) and sometimes the recreation profession benefitted indirectly from the impact that policy or organization of services had on human services in general (as in the case of Kennedy and Nixon). Regardless of the nature of the intent, without this kind of key support from medical and political leadership, the young field of therapeutic recreation would have had a difficult time in bringing its service mission to the attention of the consumer. Related to the support provided by important personages was the progress in legal precedent, legislative mandate, and funding acts, all of which were central to the development of the young therapeutic recreation profession.

TABLE 2.3 Key Proponents and Leaders of Modern Rehabilitation Services Who Evidenced an Influence on Therapeutic Recreation Development

Dorothea Dix

Brought attention to the inadequate custodial care of the institutionalized in the early 1900s; key figure in alleviating overcrowding and provision of enhanced resident services.

Paul Haun

A Physician/Advocate in the 1940s and '50s whose writings and presentations supported recreation as a therapeutic modality able to create a desirable psychological state within the patient.

Carl Menninger

A Physician/Advocate, founder of the Menninger Clinic; influential advocate during the '40s through '60s on the clinical effectiveness of recreation experiences as an adjunct to standard psychiatric practice.

Ethel Kennedy

Founder of the Special Olympics movement through the auspices of the Joseph P. Kennedy, Jr. Foundation in the early 1960s; helped to spread recreation as formal community movement throughout community-based programs for the mentally retarded.

Howard Rusk

Physician and international authority on physical rehabilitation who believed that both individual and group recreation had a direct and positive relationship upon recovery; helped to establish the credibility of recreation as an adjunctive therapy.

Richard Nixon

President of the United States, mandated in 1967 that the mentally ill and mentally retarded populations in public institutions be reduced by at least one third, thus emphasizing greater emphasis on community-based social services on a national level.

George Bush

President of the United States, signed into law on July 26, 1990, the Americans with Disabilities Act thus extending to the public sector sweeping civil rights protection guaranteeing the person's right to accessibility and useability of public buildings and services.

Source: Table 2.3 paraphrased in part from Reynolds & O'Morrow, 1985, p. 119–121, and Carter, Van Andel, & Robb, 1985, p. 35–50.

Table 2.4 provides a brief chronology and annotation of the history of important legislative mandates as they impacted the therapeutic recreation profession.

Keeping in mind the ancillary support from professional and political leaders, as well as the more global rehabilitation laws reviewed above, we can now turn our focus to the specific history of the professionalization of therapeutic recreation services. While the vast majority of contemporary history has accumulated since the 1960s we must begin literally at the turn of the century in order to retrieve all relevant events that have impacted the modern day service ethic in therapeutic recreation.

TABLE 2.4 Legislation Affecting Recreation for Special Populations

Law	Impact
The Social Security Act, 1936	A compilation of law, including numerous amendments over the last several years related specifically to the elderly and disabled, including provisions for physical education and recreation through (l) formal procedure for review of professional services, (2) establishing funds to states for self-support services for individuals, (3) grants to states for providing community-based care.
Vocational Rehabilitation Act, 1963	Training and research funds for recreation for the ill and handicapped. The first recognition by a specific federal agency of the importance of recreation services in rehabilitation.
PL 88-29 Nationwide Outdoor Recreation Plan, 1963	Directed the formulation and maintenance of a comprehensive nationwide outdoor recreation plan. The plan was completed in 1973 and included emphasis on compliance with PL 90-480 (see below). Concerns for the handicapped have been listed as a priority area.
PL 90-170 Education for Handicapped Children Act, 1967	Established the Unit of physical education and recreation for handicapped children within the Bureau of Education for the Handicapped; became the largest federal program for training, research, and special projects.
PL 90-480 Architectural Barriers Act, 1968	Simply states: "Any building or facility, constructed in whole or part by federal funds, must be accessible to and usable by the physically handicapped."
PL 91-517 Developmental Disabilities Services and Facilities Construction Act, 1971	Developmentally disabled persons are specifically defined and recreation is listed as a specific service to be included as a fundable service.
PL 93-112 Rehabilitation Act of 1973	A comprehensive revision of the 1963 Vocational Rehabilitation Act which included an emphasis on the "total" rehabilitation of the individual. Special provisions included: (l) personnel training, (2) special projects and demonstrations for making recreational facilities accessible, (3) powers to ensure accessibility compliance for parks and parklands, (4) states must develop a comprehensive plan which ensures that they comply under section 504 that individuals shall not be discriminated against solely by reason of their handicap.
PL 93-516 Rehabilitation Act Amendment of 1974	Authorized the planning and implementation of the White House Conference on Handicapped Individuals which was conceived in 1977. Recreation was cited as one of sixteen areas of concern.
PL 94-142 Education of All Handicapped Children Act, 1975	Requires a free and appropriate education for all handicapped children. Physical education is listed as a direct service and recreation as a related service.

(continued)

TABLE 2.4 Continued

Law	Impact
PL 99-457 Education of the Handicapped Act Amendment, 1986	Emphasized development of comprehensive statewide programs of early intervention services for handicapped infants, toddlers, and families. A multidisciplinary team must develop an individualized family services plan. Recreation is cited as a related service in these amendments.
PL 101-336 The Americans with Disabilities Act, 1989	Provides comprehensive guidelines on banning discrimination against people with disabilities. An omnibus civil rights statute that prohibits discrimination against people with disabilities in sectors of private and public employment, all public services (including recreation), public accommodations, transportation, and telecommunications.

Source: Table 2.4 is a revision and update of previous work by Crawford, 1985.

THE GROWTH OF THERAPEUTIC RECREATION AS A PROFESSION

The use of the word "profession" when speaking of recreational personnel and services is still a relatively new concept. We say relatively new in reference to more mature professions like medicine, law, or psychology. For a group of individuals and the skills they provide to qualify for the label of "profession" it is essential that what they do be distinguished from trade or semi-skilled services. Most believe that a true profession has as its basis a set of characteristics, or criteria, which distinguish it as a true scientific endeavor (Strong, 1982).

The approach of this section will be to discuss the evolution of therapeutic recreation as a profession as it relates to the key global criteria which constitute the definition of a scientific profession. These include: professional organizations, service motive, scientific basis, extended preparation of personnel, autonomy of judgment, and code of ethics.

Professional Organizations

These organizations make progress possible that individual practitioners could not on their own otherwise obtain. One of the most important aspects of professional organizations is providing a forum for continuing education of its members. Conventions conferences, and topical symposia enable one to keep up with the growth of the field. In a related vein, political agitation and consumer advocacy at local state and national levels are essential for the continued growth and upgrading of standards. In some ways the success of a profession in following its service ethic can be either tremendously facilitated or hindered in direct proportion to the ability of its professional body to apply political clout toward the passage of important regulations, laws, and standards.

The history of the formation of professional organizations within therapeutic recreation is relatively short and, as of recent times, circular. The problem lies in a philosophical derisiveness over what really constitutes the true service motive of the profession. As we shall see, therapeutic recreation personnel have still not solved this fundamental definition of a profession, and it continues to drive deep differences. One of the ways these differences have manifested themselves has been in the formation of different professional organizations, the coalition or merger of them into a unified whole, and the eventual break-up back into separate professional groups.

1948 At the national Congress of the American Recreation Society (ARS) the Hospital Recreation Section becomes a reality. Members predominantly represented practitioners from veterans and military hospitals who espoused a "recreation for all" philosophy, also referred to as the recreation for recreation's sake perspective, commonly referred to today as so-called "diversional programming" (Navar, 1979, p. 190).

1952 A Recreation Therapy Section is established with the Recreation Division of the American Association for Health, Physical Education, and Recreation. The primary emphasis of this membership focused on recreation and adapted physical education and sport programs in special and public schools.

1953 The National Association of Recreational Therapists (NART) is organized. This membership was comprised essentially of personnel from state hospitals and schools and was concerned with the clinical practice of therapeutic recreation, the major premise of this group being that recreation could serve as an intervention, a specific tool of treatment or rehabilitation effective in combatting problems associated with primary disabilities (Austin, 1986).

1953 The Council for Advancement of Hospital Recreation (CAHR) was formed to serve as the structure for enabling all three professional organizations (NART, HRS, and RT-AAHPER) to have a common dialogue.

1959 A merger committee within CAHR is formed to discuss a plan for growth of the profession and possible merger. After four years of work, no agreement regarding direction for the field is reached.

1966 Branch status is given to the National Therapeutic Recreation Society (NTRS) by the relatively new National Recreation and Park Association (formed in 1965). Members of NTRS constitute the combined membership of NART and the Hospital Recreation Section of ARS. The Recreation Therapy Section of AAHPER continues independently with its focus on schools and education (a mission which eventually becomes subdivided within AAHPERD among several different host organizations and professional councils). The voluntary registration plan for personnel begun by CAHR in 1956 remains intact and is administered by NTRS.

1971 The first regional training symposia for TR personnel is established—the Midwest Symposium on Therapeutic Recreation (hosted by The University of Illinois). Subsequent regional symposia are developed as the NTRS front-line of continuing education training for its membership.

1978 The Therapeutic Recreation Management School at Ogelby Park, Wheeling, West Virginia, is established as a formal post-degree in-service training alternative.

1978 NTRS Board of Directors approves and publishes Community TR standards of practice "Guidelines for Community-Based Programs for Special Populations."

1979 Clinical Standards of Practice are Published by NTRS.

1981 The National Council for Therapeutic Recreation Certification (NCTRC) becomes a completely autonomous credentialing body. From this point forward the content and process of credentialling personnel are independent of NRPA/NTRS and AALR.

1982 Residential Facility Standards of practice are published by NTRS.

1984 The American Therapeutic Recreation Association (ATRA) is founded. Fifty key founding members and leaders include several past-presidents and board members of NTRS. The focus of the new organization is to provide for more aggressive growth of clinical practice and specialization within TR.

1993 ATRA's membership eclipses that of NTRS. By January of 1995 ATRA's membership numbers swell to over 3,650 while NTRS's membership declines below 2,000. However, neither organization can claim representativeness for a workforce estimated by the U.S. Department of Labor in excess of 32,000 (Huston, 1994).

1995 For the second time in its short ten year history the ATRA membership considers a formal change in name to ARTA (American Recreational Therapy Association). The name change is considered symbolic by many of the commitment by ATRA to the "clinical" mission of therapeutic recreation. An evenly divided membership fails by ballot to pass the measure. The attempt however serves as a reminder to leadership and others of how deep and emotionally charged the philosophical division over philosophy and mission is for the general membership (Austin, 1994).

Professional Organizations Summary. The early organizations concerned with TR were composed essentially of different subspecialties of TR practitioners, each more or less concerned with its own constituency and service setting. After years of discussion and meetings, the failure of CAHR to find common ground and thus a more unified front for the three national organizations is symptomatic of how deep the philosophical divisions were. Then, remarkably, the number of groups concerned with TR shrank from three to one. (From a pragmatic viewpoint RT-AAHPER did not last long as a formal group within AAHPER after the formation of NTRS and asserted less and less influence regarding clinical practice.) Following the example set by the "parent" body of NRPA, where in 1965, five separate recreation organizations formed together into one. Within one year the three TR organizations were finally able to achieve a working alliance, and thus NTRS was established as a branch group under NRPA. Basic philosophical incompatibilities troubled NTRS, however, (as is evidenced in other sections of this chapter) most notably credentials and curricula served as focal points of derisiveness resulting in frequent and radical shifts in basic services and messages to the membership. Finally, in 1984 the beginning of the "unravelling" of the NTRS coalition gained formal momentum with the formation of ATRA. Many of the founding members of ATRA were past-presidents and former board of director's members of NTRS. Impatient with slow progress and tired of bureaucratic foot-dragging within NTRS/NRPA on key issues such as curriculum and clinical/health care delivery services, these individuals decided that the subspecialty of TR needed a more focussed organizational advocate. And so once again, the field of TR claimed more than one national organization concerned with development of the profession.

Regarding the long-term historical perspective, NTRS to date (mainly as a function of longevity) has accomplished a great deal for its membership in terms of fulfilling the criteria for a professional organization. Publishing practice standards in 1979, 1981, and 1982, establishing conventions (1971), conferences (1978), and taking the lead in consumer advocacy and political agitation with JCAH and CART (see service ethic section of this chapter), and publishing the premier scientific journal in the field (TRJ).

However, within its short ten year history ATRA has similarly accomplished a great deal. The ATRA press has placed important materials regarding TR research (Malkin & Howe, 1993), quality assurance (Riley, 1991), and clinical practice (Skalko, et al., 1995) into the professional literature. Key to this contribution has been the reemergence of a second scientific journal dedicated exclusively to TR content, the Annual in TR (1990). In addition, the further refinement of clinical practice standards across health care accreditation organizations in the 1990s (see service this section of this chapter e.g., JCAHCO 1992, CARF 1988, and Medicare/Medicaid 1993) must in the main be credited to the ATRA lobby and membership. ATRA's contribution to continuing education, as witnessed by both its national conferences (beginning in 1986) and mid-year meetings (beginning in 1987) has come at an important time as the national membership credentialed as CTRS's look for both depth of content and relative ease and efficiency in obtaining CEU credits. Finally, with the appointment of a full time executive director in the fall of 1994, ATRA became the first therapeutic recreation organization to have a full time staff member whose responsibilities are exclusively directed toward the betterment of the therapeutic recreation profession.

However, the creation of ATRA as a "specialty" organization narrowly focussed toward clinical services and health care provision is potentially problematic for TR. Not unlike an adolescent seeking to resolve an identity crisis, the TR profession is now pulled in different directions simultaneously. On the short term ATRA, as an independent and clinically focussed body, has indeed been able to make relatively swift and dramatic impacts on the delivery of clinical TR service. However, for the long haul, the profession's macropolitical clout may be damaged by membership dilution across two national groups. Short term advantages in the clinical world may prove somewhat empty if these gains are made to the detriment of the total profession's ability to present its service ethic clearly to the public. In Chapter 18 on Trends and Issues, more of the concerns regarding multinational organizations are presented.

Service Motive

Truly professional people are dedicated to a particular service motive. The improvement of society is first, and the betterment of their profession next. Traditionally then professionals have been viewed as altruistic, looking out for society (although in contemporary times this has become somewhat tarnished due to teacher and nursing strikes). When groups let their own importance or well being overshadow service, as is the case with most traditional blue collar occupations and their labor unions, then society tends to view them as a nonprofessional service provider.

What is the historical case for therapeutic recreation in demonstrating a true service ethic? Most historians of therapeutic recreation point to the organization of the Boston Sand Gardens in 1885 not only as the beginning of truly professional recreation services in the United States (Kennedy, Austin, & Smith, 1991), but also as the first true public therapeutic recreation program because of its emphasis on serving the economically disadvantaged. How did the public's view of the service motive build from this departure point? (Note: some also claim the Sand Gardens as the beginning of the American Playground Movement; Bruya and Langendorfer, 1988). A brief chronology which highlights key events related to service motive will serve to demonstrate both the diversity and relative newness of this aspect of the profession.

1893 The "Industrial Home for the Blind" in New York City was established to provide among other things recreation experiences for its clients (Avedon, 1974, p. 12).

1905 The "Lighthouse" (Another New York association for the blind) added the donation of theater and concert tickets as part of its services (Avedon, 1974, p. 12).

1913 The American Journal of Insanity details how one hospital chartered a train and took 500 patients on a picnic for curative and restorative benefits (Avedon, 1974, p. 12).

1914 The Jewish Guild for the Blind cites as one of its original purposes the provision of a recreation center (Avedon, 1974, p. 13).

1915 The director of the Vineland Institute (New Jersey) publishes an account of the use of games and play to help develop self-control, coordination, and manner in the mentally retarded (Avedon, 1974, p. 14).

1919 The American Red Cross formally organizes a division of recreation in hospitals (by 1930 there are 117 full time Red Cross hospital recreation workers) (Navar, 1979, p. 88).

1932 The White House Conference on Child Health and Protection acknowledged the need for recreation as one element essential in supplementing social reform (Carter, Van Andel, & Robb, 1985, p. 47).

1938 The term therapeutic recreation first appears in federal legislation as part of the creation of the Works Progress Administration (WPA) (Shivers & Fait, 1985 p. 7).

1944 The first Community Center entirely devoted to serving older adults was started by the New York City Department of Welfare (Avedon, 1974, p. 15)

1965 The first organized attempt to develop uniform standards of practice for the delivery of therapeutic recreation gets underway via the Council for Advancement of Hospital Recreation (CAHR).

1978 Standards of practice for the delivery of therapeutic recreation in community-based programs are printed by the National Therapeutic Recreation Society (NTRS).

1979 Standards of practice in ten specialized areas of clinical and residential service settings are formalized by NTRS.

1980 NTRS begins a dialogue with both the Joint Commission on Accreditation of Hospitals (JCAH) and the Commission on Accreditation of Rehabilitation Facilities (CARF) to see that standards of practice intended to protect the consumer become part of the standard review process of accreditation of facilities. Eventually, both bodies adopt key elements of the NTRS standards (JCAH in 1981 and CARF in 1982).

1982 The NTRS membership and board of directors formally adopt a national philosophical position statement as a declaration to the public of the mission of NTRS. It should be noted, however, that this adoption was not without controversy. Both a very low membership voting turnout and the very divided results of balloting (four different positions were voted on) contributed to post-decision derisiveness within the profession (Ollson,1989).

1988 The Council for the Accreditation of Rehabilitation Facilities' (CARF) new standards recognize the CTRS credential for the first time. Subsequently, demands on the national job market for CTRS's increase 120% over the next calendar year.

1990 The NTRS membership and board of directors formally adopt "Standards for Practice" toward the goal of assuring unified delivery of the service motive across practitioners and service settings.

1991 The American Therapeutic Recreation Association (ATRA) membership and board of directors publish their version of "Standards of Practice." The document includes twelve points and requires, among other points, the credentialing of all ATRA members through the National Council for Therapeutic Recreation Certification (NCTRC) and pledges to uphold confidentiality of clients, practice individualized treatment planning, and adhere to the ATRA Code of Ethics.

1992 The Joint Commission for the Accreditation of Health Care Organizations (JCAHO) recognizes recreational therapy within its standards as a formal rehabilitation therapy. These standards actually recognized RT along with its sister therapies: Occupational, Physical, and Speech Therapy (all members of the newly organized National Coalition of ARTs Therapies).

1995 The Comprehensive Accreditation Manual for Hospitals (CAMH) published by the Joint Commission of the Accreditation of Health Care Organizations defines for the first time recreational therapist, qualified and recreational therapy assistant/technician, qualified. The development and adoption of these definitions were a joint venture by both ATRA and NCTRC.

Service Motive Summary. As can be seen by this brief revisit to early beginnings the public demonstration of the service motive of therapeutic recreation began in an unorganized fashion. Chiefly concerned with betterment of life quality for specific disability groups, private advocacy organizations developed the first delivery of services programs. Not until the formal organization of the National Therapeutic Recreation Society (1965) did more "umbrella" or inclusive acts of advocacy take shape and push forward a well-articulated national agenda. Even then, a well-articulated national philosophy statement was not formally adopted until 1982, and shortly thereafter fractured again in 1985 with the return to multiple national organizations. The arrival of two distinct Codes of Ethics barely a year apart (one by NTRS, the other by ATRA) created a potential dualism in membership allegiance which was at best confusing and at worst divisive. As the reader should recall from the previous section of this chapter devoted to professional organizations, the quest for a national philosophy of therapeutic recreation and unified service motive remains a point of controversy, debate, and potential division within the field. Finally, in the 1990s (largely as a result of the ATRA lobby) the refinement of the professional mission in clinical and health care facilities became increasingly refined as the major national organizations in facility accreditation adopted TR standards.

Scientific Basis

Simply put, this means that there is a body of facts related to the professional practice. Not only are the governing laws and principles of a profession supposedly guided by this body of knowledge, but also the applied and practical delivery of service is governed by certain fundamental consistencies. Consistent with the acquisition of a body of knowledge is the public display or demonstration of such. Thus a body of literature as demonstrated through professional journals, books, and other publications is an index of the vitality and soundness of a profession. Without specific references to point to in defense of practices and skills, the individual practitioner lacks a professional stature.

When did the scientific basis for the provision of therapeutic recreation begin in this country? What evidence has accumulated in support of a scientific body of literature?

1919 The first "manual" concerned with recreation and illness was published "Hospital and Bedside Games" (cited in Avedon, 1974, p. 15).

1932 The use of recreation in chronic psychiatric settings is published in a text

"Emotion and Sport" (cited in Avedon, 1974, p. 15).

1932 "The Selection and Use of Games in Cases of Cardiac Insufficiency" represents the extension of recreation into the treatment of acute illness and disability (cited in Avedon, 1974, p. 15).

1932 One of the very first experimental design projects regarding recreation is completed at the Lincoln State School and Colony in Illinois. The results indicate that responses of retarded children can be significantly improved through the use of play activities (cited in Carter, Van Andel, & Robb, 1985, p. 55).

1933 The book "Psychoanalytic Theory of Play" extends the case for recreation as a part of the psychoanalytic school of psychology (cited in Avedon, 1974, p. 15).

1954 Publication of "Recreation in Treatment Centers" an annual collection of therapeutic recreation research is begun by the Hospital Recreation Section of the American Recreation Society and is published until 1969.

1955 One of the earliest university textbooks available is printed: "Recreation for the Handicapped" by Valeric Hunt (cited in Carter, Van Andel, & Robb, 1985, p. 55).

1958 The National Recreation Association commissioned a study that involved more than 6000 hospitals/institutions as the first major cataloging of personnel, content, and clients served in therapeutic recreation programming (cited in Reynolds & O'Morrow, 1985, p. 129).

1959 "Recreation in Total Rehabilitation" by Rathbone and Lucas provided one of the first comprehensive technical manuals on provision of therapeutic recreation services.

1957 A quarterly journal "Recreation for the Ill and Handicapped" is developed by the National Association of Recreational Therapists and is published until 1967.

1967 NTRS begins the publication of the "Therapeutic Recreation Journal" as a replacement journal for "Recreation for the Ill and Handicapped" (publication of TRJ continues through to present day).

1970 NTRS begins the publication of the "Therapeutic Recreation Annual" as a replacement for "Recreation in Treatment Centers" (however the TR Annual survives only through five volumes and leaves the TRJ as the only professional journal published by NTRS).

1970s A small flurry of new academic textbooks begins as curricula diversify with such works as: Frye and Peters (1972); Kraus (1973); Stein and Sessoms (1973); Avedon (1974); Shivers and Fait (1975); O'Morrow and Reynolds (1976); Peterson and Gunn, (1978); and Kaplan (1979).

1972 Frye and Peters (1972) report that one third of all studies within therapeutic recreation had been completed since 1963.

1973 Martin reported that between 1965 and 1973 a total of 210 research studies appeared either in professional journals, or conference and symposia proceedings.

1980s Clinical specialization of textbooks begins as new titles based on specific populations and models of service appear: Austin (1982); Teaff (1985); Carter, Van Andel, and Robb (1985); Kennedy, Austin, and Smith (1987) Crawford and Mendell (1987).

1986 "The Journal of Expanding Horizons in Therapeutic Recreation" is begun by the

University of Missouri as the second contemporary referred journal (TRJ being the first) dedicated exclusively to therapeutic recreation.

1990 The "Annual in Therapeutic Recreation" is published as a joint venture between the University of Missouri, the American Therapeutic Recreation Association, and the American Association of Leisure and Recreation. The "Journal of Expanding Horizons" closes after just three volumes; however, its editorial mission is refined and forms the cornerstone for the new Annual. After two years the Annual becomes the sole responsibility of ATRA.

1990s The clinical specialization of textbooks accelerates with particular focus on applied research techniques (Malkin & Howe, 1993), clinical case studies (Wilhite & Keller, 1992), assessment and evaluation (Burlingame, 1990), medications and medical terminology (Skalko et al., 1995), and quality assurance management (Riley, 1991).

1991 A national conference on therapeutic recreation research and benefits is hosted by Temple University, funded by the National Institute on Disability and Rehabilitation Research. A summary monograph is published in which a typology of six global "benefits" to TR is validated. The review of research covers over 135 studies from 1973 to 1990 across 30 interdisciplinary journals and represents the most exhaustive meta-analysis of research in TR in the history of the profession (Coyle et al., 1991).

Scientific Basis Summary. Early technical manuals based upon a mixture of theory and case study approaches slowly gave way to more rigorous scientific inquiry in the 1950s. However the real knowledge explosion within the field did not really begin until the 1960s. As increasingly diverse clinical services documented therapeutic recreation effectiveness, the design of textbooks moved from the early comprehensive approaches of the 1970s (which attempted more or less to deal with total knowledge organization) to client directed or specialized service driven approaches of the 1980s and '90s. This evolution of textbook organization documents in part the rapid expansion of the knowledge base into more specialized areas of client service and care. The organization of a second contemporary national journal by ATRA distinct from NTRS's also speaks indirectly to the expanded vitality of the literature and research base of the young therapeutic recreation profession. The meta-analysis research review completed through the Temple University grant in the early 1990s provided a much needed national template for research priorities. Prior to this document, the diverse, geographically scattered, and all too thin ranks of TR researchers had little guidance in setting research goals that would lead to national high priority outcomes for the development of the profession or in interpreting and placing their work into a cohesive and comprehensive model of TR services and benefits.

Extended Preparation of Personnel

To ensure that the body of knowledge which constitutes the profession is properly utilized, extended years of preparation and training are required. There are two subcomponents to this process. One is the challenge of obtaining specialized skills that are unique (for example the skills of surgery an M.D. must acquire, or the ability to assess psychological functioning through IQ scales that the psychologist strives for, etc.). The second is to provide for the attainment of these skills under uniform standards that culminate in the awarding of a formal degree. For most contemporary professions the baccalaureate degree is rapidly becoming inadequate, or obsolete, as evidence that one is a professional; usually at least one or more graduate or professional degrees are now required for admission to truly professional ranks (for example, although there are any number of bachelor's degrees available in psychology, one is not considered to be a "psychologist" until at least obtaining a masters or doctoral degree in the field; in fact, in most states the doctorate is required for someone to practice as and call oneself a "psychologist").

How has the field of therapeutic recreation progressed relative to the question of extended preparation of personnel?

1909 The first known course in professional recreation is taught at an institution of higher learning (Carter, Van Andel, & Robb, 1985, p. 53).

1926 The first formal training school devoted solely to the training of professional recreation personnel is established and called the "National Recreation Association's Leadership Training School" (Navar, 1979, p. 189).

1931 New York University offers the first university curriculum in recreation.

1950 The University of Minnesota offers the first university curriculum in therapeutic recreation (Navar, 1979, p. 190).

1953 A study by the Standards and Training Committee of the Hospital Recreation Section of the American Recreation Society reported 6 colleges and universities with graduate or undergraduate degrees in hospital recreation (Carter, Van Andel, & Robb, 1985, p. 53).

1961 The National Recreation Association sponsored a therapeutic recreation curriculum development conference, the first nationally organized effort to identify general competencies needed by recreation personnel in hospital settings.

1963 The Rehabilitation Services Administration of the U.S. Department of Health, Education and Welfare provided funds to selected colleges and universities for graduate study in therapeutic recreation (Reynolds & O'Morrow, 1985, p. 113).

1968 A national Recreation Education Accreditation Project (begun originally in 1963) published therapeutic recreation emphasis criteria for both undergraduate and graduate levels of study (Carter, Van Andel, & Robb, 1985, p. 53).

1969 A national study identified 28 undergraduate and 26 graduate programs in therapeutic recreation (Carter, Van Andel, & Robb, 1985, p. 53).

1975 The first standards for the accreditation of recreation curricula in colleges and universities are implemented by the National Recreation and Park Association in concert with the American Association of Leisure and Recreation. The first standards for therapeutic recreation are accepted by this body in 1976.

1979 A national study identified a total of 116 undergraduate therapeutic recreation programs and another 34 master's degree programs (Carter, Van Andel, & Robb, 1985, p. 54).

1984 A national survey by the Society of Park and Recreation Educators catalogs a total of 98 undergraduate and 55 graduate programs of study in therapeutic recreation across a total of 260 responding institutions.

1987 The National Council on Post-secondary Accreditation formally recognizes the NRPA/AALR accreditation of educational standards and programs; a kind of national "good housekeeping seal of approval" is thus extended. This event represents a landmark legitimization of the quality of post secondary curricula in therapeutic recreation.

1988 Nationwide, a total of 81 Universities are accredited based on the NRPA/AALR Council for Accreditation standards; 37 of these have TR options.

1988 In a move that "rankles" many educators the NCTRC sets forth content coursework guidelines for the review of certification eligibility of professionals. Specific course titles and content are deemed appropriate or inappropriate for both TR and general recreation/leisure studies courses. Many university and college programs are forced to re-title and re-think their content offerings in order for their graduates to be certification eligible (these standards are revised and further sharpened in 1993).

1995 The list of accredited university curricula in recreation and leisure studies grows to 94, with 39 of these having TR options.

1995 ATRA sets a focus on higher education and curriculum reform in TR as a 3-day focus for its national mid-year conference. A national panel and 65 participants debate the indicators of TR coursework content, patterns, and needs and establish a set of reform and developmental priorities for curriculum planners.

Extended Preparation of Personnel Summary. The great span of time between the early pioneering initiatives of the 1900s through 1930s and flurry of expanded activity in the 60s and 70s demonstrate well the slow and sporadic growth of the field from a service provider to professional delivery status. The contemporary identification of content for standards was a tedious and time consuming process beginning in the early 1970s and spanning some 20 plus years (in fact, it is ongoing). The difficulty of this process was due in part to the characteristically slow nature of a multi-organization enterprises (AALR and NRPA working together) but probably more a function of trying to statistically and definitively organize a very rapidly expanding field. Even so the accreditation standards as they exist today have been criticized as being based on "minimal standards"; in other words, lacking sufficient regulatory teeth to clearly distinguish between exceptional and marginal programs. Despite its many critics (and the fact that it remains a voluntary process) the national accreditation of curricula at a minimum has facilitated the following: (1) improvement in the quality of professional preparation at a national level by helping to overcome in part the diversity that has existed across curricula, (2) promotion of inter-organizational communication, and (3) assisted in building a more successful and positive image of the therapeutic recreation profession among the lay public (O'Morrow and Reynolds, 1989, p. 319). Perhaps the most dramatic catalyst to reform of TR curriculum has not come from TR educators and/or accreditation standards but from the NCTRC personnel certification standards. When faced with the unpleasant possibility of having their alumnists deemed ineligible for certification as a CTRS, many institutions who had not supported the accreditation of curricula by options were in effect "forced" to at least ensure that their course titles and content fell in line with the professionalization (and many would say clinicalization) of the TR curricula as envisioned by the NCTRC leadership. During the early period of acclimatization to the new certification standards, many educators privately and otherwise "grumbled" about the "tail wagging the dog" process of curriculum reform in TR. Still the uniform curriculum standards put in place by NCTRC have been at least as influential (if not more so) than the accreditation process itself in defining the minimum standards of personnel preparation.

Autonomy of Judgement

True professionals are granted by society the authority to exercise personal responsibility to practice in accord with professional standards of their field. In most cases society has seen fit to set up licensing or certification standards for these professions in order to protect the consumer and ensure that the individual practitioner meets acceptable standards of competency. Thus, simply fulfilling the requirement for extended preparation by getting a degree or diploma, (for example, graduating from medical school is not enough), the new professional must prove his mastery of knowledge by passing state licensing examinations before he or she is entrusted with the authority to exercise autonomy of judgment.

In therapeutic recreation the issue of autonomy of judgment has been a relatively recent one.

1944 A publication by the National Recreation Association states that "a demand had arisen for recreation leadership personnel with proper qualifications" (cited in Navar, 1979, p. 117).

1950 The state of California Recreation Commission published a book of standards for recreation personnel.

1956 The Council for Advancement of Hospital Recreation (CAHR) formulates standards for qualifying hospital recreation personnel. A national voluntary registration plan with three levels: director, leader, and aide is implemented (Carter, Van Andel, & Robb, 1985, p. 52).

1961 The American Medical Association officially designates recreation service as an allied health field (Reynolds & O'Morrow, 1985).

1965 The original voluntary registration plan developed by CAHR in 1956 is taken over by NTRS.

1969 The first extensive revision of the national registry standards for therapeutic recreation personnel takes place under NTRS administration.

1969–1980 During this period of time, no less than six revisions are made to the registration process. These were in the main reactive alterations in light of curriculum improvements and employment standards of the field (cited in Carter, Van Andel, & Robb 1985, p. 57).

1975 The state of Utah established a licensing procedure for therapeutic recreation personnel. All persons wishing to "practice" as recreational therapists must pass a state examination and be licensed to do so. This move on the part of TR leadership within Utah is taken without endorsement or consent of the national leadership. Many criticize it as premature given the relative youth of the TR profession. The state of Georgia follows suit in 1981 with a licensure law of its own.

1976 NTRS establishes the Continuing Professional Development Review Board (CPD) to review, endorse, and increase the number of therapeutic recreation training opportunities for practitioners. The goal of this Board is to maintain a competent professional work force.

1981 The National Council for Therapeutic Recreation Certification (NCTRC) is formed as an independent entity (independent of NRPA and NTRS) for the sole purpose of managing and administering the certification and re-certification of therapeutic recreation personnel.

1986 A model practice act for state organizations to utilize in planning licensure bills for their state court houses is endorsed by the NTRS.

1987 Formal commitment to a national certification exam is made by NCTRC via a signed contract with the Educational Testing Service to conduct a national job analysis survey with the membership (Sable, 1988).

1990 NCTRC in conjunction with ETS conducts the first national certification exam in therapeutic recreation. A total of 3,306 practitioners sit for the exam (96.4% pass).

1991 NCTRC publishes a three-pronged recertification program in which clinicians can maintain their credentials through a combination of retesting, continuing education experiences, and credit for employment and service to the profession. (This plan was approved in concept as early as April of 1990 but was not published until after the first administration of the certification exam. The lack of coordination or time lag in publishing the certification and recertification standards once again draws the ire of many of the membership.)

1991 The state of Georgia's licensure act for therapeutic recreation specialists passes out of existence as a function of the State's legislative sunshine provisions leaving Utah as the only state with licensure of TR practitioners.

1992 The state of North Carolina passes a title protection act, a limited form of licensure that ensures no individual can use the credentials or title of a recreation therapist unless so "licensed" to do so. The act, however, does not prevent sister disciplines from engaging in similar content practice. Thus, occupational therapists and activity directors are free to do leisure education, leisure counseling, play skill development, etc., so long as they do not call the process therapeutic recreation or claim to be recreational therapists (Olsson, 1995).

1994 NCTRC announces the phase out of the Certified Therapeutic Recreation Assistant (CTRA) program by 1999. Originally created to emulate the development of para-professional programming assistants in the tradition of sister therapies (occupational and physical therapy) a combination of low workforce interest (only 356 CTRA's throughout ten year period), lack of consensus and control regarding preparation programs, and overall cost of operation all contributed to the demise of the credential.

1995 The number of individuals credentialed as CTRSs by NCTRC grows in excess of 13,000, however, the national workforce as estimated by the U.S. Department of Labor Statistics is reported at over 32,000. Thus, to the chagrin of national leadership, only a scant 40% of those individuals employed as recreational therapists are professional enough to credential themselves through the national organization (Huston, 1994).

Autonomy of Judgement Summary. From 1956 to 1969 the voluntary registration of therapeutic recreation professionals remained essentially unchanged. The confusion that followed as a result of six changes in the period from 1969 to 1980 is better understood in light of these prior 14 years of stability. Thus, from the perspective of some, the creation of NTRS (1966) brought about radical and seemingly unending changes in organizational stability and professional identity. Dissent among the work force during this period of rapid change and resulting confusion were further exacerbated by the fact that although a formal merger of TR organizations had taken place in creating NTRS (see professional organizations section of this chapter) a merger of philosophies within the newly joined membership had not really been facilitated. Further, the move from a national registry (a simple cataloging procedure) to a certification plan (with criteria/standards and requirements) and ultimately national testing served to alienate significant portions of the membership. Many of the field's so-called "old-timers" felt intimidated and "left out" by the rapid new march toward stricter standards. Others were simply opposed philosophically to the direction and intent of the certification program. Despite allowances for non-degree professionals (grandfather clauses allowing people with work experience to qualify for professional certification) many cried elitism and refused to participate in the process.

The next logical extension of autonomy of judgment for the field, licensure, was not initially endorsed by NTRS. The states of Utah and Georgia found it necessary to act alone in the creation of their state licensure programs. Although NTRS did eventually develop a model practice act or licensure bill for states to look at, the very issue of licensure for TR professionals (the governmental definition, monitoring, and restriction of professional practice to protect the interest of the public) is viewed by many scholars as premature (Carter, 1984) and is still hotly debated. The fact that so few states have successfully addressed the issue adds to the controversy (more about the issue of licensure of TR personnel can be found in Chapter 18 on Trends and Issues).

The early history of the National Certification Exam was not without controversy. New cries of elitism once again echoed throughout the membership; some individuals and state societies even considered legal action to block implementation of the exam process. The NCTRC leadership did not help matters by providing exam access via a limited number of test sites (only 15 initial cities were involved in the initial testing leaving many individuals financially pressed due to travel/time impediments). Further, the fact that the exam process was put in place in advance of a well-articulated recertification process or plan fueled ideological arguments about the wisdom of certifying a workforce you could neither decertify for cause, or recertify with some reasonable assurance of quality. Despite these "rocky" beginnings, a critically important developmental step was taken by the TR profession in implementing the national testing standard. Therapeutic recreation had in one giant stride gained tremendous ground toward catching its sister therapies (and market place competitors) and begun in earnest the developmental transition from adolescence to young adulthood.

Code of Ethics

A true professional serves his or her constituency on the basis of a set of ethical standards and practices which govern all members. Key to this code of ethics being accepted as a valid measure of professionalism by the public is a means or mechanism for insuring compliance with the code by its practicing members. Thus not only can membership to the profession be granted on the basis of competency, but also stripped from an individual based upon his or her misconduct as related to those competencies.

1953 A committee within the Hospital Recreation Section of the American Recreation Society published a document entitled "Basic Concepts of Hospital Recreation" which among other things asserted basic responsibilities of recreators as members of an adjunctive therapy (O'Morrow, p. 119).

1973 Following a national field study, a preliminary Code of Ethics Draft is prepared by the NRPA Code of Ethics Committee.

1976 A statement of a professional ethics is finalized for three branches of NRPA including the National Therapeutic Recreation Society (Carter, Van Andel, & Robb, 1985, p. 55).

1984 NCTRC establishes an ethics board whose chief responsibility is limited to policing the credentialling process to ensure that falsification of personal data is not tolerated.

1985 ATRA establishes a national ethics committee and charges it specifically to begin work on a draft code of ethics for the organization.

1989 The NCTRC ethics board receives a name change—the new Disciplinary Action Board is asked to take on an expanded mission regarding the credentialling process, particularly as it relates to student internship sites and process.

1990 The NTRS membership and Board of Directors adopt a Code of Ethics for all practitioners to follow to ensure that certain basic human and legal rights of clients and families are protected during the delivery of therapeutic recreation services.

1990 The ATRA membership and Board of Directors approve their version of a professional Code of Ethics. Key among the eight principles the membership must swear to uphold are professional competence, client confidentiality, and informed treatment consent.

1992 ATRA establishes a national council for consumer representation. The consumer advisor council charge is to ensure that practice standards and services coincide with consumer needs.

1992 NCTRC expands in certification eligibility guidelines to require professionals to notify the national office of any indictment, charge, or criminal proceeding directly relating to the practice of therapeutic recreation. Failure to notify can result in loss of credentials or certification eligibility. In addition, acts of repeated or gross negligence, habitual use of alcohol or other substances which might impair professional judgment, and/or felony convictions or pleas of guilty as they relate to TR practice become grounds for loss of credentials.

Code of Ethics Summary. In the early 1970s through the 1980s little progress was made toward a national Code of Ethics. While a joint committee of AALR/NRPA remained active, the compliance aspect of the 1976 code remained an individual voluntary act. Suddenly in the 1990s, TR practitioners were inundated with Codes of Ethics as NTRS (1990) ATRA (1990) and NCTRC all came out with substantive documents. However, only the NCTRC standards have the benefit of a formal enforcement mechanism, and even this disciplinary process relates solely to the credentialing and/or decredentialing of practitioners for the CTRS credential. It should be noted that litigative appeals or tests regarding the NCTRC disciplinary board rulings have yet to occur (Rappaport, 1995). At any rate, since the majority of practitioners are neither members of ATRA or NTRS, or have even credentialed themselves as CTRS's much of the "professional" practice of therapeutic recreation remains unregulated. Further, since there is no formal communication at present between state credentialling bodies and the NCTRC, even sanction or loss of the CTRS credential would not prevent an individual from continuing to work within the field. The major problem with this aspect of professional development remains one of oversight and enforcement. Chapter 18 on Trends and Issues discusses further the challenge that this area of professionalism presents in the future.

SUMMARY

This chapter has presented a snapshot in time of the professional evolution of the young field of therapeutic recreation. This was accomplished by first tracing the historical roots provided by ancient civilizations where the fundamentals of specialized treatment centers, physician prescription, the case study approach, and activities applied for restorative purposes were first practiced. The leaders of the "treatment with care" era heralded not only a radical departure form the brutal treatment of medieval Europe but the beginning of the modern era of services. During the modern era, key medical and political leaders furthered the cause of therapeutic recreation. Their actions in concert with the landmark legislative acts of the '60s and '70s provided a rich medica for cultural change in the U.S. regarding philosophy and practice of rehabilitative and habilitative care.

The current status of the TR movement as a profession was reviewed by applying a chronological approach in annotating key events against a model of professionalism. Review of the TR service motive, professional organizations, scientific basis, extended preparation of personnel, autonomy of judgment, and code of ethics revealed a young field striving toward fulfillment of criteria to meet "professional" status. In Chapter 18 trends and issues that relate to further growth in these areas are addressed.

READING COMPREHENSION QUESTIONS

1. Which ancient culture was responsible for introducing the concept of medical malpractice? Which one is credited with establishing the hospital system?
2. In post-twentieth century Europe, persons from which disability group were sometimes labeled as possessed and burned at the stake?
3. What world events helped to trigger the "treatment with care" era in this country?
4. Can you name three important early leaders of the modern treatment era and briefly recount their contributions?
5. Which law required that buildings and facilities constructed with federal monies be made accessible for the handicapped?
6. In which law is recreation listed as a related service for handicapped children to receive?
7. Can you differentiate between a profession and a trade or semi-skilled group? What are the six characteristics of a profession?
8. What is considered to be the first public demonstration of the TR service motive?
9. What are the two national hospital and institutional accrediting bodies that NTRS worked with to ensure that modern standards of practice were established?
10. When did the knowledge explosion in TR take place in this country?
11. Can you define the two subcomponents to extended preparation of personnel as a characteristic of a profession?
12. Can you identify positive contributions made by national accreditation standards for TR education? What is the major criticism of these standards?
13. What is the predominant assumption behind autonomy of judgment as a characteristic of a profession?
14. Which two states have licensure laws that regulate delivery of TR services?
15. What is a controversial aspect of the current approach to certification taken by NCTRC? Why was NCTRC established?
16. What philosophical connection do the old NART and modern ATRA organizations share in common?
17. Which organization has contributed the most to political agitation and consumer advocacy for the field of TR? What are the contributions?
18. Which of the six characteristics of professionalism is the most underdeveloped within TR?

REFERENCES

Austin, D.R. (1982). *Therapeutic recreation: Processes and techniques.* New York: John Wiley & Sons, Inc.

Austin, D.R. (1986). The helping profession: You do make a difference. In A. James & F. McGuire (Eds.), *Selected papers from the 1985 southeast therapeutic recreation symposium.* Clemson University Extension Services.

Austin, D.R. (1987). Therapeutic recreation. In A. Graef & S. Parker (Eds.), *Recreation and leisure: An introductory handbook* (pp. 155–557). State College, PA: Venture Publishing, Inc.

Austin, D.R. (1994). President's message. *ATRA Newsletter,* (6), 1. Hattiesburg, MS: ATRA Press.

Avedon, E.M. (1974). *Therapeutic recreation service: An applied behavioral science approach.* Englewood Cliffs, NJ: Prentice Hall.

Bruya, L.D., & Langendorfer, S.J. (1988). *Where our children play: Elementary school playground equipment.* Reston, VA: American Alliance for Health, Physical Education, Recreation and Dance.

Burlingame, J., & Blaschko, T. (1990). *Assessment tools for recreational therapy: Red book #1.* Ravensdale, WA: Idyll Arbor Inc.

Carter, M.J. (1984). Issues in continuing professional competence of therapeutic recreators. *Therapeutic Recreation Journal, 18*(3), 7–10.

Carter, M.J., Van Andel, G.E., & Robb, G.M. (1985). *Therapeutic recreation: A practical approach.* St. Louis: Times Mirror/Mosby College Publishing.

Coyle, C., et al. (1991). *Benefits of therapeutic recreation: A consensus view.* Philadelphia, PA: Temple University Press.

Crawford, M.E. (1985). Planning for the handicapped. In R.B. Flynn (Ed.), *Planning facilities for athletics, physical education, and recreation* (3rd ed.). Reston, VA: Athletic Institute.

Crawford, M.E., & Mendell, R. (1987). *Therapeutic recreation and adapted physical activities for mentally retarded individuals.* Englewood Cliffs, NJ: Prentice Hall.

Ellis, G.D., & Witt, P.A. (1986). The leisure diagnostic battery: Past, present, and future. *Therapeutic Recreation Journal, 20*(4), 31–47.

Frye, V., & Peters, M. (1972). *Therapeutic recreation: Its theory, philosophy and practice.* Harrisburg, PA: Stackpole Co.

Gunn, S.L., & Person, C.A. (1978). *Therapeutic recreation program design: Principles and procedures.* Englewood Cliffs, NJ: Prentice Hall.

Halberg, K.J., & Howe-Murphy, R. (1985). The dilemma of an unresolved philosophy in therapeutic recreation. *Therapeutic Recreation Journal, 19*(3), 7–16.

Huston, A. (1994). Executive director's message. *ATRA Newsletter, 10*(6), 3. Hattiesburg, MS: ATRA Press.

Kaplan, M. (1979). *Leisure, lifestyle and lifespan.* Philadelphia, PA: W.B. Saunders Co.

Kennedy, D.W., Austin, D.R., & Smith, R.W. (1991). *Special recreation: Opportunities for persons with disabilities* (2nd ed.). Dubuque, IA: W.C. Brown Publishers.

Kraus, R. (1973). *Therapeutic recreation service: Principles and practices.* Philadelphia: W.B. Saunders Co.

Meyer, L. (1980). Three philosophical positions of therapeutic recreation and their implications for professionalization and NTRS. *Proceedings of the First Annual Post-Doctoral Institute* (pp. 28–42). Bloomington: Indiana University, Department of Recreation and Park Administration.

Mobily, K.J. (1983). Quality analysis in therapeutic recreation curricula. *Therapeutic Recreation Journal, 17*(1), 18–25.

National Therapeutic Recreation Society. (1982). Philosophical position statement of the national therapeutic recreation society.

Navar, N.H. (1979). *The professionalization of therapeutic recreation in the state of Michigan.* Unpublished dissertation. Bloomington: Indiana University.

Olsson, R. (1988). A survey of southeastern therapeutic recreation specialists: Philosophy, practice and education. *Journal of Expanding Horizons in Therapeutic Recreation, 3*(3), Columbia, MO: University of Missouri Press.

Olsson, R. (1995). Licensure in the 90s: A new frontier. *ATRA Newsletter, 11*(1), 11. Hattiesburg, MS: ATRA Press.

O'Morrow, G.S., & Reynolds, R.P. (1989). *Therapeutic recreation: A helping profession* (3rd ed.). Englewood Cliffs, NJ: Prentice Hall.

Rappaport, T. (1995). Personal communication with author from credentialling specialist for the NCTRC. Thiells, NY.

Reynolds, R.P., & O'Morrow, G. S. (1985). *Problems, issues and concepts in therapeutic recreation.* Englewood Cliffs, NJ: Prentice Hall.

Riley, B. (Ed.). (1991). *Quality management: Applications for therapeutic recreation.* State College, PA: Venture Publishing, Inc.

Sable, J. (1988, February/March). *NCTRC Newsletter.* Spring Valley, NY.

Skalko, T., et al. (1994). *Basic guide to physical and psychiatric medications for recreational therapy.* State College, PA: Venture Publishing, ATRA Publications.

Shivers, J.S., & Fait, H.F. (1975). *Therapeutic and adapted recreational services.* Philadelphia: Lea & Febiger.

Stein, T.A., & Sessoms, D.H. (1973). *Recreation and special populations.* Boston: Holbrook Press.

Strong, C. (1982). Characteristics of a profession. Research Design in the HPER Professions T590 Class Handout Packet. Bloomington, IN: Indiana University Press.

Teaff, J.D. (1985). *Leisure services with the elderly.* St. Louis: C.V. Mosby Co.

Wilhite, B., & Keller, J. (1992). *Therapeutic recreation: Cases and exercises.* State College, PA: Venture Publishing Co.

Wolfensburger, W. (1972). *Normalization: The principal of normalization in human services.* Toronto: National Institute on Mental Retardation.

CHAPTER 3

THE THERAPEUTIC RECREATION PROCESS

DAVID R. AUSTIN

OBJECTIVES

- Describe the TR process, including its four phases.
- Identify methods for completing client assessment.
- Understand elements of concern during the planning phase, including goals and objectives.
- Know the role of the TR specialist during the implementation phase.
- Know the purpose of evaluation in the TR process.
- Identify characteristics of therapeutic activities.

DEFINITION OF THERAPEUTIC RECREATION AND THE TR PROCESS

Therapeutic recreation is a purposeful intervention designed to help clients grow and to assist them to relieve or prevent problems through recreation and leisure. The intervention takes place through an interaction between a professionally prepared therapeutic recreation specialist and a client with whom the therapeutic recreation specialist collaborates. The therapeutic recreation process is used to achieve a higher level of health in the client.

The *therapeutic recreation process* is a systematic problem-solving procedure used by therapeutic recreation specialists to help clients improve their levels of health by meeting identified needs. During a four-phase progression, TR specialists initially assess client health status, needs, and strengths. Next, planning transpires to develop a plan of action to meet goals and objectives that flow out of the assessment phase. The planned intervention is then implemented. Finally, the effect of the intervention on goals and objectives is evaluated. The therapeutic recreation process is the essence of therapeutic recreation in that it provides a base from which all therapeutic recreation actions proceed.

The basis for therapeutic recreation practice must transcend the cognition that recreation, by its nature, is good, so it has benefit to the well-being of all persons, including those who are ill. To justify the profession of therapeutic recreation on the credo of "recreation is good for all" trivializes therapeutic recreation. As Mobily (1987) has explained, therapeutic recreation has instrumental value. Its outcomes are not "accidental and random" but rather are "purposeful and systematic." Therapeutic recreation is a means to an end—the end of health protection and health promotion to enhance the individual's quality of life. Mobily (1985) has exclaimed, "The very cognition of recreation as a means is the distinguishing feature of TR."

INTRODUCTION TO THE THERAPEUTIC RECREATION PROCESS

Purposeful intervention in therapeutic recreation is accomplished through the employment of the therapeutic recreation process. The term *TR process* may seem mysterious when first encountered. It is, however, merely a problem-solving mechanism that therapeutic recreation specialists use to help clients meet needs and thereby maintain, restore, or promote health. It involves four components: assessment, planning, implementation, and evaluation.

Therapeutic recreation specialists initially work with clients to identify their health status, needs, and strengths. This is the *assessment phase.* Possible means to meet the needs are devised during the *planning phase.* Next, the planned intervention is tried out during the *implementation phase.* Finally, outcomes are appraised during the *evaluation phase.*

Assumptions underlying the TR process are as follows:

1. The TR process provides a systematic means for organizing the delivery of therapeutic recreation services.
2. The goal of the TR process is self-actualization by maximizing human potential through the maintenance, restoration, and promotion of health leading to an optimal quality of life.
3. Rather than emphasizing what is "wrong" with the client, the TR process allows the therapeutic recreation specialist to concentrate on client strengths.
4. The client plays as large a role as possible in the TR process. The TR specialist attempts to allow as much control as is reasonable to remain with the client. The TR specialist is the client's partner who facilitates the client's progress toward meeting his or her needs.
5. The TR process helps to define the domain of therapeutic recreation practice.

The Relationship of the TR Specialist and Client

The therapeutic recreation specialist's relationship with the client is the means for applying the TR process. The TR specialist and client work together toward achievement of the client's optimal level of health. There is a mutuality in this relationship.

The relationship between the TR specialist and client is characterized by trust, mutual respect, and positive emotional feelings. The TR specialist is a person with whom the client associates positive outcomes as he or she experiences mastery, control, personal satisfaction, and feelings of effectiveness.

Effective relationships with clients are more easily achieved once we have examined our own values, beliefs, strengths, and limitations. Knowing ourselves is helpful in many ways. It helps us identify and relate more quickly to clients' problems because we can associate their problems with ones we have personally encountered. Having an awareness of our personal values and beliefs allows us to monitor ourselves so we will not attempt to force our own values and beliefs on clients. Acknowledging our strengths and weaknesses brings us to realize that, like our clients, we have strong points and limitations. Knowing our strengths, we can exploit them in helping clients. Understanding our limitations allows us to know when we have reached the limits of our helping abilities (Austin, 1991; Yura & Walsh, 1988). In short, knowing ourselves creates an awareness so that we can consciously use ourselves in therapeutic ways.

Knowing oneself also enhances the therapeutic recreation specialist's ability to foster three aspects that facilitate therapeutic relationships. These are (1) *genuineness,* or the ability to be aware of one's feelings and to be genuine in communicating these; (2) *unconditional positive regard,* or accepting another person nonjudgmentally and without conditions; and (3) *empathy,* or the ability to understand another individual so that you can "put yourself in his or her own place" (Rogers, 1961).

The therapeutic recreation process is applied both in treatment and rehabilitation. *Treatment* follows diagnosis of illness and focuses on reduction of symptoms. *Rehabilitation* is based on assessment of disability and limitations in functioning. It emphasizes the building of a full range of skills, from basic skills (e.g., grooming) to those that are more advanced (e.g., leisure and social skills) (Gudeman, 1988). Rehabilitation follows treatment in that it prepares ("re-ables") clients to function as independently as possible in the setting in which they will eventually reside.

In both treatment and rehabilitation, therapeutic recreation specialists concentrate on strengths rather than what is "wrong" with the client. Client residual abilities are brought into focus in therapeutic recreation. Therapeutic recreation specialists also attempt to allow as much control as possible to remain with the client.

Assessment

The first phase in the TR process is assessment. It is the foundation for all that follows. A sound assessment identifies the client's health status, needs, and strengths. In doing so, the assessment provides direction for the planning phase by developing pertinent data about the client. Assessment is a critical dimension because without adequate and valid data on which to base TR interventions, much time may be lost in effecting treatment and rehabilitation programs.

The therapeutic recreation specialist gathers, organizes, and analyzes assessment data. Following this, he or she must make clinical judgments as to the appropriate application of therapeutic recreation interventions in the client's treatment or rehabilitation program.

Efforts should be made to involve the client in assessment as soon and as much as possible. Some clients obviously will be unable to participate temporarily or will be able to take part only partially. Nevertheless, it is important for the therapeutic recreation specialist to develop rapport so that the client feels comfortable in sharing personal information to the best of his or her abilities. The client needs to have confidence that the information collected is to be used in a confidential manner for the sole purpose of helping him or her toward achieving optimal health.

Even when we establish excellent rapport, client assessment is not as straightforward as it might initially seem. That is, sometimes clients tell us what they believe we want to hear or what they perceive a "good" or "rational" client might say. This occurs with some regularity with chronic psychiatric clients, as we are warned by Kanter (1985), who states that professionals may focus too much on expressed wishes for independence to the exclusion of other concerns. Kanter has written:

> *While we overemphasize the expressed wishes of chronic patients for independence, we often neglect their unarticulated needs to be cared for, understood, and accepted, as well as their fear of abandonment should they actually achieve a measure of autonomy (p. 65).*

Thus, the helping professional must look past the client's verbalizations to examine behavioral expressions of needs, as well as go beyond the client to seek other sources of assessment data. Although the client is typically a chief source of information, other data sources are interviews with family members and friends, conferences with other health professionals, test results, medical records, social histories, educational records, progress notes, and team meetings.

Methods of Assessment. Observing and interviewing are the most commonly employed methods of assessment. Observations in therapeutic recreation are often done in unstructured recreational settings. These *naturalistic observations* are recorded by anecdotal notes, photographs, video, or a combination of these techniques. *Specific goal observations* take place in structured situations where the observer sets predetermined goals for the observation. For example, the therapeutic recreation specialist may structure a situation where frustration is likely to occur in order to observe the client's reaction. *Standardized* *observations* are two types. One is the standardized instrument, such as a physical fitness test. The other type is the time-interval observation where the frequency of client behaviors is recorded for predetermined times. For example, the number of aggressive acts occurring during a one-hour period could be recorded (Schulman, 1978).

Checklists and *questionnaires* are means to gain specific types of information and save time in collecting it. Clients are sometimes asked to complete checklists and questionnaires. At other times, therapeutic recreation specialists collect the data, particularly in cases where clients cannot read or write, are disoriented, or do not have the strength or inclination to fill out the forms. Even when clients complete the checklists or questionnaires, the TR specialist normally has a follow-up interview to clarify and verify the information.

The *interview* is a time to gather information about the client, clarify items not understood, and observe the client's condition and behavior. The therapeutic recreation specialist permits the client to express himself or herself freely and to have any questions answered.

The primary areas examined in interviews by the therapeutic recreation specialist are leisure interest and behaviors. The TR specialist will typically ask clients about past leisure habits, the types of activities in which they participate, with whom they usually take part, and if they can identify recreation interests they may wish to pursue in the future. Regularly used techniques to enhance the interview process are (1) open-ended questions, and (2) leisure inventories (Austin, 1991).

Open-ended questions to begin conversations might include those drawn from Yura and Walsh (1988). They follow:

Activity

- What do you do in an average day?
- Do you do anything to keep in shape?
- Do you try to keep up with local, national, or world news?

Acceptance of self and others

- What are your personal strengths? How do you feel about them?
- Have you identified limitations? What are they, and how do you feel about them?
- Describe your acceptance by family members, friends, and people with whom you work. How do you feel about their acceptance?

Appreciation

- Which of your positive qualities and accomplishments have been noticed by others?
- What type of response do you get from others in terms of their appreciation of you?

Autonomy, choice

- Would you describe yourself as being an independent person?
- When you are confronted with choices about your leisure, how do you handle these?

Belonging

- Describe your relationship with family members, friends, and co-workers.
- With whom do you have your closest relationships?
- Are you a member of any community or church groups?

Challenge

- If you had to name a challenging situation in your life, what would you say?
- Do you get satisfaction from taking on challenges?

Confidence

- In what situations do you feel most secure or sure of yourself?
- What things do you do that make you most confident? least confident?

Leisure

- What do you do for recreation and leisure? When? How often?
- What activities are most likely to make you feel refreshed?
- Are there activities you would like to try?

Personal recognition and esteem

- What do you do that brings you personal recognition and esteem?
- Who are the people who provide you with recognition?

Self-control, self-determination

- How much ability do you have to be in control of your life or be responsible for yourself?

- What within you, or outside you, gives you ability to control and determine things for yourself? What takes away control?
- How do you account for your state of health?

Self-actualization, self-fulfillment
- Are you fulfilling your goals in life?
- What do you see in your future in terms of realizing your potential?

Wholesome body image
- How do you and your body appear to you?
- How would others describe your body?

Value system
- What beliefs do you hold in terms of taking part in leisure?
- Identify beliefs you hold in regard to the worth of people and in regard to experiences in your life.

Most agencies and institutions that have therapeutic recreation services will design or adopt leisure inventories appropriate for use with their clients. It is common practice for agencies and institutions to develop leisure interest checklists. Others adopt instruments. Instruments sometimes adopted for use in TR assessment include the Mirenda Leisure Interest Finder (Mirenda, 1973), the Self Leisure Interest Profile (McDowell, 1974), the Leisure Activities Blank (McKechnie, 1974), the Avocational Activities Inventory (Overs, 1970), the Leisure Diagnostic Battery (Witt & Ellis, 1985), and the Comprehensive Leisure Rating Scale (Card, Compton, & Ellis, 1986). A number of assessment instruments are reviewed in *Assessment Tools for Recreational Therapy* (burlingame & Blaschko, 1990), sometimes referred to as "the Red Book."

General Factors to Consider in Assessment. In addition to leisure patterns and interests, a number of factors are considered in therapeutic recreation assessment. Biographical data are normally gained from the admissions report and the initial interview with the client. These data include name, address, telephone number, date of birth, place of birth, gender, marital status, ethnic groups, religious preference, primary language spoken, education, and occupation. Additional information could include socioeconomic status, coping patterns, interactional patterns, employment status, client views of illness and wellness, client's family, and client's community (Yura & Walsh, 1988).

Conclusion on Assessment. Thorough assessment forms the foundation for the planning phase. Both *subjective data* gained from the client and *objective data* from other sources are required to determine client needs and strengths. The *needs list* and *strengths list* are the basis for the individual program plan, treatment plan, care plan, educational plan, or whatever term is used to describe the document that contains the plan of action for each client. The term *individual program plan* has been adopted for use in this chapter because it is frequently employed in the therapeutic recreation literature.

Planning

Following the identification of the client's needs and strengths during the assessment phase, the therapeutic recreation specialist and client are ready to move to the second stage of the TR process, the planning phase. During this phase priorities are set; goals are formulated; objectives are developed; programs, strategies, and approaches are specified; and means of evaluation are determined. When this phase has been completed, the TR specialist and client have a personalized therapeutic recreation program designed to meet the client's needs.

The therapeutic recreation plan usually becomes a component part of the client's total individual program plan developed by an interdisciplinary team (often termed the *treatment plan*). The TR specialist typically works closely with a variety of other health professionals in determining the overall individual program plan. Group meetings are commonly held to formulate the final plan, which is then reviewed with the client.

More specifically, in the planning phase:

- Client needs and strengths are considered.
- Priorities are stipulated.

- Specific goals and objectives are stated, including the expected time for achievement.
- Specific activities or programs are selected as means to achieve goals and objectives.
- Responsibilities for helping the client are determined.
- An evaluation plan is agreed upon so both the when and how of evaluation are made clear.

Setting priorities involves an analysis of the identified needs in order to determine which needs require the professional help of the therapeutic recreation specialist and which are most urgent. The client should be included in this determination, if possible, because it is desirable to engage the client in the planning process as soon as it is practical.

Goals flow directly from the needs list. Goals reflect sought outcomes that are directed toward satisfaction of the client's needs. They are, therefore, stated in terms of the client's behavior and describe proposed changes in the individual in broad terms. Because goals describe client outcomes, they give direction to the TR specialist, client, and others in terms of knowing what results are intended from the program.

Objectives are developed to specify client behaviors related to reaching goals. Objectives enable clients to achieve goals and consequently are sometimes referred to as *enabling objectives.* Usually three to six enabling objectives are needed in order to reach a goal. Objectives, therefore, offer a means for the TR specialist and client to organize their efforts as they break goals down into manageable behaviors that direct program design and offer a basis for evaluation.

Because the needs list serves as the basis for the goals set, the strengths list is drawn from when objectives are formulated. That is, objectives take advantage of the strengths that the client brings with him or her. Strengths can range from possessing a particular leisure skill or ability to having the support of family and friends.

An illustration may add to a clearer understanding of goals and objectives. A need of a client might be to interact with others through verbal expression. This need could translate into a goal stated as: "Increases verbal interactions with others within one month." An enabling objective would be: "Answers questions posed by staff." This objective would provide direction so that the TR specialist would know to structure opportunities for this occurrence by scheduling a social type of activity in which the client has some amount of ability. The objective would also be readily measurable so it could be a basis for evaluation of progress toward the goal.

Programs flow out of the goals and objectives. Programs provide further specificity to the plan. The therapeutic recreation specialist, in conference with the client, prescribes programs or activities for client participation that offer opportunities for the sought outcomes of the plan (i.e., goals and objectives). As has been mentioned, the program area selected needs to be one in which the client has skills or the ability to develop skills.

Perhaps another example will be helpful in illustrating the program component. A client who has the goal of learning stress management techniques may be placed in a stress reduction group in which relaxation training techniques are learned and practiced. The strategy used may be to begin with the therapeutic recreation specialist initially working with the client in a small group so the client may become comfortable in doing relaxation training before moving to the regular stress reduction class that meets daily in the gymnasium with 15 clients taking part. One element of the plan would be for the TR specialist to be given the responsibility of determining, with the client, when the client was ready to enter the regular class.

Finally, once the program or activities for the client's participation have been chosen, a description of *evaluation* procedures needs to be determined. The interdisciplinary team typically determines when the client's progress will be followed (e.g., keeping daily progress notes). Depending on the outcome of the evaluation, the client's schedule of activities may be retained or revised to accommodate the needs of the client.

The planning phase culminates with the producing of the individual program plan. This plan serves as a "blueprint for action" (Yura & Walsh, 1988).

Implementation

The implementation phase is the action phase of the therapeutic recreation process. Implementation involves the actual execution of the individual program plan by the therapeutic recreation specialist and client. The TR specialist assumes responsibility for coordinating client-focused and goal-directed activities consistent with the proposed plan of action. He or she guides the client until the client can assume self-responsibility. The TR specialist also makes certain that the client's actions and responses are fully documented throughout the implementation phase.

Therapeutic recreation programs are tailored to the needs, capacities, and degree of readiness of each client. Programs focus on using existing strengths and interests as foundations for treatment/rehabilitation. Progressive, graded programs offer developmental sequencing for the acquisition of skills as the client progresses. The plan should stipulate the frequency and duration of the client's participation in each activity scheduled.

Most who have been acutely ill would agree that leisure is unattainable for persons who are severely ill. Initially, the client may engage in activities without any pretense of experiencing recreation or leisure. In fact, it would be naive to believe that clients who are seriously ill are ready or able to make self-determined choices. For example, clients with neurological dysfunction, Alzheimer's disease, or chronic depression may suffer from impaired functioning to the point that they cannot exercise freedom of choice (Shank & Kinney, 1987).

Shank and Kinney (1987) have portrayed this situation in a paper on clinical practice in TR. They have written:

If leisure is a premature issue in certain clinical situations, what should a therapeutic recreation specialist do? Without abandoning service provision to individuals with these functional limitations, therapeutic recreation specialists can use recreation activity as an intervention addressing psychosocial needs associated with the stress caused by illness or disability. In this sense, the concerns are basically "pre-leisure."

The concept of "pre-leisure" behavior is an important one in understanding clinical intervention. The very notion of leisure implies . . . freedom from control. Yet freedom from control requires psychological, social, and affective functioning at a level to insure that free choice does not result in maladaptive outcomes. The basic fact that some individuals are not in control of themselves renders the question of leisure momentarily moot. Thus the central concern becomes one of helping the individual achieve or regain those pre-leisure competencies that are the necessary foundations for subsequent leisure issues addressed at another time (pp. 68, 69).

Helplessness and despair frequently occur in clients whose coping mechanisms have been severely tested by the stress of dealing with health problems. Clients undergoing psychiatric treatment, physical rehabilitation, and nursing home care seem particularly subject to feelings of helplessness. Research by Rodin has suggested that helping people regain a sense of control over their lives offers them hope and improves their morale (Bule, 1988). Once individuals begin to experience a restoration of their morale, they develop a renewed sense of resolution or determination to conquer their health problems.

Because of the severity of the client's health condition or because of feelings of helplessness, the therapeutic recreation specialist may initially carefully select therapeutic activities that provide the structure and level of demand that can be beneficial for the client. Once the client's morale has been enhanced, he or she can move to activities that are truly recreational in nature. Recreation represents experiences that are restorative but are largely done for pleasure and enjoyment. Recreation activities are chosen by the client in close collaboration with the TR specialist. Ultimately, the client may be able to exercise perceived control by selecting leisure activities that represent growth opportunities. The highest form of therapeutic recreation participation is that which the client finds self-rewarding and is not a product of external compulsion.

The Therapeutic Recreation Specialist. Interpersonal, observational, decision-making, and technical skills are called for on the part of the therapeutic recreation specialist during the implementation phase of the therapeutic recreation process. These skills are necessary to put the program plan into action.

Interpersonal skills are particularly critical to the success of the implementation phase. Interactions need to be goal-directed and purposeful within an accepting, nonthreatening atmosphere. The significance of creating a positive climate has been proclaimed by Rogers (1980), who has written:

> *On the basis of experience I have found that if I can help bring about a climate marked by genuineness, prizing, and understanding, then exciting things happen. Persons and groups in such a climate move away from rigidity and toward flexibility, away from static living toward process living, away from dependence toward autonomy, away from defensiveness toward self-acceptance, away from being predictable toward an unpredictable creativity. They exhibit living proof of an actualizing tendency (pp. 43, 44).*

During interactions with clients, the therapeutic recreation specialist continually makes observations. Such observations document the progress of the client, as well as verify that the plan of action is correct. Client reactions are documented in the form of progress notes. If the plan is not working as expected, decisions need to be made in regard to modifying the goals and objectives or the approach to achieving the goals and objectives.

Technical skills relate to the therapeutic recreation specialist's knowledge of the properties of activities and leadership abilities in conducting activities. The TR specialist is action oriented in organizing activities, teaching activity skills, offering positive feedback, providing psychological support, and processing with clients on their participation following activities. In order to demonstrate the therapeutic use of an activity, the TR specialist must be familiar with the demands it makes on clients, as well as anticipated outcomes from participation.

Concluding Statement on Implementation. In sum, the implementation phase of the therapeutic recreation process includes the actions of the therapeutic recreation specialist in working with clients to execute the individual program plan (IPP). In doing so, it is important that the actions of the TR specialist are consistent with the IPP. The TR specialist must remain cognizant of the goal-directed nature of his or her responsibilities in conducting activities so that they are organized and carried out in a purposeful manner and do not become "activity for the sake of activity." It is equally important to the success of the implementation phase that there is adequate documentation of client actions and responses as the plan is executed. As a result of a high level of performance on the part of the therapeutic recreation specialist, it is anticipated that positive strides will be made by the client. The direction and amount of these changes are determined during the evaluation phase.

Evaluation

Evaluation is the fourth and final phase in the therapeutic recreation process. In the phase, the goals and objectives in the individual program plan are appraised. The primary question to answer in the evaluation phase is, How did the client respond to the planned intervention?

Evaluation reveals if the plan has been effective or if it requires revision. If the planned program has not had the desired effect, it needs to be modified, reimplemented, and reevaluated. This cyclic process continues as long as it is necessary.

The same methods employed in completing the initial assessment may be used in the evaluation phase. Common means of doing evaluation are to conduct a review of progress notes, interview the client so he or she may respond retrospectively following participation in the treatment/rehabilitation program, and hold an interdisciplinary team meeting to discuss the client's progress. Evaluation procedures should retrieve evaluation information from several independent sources in order to make certain that data are reliable and valid (Austin, 1991).

As has been indicated, it is essential to involve clients in all phases of the therapeutic recreation process to the fullest extent of their capacities. This principle should, of course, be followed in the evaluation phase, where clients can help the therapeutic recreation specialist to determine the effectiveness of the program in achieving sought outcomes (Austin, 1991).

SOME COMMENTS ON THE TR PROCESS

The therapeutic recreation process is an orderly, systematic means of determining a client's needs, formulating goals and objectives, establishing an action plan, implementing it, and evaluating the extent to which the plan was effective in achieving the stated goals and objectives. The basic belief that underlies the TR process is that every person has the potential for improving his or her level of health, given sound planning and proper resources.

Universal Application of the TR Process. Although the therapeutic recreation process is commonly associated with agencies and institutions that are highly clinical in nature, the TR process is not restricted to clinical settings. The use of the TR process is not confined to hospitals or treatment and rehabilitation centers. It is a systematic process that can guide therapeutic recreation in nursing homes, corrections facilities, community-based programs for persons who are disabled, or wherever recreation is used with therapeutic intent in goal-directed programs. Nor is the TR process limited to use with "special populations." It may be applied with any individual who desires to maintain or improve his or her level of health (Austin, 1991).

Direct Experience in Activities. Bandura's (1977) self-efficacy theory deals with how people enhance their perceptions of their ability to produce intended results, or to be effective in what they do. According to Bandura, individuals derive information about themselves and their ability to produce desired outcomes, or cope with situations, from four sources. These are performance, vicarious experiences, verbal persuasion, and experiencing sensations of arousal. Of these, performance (or direct experience) plays the most important role in creating feelings of self-efficacy or effectiveness. It is through direct experience in carefully chosen activities that the majority of therapeutic benefits are derived during the therapeutic recreation process. The therapeutic recreation profession has been heavily influenced by the Gestalt therapy of Frederick (Fritz) Perls, who emphasized experiencing and learning by doing (Austin, 1991), and by Carl Rogers (1980), who in his person-centered therapy stressed staying close to "the earthiness of real experience" (p. 44) within a warm, caring, and nonjudgmental atmosphere.

Activities as Modalities for Treatment and Rehabilitation. Almost any activity typically conceived to be a recreation or leisure activity may be used for therapeutic purpose within therapeutic recreation. Therapeutic media regularly employed in therapeutic recreation include play, games, sports, physical fitness activities, dance and movement, crafts, expressive arts, outdoor recreation activities, and social activities. Therapeutic recreation specialists also conduct individual and group leisure counseling in order to promote client self-awareness of leisure values and attitudes, as well as to prepare clients for community living.

Characteristics of Therapeutic Activities. In order for activities to hold the potential for therapeutic outcomes, they need to be conducted so that they possess the following characteristics. Therapeutic activities:

1. *Are goal directed.* Therapeutic recreation activities are directed toward a purpose. They are not "time fillers" but rather are done for a reason. The goal may be as general as involving the client in something outside of himself or herself, thus allowing him or her less time to dwell on problems. Or the goal may be very specific, such as gaining a particular social or leisure skill.
2. *Require active participation by clients.* Self-determination is important in the sense that clients are as active as possible in both choosing activities and having a role in affecting the outcome of the activities. Clients need to be involved to the largest extent possible in determining the activity in order to exercise control. They need to feel that their participation meaningfully affects the results of the activity in order to gain feelings of self-efficacy and competence.
3. *Have meaning and value to the client.* The client needs to learn to approach activities not as a requirement but as an opportunity to achieve an end. Therapeutic recreation specialists often process (i.e., discuss) the activity with clients following participation so that clients may gain personal awareness of behaviors, feelings, and outcomes achieved as a result of taking part.
4. *Offer potential for pleasure and satisfaction.* Ideally, the primary motivation for the client lies in the pleasurable, satisfying experience gained from participation. Even where gratification is not immediate, activities should make it possible ultimately to gain pleasure and satisfaction.
5. *Provide opportunity for mastery.* Activities need to offer the opportunity for gaining and displaying mastery. Feelings of competence lead clients to feelings of self-efficacy and enjoyment with accompanying heightened interest in the activity. Clients should not be expected to participate in activities in which they are likely to be embarrassed or to fail.
6. *Are carefully selected with the guidance of the TR specialist.* As Gump and Sutton-Smith (1955) wrote years ago: "Activities have a reality and a behavior-influencing power in their own right. An activity, once entered, will exclude some potential behaviors, necessitate other behaviors, and, finally, encourage or discourage still other behaviors." Because activities make inherent demands, the therapeutic recreation specialist needs to draw on his or her professional knowledge of activities in order to help clients select activities that will possess characteristics suitable to meet the clients' needs and that are within the clients' capabilities.

SUMMARY

The purpose of this chapter was to provide an introduction to the therapeutic recreation process as an element essential to therapeutic recreation. The TR process was defined, and each of its four components was discussed.

Also covered was the relationship of the therapeutic recreation specialist with the client. This relationship was presented as the means through which the TR process is executed. Final comments in the chapter concerned the universal application of the TR process, the emphasis on direct experience in therapeutic recreation, activities as modalities for treatment and rehabilitation, and characteristics of therapeutic activities.

READING COMPREHENSION QUESTIONS

1. Do you agree with the definition of therapeutic recreation found at the beginning of the chapter?
2. Can you explain why the TR process might be termed *the essence of therapeutic recreation?*
3. What are the four phases of the TR process?
4. Do you agree with Mobily that the distinguishing feature of therapeutic recreation is that it uses recreation as a means to an end?
5. What are the assumptions on which the TR process rests?
6. Describe how the relationship between the TR specialist and client is the means for applying the TR process.
7. Do you agree that self-knowledge is important to the therapeutic use of self? If so, what things should be explored in becoming self-aware?

8. What three aspects of relationships have been emphasized by Carl Rogers?
9. Can you differentiate between treatment and rehabilitation?
10. Describe how therapeutic recreation specialists emphasize client strengths, rather than what is "wrong" with the client.
11. Why is assessment critical to the provision of treatment and rehabilitation?
12. What is the role of the client in the TR process?
13. Why should TR specialists look beyond client verbalizations in conducting needs assessment?
14. What are data sources for assessment?
15. Describe methods that may be used in TR assessment.
16. Do you believe that the open-ended assessment questions in the chapter would be helpful to a TR specialist?
17. What are some assessment instruments used in TR?
18. What biographical data are normally collected? From what sources?
19. What are subjective data? Objective data?
20. What are some names for the document that contains the action plan or blueprint for action resulting from the planning phase?
21. What transpires during the planning phase?
22. What is the relationship between goals and objectives?
23. What is the relationship between the list of client needs and goals? Between the list of client strengths and objectives?
24. Can you describe some strengths that clients might possess?
25. Why must TR activities remain "client focused" and "goal directed"?
26. Do you agree with the content of the quotation taken from Shaken and Kinney's paper? Why or why not?
27. Can you differentiate between the expressions *therapeutic activities, recreation activities,* and *leisure activities?*
28. What skills are called for on the part of the therapeutic recreation specialist during the implementation phase?
29. Why the "big deal" about activities being conducted in a goal-directed, purposeful manner?
30. Explain why documentation is a major concern during the implementation phase.
31. In what respect may the TR process be cyclic?
32. Identify examples of methods of doing TR evaluation.
33. Can the TR process be applied outside of hospitals or treatment and rehabilitation centers?
34. What is the significance of direct experience in TR? How may Perls and Rogers have influenced TR?
35. What makes activities therapeutic?

SUGGESTED LEARNING ACTIVITIES

1. Interview three TR specialists regarding how each defines therapeutic recreation. In a 3- to 5-page paper, compare and contrast their definitions with definitions found in the TR literature. Conclude the paper with your own definition of therapeutic recreation that you have constructed after exploring the topic.
2. Review the literature for activities and exercises that could be used to help TR students increase self-awareness. Submit the one you like best to your instructor on a 5- by 8-inch card and/or read it in class.
3. Working with your instructor and classmates, contact TR agencies to obtain copies of TR assessment instruments. Place these on reserve at the library so all current and future students can have access to them.
4. Invite TR specialists from several agencies to come into your classroom to discuss (1) how they employ the TR process and (2) their perceptions of the importance of establishing and maintaining a therapeutic relationship.
5. Read over the characteristics of therapeutic activities listed in the chapter. Then, in a 3- to 5-page paper, rank these in importance and justify your ranking.

REFERENCES

Austin, D.R. (1991). *Therapeutic recreation: Processes and techniques* (2nd ed.). Champaign, IL: Sagamore Publishing.

Bandura, A. (1977). Self efficacy: Toward a unifying theory of behavior change. *Psychological Review, 84,* 191–215.

Bule, J. (1988). Control studies bode better health in aging. *The APA Monitor, 19*(7), 20.

Burlingame, J., & Blaschko, T.M. (1990). *Assessment tools for recreational therapy.* Ravensdale, WA: Idyll Arbor, Inc.

Card, J., Compton, D., & Ellis, G. (1986). Reliability and validity of the Comprehensive Leisure Rating Scale. *Journal of Expanding Horizons in Therapeutic Recreation,* 1, 21–27.

Gudeman, J.E. (1988). The person with chronic mental illness. In A. M. Nicholi (Ed.), *The new Harvard guide to psychiatry* (pp. 714–727). Cambridge, MA: The Belknap Press of Harvard University Press.

Gump, P., & Sutton-Smith, B. (1955). Activity-setting and social interaction: A field study. *The American Journal of Orthopsychiatry, 25,* 755–760.

Kanter, J.S. (1985). Psychosocial assessment in community treatment. In J.S. Kanter (Ed.), *Clinical issues in treating the chronic mentally ill* (pp. 63–75). San Francisco: Jossey-Bass.

McDowell, C.F. (1974). Toward a healthy leisure mode: Leisure counseling. *Therapeutic Recreation Journal, 8*(3), 96–104.

McKechnie, G.E. (1974). Psychological foundations of leisure counseling: An empirical strategy. *Therapeutic Recreation Journal, 8*(1), 4–16.

Mirenda, J.J. (1973). Mirenda Leisure Interest Finder. In A. Epperson et al. (Eds.), *Leisure counseling kit.* Washington, DC: American Alliance for Health, Physical Education, and Recreation.

Mobily, K.E. (1985). A philosophical analysis of therapeutic recreation: What does it mean to say "we can be therapeutic?" Part II. *Therapeutic Recreation Journal, 19*(2), 7–14.

Mobily, K.E. (1987). A quiescent reply to Lee. *Therapeutic Recreation Journal, 21*(2), 81–83.

Overs, R.P. (1970). A model for avocational counseling. *Journal of Health, Physical Education and Recreation, 4*(2), 28-36.

Rogers, C.R. (1961). *On becoming a person: A therapist's view of psychotherapy.* Boston: Houghton Mifflin.

Rogers, C.R. (1980). *A way of being.* Boston: Houghton Mifflin.

Schulman, E.D. (1978). *Intervention in human services* (2nd ed.). St. Louis: C. V. Mosby.

Shank, J., & Kinney, T. (1987). On the neglect of clinical practice. In C. Sylvester et al. (Eds.), *Philosophy of therapeutic recreation: Ideas and issues* (pp. 65–73). Alexandria, VA: National Recreation and Park Association.

Witt, P., & Ellis, G. (1985). Development of a short form to assess perceived freedom in leisure. *Journal of Leisure Research, 17,* 225–233.

Yura, H., & Walsh, M.B. (1988). *The nursing process: Assessment, planning, implementing, evaluating* (5th ed.). Norwalk, CT: Appleton & Lange.

CHAPTER 4

PSYCHIATRY AND MENTAL HEALTH

JUDY SOTTILE KINNEY
W. B. (TERRY) KINNEY

OBJECTIVES

- Understand the distinction between mental health and mental disorder within the context of our society.
- Be aware of the current classifications and characteristics of major mental disorders.
- Understand the purpose of therapeutic recreation within the context of treatment for mental disorder.
- Be aware of the relationship of therapeutic recreation to various treatment settings and to the treatment team.
- Know the process of therapeutic recreation within the context of treatment for mental disorders.

Defining what constitutes mental health and its opposite, mental disorder, has always been a difficult task. In one of the classic discussions of mental health, Hartman (1939) chose to base his explanation around the process of adaptation. He states it is the individual's adaptation to the demands of reality that determines mental health or mental disorder. While Hartman does not elaborate on the course that adaptation may take, we can assume that it is the direction of that adaptation that decides whether we will function in a mentally healthy or mentally unhealthy manner. The crucial point to consider is that we may adapt to reality by developing mentally unhealthy behavior such as withdrawal from reality.

The extent to which we can utilize our internal skills and strengths and bring to bear the various supportive elements we have at our disposal are key elements in the extent to which we can master the demands of that reality which we face. The utilization of these skills, strengths, and resources is termed **coping** (Mechanic, 1976). Coping is combined with the use of certain defenses, such as rationalization, denial, sublimation, and so on, to allow us to face challenging tasks and demands without becoming overwhelmed by anxiety. According to Mechanic (1976), "Successful application of skills and capacities (coping) requires that the individual maintain control over feelings of inadequacy and uncertainty and protect against a sense of futility" (p. 2). Through the use of defenses, the individual maintains a sense of equilibrium and esteem while attacking the demands of everyday reality in the best manner possible.

As we develop from our youngest days to our oldest days, we are faced with the issue of how we interpret and deal with reality. Part of the process of human development involves recognizing, developing, and learning how to use the judgments, skills, and internal resources we have at our disposal. These judgments, skills, and internal resources are termed **ego strengths** and it is our use of these ego strengths that determine our success in coping.

It must be remembered that the characteristics of positive mental health are the culmination of successful human development. The course of that development involves facing a series of stages (or crises) during which we face new levels of challenges and expectations. Table 4.1 shows those levels in a developmental perspective along with the key issues and ego strengths that need to be addressed and developed.

We all exhibit some characteristics of positive mental health and negative mental health depending on how well we developed our ego strengths, how strong our social support system is, and the intensity of perceived stressors. Very few of us consistently operate at a very high level of positive mental health. The actuality is that we tend to vary from day to day, and sometimes even from moment to moment.

How then, do we determine who is mentally healthy and who is mentally unhealthy? The rather vague answer is that the broad rules and expectations of our society determine our level of mental health. Part of human development is becoming acculturated—learning the expectations and rules of the culture in which we live and deciding the extent to which we wish to internalize or reject the acceptable behaviors of our society. As society changes and becomes more or less tolerant of behavior that deviates from its norms, the extent and nature of mental disorder likewise changes.

If the yardstick for mental disorder is so broadly defined and ever changing, who then needs treatment in a psychiatric program? How are people identified as requiring professional help? It must be remembered that behaviors that appear to represent mental disorder may be the result of many legitimate precipitants, for example, side effects of medication. In such a case, bizarre or deviant behavior would not be a result of mental disorder but of a physical, external problem. In order for behavior to be questioned as indicating mental disorder, that behavior must be in evidence for some duration and be consistently inappropriate over a period of time. Except in the case of individuals who cause serious harm to themselves or others, the question largely becomes individualized based on the input and influence of the individual exhibiting the behavior in question, the family, and sometimes significant others (i.e., close friends, employers, teachers, or members of the clergy). As a result of individual rights and protection, it is relatively difficult to have someone hospitalized involuntarily. Most psychiatric admissions are by voluntary means. For those individuals who make the decision to seek psychiatric treatment, there are a variety of treatment settings (e.g., in-patient, out-patient, partial hospitalization, etc.), that are available depending on the individual's needs.

CLASSIFICATION OF PSYCHIATRIC DISORDERS

Individuals undergoing psychiatric treatment, like anyone else, will exhibit a variety of behaviors that become fairly representative of their style and ability to cope with life demands and situations. Careful documentation and analysis of those particular behaviors termed **pathological**—that is, contributing to mental disorder—have enabled us to develop a classification system for diagnosing conditions of psychiatric disturbance. The consideration of both negative or pathological behavior as well as positive or behavior strengths allows clinical staff to develop **treatment protocols**—that is, interventions designed to further strengthen positive behaviors and reduce negative behaviors.

The *Diagnostic and Statistical Manual of Mental Disorders Fourth Edition* (DSM-IV) (1994) is the reference commonly used by clinicians in making diagnoses. The DSM-IV provides clear descriptions of diagnostic categories and a coding system for the assignment, treatment, and

TABLE 4.1 Developmental Levels and Associated Behaviors

Behaviors Indicating Positive Adjustment	Behaviors Indicating Negative Adjustment
Level I: The Development of Trust	
1. Invests in relationships	1. Avoids relationships
2. Has an open, nonsuspicious attitude	2. Is suspicious, closed, guarded
3. Welcomes touching	3. Is a loner and unhappy
4. Maintains good eye contact	4. Maintains poor eye contact
5. Shares self and possessions	5. Does not share self or possessions
Level II: The Development of Autonomy	
1. Is independent	1. Frequently procrastinates
2. Resists being dominated	2. Has difficulty working alone
3. Stands up for self	3. Needs much structure
4. Is assertive when necessary	4. Has difficulty making decisions
	5. Is easily influenced
Level III: The Development of Initiative	
1. Is a self starter	1. Is easily depressed
2. Accepts challenges	2. Has poor self esteem
3. Assumes leadership roles	3. Maintains poor eye contact
4. Sets goals and pursues them	4. Has low energy level
Level IV: The Development of Competence	
1. Wonders how things work	1. Is timid, withdrawn
2. Brings projects to completion	2. Is overly obedient
3. Enjoys variety of projects	3. Frequently procrastinates
4. Enjoys learning	4. Is a passive observer rather than an active participant
5. Enjoys experimenting	5. Is unsure of own ability
Level V: The Development of Identity	
1. Is comfortable with sex-role identity	1. Has doubts about sex-role identity
2. Takes active interest in social engagement	2. Lacks confidence
3. Plans for future	3. Is overly hostile to authority
4. Appropriately challenges adult authority	4. Is overly obedient
5. Is self accepting	5. Tends to be self rejecting

research analysis of various disorders. Each individual is assessed on five separate axes in order to give attention to various disorders, environmental concerns, and functional aspects that might otherwise be missed if the focus were on assessing a single presenting problem.

Since DSM-IV contains over 300 diagnoses and categories, we will discuss only those that the therapeutic recreation specialist is most likely to encounter in various treatment settings.

Schizophrenia

Schizophrenia involves highly distorted abilities in perception, thinking, emotion, speech, and physical activity. It is an altered sense of reality displayed by inconsistency in mental functions and expected actions. For example, an individual may show remarkedly **inappropriate affect**—that is, display no emotion—or even appear happy, while describing a very sad or unfortunate happening. This is the characteristic **splitting** that has led lay persons to mistakenly describe schizophrenia as "split personality."

In actuality, schizophrenia is a disturbance represented by many different causes and symptoms that result in a wide variety of clinical manifestations. This makes it an extremely difficult disorder to diagnose and requires clinicians to observe and document pathological behavior over a long period of time—at least six months. Another factor that confuses diagnosis is that individuals are not always consistent in their display of pathological behavior. The individual may be totally unable to function at one time, and a short time later, perhaps a few days or weeks later, be functioning at a fairly high level.

According to DSM-IV, the classic symptoms of schizophrenia are:

1. Hallucinations—usually of an auditory nature consisting of sounds or voices, sometimes even continuous dialogues. It is not unusual for schizophrenic persons who commit violent crimes to be obeying the voices they hear issuing them commands.
2. Delusions—false beliefs that the individual clings to despite facts or logic that prove otherwise. Usually these relate to control over one's thinking (e.g., that someone can read one's mind or control their thoughts in some way). Delusions of persecution are common with some of the sub-types of schizophrenia.
3. Emotional Disturbance—shown by the lack of affect referred to earlier.
4. Disorganized Speech—often revealed by incoherence, use of "made up" words, or thought patterns that do not logically follow one another.
5. Grossly Disorganized or Catatonic Behavior—may consist of extreme inactivity or overactivity; strange, repetitive behavior; mimicking; and stiff, machine-like behavior.

The DSM-IV identifies a number of sub-types of schizophrenia. These are:

1. Disorganized Type
2. Catatonic Type
3. Paranoid Type
4. Residual Type
5. Undifferentiated Type

Mood Disorders

These are disorders of affect—that is, emotion, and used to be referred to as affective disorders. Mood disorders are divided into depressive disorders, bipolar disorders and two disorders based on etiology—mood disorder due to a medical condition and substance induced mood disorder.

A manic episode is a markedly distinct period of elevated mood characterized by extremely high energy and activity. During this period, the individual may exhibit several of the following behaviors:

1. inflated self-esteem and grandiosity;
2. decreased need for sleep;
3. excessively talkative;
4. flight of ideas (i.e., sense of fast, racing thoughts);
5. easily distracted;
6. increased physical activity;
7. increased participation in activities that may lead to negative consequences.

A depressive episode is an intense feeling of sadness, or of not caring anymore, or of discouragement. All of us, at one time or another feel depressed. The difference between "everyday" depression and clinical depression is one of time, intensity, and degree of impact on our functioning.

A major depressive episode, according to DSM-IV, consists of evidence of at least five of the following symptoms that represent a change from previous functioning and are evidenced most of the day and nearly every day over at least two weeks:

1. depressed mood;
2. markedly diminished interest or pleasure in activities;
3. significant weight loss or gain when not dieting;
4. insomnia or oversleeping;
5. excessive or markedly decreased physical activity;
6. fatigue or loss of energy;
7. feelings of worthlessness or excessive or inappropriate guilt;
8. diminished ability to think or concentrate;
9. recurrent thoughts of death or of **suicidal ideation**—that is, thoughts of committing suicide but not having a specific plan to carry it out or making an actual attempt at carrying it out.

It should be remembered that many of the symptoms of depression (and other disorders as well) are common experiences in life for all of us. This points out the fact that individuals in psychiatric treatment are just like us—human beings, albeit ones who are having difficulty dealing with the stresses of reality at this time in their lives. The difference, according to Waldinger (1990), may be pointed out by examining the intensity, duration, and degree of disruption caused. Of central concern is whether the mood is of such length and intensity to disrupt normal activities, alter the view of reality, or place the individual or others in danger.

In some cases, individuals may experience both manic and depressive episodes—not at the same time, but as wide swings in behavior and feelings ranging from extremely manic to extremely depressed. These are called bipolar disorders, or more commonly, manic-depressive disorders. Other individuals may swing less widely in their affective shifts and exhibit the symptomatic behaviors in a much less extreme fashion. Mood swings may last for several days or months. Bipolar disorders tend to respond quite well to medication; however, a frequent problem is that individuals start feeling better and think they no longer need their medication, starting the cyclical process over again.

Anxiety Disorders

Anxiety is a commonly used term to describe "nervousness," an emotion experienced by everyone at various times. Clinically, however, anxiety takes on a much sharper focus. Anxiety can be better described as intense fear or panic; and clinically it appears where it is not justified, where there is no real reason for fear or panic. Panic attacks may result in the individual feeling a shortness of breath, dizziness, trembling, sweating, and perhaps nausea. Other feelings may be a sense of **depersonalization** (or strange sense of unreality about one's self or the environment), chest pains, a fear of dying, or a fear of "going crazy" or losing control.

In psychiatric settings, panic disorders are frequently associated with phobias. Phobias are continuous, unrealistic fears about an object, situation, or event that come to dominate an individual's thinking. Individuals become obsessed with avoiding that object, situation, or event and go to extraordinary steps to do so. Many of us experience unrealistic fears, say a fear of flying or a fear of snakes. Such a fear becomes a phobia when it causes panic to the extent that an individual becomes almost incapacitated to function.

DSM-IV discusses three broad types of phobias: agoraphobia, a fear of being caught in an open place (say outside the home) where one feels they cannot escape from the situation; social phobia, a fear of not being able to perform appropriately in social situations; and specific phobia, a fear of a generally specific object or situation (such as snakes or flying).

Obsessive-compulsive disorders are an interesting subtype of the anxiety disorders (not to be confused with obsessive-compulsive personality disorder). As an anxiety disorder, the obsessive-compulsive person experiences persistent thoughts (an obsession) that are extremely discomforting and cause a great deal of anxiety. For example, the individual may have thoughts about killing his or her own child, something that they recoil from in horror but cannot stop thinking about. The compulsion is a particular behavior, or routine that helps the individual control the unpleasant obsession. Compulsions tend to reflect fairly rigid, time consuming behaviors that serve to "cleanse" the individual of those terrible thoughts. Continuous cleaning of a house or apartment for hours on end, over and over; or a long and tedious ritual of hand washing are examples. Of course the compulsions do not completely control the obsession and the individual becomes locked into a frightening cycle of increased compulsive, ritualistic behavior.

Post traumatic stress disorder occurs when an individual is exposed to an extremely traumatic stressor whereby the experience places the individual in danger of serious harm or death, or the individual witnesses another individual being harmed or killed. The individual's response to this event or series of events is an intense fear, horror, or feeling of helplessness. Symptoms resulting form the trauma include continually reliving the event (i.e., dreams, recollections), avoiding anything related to the event, and increased arousal (i.e., difficulty sleeping, outbursts of anger, exaggerated startle response, etc.).

Personality Disorders

Many behaviors associated with this category bear a resemblance to other categories discussed. Obsessive-compulsive behaviors, paranoid behaviors, and mood related behaviors are part of personality disorders as well as other categories. The primary difference is one of level and degree of dysfunction. The personality disorders are lifelong patterns of maladaptive behaviors with onset in adolescence or early adulthood. While many people suffering with psychiatric problems are truly suffering—they know something is very wrong with them—the person with a personality disorder tends to view his or her behavior as healthy, not deviant. Thus the problems they create are someone else's, not theirs. Individuals with personality disorders do not tend to voluntarily seek help. Instead they wind up being coerced into treatment by family members and become very reluctant clients. These individuals typically behave in ways that make people very angry. They always know what "buttons to push" and seem to be masters at manipulating others. Obviously, they are very difficult to treat, and the failure rate with them is extremely high.

DSM-IV describes the following personality disorders:

- Antisocial personality
- Avoidant personality
- Borderline personality
- Dependent personality
- Histrionic personality
- Narcissistic personality
- Obsessive-compulsive personality
- Paranoid personality
- Schizoid personality
- Schizotypal personality

DSM-IV clusters these personality disorders by similarity in behaviors but cautions that these "clusters" are controversial. Cluster A includes the paranoid, schizoid, and schizotypal personality disorders as individuals who appear odd or eccentric. Cluster B includes antisocial, borderline, histrionic, and narcissistic personality disorders as individuals who appear dramatic, emotional, or erratic. Cluster C includes avoidant, dependent, and obsessive compulsive personality disorders as individuals who appear anxious or fearful.

Only one disorder, borderline personality, will be described in any detail since that particular disorder appears to be significantly increasing in incidence. Borderline individuals have a number of strengths that make them initially appear to be high functioning. As you become more familiar with the true character of the individual, however, a number of typical problem behaviors emerge. The most typical pathological defense utilized by the borderline is **splitting.** As a result of ". . . a developmental failure to integrate and to

accept positive and negative feelings about himself, (the individual) divides his world into either good and nurturing objects or punitive and rejecting objects" (O'Brien, Caldwell, & Transeau, 1985). The individual sees the world and himself/herself in all good or all bad terms. In order to protect himself or herself internally, the individual projects the bad parts of himself/herself onto others and reacts to those now externalized bad things with tremendous anger. The borderline person frequently does not feel alive and constantly seeks stimuli to reassure himself/herself of his or her existence. The borderline person also has a tremendous need to control his/her environment and develops tremendous manipulation skills and becomes involved in destructive "people games," pitting staff against staff or patient against patient. **Slashing**—the act of cutting yourself purposely, but not serious enough to be considered suicidal—is a frequent behavior of some borderlines. This cutting is both a manipulative behavior and an attempt to affirm that you are alive by seeing your own blood and feeling the wound. Other characteristics may include being impulsive in a self-destructive manner (e.g., engaging in frequent, inadvisable sexual involvements without considering the consequences), a fear of being alone, engagement in stormy interpersonal relationships that are intense and unstable, and marked shifts in mood.

Because the borderline personality engages in such manipulation, it is very difficult for staff to form the type of relationship needed to create clinical progress. Consequently, treatment is frequently unsuccessful with the client leaving the program feeling as though he or she were the victim of uncaring and incompetent staff. The borderline individual typically experiences many repeated hospitalizations with intermittent times of relatively stable functioning.

Eating Disorders

Eating disorders are predominantly diagnosed in women (90% of all eating disorder diagnoses) in industrial nations. Eating disorders are a severe disturbance in eating patterns or behaviors. The individual's body image is distorted in both issues of weight and shape. There are two major types of eating disorders: **anorexia nervosa** and **bulimia nervosa.**

Anorexia nervosa is a refusal for the individual to maintain body weight that is appropriate to his or her height and build. The prevalence of anorexia nervosa is approximately 0.5% to 1.0% of the general population. The average age of individuals suffering from this diagnosis is 17 years old. Individuals often express feelings of ineffectiveness, a need to control their environment, and inflexible thought processes. Two specific types have been added to this diagnosis since the previous DSM version: Restricting (the individual does not regularly engage in the binge-purge cycle) and Binge-Eating/Purge type (the individual regularly engages in the binge or purge cycle). This type should not be confused with bulimia nervosa; the major difference is that these individuals are not able to maintain their normal body weight whereas those with Bulimia Nervosa are able to maintain normal body weight.

Individuals diagnosed with **bulimia nervosa** are able to maintain body weight at, or above, the normal weight for their size and shape. These individuals partake in binge eating and then use inappropriate methods to prevent any weight gain from these eating binges. In order for an individual to be diagnosed with bulimia nervosa, these behaviors (binges and purges) have to occur at least two times a week for three months. Stress, feeling depressed, hunger following a period of dieting, or lack of control over a situation can trigger a binge episode. There is a recurrent use of unhealthy methods to prevent weight gain resulting from a binge episode. Unhealthy methods include vomiting (purging), use of laxatives, fasting, or excessive exercise.

Two specific types have been added to this diagnosis since the DSM-IIIR revision: Purging (the individual utilizes the methods of vomiting and laxatives to prevent weight gain) and Nonpurging (the individual utilizes fasting and/or excessive exercise to prevent weight gain).

PREVALENCE OF MENTAL DISTURBANCE

The most ambitious attempt to determine prevalence rates has been made by the Epidemiologic Catchment Area (ECA) program which has been surveying individuals in communities across the country. ECA surveyors in each of the communities randomly interviewed individuals regarding the prevalence of symptoms from 15 of the major diagnoses of DSM version III. Findings revealed that from 29 percent to 38 percent of people interviewed had experienced at least one of the 15 disorders during their lifetime. An average of the three sites yields a prevalence rate of 33 percent, which indicates that one in three individuals has experienced such disturbance. Alcohol and/or drug abuse was the most common disorder (16.7%), followed by anxiety disorders (15.5%), mood disturbances (7.8%), and personality disorders (2.6%) (Robins et al., 1984). Given the difficulties in determining accurate recall of symptoms, it can be assumed that these prevalence rates are on the conservative side. While specific symptomatology will vary from region to region, it can be seen that the total number of individuals experiencing psychological disturbance is a distressingly high number.

Lest these numbers should mislead the student into thinking that everyone in his or her classroom belongs in a psychiatric hospital, it should be pointed out that these figures do not reflect level of functioning. That is, the presence of psychiatric symptomatology does not automatically necessitate treatment. As pointed out in the beginning of this section, most everyone has problems of one nature or another, but it is the degree of impairment that really precludes outside assistance. A recent newspaper health and science note made the following point concerning psychiatric diagnoses:

> **Crazier than ever**
> *Are you crazy? Well, not crazy exactly but—shall we say—a victim of a condition, a syndrome, a mental disorder? According to DSM-IV, if you've got a heartbeat, you probably are. DSM-IV is the newest edition of the Diagnostic and Statistical Manual of Mental Disorders, the shrink's bible. It includes more than 300 mental disorders, more than three times the number in the first edition, published in 1952, the Hartford Courant reports. Among them are the "Disorder of Written Expression," which afflicts people who can't write well (Schogol, 1994).*

PURPOSE OF THERAPEUTIC RECREATION

Within the realm of psychiatric rehabilitation, therapeutic recreation reflects the characteristics of the three levels of service delivery defined by Peterson and Gunn (1984); that is, rehabilitation, education, and participation. A comprehensive therapeutic recreation program would direct attention to those three levels depending on the extent of staff resources, agency support and client needs.

The recreation participation component provides clients with the opportunity to participate in freely-chosen activities that are similar to activities and opportunities outside the treatment setting. This experience duplicates all the beneficial outcomes of recreation participation for anyone: it is fun, enjoyable, makes people feel better about themselves, and provides the opportunity to feel in control; that is, individuals choose whether to participate, with whom, when, and how much. There are other benefits of a more therapeutic nature, also. Clients get to "try out" new behaviors or ways of interacting with others in a relatively safe environment and they get to "be themselves" in a setting where everything is not always clinically examined for its significance and meaning. Recreation participation has the potential to improve the client's currently perceived quality of life, as well as help the client to feel better about being in the treatment program, and perhaps be more accepting of the clinical interventions of other areas of treatment.

The leisure education component serves to address leisure related skills, attitudes, and knowledge (Peterson & Gunn, 1984). Whereas the role of the therapeutic recreation specialist in the participation component is one of organizer and leader, the role in the leisure education component is one of educator and group facilitator. Both the participation and education components are geared towards somewhat less tangible and observable outcomes. Attitudes and values are difficult to observe and measure directly. The nature of their benefits tends to be largely internal and very much under the control of the client.

For this and other reasons, there is a great deal of emphasis within the field of psychiatric treatment on the rehabilitation, or therapy, component of therapeutic recreation service delivery. This is what Shank and Kinney (1987) refer to as the clinical context. It is a situation where the client experiencing disturbed mental processes is recognized as an individual involved in a health crisis, a situation where clinical interventions are required to *help the individual free himself from the constraints that are limiting his personal growth and healthy choices of behavior.*

The health crisis is a result of an individual's coping style being inadequate or inappropriate for the demands of a particular situation. Disorganization or disequilibrium results with consequent increased stress placed on coping resources. This disorganization means that the individual is now dealing with reality at a lower level of effectiveness than previously. As further crises develop, the individual, with reduced effectiveness, experiences increased stress and disequilibrium. For some individuals this cycle represents a continuing downward cycle until some sense of stability prevails. At the total extreme, stability may be maintained by withdrawal from reality. It is the purpose of the therapy component to work with the entire treatment team to disrupt this downward spiral, reinforce those effective coping behaviors that are working, develop new coping behaviors, and help the individual become more effective in dealing with life crises.

Treatment in therapeutic recreation may be individual or small-group oriented, depending on the needs of the client and the resources of the agency. Most of these interventions tend to be group oriented. If these therapeutic recreation groups are to be effective as clinical interventions, then it is necessary for them to meet certain requirements.

1. The group must be conceptualized to meet the specific needs of particular clients.
2. Specific referral criteria for admission to the group must be clearly identified, along with the purpose of the group, objectives and/or planned outcomes, and a description of how the group will function.
3. The functioning of the group is supported by the clinical milieu—that is, it is accepted by other therapies as a legitimate and important part of the treatment environment, clients are encouraged to attend, and non-participation becomes a concern for all staff to explore with the client.

This type of clinical group differs from the purely recreational group in that it allows for the principles of group process to evolve. In other words, the group, through natural evolution (and the therapist's interventions) takes on a life and characteristics that reflect its members typical interactions with other elements of life. To make a contrast, a recreation participation group—a library discussion group that meets periodically with attendance dependent only upon interest—may have a completely different set of individuals at each meeting. Consequently there is little opportunity for intense group process to occur. While this library group may meet some of the purely recreational needs of clients, it stands little chance of serving as a therapy group.

COMMON SERVICE SETTINGS

The individual experiencing disturbed mental processes has a variety of alternatives for treatment. The choice of alternative depends on a number of factors including finances (or health insurance), family and work concerns, and the degree to which the individual is able to function or not function in his or her current environment. Typical settings include in-patient, out-patient, partial or day settings, transitional settings, and individualized settings with one's own counselor or therapist. The significant aspect of these settings is one of structure. The individual who is experiencing psychological discomfort but remains functioning at a reasonable level probably requires only periodic meetings with a psychologist, psychiatrist, or other licensed and certified therapist. As individuals regress in functional abilities, the choice becomes settings with increased structure and number of staff. In-patient, day settings, and transitional settings are those most likely to employ therapeutic recreation specialists.

Within those settings the preferred approach is some variation of the team treatment concept whereby representatives from various disciplines meet as a group to plan an integrated treatment program. Typically, a treatment team consists of representatives from nursing, psychiatry, psychology, social work, and therapeutic recreation (or one of the other activity therapies). This team is responsible for an assigned group of clients and coordinates the various therapies in an individualized fashion. Often the team meets several times each week and discusses the progress of various clients. Team meetings provide the opportunity to review clients on a routine basis as well as an "as needed" basis, particularly when difficulties arise.

Information is taken back by the therapeutic recreation specialist to be shared with relevant workers in therapeutic recreation staff meetings. Thus, each staff member may be a representative to a different treatment team, as well as a member of the therapeutic recreation staff. This information sharing is a two-way process with staff who interact with the client providing information to the primary therapeutic recreation specialist who, in turn, provides information to the treatment team. Conversely, thoughts and direction about the best way to interact with a client come down from the treatment team and back to the many individual staff who see the client. It is this coordination that is the heart of the **milieu therapy concept** whereby everything in the client's environment becomes oriented to a consistent treatment approach (Gunderson, 1978).

Within psychiatric settings, many agencies have opted to administratively combine a number of therapies that utilize similar modalities into one activities therapy department. Such departments may house specialists from art, dance/movement, horticulture, music, occupational therapy, and therapeutic recreation. The way such departments function varies a great deal. Some function as discreet sub-units and attempt to hang on to their unique identities, while some merge into one cohesive group and attempt to utilize each individual's unique talents in a way that best serves the total unit.

CURRENT BEST PRACTICES AND PROCEDURES

Assessment

Assessment is the initial determination of a client's strengths and weaknesses regarding optimal leisure functioning and is used to establish treatment objectives within therapeutic recreation and to provide data to the treatment team for the establishment of overall treatment goals. It needs to be made very clear that although the purpose of therapeutic recreation assessment is relative to optimal leisure functioning, many of the elements of that assessment will be concerned with the same aspects of mental status that most other disciplines consider. This is not a redundancy. When different assessments look at similar behaviors, they are looking at them under different conditions and expectations. The environment of a psychiatrist's office and a recreation workshop are very different. Consequently, the sharing of this data allows for the treatment team members to validate (confirm) their own thoughts regarding the client or to question their own findings regarding the client. Given the difficult nature of defining exactly what is psychological disorder, this consensual process is very important.

Because of this, there are a number of universal characteristics of psychological process that the therapeutic recreation specialist wants to constantly monitor. These are relevant to the

mental status examination which is: (1) the process of gathering information regarding a client's state of mind during observations and interactions with that client; and (2) a standard section of the client's medical chart. Waldinger (1990) provides an excellent discussion of these assessment concerns which follow.

Therapeutic recreation specialists need to differentiate between thought content, thought process, and thought disorder. **Thought process** is the manner in which a client puts ideas and thoughts together; **thought content** is the ideas the client projects; and a **thought disorder** "is a disturbance of content or process, or of both" (Waldinger, 1990, p. 63).

Relative to **thought process,** Waldinger identifies the following for assessment concern:

1. *Rate and flow of ideas.* This includes racing thoughts—a feeling of being flooded with thoughts, retarded or slow thought; circumstantially-delayed, indirect thoughts; blocking—an interruption in the flow of thought; and perseveration—the repeating of the same verbal responses over and over.
2. *Associations.* These are the connections between various ideas. Various disturbances with associations may include loose associations—switching subjects in discussion where there appears no logical connection between the subjects; flight of ideas—rapid switching from one idea to another; and tangentiality—answering questions in a very roundabout manner.

Concerning **thought content,** Waldinger identifies the following for assessment concern:

1. *Delusions.* These are false beliefs that the person tenaciously hangs on to despite all evidence to the contrary. They may include delusions of grandeur—delusions of one's importance; delusions of persecution—delusions that one is the target of planned abuse or oppression; delusions of control—thinking that one's thoughts are somehow being controlled by someone or something else; somatic delusions—beliefs that involve some part of the body (e.g., that a particular mark on the body means that the person is of some cosmic importance); thought broadcasting—the belief that others can read your mind; ideas of reference—beliefs that unrelated events bear some special meaning specifically for the individual (e.g., that an actor in a movie is giving you a personal message);
2. *Depersonalization*—a strong sense of unreality about the environment and the self;
3. *Preoccupations*—obsessive thinking regarding death; and
4. *Suicidal and homicidal ideation*—thoughts of physical injury or death to oneself or someone else.

Other aspects of mental status which the therapeutic recreation specialist should be concerned about include various hallucinations—strange and inappropriate perceptions the client experiences, including auditory, visual, olfactory (smell), and gustatory (taste) hallucinations; level of consciousness—that is, alertness; orientation to time, place, and person; concentration; memory; judgment; and insight—that is, the client's awareness of his or her own disturbed thought and reasons for that disturbed thought.

Table 4.2 presents an outline recommended for assessments by therapeutic recreation specialists. It should be noted that there are few standardized instruments available for assessment in therapeutic recreation. The principle approach is to design activities and tasks that will require the client to demonstrate the skill or behavior to be assessed. As the specialist views those behaviors of concern, he or she makes a judgment as to the degree of function or dysfunction of those behaviors. Finally, the specialist seeks to validate or deny his or her interpretations through input from the client and other treatment team members.

Planning

Results of the assessment and input from other sources, including the client, become the basis for selection of goals and objectives to be addressed. Ideally, this is a process that is done with the client; however in some cases a client's functioning may be so impaired that planning will have to be done for the individual. In many cases the focus of the treatment plan will include targets of change other than the client. Maladaptive behavior may be

TABLE 4.2 Therapeutic Recreation Assessment Format

I. Personal Presentation	
Appearance	Reality orientation
Physical mannerisms	Motor behavior
Eye contact	Impulse control
Quality of speech	Affect
Comfort level	Insight
Thought pattern	
II. Task Performance (Includes individual and group, structured and unstructured)	
Ability to follow directions	Problem solving/Decision making
Organization	Task completion
Attention span	Quality of effort
Follow-through	
III. Interpersonal Skills	
Reaction to authority figures	Resistance/Compliance
Resistance/Compliance	Assumption of group role
Competitiveness and reaction to competition	Dependence/Independence
Cooperation and sharing	Responsibility
	Interpersonal space
IV. Physical Skills	
Fine motor	Endurance
Gross motor	Mobility
Balance	Coordination
Strength	Flexibility
Agility	Aerobic fitness
V. Leisure Pattern	
History	Motivations
Knowledge	Barriers
Interests and involvement	Lifestyle organization
Attitudes and values	

Source: Adapted from Kinney (1980, pp. 42–45) and Carter, Van Andel, & Robb (1985, p. 236).

the legitimate result of an unhealthy environment. To change an individual's behavior and send that person back to the same environment is attacking only part of the problem.

The treatment plan, therefore, should consider and address goals relevant to the individual, the physical environment, and the social environment (Howe-Murphy & Charboneau, 1987). Goals targeted within therapeutic recreation will vary, depending on the mission of the agency and the perspective of therapeutic recreation as a treatment modality. Another important factor affecting goal planning is the length of time the client is expected to be affiliated with the agency. Third party insurers dictate the length of time they are willing to cover and that time factor becomes a very large factor in treatment planning.

Implementation

Figure 4.1 illustrates how the clinically designed group becomes treatment. Beginning at the innermost level, the group consists of a number of clients (selected for some particular reason relevant to the anticipated outcomes) and a therapeutic recreation specialist. Each client relates to the group on three levels reflected by the triangle: Individual level—thoughts and behaviors regarding the self; Interpersonal level—the thoughts and behavior reflected through interactions with two or more individuals; and Group level—thoughts and behaviors that reflect the collective thoughts and behaviors of the group (Ward, 1985). These individuals function within the structure of a specific recreational activity selected to help the group address its ultimate purposes. This activity serves as a stimulus which elicits behaviors at all three levels, sometimes at the same time. This group and recreational activity occurs within a particular environment which also affects thoughts and behaviors.

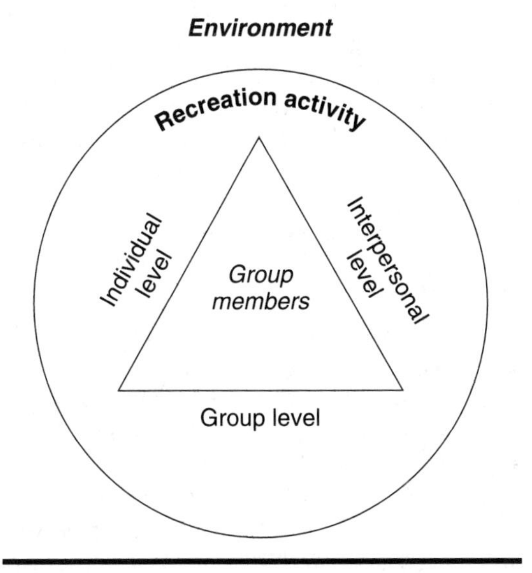

FIGURE 4.1 Context of Therapeutic Group Activity

Within this mix, the therapeutic recreation specialist interjects his or her group process skills which are targeted at one or more of the three levels and are designed to help the group evolve and overcome identified problem areas. Examples of a therapeutic recreation specialist's verbal comments at each level might be:

- Individual level—"Bill, you continue to picture yourself as an incompetent person, yet your contributions to the group project today were invaluable."
- Interpersonal level—"You know, Bill and Mary, the two of you have become increasingly supportive of each other in your attempts to reach out to others more. To what do you attribute that?"
- Group level—"I sense quite a lot of tension over the fact that we are planning to move on to a project that will involve a lot more commitment from each of us. How do you think that tension reflects how we feel about ourselves as a group?"

The careful planning of interventions and their settings and the "on the spot" group process skills of the therapeutic recreation specialist allow the group to become more cohesive and more willing to confront each other or support each other as the need requires. As a group becomes cohesive, there are a number of naturally occurring therapeutic factors that the therapeutic recreation specialist wants to attempt to enhance. Yalom (1985) has identified eleven therapeutic factors that exist in cohesive treatment groups. These are:

1. **1.** Instillation of hope—the belief that we can get better and that no matter how bad the situation, there is hope for a better life.
2. **2.** Universality—the recognition that we are not alone; other people have similar problems and we do share much in common with each other.
3. **3.** Imparting of information—the teaching of skills, giving of advice, and other events of an instructive nature.
4. **4.** Altruism—the giving to others and the sense of positive esteem that results from helping someone else.
5. **5.** Corrective recapitulation of the primary family group—in many respects a cohesive group

represents a family, and the interactions of group members tend to reflect somewhat similar interactions they experienced with their first and primary group, their own family. The exploration of those pathological interactions within the cohesive group allows for "corrective" action to occur.

6. Development of socializing techniques—the learning through role playing, observing others, or through feedback from others, the effects that one's social behaviors have on others, and learning how to improve social interactions.
7. Imitative behavior—seeing how others in the group behave in certain situations and picking up some of those behaviors to "try out" in our own interpersonal interactions.
8. Interpersonal learning—the reconstruction and examination of relationships and interactions within the group that typify relationships and interactions outside the group. The interventions of the group leader and members allow individuals to realize how they have been contributing to their problems and subsequently change their behavior (Waldo, 1985).
9. Group cohesiveness—the "togetherness" of the group; also, the recognition of group norms and conformance to those norms.
10. Catharsis—the good or "cleansing" feeling that results from expressing some emotion that one has had difficulty previously expressing.
11. Existential factors—a broad group of factors that generally result in an acceptance of life as it is, and the recognition that each person is ultimately responsible for his or her own life.

It is these therapeutic factors that determine how the therapeutic recreation specialist designs and guides the therapeutic recreation group toward its goals. Clearly, the therapeutic recreation specialist must have an excellent grasp of group dynamics and group process as well as an understanding of the psychodynamics of human thinking and functioning.

Evaluation Procedures

Evaluation is the analysis of data to determine the extent to which an individual or group of clients has progressed toward their identified goal(s). While evaluation is typically an ongoing process, it involves several levels of input. The therapeutic recreation specialist, in working with groups, helps members set individual as well as group goals. It is helpful to the group process to periodically have the group spend time discussing progress and providing feedback to each other. Thus client self-evaluation is an important source of input.

Information from others is extremely valuable in gathering evaluation data. Such information may come from other staff working with the client (this information is usually transmitted through treatment team meetings), from family or other significant individuals in the clients' life, and from the clients' medical chart (Posavac & Carey, 1985).

Within the psychiatric setting there is an additional form of evaluation that is particularly helpful to the specialist. This is the practice of **clinical supervision.** Clinical supervision is a process whereby one therapist (usually of senior standing and experience) helps another therapist develop their clinical skills through an intensive, interpersonal approach (Critchley, 1987). While one focus of clinical supervision is to analyze difficulties that the therapist may be having with a particular client (Platt-Koch, 1986), another may be to help a therapist recognize the progress a client is making in the interventions the therapist is structuring. Thus, clinical supervision can be a helpful process of evaluating client movement and the appropriateness of certain interventions.

APPLICATION OF THE TR PROCESS

CASE STUDY

Wilbur, at the time of admission, was a 27-year-old white male with a primary diagnosis of schizophrenia, further complicated by diabetes. The psychological evaluation indicated evidence of delusions of grandeur and paranoia. His IQ was normal to high normal. He has had numerous psychiatric admissions at other facilities, but this was his first admission to this facility. Wilbur's activity of daily living skills were poor; his appearance was disheveled; he wore multiple-layered clothing; and he had poor hygiene habits. He did not follow his diabetic diet which lead to several health crises (i.e., insulin shock, rehospitalization, etc.).

The therapeutic recreation evaluation revealed a poor work history, pattern of severe isolation, poor interpersonal skills, short attention span, and poor insight into his illness or how others perceive him. His goal in life was to be a rock star.

One of the treatment goals for Wilbur focused on building social interaction skills. This group emphasized learning to tolerate other people in a group setting; speaking/acknowledging others; making suggestions and/or expressing opinions; and learning to make compromises.

Wilbur's progress was slow and often delayed. In the initial stages of participation, he was unable to consistently attend groups, was resistant to suggestions in regards to interactions with other group members, unwilling to participate in activities, and quit the activity when frustrated. He eventually progressed to the point where he met the criterion for discharge from the group as initially designed with his input:

1. Ability to consistently attend the group three times a week for four weeks (12 consecutive sessions);
2. Verbally express a minimum of two suggestions per group for a week;
3. Independently initiate conversation with another group member (not staff);
4. In stressful situations, discuss any problems/conflicts and make compromises two out of three times; and
5. Demonstrate ability to encourage other group members to participate in an activity.

Eight weeks after Wilbur was in the recreation therapy group and demonstrated the ability to tolerate working with others and was somewhat consistent in attending, he was referred to the work skills program, the next step in his rehabilitation.

Trends in Mental Health Care

Traditionally, the treatment for individuals with mental illness has occurred in settings that were restrictive in nature (usually inpatient hospital stays) (Bickman et al., 1992; Cohen et al, 1992; Frank & Deva, 1992). Hospitals are considered the most restrictive and most costly settings in which to provide mental health services (Frank & Deva, 1992). Over the past twenty to thirty years there have been dramatic changes in the delivery of care, including the types of services provided to individuals with a mental illness.

The current focus is directed toward a **continuum of services** that, for the most part, is community based. The type of service recommended for any individual should be the least restrictive setting as his or her condition will allow. This should be determined by a clinical assessment of the individual's current level of functioning. At the most restrictive end of this continuum, **inpatient stays (hospitalizations)** should only be used for individuals who require 24-hour supervision to ensure the safety of themselves or others (i.e., making direct threats to harm self; violent, unpredictable behavior, etc.). At the opposite end of the continuum, the least restrictive setting, are **outpatient services** which are provided while the individual is living independently in the community. Until recently, these two services were the most predominant forms of treatment available. Other services in the continuum, usually referred to as **intermediary services,** were sparse, and waiting lists into these programs necessitated prolonged hospital stays. Hospitalized individuals in need of a less restrictive setting could not be discharged because the level of services needed to maintain the individual in the community were not available.

One factor that has been a catalyst in the campaign towards improving and increasing the number and type of intermediary services has been cutbacks and/or reductions in health insurance coverage. The demand for these services has highlighted the fragmentation of services available to individuals with a mental illness (Cohen et al., 1992). This has necessitated an increase in the types and numbers of programs available that provide intermediary services. The types of services listed below represent a continuum of mental health services that are currently available.

Depending on the needs of an individual, he or she can move in either direction on the continuum of services model (see Table 4.3).

Inpatient hospitalization is considered to be the most restrictive and costly of services. As stated above, only those assessed to be a danger to themselves or others and who require 24 hour supervision should be admitted for an inpatient stay. **Partial hospitalization** is an intermediary service that provides the structure and continuity of intensive hospital services for the individual ready for discharge. Typically individuals participate in hospital services during the day and return to their home or other community living arrangements during the evening and night. **Pre-discharge programs** allow hospitalized individuals to participate in a community-based day treatment program, which is a less intensive program than a hospitalization, while maintaining their residence in the hospital. The purpose of such a service is to assess whether the individual can be maintained and achieve success in a less restrictive environment. It also provides a successful transition from the hospital into such a program. Typically the individual participates in such a program for one to two weeks prior to discharge from an inpatient stay. This service is typically utilized for the more chronically ill adult population. A transition period assists in reducing the anxiety and fear that is usually experienced when they anticipate leaving one program and starting another.

Specialty Centers. **Crisis centers** are available in some states. These centers typically offer short-term, crisis stabilization for those who require intensive, 24-hour services, with the goal of reducing their need for more extensive and restrictive hospital stays. With the current changes in health care, even what was considered to be short-term treatment (one month) is being restructured. Now some individuals admitted to a crisis center may stay for as short a time as one to two days for an evaluation, while others may require longer periods of crisis intervention (average is usually two weeks). As soon as the problems presented at admission have been stabilized, the individual is referred to a less restrictive setting/program. **Drug and alcohol centers** offer specialized 28-day programs for those individuals with addictions to drugs and/or alcohol.

Residential Services. **Community based supervised residences** (group homes) provide 24-hour supervision with less intensive and more limited scope of services provided for the individual. The supervised residence provides structure and training for individuals who can not live independently in the community. Individuals do not need the intensity of inpatient services but need to learn independent life skills (for adults). These services have been provided by mental health workers who supervise and train individuals with a mental illness in areas such as personal hygiene, cooking, budgeting of money, use of leisure time, etc. Residential services continue to exist today and have homes that not only serve adult populations but also children and adolescent group homes, which are separate services. For children/adolescents, community-based supervised residences provide training and therapy surrounding issues and behaviors that prevent the children from returning to their familial homes. In addition, children receive assistance and training in activities of daily living, problem resolution, etc. Children and adolescents also attend school and partial care programs while at the residence. There are varying degrees of services provided by community-based supervised residences. Some are considered post 28-day programs for those individuals who have been recently discharged from a hospital setting and need a short-term structured setting prior to returning to the community independently. Other residences provide a more long-term, less intensive service for those determined to need this type of service. **Semi-independent apartments** are another type of residential service that is less restricted than the supervised residences. The individual maintains an apartment independently or with a roommate.

TABLE 4.3 Continuum of Services

Setting	Service	Typical programs	Description
Least Restrictive to Most Restrictive	Outpatient	Individual Couples Family Intensive Outpatient	Weekly to monthly visits 50–60 minute sessions Short-term—usually 6–12 sessions
	Home-based	Short-term crisis intervention Intermediary crisis intervention Long-term crisis intervention Specialized Foster Care	One to three times a week in home Link families to community services Six weeks to over 6 months linkage training parents/guardians and families
	Day Treatment/ Partial Care	Child Partial Care Adolescent Partial Care Adult Partial Care Vocational Rehabilitation/Work Adjustment Supported Employment	Youth programs after school for 3 to 6 hours a day up to 5 days/week Adult programs—up to 5 hours/day up to 5 days/week Provides therapy groups, individual therapy, case management services
	Residential Services	Community-based supervied residential services Semi-independent residences Boarding Homes	Provides up to 24 hour supervision Group home setting Provides instruction in activities of daily living Ranges from 28 days to approximately year
	Crisis Centers	Usually 28-day stabilization	24-hour crisis intervention
	Inpatient Services	Full hospitalization Partial hospitalization Day hospital Predischarge programs	24-hour supervision Intensive inpatient therapy both group and individual

The individual receives limited services such as reviews/visits by mental health workers to evaluate the progress that the client is making and to provide counseling and education in those areas that prevent the client from independent living.

Day Treatment. **Partial care programs** are offered five days a week for five or more hours a day. These programs are available for those individuals who live in community-based supervised residential facilities (i.e., group homes) and those who live in the community yet need the structure of a day treatment or partial care program to maintain and improve their level of independent living. Services tend to be more lengthy, with some individuals participating in treatment for approximately six months. Individuals attending these programs receive case management services, individual and group therapy, medication monitoring, and psychoeducational services. Depending on the progress made during the program, these individuals typically attend two, three, or five days a week. Day treatment programs are offered for adults, adolescents, and children. Due to the developmental differences of these three populations, the nature and focus of the services differ. For adults, the focus is on learning independent living and vocational skills. Child and adolescent day treatment programs are typically held after school and provide intense structured services including social interaction skills, independent living (when appropriate), individual and group therapy, family therapy, school, etc. The purpose is for the child to develop insight into his or her behaviors, to improve their judgment, decision-making abilities and problem resolution skills with the goal of the child's successful re-entry into the home and community. **Vocational training programs** are offered for adults usually as the next step in the day treatment process, although it is not necessary to have attended a day treatment program to receive these services. This is usually at least a two-part process for those who will be able to maintain a job in the community. The first step would be for clients to work in simulated or controlled work environments. Often the program provides job training at the site. This can involve secretarial skills, maintenance jobs, food service, and housekeeping tasks. Typically the clients perform the services at the program and are supervised by a vocational counselor. Issues of attendance, timeliness, personal hygiene, social interaction, attention to detail and following directions are addressed. The next step would be supported employment whereby job interview skills are taught and assistance in applying and interviewing for jobs in the community is available. Assistance, job coaching, and support once a job has been secured are also available to the individual.

Home-based services are family-based interventions that are provided primarily within the home setting. Those eligible for services are usually identified as being in danger of out-of-home placement. The purpose of these services is to strengthen the family, prevent separation, link the family with community services, and develop and strengthen the family's healthy coping skills (Stroul & Goldman, 1990, p. 200). There are basically three types of home-based services: long-term services which are provided from nine to eighteen months; midrange services which are provided from three to nine months; and short-term, crisis intervention programs which serve families for up to three months. **Community mobile outreach** programs are becoming an important service in the continuum of care. Professionals, often in teams, respond to psychiatric crisis situations with the goal of stabilizing the individual and family. Typically, the outreach staff respond to crisis situations as they arise, on an around-the-clock basis. Once the crisis situation in the home has stabilized, this program typically follows the family for four to six weeks, provides counseling, and links the individual and family with community providers prior to discharging the family from its services. The goal of this service is family preservation and prevention of out-of-home placement for the individual and family in crisis. **Specialized foster care** programs are offered for foster care parents and families who have a child/adolescent with a mental illness placed temporarily in their care. Specially trained professionals provide services aimed at integrating the child into the home. This program provides support and education to the foster family regarding the behaviors and treatment issues involved with the foster child.

Outpatient services are now considered to be intensive but short-term. Services can include individual, couples, or family therapy, or a combination of any of the three services. Sessions typically last one hour and the client usually is scheduled for a predetermined number of visits which is determined by the individual's insurance company. **Intensive outpatient services** are offered three to six times a week for three to five hours a day. This program provides those individuals discharged from a hospital stay with a program that offers intensive therapy for a brief period of time. Often these programs are run in the evening so that the individual can restart work and attend the program after work hours. The program provides support for recently discharged individuals as they make the necessary adjustments in their work and family lives. These programs offer individual and group therapy and medication-monitoring services. Intensive outpatient services tend to serve high functioning clients who have experienced acute psychiatric crises. **Drop in programs** are another service in the continuum that are offered to individuals who do not need the structure of a daily or weekly program. These programs often operate in the evenings or weekends and allow individuals to attend when they determine that they could benefit from the support offered from such a program. Typically these programs offer group and individual counseling.

SUMMARY

This chapter has described the difficult task of defining what constitutes mental disorder. In a sense, we define it as not having mental health. If one looks at mental health as having the ability to cope with the life stresses of reality, it becomes easier to see what specific characteristics are involved. Individuals learn to cope by utilizing various defense mechanisms to protect the psychological self from stress. At the same time, individuals bring to bear the cognitive and emotional skills they have to either adapt to stress and crisis or to reach out and change things so that their stress is reduced. People experiencing mental disorder are overwhelmed by the stress of their situations because their defenses and ego strengths cannot meet the demands of those situations. Consequently, they experience psychological pain, much as we feel physical pain, and sometimes develop behaviors that put them further at odds with society's accepted behavior.

The *Diagnostic and Statistical Manual of Mental Disorders Fourth Edition* (DSM-IV, 1994) provides a basis for examining behaviors associated with mental disorder and categorizing them for purposes of understanding. This chapter discussed only those most prevalent which the therapeutic recreation specialist may encounter: schizophrenia, mood disorders, anxiety disorders and phobic neuroses, personality disorders, and eating disorders.

Individuals experiencing mental disorder have a variety of alternatives in seeking treatment. The setting in which the therapeutic recreation specialist is most likely to be involved is where a team of health care professionals design and supervise the various treatment interventions. The therapeutic recreation specialist may be involved in services that are primarily oriented to either recreation participation, education, or rehabilitation (therapy).

When engaged in delivering therapy services, the specialist usually is involved in the development of therapeutic recreation groups. The specialist utilizes his or her understanding of individual psychodynamics, group process, and various activities to help the group become cohesive and engage in a level of interaction that is appropriate for the individuals in the group. Through the processing of interactions and feelings, group members learn how their behavior affects themselves and others, and gradually recognize that their behaviors within the group are typical of their behaviors outside of the group.

SUGGESTED LEARNING ACTIVITIES

1. Pick an activity to focus on, such as eating in a restaurant or playing volleyball; identify possible behaviors that might be exhibited in that activity by: a depressed individual, a very passive individual, an aggressive individual.
2. Debate, within a group, whether de-institutionalization has helped or hindered the cause of mental health advocacy.
3. Research how different societies and cultures deal with mentally ill individuals. What are the similarities and differences to our societal approach?
4. Visit different settings which treat mental illness (e.g., a state hospital, private inpatient hospital, day care hospital, etc.), and discuss the differences in approaches.
5. Draw a "time line" with a ruler, 10 inches long; mark it off into one inch intervals. Now draw a "high point line" three inches above your time line, and a "low point line" three inches below your time line. You should have three parallel lines. Label the one inch spaces on your time line by years going back over your previous ten years. Now graph your own emotional highs and lows for the previous ten years. Take selected spots and examine what was going on in your life at the time; how were you contributing to the feelings? What kind of environmental or external support did you have at the time? What behaviors did you utilize, particularly at the low points, to help yourself through those difficult times? Was your overall behavior different between the high spots and the low spots?
6. Interview someone else who understands the "time line" process and agrees, using a similar technique described in #5. Use helpful questions to attempt to understand their behavioral profile and the internal and external things that contributed to the situation.

REFERENCES

Bedell, R. J. (Ed.). (1994). *Psychological assessment and treatment of persons with severe mental disorders.* Bristol, PA: Taylor & Francis.

Bickman, L., et al. (1992). Evaluation planning for an innovative children's mental health system. *Clinical Psychology Review, 12,* 853–865.

Carter, M. J., et al. (1985). *Therapeutic recreation: A practical approach.* St. Louis: Times Mirror/Mosby College Publishing.

Cohen, R., et al. (1992). Implementing a responsive system of mental health services for children. *Clinical Psychology Review, 12,* 819–828.

Critchley, D. L. (1987). Clinical supervision as a learning tool for the therapist in milieu settings. *Journal of Psychosocial Nursing, 25*(8), 18–21.

Frank, R. G., & Deva, C. S. (1992). Insurance, system structure, and the use of mental health services by children and adolescents. *Clinical Psychology Review, 12,* 829–840.

Gunderson, J. G. (1978). Defining the therapeutic processes in psychiatric milieus. *Psychiatry, 41,* 327–335.

Hartman, H. (1939). Psychoanalysis and the concept of health. *International Journal of Psychoanalysis, 20,* 308–321.

Howe-Murphy, R., & Charboneau, B. G. (1987). *Therapeutic recreation intervention: An ecological perspective.* Englewood Cliffs, NJ: Prentice Hall, Inc.

Kinney, W. B. (1980). Clinical assessment in mental health settings. *Therapeutic Recreation Journal, 14*(4).

Mechanic, D. (1976). Stress, illness, and illness behavior. *Journal of Human Stress, 2*(6).

O'Brien, P., Caldwell, C., & Transeau, G. (1985). Destroyers: Written treatment contracts can help cure self destructive behaviors of the borderline patient. *Journal of Psychosocial Nursing, 23*(4).

Peterson, C. A., & Gunn, S. L. (1984). *Therapeutic recreation program design principles and procedures* (2nd ed.). Englewood Cliffs, NJ: Prentice Hall, Inc.

Platt-Koch, L. M. (1986). Clinical supervision for psychiatric nurses. *Journal of Psychosocial Nursing, 26*(1), 7–15.

Posavac, E. J., & Carey, R. G. (1985). *Program evaluation methods and case studies.* Englewood Cliffs, NJ: Prentice Hall, Inc.

Robins, L. N., et al. (1984). Lifetime prevalence of specific psychiatric disorders in three sites. *Archives of General Psychiatry, 41,* 949–958.

Shank, J., & Kinney, T. (1987). On the neglect of clinical practice. *Philosophy of therapeutic recreation ideas and issues.* Alexandria, VA: National Therapeutic Recreation Society of the National Recreation and Park Association.

Schogol, M. (1994, October 3). Personal briefing: Crazier than ever. *Philadelphia Inquirer,* p. G1.

Stroul, B. A., & Goldman, S. K. (1990). Study of community based services for children and adolescents who are severely emotionally disturbed. *Journal of Mental Health Administration, 17,* 61–77.

Tyrer, P., & Casey, P. (Eds.). (1993). *Social function in psychiatry: The hidden axis of classification exposed.* Petersfield, UK: Wrightson Biomedical Publishing LTD.

Waldinger, R. J. (1990). *Psychiatry for medical students* (2nd ed.). Washington, DC: American Psychiatric Press, Inc.

Waldo, M. (1985). A curative factor framework for conceptualizing group counseling. *Journal of Counseling and Development, 64,* 52–57.

Ward, D. D. (1985). Levels of group activity: A model for improving the effectiveness of group work. *Journal of Counseling and Development, 64,* 59–63.

Yalom, I. D. (1985). *The theory and practice of group psychotherapy* (3rd ed.). New York: Basic Books, Inc.

CHAPTER 5

CORRECTIONS AND SOCIAL DEVIANCE

GAIL E. McCALL

OBJECTIVES

- Identify the most common types of settings in which the incarcerated population may receive therapeutic recreation services.
- Identify the classification types of inmates.
- Understand the current recreational philosophy and practices used in correctional facilities.
- Describe the history of correctional recreation in the United States.
- Discuss the two-pronged approach to the delivery of leisure services in correctional settings.
- Identify and discuss the goal and the projected outcome of the therapeutic recreation process on offenders.

INTRODUCTION TO CORRECTIONS

In 1993 (the last year with complete statistics) crime cost United States governments (federal, state, and local) $674 billion. Collins (1994) stated that injuries to victims of drunk drivers cost $110 billion; police protection, prison systems, and legal and judicial costs—$78 billion; the medical and mental health care costs as well as lost wages (not counting police, court, or incarceration costs) for drug abuse—$40 billion, etc. If you count all associated costs of crime such as a victim's loss of life and goods, welfare for the families whose breadwinner is in prison, the cost of personal protection systems (car alarms and home burglar systems), etc., the cost by the year 2000 could be a staggering $l trillion. Crime is not only the largest business in the United States, it is also the largest growth industry. Who is paying for crime? It is not the criminal. It is the average hard-working American taxpayer.

Initially, prisons were designed only to keep criminals away from society so they could not harm another innocent person. Prisons were primarily used to hold people awaiting trial, or to hold those sentenced until a death penalty could be executed. One of the first holding facilities in the United States was the Walnut Street Jail in Philadelphia, established in 1790. These early facilities primarily provided individual detention cells (6 × 8 feet) with a wooden bench for sleeping, a bucket for human waste, a Bible for reading to help the individual turn his life around, and bread and water for nourishment; punishment and retribution were the order of the day.

Two hundred years later "Lawmakers have discovered that bashing prison inmates is the season's easiest and most disingenuous way to exploit voters' anti-crime sentiment" (Reibstein, Carroll, & Bogart, 1994). The Mississippi state legislature voted in August, 1994, to remove television, air conditioning and weightlifting equipment from all state correctional facilities and to dress inmates in striped uniforms. In October, 1994, the Arizona state legislature demanded that $900,000 worth of weightlifting equipment be removed from its state correctional system. In February, 1995, the Washington state legislature was entertaining the idea of banning coffee and cigarettes from all of its correctional facilities. Jonathan Turley, director of the Prison Law Project, was quoted in *Newsweek* "It's difficult to imagine a measure draconian enough to satisfy the public desire for retribution" (Reibstein, Carroll, & Bogart, 1994).

Prisons have proven to be a 200-year-old failure. The fortress prisons that we have seen over this period of time are overcrowded, unclean, ungovernable, and unhealthy. Reassessment of old methods and structures critically challenge the corrections system of today and of the future. If current legislative mandates continue for punitive measures only, the prison riots of the 1970s and early '80s will be only a minor occurrence compared to what is likely to happen in the future.

The Attica prison uprising in 1971, the burning of the Kansas State Prison in 1973, the takeover of the Washington State Penitentiary in 1979, and the prison riot at the New Mexico State Prison in 1980 raise some difficult philosophical and practical questions regarding practices in prisons and correctional institutions. In the 200 year history of American prisons, we have seen the theoretical pendulum swing from strict hard labor–solitary confinement to liberal policies that allow inmate groups to govern many areas of their existence.

Fogel (1974), in his editorial *Reappraising the Fortress Prison,* indicates that "we still have a system where a 'good' convict makes a lousy citizen and a 'lousy' convict may have what we look for in a good citizen. Consider what a prison requires of a man: routinization, no real responsibility, no family life, no new horizons or initiative, a minutely structured life. On the other hand, an employer seeks: creativity, initiative, a stable family life, flexibility, and a moderate risk-taker. Convicts who act in this latter fashion frequently end up in the 'hole' in a prison."

We should have learned over the past 200 years that neither severe treatment nor leniency are the answers to returning responsible, productive people to society. Finding a common ground somewhere in between is the answer. We must be compassionate, yet strict; humane yet rigorous; have high expectations, yet allow time to learn and achieve; and finally, have the opportunity to apply what has been learned in the institution to the outside world without the stigma of the correctional system. The only answer to recidivism is to develop programs within the correctional system that will prepare the incarcerated person for reentry into society. Therapeutic recreation is one of the most important programs to achieving successful results with correctional populations.

A Brief History of Correctional Recreation

Prior to 1900, there was little or no recreation in prisons. Some prisons had a prison library which certain inmates were permitted to use. In one prison, there was no Sunday recreation, but on holidays the prisoners were allowed to play football in a vacant part of the yard. In another, black inmates were permitted to sing and improvised a concert (Byers et al., 1983).

Little progress was made in recreation until the 1930s. Research indicates that in fifty institutions surveyed, there was a wide range of recreation programs of some kind (Neal, 1972). The next major leap in correctional recreation came in the early 1950s. At a conference entitled "Recreation in Correctional Institutions," a series of recommendations were made that included one stating that *recreation must be a distinct part of the correctional process* (Hormachea, 1981).

In 1966, at the American Correctional Association congress, a panel addressed the effectiveness of recreation in a correctional system. In a world of rapid pace and social change, the importance of recreation in preparing an inmate for the world outside was recognized (Wilkinson & Doggett, 1966).

After limited progress in the '60s, a new wave of interest and initiative began in the 1970s.

The role of recreation in corrections was discussed at the 1971 National Recreation Congress. The destruction and violence witnessed during the prison riots at Attica in 1971 shocked most Americans. One of the principle demands of the inmates at Attica was more recreation time and better resources (Bodillo & Haynes, 1971).

While recreation in correctional institutions improved in the 1980s, most institutions were concentrating on highly organized team sport activities such as football or basketball which gave little carryover value. On an average, only 61 percent participated in athletic offerings (Crutchfield, Garrette, & Worrall, 1981). It should be noted that, while team sports and "pumping iron" were the norm, diverse programs on the cutting edge at that time were also being offered (Garibaldi & Moore, 1981).

The end of the '80s and the beginning of the '90s have seen recreation as an integral part of most inmates' way of life. The programs today are not just sports and athletics which cater to a certain segment of the incarcerated population. Today in some institutions you will find ropes courses in correctional boot camps, educational training on nutrition and athletic performance, pet therapy, music therapy, photography, and more (N.C.R.A. Conference program, 1991).

INTRODUCTION TO SOCIAL DEVIANCE

Socially deviant behavior is a precursor to criminal behavior. In order for a behavior to be deviant, it must vary from an established standard. Deviant behavior means that someone violates the laws or norms of the greater society and thus infringes upon the set standards. Social deviance as it relates to correctional populations has three very distinct characteristics: *sociocultural implications, sociological implications,* and *psychological implications.*

Sociocultural Implications

In a society where diversity and freedom are the very roots of existence, sociocultural differences are an absolute given. American society is made up of hundreds, if not thousands, of broadly differing cultural influences that deal with race, ethnicity, religion, sexuality, age, economic status, etc. Each person is influenced by many subcultures at any one time (see Figure 5.1). If the subcultures' rules are compatible with the larger, or dominant, society, then there is no conflict and thus no social deviation. However, if the rules of the various subcultures the individual belongs to are in conflict with the greater society, then we have social deviance. Because the rules of the subculture are closer to the individual than the laws of the larger society, there is conflict between the values of the subculture and the laws of the land. We take on the characteristics of the culture(s) we live in (Capuzzi & Gross, 1992).

Individuals live on a minute-by-minute basis in their various subcultures and, therefore, gain all of their recognition and identity from the subcultures. In order to survive emotionally and psychologically, the individual must continue to satisfy the needs of the subculture to secure a permanent and secure place within the group, regardless of the overall consequences of his behavior. The

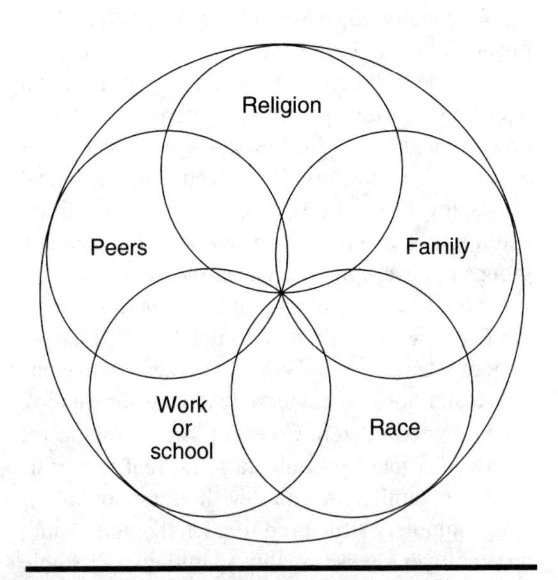

FIGURE 5.1 Sociocultural Clusters of the Individual

individual is caught in conflict between the acceptance of his subculture and obeying the laws of the greater society. The subculture wins this battle 98 percent of the time (Capuzzi & Gross, 1992).

It is impossible to rehabilitate this part of a person's existence. As long as the individual must find his acceptance within the subculture, he will not abide by the laws of the overall society. If rehabilitation is to take place, the individual must be removed from subcultures that are in conflict with the laws of society.

Sociological Implications

Sociological implications begin with the way society builds its social order. This social order can be found in a society's *folkways, mores, and laws. Folkways* are the traditional social customs of a group; these are called the "shoulds." In order to be a good group member you "should" follow the rules. *Mores* are fixed, morally binding customs or moral attitudes of a group; these are called "musts." In order to be accepted as a good group member you "must" stringently follow the moral customs of the group. *Laws* are rules of conduct prescribed by a controlling authority; these are the "have to's." If the individual does not obey the law, then he is punished by loss of privileges. Laws are the end result of folkways becoming so important to social order that they become mores, and finally, when the mores provide enough pressure to make individuals conform to the group's wishes, they then become laws.

Another sociological factor is *social hardness.* This phenomenon comes about over a very long period of time. This is a common characteristic of the socially deviant. Social hardness is the result of repeated rejection, disappointment, and distrust that usually starts during childhood. The individual is told repeatedly that he will never amount to anything (a self-fulfilling prophecy), and over a period of time he begins to believe that he is a nobody. People promise they will do things or be there for him, but when he needs them, they are not. This brings about a rigid "self-reliance" that the individual develops as a self-defense. He will count on only those things he can do for himself. This person is often arrogant, selfish, opinionated, and a loner. He will not trust the recreation therapist or, in many cases, even give that person a chance to discuss what his future might hold (assessment).

Social values are probably the biggest key to social deviance. Values are personal beliefs that are based on strongly held notions of right and wrong. *All* individuals in correctional populations have poorly developed value systems or value systems that are not compatible with the norms of society. We know value systems are affected by many factors: the home, family, culture, school, religion, and peer group, to name a few.

Another sociological implication arises from *social systems within the home.* We are a nation of nomads. We are born in one part of the United States, educated in another, and work in yet another. We meet and marry people from different backgrounds and from opposite ends of the country. Conflict arises when the social order from one cultural influence meets a different social order. We cannot agree on the proper way to rear children, whether to squeeze the toothpaste tube from the middle or the end, or even if Sunday dinner should be at 2:00 P.M. as it was in her family or at 5:00 P.M. as it was in his. Our society tries to merge divergent cultures into compatible families and often the result is divorce and single parent families. Working or single parents often provide latchkey children with little or no supervision. With time on their hands and no one around, teens get into trouble, which leads to an escalating crime rate among children and adults.

Still another sociological factor is *peer pressure;* this is very closely related to sociocultural pressure. Peer pressure has a very strong influence on the individual. If peers are involved in an activity, regardless of its importance to the individual, the individual must become involved or lose the position within the peer group (DuBray, 1992).

Socioeconomic class is another sociological implication that has a great impact on the socially deviant population. There seems to be a disproportionate number of people from the lower socioeconomic groups represented in correctional populations (Bashford, 1995). Survival and value systems that do not fit the mainstream of society seem to have a great deal to do with this group's non-conformity to the rules of society.

And finally, we know that *social systems change faster than the laws*. Before a law can be downgraded from a law to more or folkway, a majority of society must not see that weakening the law would be a threat to the survival of the society. An example of this would be marijuana laws. Long before marijuana possession was downgraded from a felony to a misdemeanor, people were risking its use because the majority of Americans did not see marijuana as a major health hazard or threat to society. The sentiment was that stopping marijuana use was not as important as stopping murder. This is a case of society changing faster than the laws (Bersani, 1970).

Psychological Implications

Psychological implications deal with the mental, emotional and behavioral problems of the socially deviant. We find two distinct personality types within the psychological area, *psychopathic* and *sociopathic*.

Someone with a *psychopathic personality* is usually very normal in appearance; however, he has emotional and behavioral dysfunction. He has a clear perception of reality but he feels no social or moral obligation to society. The instant personal gratification of his desires is his only guide. He knows right from wrong but has no guilt because his need justifies his actions. Often persons with psychopathic personalities commit heinous crimes.

The person with a *sociopathic personality* often displays asocial or antisocial behaviors. He is seldom confused with a normal person and often reacts out of unabashed desires, regardless of social consequence. This person is often reclusive and lacks social skills. He is maladjusted and requires a great deal of the recreation therapist's attention.

If a person does not fit into either of these categories, then he is thought to have normal psychological fields. The normal psychological pressures that affect all people have a similar effect on those who display socially deviant behaviors. *Self-concept* (see Figure 5.2) affects everyone. However, because the socially deviant suffer from so many of the above-mentioned problems (sociocultural, sociological) they tend generally to have *very* poor self-concepts.

The development of positive self-concepts is a major function of therapeutic recreation. The recreation therapist must plan and develop activities that can build self-esteem, self-worth, and self-image in all correctional populations.

Another psychological implication for the socially deviant is the *psychological pressure of the corrections system which causes temporary conformity* of the individual during incarceration. Here the individual learns the very narrow confines of the system and what is expected of him. He temporarily conforms to the system and becomes what the system calls a "model inmate." However, these changed behaviors are not internalized, and when the individual returns to society he reverts to his deviant behaviors. This is one of the major reasons that the socially deviant return over and over to the corrections system. The recreation therapist has an opportunity to help the individual recognize and internalize the changes he has made in order to take them with him after incarceration.

The socially deviant often display what is known as the *persecution complex*. The individual feels that everyone is against him. No one wants to see him succeed. He often gives excuses, for example that his parents divorced and he had

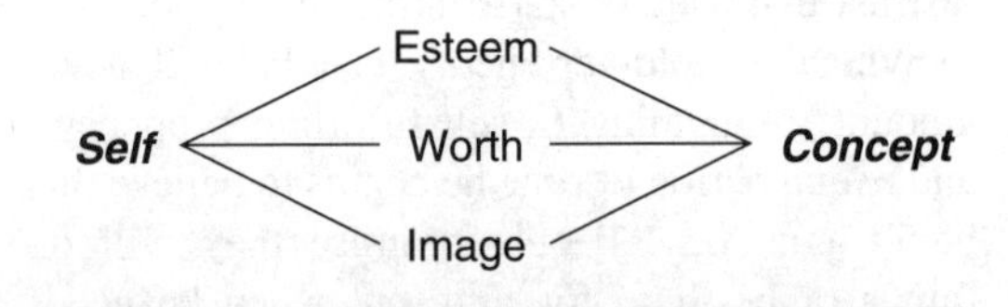

FIGURE 5.2 Major Components of Self-Concept for Socially Deviant Individuals

to drop out of school to help his mother support the family. This is usually untrue, but he uses it as an excuse for his failure. He also feels the system—schools, employers, police, courts, and so on—have always set up insurmountable obstacles for the sole purpose of seeing him fail. The person with a persecution complex is someone the recreation therapist can help immensely. This person needs multiple successful experiences to recognize that his efforts are what bring about success, rather than believe he is denied success by some imagined barrier.

Yet another psychological barrier for the socially deviant is what is known as *low-tolerance* or *low-threshold.* Socially deviant individuals are often easily angered; they often overreact to minor situations. The recreation therapist has a unique opportunity to help these individuals learn "anger management and aggression control" and tolerance through participation in leisure activities (Klare, 1973).

Leisure skills development and the management of leisure time are important issues in helping the socially deviant reenter society. Of all the adjunctive therapies and programs in the correctional system, none is as important as helping individuals utilize their leisure time in a healthy and acceptable manner. Since 90 to 95 percent of all crimes are committed during leisure, we in the leisure field must unlock the secret to acceptable leisure pursuits for the socially deviant.

TERMINOLOGY

It is essential for the reader to become acquainted with the various terms that are used in the socially deviant and correctional fields. Two broad and general terms that are used to distinguish the severity of the crime and to give some general information about the personality type of the person committing the crime are ***nonviolent*** and ***violent.***

Nonviolent

A nonviolent crime is a crime that is perpetrated against property, that is, a crime that does not have a victim but does result in the loss of something valuable to the original owner, such as a car, a stereo, money, or some other object. In terms of recreation, people who commit nonviolent crimes most often choose leisure activities that can be done alone or with one other person.

Violent

A violent crime is the most severe crime in our society because it has a victim or a potential victim. A murder has a victim and thus is a violent crime. However, an armed robbery, one that does not result in a loss of life, is also a violent crime because there is a *potential* victim. If the robbery attempt had not gone well for the perpetrator, then a death may have occurred. Other examples of violent crimes are rape, assault and battery, manslaughter, and kidnap. In terms of recreation, people who commit violent crimes most often choose leisure activities where they can be the center of attention or show off. They like to draw attention to themselves. They like a challenge and an opportunity to excel.

Felony	A serious crime that is punishable in a state facility for one year or more.
Misdemeanor	A less serious crime that is punishable in a county or local facility (jail) for one year or less.
Probation	A preincarceration experience. The court sentences the offender to probation in lieu of going to prison.
Parole	A postincarceration experience. After the offender has served a substantial portion of the sentence imposed by the court, he is released back to the community on a trial basis.
Incarceration	The act of placing someone in confinement or prison.
Institutionalization	A person becomes so dependent on the institution to

satisfy his needs that he cannot survive psychologically, physically, or emotionally without the institutional setting.

Peaking — The moment that a person realizes that it is he that must change, not society or those around him. It is that time when he can finally redirect himself to make permanent attitude and value changes.

Threshold — A point, above or below, at which a person exceeds the norm of acceptable behavior.

Open population — Refers to those inmates who can move freely within the open confines of the correctional facility.

Administrative confinement — Refers to the individual detention or confinement of an inmate because he seriously violated the rules of the institution, or he has asked for protection from other inmates.

Death row — The individual detention of persons awaiting execution. These inmates are housed in a separate area of the institution.

CLASSIFICATION OF OFFENDERS

Juvenile offenders — Those individuals committing one of the two classified acts considered a juvenile offense. (1) *A delinquent act* is considered to be a serious offense by a juvenile. Had the juvenile been an adult, he would be charged with a criminal act. (2) *A status offense* is only a crime if you are a juvenile; the offenses are truancy or running away from home. An adult cannot commit a status offense.

Maximum security or close custody — These terms are used interchangably; they both refer to the same type of monitoring required of inmates who are difficult to manage. This type of offender is usually housed in prisons or correctional institutions. The recreation opportunities offered to this classification of inmate must meet the six criteria discussed in the limitations section.

Medium custody — An inmate in this classification usually has been in the institution long enough for the staff to observe his behavior and to classify him as someone who does not pose a security threat (particularly when he is participating in programs in the open population with other inmates). He is usually able to give some self-direction with regard to his leisure pursuits and choices.

Minimum custody — This classification of inmate is the lowest custody level of inmates held within the compound. He may move about the institution freely. He has access to all of the resources in the recreation therapy department. He has been in the institution long enough to be evaluated several times and has built trust with the staff. He does not pose a security threat to the institution.

Trustee or work release — These are not the same, but their classification is the lowest possible within the correctional system. Both of these inmates may move from inside the institution to the outside world and then back again. These inmates have access to all recreational opportunities.

DESCRIPTION OF LIMITATIONS

There are obvious limitations imposed by the nature of incarceration. The inmates, as do all people, have their own strengths and limitations. Individuals incarcerated in the nation's facilities have committed crimes from murder to trespass, but they often share a disturbingly similar background.

Justice Department surveys found that less than one third grew up with both parents. More than half had family members who had been in jail. Drugs were also a common factor. More than 60 percent of jailed juveniles said they used drugs regularly, and almost 40 percent were high when they committed crimes (Meddis & Edmonds, 1994).

In order for leisure services to be introduced into any correctional setting they must meet certain very strict criteria. (1) The activities must be nonviolent in nature. (2) They must be conducted in small or limited space. All space in closed compounds or facilities with perimeter fencing is at a premium and recreation is only alloted a limited amount of this space. (3) Recreational activities must be inexpensive because funding is usually generated from nonappropriated funds, such as canteen or telephone revenues. Correctional dollars traditionally go for security and maintenance, not programs. (4) Recreation programs must not offend the public. If the public cannot afford a swimming pool or tennis court in their backyard, then they do not feel that inmates deserve one in their backyard either. (5) The recreation program cannot create a security problem for the institution. If an activity is too raucous or boisterous and the inmates become agitated or overwrought, then the security staff complain that they have to increase personnel to prevent a possible riot or disturbance. Events that include running or objects such as bats and balls that could be used as weapons can present a potential problem. A large number of inmates in a small space can also be a potential danger to security. (6) Recreation programs must serve a large number of inmates at one time. Staff is limited and time that is available for participation is also limited; therefore, those who want to participate must do so in large groups.

The therapeutic specialist must always keep the above limitations in mind and be ready to adapt programs and activities when necessary.

PURPOSE OF THERAPEUTIC RECREATION

The purpose of therapeutic recreation in correctional settings is to help inmates develop new leisure skills that will assist them in reentering the community upon their release. Therapeutic recreation must help the inmate develop an awareness of how recreational activities can help him deal with difficult situations through anger management and aggression control. Participation in leisure activities is therapeutic to the extent that it enables an inmate to make attributions of leisure behavior to personal abilities and improves self-perception of personal capabilities. In addition, recreation must create opportunities within the institution for inmates to release the daily tensions of incarceration.

The therapeutic recreation model that we find in correctional settings today consists of what is known as the ***Leisure Education Model.*** The Leisure Education Model was first developed as a response to the federal grant program, "Project Culture," that was conceived by the American Correctional Association and funded by the Law Enforcement Assistance Administration (Nicolai, 1981). The word CULTURE is an acronym for **C**reative **U**se of **L**eisure **T**ime **U**nder **R**estricted **E**nvironments. This demonstration project had a profound effect on the acceptance of *leisure* as a therapeutic modality within correctional settings. The leisure education model has since been used in many states by many different types of institutions and has been refined over the years. Figure 5.3 illustrates the various components that comprise leisure education in the correctional setting.

Therapeutic recreation in a correctional setting begins with leisure education. Through class instruction, the individual is exposed to the role that recreation has played and will continue to play in his life. He learns how leisure experiences can enhance the quality and increase the number

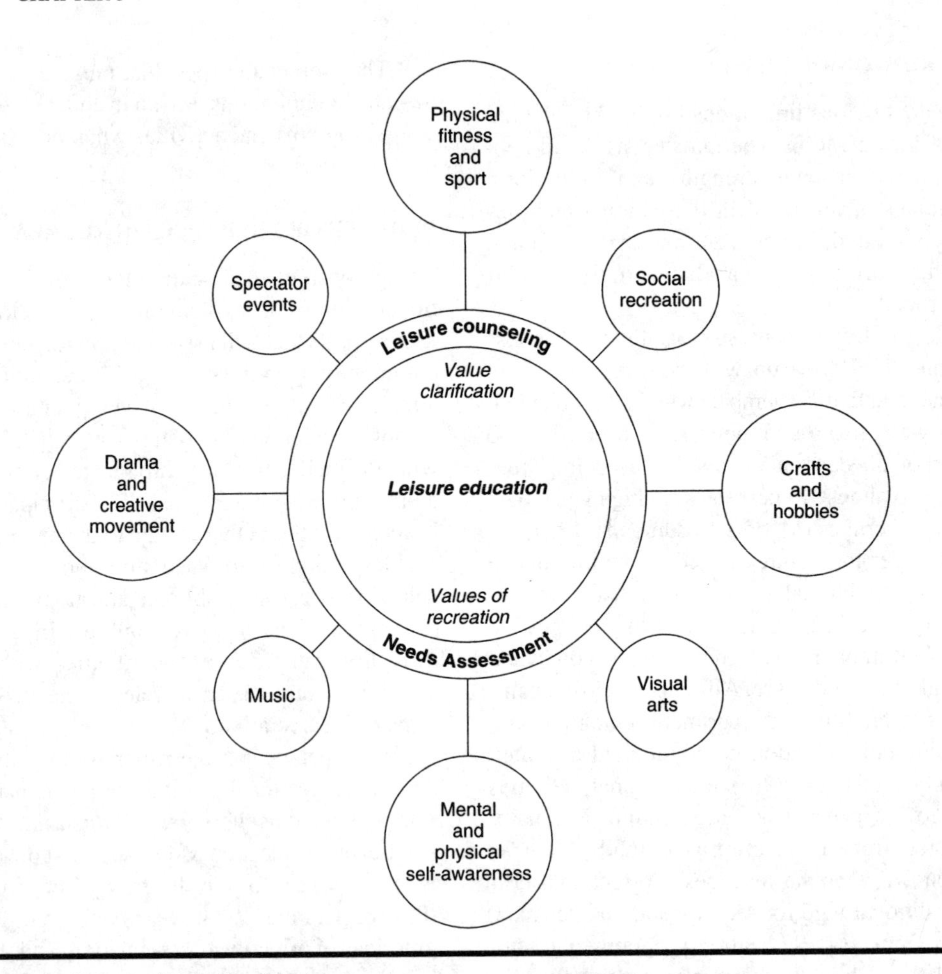

FIGURE 5.3 Leisure Education Model

of options available to him. After the impact of leisure has been discussed, and the inmate clearly understands the concepts of leisure education, the leisure education program moves into the next phase—value clarification.

Value clarification enables each inmate to identify his need for praise, belonging, and acceptance. Self-esteem, self-concept, self-control, self-image, and self-worth are also a necessity. These values, as well as methods for achieving and satisfying them, should be discussed at length. For example, the inmate should understand that all people have a need for praise. The individual who does not receive praise or recognition from a job well done or from an act of kindness should pursue leisure activities that have the potential to satisfy this need. If the problem is self-control, leisure education and value clarification should help the individual to recognize uncontrolled temper and to learn activities which use hostile energy positively and divert attention from further negative action. Recognizing personal needs and the way that leisure can help in satisfying these needs is the objective during the value clarification phase of the model.

Compiling a "needs assessment inventory," including both past leisure history and future desires for leisure activity, is the next step in leisure education. Several inventories may be used, such as McKechnie's (1974) *Leisure Activities Blank,*

McCall's (1977) *Leisure Interest Inventory,* and Ellis & Niles's (1985) *Brief Leisure Rating Scale.* Understand that these tests or inventories should not be administered before the leisure education and value clarification components of the program. If the inventories are administered first, the inmate will make choices based on perceived likes and dislikes rather than on activities having a potential for satisfying a need or a value. Two separate areas of the individual's leisure should be revealed by the needs assessment. First, it should reveal *recreation pursuits,* activities, and frequency of participation prior to incarceration. Second, the assessment should reflect the individual's *leisure interests,* activities the individual would enjoy but in which, for whatever reason, he has never participated. There are many reasons an individual may not have attempted a leisure activity in the past. Facilities may not have been available or the individual may have lacked the necessary skills. An activity may have been too expensive. Once the assessment has been completed, TR personnel should carefully evaluate the identified recreation pursuits and leisure interests and then help the individual balance leisure activities previously pursued with new activities, thus helping the inmate develop new leisure perspectives.

The final step in the model is to provide leisure counseling and opportunities for skill acquisition, two areas which go hand in hand. As the individual becomes involved in the leisure service program, a TR specialist should help the inmate discuss his satisfactions or dissatisfactions with current activities. The inmate should be encouraged to stop participation in an unsuitable activity and pursue another of greater benefit.

It should be remembered that the purpose of therapeutic recreation in a correctional setting is three-fold: *diagnostic, treatment,* and *diversion.* The first, *diagnostic,* is the part of the therapeutic model that evaluates the individual and considers all facets of his existence. Diagnosis must look at past behaviors and evaluate whether or not leisure choices have been a factor in an individual's deviant acts. Diagnosis must also address the type of crime—violent or nonviolent.

The second component, *treatment,* is designed to take the facts gathered during diagnosis and assess what part leisure can play in helping the individual become a normal productive citizen. Sometimes we see that the type of deviancy can be related to leisure choices. We know that individuals who commit violent crimes choose leisure activities that are often violent in nature and that will allow the person to be the center of attention. Nonviolent criminals select activities that allow anonymity and do not require others to participate. Treatment, then, should include helping the violent individual select leisure pursuits that will meet his needs yet will require him to be the center of attention. Treatment should help the nonviolent offender pursue activities that will help him build social confidence and expand his social circle.

The third component, *diversion,* is that portion of the recreation program that allows the inmate to release anger and frustration and, at least for a few moments, forget the harshness of incarceration. Diversion will be discussed at length in the section on the Two-Pronged Approach on page 89.

COMMON SERVICE SETTINGS

There are a myriad of settings in which we find correctional therapeutic recreation. These settings are usually distinguished by age (juvenile or adult), sex, criminal or behavioral classification (custody), or institutional size.

Juvenile detention centers may be locally (city or county) or state operated facilities. The city or county operated facilities are designed to hold juveniles awaiting trial or serving very short sentences after their trial. These facilities provide food, shelter, clothing, education, and recreation. Recreation in this setting is seldom therapeutic in nature. These facilities seldom have designated recreation areas. Recreation activities are offered solely for the juveniles to release tension and energy. State operated juvenile facilities are designed for the long-term incarceration of young offenders. Besides food, they offer shelter, clothing, extensive educational programs, vocational education, counseling, and therapeutic recreation programs to assist juveniles with their reentry into society. These facilities often have large designated areas for recreation, both in the living units and on the general compound.

Jail is a locally (city or county) operated facility that is designed primarily as a holding facility for adult offenders awaiting court dates or trials. These facilities have very limited program offerings because they are designed for short-term stays. An offender might be in this facility for as little as 24 hours or as long as 364 days. Recreation is planned primarily as a diversion from the daily pressures of incarceration. Because the offender's stay in this type of facility is so short, there is not a time frame to incorporate therapeutic principles into the program.

There is usually only one *prison* per state. This facility will always include the death chamber if the state has a death penalty statute. This facility is designed as a *maximum custody* facility only. Only the most hardened criminals or those inmates who pose an escape risk are sent to this facility. A prison's **number one** priority is security; nothing goes on in the facility that would threaten security. The **number two** priority is maintenance—providing food, shelter, clothing, and medical care for inmates. The **number three** priority is the provision of programs. The inmates in the prison population are usually serving long sentences, and therefore programs are important to assist them with productively utilizing their time. Programs in prison are usually very conservative because of the custody problem and the length of the offender's sentence. These programs should be designed to help the inmate acquire new skills as well as cope with the pressures of incarceration.

Correctional institutions are designed as long-term holding facilities. Inmates in these facilities are serving sentences from one year to life; however, the average sentence is usually four years or more. The **number one** priority in a correctional institution is programs. Since most of the inmates in these institutions are released back into society, it is imperative that a wide range of treatment modalities be offered. Inmates must acquire occupational skills, either vocational or academic, that have a good market value on the streets. They must have access to counseling, both psychological and sociological, to help them handle their inability to cope in an open society. They must have extensive access to recreation therapy in order to develop new leisure skills that can help them establish new friends and social circles once they are released. The **number two** priority is security. Since most inmates in correctional institutions are either in close or medium custody, no program should be a serious threat to the security of the institution. The **number three** priority is maintenance. The institution has an obligation to provide food, shelter, clothing, and medical care.

Treatment centers are designed to deal extensively with the treatment of serious behavior problems. These are often sex offender institutions or facilities primarily designed to deal with offenders who have serious psychological problems. There are usually medical treatment teams in these institutions, and they have many facilities for the necessary programs. The **number one** priority of these institutions is the treatment of the inmate's dysfunction. The **number two** priority is programs. With the exception of the most seriously disordered inmate, all inmates are released from these institutions. Sometimes the inmates are released to other correctional facilities, but usually they are released directly into society. It is essential that all treatment modalities be available in this type of facility. Recreation is one of the most important adjunctive therapies, since it helps the person redevelop his life structures and habits. The recreation therapist is an integral member of the treatment team. The **number three** priority is maintenance of the individual, and the **number four** priority is security. Security, of course, is important, but it cannot supersede the value of treatment programs.

Community release centers are prerelease facilities. These facilities are designed as "step down" institutions to allow the inmate to reintegrate slowly into society. Usually about six months before an inmate is to be released, he is assigned to a community release center where he can leave for an eight-hour period to work at a job in the community. The remainder of the 24-hour period is spent inside the institution. The **number one** priority is job/life skills. The inmate is assisted in finding a job. He must attend classes such as money management and Alcoholics Anonymous (if he had a drinking problem prior to incarceration), and a myriad of other self-help programs. The **number two** priority is programs such as attending community college classes, attending leisure education classes, and any other program that might help his reentry into society. The **number three** priority is maintenance of the individual, and the **number four** priority is security. Security is usually not a problem, since the inmates are so close to release; it would be foolish to walk away from the facility and then receive a mandatory sentence for escape.

CURRENT BEST PRACTICES AND PROCEDURES

The correctional recreation programs that are currently being offered in correctional settings today are either totally diversionary, that is, devoid of any therapeutic value, or they are a combination of therapeutic recreation and diversion. Diversion programs are primarily designed to allow inmates to burn off excess energy and hostility in a controlled environment. These programs are usually planned by correctional staff or professional staff who do not have therapeutic recreation degrees or training. A diversionary program usually consists of weightlifting, body building, team sports such as basketball, football, volleyball, or softball, and, if space, staff, and budgets allow, even arts and crafts, and hobbies. These programs serve a useful purpose by helping the institution manage inmates by allowing them to "blow off steam" in a socially acceptable manner that might otherwise be vented as hostility toward other inmates or staff. These recreation programs offer little or no carryover value to the outside world and are not thought of as therapeutic.

The following ***leisure restructuring*** model has been used in many states and in many different types of institutions. This part of the leisure restructuring model is called the ***Two-Pronged Approach*** (see Figure 5.4). This system relies heavily on the *Leisure Education Model* (Figure 5.3) that was discussed earlier.

The first part of the Two-Pronged Approach, the delivery of leisure services within prisons and correctional institutions, exclusively addresses the release of daily tensions generated as a result of the unnatural incarceration environment. An individual placed in a single-sex institution loses all freedom of choice in what he does, what he wears, what he eats, and with whom he associates. Deprived of these choices, tensions build which may lead to open and hostile violence that often ends in prison riots.

As an integral part of the correctional system, the recreation and leisure service program contributes to the process of relieving tension by providing therapeutic programs. A goal of the programs is to provide opportunities to vent pent-up energies and tension in a healthy and acceptable manner.

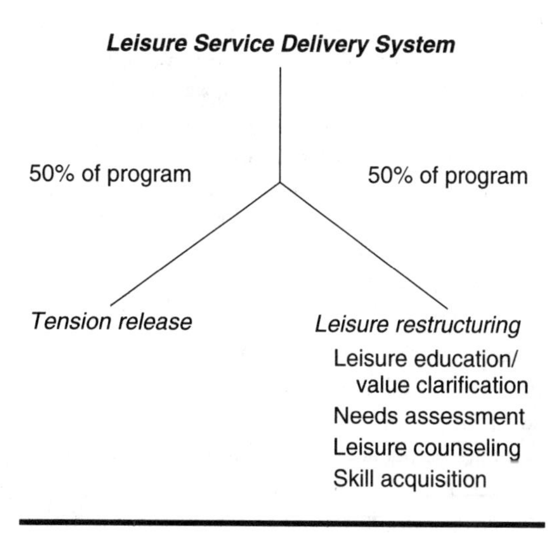

FIGURE 5.4 Two-Pronged Approach for Delivering Leisure Services

The second aspect of the Two-Pronged Approach in the delivery of leisure services in restricted environments is the process of leisure restructuring. Restructuring includes leisure education/value clarification, needs assessment, leisure counseling, and skill acquisition. Leisure restructuring does not deal exclusively with the leisure needs of the individual but more broadly addresses the individual as a multifaceted member of society. Each individual has unique needs and problems that must be dealt with in an understanding manner. The recreation therapist must combine his/her knowledge of the individual with that of the other members of the treatment team (psychologist, sociologist, medical staff) in order to treat the whole individual and assist with his reentry into society. The leisure education/values clarification, needs assessment, leisure counseling, and skill acquisition portions of leisure restructuring were discussed at length in the Purpose of Therapeutic Recreation section earlier in this chapter.

Finally, recreational services are delivered in three different settings within prisons and correctional institutions. The first is called *open population,* which refers to the status of the inmate's custody and where he lives within the institution. Most recreation programs are delivered in the open population setting. Programs in open population include "in-cell" and "out-of-cell" activities. These programs may be found anywhere in the prison or correctional compound. The second is called *administrative confinement.* This type of confinement requires that all recreational activities, except for one hour outdoors per day, be carried out within the cell. The inmate is locked up 23 hours per day either because of disruptive behavior or to protect him from harm in the open population. Third, leisure services are delivered to *death row.* The activities usually found on death row are diversionary. These inmates have no reason to learn activities that would have carryover value to the outside world. The activities primarily consist of reading, playing cards, writing, watching television, and other sedentary in-cell activities. In most states, these inmates may leave their cells only for showers and meetings with attorneys. They are allowed out-of-cell for one hour, three times a week, to participate in physically active activities; however, they do so outside in a *very* secure area by themselves.

APPLICATION OF THE TR PROCESS

The incarcerated segment of the general population is a unique group in terms of their confinement at this time of their lives. While many of their backgrounds may be similar, they vary greatly in terms of individual interests and experiences. The following case study provides an illustration of the TR process in a correctional population.

CASE STUDY

Steve was a 15-year-old white male at the time of his arrest. He previously had been arrested seven times. He is from an upper-middle class home where both of his adoptive parents hold Ph.D.'s, and both are employed. He is the oldest of three children. His two siblings are biological offspring of his parents. His arrests include breaking and entering, trespassing, and armed robbery. Steve has been sentenced to a diversion program in his community.

Assessment

Steve was given several assessments including the McCall Leisure Interest Inventory, Leisure Diagnostic Battery, and the Leisure Activities Blank. In addition to the findings from these inventories, the TR specialist also gleaned information from the Coopersmith Self-Esteem Inventories administered by other members of the treatment team. The lack of self-esteem is seen as a common thread in most of today's inmates. Research has indicated that the primary common factor among cases involving drug problems, delinquency, and teenage pregnancy is that the majority of the people have no sense of self-worth (Jackard, 1988).

Through assessment and personal interviews, it is learned that Steve is doing poorly in school. He has no positive extracurricular activities and usually "hangs out" with a group of teens his age or older. Most of the members of his group also have an arrest record. He has poor self-esteem and is not interested in many leisure activities. What interests he does have include risky and challenging pursuits. He has a fascination with planes and would like to learn to fly. Since his financial resources include an upper middle-class family and he has not been incarcerated, the TR specialist will pursue this interest.

Planning

Long-term goal: To enhance and improve Steve's self-concept and image through the development of new leisure behaviors and skills.

Short-term goals: (1) to assist Steve in developing ways to improve his sense of self-worth; and (2) to provide opportunities for Steve to participate in his leisure interest.

Objectives: Steve will be given opportunities to learn to fly an airplane in order to: (1) give him a new group of friends with whom to identify; (2) reinforce his feelings of self-worth; (3) build a positive relationship with his parents and siblings; and (4) encourage independence, self-direction, and strength of character through the provision of decision-making skills.

Content: Steve will verbally express his appreciation and enjoyment of his leisure pursuit. He will be encouraged to plan ahead for his next recreation session. He will maintain open communication with his TR Specialist and his family.

Process: The TR Specialist will: (1) provide backgound information to his flight school instructor; (2) encourage Steve to attend all lessons; (3) hold sessions with Steve to assess progress with skills and character building; and (4) keep weekly contact with Steve's family and flight school.

Implementation

Steve will attend school daily and keep his grades at least C or better. He will also attend his flight school in the afternoon three times a week. Recreation Therapy will provide reinforcement for his change in attitude and his skill performance. Records of his moods and behaviors will be maintained.

Evaluation

The effectiveness of the leisure counseling will be determined by the continued progress of the client. The client will serve as documentation as to whether or not the goals and objectives are being met. Steve's teachers, both school and flight, should be contacted for their review of his progress and program design. Comprehensive review should also include Steve's family.

TRENDS AND ISSUES

After the 1994 elections conservative state and federal legislatures are requiring, not requesting, correctional facilities to reflect the punitive nature of incarceration. With this prevailing sentiment comes the dilemma of providing therapeutic recreation programs that cannot be perceived as being fun, entertaining, or enjoyable. In short, recreation facilities and programs in correctional settings are viewed by the public as creating a resort atmosphere in prison. The correctional therapeutic recreation specialist in the future will have a *major* public relations responsibility to educate both legislators and the public on the value of restructuring inmates' leisure behaviors in order to help them become safe and productive citizens.

The percentage of women in the correctional system is increasing more rapidly than the percentage of men. Women in confinement are often denied the same access to recreational services as their male counterparts. "Men in the most restrictive settings have more access to the outdoors in one day than all women have in a normal week" (Street, 1991). One court found it necessary to tell the state that "access to showers, beauty culture, sewing, and laundry rooms to engage in passive activities is not . . . meaningful recreation" for female prisoners (Street, 1991). The therapeutic recreation specialist must develop programs that will assist women in realizing the importance of developing leisure skills that can help them return to society in a more acceptable manner.

The 28th Annual National Correctional Recreation Association conference in Seattle in March, 1995, addressed the issue of trends in the correctional recreation field. The major trends that were identified at the conference were: (1) the establishment of more and better health and wellness programs for both inmates and staff; (2) improving the public image of correctional recreation; (3) recreation programs must address the issue of recidivism; (4) inmates must learn useful skills within the institution that they can use for life after prison; (5) flexible programming to allow a greater variety to help deal with the diversity of inmates currently incarcerated; (6) develop more and better programs for special needs inmates such as mentally ill and physically handicapped; (7) prepare for more older inmates because of the "three strikes and you are out" laws that will keep more inmates in prison for their later years in life; (8) utilizing qualified volunteers to help provide more recreation staff; and (9) funding.

Many recreation programs in prison now, and certainly in the future, will be funded by inmate participation fees. Inmates will pay for their own programs and not have the use of tax dollars for these services (McCall, 1995).

SUMMARY

It is clear that the criminal justice and correctional system of the past 200 years has failed to reduce crime and keep our society safe. The average tax-paying American is demanding that politicians, lawmakers, and the criminal justice system stop recidivism and the vicious cycle of the revolving door in prisons. It is also known that most crimes are committed during leisure, and that the misuse of leisure often leads to crime.

As the inmates move from incarceration into the outside world, it is necessary for them to have the concepts, values, and skills TR professionals have given them, as well as the assurance that they know what is socially acceptable behavior. It is up to us as TR specialists to be part of the treatment process that promotes positive change and, ultimately, inmate inclusion in the mainstream. The goal is to return individuals to society who can function properly and productively in all facets of their lives: work, family, and leisure.

READING COMPREHENSION QUESTIONS

1. What is the primary purpose of therapeutic recreation in a correctional setting?
2. Why is the public perception of recreation in correctional settings so negative?
3. What are some environmental conditions that may contribute to socially deviant behavior?
4. What is the necessity for the breakdown of minimum, medium, and close custody facilities?
5. Debate the issue of public versus private correctional facilities.
6. Discuss a current trend for juvenile correctional facilities.
7. Debate the issue of mothers being allowed to keep their babies in prison.
8. What is the purpose of the two-pronged approach in delivering leisure services to correctional settings?
9. Does the nature of the offense play a part in the kind of recreation activity the inmate selects?
10. Are there significant differences in women's and men's prisons with regard to recreation?
11. Why are some recreation adaptations or modifications necessary in the correctional setting?
12. Can you define social deviance?

SUGGESTED LEARNING ACTIVITIES

1. Participate in a planned visit to a jail, a work release center, and a prison.
2. Visit a "boot-camp" for juvenile offenders.
3. Plan a therapeutic recreation program for a juvenile, women's, and men's facility for a week.
4. Participate in a debate on any controversial inmate topic. Some suggestions are: (1) mothers keeping their babies when they are born in prison; (2) conjugal visits for minimum security inmates; (3) public versus privately operated correctional facilities; (4) juveniles being tried as adults; or (5) is capital punishment a deterrent to crime?
5. Interview two inmates with regard to their recreation/leisure activities while incarcerated. One inmate should not have served more than a two-year incarceration while the other should have served at least ten years.
6. Visit the recreation area in a long-term facility in your locality. Inventory the services provided (how many are therapeutic in nature?), the personnel provided, and the related costs.
7. Interview a recreation therapist in a correctional setting. Find out the percentage of participating inmates for different recreation programs in the facility.

REFERENCES

Bashford, S. (1995, January 24). Young criminals and the system. *The Florida Times Union,* A 5.

Bersani, C. A. (1970). *Crime and delinquency.* London: The Macmillan Co.

Bodillo, H., & Haynes, M. (1971). *A bill of no rights.* New York, NY: Overbridge & Lozard.

Byers, et al. (1983). Special privileges, recreation, etc. In *The fourth report of proceedings of the National Prison Association Congress in Saratoga Springs.* New York: C.G. Burgoune's Quick Print.

Capuzzi, D., & Gross, D. R. (1992). *Introduction to group counseling.* Denver, CO: Love Publishing Co.

Collins, S. (1994, January 17). Government and the cost of crime. *U.S. News & World Report,* 29–30.

Crutchfield, E., Garrette, L., & Worrall, J. (1981, February). Recreation's place in prisons: A survey report. *Parks and Recreation, 16*(2), 35–41.

DuBray, B. J. (1992, March/April). Pushing for positive peer influence in Missouri. *Student Assistance Journal,* 27–29.

Ellis, G. D., & Niles, S. (1985). Development, reliability, and preliminary validation of a brief leisure rating scale. *Therapeutic Recreation Journal, 19,* 50–61.

Fogel, D. (Ed.). (1974). Recreation in corrections {Special issue}. *Parks and recreation, 9*(9), 17.

Garibaldi, M., & Moore, M. (1981, April). The treatment team approach. *JOPERD,* 28–32.

Hormachea, C. (1981, February). New slants on old correctional recreation ideas. *Parks and Recreation,* 31.

Jackard, C. R. (1988). Reaching the under-challenged, marginal or at-risk student. *The Clearing House, 62*(3), 128–130.

Klare, H. J. (1973). *People in prison.* New York: Putnam Publishing.

McCall, G. E. (1977). *McCall leisure interest inventory.* Unpublished doctoral dissertation. Bloomington, IN: Indiana University.

McCall, G. E. (1995). *Trends in correctional recreation.* Educational session presented at the 28th Annual National Correctional Recreation Association conference, Seattle, WA.

McKechnie, G. E. (1974). *Manual for the leisure activities blank.* Palo Alto, CA: Consulting Psychologists Press.

Meddis, S., & Edmonds, P. (1994, September 28). The ties of crime: Kin, drugs, race. *USA Today,* 11A.

National Correctional Recreation Association Conference Program. (1991). *Focus on the future,* Orlando, Florida.

Neal, L. E. (1972). Prison reform: An historical glimpse at recreation's role. *Therapeutic Recreation Journal, 3,* 105.

Nicolai, S. (1981, April). Rehabilitation and leisure in prisons. *JOPERD,* 33.

Reibstein, L., Carroll, G., & Bogert, C. (1994, October 17). Back to the chain gang? *Newsweek,* 87–90.

Street, L. G. (1991, Winter). Despair and disparity in Florida's prisons and jails. *Florida State University Law Review, 18*(2), 529.

Wilkinson, F., & Doggett, L. (1966). Effectiveness of recreation in a correctional system. In *Proceedings of the ninety-sixth congress of the American Prison Association* held in Baltimore, Maryland August 28–September 1, Washington: Shoreham.

Witt, P. A., et al. (1982). *The leisure diagnostic battery: Background, conceptualization, and structure.* Denton, TX: North Texas State University, Division of Recreation and Leisure Studies.

CHAPTER 6

SUBSTANCE ABUSE

ROBIN KUNSTLER

OBJECTIVES

- Define the terms used to describe drug and alcohol abuse.
- Comprehend the scope of drug and alcohol abuse.
- Describe the effects of drug abuse.
- Explain the purposes of TR in substance abuse treatment.
- Describe TR programs to be used with substance abusers.
- Differentiate among types of common service settings.
- Know typical treatment approaches used in different settings.
- Identify areas of client functioning to be assessed.
- Explain how client needs can be met through specific TR activities.
- Justify TR interaction techniques to be used during program implementation.
- Explain the role of evaluation in treatment process.
- Demonstrate ability to apply the TR process to a case study.
- Evaluate social and economic trends and issues as they influence drug abuse and alcoholism and their treatment.
- Demonstrate awareness of research findings related to therapeutic recreation and substance abuse treatment.

A drug can be defined as any chemical substance that can be absorbed into the body. It can be either a medicine or a substance, usually taken voluntarily, that produces a temporary, usually pleasurable effect.

Most *psychoactive drugs* are used for the changes they produce in how a person feels, thinks, or behaves. Psychoactive drugs affect the brain directly by changing one's perceptions, or how the brain interprets the messages it receives. The drug causes the brain to read "painlessness" for "pain," as an example. Abuse of drugs is a major health problem for millions of users, their families and friends, and affects society as well.

The following are commonly used terms to describe problems with drug and alcohol use:

1. substance or drug abuse is the repeated use of a drug that results in physical, mental, emotional, or social impairment of the user.
2. chemical or drug dependence refers to a state of psychological and/or physical need for a substance, usually characterized by compulsive use, tolerance, and physical dependence manifested by withdrawal sickness.

3. tolerance is reduced sensitivity resulting in the need for increased dosage to achieve the desired drug effect.
4. addiction is a pattern of behavior characterized by an overwhelming involvement with using a drug and securing its supply, despite adverse consequences associated with use of the drug, and with a significant tendency to relapse after quitting or withdrawal.

Drug and alcohol abuse is a major health problem in the United States. There are more deaths, illnesses, and disabilities from substance abuse than from any other preventable health condition. Of the 2 million deaths in the United States each year, more than one in four is attributed to the use of alcohol, illicit drugs, or tobacco. Between 25 and 40 percent of all general hospital patients are there because of complications related to alcoholism. Drug abuse is also related to criminal behavior. At least half of all people arrested for major crimes, including homicide, theft, and assault, were using illicit drugs at the time of their arrest.

The most prevalent form of drug abuse is alcoholism. As many as 14.5 million Americans are thought to be problem drinkers or alcoholics, and some estimates go as high as 28 million. Their alcohol problems affect an additional 56 million people, half of whom are children of alcoholics. One in three families is affected by a problem drinker. Children in alcoholic families exhibit emotional and adjustment difficulties including aggressive behavior, difficulties with peers, hyperactivity, and poor school adjustment.

Substance abuse continues to be a problem for teenagers. The 1994 annual survey for high school drug use showed an increased use of marijuana, cocaine, and other illegal drugs. The age when young people first start using alcohol and other drugs is a powerful predictor for later substance abuse, especially if use begins before age fifteen. Problems typically become apparent by the age of twenty. By the eighth grade 70 percent of adolescents have consumed alcohol.

For most problem drinkers under the age of thirty-five, alcohol is used in combination with other drugs. It is often used after cocaine. Twenty-two million Americans have tried cocaine at least once. In 1988, 862,000 Americans were estimated as heavy cocaine users, meaning at least once a week. This number declined to 625,000 in 1991. In 1991, 3 million reported using cocaine once in a one-month period.

"Crack," an extremely addictive, inexpensive, and readily available form of cocaine, became a severe problem in the mid-1980s. Cocaine addiction is associated with crime, homelessness, and hospital emergencies.

Three and a half million Americans have reported occasional use of heroin; between 500,000 and 700,000 are heroin addicts. This number has been fairly constant since the early 1970s. In the early 1990s there was a reported increase in heroin use due to increased purity, lower prices, and the fact that it could be smoked rather than injected. Fear of contracting HIV, the virus that causes AIDS, led injecting drug users to seek out other forms of ingesting drugs. Death from AIDS is the fastest-growing cause of death among injecting drug users.

Seven million Americans use sleeping pills once a week or more. Although these drugs are medically prescribed, taking a tranquilizer for more than four to six weeks carries the risk of dependency. In fact, more people die from prescription drugs each year than from all illegal substances combined (Gold, 1986).

CLASSIFICATION OF DRUGS

The most common categories of illicit drugs include narcotics (heroin, morphine, codeine), stimulants (cocaine, crack, amphetamines), depressants (alcohol, barbiturates, benzodiazepines, methaqualone) and hallucinogens (LSD, PCP, peyote). Addiction can occur to one or a combination of drugs that affect the central nervous system.

Drugs can be classified by their effects on the central nervous system (CNS). CNS depressants and CNS stimulants have generalized effects on the brain. The depressants slow down heart rate, pulse, and breathing. They have a relaxing or tranquilizing effect and may produce sleep. These include alcohol, barbiturates (phenobarbital, seconal), sedatives, benzodiazepines (minor tranquilizers such as Librium, Valium, dalmane, and Xanax) and small doses of marijuana or hashish. The stimulants speed up functioning, producing alertness and excitability. These include amphetamines, cocaine, caffeine, and nicotine.

Other drugs have localized effects on the brain. One group is known as limbic depressors, because they slow down the portion of the brain that controls emotional functions. These drugs are antipsychotics or major tranquilizers (thorazine, Mellaril, Stelazine, prolixin and Haldol), antidepressants (Elavil, Tofranil, Prozac), and lithium. The narcotics, such as heroin, morphine, codeine, opium, Darvon, and demerol, decrease pain. The last group is the psychedelics that destort thoughts and sensory processes, and can induce a psychosis-like state with illusions and hallucinations. LSD, mescaline, psilocybin, PCP, and large doses of cannabinoids are in this group.

Some drugs, such as caffeine, are freely available. Nicotine and alcohol are considered more harmful, and their use is discouraged, but not prohibited. Barbiturates, amphetamines and tranquilizers have legitimate medical uses as well as significant potential for harm. Marijuana and heroin are considered to be harmful to individuals and society and their medical use is largely unexplored. However, marijuana and LSD have the lowest ratings for posing hazards to the individual and society; whereas alcohol has the highest rating for its potential risks.

When does use become abuse? According to the American Psychiatric Association, substance abuse is distinguished from normal use by three criteria: (1) pattern of pathological use: lack of control over how much of the substance is used and when it is used; (2) impairment in social or occupational functioning caused by the pattern of pathological use; and (3) pattern of abuse continues for at least one month.

Figure 6.1 depicts the progression of drug use/abuse.

An individual who uses a drug may not necessarily progress beyond any one of the stages. Progress depends on several factors such as predisposition to a drug problem based on heredity, physiology, psychology and/or socioculture; the drug itself: which one, dosage, potency, availability, and how it's used (orally, intravenously, etc.), and the enabling system of one's own attitudes and attitudes of family, friends, and society. Successful treatment of addiction requires understanding why a drug is more addictive in one society than another, for one individual and not another, and addictive for the same individual at one time and not another (Peele, 1985).

DESCRIPTION OF LIMITATIONS

All drug abusers may be victims of their own neglect in terms of personal health and self-care. They may delay obtaining proper medical treatment. Disorientation, confusion, and fear of withdrawal from the drug often characterize the condition of abusers when they enter treatment. Drug-induced psychosis may occur as a result of long-term abuse of alcohol, depressants, and stimulants. It is characterized by loss of contact with reality, disorganized thought processes, hallucinations, and withdrawal from the outside world.

Heavy drinking is related to gastrointestinal disorders, malnutrition, high blood pressure, lowered resistance to disease, heart disease, and cirrhosis of the liver which kills 30,000 Americans each year.

Alcoholics may suffer blackouts, seizures, and chest pains. They may have brain damage from injuries sustained in falls or from banging

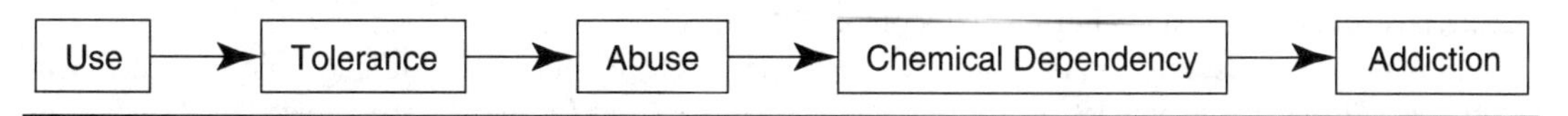

FIGURE 6.1 The Progression of Drug Use/Abuse

their heads. Some alcoholics may be taking Antabuse, a medication that causes violent illness if alcohol is ingested.

Chronic heroin users can be suffering from malnutrition, high blood pressure, or diabetes. They may have a history of hepatitis, broken bones, and various infections. Injection drug users may be infected with the Human Immunodeficiency Virus (HIV) which causes AIDS and make the HIV+ person susceptible to life-threatening illnesses. Tuberculosis is also on the rise among substance abusers. Cocaine abusers often suffer from exhaustion and experience restlessness, anxiety, and irritability.

The therapeutic recreation specialist must be aware of the possible medical and/or physical complications that may affect clients' recreation participation.

PURPOSE OF THERAPEUTIC RECREATION

Therapeutic recreation has an important role in drug abuse treatment and rehabilitation because of the emphasis on treating the whole person and changing his or her lifestyle. A primary function of the TR specialist is to help the client find healthy means to satisfy the needs previously met through drug-taking. Carruthers and Hood (1994) reported that people have certain expectancies from their substance abusing. They expect a sense of disengagement in their leisure, in other words, an escape from preoccupation and worries to feelings of social comfort and assurance, involvement, spontaneity, and less self-consciousness.

The benefits generally associated with taking drugs are: (1) people feel good; and (2) the reduction of frustrating or stressful conditions. The abilities to experience fun and pleasure and feel capable and in control of their lives are often lacking in the drug abuser. TR can help people feel good and to learn new ways to relieve stress and anxiety. Clients need to develop interests to pursue post-treatment that do not involve contact with drugs, drug users, and the drug-abusing environment. TR can contribute to overall treatment by creating an atmosphere that is positive and therapeutic, offering an avenue for developing stress management and social skills and providing leisure education. A well-planned TR program provides opportunities to develop these abilities and experience them in personally satisfying and meaningful leisure pursuits. According to Rancourt (1991), TR can address specific problems of substance abusers, facilitate new learning related to social and free time choices, and provide a natural, but supportive environment to practice new skills and pursue positive alternative ways of behaving. Individuals who are exposed to leisure alternatives in the community are more likely to use them after discharge (O'Dea-Evans, 1990).

Providing a nonpunitive and confidential atmosphere in which clients are treated with dignity and respect, and where staff serve as positive role models of effective functioning without the use of drugs, is the first objective of the TR program. As a TR professional you should be straightforward and nonjudgmental in your concern. However, drug abusers are known to be manipulative. Set limits on acting-out behaviors while allowing them to express their feelings in a safe context. Community meetings and client responsibility to monitor the environment for drugs are recommended. Clients have a need for structure that can be provided by a comprehensive program that allows for choice within the restrictions imposed by the treatment setting. For example, if clients must attend all programs including TR, allow them choice by having them select the specific game or craft for the group, select an individual quiet activity to do in the same room, or choose to be a spectator. Contract with them (have them make an agreement with you) that they can choose this alternative for a period of time (such as three days or two consecutive sessions). In this way, they are given control over their own behavior within the structured setting but are being supported that they can eventually make a more positive, healthy decision.

Developing a trust relationship with the client is essential for the TR specialist. The TR specialist should be able to participate with clients in recreation with joy and a sense of fun, presenting himself or herself as a positive role model. Addicts may feel guilty about having fun if they do not feel they deserve it. Diffley (1991) recommends physical exercise and fitness, including running, aerobics, calisthenics, and weight training as activities in which a client can gain control over his or her body and develop a more internal locus of control. Group activities such as playing on a sports team, singing in a chorus, or painting a mural contribute to social skill development, group cohesiveness and peer relationships. Cooperative games such as New Games are other means to achieve this. Art therapy facilitates expression of feelings and a sense of accomplishment; as does horticulture, which also provides intellectual stimulation and a sense of responsibility for something outside the self. One other program that may not be available in all treatment settings is outdoor adventure programming which builds self-confidence, problem-solving ability, and trust in an exhilarating atmosphere.

Clients need to develop feelings of competence and control through learning social skills, coping techniques, and decision-making processes. The addict's behaviors often include impulsiveness, low frustration tolerance, a tendency to place blame for their situation on persons and circumstances outside of themselves, denial, rationalization, and manipulativeness. To change these behaviors involves development of self-awareness, personal efficacy, and satisfying alternatives to drug abuse. Therapy works best when it requires clients to change attitudes, practice skills and make life changes, and when it attributes these changes to the client (Peele, 1985). The goals of TR are similar to the goals of recovery. In TR, we also work on increasing self-awareness, self-efficacy, and developing self-rewarding recreation experiences.

In recovery, and individual must come to believe an addiction is hurting them and wish to overcome it. Next, they develop enough feelings of efficacy to manage their withdrawal and life without the addiction. Lastly, they need to find sufficient alternative rewards to make life worth living without the addiction. A comparison of these two sets of goals reveals how relevant TR is in the recovery process.

Sessions in relaxation techniques, assertiveness training, social skills training, exercise and fitness, as well as participating in the planning, organizing, and operation of the activities, can help addicts learn more about themselves and acquire methods to function without drugs. Honest, supportive feedback is essential to helping them identify their gains in these areas. They can build their self-esteem through completion of success-oriented recreation experiences for which they receive praise. Addicts function in the "here and now," so they need to plan for today and work on today's goals, not for a distant future (even tomorrow) that is out of their control. Encourage them to receive feedback from their peers as well as from staff. It is important for substance abusers in treatment to increase their ability to express themselves, to break the denial of their addiction and to begin to identify with others. As a TR specialist you can encourage their honest expression of feelings and facilitate the development of group cohesiveness.

Documented benefits of therapeutic recreation with substance abusers include social functioning through enhancement of social skills, development of social support networks and enhancing basic communication skills; stress management through relaxation, physical exercise and fitness, and anxiety management; and development of leisure and recovering lifestyle. This last area includes: coping skills, chemical free alternatives, balanced lifestyle, structuring free time, alleviating boredom and/or providing alternatives to boredom, experiencing pleasure and enjoyment, developing leisure skills, developing problem solving and decision-making skills, and community reintegration. Despite these known benefits, TR as a treatment modality is underutilized in substance abuse treatment programs. However, in a study of one hundred substance abuse treatment programs, Malkin, Voss, Teaff and Benshoff (1993/94), found that over three-quarters offered physical fitness, leisure education, and stress management programs on at least a once-a-week basis. This is an encouraging development, as the recognition of the importance of addressing lifestyle issues of substance abusers grows.

Developing a satisfying leisure lifestyle through assessment of leisure interests, acquiring leisure skills, and engaging in leisure pursuits is essential to successful post-treatment functioning. Addicts improve when their relationships to work, family and other aspects of their environment improve. They can give up rewards they get from their addiction when they believe they will find superior gratification from other activities in their regular lives (Peele, 1985). A leisure education program that includes daily enjoyable recreation participation can demonstrate to the drug abuser that there are healthy sources of gratification available *every day.* Discussion of reasons why clients drink or take drugs, the results of substance abuse, and alternative coping mechanisms can help clients choose healthy outlets. Identifying barriers to leisure participation, discussing societal expectations of behavior, clarifying personal values, and choosing among alternatives are particularly suitable leisure education activities. Determining leisure interests through self-assessment and activity inventories, developing leisure participation skills, and participating in a variety of realistic activities to be pursued alone, at home, and with one's family are components of leisure education. The TR program can provide an environment in which to try out these newly acquired behaviors. TR encourages participation in non-drug activities that helps abusers cope and/or obtain enjoyable states, reducing reliance on drugs for the same effect. This power of the recreation or leisure experience can be understood through a discussion of Csikszentmihalyi's (1990) theory of "flow" in which the recreation experience can be seen to possess the same qualities as flow.

Flow is a state of optimal psychological arousal resulting from intrinsically motivated participation in activities where the challenge in the environment and the skills of the individual are ideally matched. It is characterized by joy, creativity, and total involvement. Flow and drug-induced states both result in increased euphoria, self-esteem, stress reduction, and leisure satisfaction. During recreation, unlike when we are under the influence of drugs, we are in control of our minds and actions.

Recreation activities are designed to make flow easier to achieve. They require skills for participation, have rules and goals, provide immediate and concrete feedback, and offer novelty and opportunities to experience control; even as we enjoy the altered perceptions and alternative realities that recreation experiences offer. Think of spinning on a merry-go-round, skydiving, acting in a play, or traveling to an exotic locale. Recapturing a sense of playfulness and feelings of empowerment are essential to recovery.

The goal of treatment for substance abusers is to change one's lifestyle and abstain from the use of problem substances. This involves choosing nonchemical alternatives to meet needs, relapse prevention skills, improved social functioning and building self-esteem. Recovery requires that abusers find new ways to have fun, relax, deal with stress, and experience satisfaction.

COMMON SERVICE SETTINGS

Scientists are still debating how best to treat substance abuse. The National Institute on Alcohol Abuse and Alcoholism began a research program in 1987 to compare effectiveness of inpatient and outpatient treatment, especially in light of increasing drug abuse and rising treatment costs.

Treatment can take place in a variety of settings. The severity of addiction should be considered in choosing a treatment setting. Schnoll (1986) describes four treatment settings:

An *acute-care hospital program,* often in a major medical center, that provides assessment through observation and use of diagnostic tests; stabilization of patient's conditions, and a safe, medically approved method of withdrawal from the drug. Patients are helped to realize the severity of their problem, are educated about the nature of addiction, and are encouraged to continue treatment. Individual and group therapy, vocational rehabilitation, and peer support are offered. The length of stay is typically three to thirty days.

Residential care is less intensive than acute care and provides less medical care, but offers maximum structure and more counseling. There are five types of residential care. (1) The first is hospital-based, offering three to four weeks of standardized treatment. (2) Free-standing facilities, the second type, are independent of hospitals with a positive, retreat-like atmosphere, vocational and educational counseling, and a length of stay of over one month. (3) The first therapeutic community, Synanon, was established in 1959. This is a long-term (six to twenty-four months) residential program with a self-help and psychological focus on restructuring the addict's personality, character, and lifestyle. Usually staffed mostly by recovering addicts, it offers a rigidly structured program with punishments and rewards and an emphasis on confrontation. (4) Halfway houses are communal living situations that provide a transition between a twenty-four-hour-a-day treatment environment and independent living. (5) Detoxification centers provide food, clothing, shelter, and medication for a one to five-day period as they oversee safe withdrawal from drugs. Eight percent of all treatment is long-term residential care.

Partial hospitalization is for those clients needing structure but who can live at home, work, or attend school. Services include self-help, education, and individual, family, and group therapy.

Outpatient services offer a wide variety of programs. They can provide methadone maintenance, medication, milieu therapy, self-help, psychotherapy, and relaxation training. About 82 percent of addiction treatment is on an outpatient basis. An outpatient has the opportunity to practice healthy behaviors in the everyday environment.

CURRENT BEST PRACTICES AND PROCEDURES

Historically, treatment for drug abusers began with two federal prison farms in Lexington, Kentucky (1935), and Fort Worth, Texas (1938). Those convicted of the "crime" of addiction (officially, the drug addict was viewed as a criminal) were sent to these hospitals for detoxification and prolonged isolation from the environment in which the addiction occurred. But this approach was not successful because patients had severe difficulty readjusting to their communities. Most addicts returned to addiction after discharge. The need for preparation to return to the community was finally recognized in 1952, when Riverside Hospital in New York City began a program to treat juvenile drug addicts with an emphasis on readjustment to the home community.

In the 1960s reports that heroin addicts could be treated successfully with methadone, a synthetic morphine substitute, led to the establishment of methadone treatment programs in many cities. These provided alternatives to the mostly unsuccessful treatment programs that emphasized abstinence. It was hoped that the rise in urban street crime committed by heroin addicts, or "junkies," could be reduced by methadone treatment. However, federal officials were reluctant to be supportive, as many saw it as substituting one addiction for another. The advantage of methadone use was that clients appeared more alert, energetic, and motivated; it can be taken orally and its effects last up to twenty-four hours.

In the early 1970s drug treatment programs were expanded, in great part due to the returning Vietnam veterans who reportedly had high levels of drug addiction. The Veterans' Administration expanded its programs. However, the fears of numbers of addicted veterans trained in warfare returning to the United States did not materialize. In the late 1970s, U.S. President Jimmy Carter called for programs to treat abusers of barbiturates, amphetamines, and combinations of drugs, including alcohol.

Treatment always begins with detoxification and medical care to restore physical health. Detoxification is the metabolism and excretion of drugs from the body, which can take from hours to weeks. Although therapeutic programs may be offered, their intensity increases after "detox."

A popular treatment model is the milieu therapy approach, in which all aspects of the treatment environment contribute to the client's care. This usually includes group therapy, individual psychotherapy, an emphasis on social skills development, and availability of support groups such as Alcoholics Anonymous (AA) and Narcotics Anonymous (NA). Other services, such as vocational rehabilitation, social services, occupational therapy, therapeutic recreation, creative arts therapy, and family therapy have become more popular as rehabilitation philosophy takes the holistic view of client needs. Frequently, treatment is delivered by the interdisciplinary team. The community reinforcement approach recognizes the importance of providing help from a clinician in the community to assist clients in finding employment, improving family and marital relationships, and enhancing social skills.

Alcoholics Anonymous (AA) is the most famous form of treatment for drug abusers. A voluntary fellowship of problem drinkers who help one another to maintain sobriety, it was begun in 1935. There are 1.5 million members worldwide. In New York City alone there are 1,826 weekly meetings. About 60 percent of those who attend AA stay as members. Anyone can join by just walking into a meeting. Philosophically, members recognize they cannot refrain from drinking on their own and need to talk about it with others. Meetings are loosely structured and members provide support to each other to stay sober. Today, more and more members are addicted to other drugs in addition to alcohol, or just to other drugs alone. But they feel AA provides the support to refrain from substance abuse. AA is a fellowship of alcoholics (and others) who believe that maintaining a life of sobriety depends on admitting that they no longer have control over alcohol and the surrender to a power (spiritual or personal) that is greater than themselves. Some experts point out that there is no empirical evidence to prove AA is effective. However, many feel AA and NA are significant factors in maintaining their recovery from substance abuse. An interesting discrepancy is that the research supports the use of certain treatment approaches as effective in working with substance abusers; yet, the most commonly used methods differ from these. Behavioral self-control training, community reinforcement, material and family therapy, social skills training, and stress management are recommended in the research literature. But the treatments of choice continue to be Alcoholics Anonymous, alcoholism education, confrontation, Antabuse, group therapy, and individual counseling.

Assessment

Assessment procedures for drug abusers follow the same basic principles and guidelines used for other groups. Techniques of observation and interview, as well as reports from family, friends, and other treatment staff, are utilized. During their initial assessment, drug abusers may be in poor health due to their lifestyle. Their reactions and reflexes are slower than normal, and their coordination is poorer. Therefore, TR specialists should plan to reassess the client after detox and when his or her health status stabilizes. Particular attention should be given to the client's stress management, social, and leisure skills.

The first observation is usually of the client's physical appearance. What is his or her level of self-care and grooming? Adjustment to the treatment environment and program are frequently difficult. Is the client familiar with any stress management techniques such as yoga, relaxation, exercise, or other fitness activities that he or she can practice? How developed are his or her verbal and nonverbal communication skills? How does he or she relate to peers and to authority figures? To what degree does he or she exhibit motivation and tolerate frustration? How is his or her impulse control? What is the client's ability to express feelings and make decisions? Does he or she possess a repertoire of cooperative, competitive, and solitary play skills? Can the client function effectively as a group member?

Assessment of leisure functioning include prior interests, activity skills, awareness of leisure, leisure barriers, and knowledge of community resources. Try to determine what needs the drug satisfies in order to use recreation instead to satisfy those needs. Clients should participate actively in the definition of the problem, goal-setting, selection of intervention strategies, and evaluation of progress.

The Leisure Diagnostic Battery (Witt & Ellis, 1985) has been used as an assessment tool with this population. The subscales of perceived competence and barriers would be particularly appropriate. The Leisure Satisfaction Scale (Ragheb & Beard, 1980) has been used as well (Mattiko, 1994). These tools can add to the data collected by the TR specialist as well as provide indicators of progress and change if used as a post-test measure.

Planning

Substance abusers need to be in control of their treatment, not just recipients of treatment services. Therefore, activities in therapeutic recreation programs for drug abusers should be planned with the client and based on the client's needs, behaviors, and personality. The client's own statement of his or her problem and goals should be of utmost consideration. By addressing the issues with which the client is most preoccupied, progress moves faster and the client is more willing to participate in treatment. For the drug abuser, a new way of life is necessary, one that encompasses new skills and abilities.

Earlier research on substance abusers reported that they had empty leisure lifestyles and were passive and sedentary in their pursuits. More recent work has shown that substance abusers do participate in recreation activities, but do not receive much satisfaction from their participation. They also have skills that can be incorporated into sober lifestyles. Rancourt (1991) studied women substance abusers who recognized that recreation and leisure activities were very important in their treatment and could help them reduce stress or boredom and experience fun. However, addiction is a powerful experience and recovering alcoholics and drug addicts will need to experience intensity or flow in their leisure pursuits to combat the craving for abused substances.

Treatment can provide opportunities to practice normal, daily activities such as household living, family recreation, and having fun. Through role-playing, for example, addicts can view their needs and behaviors in different ways and try out new skills and methods of interacting.

Addicts have a great need for acceptance and attention. Provide this with a smile, a touch, or praise about their involvement or participation. At times, redirect this need toward interaction with their peers or to continuing their work on a project on their own. Activities such as New Games, that emphasize cooperation instead of competition, offer group emotional support and trust. Working collectively on a group project such as a mural painting, music performance, or a play production can also promote trust and cooperation.

Addicts need to build enjoyable and creative activities into their daily routine. Programs such as exercise, yoga, relaxation, and fitness should begin almost immediately as they aid in treatment as well as have long-term benefits. Francis (1991) particularly recommends meditation as a means for recovering substance "misusers" to achieve flow.

Participation in physical fitness activities is shown to increase sobriety rates. One study found that college students who were heavy drinkers were able to reduce their alcohol consumption by 30 to 40 percent when they either did aerobic exercise or practiced meditation. Those who did both regularly reduced alcohol intake by 50 to 60 percent (Kutner, 1987).

Other beneficial activities are walking, swimming, bike riding, weight lifting, sports such as basketball, assertiveness training, group brainstorming, and discussion groups. Women abusers particularly need discussion groups led by women.

Outdoor activities seem to enhance feelings of freedom and enjoyment. Organizations such as Outward Bound stress the natural highs that come from rock climbing, mountaineering, and wilderness survival which can contribute to the development of self-esteem and feelings of self-worth. These and other high risk and challenge activities provide excitement through nondrug means.

Drug-oriented lifestyles provide excitement and dreams that must now be experienced in other ways. Trips, parties, the arts, and nature are possible choices.

Outlets for inner anger and hostility can be released through volleyball, ping pong, bowling, woodworking and clay work. Discussions can follow these activities that focus on clients' feelings and the means of expressing them. If clients feel an activity has worked for them, they can learn more about the resources necessary to incorporate it into their leisure lifestyle.

Drug abusers are often noted for their impulsiveness. This can be controlled through activities that take time to complete, such as candle-making and relay races, so they can slowly experience delayed gratification. For those who never put impulses into action, beginning to act is a form of control.

Consideration in TR programming should be given to active participation and skill acquisition as these approaches have the greatest potential to enhance personal competence. Opportunities for choice, control, and challenge are powerful experiences and facilitate the possibility of flow occurring (Aguilar & Munson, 1994).

Leisure education is, of course, an essential part of the TR program. Exploring perceptions of and attitudes toward leisure and free time, examining personal barriers to leisure participation and developing strategies to overcome these barriers, identifying interests, and building activity skills are important components of leisure education. Family recreation can provide a positive, healthy form of family interaction.

Two leisure education programs have been presented recently that seem to have positive results and potential for other substance abusers. Mattiko (1994) focused on relapse prevention skills according to the type of alcoholic. Two types of alcoholics have been described; the Type 1 who appears controlled on the surface but is hiding a great deal of anger; and the Type 2 who tends to be a multiple drug user and has a history of antisocial behavior such as multiple marriages, debts, and stealing. The Type 1 benefits from interpersonal skills training focusing on identification of emotions, how to control anger/frustration, how to communicate feelings, and learning outlets to manage stress. The Type 2 needs to learn basic life skills of how to obtain housing, employment, carry out ADL skills, and how to be involved in leisure. This typology can be useful in individualizing treatment and preparing clients for their future without drugs.

Carruthers and Hood (1994) developed a brief leisure education program of four sessions, recognizing the reality of short-term treatment. Leisure is a high-risk situation where substance abuse can occur due to boredom. Clients are guided to recognize negative thoughts that might lead to abusing and change these thoughts in order to enhance their ability to the present. Homework is given.

Without predischarge counseling and the development of referrals for the continuation of satisfying leisure activities, the effectiveness of TR treatment is diminished. The TR specialist should provide transitional TR services following the client into the community to offer counseling, evaluation, and cooperation with community agencies.

Implementation

In implementing the TR program, as with overall treatment and rehabilitation, a multimodality approach is more efficient than a one-dimensional approach (Craig, 1985), because there is no one strategy or technique that works best with *all* patients. The key to effective treatment is to match individual clients with the intervention most appropriate for them. Therapy succeeds when it increases people's sense of their strength to withstand uncertainty and discomfort as well as to generate positive rewards for themselves (Peele, 1985). Opportunities to explore possible rewards and feedback given in a supportive, structured environment should be provided. Clients should participate in conducting activities as well as planning them. This gives them more of an investment in the program, makes them aware of problems involved in programming and gives them opportunities to do something worthwhile by assisting the TR specialist (Earle, 1981).

Implementation begins with the initial contact between the TR specialist and the client. This meeting is the first step in establishing a relationship that may prove to be a factor in clients staying in treatment. It is important for the TRS to be "authentic" with clients, to be on their level, and share the human experience of facing challenges in one's life. Clients need to recognize that all people share the same feelings and struggles. This helps counteract feelings of isolation and loneliness. It is acceptable to self-disclose appropriately, to share your experiences in a way that builds rapport and trust. You do not self-disclose to seek help from your clients, but to support them in their efforts to get well (Carruthers & Hood, 1994).

Encourage clients to utilize recreation activities as stress reduction aids and to identify realistic, constructive leisure pursuits in which they can participate immediately. Promote group cohesiveness and trust in the relaxed atmosphere of the recreation setting. In this setting, clients can be encouraged to take responsibility for their own behavior and to monitor the behavior of their peers. Set limits, but be sure they understand the rules and why they exist, or they may not follow them. Offer realistic praise and reinforcement in order to assist them in the development of a healthy leisure lifestyle.

EVALUATION PROCEDURES

Evaluation is an especially critical function of the TR specialist with this population because you are monitoring changes in the course of the illness, as well as treating leisure dysfunction. Careful observation of client's behaviors and recording of their expressed feelings is necessary. It may be, as indicated by Hemingway (1993), that clients are more talkative during recreation activities than at other times. The TR specialist is responsible for providing input at interdisciplinary team meetings, revising clients' care plans according to their changes and progress, and doing accurate, explicit documentation. It is also important to utilize clients' self-reports on drug use, leisure participation, and their feelings and reactions to these experiences. The clients should be made aware of the TR specialist's evaluation of their progress as well as be asked to reflect on their own perceptions of their progress.

APPLICATION OF THE TR PROCESS

The following case will be used to illustrate the application of the therapeutic recreation process with a drug abuse client. The four steps in the process are assessment, planning, implementation and evaluation. Following the presentation of the case, each step will be discussed as applied to the case.

CASE STUDY

The client, David, is a 26-year-old single white male admitted for detoxification from cocaine. He was employed as an accountant until three months ago. He lives with two male roommates in a rental apartment in New York City. Both parents and a 23-year-old brother live nearby. His medical doctor referred him for admission to this 30-day inpatient treatment unit.

Prior to meeting the client for the assessment interview, the TR specialist should review the following information from the client's chart: physical and mental status, duration of substance abuse functional limitations resulting from abuse, family social history, results of neurological and psychological tests, educational and occupational background, purposes and results expected from treatment, and general goals that have been established.

During the initial client contact, the TR specialist should begin developing a rapport with the client. Building a trust relationship is the key to successful involvement of the client in the TR programs, as well as an important factor influencing his or her attitude toward overall treatment. The TR specialist should display warmth, genuine interest, and concern when greeting the client, but not be overwhelming. The TR professional should state his or her name, offer a nonthreatening handshake, and explain the purpose of the visit. At this time the TR specialist can begin to observe the client's physical appearance, body language, and communication skills. Other key areas to assess are the client's leisure history, including past and present leisure interests and recreational pursuits, participation patterns (with whom did he or she participate in recreation, how often, where, etc.), attitude toward leisure, and attitude toward and feelings about self and treatment. The client should be encouraged to explore what he or she could gain from the TR program.

In David's case, the TR assessment yielded the following information: during interview, client was very talkative, but rambling, and then would lapse into silence. He would then begin talking abruptly. His eyes darted around the room. Did not look at TR, although welcomed TR into his room and invited TR to sit down. He complained of fatigue and could not focus on discussion. TR terminated interview after ten minutes, after obtaining client's agreement to meet again in two days.

Client was seen second time for reassessment as scheduled. He was subdued, sat in chair, spoke slowly, answered TR's questions. Although eye contact was still poor, eyes were downcast rather than darting. Client was neat and well-groomed, although appeared fatigued (occasionally stifled yawn, slowed speech). Told TR he was socially active in college, attending parties and dating casually within a large group of friends. Volunteered the information that he dabbled in smoking marijuana and drinking. He did not perceive that behavior as a problem at the time. His family recreated together playing tennis and taking summer vacations, but each member also pursued independent interests. After college graduation, client moved in with roommates, got a job as an accountant, attended night school for an MBA, and became active in a late night social life. His experimentation with cocaine led to increased involvement, he stopped attending school, his work behavior was affected. His roommates finally convinced him to seek help. During the discussion with TRS David indicated that his primary goal was to "relax and feel better." He was unsure how he had "ended up like this." He made two vague statements about "letting down my family," but "what do they want from me that I haven't done?" He agreed to review the TR plan to see if he would be willing to follow it.

Following assessment, the TR specialist draws up an individualized plan of treatment for the client that includes goals and therapeutic recreation. David's treatment goals are:

1. Establish a trust relationship with TR specialist.
2. Utilize personal relaxation technique.
3. Improve physical fitness.
4. Develop outlet for self-expression.
5. Identify satisfying leisure interest.
6. Improve cooperative relationships with others.
7. Identify and appropriately express feelings.

To attempt to meet the goals, the following schedule was made for David and presented to him by the TR specialist for his agreement to participate:

Daily A.M. yoga for relaxation and fitness
Tues. A.M. bowling for fitness and leisure
Thurs. A.M. swimming interest development
Fri. a.m. discussion group, "Feelings"
Mon. and Wed. P.M. leisure education—focus on perceptions of leisure and alternative recreation choices.
Evenings—social recreation such as word games, New Games and parties for relaxation and cooperation.
Weekend—camping trip on third weekend for trust, cooperation, self-expression and leisure interests.
Client's choice—daily arts and crafts, coffee hour and weekly movies or music as desired.

Implementation

David has agreed to and signed a TR plan. As treatment progresses, feelings of anger and hostility may surface. Intervention techniques include limit-setting, redirecting dependency needs toward task at hand or peer interaction, encouraging taking responsibility during activities, and offering praise, support, and constructive feedback. Client's motivation may lag. He should be reminded that he has agreed to this plan of care. Encourage him to discuss feelings about treatment. Offer creative arts as means to express feelings. This is not required in care plan because client should experience the freedom to express self this way.

Client's self-image is badly shaken. Keeping score in bowling and word games and planning for camping trip are responsibilities that build on his previous skills. He needs to restore his emotional strength. His previous interests included sports, dining out, TV, movies, and reading. Explore his perception of leisure as an opportunity to express and fulfill self. Encourage experimentation with various media such as painting, ceramics, poetry, singing, and playing musical instruments. He needs to identify "healthy" friends with common interests. Invite family to unit party after three weeks.

Evaluation

Evaluation is made during and at the termination of treatment. Observations of David during treatment revealed that he was becoming more stable but was still quiet in groups and slightly suspicious of others' intentions. During the first week of treatment he needed encouragement to carry out his TR plan. Although his recreation interests were more individual, such as painting daily, he participated in group sing-along on Friday nights and was helpful to other patients, especially elderly alcoholics who were less physically capable. During leisure education sessions he expressed that his lifestyle needed changing so he could avoid stressful situations. During weekend camping trip he participated in New Games and cooperative cooking and clean-up tasks. Upon return to unit he seemed more relaxed and laughed a few times.

Client is making progress toward goals, he is responsive to TR and open about feelings within the context of a professional relationship. He utilizes deep breathing learned in yoga to relax. His physical health has improved as a result of hospital care; swimming and bowling have contributed to this. He developed a strong interest in painting as a means of self-expression. Several of these activities can become part of his new leisure lifestyle. He is cooperative with others. However, he still appears to have feelings which need to be expressed verbally and a need to develop more trusting relationships with others.

Discharge Plan

The discharge plan is critical to maintaining and building on the progress made in treatment. On the recommendation of the treatment team, David is being referred to an outpatient day program for thirty days. He has agreed to attend Narcotics Anonymous meetings, and wants to seek a new job in a smaller company. It is unclear at this time if and when he will do this. He plans to buy painting supplies and continue some form of aerobic exercise. He wants to spend more time with his brother. He says he will use yoga as a relaxation tool. Values clarification will be a part of his outpatient treatment.

David's case represents one type of drug abusing client. A person from a poor background who had limited education, work experience, and family and social resources would probably need longer treatment, along with educational, vocational, and life skills training. The dual-diagnosed client with mental illness and chemical addiction (MICA) is particularly difficult to treat. Often, the MICA client has had such a longstanding problem that he or she has few personal, social, and community resources to draw upon to meet the goals of treatment: achieving abstinence, maintaining sobriety, reducing recidivism, and increasing quality of life post-discharge (Hood & Mattiko, 1991). Their behavior in the past may have alienated family and friends. They have had many failures and few positive memories or experiences to draw upon for the future. They usually suffer from very low self-esteem and engage in self-defeating, sabotaging behaviors to confirm their own worst opinion of themselves. This is a chronic problem and treatment is frequently long-term and involves repeated admissions. It is often unclear what came first, the mental illness that the individual attempted to treat with drugs and became addicted; or the drug abuse that led to mental illness such as psychosis or depression.

MICA clients need support for the part of themselves that wants help and is currently in treatment. Even talking with the TRS is a positive step for which they should receive positive feedback. While support and encouragement for any small effort is important, so is limit setting and encouraging personal responsibility. The TRS may want to set one goal at a time, perhaps in the area of a personal stress management technique that can be beneficial to the client for even a brief period. Unfortunately, dual-diagnosis is a growing problem.

The lifestyle of the addict includes not only the habit of drug use, but patterns of language, ethics, and behavior. Changing to a healthy lifestyle includes awareness of one's addiction and the necessity of change, as well as learning to accept and understand one's feelings and developing appropriate nondrug-taking coping mechanisms.

TRENDS AND ISSUES

Substance abuse has been called the nation's number one health problem. Although the overall use of alcohol, illicit drugs, and tobacco has decreased in the United States, heavy use has been more stable. Within the last thirty days, 13 to 14 million Americans have used and illegal drug, 28 million within the last year.

Americans are increasingly aware of the risks associated with substance abuse, although many young people do not believe heavy use is that risky. A great deal of attention is being paid today to prevention of adolescent substance abuse. Interventions focus on alternative activities, use of free time and identifying stressors in one's personal life. Leisure education and plentiful, satisfying recreational opportunities are increasingly being used in educational programs for youth as deterrents to drug abuse. Many communities have formed coalitions that focus on prevention and early intervention for youth. These include education on consequences and risks of drug use, building self-esteem, developing skills to avoid drug use, and alternative activities. Local park and recreation departments are beginning to participate in local community programs to deter adolescent drug use.

Other subgroups with unique issues related to substance abuse include the elderly who may misuse prescribed medications and alcohol; people with disabilities; people who are homeless; and children born with fetal alcohol syndrome, HIV, or addiction to heroin or cocaine. There continues to be a need for treatment tailored to women's needs that includes day care for their children, job skills training, and frank discussion of issues such as sexuality. In addition, with the increased recognition of multiculturalism and appreciation of cultural diversity, this aspect of clients' lifestyles is also being recognized as a factor to consider in treatment.

Substance abuse treatment programs are focusing more on the well-being of the total patient rather than just targeting functional sobriety. This includes fitness and health promotion, nutrition, exercise for physical and psychological benefits and stress management (Fridinger & Dehart, 1993) as important aspects of recovery. Unfortunately, many people who need treatment do not receive it. About 5 million drug abusers and 18 million alcoholics need treatment, but do not receive it due to a lack of treatment spaces, funding or realization that they need it. In prison, where there are increasing numbers of people arrested for drug convictions, less than 10 percent receive treatment services.

The Protocol Committee of the American Therapeutic Recreation Association is conducting a delphi study to determine treatment needs of alcoholics. The Benefits of TR Conference held in 1991 developed a research agenda to investigate the relationship and contribution of therapeutic recreation to substance abuse treatment and successful recovery. Also, there appears to be a trend toward including TR as active treatment, requiring physician's orders for client participation (Malkin et al., 1993/94). But most importantly, the emphasis on a healthy lifestyle and community reintegration points to a major role for therapeutic recreation in substance abuse treatment.

SUMMARY

Drug and alcohol abuse is a serious social and health problem in the United States. Millions of Americans are adversely affected by the consequences of drug abuse. There is a severe shortage of substance abuse treatment services, although the public has consistently thought that too little is being spent on treatment. There is still much controversy over whether or not substance abuse is a crime or a disease. Another issue that needs to be addressed is the legalization of drugs and what effect that would have on drug use, abuse, crime, and other social problems.

Therapeutic recreation has an essential role in substance abuse treatment with its focus on lifestyle changes, social skills, stress management, and leisure experiences. The TR specialist can help the client identify healthy means of satisfying needs previously met through drugs and experience feelings of fun and achievement through leisure participation.

READING COMPREHENSION QUESTIONS

1. Define the terms used to describe problems with drug and alcohol abuse.
2. Describe the scope of drug and alcohol abuse in our society.
3. What are the effects of different drugs on the central nervous system?
4. What are the possible health problems of a drug abuser or alcoholic upon admission to a treatment setting?
5. Discuss the role of therapeutic recreation in drug abuse treatment and rehabilitation. What is the relationship of therapeutic recreation to recovery?
6. What is Csikszentmihalyi's theory of flow? How does it relate to therapeutic recreation and substance abuse?
7. What contributions can leisure education make to the treatment of a recovering substance abuser?
8. Describe common service settings for substance abuse treatment.
9. What are current treatment methods for substance abuse?
10. Explain the TR assessment process as applied in substance abuse treatment.
11. Give specific examples of client behaviors and needs and types of TR programs and interventions to address these.
12. Name several assessment tools that can be utilized.
13. How does the MICA client differ from other substance abusers?
14. Analyze current trends in the area of substance abuse for their impact on TR's role in treatment.
15. Appreciate the role of research in furthering TR's understanding of, and contribution to, treatment through presentation of research findings.

SUGGESTED LEARNING ACTIVITIES

1. Invite to class a TR specialist working with substance abusers to discuss their needs and behaviors and types of TR programs that are effective in treatment.
2. Attend an Alcoholics Anonymous or Narcotics Anonymous meeting. Discuss your observations and reactions in class.
3. In small groups of students, discuss how you feel about recreational drug use and drinking. When does use become abuse? Do you think alcoholism and drug abuse are crimes or diseases?
4. Define the following in your own words: social drinker, heavy drinker, problem drinker, alcoholic. Compare with other students.

5. Reflect on your personal stress management techniques. Do you drink or take drugs, including nicotine and caffeine to cope? What other means can you use instead?
6. What problems do you see with drug and alcohol abuse on your campus and in your community? Write a short paper on the role of school and community recreation services in addressing these problems.
7. Develop a community resource file of recreation programs that can serve as alternatives to drug-abusing behavior by youth and adults.
8. Brainstorm societal factors that might affect the level of drug and alcohol abuse, both positively and negatively, and the role of the therapeutic recreation profession in preventing and alleviating abuse.
9. Debate: all drugs should be legalized to reduce crime and channel resources toward deterring and treating abuse.
10. Look through newspapers and magazines to see how drinking and drug taking are portrayed in news stories and advertisements. Watch television programs and movies that involve characters using substances. What influence does the media have on our attitudes and behaviors?
11. Participate in a class discussion on flow. When do you experience feelings of flow? Describe what you are doing and how it makes you feel.

REFERENCES

Aguilar, T., & Munson, W. (1992). Leisure education and counseling as intervention components in drug and alcohol treatment for adolescents. *Journal of Alcohol and Drug Education, 37*(3), 23–34.

Carroll, C. (1993). *Drugs in modern society* (3rd ed.), Dubuque, IA: William C. Brown, Inc.

Carruthers, C., & Hood, C. (1994, September). *A model leisure education program for substance abusers: Implementation and evaluation.* Paper presented at the annual conference of the American Therapeutic Recreation Association, Orlando.

Coyle, C., Kinney, W.B., Riley, B., & Shank, J. (1991). *Benefits of therapeutic recreation: A consensus view.* Ravensdale, WA: Idyll Arbor, Inc.

Craig, R. (1985). Multimodal treatment package for substance abuse treatment programs. *Professional Psychology: Research and Practice, 16*(2), 271–285.

Csikszentimihalyi, M. (1990). *Flow: The psychology of optimal experience.* New York: HarperCollins.

Diffley, P. (1991, August). *Therapeutic recreation in a residential treatment setting.* Paper presented at the World Conference of Therapeutic Communities, Montreal.

Earle, P. (1981). *A leisure education notebook for community alcohol programs.* Eugene, OR: Parks and Recreation Department.

Francis, T. (1991). Meditation as an alternative to substance misuse: A current review. *Therapeutic Recreation Journal, 25*(4), 50–60.

Francis, T. (1991). Revising therapeutic recreation for substance misuse: Incorporating flow technology in alternatives treatment. *Therapeutic Recreation Journal, 25*(2), 41–54.

Fridinger, F. & Dehart, B. (1993). A model for the inclusion of a physical fitness and health promotion component in a chemical abuse treatment program. *Journal of Drug Education, 23*(3), 215–222.

Hemingway, V. (1993). Therapeutic recreation services for a chemically dependent client. *Therapeutic Recreation Journal, 27*(2), 126–130.

Hood, C., & Mattiko, M. (1991). Summary of chemical dependency consensus group. In C. Coyle, W.B. Kinney, B. Riley, & J. Shank (Eds.), *Benefits of therapeutic recreation: A consensus view.* Ravensdale, WA: Idyll Arbor, Inc.

Institute for Health Policy. (1993). *Substance abuse: The nation's number one health problem.* Princeton: The Robert Wood Johnson Foundation.

Kunstler, R. (1993). TR's role in the treatment of substance abuse. *Parks and Recreation, 27*(4), 58–60.

Kutner, L. (1987, December 10). Parent and child. *The New York Times,* C8.

Malkin, M., Voss, M., Teaff, J., & Benshoff, J. (1993/94). Activity and recreational therapy services in substance abuse treatment programs. *Annual in Therapeutic Recreation, 4,* 40–50.

Mast, E. (1987). Sobriety: An elusive concept. *Therapy 'N' Games, 1*(1), 1–4.

Mattiko, M. (1994, September). *Perceived freedom and leisure satisfaction of type 1 and type 2 alcoholic inpatients.* Paper presented at the annual conference of the American Therapeutic Recreation Association, Orlando.

O'Dea-Evans, P. (1990). *Leisure education for addicted persons.* Algonquin: Peapod Publication.

Peele, S. (1985). *The meaning of addiction: Compulsive experience and its interpretation.* Lexington, MA: D.C. Heath.

Ragheb, M.G., & Beard, J.G. (1980). Leisure satisfaction: Concept, theory and measurement. In S.E. Iso-Ahola (Ed.), *Social psychological perspectives on leisure and recreation.* Springfield, IL: Charles C. Thomas.

Rancourt, A. (1991). An exploration of the relationships among substance abuse, recreation, and leisure for women who abuse substances. *Therapeutic Recreation Journal, 25*(3), 9–18.

Rancourt, A. (1991). The benefits of therapeutic recreation in chemical dependency. In C. Coyle, W.B. Kinney, B. Riley, & J. Shank (Eds.), *Benefits of therapeutic recreation: A consensus view.* Ravensdale, WA: Idyll Arbor, Inc.

Schnoll, S. (1986). *Getting help: Treatment for drug abuse.* New York: Chelsea House Publishers.

Witt, P. & Ellis, G. (1985). Development of a short form to assess perceived freedom in leisure. *Journal of Leisure Research, 17,* 225–233.

CHAPTER 7

AUTISM

BARBARA A. HAWKINS

OBJECTIVES

- Describe the DSM-IV diagnostic criteria applied in the identification and assessment of autism.
- Recognize behavioral characteristics of persons having autism.
- Identify state-of-the-art procedures used in the assessment of autism for programming purposes.
- Describe the impact of autism on and the scope of services needed by families of persons with autism.
- Discuss intervention procedures and the role of therapeutic recreation services in the social and behavioral habilitation of persons with autism.
- Describe community preparation and inservice training strategies necessary to support community integration and inclusion of persons with autism.
- Recognize best practices in program implementation and evaluation for persons with autism.

DEFINITION OF AUTISM

Autism, a little understood and highly perplexing developmental disability, is most accurately described as a collection of symptoms that, when taken as a group, describe a syndrome. Autism is a complex disability that affects the individual, his or her family, caregivers, and professionals who seek to provide appropriate diagnosis and interventions in the treatment of this lifelong, pervasive developmental disorder.

Until the early 1940s when Leo Kanner first systematically observed and described the autistic syndrome, little was known about the disorder, and even less information was available regarding the treatment or management of autism. Kanner described children with autism as primarily exhibiting the following qualities: inability to develop normal social relationships, delay in speech development, noncommunicative use of speech (echolalia), insistence on sameness, stereotypical play, lack of imagination, pronominal reversal, strong rote memory, normal physical appearance and the appearance of the disorder's symptoms in infancy (Rutter, 1978). In the 1950s, the common mistaken approach to the diagnosis of autism was to confuse the disorder with psychological disturbances (i.e., schizophrenia). At that time, the treatment of choice was rooted in psychotherapy. More current research, however, supports the theory that autism is a pervasive developmental disability related to the central nervous system, rather than a psychological illness. Throughout the past five decades many names have been given to autism, including Kanner's syndrome (Kanner, 1943), childhood autism (Wing, 1980, 1985), infantile autism (Rutter, 1978), and childhood psychosis (Fish & Ritvo, 1979).

Autism is difficult to diagnose because of the complexity of the syndrome coupled with the lack of specific tests for the disorder (Gillberg, 1989; Freeman & Ritvo, 1981). The American Psychiatric Association's, *Diagnostic and Statistical Manual of Mental Disorders, Fourth Edition (DSM-IV)* (1994), is the foremost reference utilized in describing that criteria that are applied in a diagnosis of autistic disorder. The DSM-IV criteria are as follows:

- Qualitative impairment in social interaction.
- Qualitative impairments in communication.
- Restricted repetitive and stereotyped patterns of behavior, interests, and activities.
- Delays or abnormal functioning in at least one of the following areas, with onset prior to age 3 years: (1) social interaction, (2) language as used in social communication, or (3) symbolic or imaginative play (pp. 70–71).

The Autism Society of America, Inc., (ASA) offers a similar description of the definitional criteria for autism:

- Onset before 30 months.
- Disturbance of response to sensory stimuli.
- Disturbance of speech, language, cognition, and nonverbal communication.
- Disturbance of capacity to relate appropriately to people, events, and objects.
- Disturbance of developmental rates and sequences (Dalrymple, 1987).

Children diagnosed as having autism exhibit a profound inability to develop appropriate or normal social relationships with other people. Distinct to autism is the delay or deviance in language development, as well as an "insistence on sameness" and stereotypical behavior patterns (American Psychiatric Association, 1994; Rutter, 1987). Other common symptoms associated with autism are hyperactivity, compulsive behaviors, sleep problems, food obsessions, ritualistic behaviors, abnormal perceptual responses (hyposensitivity and hypersensitivity), self-stimulation, and self-destructiveness (Coleman, 1985; Coleman & Gillberg, 1992). Symptoms are unevenly distributed across individual cases and development such that, although all the symptoms reflect the disorder, they rarely all exist in every person having autism.

As frequently found in other disorders, autism can occur concurrently with other disabilities. Approximately 75 percent of the population with autism also have mental retardation (American Psychiatric Association, 1994; Rutter, 1978; Wing, 1978). About half of the individuals with autism and mental retardation have cognitive functioning at or less than 50 IQ (Coleman & Gillberg, 1992; Gillberg, 1989). In addition, one-quarter to one-third of all children with autism will develop epileptic seizures by adolescence (Coleman & Gillberg, 1992; American Psychiatric Association, 1994).

Autism is a disorder that occurs in approximately four to five cases per 10,000 people and occurs more frequently in males than females, at a ratio of one girl to every four boys (Coleman & Gillberg, 1992). Other than these incidence patterns, there appears to be no other significant pattern to its occurrence. Autism is found throughout the world among individuals of all socioeconomic and racial strata (Paluszny, 1979). Although there is no known cure for autism, people with autism do not get worse. Properly designed intervention programs can reduce the severity of the disorder on functional behavior.

CLASSIFICATION OF AUTISM

Along with general agreement on the overall definitional criteria for autism, a system of classification of the disorder has been developed. This classification entails a multiaxial system of various elements used in the diagnosis of autism (Schopler & Mesibov, 1992, 1994; Rutter & Schopler, 1978). For research and clinical purposes, independent axes are used to clarify the differential diagnosis of autism from other disabilities or conditions. Application of the multiaxial coding system will indicate a diagnosis of the behavioral syndrome of autism on one axis and the description of intellectual impairment (mental retardation) on a second axis; a third axis will indicate factors associated with medical conditions (such as phenylketonuria); and a fourth axis will describe the psychosocial situation. This system reduces ambiguity and enhances clarity of different elements (axes) in diagnosis.

Research has shown autism to be related to specific deficits in cognition that involve central coding processes and language (Schopler & Mesibov, 1992, 1994; Schopler, 1966). Therefore, the application of a multiaxial approach to classification and diagnosis differentiates autism from the presence or absence of mental retardation.

Autism also has been previously confused with childhood schizophrenia; however, the multiaxial system provides clarification to this potential point of confusion. Research evidence (Rutter, 1968, 1971, 1972) substantiates important distinctions regarding the course of autism and schizophrenia such that they should be regarded as separate disorders. The same differentiation has been determined for autism and neurosis; therefore, the multiaxial system is useful in distinguishing between autism and other childhood disorders (American Psychiatric Association, 1994). In summary, significant progress has been made in the definition of autism and the development of a multiaxial system for distinguishing autism from other disorders such as schizophrenia, mental retardation, or other psychosocial conditions.

DESCRIPTION OF LIMITATIONS

As with all people, individuals with autism have their own strengths and limitations. There are limitations that are inherent in the disability, such as deficits in social behavior, communication, and learning skills. Table 7.1 illustrates common behaviors related to these limitations as they appear in people with autism (Dalrymple, 1987).

In addition to these limitations, people with autism often experience other factors that inhibit normal activity. Two of these factors are seizure disorders and pharmacologic treatments. As mentioned previously, one quarter to one third of all autistic children develop epileptic seizures before adolescence. Although there is little research in this area, various types of seizures have been documented in individuals with autism (Coleman & Gillberg, 1992). Seizures can be of the generalized motor type or sudden episodes, as in periods of blank staring or as associated with abnormalities in specific behavior (Dalldorf, 1983).

Although there is no evidence that medication can reduce or reverse the symptoms of autism, many individuals with autism are on medication to treat associated problems (Gualtieri, Evans, & Patterson, 1987). These difficulties include hyperactivity, withdrawn states, sleep disturbances, aggression, agitation, self-injurious behaviors, and seizure disorders (Dalldorf, 1983; Gualtieri, Evans, & Patterson, 1987). Several classifications of medications have been used with people who have autism, including neuroleptic drugs to control overactive and aggressive behaviors, and anticonvulsant drugs to control seizures (Gualtieri, Evans, & Patterson, 1987). A number of side effects can be associated with each of these types of medication, including cognitive impairment and tardive dyskinesia from the neuroleptic medications, and negative cognitive and behavioral effects from anticonvulsants (Gualtieri, Evans, & Patterson, 1987).

Gualtieri and his colleagues (1987) pointed out that few physicians have adequate training or knowledge to administer these types of medications properly to people with autism because of the complexity and low incidence of the disorder. Additionally, little research has been done with autistic people in such areas as long-term and interactive effects of multiple medications. Therefore, careful monitoring of medications must be

TABLE 7.1 Common Behaviors Associated with Autism

Social Behavior	Communication Behavior	Unusual Behavioral Characteristics	Learning Characteristics
Relates to people with difficulty	Develops and understands gestures poorly	Acts deaf and/or very sensitive to some sounds	Develops unevenly within and across skills areas
Has strange fears	Speaks infrequently or not at all for 50% or more of the time	Resists change in routine	Resists change in learning environment; perseverates
Lacks understanding of social cues	Has difficulty understanding abstract concepts	Lacks fear of real danger	Has difficulty with unstructured time and waiting
Avoids or has odd use of eye contact	Has problems answering even simple questions	Exhibits repetitive body movements such as rocking, pacing, hand flapping	May not generalize skills to other areas and places
Wants to be alone frequently	Lacks comprehension of content and timing of communication	May stare or fixate on objects	Has difficulty with abstract concepts
Develops strong inappropriate attachment to objects	Perseverates on one topic; rambles	Explores environment by inappropriate methods such as licking, smelling, handling	Overselects one or more stimuli with failure to understand the whole
Giggles, laughs, screams inappropriately	Follows a line of exchange with difficulty	Perseverates on or has short attention to task	Exhibits impulsivity and inconsistency
Lacks imaginative play	Has difficulty communicating socially	Uses peripheral vision rather than straight on vision and/or avoids looking	Needs to be taught to make choices, decisions, and plans
Often uses toys in odd ways such as lining up, spinning, etc.	Initiates communication infrequently	May avoid human contact in favor of touching objects	Relies on cues and learned routines often
Lacks understanding of how others feel	May run, aggress, or be self-injurious to express frustration		Usually is not competitive
Expresses emotions inappropriately and has narrow range			
Lacks social/sexual understanding			

Source: Reprinted with permission from N. J. Dalrymple: *Introduction to Autism,* 1987. Bloomington, IN: Institute for the Study of Developmental Disabilities.

considered when programming for the person who has autism to ensure proper health and to determine whether specific behaviors are associated with the medication, with the disability, or with the intervention that is being introduced.

Strengths

Although the preceding list of limitations may cause the service provider to wonder what the person with autism *can* do, there are a number of strengths that, with proper motivation, can be used to enhance program effectiveness. These strengths include stamina, well-developed gross and fine motor skills, enjoyment of routines, good long-term memory, accuracy, and "splinter skills" (Dalrymple, 1987). Frequently observed in autistic persons are qualities that are both identifiable with the disorder and, under certain circumstances, are considered to be assets. The ability to stay on task until it is completed, to withstand constant monotonous routines, and to perform the same task repeatedly with accuracy (once it is learned) may be a consequence of the disorder that can be a great strength. In addition, many people having autism display unusual talents, such as facility with numbers, calendar skills, music abilities, art, and fine motor precision skills. These talents must not be overlooked in gaining a more complete understanding and appreciation of the person who has autism.

PURPOSE OF THERAPEUTIC RECREATION

Since Kanner's historic case study work in which he detailed salient attributes of the autistic syndrome, a large new body of work has been proliferated about children with this pervasive developmental disorder. Most recently, concern has begun to extend beyond childhood autism and to confront the changes in adults.

Typically, physicians, psychologists, speech clinicians, educational consultants, social workers, and other allied health professionals (i.e., nurses, occupational therapists, physical therapists) have been the primary professionals to come in contact with, diagnose, and treat children with autism. Therapeutic recreation specialists have had minimal roles in the past; however, their professional involvement in the care and treatment of persons with autism has expanded in recent years as a significant number of individuals with autism have remained in the community as opposed to being institutionalized. As residents in institutions, people with autism historically have had opportunities to participate in recreation services but probably not as a significant part of their written treatment plan. The role of a variety of disciplines, including therapeutic recreation, in the interdisciplinary treatment process has greatly expanded as a clearer delineation of the contribution these services make to habilitation has been demonstrated.

General Approaches to the Treatment of Autism

Lifelong habilitation is the ongoing mission of intervention programming for persons with autism. Habilitation can be simply described as a process of gaining the necessary skills required to function as independently as possible, given the constellation of individual strengths and deficits. As a consequence of a significant amount of research on program design in the area of autism, general habilitation areas have emerged to include behavior management, socialization, communication, and learning (Dalrymple, 1991; Donnellan, 1980; Koegel, Rincover, & Egel, 1982; Lovaas, 1981). Because of profound deficits and anomalies in the sequence of normal development, several disciplines join together to design and implement the intervention program. Each discipline focuses on a common set of goals to enhance habilitation. The preferred treatment strategy involves an *integrated triad approach,* which combines the utilization of the behavioral, functional, and developmental approaches to skill development (Donnellan & Kilman, 1986).

The *behavioral approach* to intervention provides the methodology (or "how to") needed to affect skill development (Schopler & Mesibov, 1994; Koegel, Rincover, & Egel, 1982; Lovaas,

1981). Important characteristics of the behavioral approach include the following:

1. Definable, observable, and measurable responses that are predicated on goals and objectives that indicate present, as well as postintervention, levels of functioning.
2. Accountability through objective and reliable evaluation procedures that are amenable to modification and revision as needed in order to support educational efforts and success.
3. Flexibility in terms of the variety of data that can be meaningfully applied and used.
4. Power and effectiveness in teaching a variety of skills to persons with autism (i.e., the application of incidental teaching, time delay, and the technique of shaping).
5. Power and effectiveness in managing behavior (i.e., nonaversive technology for managing social behaviors) (Donnellan & Kilman, 1986).

The *functional approach* (Brown et al., 1979; Brown, Nietupski, & Hamre-Nietupski, 1976; Donnellan, 1980) provides the content to be taught (otherwise known as the "what" to teach). The functional skills approach to intervention programming is predicated on the question, "What does this individual need to know in order to function in his or her current environment or in preparation for functioning in a subsequent environment?" A functional skills approach safeguards against persons with autism being taught meaningless tasks in relationship to the skills that are needed for the particular age, residential setting, family/caregiver situation, and community context (Donnellan, 1980). The functional approach focuses on the natural context rather than in an artificial learning environment. For example, riding the bus is not taught in a classroom using a prop bus; rather, it is taught using the actual bus and bus route on which the person is expected to use in every day life. A functional skills approach reduces difficulties associated with task generalization, which is typically problematic for the person with autism, while capitalizing on the requisites, cues, and consequences of the natural context for the skill being taught (Brown, Nietupski, & Hamre-Nietupski, 1976).

The *developmental approach* focuses on the individual's present ability repertoire as applied to the task to be taught (Wood, 1975). Information about the person's abilities in relation to the developmental continuum provides the baseline for determining what the person already knows, as well as how to accommodate the environment to enhance learning of other tasks through use of present skills (Piaget, 1960; Schopler, Reichler, & Lansing, 1980).

The combined triad-based approach (behavioral, functional, developmental) is the preferred methodology for planning and implementing treatment programs for persons with autism. The application of a triadic approach will enhance the potential for success in habilitation programming throughout the life course and across the varied settings in which services are delivered to persons with austism.

Common Habilitation Objectives

Habilitation objectives designed for people with autism are usually based on a set of primary needs (cognitive, social, behavioral, and communicative) for this population. It is important to emphasize that specialized programming will not cure autism; it is a severe, pervasive disorder that requires lifelong treatment and support. In spite of the severity of the disability, people with autism can learn functional skills, and higher-functioning (intellectually) people can learn to live independently as adults. Each person with autism is unique, so programs must be designed to meet individual needs ranging from specialized programming to generic programs (in the case of public school, regular classes).

Common treatment objectives include the development of interactive social and communication skills, appropriate social behavior, and community living skills (e.g., leisure, vocational, and home-life skills). Opportunities to participate in programs are important considerations in the treatment of autism. Because nearly all persons with autism exhibit difficulty in generalizing, treatment programming should be designed for implementation in the actual context in which the autistic person is expected to perform the skill (Olley, 1986).

Planning for behavior management is a particularly important aspect of treatment programming for persons with autism (Dalrymple, 1991; Favell, 1983). Frequently, failure to learn or function appropriately is due to behavioral interference. The selection of the appropriate behavior management strategy in any given situation also should take into consideration environmental modifications to support the person's ability to behave accordingly (Amado, 1988). Frequently, the manner in which the environment is designed will reduce behavior problems. The environment should offer consistency and structure, and should focus on a functional skills program.

The Role of the Family in Intervention

Mesibov (1983) noted the need to define more clearly the family's role in the treatment of persons with autism. The value of family involvement has been demonstrated with some concern noted regarding the abilities of families to sustain their involvement throughout the lives of their children (Schopler & Mesibov, 1984; Schopler & Reichler, 1971; Sullivan, 1977; Wing; 1985). Therefore, although families may be more involved when their children with autism are young, other avenues for their participation in treatment should be delineated as their children mature to adulthood (Mesibov, 1983). These avenues might include advocacy for needed services, self-help support network building, long-range financial planning, and other legal arrangements.

DeMyer and Goldberg (1983) noted the primary adverse effects of autism on family life to be first and foremost a total loss of family recreation because of the totality of demand in caring for a child with autism. This situation does not ease with time, and families often express fatigue and burnout by the time their son or daughter reaches adolescence. Financial drain, along with strain in the emotional/mental health status of parents, is another adverse outcome of caring for a son or daughter with autism. Illustrative of a contributing factor to financial loss is the mother's inability to work outside of the home to supplement income. Being able to find care for children with autism is difficult and typically is impossible. When mothers can manage to work outside of the home, most of the extra income is dispensed in the care and treatment (including private residential placement) of the son or daughter with autism. Feelings of depression, grief, and burnout are common among families with an autistic member.

Additional adverse effects for parents include diminished physical health, difficulty meeting the needs of siblings, loss of friendships and neighborhood relationships, increased tensions among siblings, and strained marital relationships. It is an accepted fact that the family lifestyle will alter markedly in the presence of a son or daughter with autism in order to accommodate the range of symptoms associated with the disorder (DeMyer & Goldberg, 1983).

The treatment strategy for families involves providing social and emotional support services, services to assist with the autistic child's growth and development, and services to enable the family to experience growth. Approaches that have been successful in meeting family needs include parent training, parent and sibling support groups, and accessible respite care programs.

The Role of TR in Social and Behavioral Treatment

Deficits in appropriate social and behavioral skills in persons with autism have been described as a major contributor to failure in family life, school life, and vocational placements (Henning & Dalrymple, 1986). Social skill deficits alone are characteristic and pervasive attributes of the disorder and, thus, require special attention in programming (Schmidt, McLaughlin, & Dalrymple, 1986; Henning, et al., 1982). Mesibov (1986) noted that specific programs addressing sociability in persons with autism are needed. Based on the widely accepted role of leisure and recreation in social development, it is appropriate to apply therapeutic recreation as a treatment modality in the development of social skills by autistic persons (Wehman, 1977, 1983; Wehman & Schleien, 1980, 1981).

Therapeutic recreation programs designed to address social skills and behavior deficits should first establish overall program priorities. Commonly, these priorities will emerge from an interdisciplinary team assessment of the person's strengths and needs, as well as known priorities generally associated with autism. Targeted deficits should be responsive to remediation. Other considerations when selecting social and behavioral skills for programming should include sensitivity to age appropriateness, family preferences, learning style, sensory considerations, current developmental level, program resources, and community resources (Henning & Dalrymple, 1986).

The role of therapeutic recreation is to support global treatment goals in behavior management, socialization/social skill development, and leisure skill development. An emphasis is placed on those social, behavioral, and leisure skills that are age appropriate and will be used throughout the life course (Schleien, Kiernan, & Wehman, 1981; Wuerch & Voeltz, 1982).

Treatment objectives that are applicable in therapeutic recreation programming include the following:

1. Teaching functional academic skills such as money skills, time skills, reading, and giving/requesting information.
2. Teaching self-care skills such as personal grooming, socially appropriate manners, appropriate sexual behavior, and care of personal belongings.
3. Teaching interpersonal skills such as cooperation, appropriate ways of interacting socially with others within situational context (handshake, hugs, etc.).
4. Teaching social communication skills such as proper greetings, use of personal names when greeting or requesting attention, requesting permission to borrow others' possessions.
5. Teaching specific leisure skills such as playing games following rules and etiquette, choosing independently from leisure activity options, recognizing and distinguishing picture cues of leisure activities and work activities.
6. Teaching community living skills such as ordering food and eating properly at a restaurant, shopping skills, and using public transportation (Henning & Dalrymple, 1986).

Therapeutic recreation can make its greatest contribution in the treatment of people who have autism when the focus is on social and behavioral skills development, using leisure activities as the modality for goal attainment. In some ways, therapeutic recreation services offer a superior avenue for supporting social and behavioral skills development because leisure activities are recognized as fun and pleasurable experiences (Wehman & Marchant, 1978; Schleien & Ray, 1988). Most people with autism have recreation activity preferences, and involvement in these activities can supplant less stimulating ways of achieving skill development.

COMMON SERVICE SETTINGS

Probably one of the most noteworthy advancements in the area of autism is the movement toward the community integration and inclusion of persons with this disability. However, describing common service settings for persons with autism is problematic at best. Schopler and Mesibov (1992, 1994) noted the lack of appropriately designed community-based program alternatives that meet the habilitation needs of this population. Unfortunately, this situation has made little progress in recent years. Children and adults with autism have difficulty finding residential alternatives outside of the family and institutional contexts. Vocational training programs and employment options also present limited capacity to meet the social, behavioral, communicative, and cognitive needs of autistic persons. Children with autism are entitled to educational services under Public Law 94-142, but only a few teachers have the knowledge and skills needed to teach children with autism in regular classrooms.

Probably the most useful way of conceptualizing service settings for persons with autism is to focus on the major settings in which the habilitation plan is implemented. Individual educational or habilitation plans are implemented across home (residential context), school or work, and recreation. The variety of settings in which the individual will have habilitation goals and objectives implemented in programmed activities will be dependent upon whether the basis of residential placement is with the family, community-based alternative (e.g., group home), or institution. Probably the most critical issue for persons with autism is the preparation of community programs to understand and accept the behaviors commonly associated with this disorder.

Because broad-based knowledge about autism and the subsequent development of appropriate programming strategies for persons with autism are still unfolding, it is understandable that progress in the evolution of common service settings is less well developed than in other areas (e.g., geriatric services, substance abuse). There are curriculum materials and teaching environments that demonstrate effective strategies for teacher and learner education (i.e., the **T**reatment and **E**ducation of **A**utistic and related **C**ommunication Handicapped **C**hildren—TEACCH—program at the University of North Carolina) (Mesibov, Schopler, & Sloan, 1983). Benhaven also offers an example of a specialized day and residential school facility that provides an intensive program for children and adults (Lettick, 1983).

Parent advocacy efforts continue to impact the availability of program and treatment options for autistic persons. For example, the Jay Nolan Center in Newhall, California, was developed from the consumer-based activities of the Los Angeles Chapter of the National Society for Autistic Children (LaVigna, 1983). This center demonstrates a continuum of residential, recreational, vocational, and educational services for persons with autism and their families. The services and programs provided are based on normalization, community integration, and inclusion principles. As parents and professionals gain better understanding and skills in the treatment of autism, it is hoped that future strides in the availability and use of community-based programs will evolve.

CURRENT BEST PRACTICES AND PROCEDURES

The diagnosis of autism has had a history of confusion because of misinterpretation of symptoms with other disorders (e.g., schizophrenia, mental retardation, Rett's Disorder, Childhood Disintegrative Disorder) (American Psychiatric Association, 1994). Today, a differential diagnosis can be made through the application of criteria and instruments that have significantly enhanced the identification of clients with autism. The ASA and the American Psychiatric Association provide criteria for making a diagnosis. These criteria are (1) onset before the age of thrity-six months; (2) disturbance of response to sensory stimuli; (3) disturbance of speech, language, cognition, and nonverbal communication; (4) disturbance of capacity to relate appropriately to people, events, and objects; and (5) disturbance of developmental rates and sequences (American Psychiatric Association, 1994; Dalrymple, 1987). Although these criteria are useful in the process of making a diagnosis, problems associated with distinguishing autism from other disorders may require a multiaxial approach as previously discussed. The Childhood Autism Rating Scale (CARS), which is comprised of fifteen scales, can be widely applied for determining the diagnosis of autism (Schopler et al, 1980).

Assessment

Current best practices in the identification, assessment, and treatment of persons with autism rely heavily on the use of an interdisciplinary approach. This approach incorporates the expertise of several professionals in the assessment of functioning, the formulation of the diagnosis of autism, and the development of an individual program plan. Maximum benefits for the person with autism and his or her family have the greatest potential when the interdisciplinary approach is pursued. Typical areas represented in the interdisciplinary approach include education, social work, audiology/speech and language, medicine, recreation therapy, occupational/physical therapy, and psychology. Each of these disciplinary areas relates closely with characteristics of the autistic disorder.

Illustrations of the different disciplinary roles are as follows. Based on deficits in cognition that affect learning, it is appropriate that education play a role in identification, assessment, and treatment of cognitive function. Social work will assist with family education and adjustment. Audiology, speech, and language specialists will be interested in the total communication development of the individual. The physician may be the first professional to recognize problematic development that suggests the autistic disorder in the young patient, as well as to provide pharmacologic interventions when indicated. The psychologist will supply important evaluative information on social and cognitive development as compared to normal developmental markers. The therapeutic recreation specialist will assess functional social skills and recreational interests that will enhance participation in community-based activities. The occupational/physical therapist will provide additional information on perceptual problems and motor function. It is readily apparent from this sampling of disciplinary involvement that the interdisciplinary approach will provide greater depth and breadth in understanding the needs and strengths of the individual who has autism.

Currently, assessment instruments and procedures for young children through to adolescence and adulthood are available. Unfortunately, very few middle-aged or older adults are likely to be living in community-based residential alternatives; thus, there is a shortage of assessment information that is applicable to older adults, nor is there certainty of its value at this time in the life course.

Illustrative of an appropriate assessment instrument for young children with autism is the PEP (Psycho Educational Profile) developed at the Division for TEACCH at the University of North Carolina (Schopler & Reichler, 1979). The instrument is a behaviorally based tool for application with autism that produces highly useful information for individual program planning. Using a Pass-Fail-Emerging scoring system, the PEP assesses ten areas of functioning: perception, imitation, fine motor skills, gross motor skills, eye-hand integration, expressive language, cognitive performance, self-help skills, behavior problems, and social skills (Mesibov, Schopler, & Sloan, 1983). The PEP has demonstrated success in the identification and assessment of autism because it minimizes the use of language, it provides the time needed for completing tasks, it presents materials in an attractive manner for young children, and it allows for flexible administration. Worldwild use of the PEP has produced test results for children who were previously reported to be untested (Schopler & Reichler, 1979).

Whereas the PEP was specifically designed for young children, an assessment process appropriate to the needs of autistic adolescents and young adults was also developed at TEACCH. The Adolescent and Adult Psycho Educational Profile (AAPEP) applies more relevant tasks to the needs and goals of adolescents and young adults (Mesibov, Schopler & Schaffer, n.d.). AAPEP is divided into six overlapping functional areas encompassing vocational, independent functioning, leisure, functional communication, and interpersonal behaviors that are assessed on three scales. A direct Observation Scale is administered clinically by a therapist, and the Home Scale and the School/Work Scale are based on behavioral reports made by primary caregivers in each context. The AAPEP uses the same Pass-Fail-Emerging scoring system as does the PEP and is targeted for use with the presence of moderate to severe mental retardation. The integrated results of the three scales form the basis of individual program plan development.

Important features of both the PEP and the AAPEP are the minimal use of verbal language-based directions, the significant application of the "emerging" score for identifying the possession of some skills necessary to complete a task, flexible administration, and the allotment of adequate time to complete test items. A significant difference between PEP and AAPEP is that the former is based upon developmental levels and the latter on criterion referencing.

It is important to note that members of the interdisciplinary assessment team will, by choice, implement a variety of assessment instruments associated with their individual disciplinary areas. Thus, the PEP and AAPEP are illustrative of one methodology in the assessment of program needs and the evaluation of progress with persons who have autism.

Planning

The basis for program design for autistic people focuses upon the characteristic deficits associated with the disorder as they appear in individuals based upon the interdisciplinary team assessment. These characteristics fall under four areas: behavioral, communication, learning, and social and interpersonal skills.

The unusual behaviors generally exhibited by persons with autism is one of the most notable characteristics of the disorder and thus, they require special program planning. The success or failure of programming in other areas often depends upon the effectiveness of the behavior management plan for the client. People with autism do not perceive the world in the same manner as do nondisabled people. Therefore, sensory stimuli can often evoke unusual behaviors in persons with autism. The behaviors most often encountered in people with autism include ritualistic and compulsive behavior, staring or visual fixation on objects, perseveration, avoidance of human contact, aggression, lack of self-control, insensitivity or oversensitivity to sounds, and inappropriate interaction with environment (e.g., licking) (American Psychiatric Association, 1994; Dalrymple, 1987; Gillberg, 1989; Mesibov, 1983).

Communication skills are central to the autistic person's ability to relate to those around him or her; therefore, the individual treatment plan will probably contain programmatic accommodations and objectives targeted at the development of communication skills. Common deficits include poor or no spoken language skills; perseveration on words or topics; infrequent initiation of communication; and exhibited difficulty in comprehending abstract concepts, in following a line of exchanges, and in answering questions even when they are simple (American Psychiatric Association, 1994; Dalrymple, 1987).

Learning difficulties for persons with autism are compounded by the presence of mental retardation. Typical deficits in learning skills include the inability to generalize skills; difficulty with unstructured or extra time; difficulty changing learning environments; tendencies to perseverate; overselection of stimuli; uncompetitiveness; impulsivity; inconsistency; difficulty with the abstract; and reliance on routine, prompts, and cues (Dalrymple, 1987).

The social and interpersonal skills of persons with autism are foremost areas in which therapeutic recreation services can make a contribution. Persons with autism relate poorly to people. They have strange fears, tend to avoid eye contact or use it oddly, often want to be alone, demonstrate strange and inappropriate social behavior (giggling, screaming), and lack empathy or an understanding of how another feels. The use of toy and play materials often will be odd. Difficulty with social and interpersonal behavior is present for all persons with autism (Amercian Psychiatric Association, 1994; Dalrymple, 1987). Leisure activities and therapeutic recreation have the potential, therefore, to occupy a significant place in the planned intervention strategy that addresses social skills.

Implementation

People with autism have difficulty generalizing skills across settings and materials. Therefore, the development of a leisure and social skills program that is based upon the overall functional life skills of the individual is the preferred implementation strategy. This strategy will be enhanced through the selection of skills that consider (1) age appropriateness and frequency of involvement by nondisabled age cohorts, (2) family preferences, (3) community resources, and (4) client's characteristic strengths and needs (Henning & Dalrymple, 1986; Wuerch & Voeltz, 1982).

An important element in program implementation for this population is the need to include a behavior management plan based on the presence of aggressive or inappropriate behaviors. The program implementation plan should include person-specific behavior management strategies and contingencies so that managing behavior does not overshadow the original intent of the program and habilitation objectives. Examples of behavior management considerations include identifying the antecedents to behavioral problems, understanding how to make environmental modifications, understanding the use of natural consequences, being capable of helping the individual to manage behavior with prompts and cuing, and identifying desired reinforcers for appropriate behaviors (Amado, 1988; Dalrymple, 1991; Favell, 1983).

Wehman (1983) identified the characteristics of an appropriately designed leisure skills program for autistic persons as including (1) normalization and social integration as a philosophical base; (2) the capacity to modify equipment, facilities, rules, and skill sequences as needed; (3) a behavioral base to skill training; and (4) teaching skills where they will be used. The optimal service delivery model is one in which the community is prepared to accept participation by the person with autism. A skilled therapeutic recreation specialist will serve as a consultant on the treatment team in relation to assessment, selection of age-appropriate skills, adaptation of the environment and/or skill, instruction, community preparation, and evaluation.

Evaluation

The evaluation of client progress is difficult in the treatment process of persons with severe disability. Gains often take a long time to produce in terms of measurable change, yet even the smallest success may be very important toward attaining individual potential.

Brookhiser and Dalrymple (1987) developed a computer-based model for tracking the behaviors and capabilities of persons with autism based on each individual's educational (habilitation) plan goals and objectives. Through the application of this sophisticated system, individual behaviors and capabilities can be monitored and evaluated across all program environments (home, school/work, recreation, and community). A system of data documentation and management that tracks behaviors and outcome performance across time and all program environments has the greatest promise for providing useful evaluation data in the treatment of complex disorders such as autism.

APPLICATION OF THE TR PROCESS

The uniqueness of each individual with autism is a noteworthy aspect of this pervasive developmental disorder. It is inappropriate, therefore, to draw generalizations for all people with autism from an individual characterization other than providing reinforcement for the general characteristics of the disorder. Specifically, these characteristics include profound disturbances in the development of appropriate social, behavioral, and communicative skills. The following case study provides illustration of the manifestation of these disturbances, as well as glimpses of splinter skills that also may be present in persons with autism.

CASE STUDY

Joan is a 23-year-old female who is presently residing in an acute care mental health facility. She previously had been living at home while waiting for placement in a group home. Her parents live in the same community as the facility. Her father is employed at a local retail firm, and her mother has been the primary homemaker for the family. Joan has two older siblings—a married brother and a sister with a professional career.

Assessment

Joan was reported (by mother) to be a good baby in that she did not frequently cry for attention. She walked independently at 11 months and babbled a few single words between the first and second birthday. At age 5, Joan was putting two words together. She was a head banger, crib rocker, and slept less than other children as a young child.

Joan has a history of biting herself. She also showed a particular interest in whirling objects. At 5½ years of age, she was formally evaluated and identified as having autistic disorder with mild to moderate mental retardation. She also developed seizure disorder shortly after the diagnosis of autism was made. The seizure disorder has been controlled with medications since its onset. During early adolescence, Joan's self-injurious behaviors were extinguished, while her functional communication and vocational skills were developed.

Joan suffers from constipation and seems to like salty foods. Often, she eats enormous amounts of food.

Since Joan's eligibility for public educational programming ended, she has been employed in several sheltered workshops. Each of these placements has ended in her removal from the program because of interfering and aggressive social behaviors. She was unable to work continuously without direct adult supervision and cuing.

Joan has other skills that can be developed for their potential to support vocational placement. She demonstrates a remarkable ability to participate in a variety of housekeeping chores, including cooking and cleaning.

Joan's special talent is music; she can play the piano quite well and likes listening to the radio. Past records show that her behavior management is assisted by engaging her in activities such as rug hooking and music.

Present behaviors: Joan is on a focused program to bring her behavior under control. Little else can be accomplished until she is settled down regarding residential and vocational placement. She has been preoccupied with self-injurious behaviors and a pronounced regression to past behaviors (i.e., biting herself). This period in Joan's life is one of the most turbulent and distressing because of the lack of community residential alternatives and suitable vocational placements that match her needs and strengths.

Current pharmacologic intervention is the use of Haldol to reduce agitation and activity level, and Tegretol for seizure disorder. Previous medications include Stelazine and Mellaril.

Planning

Long-term goal: To seek stable daily leisure activities that are independent of the residential location and that support Joan's needs for restorative leisure behaviors.

Short-term goals: (1) To assist Joan in using leisure interests to cope with present mental distress. (2) To assist Joan in using past leisure skills to add predictability and routine to the present situation.

Objectives: Joan will participate in daily therapeutic recreation programming to (1) provide an expected routine to each day, (2) assist in releasing tensions associated with the temporary nature of the current residential situation, and (3) provide opportunities to demonstrate acquired leisure skills successfully.

Opportunities to take Joan into the community for leisure activities will be sought as reinforcers to community living skills that she previously demonstrated.

Content: Joan will verbally indicate leisure activities she enjoys and will be encouraged to plan ahead for the next therapeutic recreation session. Her awareness of the pleasure and satisfaction derived from leisure participation will be observed and recorded.

Process: (1) To sensitize mental health facility staff to the leisure needs, interests, and skills that Joan possesses. (2) To encourage facility direct care staff to use relaxation activities to calm and focus Joan's attention on positive skills. (3) To request direct care staff to schedule daily routine times for independent leisure activity beyond those associated with therapeutic periods.

Implementation

Joan will participate in daily recreation therapy as well as have opportunities to participate in activity preferences during unscheduled free or downtime. Recreation therapy will focus on providing reinforcement for skill performance and daily routines in leisure activity. Participation and anecdotal records will be maintained by the TR specialist and direct care staff.

Evaluation

Behavioral data will be maintained on a daily basis for Joan. Targeted interfering behaviors (e.g., self-biting), situational antecedents, and consequences will be observed and recorded. Progress on therapeutic recreation interventions for controlling interfering behavior will be reviewed and evaluated for change or modification in the individual treatment plan. As residential and vocational placement is identified for Joan, her therapeutic recreation program will be reviewed as part of the development and implementation of her overall individual habilitation plan.

TRENDS AND ISSUES

The trend in services to persons with severe disabilities such as autism is to support programming within the community and thus advance the concepts of normalization and inclusion. However, persons with severe disorders such as autism have yet to be fully and effectively socially integrated into community, school, vocational, and recreational programming settings. For persons with autism, social integration and inclusion require careful planning, systematic implementation, and sustained efforts in order to ensure success for both the autistic person, as well as other community members. One clear goal that is necessary to advance community inclusion is the availability of systematically planned and implemented age-appropriate experiences with chronological age peers (Schleien & Ray, 1988; Schleien et al., 1987; Wuerch & Voeltz, 1982). It is important to note that research findings are mixed on the influence that normalized, community-based settings have on improved recreational functioning of persons who have severe disability.

In therapeutic recreation service, as with other professional services, there are numerous issues related to successful community integration and inclusion of people with autism. An important issue to be addressed is the limited level of training in the treatment of autism that is available to community-based service providers. In addition to having a basic knowledge of behavior management techniques in order to provide effective motivation and reinforcement, the community-based professional will need training in the use of alternative communication techniques. People with autism often have severe limitations in expressive and receptive communication skills, as well as their language comprehension. Some training in communication strategies is necessary in order to provide effective programming in support of community inclusion goals.

As community-based recreation program opportunities expand for persons with autism, the potential arises for new roles in service delivery to emerge (Reynolds, 1981). These roles encompass the following:

- Decreasing the number of special events that reach large groups and increasing individualized programming.
- Moving away from the clinical medical model of service delivery.
- Using behavior management techniques that are commensurate with normalization practices.
- Adopting advocacy roles and providing liaison with community programs to ensure access.
- Transferring training and skills from the specialist to the general community recreation leader and family members.

Although these changing roles seem far off in the distance for professionals serving individuals with autism, the intent of enabling the community to accept people with severe disabilities lies at the heart of the trend promoting inclusive communities, a trend that is clearly here to stay. Preparing the service delivery system, as well as other constituents who use leisure services, to understand, accept, and assist in meeting the needs of persons with autism perhaps is one of the greatest challenges for the field.

SUMMARY

Perhaps one of the most frustrating aspects of dealing with people who have autism is the perplexing nature of the disorder. Designing interventions that eventually produce habilitative results, but only after long periods of programming, often leaves caregivers with a sense of burnout and exhaustion. Meeting the needs of persons with autism across the life span will bring a myriad of professionals in contact with the disabled individual and his or her family. The pervasive nature of this disorder will necessitate professional fortitude. Thus, only a select few will probably choose to become professionals working with people who have autism. For the few who do opt to work with these individuals, a cycle of inservice training will be needed to fortify energies in the face of rising feelings of burnout. People with autism need extra special caregivers who are open to change and growth, and who demonstrate adaptability (Smith, 1990; Wing, 1985).

For those therapeutic recreation specialists working with people who have autism and their families, the rewards may be greater than in other areas of human service. Persons with autism are capable of learning and participating in a wide variety of leisure activities that bring both habilitative functions, and moments of joy and pleasure in an otherwise confusing world of demands and disorder. In this respect, the opportunity to develop socially appropriate and fun-oriented behaviors through participation in recreation may be the single most important contribution of therapeutic recreation in the treatment of autism.

READING COMPREHENSION QUESTIONS

1. Describe the American Psychiatric Association's current (DSM-IV) criteria that are applied in the identification and diagnosis of autism.
2. What are six disciplines that might cooperate to complete an interdisciplinary assessment of a person suspected of having autism?
3. Explain why there is a lack of understanding about the syndrome of autism.
4. Describe common behavioral characteristics that are often associated with autism.
5. Explain the role that therapeutic recreation can play in the treatment of persons who have autism.
6. Describe the potential impacts that trends in community integration and inclusion for persons with severe disabilities may have on therapeutic recreation services to persons with autism.

SUGGESTED LEARNING ACTIVITIES

1. Invite a parent of a child with autism to visit your class and discuss his or her experience of living with an autistic son or daughter. Follow up the parent-visit class session with a separate class discussion period to explore students' perceptions of parent adjustment, grief, guilt, and family life dynamics that are a consequence of the presence of the autistic family member.
2. Prepare a short analytical paper on the role of leisure in the development of social skills in persons with autism.
3. Hold a small group discussion in which you identify and review the primary issues associated with normalization, community integration, and community inclusion for persons with autism.
4. Develop a list of behavioral characteristics of persons with autism. Visit a large public area (e.g., shopping mall) and while there, apply your checklist randomly to people you observe in the setting. Share your findings in class.
5. Visit an agency that serves persons who have autism and assist the TR professional. Give a report in class on your experience.

REFERENCES

Amado, R.S. (1988). Behavioral principles in community recreation integration. In S. J. Schleien & M.T. Ray (Eds.), *Community recreation and persons with disabilities: Strategies for integration* (pp. 79–90). Baltimore: Paul H. Brookes.

American Psychiatric Association. (1994). *Diagnostic and statistical manual of mental disorders* (4th ed.). Washington, DC: American Psychiatric Association.

Brookhiser, J.K., & Dalrymple, N.J. (1987). A microcomputer-based system for profiling behaviors and capabilities of individuals with autism or severe learning and behavioral handicaps. In K.L. Mayfield & G.G. Yajnik (Eds.), *Proceedings of the Second Annual National Symposium Information Technology as a Resource to Health & Disability Professionals, 1,* 205–220. Columbia, SC: University of South Carolina.

Brown, L., et al. (1979). A strategy for developing chronological age-appropriate and functional curricular content for severely handicapped adolescents and young adults. *Journal of Special Education, 13,* 81–90.

Brown, L., Nietupski, J., & Hamre-Nietupski, S. (1976). The criterion of ultimate functioning and public school services for severely handicapped students. In M.A. Thomas (Ed.), *Hey, don't forget about me: Education's investment in the severely, profoundly and multiply handicapped* (pp. 2–15). Reston, VA: Council for Exceptional Children.

Coleman, M. (1992). The autistic syndromes. In A.M. Donellan (Ed.), *Classic readings in autism* (2nd ed.) (pp. 370–382). New York: Teachers College Press.

Coleman, M., & Gillberg, C. (1985). *The biology of the autistic syndromes.* New York: Praeger.

Dalldorf, J.S. (1983). Medical needs of the autistic adolescent. In E. Schopler & G.B. Mesibov (Eds.), *Autism in adolescents and adults* (pp. 149–168). New York: Plenum Press.

Dalrymple, N.J. (1991). *Helping people with autism manage their behavior.* Bloomington, IN: Indiana University, Institute for the Study of Developmental Disabilities.

Dalrymple, N.J. (Ed.). (1987). *Introduction to autism.* Bloomington, IN: Indiana University, Institute for the Study of Developmental Disabilities.

DeMyer, M.K., & Goldberg, P. (1983). Family needs of the autistic adolescent. In E. Schopler & G.B. Mesibov (Eds.), *Austism in adolescents and adults* (pp. 225–250). New York: Plenum Press.

Donellan, A.M. (1980). An educational perspective of autism: Implications for curriculum development and personnel development. In B. Wilcox & A. Thompson (Eds.), *Critical issues in educating autistic children and youth* (pp. 53–88). Washington, DC: U.S. Department of Education, Office of Special Education.

Donnellan, A.M., & Kilman, B.A. (1986). Behavioral approaches to social skill development in autism. In E. Schopler & G.B. Mesibov (Eds.), *Social behavior in autism* (pp. 213–236). New York: Plenum Press.

Favell, J.E. (1983). The management of aggressive behavior. In E. Schopler & G.B. Mesibov (Eds.), *Autism in adolescents and adults* (pp. 187–222). New York: Plenum Press.

Freeman, B.J., & Ritvo, E.R. (1981). The syndrome of autism: A critical review of diagnostic systems, follow-up studies, and the theoretical background of the behavioral observation scale. In J.E. Gilliam (Ed.), *Autism: Diagnosis, instruction, management, and research* (pp. 17–63). Springfield, IL: Charles C. Thomas.

Gillberg, C. (Ed.). (1989). *Diagnosis and treatment of autism.* New York: Plenum Press.

Gualtieri, T., Evans, R.W., & Patterson, D.R. (1987). The medical treatment of autistic people: Problems and side effects. In E. Schopler & G.B. Mesibov (Eds.), *Neurobiological issues in autism* (pp. 373–388). New York: Plenum Press.

Henning, J., & Dalrymple, N.J. (1986). A guide for developing social and leisure programs for students with autism. In E. Schopler & G.B. Mesibov (Eds.), *Social behavior in autism* (pp. 321–350). New York: Plenum Press.

Henning, J., et al. (1982). *Teaching social and leisure skills to youth with autism.* Bloomington, IN: Indiana University Developmental Training Center.

Kanner, L. (1943). Autistic disturbances of affective contact. *Nervous Child, 2,* 217–250.

Koegel, R.L., Rincover, A., & Egel, A.L. (Eds.). (1982). *Educating and understanding autistic children.* San Diego: College Hill Press.

Lavigna, G.W. (1983). The Jay Nolan Center: A community-based program. In E. Schopler & G.B. Mesibov (Eds.), *Autism in adolescents and adults* (pp. 381–410). New York: Plenum Press.

Lettick, A.L. (1983). Benhaven. In E. Schopler & G.B. Mesibov (Eds.), *Autism in adolescents and adults* (pp. 355–379). New York: Plenum Press.

Lovaas, O. (1981). *Teaching developmentally disabled children.* Baltimore: University Park Press.

Mesibov, G.B. (1983). Current perspectives and issues in autism and adolescence. In E. Schopler & G.B. Mesibov (Eds.), *Autism in adolescents and adults* (pp. 37–53). New York: Plenum Press.

Mesibov, G.B. (1986). A cognitive program for teaching social behaviors to verbal autistic adolescents and adults. In E. Schopler & G.B. Mesibov (Eds.), *Social behavior in autism* (pp. 265–283). New York: Plenum Press.

Mesibov, G.B., Schopler, E., & Schaffer, B. (n.d.). *Adolescent and adult psychoeducational profile.* Chapel Hill, NC: University of North Carolina.

Mesibov, G.B., Schopler, E., & Sloan, J.L. (1983). Service development for adolescents and adults in North Carolina's TEACCH program. In E. Schopler & G.B. Mesibov (Eds.), *Autism in adolescents and adults* (pp. 411–432). New York: Plenum Press.

Olley, J.G. (1986). The TEACCH curriculum for teaching social behavior to children with autism. In E. Schopler & G. B. Mesibov (Eds.), *Social behavior in autism* (pp. 351–373). New York: Plenum Press.

Paluszny, M.J. (1979). *Autism: A practical guide for parents and professionals.* Syracuse, NY: Syracuse University Press.

Piaget, J. (1960). The definition of states of development. In J. Tanner & B. Inhelder (Eds.), *Discussions on child development* (pp. 116–135). New York: International Universities Press.

Reynolds, R.P. (1981). Normalization: A guideline to leisure skills programming for handicapped individuals. In P. Wehman & S. J. Schleien (Eds.), *Leisure programs for handicapped persons* (pp. 1–13). Baltimore: University Park Press.

Rutter, M. (1968). Concepts of autism: A review of research. *Journal of Child Psychology and Psychiatry, 9,* 1–25.

Rutter, M. (1971). The description and classification of infantile autism. In D.W. Churchill, G.D. Alpern, & M.K. DeMyer (Eds.), *Infantile autism.* Springfield, IL: Charles C. Thomas.

Rutter, M. (1972). Childhood schizophrenia reconsidered. *Journal of Autism and Childhood Schizophrenia, 2,* 315–337.

Rutter, M. (1978). Diagnosis and definition of childhood autism. *Journal of Autism and Childhood Schizophrenia, 8,* 139–161.

Rutter, M., & Schopler, E. (Eds.). (1978). *Autism: A reappraisal of concepts and treatment.* New York: Plenum Press.

Schleien, S.J., Kiernan, J., & Wehman, P. (1981, February). Evaluation of an age-appropriate leisure skills program for mentally retarded adults. *Educational Training of the Mentally Retarded,* 13–19.

Schleien, S.J., et al. (1987). The effect of integrating children with autism into a physical activity and recreation setting. *Therapeutic Recreation Journal, 21*(4), 52–62.

Schleien, S.J., & Ray, M.T. (1988). *Community recreation and persons with disabilities: Strategies for integration.* Baltimore: Paul H. Brookes.

Schmidt, G., McLaughlin, J., & Dalrymple, N.J. (1986). Teaching students with autism: A sport skill specialist's approach. *Journal of Physical Education, Recreation, and Dance, 57*(7), 60–63.

Schopler, E. (1966). Visual versus tactual receptor preference in normal and schizophrenic children. *Journal of Abnormal Psychology, 71,* 108–114.

Schopler, E., & Mesibov, G.B. (Eds.). (1984). *The effects of autism on the family.* New York: Plenum Press.

Schopler, E., & Mesibov, G.B. (Eds.). (1992). *High functioning individuals with autism.* New York: Plenum Press.

Schopler, E., & Mesibov, G.B. (Eds.). (1994). *Behavioral issues in autism.* New York: Plenum Press.

Schopler, E., & Reichler, R.J. (1971). Parents as cotherapists in the treatment of psychotic children. *Journal of Autism and Childhood Schizophrenia, 1,* 87–102.

Schopler, E. & Reichler, R.J. (1979). *Individualized assessment for autistic and developmentally disabled children: Psychoeducational profile,* Vol. I. Baltimore: University Park Press.

Schopler, E., et al. (1980). Toward objective classification of childhood autism: Childhood autism rating scale (CARS). *Journal of Autism and Developmental Disorders, 10,* 91–103.

Schopler, E., Reichler, R.J., & Lansing, M. (1980). *Individualized assessment and treatment for autistic and developmentally disabled children: Teaching strategies for parents and professionals,* Vol. II. Baltimore: University Park Press.

Smith, M.D. (1990). *Autism and life in the community.* Baltimore: Paul H. Brookes.

Sullivan, R.C. (1977). Parents speak. *Journal of Autism and Childhood Schizophrenia, 7,* 287-288.

Wehman, P. (Ed.). (1977). *Recreation programming for developmentally disabled persons.* Baltimore: University Park Press.

Wehman, P. (1983). Recreation and leisure needs: A community integration approach. In E. Schopler & G.B. Mesibov (Eds.), *Autism in adolescents and adults* (pp. 111–132). New York: Plenum Press.

Wehman, P., & Marchant, J. (1978). Improving free play skills of severely retarded children. *American Journal of Occupational Therapy, 32*(2), 100–172.

Wehman, P., & Schleien, S.J. (1980). Assessment and selection of leisure skills for severely handicapped persons. *Education and Training of the Mentally Retarded, 14*(3), 36–42.

Wehman, P., & Schleien, S.J. (1981). *Leisure programs for handicapped persons: Adaptations, techniques, and curriculum.* Baltimore: University Park Press.

Wing, L. (1978). Social, behavioral, and cognitive characteristics: An epidemiological approach. In M. Rutter & E. Schopler (Eds.), *Autism: A reappraisal of concepts and treatment.* New York: Plenum Press.

Wing, L. (1980). *Early childhood autism* (2nd ed.). Oxford: Pergamon Press.

Wing, L. (1985). *Autistic children: A guide for parents* (2nd ed.). New York, NY: Brunner/Mazel.

Wood, M.M. (Ed.). (1975). *Developmental theory.* Baltimore: University Park Press.

Wuerch, B.B., & Voeltz, L.M. (1982). *Longitudinal leisure skills for severely handicapped learners: The Ho'onanea curriculum component.* Baltimore: Paul H. Brookes.

CHAPTER 8

MENTAL RETARDATION

JOHN DATTILO

OBJECTIVES

- Understand the following terms and phrases: mental retardation, significantly subaverage intellectual functioning, intelligence quotient, adaptive skills, developmental period, and developmental disability.
- Describe ways of classifying people with mental retardation and the implications of these classifications on their lives.
- Describe the importance of treatment in providing comprehensive therapeutic recreation services to people with mental retardation.
- Understand the components of leisure education and their relevance to people with mental retardation.
- Explain the concepts of least restrictive environment, deinstitutionalization, normalization, integration, inclusion, and their role in determining the best transition setting for administering therapeutic recreation services to people with mental retardation.
- Understand the procedures of preference analysis, activity analysis, environmental analysis, and task analysis, and their role in the assessment and planning phases of therapeutic recreation services.
- Discuss the importance of partial participation, reciprocal communication, cooperation and competition, behavior modification, instructional prompts, practice and repetition, and generalization training.

When relating to people who have been grouped together, for whatever reasons, it is important to consider these individuals as people first and then, if relevant, consider their group affiliation. It is much easier to interact with a person if we initially concentrate on the similarities we share with this person rather than the differences. Therefore, as you read this chapter, as much as possible try to avoid the tendency to make stereotypic generalizations about people who, in addition to many of the other characteristics that affect their individuality (i.e., sense of humor, reliability, and honesty), happen to be identified as having mental retardation. In addition, attempts have been made to use sensitive terminology described by Dattilo and Smith (1990), and later, Dattilo (1994), that is reflective of numerous policies such as those put forth by the federal government and editorial suggestions endorsed by the *Therapeutic Recreation Journal.*

Reschly (1992) reported that the concept of "mental retardation" has experienced many changes in definition and classification over the past four decades. The changes have occurred because professionals have continuously tried to improve their understanding of the condition of mental retardation and subsequently produced effective services.

Schalock and colleagues (1994) observed that since 1983, when the last terminology classification manual was produced by Grossman (1983), there has been a paradigm shift resulting in "the conception of mental retardation not as an absolute trait expressed solely by the person, but as an expression of the functional impact of the interaction between the person with limited intellectual and adaptive skills and that person's environment" (p. 181). The change in the way mental retardation is conceptualized stipulates that services are provided in typical integrated environments that contain necessary supports based on the strengths and capabilities of the person with the purpose of empowering the individual to function within our society (Smull & Donnehey, 1993). Schwartz (1992) observed that the new definition of mental retardation redefines services for these individuals; these services should now reflect person-centered planning and functional supports within the community.

The American Association on Mental Retardation (AAMR) (1992) reported that the current conception of mental retardation focuses attention on the capabilities of the person related to limited intelligence and adaptive skills, the environment in which people with mental retardation live, and the presence or absence of the supports needed for them to live a meaningful life. When conceptualizing mental retardation, the AAMR (1992) recommended the use of a three-step process involving:

1. definition and diagnosis,
2. classification and description, and
3. profile and intensities of needed supports.

The three areas are addressed in the following section of the chapter.

DEFINITION OF MENTAL RETARDATION

According to the AAMR (1992) "mental retardation" is characterized by:

1. significantly subaverage general intellectual functioning,
2. resulting in or associated with concurrent impairments in at least two adaptive skill areas, and
3. manifested before the age of 18 (during the developmental period).

A description of each of the three components of the definition is provided below.

Intellectual functioning. Identification of "significantly subaverage intellectual functioning" occurs when a person receives a score on standardized measures of intelligence quotient (IQ) that is below the score of the average person taking the test to such a degree (two standard deviations) that society has determined this person requires assistance in development beyond what is typically provided by the family and community. The average intelligence quotient has been determined to be a score of approximately 100. A score below approximately 70–75 results in a significantly subaverage intellectual functioning. Although IQ and intelligence are frequently used interchangeably, it is important to remember that these concepts are not synonymous. The IQ score is only an estimate of an individual's rate of intellectual development as compared with the average rate for same-age peers (Gottlieb, 1987).

Although various instruments have been developed that attempt to compensate for particular disabilities (e.g., Peabody Picture Vocabulary Test), a person's lack of performance on a particular standardized measure of IQ can be the result of many factors other than actual intelligence. For instance, some people may not have been exposed to the items presented on the test due to cultural and environmental differences. Perhaps other people may have difficulty communicating their responses due to physical or neurological impairments. Other individuals could be experiencing pain and sickness. In addition, the attitudes of the examiner and examinee can also influence test scores (Zigler & Butterfield, 1968). The aforementioned situations may reduce the performance of a person on an intelligence test and perhaps bring into question the reported scores. The reader is referred to the text by Jensen (1980) entitled *Bias in Mental Testing* for an extensive review of the debate focusing on the validity and utility of intelligence testing.

Adaptive skills. "Adaptive skills" are a collection of competencies which allows for individuals' strengths, as well as limitations, to be defined. The specific adaptive skill areas identified by the AAMR (1992) include:

1. communication,
2. self-care,
3. homeliving,
4. social,
5. community use,
6. self-direction,
7. health and safety,
8. functional academics,
9. leisure, and
10. work.

To be prepared to meet the demands of the specific adaptive skill area identified as leisure, it is helpful to understand all the adaptive skills areas because they are interrelated. Therefore, because leisure was recognized as an adaptive skill area in which significant functional impairment would contribute to the identification of an individual's need for services (Steffens et al., 1993), for the purposes of this chapter the adaptive skill area of leisure will be highlighted. The AAMR (1992) described the adaptive skill area leisure as:

> *the development of a variety of leisure and recreational interests (i.e., self-entertainment and interactional) that reflect personal preferences and choices and, if the activity will be conducted in public, age and cultural norms. Skills include choosing and self-initiating interests, using and enjoying home and community leisure and recreational activities alone and with others, playing socially with others, taking turns, terminating or refusing leisure or recreational activities, extending one's duration of participation, and expanding one's repertoire of interests, awareness, and skills. Related skills include behaving appropriately in the leisure and recreation setting, communicating choices and needs, participating in social interaction, applying functional academics, and exhibiting mobility skills (p. 41).*

Developmental period. According to AAMR (1992, p. 9), mental retardation begins in childhood when "limitations in intelligence coexist with related limitations in adaptive skills. In this sense, it is a more specific term than developmental disability because the level of functioning is necessarily related to an intellectual limitation."

The "developmental period" refers to the time after conception when growth and change occur at a rapid rate. This rate of development typically begins to slow as the person enters adulthood (identified as age 18, 21, or 22). Mental retardation is one particular type of developmental disability. A developmental disability, as reported in Public Law 95-602 enacted in 1978, refers to a severe, chronic disability that:

1. is attributable to a mental and/or physical impairment,
2. is manifested before age 22,
3. is likely to continue indefinitely, and
4. results in substantial functional limitations (Grossman, 1983).

Although the age of 22 has been identified as the age for which eligibility of services under The Developmental Disabilities Act is discontinued, the oldest a person can be to receive a diagnosis of mental retardation is 18 years (AAMR, 1992).

AAMR's (1992) definition of **mental retardation** contains the following underlying assumptions:

1. mental retardation is not a general phenomenon,
2. intelligence, as defined by tests, has limited use,
3. no behavior clearly defines potential,
4. adaptive behavior can be assumed,
5. development is lifelong,
6. educate people and avoid testing them, and

7. mental retardation is most meaningfully conceptualized as a phenomenon existing within the society which can only be observed through the depressed performance of some of the individuals in that society.

Therefore, although the phrase "mental retardation" is used throughout this section, the label alone means very little. The unique profile of cognitive, adaptive, educational, and recreational ability, as well as the health status associated with each person is critical for appropriate planning and implementation of effective services (Woodrich & Joy, 1986).

When therapeutic recreation specialists are working with people with mental retardation, they may examine the results of these people's scores on standardized measure of IQ, adaptive behavior scales, and other assessments and determine that the person with mental retardation has significant problems as well as limited potential for growth and development. If this conclusion has been drawn, with the focus of the problem on the individual with mental retardation, the specialist's work has ended. However, if therapeutic recreation specialists view people with mental retardation as having the potential for growth and development, then these specialists have before them a lifetime of challenges as they continuously attempt to determine the most effective and efficient procedures to assist these individuals in achieving their maximum potential.

CLASSIFICATION SYSTEM FOR MENTAL RETARDATION

According to Dattilo (1994), more important than the definition of mental retardation is the classification of mental retardation established by AAMR (1992); that is to say that mental retardation refers to a level of functioning which requires from society significantly above average training procedures. Therefore, the person with mental retardation is classified by the extent of support required for the person to learn, and not by limitations to what the person can learn. The height of a person's level of functioning is determined by the availability of training technology and the amount of resources society is willing to allocate and not by significant limitations in biological potential.

The intensity levels of support have been defined and described by the AAMR (1992) as:

1. intermittent supports that are provided as needed,
2. limited supports that are limited in time, but consistent across time rather than intermittent,
3. extensive supports are not limited in time and are provided on a regular basis in some environments such as the home, and
4. pervasive supports that are constant, intense, and have the potential to sustain life.

According to AAMR (1992, p. 34):

> *The concept of needed supports reflects the contemporary perspective regarding the expectation for growth and potential of people; focus on personal choice, opportunity and autonomy; and the need for people to be both in and of the community. This step applies the zero reject model in which all people are given the supports necessary to enhance their independence/interdependence, productivity, and community integration.*

This classification system represents a shift toward understanding mental retardation as a multidimensional concept that requires comprehensive assessment, rather than reliance on intelligence tests as the primary indicator of mental retardation. In addition, the classification system removes the previous IQ-based levels of mild, moderate, severe, and profound mental retardation. The classification system has also eliminated identification of people with mental retardation by mental age. The Stanford-Binet Intelligence Scale, developed by Terman (1916), calculated IQ scores by dividing the "mental age," derived from the test, by the chronological age and multiplying by 100. Dattilo and Smith (1990) and Baroff (1986) suggested that practitioners avoid using the phrase "mental age" because the label tells the practitioner nothing about the particular pattern of the person's cognitive strengths and weaknesses.

SUPPORTS NEEDED FOR PEOPLE WITH MENTAL RETARDATION

Once individuals are diagnosed as having mental retardation and their classification identified, the kind and intensity of needed supports are determined across the four dimensions of:

1. intellectual functioning and adaptive skills,
2. psychological/emotional considerations,
3. physical/health/etiology considerations, and
4. profile and intensities of needed supports (AAMR, 1992).

According to the AAMR (1992), the dimension of intellectual functioning and adaptive skills, considers the individual's strengths and weaknesses in all the adaptive skill areas: communication, self-care, home living, social skills, community use, self-direction, health and safety, functional academics, leisure, and work. The results of testing (e.g., Stanford-Binet Intelligence Scale) and observation are used to describe the individual's intellectual functioning, and existing limitations in the adaptive skill areas.

The next dimension, psychological and emotional considerations, is essential for determining functionality, adaptive skill areas, environments, and appropriate supports, since as many as one third of all noninstitutionalized individuals with mental retardation are also diagnosed as having mental illness. Psychological and emotional considerations are described using behavioral observations, clinical assessments or formal diagnosis based on the most current edition of the American Psychiatric Association's *Diagnostic and Statistical Manual of Mental Disorders* (AAMR, 1992).

The importance of health, physical functioning, and etiology (the cause or origin of the mental retardation) is reflected by the third dimension (AAMR, 1992). Like all other individuals, people with mental retardation can be greatly affected by their state of health. For example, a person with mental retardation who is in great health with good physical abilities might participate successfully in school sports with his/her same age peers who do not have mental retardation. However, another person with mental retardation might also be affected by cerebral palsy. This individual might have restricted mobility, have little or no spontaneous movement, and be unable to chew or swallow. Because of these physical problems, they may have related health problems such as susceptibility to recurrent infections, nutritional deficits, and orthopedic disorders including fractures and scoliosis (AAMR, 1992). Most individuals with mental retardation fall in between these two extreme cases. In addition, "These health problems are not inherently different from those of people who do not have mental retardation. The effects of these problems may, however, be different because of environments, coping limitations, and impediments in health care systems" (AAMR, 1992, p. 62). Furthermore, according to the AAMR (1992), etiology is important because it may be associated with health-related problems that affect physical functioning. Moreover, early diagnosis of the etiology may allow the individual to receive treatment that might prevent or minimize mental retardation.

Environmental considerations, the fourth dimension, focus on the person's environment and considers the influence that environmental factors have on a person's growth, development, well-being, and satisfaction (AAMR, 1992). In particular, this dimension analyzes two aspects of the environment: current settings and characteristics of optimum settings. The current settings aspect requires evaluation of the person's current living, education, and employment environment to determine:

1. the level of integration,
2. level of participation,
3. intensities of needed supports, and
4. hours of service per month (AAMR, 1992).

To determine the characteristics of optimum environmental settings for people with mental retardation, the AAMR (1992) suggested evaluating:

1. community presence,
2. choice,
3. competence,
4. respect, and
5. community participation.

Frequently, practitioners mistakenly treat a person with mental retardation as a child. A problem occurs when an adult who happens to have mental retardation is compared to a child because he or she performs some skills (e.g., reading) at a level similar to some children. Because the adult with mental retardation has many more years of experience at living and has developed a variety of skills, the comparison to a child is misleading. Therapeutic recreation specialists must avoid viewing adults with mental retardation as children and instead give them the respect provided to other adults in our society. This view of people with mental retardation will encourage professionals to develop recreation programs that are appropriate for the age of the participants and do not require people with mental retardation to compromise their dignity.

Information related to definitions, classifications, and necessary supports associated with mental retardation has been presented. For a more detailed description of terminology related to mental retardation, the reader is encouraged to consult the text *Mental Retardation: Definition, Classification, and Systems of Support* (AAMR, 1992). To obtain historical information about the development of mental retardation, refer to the text by Trent (1994), *Inventing the Feeble Mind: A History of Mental Retardation in the United States.*

DESCRIPTION OF LIMITATIONS

Mental retardation is associated with more than 200 known medical entities, including genetic defects, chromosomal disorders, infections during pregnancy, accidental poisonings and injuries, metabolic disorders, and central nervous system infections (Gottlieb, 1987). However, Carter, Van Andel, and Robb (1985) identified research indicating that the present known number of causes, nearly 300, represents only one-third of those possible. According to the authors, there is rarely one cause or simple explanation of mental retardation.

Mental retardation occurs as a result of biomedical, social, behavioral, and educational types of factors. The timing of the occurrence of these causal factors also plays a role, affecting individuals with mental retardation, their parents, or both. This causal aspect is termed "intergenerational" because the factors that influenced one generation affect the outcomes on the next generation (AAMR, 1992). However, for approximately half the people with mental retardation, more than one possible causal factor is responsible; and often mental retardation is the result of the cumulative or interactive effects of two or more factors (AAMR, 1992). Moreover, for 30 to 50 percent of the cases, the cause is idiopathic. The term *idiopathic* indicates the cause is unknown.

There are instances of mental retardation that are determined at conception due to hereditary disorders (i.e., phenylketonuria) or to chromosomal abnormalities (i.e., Down's syndrome). In addition to these two forms of biological causes, mental retardation may be biologically developed after conception during the prenatal period (before birth), perinatal period (immediately preceding or during birth), or postnatal period of development (following birth). Approximately 90 percent of people who acquire mental retardation through biological reasons develop their disability during the prenatal period of development and manifest the condition at birth or early infancy (Grossman, 1983). The following are problems that can occur during the prenatal period of development that may result in mental retardation: diseases (e.g., syphilis, rubella); nutritional deficits; infections (e.g., encephalitis); toxemia (i.e., poisonous drugs such as alcohol or lead); and radiation in large doses. Many of the conditions that can occur during the prenatal period may result in prematurity and low birth weight. In addition to prematurity and low birth weight, other possible perinatal conditions causing mental retardation may include trauma, infection, anoxia (oxygen deprivation), and the development of antibodies by the mother (RH incompatibility). Following birth, mental retardation appears primarily to occur as a result of malnutrition, trauma (i.e., automobile collisions, child abuse), or poisoning (i.e., lead encephalopathy). A variety of conditions that can contribute to the occurrence of mental retardation have been identified; however, for about half the cases the reasons for the development of mental retardation are yet unknown (McLaren & Bryson, 1987).

PURPOSE OF THERAPEUTIC RECREATION

The purpose of therapeutic recreation is to facilitate the development, maintenance, and expression of an appropriate leisure lifestyle for the person with physical, mental, emotional, or social limitations (National Therapeutic Recreation Society [NTRS], 1982). The phrase *leisure lifestyle* refers to the day-to-day behavioral expression of one's leisure-related attitudes awareness, and activities revealed within the context and composite of the total life experience (Peterson, 1981). Therapeutic recreation places special emphasis on the development of an appropriate leisure lifestyle as an integral part of independent functioning (American Therapeutic Recreation Association [ATRA], 1984). According to Peterson and Gunn (1984), the most essential aspect of the definition is the focus on day-to-day behavior expression, in that it implies that leisure lifestyle is a routine engaged in as a part of the individual's daily existence. Therefore, specialists should provide comprehensive therapeutic recreation services for people with mental retardation to develop leisure-related skills that allow them to enhance the quality of their life each day. Three specific areas of professional service are used to provide this comprehensive leisure ability approach that facilitates appropriate leisure lifestyles: therapy (treatment), leisure education, and recreation participation (NTRS, 1982).

Treatment

Because people with mental retardation have impaired intellectual functioning, it is extremely important for therapeutic recreation specialists to develop interventions and treatments that assist these individuals in developing functional skills necessary for participation in leisure pursuits. Therapeutic recreation involves the application of appropriate leisure intervention strategies to promote independent functioning for people with a variety of disabling conditions (ATRA, 1984). It is apparent that interventions encouraging the development of cognitive skills such as understanding and remembering rules and procedures, concentrating on the task, maintaining scores, and following directions should be the focus of therapeutic recreation treatment for people with mental retardation. However, it is also important for therapeutic recreation specialists to remember to develop strategies that increase physical, social, and emotional development related to leisure participation.

Leisure Education

Leisure education provides a vehicle for developing an awareness of leisure activities and resources and for acquiring skills requisite for participation throughout the life span (Howe-Murphy & Charboneau, 1987). As a result of leisure education, individuals will be able to enhance the quality of their lives in leisure; understand the impact of leisure on the quality of their lives; and have knowledge, skills, and appreciations that enable broad leisure skills (Mundy & Odum, 1979). According to Dattilo and Murphy (1991), an effective leisure education program for people with mental retardation should include, but not be limited to, the following components:

1. awareness of self in leisure,
2. self-determination in leisure,
3. leisure appreciation,
4. leisure decision-making skills,
5. knowledge and utilization of leisure resources,
6. social interaction skills, and
7. recreation activity skills.

For a detailed presentation of leisure education program planning please refer to the text by Dattilo and Murphy (1991) *Leisure Education Program Planning: A Systematic Approach.*

Recreation Participation

Wehman and Schleien (1981) asserted that the ultimate goal of any leisure education program is to facilitate self-initiated independent use of free time with chronologically age-appropriate recreation activities. According to Dattilo (1994), some families and professionals make choices for people with disabilities rather than allowing participants to decide for themselves. Individuals' opportunities to express personal interests and preferences have been prevented by people who incorrectly assume that people with disabilities are incapable of making informed choices (Kishi et al., 1988). Therefore, the importance of recreation participation in the lives of people with mental retardation relative to having opportunities to make choices and decisions as well as being able to participate in age-appropriate recreation activities will be presented.

Choice. As previously discussed, when providing therapeutic recreation services to people with mental retardation, it is important to develop functional skills through leisure education. Although these actions are important, they are not sufficient when attempting systematically to enhance the leisure lifestyles of individuals with mental retardation (Wuerch & Voeltz, 1982). Dattilo (1986) noted that a person may not encounter the freedom of choice associated with the leisure experience when involved in therapy or structured leisure education. However, freedom of choice is vital to the pursuit of enjoyable, satisfying, and meaningful experience and, according to Hawkins (1993), personal autonomy for people with disabilities has become recognized as an essential aspect of independent functioning and self-reliance. Therefore, opportunities for choice, often associated with recreation participation, must be systematically provided (Dattilo & Rusch, 1985).

Decision Making. If one of the goals of therapeutic recreation is to foster independence, it is imperative that the ability to make appropriate decisions regarding specific tasks be encouraged during recreation participation (Dattilo & Murphy, 1987a). Dattilo and Schleien (1994) provided the following example to illustrate this point. Anne's favorite recreation activity is doing art work. When she attends her art class she is encouraged to select the paper she will use; she chooses between different colors, sizes, and textures. In addition, she decides to use watercolors today rather than chalk or markers. After she has her materials, Anne is invited to position her easel where she prefers and begins her chosen project while carefully selecting her color scheme. According to Dattilo and Murphy (1987a), an intended benefit of recreation participation is an increase in personal effectiveness that can result from the making of timely and correct decisions. People with mental retardation who do not possess the appropriate appraisal and judgment skills needed for activity involvement will be more likely to acquire these skills if they participate in actual recreation activities.

Age-Appropriate Participation. It is extremely important for individuals with mental retardation to develop age-appropriate, community-based leisure skill repertoires that facilitate successful integration into the community (Schleien, Tuckner, & Heyne, 1985). Ray and Meidl (1991) encouraged professionals to treat participants with disabilities as they would others their age by expecting them to be as independent as possible, encouraging others to interact with them, supporting and assisting only when necessary and encouraging accomplishments. It is helpful to compare a participant's abilities to what is expected of all participants and, if there are aspects of the activity that a person cannot perform independently, problem-solve to determine what types of supports are needed (Ray & Meidl, 1991).

Using age-appropriate materials and methods, accommodating for individual patterns of development, learning through interacting with peers, and teaching within natural environments and meaningful routines are emphasized when providing services that include people with disabilities (Hanline & Fox, 1993). Therefore, therapeutic recreation specialists should encourage people with mental retardation to acquire leisure skills that are age-appropriate and comparable to their peers. Practitioners are encouraged to teach only those leisure skills that have the potential of being performed in the presence of, or in interaction with, peers without disabilities (Schleien & Ray, 1988). Because some people with mental retardation may have inaccurate perceptions of their own capabilities, Kennedy, Austin, and Smith (1987) suggested that therapeutic recreation specialists assist participants in selecting activities that are age-appropriate.

COMMON SERVICE SETTINGS

The majority of people with mental retardation reside either in residential training centers, in group homes within the community, with their families at home in their community, or on their own in the community. Regardless of where the person lives, there are important concepts that therapeutic recreation specialists must consider when determining the best environment for the provision of leisure services. The following concepts are presented to encourage therapeutic recreation specialists to establish the most appropriate service setting for people with mental retardation:

1. least restrictive environment,
2. deinstitutionalization,
3. normalization,
4. integration,
5. inclusion, and
6. transition.

Least Restrictive Environment

It is important that therapeutic recreation specialists support efforts encouraging people with mental retardation to reside and receive services in an environment that is as least restrictive to their life as possible. The concept of "least restrictive environment" involves people with mental retardation living as normally as possible and receiving appropriate services in the least separate or most integrated setting.

To determine the least restrictive recreation environment for people with mental retardation, Brown et al. (1979a) encouraged practitioners to delineate the current and subsequent chronological age-appropriate recreation community environments that are:

1. currently available and used in the community by people both with and without disabilities,
2. available and used in other communities by people both with or without disabilities, and
3. used by peers without disabilities that are potentially available and usable in the community.

Once these three steps have been completed, the therapeutic recreation specialist can access the environments that best represent the least restrictive environment for a person with mental retardation residing in a specific community.

Deinstitutionalization

The philosophy of least restrictive environment has led to the deinstitutionalization of people with mental retardation. Deinstitutionalization as a concept affecting people with mental retardation gained recognition during the sixties, acquired greater support during the seventies, and has now become a national professional goal (Scheerenberger, 1987). Scheerenberger described the philosophy of deinstitutionalization as seeking greater emphasis on freedom, independence, individuality, mobility, personalized life experiences, and a high degree of interaction in a free society. Although for at least a decade our rhetoric has called for deinstitutionalizing people with mental retardation and the creation of community-based services, the development of these services has lagged (Baroff, 1986). Therefore, every attempt should be made to provide recreation services for people with mental retardation in an integrated fashion within the community.

Normalization

The introduction of the principle of normalization by Nirje nearly two decades ago has become the primary philosophical orientation guiding the development and delivery of community-based services for people with disabilities (Schleien & Ray, 1988). Normalization is defined as the process that involves making available for people with mental retardation patterns and condition of everyday life that are as close as possible to the norms and patterns of the mainstream of society (Nirje, 1969). Wolfensberger (1972) broadened Nirje's definition of normalization to include the use of means that are as culturally normative as possible, and to establish and/or maintain personal behaviors and characteristics that are as culturally normative as possible. Therefore, normalization involves placing a high value on the life, rights, and dignity of citizens with disabilities (Lakin & Bruininks, 1985). The integration of people with disabilities into community recreation programs is essential if the process of normalization is to be completed (Schleien & Ray, 1988).

Integration

When people are grouped together and then separated from others, for whatever reason, the differences between the groups, rather than their similarities, appear to become the focus of attention. In effect, when people are separated from other people in a society, they do not experience equal opportunities to receive services. Although integration has been described as consisting of those practices that maximize a person's participation in the mainstream of society, integration is only meaningful if it involves social integration and acceptance, and not merely physical presence (Wolfensberger, 1972).

Hutchison and Lord (1979) described integration of people with disabilities into recreation activities as:

1. experiencing participation and enjoyment similar to peers who do not possess disabilities,
2. upgrading skills and confidence,
3. participating in community activities of their choice, and,
4. encouraging self-confidence and the perception of dignity.

Schleien and Ray (1988) encouraged practitioners to set the stage for integrated recreation by implementing the following strategies:

1. develop communication linkages between people and agencies concerned about community leisure services,
2. conduct surveys of architectural accessibility of leisure service settings, and
3. provide comprehensive staff in-service training.

The potential advantages of integration of people with mental retardation into recreation activities in the community are not limited to the people with disabilities (Howe-Murphy & Charboneau, 1987). After participating in experiences involving systematic interaction with people who possess disabilities, individuals without disabilities have demonstrated an increase in positive attitudes toward people with disabilities (Donder & Nietupski, 1981; Fenrick & Petersen, 1984; McHale & Simeonsson, 1980).

Inclusion

Inclusion is about ensuring choices, having support, having connections, and being valued (Moss, 1993). To illustrate these characteristics, Moss (1993) stated, "I can make many of the choices I do because I have friends and family and community to support me in those choices" (p. 1). Implied in the concept of inclusion is the importance of support. To emphasize the importance of support, Hutchinson and McGill (1992, p. 9) stated that: "Supporting people in developing leisure identities contributes to helping them find the 'essence of community'."

Ferguson et al. (1992) called for "inclusion" for people with disabilities, with all its implications of being socially connected, exchanging and sharing responsibilities. If inclusion is to mean anything, it must mean that people with disabilities become full, active, learning members of the community (Ferguson et al., 1992). The reader is referred to the text *Inclusive Leisure Services: Responding to the Rights of People with Disabilities* by Dattilo (1994) for a detailed presentation of inclusion.

Transition

According to Dattilo and St. Peter (1991), the Office of Special Education and Rehabilitation Services transition model emphasized the transition of high school students with disabilities to post-school employment with varying levels of support. This transition model was revised by Halpern (1985) to include the dimensions of residential environment, employment, and social and interpersonal networks. Together, these three dimensions can support successful community adjustment. As such, transition can be used as a label for the process of moving from being in school to living actively in the community (Dattilo & St. Peter, 1991).

The emphasis of transition for adults with mental retardation has typically been focused on school to integrated community employment (Dattilo & St. Peter, 1991). However, as Dattilo and St. Peter (1991) reported, although community adjustment requires support in the form of social and interpersonal networks including friendships that are often acquired and maintained in leisure settings, training and support services for nonwork educational outcomes such as success in integrated adult leisure environments has received little attention. In addition, while social skills and interpersonal networks are essential to virtually everything we do, they are frequently not learned or developed casually by individuals with mental retardation (St. Peter et al., 1989). As such, therapeutic recreation specialists who provide community recreation activities involving interactions with peers without disabilities are "the most natural means of transition training for working toward meaningful mastery of interpersonal skills" (Dattilo & St. Peter, 1991, p. 421).

CURRENT BEST PRACTICES AND PROCEDURES

The remediation of learning difficulties associated with mental retardation necessitates the use of a spectrum of educational strategies (Gearheart, 1987). Austin (1982) described therapeutic recreation as being characterized by eclecticism, or the utilization of approaches and techniques drawn from several sources. Therefore, therapeutic recreation specialists are encouraged to use a variety of assessment, planning, implementation, and evaluative strategies in order to facilitate leisure participation resulting in enjoyment and satisfaction for people with mental retardation.

Assessment and Planning

Kennedy, Austin, and Smith (1987) observed that the wide range of behaviors and abilities of people with learning impairments, such as mental retardation, necessitates careful consideration of each person's recreation abilities and the avoidance of assumptions of the individual based on categorical designation. Gearheart (1987) stated that significant improvement is often observed when a combination of approaches are employed based on valid assessment data and reasonable planning. To encourage therapeutic recreation specialists working with people with mental retardation to plan comprehensive assessment procedures, the following areas of analysis will be presented:

1. preference,
2. activity,
3. environment, and
4. task.

Preference Analysis. An initial step in providing opportunities for individuals with mental retardation to participate in chosen leisure experiences is the assessment of an individual's preferences (Dattilo, 1986). These preferences should be a major concern in the development of recreation programs for people with mental retardation. When attempting to provide opportunities for the expression of preferences and the making of choices, Newton and colleagues (1991) suggested that professionals determine the person's preferences, and create supporting opportunities for the person to choose among preferred options. Given the importance of choice and preference, more attention must be devoted to developing simple, valid strategies for assessing the preferences of people with severe disabilities (Newton et al., 1991). Newton and colleagues (1991) stated that whether such assessment is accomplished via participant's self-reports or via the outcomes of multiple choice-making opportunities, we should attempt to develop ways to validly and reliably assess preferences of participants.

Each day presents many opportunities for participants to express preferences and make choices about their activities, activity "instances" (e.g., playing the "Space Invaders" video game vs. the "Super Mario Brothers" game), community locations where activities are to be performed, activity companions, days and times when the activities are to be performed, and so on (Newton et al., 1991). To respond to the needs of people with disabilities, Newton et al., (1991) suggested that professionals assess participants' preferences, develop strategies for determining the *most* preferred activities, and assess the relationship between preferences honored in planning and preferences honored in daily life. Once assessment of their preferences has occurred, individuals with mental retardation can experience enjoyment and control through participation in a preferred activity (Dattilo, 1988).

Activity Analysis. After assessment information concerning the abilities of people with mental retardation has been collected, it is important for therapeutic recreation specialists to analyze the recreation activities. This analyzation will permit specialists to match the appropriate activity with the individual participants. If there is a discrepancy between the requirements of the activity and the skills of the individual, therapeutic recreation specialists will be able to determine activity modification procedures or instructional strategies to teach the individual the necessary participatory skills. The procedure for breaking down and examining an activity to find inherent characteristics (physical, mental, affective, and social) that contribute to program objectives is termed *activity analysis* (Peterson & Gunn, 1984). The reader is referred to the text by Peterson and Gunn (1984), *Therapeutic Recreation Program Design*, for an example and description of an activity analysis rating form.

Environmental Analysis. It is useful for the therapeutic recreation specialist to examine the total environment in which the person with mental retardation will attempt to participate in a recreation activity. Environmental analysis inventories provide the therapeutic recreation specialist with a systematic approach to analyze the leisure context and facilitate leisure involvement for people with mental retardation (Certo, Schleien, & Hunter, 1983). Use of the inventory helps heighten public awareness and increases the level of sensitivity of all people involved in the process of integrating community leisure services (Schleien & Ray, 1988). The reader is referred to the text by Schleien and Ray (1988) entitled *Community Recreation for Persons with Disabilities* for a detailed description and examples of environmental analysis inventories.

Task Analysis. Wuerch and Voeltz (1982) defined tasks analysis as the identification of all the necessary participant responses or component skills and the sequence in which these responses or skills must occur for successful participation. The use of task analytic assessment procedures has been suggested as an alternative approach for assessing performance of individuals with mental retardation (Vallet, 1972). Task analysis is not a statement of how to assess, but rather a statement of what is to be assessed (Williams & Gotts, 1977). The task analysis procedure involves the description of the tasks associated with a recreation activity to be performed during the testing procedure and allows the therapeutic recreation specialist to analyze critically the content of the skills used during the assessment process (Dattilo, 1984). Once a task has been described in observable and measurable terms and identification and sequencing of component skills completed, the client is encouraged to perform the task associated with the recreation activity. Assistance may be provided by the therapeutic recreation specialist to allow the person with mental retardation to complete the task. However, Knapczyk (1975) suggested that the assistance provided by the practitioner should be provided only when the person has made an unsuccessful attempt at performing the task in the specified time. It is critical when using this assessment procedure that therapeutic recreation specialists record the type and degree of assistance that was needed for the person with mental retardation to complete the task associated with the recreation activity.

Implementation

In general, when comparing people with mental retardation to those individuals not identified as having a disability, individuals with mental retardation tend to perform well on practical and concrete types of tasks and less well on those that require primarily verbal reasoning and judgment (Baroff, 1986). Ramifications of mental retardation are observed when individuals attempt to complete developmental tasks expected of their same-age peers. These age-appropriate developmental tasks require demonstration of maturation, learning, and social adjustment. Baroff observed that in the earlier years of development, a slower rate of maturation is reflected by lags in the development of skills related to motor performance, communication, cognition, self-help, and socialization. As a result of these delays, people with mental retardation may encounter a greater number of failures than their same-age peers when attempting to participate in recreation activities. To implement therapeutic recreation services for people with mental retardation that foster success and development, the following strategies appear useful:

1. partial participation,
2. reciprocal communication,
3. cooperation and competition,
4. behavior modification,
5. instructional prompts,
6. practice and repetition, and
7. generalization training.

Partial Participation. Individuals with mental retardation are often excluded from a wide range of recreation activities due to their assumed inability to perform complete skill sequences independently and in the correct order (Ford et al., 1984). However, an individual who is deemed unable to engage in an activity independently should not be denied the opportunity for partial participation (Brown et al., 1979b). These individuals should be provided the opportunity to participate in environments in which their skills will be used rather than in artificial settings (Krebs & Block, 1992). Partial participation involves the use of adaptations, and provides assistance needed to facilitate leisure participation. Thereby, the right of people with mental retardation to participate in environments and activities without regard to degree of assistance required is affirmed (Baumgart et al., 1982).

Adaptations to enhance participation or to make partial participation possible include:

1. providing personal assistance,
2. adapting activities by changing materials, modifying skill sequences, altering rules, and using adaptive devices and alternative communications systems, and
3. changing physical and social environments to promote friendships.

Through partial participation, individuals with disabilities may experience the exhilaration and satisfaction associated with the challenge inherent in a particular recreation activity (Dattilo & Murphy, 1987a).

Reciprocal Communication

It may take some people with mental retardation considerable time to formulate and communicate their thoughts. Often, professionals do not provide them with adequate time to formulate a communication turn (Dattilo, 1994). According to Dattilo (1994), this unwillingness to wait for people to take their turn results in the professional taking control of the conversation and, often, the entire situation.

Dattilo and colleagues (Dattilo & Camarata, 1991; Dattilo & O'Keefe, 1992) demonstrated that simply providing people with limited communication skills with an alternative form of communication was not sufficient to shift them away from the conversational role of respondent; rather, specific attention to responding to conversational attempts was needed. Since the ability to choose to initiate involvement is critical to the leisure experience, people with mental retardation should be encouraged to initiate interactions and share conversations. Dattilo (1993) reported that construction of a supportive environment that is responsive to the communicative attempts of these people is important. Based on the findings of Dattilo and Light (1993), a supportive environment is created when professionals:

1. approach the person,
2. attend to the person, and
3. wait at least ten seconds for that person to initiate interaction.

If people with mental retardation do make a communicative initiative, therapeutic recreation specialists can reinforce these attempts by providing people with objects they have requested, returning greetings to people, and extending and expanding their comments. However, if the person does not initiate interaction, specialists are encouraged to ask open-ended questions beginning with "what" and "how" as opposed to those questions that force people into a yes/no response. In conclusion, Wilcox (1993) reported on the importance of consistently recognizing a person's communicative attempts and responding in a contingent, appropriate and consistent manner.

Cooperation and Competition. In an attempt to provide people with mental retardation with recreation activities that encourage success, the therapeutic recreation specialist should include those activities that encourage cooperation and indirect competition. According to Fait and Billing (1978), competition against a record or previous achievements is termed *indirect competition* as opposed to *direct competition,* which requires a rivalry between opposing forces in which the interests of both are not mutually obtainable. Based on these definitions, Dattilo and Murphy (1987b) recommended the redirection of an emphasis from direct competition and winning, to learning and development fostered by indirect competition. In this way, participants will be encouraged to "celebrate" their abilities and skills rather than compare them with others (Farrington, 1976). The challenge that therapeutic recreation specialists should instill in the participants with mental retardation is to develop and grow through indirect competition and cooperation rather than defeat or destroy through direct competition.

Behavior Modification. Behavior modification is a systematic, evaluative, performance-based method for changing any observable and measurable act, response, or movement by an individual (Dattilo & Murphy, 1987b). The authors contend that an understanding of introductory techniques of behavior modification can provide therapeutic recreation specialists and other professionals with helpful facilitation procedures in the provision of leisure services. Therapeutic recreation services incorporating behavior modification techniques promote a hopeful view that emphasizes the learning capabilities of people with mental retardation and recognizes possibilities for growth and development in recreation (Raw & Errickson, 1977). Trap-Porter and Perry (1982) suggested that therapeutic recreation specialists, especially those providing services to people with mental retardation, should receive comprehensive training in behavior modification principles. The reader is referred to the text by Dattilo and Murphy (1987a) entitled *Behavior Modification in Therapeutic Recreation* for additional information.

Instructional Prompts. Instructional prompts refer to information provided before an action is performed (Wuerch & Voeltz, 1982). Falvey et al. (1980) stated that instructional cues are an addition to information naturally provided by the environment. Frequently, those prompts that are concrete have been found to be useful to demonstrate or model the appropriate leisure behavior. If direct physical guidance is needed, Donnellan and colleagues (1986) suggested a physical prompt-fade strategy that can involve a hand-over-hand procedure. Therapeutic recreation specialists are encouraged to allow the participant with mental retardation to perform as much of the task as possible, and only provide light physical assistance as needed. This procedure also has been described as a graduate-guidance technique that involves the fading of more restrictive physical cues and replacing them with less assistance. Additional prompts such as verbal, gestural, and visual also may be used by the therapeutic recreation specialist. Visual cues can be in the form of symbols, colors, or words positioned within view of the participant to permit the individual to learn or remember the proper procedure for participation. Finally, therapeutic recreation specialists can provide assistance to the person with mental retardation simply by arranging the environment to remind the person of necessary steps for activity involvement.

Practice and Repetition. Baroff (1986) identified problems in acquisition of information by people with mental retardation that results in the need for greater repetition of experiences and more frequent explanations of the principles being presented. Therefore, therapeutic recreation specialists may wish to incorporate numerous opportunities for people with mental retardation to practice leisure skills. Additional opportunities to practice the leisure skills could be facilitated by providing longer time segments for acquisition of skills. In addition, the task analysis procedure, previously discussed, will provide sufficient information to allow the therapeutic recreation specialist to teach people with mental retardation small concrete steps.

Generalization Training. Dattilo and Murphy (1987a) defined the term *generalization* as the display of a specified behavior over time, in a variety of situations and settings, across different people, or with similar materials. According to Dattilo and Murphy, generalization also can involve the exhibition of various related behaviors that are similar to the target behavior. Frequently, the knowledge that people with mental retardation acquire tends to be specific to the situation in which it was learned rather than generalized to related environments.

The more similar two situations, people, or materials are, the more likely it is that the behavior will generalize (Dattilo & Murphy, 1987a). According to the authors, one way for therapeutic recreation specialists to encourage generalization is to conduct training and practice sessions in an environment that is as similar as possible to the environment where the behavior is ultimately performed. Once a person with mental retardation has learned a leisure skill, the therapeutic recreation specialist should then gradually decrease the amount and rate that a particular reward is being administered. Therefore, as the specialist decreases the reward, the participants will be required to exhibit more of the desired leisure skill for a longer period of time to receive the same reward. In addition, it is important for the therapeutic recreation specialist to use rewards that are naturally occurring within the environments where the leisure skill is intended to be performed, because if the rewards used during the teaching of the skill are not available in other situations, the likelihood of generalization is reduced.

Evaluation

The process of collecting and analyzing information about people and programs is a critical task of the therapeutic recreation specialist. In response to the unique problems created by the application of therapeutic recreation programs in a variety of settings and situations, the specialist should possess an assortment of evaluation skills. Observational strategies appear to be the most reliable method of evaluation for individuals with mental retardation. Pelegrino (1979) stated that observational procedures are the primary method to obtain information on what is actually happening in a situation.

Therapeutic recreation specialists should employ an individualized evaluation strategy to examine accurately the impact of services on participants. One methodology that allows practitioners to evaluate the effect of interventions on the individual is the application of single-subject designs (Dattilo & Nelson, 1986). Single-subject evaluation requires an extensive examination of each individual, using multiple measurements to verify the functional relationship between a therapeutic recreation program and its effect on the individual with mental retardation. However, Dattilo, Gasts & Schleien (1993) reported that single-subject designs provide a feasible procedure for therapeutic recreation specialists to implement. According to Dattilo (1987) single-subject evaluation represents a viable method for making informed decisions about the quality of a therapeutic recreation program and provides the context for understanding the behavioral dynamics of individuals.

APPLICATION OF THE TR PROCESS

CASE STUDY

James is a 33-year-old man who enjoys spending his free time socializing with his friends and family. Although James has an excellent sense of humor, he needs to develop more social interaction skills. In addition, he has encountered difficulty in attempting to initiate participation in preferred recreation activities. As a result of his severe mental retardation, James has limited expressive communication skills. James's parents have been extremely supportive of him; however, at times they have tended to be somewhat overprotective.

James has registered to participate in a leisure education class offered by the community recreation and parks department. Based on the model presented by Dattilo and Murphy (1991) and adapting specific programs contained in their text, the therapeutic recreation specialist has developed the following comprehensive leisure education program. The program is designed to provide James with long-range leisure instruction intended to allow him to participate with his family and friends in integrated recreation programs within his community.

Awareness of Self in Leisure. In order for James to make appropriate choices about recreation participation, it is vital that he possess knowledge of himself relative to his preferences (Montagnes, 1976). It is important for James to gain a realistic view of his abilities as well as his limitations. It is also helpful for him to examine his preferences and desires relative to leisure participation. Reflecting on past leisure pursuits may permit James to gain insight into his skills. Analyzation of his current leisure involvement should assist him in identifying activities he enjoys as well as determining barriers he would like to overcome. To enhance motivation to participate in leisure education, the therapeutic recreation specialist will encourage James to look beyond his past and present leisure participation patterns and begin to consider areas for future discovery.

Leisure Appreciation. To gain an awareness of leisure, it is useful for James to develop an understanding of the concepts of leisure and leisure lifestyle. If James begins to understand these concepts, his ability to participate in recreation activities that result in satisfaction and enjoyment will be enhanced. Because James has been overprotected, his ability to take personal responsibility for his own leisure involvement has been reduced. Therefore, the leisure education for him will be designed to teach James to take responsibility for his leisure lifestyle. By focusing on leisure awareness, James should begin to develop a sensitivity for the uniqueness of leisure. In addition, it is important for him to understand the outcomes of his leisure participation. Finally, it is useful for James to be aware of the numerous possibilities that can facilitate the leisure experience.

Self-Determination in Leisure. Witt, Ellis, and Niles (1984) emphasized the need for therapeutic recreation specialists to provide leisure education services that promote an individual's perception of leisure control, leisure competence, and intrinsic motivation to facilitate the person's sense of freedom of choice. This recommendation was based on the arguments presented by many contemporary theorists for the inclusion of choice in definitions of leisure (Csikszentmihalyi, 1975; Iso-Ahola, 1980; Neulinger, 1982). Therefore, the therapeutic recreation specialist will attempt to incorporate the notion of choice into the leisure education program designed for James. It is hoped that the demonstration of choice through selection will encourage James to initiate activity spontaneously, interact with elements of the environment, and assert a degree of control over his surroundings (Dattilo & Barnett, 1985). For further assistance with meeting the unmet leisure education needs of people with severe mental retardation, the reader is referred to the text by Schleien et al. (1994) entitled *Lifelong Leisure Skills for Persons with Developmental Disabilities.*

Leisure Decision Making. James has encountered difficulty in making decisions related to many aspects of his life. This problem is evident in relation to his leisure lifestyle. Based on observations that people with mental retardation frequently fail in their attempts to adjust to community living as a result of inappropriate use of their free time, Hayes (1977) recommended that therapeutic recreation specialists teach the decision-making process and encourage the selection and participation in appropriate recreation activities. Therefore, the therapeutic recreation specialist will teach James the decision-making process.

Knowledge and Utilization of Leisure Resources. According to Overs, Taylor, and Adkins (1974), difficulty in making appropriate leisure choices may result from people's lack of knowledge of leisure resources. Knowledge of leisure resources and the ability to use these resources appear to be an important factor in the establishment of an independent leisure lifestyle (Peterson & Gunn, 1984). Therefore, Dattilo and Murphy (1987a) recommended that therapeutic recreation specialists teach participants not only how to participate in an activity but also how they can answer questions such as:

1. where can one participate?
2. are there others who will participate?
3. how much will participation cost?
4. what type of transportation is available? and
5. where could a person learn more about a particular recreation activity?

The therapeutic recreation specialist will implement the leisure education program described in Joswiak's (1989) text entitled *Leisure Education: Program Materials for Persons with Developmental Disabilities* and will teach James to become more aware of the leisure resources available to him.

Social Interaction Skills. One of the major deficits experienced by James that prevents him from developing a satisfying leisure lifestyle is related to social interaction skills. In fact, a defining characteristic of mental retardation has become a deficiency in social skills (AAMR, 1992). Frequently, James has been identified as being mentally retarded, not because people observed his inability to perform some cognitive or physical skill but as a result of his display of inappropriate social behaviors. The absence of social skills is particularly noticeable during leisure participation (Marlowe, 1979) and frequently leads to isolation and an inability to function successfully (O'Morrow, 1980). Therefore, the development of social skills used in leisure situations appears to be important to James because the acquisition of these skills facilitates integration (Keogh et al., 1984). The development of meaningful friendships and effective social interaction skills can be taught to James through a systematic leisure education program.

TRENDS AND ISSUES

The trends and issues related to leisure services for people with mental retardation are as follows:

- Focus on individual's similarities as opposed to differences.
- Implement services including treatment, leisure education, and recreation participation.
- Provide opportunities to make leisure choices and decisions.
- Develop age-appropriate recreation activities.
- Support the provision of leisure services in the person's least restrictive environment.
- Encourage the deinstitutionalization movement.
- Provide leisure programs demonstrating the normalization principle.
- Develop strategies that facilitate integration into community recreation activities.
- Incorporate assessment, planning, implementation, and evaluation into programming.
- Implement preference, activity, environmental, and task analysis assessment procedures.
- Facilitate the opportunity for at least partial participation.
- Provide recreation activities that involve cooperation and indirect competition.
- Use behavior modification in applied settings to facilitate positive leisure involvement.
- Systematically administer instructional prompts to develop a repertoire of leisure skills.
- Provide opportunities for practice and repetition of leisure participation.
- Develop procedures to encourage generalization of leisure behaviors.
- Use observational strategies to evaluate performance in recreation activities.
- Implement single-subject research designs to examine the impact of leisure services.

SUMMARY

This chapter was developed with the intent of encouraging the reader to gain an understanding of mental retardation, significantly subaverage intellectual functioning, intelligence quotient, adaptive skills, developmental period, and developmental disability. Ways of classifying people with mental retardation and the implications of these classifications on their lives were also highlighted. The reader was presented with information on the causes of the limitations associated with mental retardation. Therapeutic recreation and leisure lifestyle were described in relation to people with mental retardation. The importance of treatment in providing comprehensive therapeutic recreation services to people with mental retardation was emphasized. The chapter also contained information describing the components of leisure education (self-awareness, leisure competence, leisure awareness, decision making, knowledge of leisure resources, and social interaction skills) and their relevance to people with mental retardation. Strategies for incorporating opportunities for choice and decision making as well as encouraging age-appropriate involvement in recreation participation for people with mental retardation were presented. The reader was introduced to the concepts of least restrictive environment, deinstitutionalization, normalization, integration, inclusion, and transition, and their role in determining the most appropriate setting for administering therapeutic recreation services to people with mental retardation. Specific techniques such as preference analysis, activity analysis, environmental analysis, and task analysis, and their role in the assessment and planning phases of therapeutic recreation services for people with mental retardation were described. A major portion of the chapter was devoted to identifying and describing the procedures of partial participation, cooperation and repetition, and generalization training when implementing therapeutic recreation programs for people with mental retardation. The chapter also contained a description of the value of behavioral observation and single-subject designs when evaluating therapeutic recreation services designed for people with mental retardation. A specific application of the therapeutic recreation process for an individual with mental retardation was subsequently provided in the chapter. Finally, the chapter concluded with the identification of trends and issues affecting therapeutic recreation services for people with mental retardation.

READING COMPREHENSION QUESTIONS

1. What is meant by mental retardation?
2. What is the difference between the phrases *developmental disability* and *mental retardation?*
3. What are the four dimensions used to classify and determine supports that may be needed by people with mental retardation?
4. Why is the practice of classifying people with mental retardation based on mental age a problem?
5. What are some conditions that may cause mental retardation?
6. What are the three specific areas of professional service that are used to provide a comprehensive leisure ability approach for people with mental retardation?
7. Why is it important to incorporate opportunities for people with mental retardation to demonstrate choices, make decisions, and learn age-appropriate skills when participating in recreation participation programs?
8. What is meant by the following: least restrictive environment, deinstitutionalization, normalization, integration, inclusion, and transition? Why are these principles important to consider when providing recreation services for people with mental retardation?
9. Why should you encourage the integration of people with mental retardation into community recreation programs?
10. Who benefits from the inclusion of people with mental retardation into community programs?
11. Why is it useful to conduct a preference analysis when providing comprehensive leisure programs for people with mental retardation?
12. What is meant by the phrase *task analysis?* Why is it useful to employ task analytic assessment procedures prior to providing leisure services for people with mental retardation?
13. Why is it valuable to adopt the philosophy of partial participation that encourages people with mental retardation to participate actively in recreation activities?
14. What is meant by the phrase *indirect competition?* Why should indirect competition and cooperation be incorporated into recreation programs for people with mental retardation?
15. What is meant by the word *generalization?* Why is it useful systematically to promote the generalization of leisure skills acquired by individuals with mental retardation?
16. What are some components of a comprehensive leisure education program that should be addressed when developing lifelong leisure skills for people with mental retardation?

SUGGESTED LEARNING ACTIVITIES

1. Attend a meeting of your local chapter of the Association for Retarded Citizens. Take notes at the meeting and write a brief report describing what you learned.
2. Contact your community recreation and parks department to determine if any individuals with mental retardation participate in an integrated recreation event. If so, participate in the activity and attempt to get to know the people.
3. Develop an outline of a comprehensive leisure education program that you would develop if you were planning to teach a variety of people, including those with mental retardation.
4. Choose a friend, family member, or acquaintance. Attempt to communicate to the person the advantages associated with integrating people with mental retardation into community recreation programs.
5. Practice using appropriate terminology when talking about people with mental retardation as suggested by Dattilo and Smith (1990) and Dattilo (1994).
6. Interview a person with mental retardation and determine his or her leisure interests and desires. Discuss ways that the person may be able to meet the identified needs by accessing community recreation resources.

REFERENCES

American Association on Mental Retardation. (1992). *Mental retardation: Definition, classification, and systems of supports* (9th ed.). Washington, DC: American Association on Mental Retardation.

American Psychiatric Association. (1987). *Diagnostic and statistical manual of mental disorders: DSM-III-R.* Washington, DC: American Psychiatric Association.

American Therapeutic Recreation Association. (1984). ATRA. Washington, DC: American Therapeutic Recreation Association.

Austin, D. R. (1982). *Therapeutic recreation: Processes and techniques.* New York: John Wiley & Sons.

Baroff, G. S. (1986). *Mental retardation: Nature, cause, and management* (2nd ed.). Washington, DC: Hemisphere.

Baumgart, D., et al. (1982). The principle of partial participation and individualized adaptations in educational programs for severely handicapped students. *Journal of the Association for the Severely Handicapped, 7*(2), 17–27.

Brown, L., et al. (1979a). A rationale for comprehensive longitudinal interactions between severely handicapped and nonhandicapped students and citizens. *AAESPH Review, 4*(1), 3–14.

Brown, L., et al. (1979b). Using the characteristics of current and subsequent least restrictive environments in the development of curricular content for severely handicapped students. *AAESPH Review, 4*(4), 407–424.

Carter, M. J., Van Andel, G. E., & Robb, G. M. (1985). *Therapeutic recreation: A practical approach.* St. Louis: Times Mirror/Mosby.

Certo, N. J., Schleien, S. J., & Hunter, D. (1983). An ecological assessment inventory to facilitate community recreation participation by severely disabled individuals. *Therapeutic Recreation Journal, 17*(3), 29–38.

Csikszentmihalyi, M. (1975). *Beyond boredom and anxiety.* San Francisco: Jossey-Bass.

Dattilo, J. (1994). *Inclusive leisure services: Responding to the rights of people with disabilities.* State College, PA: Venture Publishing Co.

Dattilo, J. (1993). Facilitating reciprocal communication for individuals with severe communication disorders: Implications to leisure participation. *Palaestra, 10*(1), 39–48.

Dattilo, J. (1988). Assessing music preferences of persons with severe disabilities. *Therapeutic Recreation Journal, 22*(2), 12–23.

Dattilo, J. (1987). Encouraging the emergence of therapeutic recreation research practitioners through single-subject research. *Journal of Expanding Horizons in Therapeutic Recreation, 2,* 1–5.

Dattilo, J. (1986). Single-subject research in therapeutic recreation: Implications to individuals with limitations. *Therapeutic Recreation Journal, 20*(2), 76–87.

Dattilo, J. (1984). Therapeutic recreation assessment for individuals with severe handicaps. In G.L. Hitzhusen (Ed.), *Expanding horizons in therapeutic recreation* (Vol. 11, pp. 146–157). Columbia, MO: Curators University of Missouri.

Dattilo, J., & Camarata, S. (1991). Facilitating conversation through self-initiated augmentative communication treatment. *Journal of Applied Behavior Analysis, 24*(2), 369–378.

Dattilo, J., & O'Keefe, B. M. (1992). Setting the stage for leisure: Encouraging adults with mental retardation who use augmentative and alternative communication systems to share conversations. *Therapeutic Recreation Journal, 26*(1), 27–37.

Dattilo, J., & Barnett, L. A. (1985). Therapeutic recreation for persons with severe handicaps: An analysis of the relationship between choice and pleasure. *Therapeutic Recreation Journal, 21*(3), 79–91.

Dattilo, J., Gast, D., & Schleien, S. (1993). Implementation of single-subject designs in therapeutic recreation research. In M. J. Malkin & C. Z. Howe (Eds.). *Research in therapeutic recreation: Basic concepts and methods* (pp. 181–202). State College, PA: Venture Publishing Co.

Dattilo, J., & Light, J. (1993). Setting the stage for leisure: Encouraging reciprocal communication for people using augmentative and alternative communication systems through facilitator instruction. *Therapeutic Recreation Journal, 27*(3), 156–171.

Dattilo, J., & Murphy, W. D. (1991). *Leisure education program planning: A systematic approach.* State College, PA: Venture Publishing Co.

Dattilo, J., & Murphy, W. D. (1987a). *Behavior modification in therapeutic recreation.* State College, PA: Venture Publishing Co.

Dattilo, J., & Murphy, W. D. (1987b). Facilitating the challenge in adventure recreation for persons with disabilities. *Therapeutic Recreation Journal, 21*(3), 14–21.

Dattilo, J., & Nelson, G. (1986). Single-subject evaluation in health education. *Health Education Quarterly, 13*(3), 249–259.

Dattilo, J., & Rusch, F. (1985). Effects of choice on leisure participation for persons with severe handicaps. *Journal of the Association for Persons with Severe Handicaps, 10,* 194–199.

Dattilo, J., & Schleien, S. J. (1994). Understanding the provision of leisure services for persons with mental retardation. *Mental Retardation, 32*(1), 53–59.

Dattilo, J., & Smith, R. (1990). Communicating positive attitudes toward people with disabilities through sensitive terminology. *Therapeutic Recreation Journal, 24*(1), 8–17.

Dattilo, J., & St. Peter, S. (1991). A model for including leisure education in transition services for young adults with mental retardation. *Education and Training in Mental Retardation, 26*(4), 420–432.

Donder, D., & Nietupski, J. (1981). Nonhandicapped adolescents teaching playground skills to their mentally handicapped peers: Toward a less restrictive middle school environment. *Education and Training of the Mentally Retarded, 16,* 270–276.

Donnellan, A. M., et al. (1986). *Progress without punishment: A staff training manual of non-aversive behavioral procedures.* Madison, WI: University of Wisconsin.

Fait, H. F., & Billing, J. E. (1978). Reassessment of the value of competition. In R. Martens (Ed.), *Joys and sadness in children's sports* (pp. 98–105). Champaign, IL: Human Kinetics.

Falvey, M., et al. (1980). Strategies for using cues and correction procedures. In W. Sailor, B. Wilcox, & L. Brown (Eds.), *Methods of instruction for severely handicapped students.* Baltimore: Paul H. Brookes.

Farrington, P. (1976). Games. In A. Fluegelman (Ed.), *The new games book* (p. 10). Champaign, IL: Doubleday.

Fenrick, N., & Petersen, T. K. (1984). Developing positive changes in attitudes towards moderately/severely handicapped students through a peer tutoring program. *Education and Training of the Mentally Retarded, 19,* 83–90.

Ferguson, D. L., et al. (1992). Figuring out what to do with the grownups: How teachers make inclusion "work" for students with disabilities. *Journal of the Association for Persons with Severe Handicaps, 17*(4), 218–226.

Ford, A., et al. (1984). Strategies for developing individualized recreation and leisure programs for severely handicapped students. In N.J. Certo, N. Haring, & R. York (Eds.), *Public school integration of severely handicapped students: Rational issues and progressive alternatives* (pp. 245–275). Baltimore: Paul H. Brookes.

Gearheart, B. R. (1987). Educational strategies for children with developmental disabilities. In M.I. Gottlieb & J.E. Williams (Eds.), *Textbook of developmental pediatrics* (pp. 385–397). New York: Plenum Medical.

Gottlieb, M. I. (1987). Major variations in intelligence. In M. I. Gottlieb & J. E. Williams (Eds.), *Textbook of developmental pediatrics* (pp. 127–150). New York: Plenum Medical.

Grossman, H. J. (Ed.). (1983). *Classification in mental retardation.* Washington, DC: American Association on Mental Deficiency.

Halpern, A. S. (1985). Transition: A look at the foundations. *Exceptional Children, 51*(6), 479–486.

Hanline, M. F., & Fox, L. (1993). Learning within the context of play: Providing typical early childhood experiences for children with severe disabilities. *The Journal of the Association for Persons with Severe Handicaps, 18*(2), 121–129.

Hawkins, B. A. (1993). An exploratory analysis of leisure and life satisfaction of aging adults with mental retardation. *Therapeutic Recreation Journal, 26,* 98–109.

Hayes, G. A. (1977). Professional preparation and leisure counseling. *Journal of Physical Education and Recreation, 48*(4), 36–38.

Howe-Murphy, R., & Charboneau, B. G. (1987). *Therapeutic recreation intervention: An ecological perspective.* Englewood Cliffs, NJ: Prentice Hall.

Hutchison, P., & Lord, J. (1979). *Recreation integration: Issues and alternatives in leisure services and community involvement.* Ottawa, Ontario: Leisurability Publications, Inc.

Hutchison, P., & McGill, J. (1992). *Leisure, integration and community.* Concord, Ontario: Leisurability Publications, Inc.

Iso-Ahola, S. E. (1980). *The social psychology of leisure and recreation.* Dubuque, IA: William C. Brown.

Jensen, A. R. (1980). *Bias in mental testing.* New York: The Free Press.

Joswiak, K. F. (1989). *Leisure education: Program materials for persons with developmental disabilities.* State College, PA: Venture Publishing, Inc.

Kennedy, D. W., Austin, D. R., & Smith, R. W. (1987). *Special recreation: Opportunities for persons with disabilities.* Philadelphia: Saunders College Publishing.

Keogh, D. A., et al. (1984). Enhancing leisure skills in severely retarded adolescents through a self-instructional treatment package. *Analysis and Intervention in Developmental Disabilities, 4,* 333–351.

Kishi, G., et al. (1988). Daily decision-making in community residences: A social comparison of adults with and without mental retardation. *American Journal on Mental Retardation, 92,* 430–435.

Knapczyk, D. R. (1975). Task analytic assessment of severe learning problems. *Education and Training of the Mentally Retarded, 10,* 74–77.

Krebs, P. L., & Block, M. E. (1992). Transition of students with disabilities into community recreation: The role of the adapted physical educator. *Adapted Physical Activity Quarterly, 9*(4), 305–315.

Lakin, K. C., & Bruininks, R. H. (Eds.). (1985). *Strategies for achieving community integration of developmentally disabled citizens.* Baltimore: Paul H. Brookes.

Marlowe, M. (1979). The game analysis intervention: A procedure to increase the peer acceptance and social adjustment of a retarded child. *Education and Training of the Mentally Retarded, 14,* 262–268.

McHale, S. M., & Simeonsson, R. J. (1980). Effects of interaction on nonhandicapped children's attitudes toward autistic children. *American Journal of Mental Deficiency, 85,* 18–24.

McLaren, J., & Bryson, S. E. (1987). Review of recent epidemiological studies of mental retardation: Prevalence, associated disorders, and etiology. *American Journal of Mental Retardation, 92*(3), 243–254.

Montagnes, J. A. (1976). Reality therapy approach to leisure counseling. *Journal of Leisurability, 3,* 37–45.

Moss, K. (Ed.). (1993). *P.S. News, 5*(1).

Mundy, J., & Odum, L. (1979). *Leisure education: Theory and practice.* New York: John Wiley & Sons.

National Therapeutic Recreation Society. (1982). *Philosophical position statement of the National Therapeutic Recreation Society.* Alexandria, VA: National Recreation and Park Association.

Neulinger, J. (1982). *The psychology of leisure: Research approaches to study of leisure* (2nd ed.). Springfield, IL: Charles C. Thomas.

Newton, J. S., Horner, R. H., & Lund, L. (1991). Honoring activity preferences in individualized plan development: A descriptive analysis. *Journal of the Association of Severe Handicaps, 16*(4), 207–221.

Nirje, B. (1969). The normalization principle and its human management implications. In R. Kugel & W. Wolfensberger (Eds.), *Changing patterns of residential services for the mentally retarded.* Washington, DC: President's Committee on Mental Retardation.

O'Morrow, G. S. (1980). *Therapeutic recreation: A helping profession.* Reston, VA: Reston.

Overs, R. P., Taylor, S., & Adkins, C. (1974). Avocational counseling for the elderly. *Journal of Physical Education and Recreation, 48*(4), 44–45.

Pelegrino, D. A. (1979). *Research methods for recreation and leisure: A theoretical and practical guide.* Dubuque, IA: William C. Brown.

Peterson, C. A. (1981, September). *Leisure lifestyle and disabled individuals.* Paper presented at Horizons West Therapeutic Recreation Symposium. San Francisco, CA.

Peterson, C. A., & Gunn, S. L. (1984). *Therapeutic recreation program design: Principles and procedures* (2nd ed.). Englewood Cliffs, NJ: Prentice Hall.

Raw, J., & Errickson, E. (1977). Behavioral techniques in therapeutic recreation. In T. Thompson & J. Grabowski (Eds.), *Behavior modification of the mentally retarded* (pp. 379–395). New York: Oxford University Press.

Ray, T., & Meidl, D. (1991). *Fun futures: Community recreation and developmental disabilities.* St. Paul, MN: SCOLA of Arc Ramsey County.

Reschly, D. J. (1992). Mental retardation: Conceptual foundation, definitional criteria, and diagnostic operations. In S. R. Hynd & R. E. Mattison (Eds.), *Assessment and diagnosis of child and adolescent psychiatric disorders. Vol. II: Developmental disorders.* Hillsdale, NJ: Erlbaum.

Schalock, R. L. et al., (1994). The changing conception of mental retardation: Implications for the field. *Mental Retardation, 32*(3), 181–193.

Scheerenberger, R. C. (1987). *A history of mental retardation: A quarter century of promise.* Baltimore: Paul H. Brookes.

Schleien, S. J., Meyer, L. H., Heyne, L. A., & Brandt, B. B. (1994). *Lifelong leisure skills and lifestyles for persons with developmental disabilities.* Baltimore: Paul H. Brookes.

Schleien, S. J., & Ray, M. T. (1988). *Community recreation and persons with disabilities: Strategies for integration.* Baltimore: Paul H. Brookes.

Schleien, S. J., Tuckner, B., & Heyne, L. (1985). Leisure education programs for the severely disabled student. *Parks and Recreation, 20,* 74–78.

Schwartz, D. B. (1992). *Crossing the river: Creating a conceptual revolution in community and disability.* Brookline, MA: Brookline.

Smull, M. W., & Donnehey, A. J. (1993). The challenges of the 90s: Increasing quality while reducing costs. In V. J. Bradley, J. Ashbough, & B. Bailey (Eds.), *Creating individual supports for people with developmental disabilities: A mandate for change at many levels.* Baltimore: Paul H. Brookes.

St. Peter, S. M., et al. (1989). Social Skills. In A. Ford et al. (Eds.), *The Syracuse community-referenced curriculum guide* (pp.171–188). Baltimore: Paul H. Brookes.

Steffens, K., et al. (1993). Leisure as an adaptive skill area. *American Association of Mental Retardation Leisure and Recreation Division Newsletter, 5*(2), 2–4.

Terman, L. M. (1916). *The measurement of intelligence.* Boston: Houghton Mifflin.

Trap-Porter, J., & Perry, W. J. (1982). Moving from a medical to a behavioral model: Can therapeutic recreation learn from special education? *Education and Training of Children, 5*(3), 297–301.

Trent, J. W. (1994). *Inventing the feeble mind: A history of mental retardation in the United States.* Berkeley, CA: University of California Press.

Vallet, R. E. (1972). Developmental task analysis and psycho-educational programming. *Journal of School Psychology, 10,* 127–134.

Wehman, P., & Schleien, S. J. (1981). *Leisure programs for handicapped persons: Adaptations, techniques, and curriculum.* Baltimore: University Park Press.

Wilcox, M. J. (1993). Partner-based prelinguistic intervention: A preliminary report. *OSERS News in Print, 5*(4), 4–9.

Williams, W., & Gotts, E. A. (1977). Selected considerations on developing curriculum for severely handicapped students. In E. Sontag (Ed.), *Educational programming for the severely and profoundly handicapped.* Reston, VA: The Council for Exceptional Children.

Witt, P. A., Ellis, G. D., & Niles, S. H. (1984). Leisure counseling with special populations. In T.E. Dowd (Ed.), *Leisure counseling: Concepts and applications.* Springfield, IL: Charles C. Thomas.

Woodrich, D. L., & Joy, J. E. (1986). *Multidisciplinary assessment of children with learning disabilities and mental retardation.* Baltimore: Paul H. Brookes.

Wolfensberger, W. (1972). *The principle of normalization in human services.* Toronto: National Institute on Mental Retardation.

Wuerch, B. B., & Voeltz, L. M. (1982). *Longitudinal leisure skills for severely handicapped learners: The Ho'onanea curriculum component.* Baltimore: Paul H. Brookes.

Zigler, E., & Butterfield, E. C. (1968). Motivational aspects of changes in IQ test performance of culturally deprived nursery school children. *Child Development, 39,* 1–14.

CHAPTER 9

SEVERE MULTIPLE DISABILITIES

STUART J. SCHLEIEN
MAURICE K. FAHNESTOCK

OBJECTIVES

- Understand the definition of *severe multiple disability* and the problems in defining this population.
- Identify typical repertoires and needs of persons with severe multiple disabilities.
- Identify and provide a rationale for specific goals of the therapeutic recreation process as they relate to persons with multiple and significant needs.
- Understand the importance of selecting age-appropriate and functional leisure skills for instruction.
- Understand various behavioral methods for systematic leisure skills instructional programming.
- Recognize leisure-related support skills necessary for participation in select activities.
- Understand the rationale for inclusive recreation programming.
- Identify typical barriers to quality social inclusion and understand how to assess and enhance an individual's social network.

DEFINITION OF SEVERE MULTIPLE DISABILITIES

To what group of individuals does the term *severe multiple disability* refer? This question is not easily answered and requires an analysis of the factors influencing such a definition.

A review of the terms currently being used by professionals reveals an inconsistency in defining a specific population (Fredericks, 1987). Perhaps the single greatest factor influencing this inconsistency is the process of definition. Definitions have been created based on the interests of the particular agency serving the individual with a severe multiple disability. This type of

Note: The development of this chapter was partially supported by Grant Project No. H029D20002 funded by the Office of Special Education and Rehabilitative Services and Cooperative Agreement No. H133B30072 funded by the National Institute on Disability and Rehabilitation Research, both of the U.S. Department of Education. The content and opinions expressed herein do not necessarily reflect the position or policy of the U.S. Department of Education, and no official endorsement should be inferred.

influence has resulted in an abundance of terms, all somewhat workable but limited by an unclear variation in who exactly is being included or excluded.

The components of this definition problem are displayed in Figure 9.1. Two types of descriptive terms have emerged. There are generic descriptions that attempt to describe the population in a broad sense. These terms include such descriptions as persons with dual sensory impairments and profound disabilities. The second type of terms used are those that describe by referring to a specific disability. Examples of this kind of description include persons who are profoundly mentally retarded and cerebral palsied–deaf. The abundance of terms is created by four types of influencing agencies, each of which adopts its own definition. These agencies are categorized as residential/community living, vocational, recreational, and educational.

The problem of definition is made apparent by comparing the definition of *severely handicapped* as determined by the Rehabilitation Services Administration and the Office of Special Education Programs. Both agencies describe an individual with a disability that seriously limits functional ability, but this functional ability is assessed in regard to the intensive support needed to meet either vocational objectives or educational objectives, respectively. Defined in this way, two distinctly different definitions are created. The result is that a person with a severe handicap is

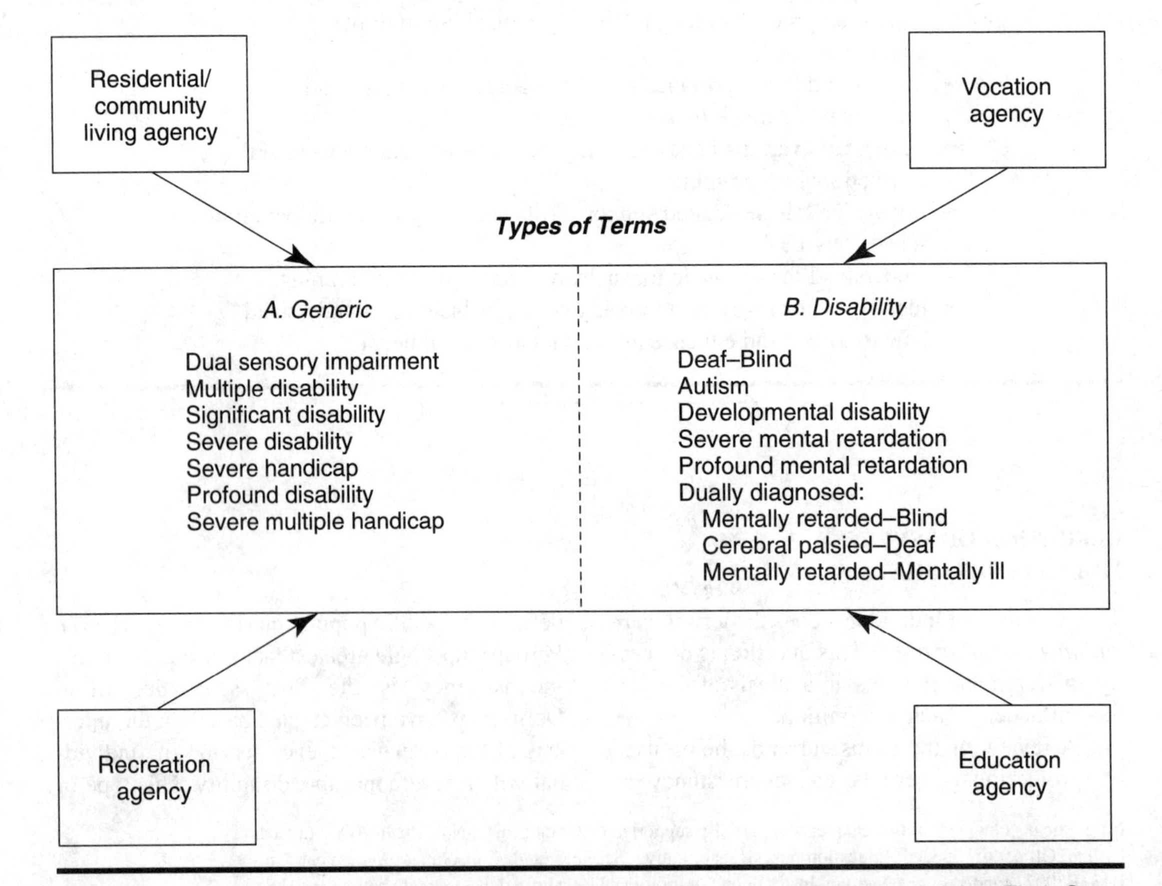

FIGURE 9.1 The Definition Problem and the Four Types of Influencing Agencies that Adopt Their Own Definition

categorized by the type of service the agency provides (Bellamy, 1985).

A definition problem also arises when the population is described by the individual's specific disability. This method may exclude some individuals from service by being too limited as to who is included under that disability. For example, the assessment label *deaf–blind* refers not only to those individuals who are deaf and blind, but to those who are visually and auditorially impaired. This includes those individuals categorized as blind/severely hearing impaired, or severely hearing impaired/severely vision impaired. Another factor entering into this characterization is that many individuals who are deaf-blind are either mentally retarded or are functioning in the range of mental retardation. Through this example it becomes evident that the term *deaf–blind* may not accurately reflect the dynamics of this population (Barrett, 1987; Fredericks & Baldwin, 1987).

This definition problem establishes the need for a definition that can include the numerous low incidence populations and all their variable characteristics. The following definition attempts to satisfy this need by being general enough to include the variance of this population, yet specific enough to be a viable definition for those servicing this population. Severe multiple disability refers to those individuals with a profound disability or with a combination of disabilities that so limit their daily activities that they require services and programming that is more innovative, extensive, and intensive than common programming for individuals with disabilities provides. This population is characterized as, but not exclusively, nonambulatory, nonindependently mobile, needing to be fed, needing assistance in toileting, and needing daily occupational or communication therapy (Covert, 1987; Fredericks, 1987).

Recreation Participation: Current Repertoires and Needs

Participation in leisure/recreation/social activities is an important aspect of life in our society. When such activities meet individuals' needs, the activities promote physical health and conditioning, provide opportunities to develop social relations, and lead to the development of new skills. Unfortunately, leisure services have had relatively low priority in programs for persons with severe multiple disabilities, until recently when specific leisure skill training techniques and curricula incorporating behavioral interventions, in conjunction with purposeful environmental arrangements, were developed. The neglect of relevant programming and services for this population is particularly unfortunate because appropriate participation in leisure activities is an important aspect in their successful community adjustment (Cheseldine & Jeffree, 1981; Hayden et al., 1988), is associated with the development of collateral skills (Meyer et al., 1985; Schleien, Kiernan, & Wehman, 1981; Vandercook, 1991), and the reduction of maladaptive behaviors (Adkins & Matson, 1980; Favell, 1973; Schleien, et al., 1995).

Unfortunately, a discrepancy exists between what is known about the short- and long-term benefits of participation in leisure activities and the current status of services to persons with severe multiple disabilities. For these individuals to maximally participate in community recreation activities alongside their nondisabled and less disabled peers, specific leisure skill instruction in home, school, and community environments, and specific provisions by communities to incorporate them into recreation activities are necessary.

Before any attempts are made to design, deliver, and evaluate appropriate therapeutic recreation services, it is necessary to describe common characteristics of persons with severe multiple disabilities. In any investigation into their community adaptation and overall wellness, it is necessary to understand their current participation in leisure and social activities, ability to occupy themselves during discretionary time, make choices, and other primary variables that seem to influence participation.

A brief review of typical repertoires and skill deficits in persons with severe multiple disabilities as they concern therapeutic recreation service delivery could include the following variables: (1) leisure skill repertoires, (2) choice making and self-initiated behavior, (3) social skills and other leisure-related support skills, (4) maintaining and generalizing skills, and (5) community participation and social inclusion. It is necessary to recognize that different individuals within the broad category of severe multiple disabilities (persons who are often grouped homogeneously) have separate programming needs. Individuals will differ markedly in their motor, social, cognitive, and affective abilities. For example, an individual who is moderately retarded and uses a wheelchair has substantially different abilities and needs than an individual who is labeled autistic with a visual impairment. Therefore, it is always necessary to approach service delivery in an individualized manner, in an attempt to satisfy personal needs and preferences. Due to the risk of thinking stereotypically, one is cautioned not to overgeneralize when designing programs for individuals with severe multiple disabilities.

Leisure Skill Repertoires. A major factor for the relatively little attention given to teaching leisure skills for home and community settings to persons with severe multiple disabilities is their serious skill deficits. Skill deficits could include two general skill areas of interaction—with objects and with people. Current habilitative and educational technology has not yet advanced to the point where professionals could determine reliably how many skills could be acquired or environments accessed. Professionals engaged in leisure skill instruction with persons with severe multiple disabilities face a variety of challenges in expanding their repertoires. Barriers center around three basic concerns: (1) specific skill deficits, (2) limited instructional materials, and (3) environmental barriers/resistance (Schleien, et al., 1990; Wehman, 1979; Wehman & Schleien, 1981). Although a totally independent leisure lifestyle, including independent functioning in community leisure environments, may be unrealistic, these individuals are capable of considerably more complex skills than they typically have performed.

Lagomarcino and colleagues (1984) demonstrated a method of training an intermediate community living skill to institutionalized teenagers who were severely and profoundly retarded. Appropriate dancing performance of noninstitutionalized persons who were mildly and moderately retarded served as the empirical norm for their instructional programs. By using behavioral interventions, other attempts to remediate play problems and address leisure education needs have been successful. Procedures such as contingent reinforcement, task analysis, careful selection of activities, cooperative learning, skill modifications, and pairing individuals in environments with nondisabled peers have been successful to teach a variety of age-appropriate leisure skills to children and adults with severe multiple disabilities. Examples include miniature golf (Banks & Aveno, 1986), pinball (Hill, Wehman, & Horst, 1982; Horst et al., 1980), video games (Powers & Ball, 1983; Sedlak, Doyle, & Schloss, 1982), darts (Schleien, Wehman, & Kiernan, 1981), photography (Wehman, Schleien, & Kiernan, 1980), and functional use of a community recreation center (Schleien & Larson, 1986).

Choice Making and Self-Initiated Behavior. Recreational activities, generally, are considered to involve the performance of particular behaviors that are not work related, are enjoyable, and are ones that the individual chooses to do. Dattilo and Barnett (1985) suggested that the omission of choice in the participation process actually prevents individuals from genuine leisure experiences. Recreational activities are often selected by therapeutic recreation specialists, special education teachers, and care providers on behalf of persons with severe multiple disabilities. Common practice is to identify the chronological age, physical characteristics, and current functioning level of the individual, and subsequently select an activity for instruction based on this information only (Schleien, et al., 1995; Wehman & Schleien, 1981). Designers of leisure skills curriculum are accustomed to making decisions in the planning process, and, consequently, may lack the inclination or skills to honor preferences of the participant (Putnam, Werder, & Schleien, 1985).

Persons with severe multiple disabilities present very few functional preferences (Dattilo & Mirenda, 1987). Selecting leisure skills for instruction based on their present leisure preferences could result in nonfunctional activities such as increasing rates of stereotypic behavior and participation in age-inappropriate activities. This highlights a frequent problem encountered by therapeutic recreation specialists, teachers, and care providers attempting to select skills or activities for instruction. Individuals with severe multiple disabilities generally demonstrate few activity or object preferences reliably. Of these preferences that are reliably demonstrated, few can be incorporated into functional, age-appropriate, and socially appropriate leisure skills. In addition, because very few individuals possess extensive formal communication skills, determining whether particular leisure skills are enjoyable becomes even more subjective and suspect than it is with verbal individuals (Dattilo & O'Keefe, 1992).

From a slightly different perspective, there are those persons with severe multiple disabilities who frequently smile and laugh, and, as an example, seem to enjoy holding hands and "dancing" in a circle around a phonograph playing an archaic folk song sung in an unfamiliar language. As a result of their supposed expression of enjoyment, we become complacent, believing we have identified an appropriate leisure skill. Teaching this same group of individuals to use a local nightclub in a socially appropriate manner may produce an equivalent amount of smiles and laughs. Questions that need to be answered include: Why are these age-appropriate correlated leisure skills so infrequently attempted? and, Why are these age-inappropriate and nonfunctional skills so frequently encountered? Interestingly, Matthews (1982) found many similarities in recreational preferences of children with and without mental retardation, suggesting that chronologically age-appropriate and inclusive activities are feasible. Others have discovered that persons with developmental disabilities have interests in the same general outdoor activities and adventure activities as nondisabled persons (Schleien, et al., 1993). West (1981) found activities of hiking, camping, and other outdoor education pursuits to be preferred over the typical indoor activity offerings. Indeed, many activities which have typically been associated with persons with severe multiple disabilities have been stereotyped including inaccurate ideas of what these individuals might be able to participate in or enjoy.

If we attend to factors such as potential for social inclusion, age appropriateness of the skill, adaptability, and nondisabled performance standards when selecting activities, it will become easier to refrain from the shortsighted selections that often accrue from too close an adherence to enjoyment or convenience factors.

A primary focus of any leisure skill program is to provide the participant with as many alternatives as possible. This outcome will become realistic only when the individual has acquired the necessary skills to exercise meaningful choices and when materials and activities are made available.

Social Skills and Other Leisure-Related Support Skills. Persons with severe multiple disabilities rarely act on play materials in self-initiated or constructive ways without large amounts of instruction and prompting. This lack of spontaneity may be attributable to not having previously experienced the reinforcing characteristics of play. Also, a lack of sensory awareness or a failure to respond or attend to the materials presented may result in passive and stereotypic behavior. By acquiring a variety of play skills that require the same basic types of fine and gross motor movements, the individual's general development would be enhanced, and he or she would concurrently be gaining a larger repertoire of leisure skills (Wehman & Schleien, 1981). Also, such a positive experience and the development of a leisure repertoire can have a positive influence in the areas of cooperation, social skills and social adjustment, and, ultimately, development of friendships and inclusion into the community (Green & Schleien, 1991; Vandercook, 1991).

Maintaining and Generalizing Skills. Even those individuals who successfully acquire leisure skills often have a difficult time generalizing these skills to other environments. Transfer of training is an area in which most people with severe multiple disabilities require additional programming or systematic transitioning. Research indicates that older individuals with developmental disabilities, and those persons who are more significantly disabled have an even more difficult time generalizing to other nontrained environments and situations (Schleien et al., 1988). The greater the alteration of the environmental conditions from the original training site, the less transfer of training that will occur. For example, an individual who has acquired electronic pinball game skills at a video arcade may not exhibit similar competencies on another pinball machine that makes different sounds (Hill, Wehman, & Horst, 1982).

In addition to generalization being of primary concern, it should not be assumed that the individual will continue to engage in the newly acquired activity after formal training has been terminated. Unless the activity itself is highly preferred and the individual can maintain appropriate play behavior, it is unlikely that he or she will continue to select and participate in the activity in the future. An ideal way to promote maintenance of recreational activities is to provide experiences that are so enjoyable that the participant is eager to engage in these activities without external prompting or encouragement (Schleien et al., 1995; Wehman & Schleien, 1981). Also, it is suggested that by varying the instructional conditions (e.g., using different instructors or settings) and encouraging the involvement of parents or care providers who are knowledgeable of the instructional procedures, transfer of training and the durability of the skill could be enhanced (Schleien, et al., 1995).

Community Participation and Social Inclusion. A historical look at the kinds of community recreation programs that have generally been made available to children and adults with severe multiple disabilities reveals a substantial gap between the services needed and those available. The recreation programs offered for school-age children, for example, have focused on a small set of activities so predominant in this area that they have become stereotyped. These include bowling, swimming, arts and crafts, field trips, and car rides (Hayden et al., 1992; Schleien & Werder, 1985). Summer programs offer a similarly restricted range of options. Most typically, children and youth with severe multiple disabilities may attend a handicapped-only camp (which itself is labeled with a "handicappism" such as "Camp Helping Hands") for from one to two weeks during summer vacation. Finally, even those recreation events that might be available in community settings require that persons with disabilities be segregated from those who are not disabled or, when interactions with nondisabled persons do occur, that they participate in "integration" experiences characterized by strictly hierarchical role relationships. In these relationships, the person without a disability serves as the helper and the individual with significant disabilities receives the help (Rynders & Schleien, 1991; Schleien & Meyer, 1988).

Just as community participation involves mastering certain skills and activities in the vocational and domestic living domains, the ability to deal constructively with free time has been considered an important predictor of successful community adjustment (Gollay, 1981; Intagliata, Willer, & Wicks, 1981; Schleien et al., 1995; Schleien & Ray, 1988). There is evidence that difficulties in dealing positively with free time—such as a coffee break at work or evenings in a group home—will impede the success of a community placement, even when the individual has otherwise mastered specific job and domestic living skills (Birenbaum & Re, 1979). Additionally, persons with severe multiple disabilities who are living in a community facility have minimal contact with nondisabled people in their neighborhoods, and may actually decrease their involvement in community activities over time (Birenbaum & Re, 1979; Hayden et al., 1992; Salzberg & Langford, 1981). Thus, despite the fact that a community-based residential facility could provide increased potential for the development of a more typical lifestyle, it by no means guarantees one.

Various authors have emphasized the importance of providing systematic instruction to address leisure education needs, and argued that the learning characteristics of persons with significant disabilities require that this instruction focus directly on criterion activities and situations as they actually occur in community environments (Ford et al., 1984; Schleien et al., 1995; Schleien & Ray, 1988; Voeltz, Wuerch, & Wilcox, 1982). Within the last few years, human service professionals have attempted to provide services to individuals with significant disabilities in community and other noninstitutional settings. The least restrictive environment (LRE) is commonly used to describe this service emphasis. The LRE doctrine as applied to leisure and discretionary time use is defined as the acquisition and performance of leisure skills by persons with severe multiple disabilities in typical community environments.

The social inclusion of individuals with severe multiple disabilities is becoming an important area of study. Social inclusion is defined through the eyes of the individual and those around him or her as to whether he or she feels welcome and is a part of the group. Social inclusion implies that the people surrounding the participant also see that individual belonging to the group. This definition is a step beyond community integration, or the mere presence of an individual in the community, and addresses the social environment in which the individual is participating. The focus of social inclusion is on the recreation experience of the individual and his or her perception of that experience, and the perceptions of membership and belonging made by his or her peers. An important distinction is made between *presence* and *belonging* because it changes the role of the intervention—from addressing the individual's skill development and physical access to interventions altering the social environment that surrounds the individual (Schleien et al., 1990).

Until recently, insufficient attention has been devoted to gaining an understanding of the personal and environmental factors that are critical to the development and maintenance of social relationships and networks of persons with severe multiple disabilities. We know little about the nature of relationships that are formed by such persons or the environmental factors that influence these interactions. A review of the available literature, however, does allow one to draw some tentative conclusions.

We know that limited community participation and relatively high degrees of social isolation are common themes in the lives of such individuals (Bogdan & Taylor, 1987; Crapps, Langione, & Swaim, 1985; Green & Schleien, 1991; Lakin et al., 1992) and that physical integration does not guarantee that persons with significant disabilities will establish and maintain desired social and interpersonal contacts with members of the community (Abery, et al., 1989; Abery et al., 1990; Bercovici, 1981; 1983; Bruininks, Thurlow, & Lange, 1987; Bruininks, Thurlow, & Steffans, 1988; Green & Schleien, 1991; Hill et al., 1989; Hill, Rotegard, & Bruininks, 1984; Meyer, McQuarter, & Kishi, 1984; Rosen & Burchard, 1990).

The social networks of persons living within the community usually include parents, siblings, fellow residents, professionals, and typical members of the community. Their social networks are typically much smaller than those of their peers without disabilities and contain fewer reciprocal social relationships. Community activities, while relatively frequent, appear to take place primarily in large groups with fellow residents under the direct supervision of staff (Certo, Schleien, & Hunter, 1983; Rosen & Burchard, 1990). Social contact between persons with severe multiple disabilities and individuals besides staff or other residents occurs infrequently (Crapps & Stoneman, 1989; Donegan & Potts, 1988; Schalock & Lilley, 1986).

People with severe multiple disabilities appear to have few intimate relationships with persons without disabilities (Todd, Evans, & Beyer, 1990). This general lack of friendship with peers characterizes the lives of many, whether they are receiving community-based services or are living at home with their families (Lakin et al., 1992). Furthermore, research results suggest that when persons with significant disabilities actually manage to establish social relationships with members of the community they often have a difficult time maintaining them (Green & Schleien, 1991; Kennedy, Horner, & Newton, 1989; Zetlin & Murtaugh, 1988).

This overview of the typical characteristics, behavioral repertoires, and the level of community participation and social inclusion of persons with severe multiple disabilities was intended as a preface to a comprehensive discussion of "best practices" in therapeutic recreation. It is believed that the capabilities and learning potential of children and adults with severe multiple disabilities far surpass the traditional levels of competencies that have been reached in the past. If leisure skill programs are designed and implemented carefully, and if they incorporate personal preferences, sound behavioral principles, and occur throughout the individual's lifespan, there is little doubt that these individuals will demonstrate that they, too, can participate successfully in many age-appropriate leisure environments and activities.

PURPOSE OF THERAPEUTIC RECREATION

Because persons with severe multiple disabilities have traditionally received little attention in the area of leisure, there happens to be an abundance of "dead time" or unoccupied time (Schleien, Heyne, & Dattilo, 1995; Schleien et al., 1995) in their daily lives. Many individuals participate in passive and sedentary activities throughout the day such as watching television or listening to music. Unfortunately, many of these individuals lack the means, skills, and opportunities to participate in more active and varied leisure pursuits. Inappropriate behaviors are often exhibited excessively by these individuals during this unoccupied time (Schleien et al., 1995; Voeltz, Wuerch, & Wilcox, 1982; Wehman, & Schleien 1981).

Therapeutic recreation offers persons with severe multiple disabilities opportunities to learn appropriate and functional leisure skills that will expand their leisure repertoires and help them become more independent. The therapeutic recreation specialist must consider individualized needs and preferences of participants while implementing systematic instruction that will promote acquisition, maintenance, and generalization of lifelong leisure skills. Therapeutic recreation goals may also include environmental interventions that attempt to ensure the social inclusion and membership of individuals with severe multiple disabilities within groups of people participating in community recreation. These goals are developed with the concept of normalization in mind and may include the following:

Increased Exploration and Manipulation of Environment. Limited mobility or deficits in one or more sensory areas prevent many individuals from actively becoming involved in and familiar with their environment. For individuals who are severely motorically impaired, exploration and manipulation can often be facilitated by using computer and microswitch technology which can be individualized according to an individual's abilities (Dattilo & Barnett, 1985; York, Nietupski, & Hamre-Nietupski, 1985; York & Rainforth, 1995).

Increased Range of Lifelong Leisure Skills. Expanding one's leisure repertoire can provide opportunities to enjoy a greater variety of chronologically age-appropriate activities that could lead to a better quality of life and increased involvement with peers who are both disabled and nondisabled.

Increased Independent Leisure Behavior. It may be true that persons with severe multiple disabilities may never be totally independent; however, interdependence is also a normalizing principle. The therapeutic recreation specialist can help an individual become more independent while learning appropriate ways of becoming interdependent. Once an individual has acquired a leisure skill, he or she can then learn to identify and initiate preferred activities. Adaptive equipment and strategies for partial participation could be helpful in facilitating interdependent and independent participation (Rynders & Schleien, 1991).

Increased Socialization and Cooperation Skills. A majority of people with severe multiple disabilities do not have well-developed interaction and socialization skills. Cooperatively structured leisure activities can help individuals learn to interact appropriately and effectively with people around them (i.e., parents, care providers, neighbors or other persons in the community, and peers who are both disabled and nondisabled) (Rynders et al., 1993). Without interaction and socialization skills, it is difficult to develop friendships and perform successfully across most environments (e.g., vocational, recreational).

Increased Collateral or Support Skills. Developing collateral or support skills is essential for maintaining almost any leisure skill. Few leisure skills are performed in isolation without the use of these support skills. Some interconnected areas include skills in self-care, money management, communication, motor, and cognition/attention span skills. An individual's affect (i.e., enthusiasm shown through facial expressions and vocalizations) can also be positively influenced and facilitative during participation in recreational activities (Kibler, 1986; Powers & Ball, 1983). Several researchers have found that as leisure-related support skills are developed, inappropriate behaviors often decrease in frequency (Alajajian, 1981; Favell, 1973; Schleien, Kiernan, & Wehman, 1981).

Increased Self-Concept and Self-Esteem. A low self-concept or low self-esteem is often attributable to a feeling of helplessness due to repeated failures and lack of choice (Seligman, 1975). Leisure skills should be taught in such a manner as to help the participant experience success often, especially during the initial stages of skill acquisition.

Increased Opportunities to Perform Acquired Skills. Following skill acquisition, it is essential that the learner be able to practice those skills frequently. Horner, Williams, and Knobbe (1985) found that individuals with significant disabilities needed at least two opportunities per month to maintain performance of newly acquired skills. Increased opportunities in slightly different settings could also enhance generalization to nontrained environments and facilitate community adjustment (Goetz, 1987; Voeltz, Wuerch, & Wilcox, 1982).

Increased Social Inclusion. Although greater numbers of individuals with severe multiple disabilities are living in the community today than ever before, they are often isolated and separated by their lack of leisure skills and by a lack of environments that are welcoming and supportive (Hayden, et al., 1992). Environmental interventions that include cooperative skills training of peers, sociometric restructuring of social environments, circle of friends training, and preparation of activity leaders can lead to richer social networks (Rynders & Schleien, 1991; Schleien et al., 1990).

COMMON SERVICE SETTINGS

Traditionally, individuals with developmental disabilities, especially those with severe multiple disabilities, were generally ignored by society and not considered worthy of membership. Prior to 1800, society did little in the way of systematic study, treatment, or care of these individuals. The real beginnings of therapeutic treatment and services took place in the early 1800s when education and political reform became widespread. The first successful public residential institutions serving persons with developmental disabilities were established, and schools throughout Germany, France, and the United States were created.

With the exception of an occasional after-school recreation program sponsored by a municipal park and recreation department, therapeutic recreation services in hospitals and state institutions, or a segregated camp that offered individuals with severe multiple disabilities an opportunity to participate, few programs had been made accessible. It was not until the 1970s (i.e., the "Decade of the Disabled") that monumental civil and human rights advances by people with significant disabilities were achieved. The 1973 Rehabilitation Act (PL 93-112), one of the most significant landmarks in the struggle for equality for all individuals, made it illegal for any agency or organization that receives federal funds to discriminate against persons with disabilities solely on the basis of his or her disability. Also, the Education for All Handicapped Children Act of 1975 (PL 94-142) and its recent amendments, including the Individuals with Disabilities Education Act (IDEA) (PL 101-476), addressed the need to provide inclusive leisure services to all people with disabilities, mandating services in least restrictive environments.

In 1990, the Americans with Disabilities Act (PL 101-336) comprehensively eliminated discrimination against persons with disabilities in the areas of employment, transportation, public accommodations, public services, and telecommunications. All areas of public accommodation, including recreational areas and programs, are to be made accessible, and nondiscriminatory practices are to be implemented.

During the past fifteen years, residential services for people with severe multiple disabilities have undergone a substantial shift in direction. Several thousand individuals each year have moved from large, public residential facilities to smaller residential programs in community settings. These smaller community facilities have experienced dramatic decreases in numbers of residents, averaging sixteen residents per agency as compared to an average of twenty-five residents in 1978 (Hill, Lakin, & Bruininks, 1984). If these trends toward smaller numbers and movement to community settings continue, then community programs will be offering services to increasing numbers of people with significant disabilities, because these people constitute the majority of those still residing in the large public and private facilities (Hauber et al., 1984). The next section of this chapter addresses best practices in the therapeutic recreation process that promote a continuing movement of persons with severe multiple disabilities toward less restrictive living, learning, and participating in recreational environments.

CURRENT BEST PRACTICES AND PROCEDURES

Needs/Preference Assessment

A needs assessment is vitally important when working with individuals who are severely multiply disabled. The assessment provides information which helps the therapeutic recreation specialist identify activities and materials that will best meet the participant's lifelong leisure needs. Many authors (Crawford, Griffen, & Mendell, 1978; Orelove & Sobsey, 1987; Schleien et al., 1995; Schleien & Ray, 1988; Voeltz & Wuerch, 1981; Wehman & Schleien, 1980) have identified key areas to address within a needs assessment. The first area includes general background information (e.g., age, abilities, physical characteristics) about the individual. An assessment of the appropriateness and functionality of the targeted activities should be part of the second component. The third area could feature an environmental analysis which helps identify component tasks required to complete an activity and the individual's current level of proficiency relative to those tasks. The final area of assessment could include an analysis of the individual's social inclusion within the program along with the attitudes and responses of the peer participants and agency staff toward the individual with a severe multiple disability. These assessments seek to understand their levels of welcoming and accommodation, and what could be done to help the individual succeed.

First, it is useful to gather information concerning the participant from a variety of sources.

Care providers, family members, teachers, related services personnel, and other support staff can contribute pertinent information concerning (1) the individual's family background, physical and medical needs (e.g., physical/motor characteristics and limitations, sensory disorders, seizure disorders, lung and breathing control), (2) educational needs (e.g., appropriate handling and positioning techniques, methods of communication), (3) social/emotional needs (e.g., types of reinforcers that are effective, personal preferences, means of selecting items), (4) family and individual leisure preferences and activities that family members commonly engage in during their discretionary time, and (5) information regarding client resources (e.g., activities and materials that are available to the participant on a regular basis, and agencies and activities in the community that are used by the family) (Rynders & Schleien, 1991; Schleien et al., 1995; Wehman & Schleien, 1981). Specific needs assessment inventories available include the "Client Home Environment Checklist" (Wehman & Schleien, 1981), "Home Leisure Activities Survey" (Schleien et al., 1995), and the "Participant Interest Survey" (Schleien et al., 1995).

A second area of assessment could address the appropriateness and functionality of activities relative to the needs of the individual with regard to the principle of normalization. Functional skills are those that the person is frequently asked to demonstrate in daily life whether it be in the home, job site, or community. A nonfunctional skill is one that has a "low probability of being required by daily activities" (Brown et al., 1979). The age appropriateness of an activity is assessed by determining whether nondisabled same-age peers typically engage in that activity.

Voeltz and Wuerch (1981) developed a checklist (recently revised by Schleien et al., 1995) that allows for the systematic evaluation of activities "in relation to the person's characteristics and needs" (p. 27). Three elements make up the "Leisure Activity Selection Checklist." The first element, *lifestyle,* addresses concerns for socially appropriate or socially valid activities. Questions in this area focus on whether nondisabled peers would be interested in and engage in the activity, how many people could use this activity, and whether the activity is potentially lifelong in nature. The second element, *individualization,* addresses the adaptability of the activity as it relates to the participant's unique and ever-changing needs and preferences. The third of the checklist addresses *environmental aspects* of the activity, including availability, durability, safety, intrusiveness, and expense.

A third area to be addressed in a needs assessment inventory concerns an individual's level of proficiency when engaged in a particular activity. An environmental analysis inventory (Belmore & Brown, 1976; Certo, Schleien, & Hunter, 1983; Schleien & Ray, 1988) can be conducted to determine the specific components of the activity that the individual has already mastered and those requiring additional training. Certo, Schleien, and Hunter (1983) stated that this inventory is "a systematic method of conducting an observation of an event as it occurs in a natural setting under typical conditions" (p. 33). The environmental analysis inventory is helpful in developing instructional sequences and identifying their component tasks. In addition, it identifies the individual's proficiency relative to the recreation activity and highlights further instruction needs. The inventory could be instrumental in identifying appropriate instructional strategies as well as adaptations that enhance participation.

A fourth area of assessment could be the social inclusion of the individual, addressing the question, how welcome and how much a part of the group is he or she? There are two basic types of assessments that yield different types of social inclusion information. To understand how socially isolated or connected an individual is, a MAPS or Circle of Friends diagram may be constructed (see Figure 9.2). A social atom diagram documents relationships in a similar fashion, but is constructed slightly differently (see Figure 9.3). The MAPS and social atom diagrams identify all of the people and where they exist within an individual's social network at a particular time. These diagrams offer snapshots of an

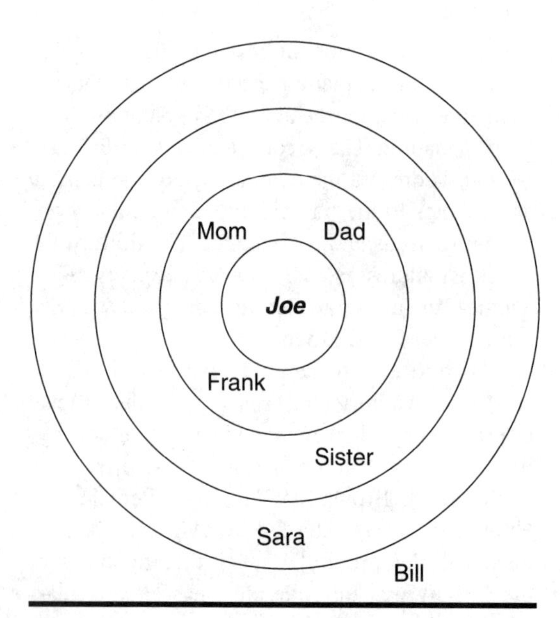

FIGURE 9.2 "Circle of Friends" Diagram

individual's social network that can be used for assessment and evaluative purposes.

A second type of social assessment is a sociometric assessment. This assessment documents all of the social relationships, both positive and negative, that exist within a group, at a particular time, as well as the existence of relationships that are defined by a social criterion (e.g., With whom would you choose to canoe?; Whom would you select to be your friend?). This is an assessment of the social environment; that is, the attitudes toward connectedness and friendship of the participants. It can help the therapeutic recreation specialist understand the cohesiveness of the group, whether or not there are isolated or rejected members, and the existence of cliques or subgroups.

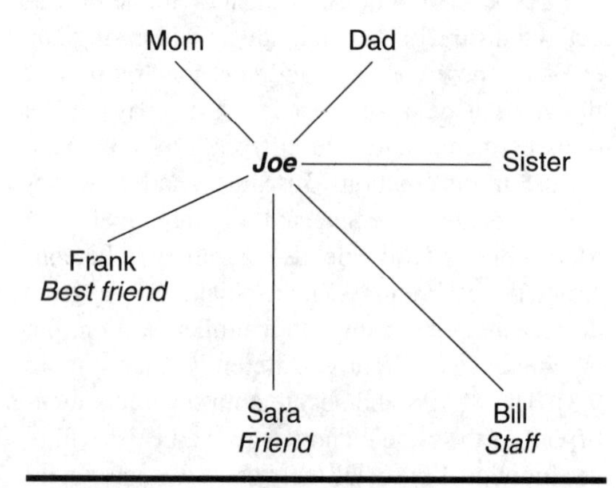

FIGURE 9.3 Social Atom Diagram

Skill Selection Guidelines/ Functional Curriculum

Following the initial needs assessment, the therapeutic recreation specialist must select the most important skills to be targeted for instruction. Most professionals agree that the leisure skills selected must be functional and chronologically age appropriate (Fardig, 1986).

As explained earlier, functional skills are those needed daily for routine tasks and are natural to an individual's environment. These skills help an individual function as independently as possible in typical settings. When developing a leisure skills curriculum, one can assess its worth or validity by determining the functionality of the curricular activities. For example, a nonfunctional skill could be the development of the participant's grasp and release skills by instructing the individual to push a medicine ball, an activity not commonly performed by peers without disabilities. A functional alternative could be to teach the individual to grasp and turn a doorknob to help him or her access other rooms and environments. It is essential to understand, however, that functional curricular materials themselves are insufficient if the skills are not chronologically age appropriate as well (Brown et al., 1979).

Collateral Skill Development/Infusion Chart

One of the principal outcomes of leisure skills instruction may be its contribution to collateral skill development. In addition to providing pleasurable activity and entertainment, participation in recreational activities could enhance development in social, emotional, psychological, communication, problem solving, motor, and other collateral skills because it allows for continued practice of newly acquired skills in positive and naturally occurring contexts. Vandercook (1991) reported that as persons with significant disabilities became more proficient in two recreational activities (i.e., pinball, bowling), their social repertoires became more sophisticated. A likely hypothesis for this phenomenon is that greater skill with the mechanics of a recreational activity allows individuals more freedom to expend greater efforts monitoring their social behavior. If social competencies can be improved "incidentally" within the context of age-appropriate recreational activities, valuable intervention time could be saved and social competencies could accrue within the context of activities in which they are expected to be expressed.

Although few empirical investigations supporting the development of skills in other curriculum areas through play by persons with severe multiple disabilities are conclusive or exist at all, these potential outcomes are compelling. For example, in a well-designed play setting, a child is able, and encouraged, to perceive himself or herself in positive ways. Research has shown that play experiences enable the child to perceive a more positive body image and self-image (Verhoven, Schleien, & Bender, 1982). As self-image is cultivated, social and personal security increases. Possibly for the first time in the individual's life he or she is perceiving himself or herself as more competent. This type of environment could provide a setting for accomplishment to balance the feelings of learned helplessness or inferiority, which many persons with severe multiple disabilities experience through repeated failure (Dattilo & Rusch, 1985; Seligman, 1975).

Other collateral skills that could be acquired within the context of a leisure program include increased communication and language skills (Bates & Renzaglia, 1982; Rogow, 1981), various social skills such as cooperation and relationship building (i.e., making friends), taking turns and sharing materials (Green & Schleien, 1991; Kibler, 1986; Schleien, Heyne, & Dattilo, 1995), and manipulation of materials and motor skills (Orelove & Sobsey, 1987; Sherrill, 1986; York & Rainforth, 1995). Other life domains could also be addressed during recreation activities. For example, if an individual with severe multiple disabilities was to participate in a horseshoe activity, he or she would need to learn about appropriate clothing (i.e., activity of daily living), necessary motor skills involved in grasping and pitching horseshoes (i.e., gross and fine motor skills), and a method of scoring and measuring (i.e., functional academics/math).

Acquisition of appropriate object manipulation skills has been linked with significant reductions in inappropriate behaviors (Favell, 1993). Similarly, as students with severe sensory impairments and cognitive impairments improved their physical fitness through a jogging program, a reduction of self-abusive and self-stimulatory behaviors has occurred (Alajajian, 1981).

Instructional Programming

Following the critical processes of assessment and skill selection, the therapeutic recreation specialist must decide on a systematic method of instructing the targeted leisure skills.

Task Analysis. Task analysis is frequently used when teaching leisure skills to persons with severe multiple disabilities. By depicting component steps of an activity that are easily teachable and observable, task analysis instruction has several advantages. First, it serves as an assessment tool that provides skill proficiency information. Second, a task analysis individualizes a program, allowing for adaptations to be made based on the learner's needs and abilities. Third, it provides a teaching sequence that can be used consistently by multiple trainers (Wehman & Schleien, 1980; 1981).

Schleien et al., (1981) taught a woman who was profoundly retarded three cooking skills (i.e., uses of an oven—boiling, baking, broiling) using a task analytic approach. Using a similar procedure, Storey, Bates, and Hanson (1984) taught coffee-purchasing skills across several community environments to adults with significant disabilities.

Shaping and Chaining. A task analysis approach is usually implemented through a variety of behavior-shaping and chaining procedures. Shaping consists of the instructor reinforcing approximations toward the desired or final behavior rather than reinforcing the final response itself. For example, the learner could purchase a snack from a vending machine by using extensions on the push buttons. This adaptation could gradually be reduced as the response becomes more accurate until the participant is manipulating standard size buttons on the vending machine. At this time, previously reinforced approximations are ignored. Chaining, on the other hand, involves the sequencing of the responses within the task. In a forward chain, the learner is initially instructed on the first step of the task analysis (i.e., locate vending machine) and then guided through the remainder of the steps. In a backward chain, instruction is initially provided on the final step in a response sequence (i.e., consume snack item) until that step is mastered. The remaining steps are then taught in reverse order, one at a time, always including the previous step in the instructional sequence. In this manner, the participant enjoys the naturally reinforcing consequences of the activity early on in the instructional process, which enhances the learning process.

Cue Hierarchy and Prompting System. Cues and prompts are intricate parts of instructional programs that attempt to elicit behaviors before they are mastered. Prompts (usually arranged in a hierarchy of least-to-most intrusive) are used to develop new behaviors or correct undesirable ones. Cues and prompts may include physical guidance, modeling appropriate behaviors, gestures, and verbal direction. They should be faded shortly after the learner masters a specific response so that dependency on the instructor does not become a problem. Fading requires the gradual removal of the guidance as the learner becomes more competent. A desirable outcome of instruction is to have the recreation materials become the natural or environmental cues that elicit appropriate and independent leisure behavior.

When comparing two different prompting procedures (i.e., antecedent and correction procedures), Day (1987) and McDonnell (1987) found that prompting strategies were more effective when delivered prior to (i.e., antecedent procedure) an erroneous response (similar to an "errorless learning" approach) rather than when they were presented following an incorrect response (i.e., correction procedure).

Prompting strategies have been major components of behavioral packages effective in teaching persons with severe multiple disabilities a variety of skills, including communication skills and leisure behaviors (Meehan, Mineo, & Lyon, 1985), coffee-purchasing skills in the community (Storey, Bates, & Hanson, 1984), and reciprocal social interactions between siblings with and without disabilities (James & Egel, 1986).

Reinforcement. A reinforcement component is usually included in leisure skill instructional procedures. Reinforcers are events that occur following a desired response, which increase the likelihood that the behavior will occur again. Individuals with severe multiple disabilities characteristically do not find many events reinforcing. Using effective reinforcers contingently and more frequently may be necessary to promote learning. Commonly used and effective reinforcers are learner specific and may include food items, praise, attention, switch-activated buzzers, vestibular reinforcers, and access to favorite recreational materials (Sandler & McClain, 1987). Reactive recreational materials such as Simon, pinball, video games, cameras, remote control vehicles, musical instruments, and vending machines that result in sensory feedback provide participants with natural reinforcers. Secondary reinforcers (i.e., those not necessarily associated with the activity) could also be effective when used contingently in a behavior-specific manner.

Adaptations/Modifications

Individuals with severe multiple disabilities often have difficulty exploring and manipulating their environments because of physical, cognitive, and/or sensory limitations. Oftentimes, selecting materials and activities that are reactive in nature (i.e., producing sound, motion, visual, tactile sensations) facilitates manipulation of recreational materials (Bambara et al., 1984; Wehman & Schleien, 1981). Therefore, it is an important task to identify materials and activities that are optimal for leisure instruction. In most instances, it is possible to adapt existing materials and activities (Dixon, 1981; Garner & Campbell, 1987) to increase participation and independence. Different methods of adapting materials and activities could include: (1) materials and equipment adaptations, (2) rules and procedural modifications, (3) skill sequence changes, (4) environmental modifications, and (5) lead-up activities. Refer to Wehman and Schleien (1981) for a detailed discussion of these adaptation methods.

Also, partial participation is a proposed way of assuring that persons with severe multiple disabilities will participate in activities that require skills beyond their abilities (Baumgart et al., 1982). Partial participation could be achieved when individuals are assisted by nondisabled peers, including volunteer advocates (Ray et al., 1986) and peer companions (Rynders & Schleien, 1991), and when cooperative grouping arrangements and cooperative learning activities (Rynders et al., 1980; Rynders et al., 1993) are implemented.

Maintenance and Generalization

A desired outcome of leisure skills instruction is for the newly acquired skills to remain part of the learner's repertoire over long periods of time following instruction. Also, it is important that the individual have the ability to transfer these skills across several environments, people, and materials.

Numerous researchers (Banks & Aveno, 1986; Crawford, 1986; Horner, Williams, & Knobbe, 1985; James & Egel, 1986; Schleien et al., 1981; Schleien, Certo, & Muccino, 1984; Sedlak, Doyle, & Schloss, 1982; Singh & Millichamp, 1987; Storey, Bates, & Hanson, 1984) have demonstrated that even though people with significant disabilities have difficulty maintaining and transferring skills, it is possible to promote maintenance and generalization by implementing particular instructional methods.

Performance repetition of the acquired skill affects skill maintenance. Horner, Williams, and Knobbe (1985) discovered that maintenance of a skill required at least two performance opportunities per month following acquisition training. Skills can be maintained when networking transpires between families/care providers, professionals, and key servicing agencies. As parents and residential staff assume more active roles in leisure skills instruction, there is greater likelihood that individuals will be provided with additional opportunities to practice and perform these skills in nontrained and inclusive community settings.

Another method of promoting skill generalization and maintenance is to use naturally occurring reinforcers during instruction. Reactive recreational materials and activities contain naturally occurring reinforcers that have the potential to promote and maintain independent leisure behavior.

A third method to enhance skill generalization and maintenance is to vary the conditions of skill performance. Coffee purchasing (Storey, Bates, & Hanson, 1984), bowling (Schleien, Certo, & Muccino, 1984), and cooking skills (Schleien et al., 1981) were instructed using task analyses and graduated prompting. The participants were offered opportunities to perform the acquired skills in multiple environments with less intrusive prompts as they became more proficient. This set of procedures resulted in successful generalization to nontrained environments. Lagomarcino et al. (1984) manipulated the training conditions by using multiple trainers. This strategy resulted in the participants learning to perform dance skills in the presence of many different individuals.

Environmental Interventions

There are two useful environmental intervention processes that can be used in leisure settings to enhance the social inclusion of participants. The first strategy, sociometry, is a group restructuring process (Moreno, 1984). The second strategy, "Circle of Friends" or MAPS, is an individual focused process (O'Brien et al., 1989).

Sociometry. The sociometric process identifies qualitative social dimensions within a given group of individuals. The social dimensions include group cohesiveness, the existence of subgroups or cliques, interpersonal attractions and rejections between members, and the social ranking of each group member by his or her peers. Beyond the study of group structure, this technique is valuable as a means to assess and promote the inclusion of individuals within a given group.

The sociometric process allows a recreation service provider to assess a group and identify isolated and excluded members. The facilitator can then restructure and reintegrate these individuals into the group by using an empowerment process. Each group member is empowered to restructure the group through the use of a social criterion. Social criteria are carefully constructed questions that request, confidentially, specific information concerning the individual's social relationships. This information can be used to alter grouping arrangements (e.g., seating arrangements, partner arrangements, teammates) to enhance the social dynamics of the group. Sociometric information is descriptive of the social structures within the group. However, it is not prescriptive as to how exactly a group should be restructured or how to intervene with an isolated or rejected individual. Furthermore, sociometric measurements are conducted to evaluate the inclusion of the originally isolated and excluded group members. The sociometric regrouping process should be ongoing throughout the life of the group to ensure the most positive group structure and to continue to empower members to enhance their own social experiences.

The following six rules for using the sociometric process were suggested by Moreno (1984) and Hare (1976): (1) the limits of the group in which the test is given should be indicated (describe who can be chosen); (2) there should be unlimited choices of other persons (select as many peers as appropriate); (3) individuals should be asked to choose and reject other group members with a specific criterion in mind (choose people based on criterion/question offered); (4) the results of the sociometric test should be used to restructure the group (group should be reorganized by placing people together who have chosen each other); (5) opinions should be given in private; and (6) questions should be phrased in a way that all members can understand.

An example of a sociogram is illustrated in Figure 9.4. This sociogram depicts a group of children participating in a scout troop. The recreation leader is undertaking the sociometric process in order to more fully understand the social dimensions within the group and to empower the scouts to select their campsite partners. Specific criteria used included "With whom would you like to set up a campsite?" and " With whom do you not want to set up camp?" The pool of individuals to select from included all of the scouts who registered for the trip. Each scout filled out a 3" × 5" card containing his or her responses to the questions, which were collected by the leader. (Adaptations to the sociometric process can be made, such as using pictures of fellow classmates, so that participants with sig-

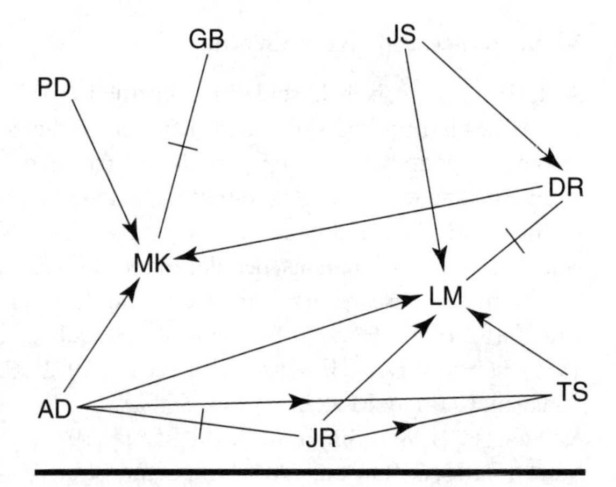

FIGURE 9.4 Original Scout Troop Social Structure

nificant disabilities or those with poor expressive language can also express their social choices [Hart, 1976].) The leader then proceeded to construct a sociogram using the initials of each scout and arrows to indicate direction of choices. Where two scouts selected each other, arrowheads were eliminated and a slash marked across the line. If a scout indicated that he or she did not wish to camp with a particular individual, a dashed line with an arrow recorded the rejection.

The sociogram in Figure 9.4 indicates that the scout troop had the following characteristics: (1) two "stars" existed, LM and MK; they were the most frequently chosen, with five and four members selecting them, respectively; (2) three "mutual attractions" existed between GB-MK, LM-DR, and AD-JR; (3) two "isolates" were present, PD and JS—they were not selected by the others; and (4) one member, TS, was rejected and not chosen.

To restructure this troop, the leader would begin by focusing on the rejected and isolated members, TS, PD, and JS. Since these individuals were the most vulnerable to being left out, the leader matched them with their first choices and away from those who rejected them. The remaining scouts were then placed. Other types of interventions may also be considered by the leader such as social and leisure skills instruction, to meet the needs of the isolates. A restructuring of the troop into two distinct groups that contain positive social relationship structures is illustrated in Figure 9.5.

The leader can check on the success of the new groupings by conducting informal interviews and by observing interactions between the scouts. Following the camping experience, the leader can evaluate this restructuring through observations, personal interviews, and by conducting follow-up sociometric measurements.

Circle of Friends. Sometimes an individual has great difficulty gaining access to a group, possibly because of the presence of a significant disability. In such a case, it may be useful to use the "Circle of Friends" intervention process. This strategy

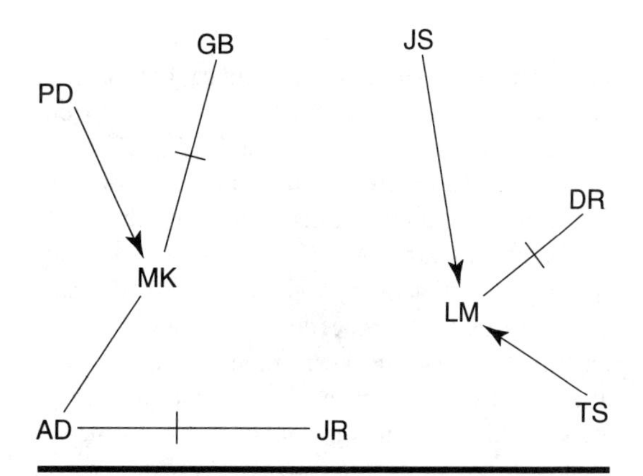

FIGURE 9.5 Scout Troop Restructured into the Campsite Groups

prepares a small group of peers or a "circle of friends" to assist the individual or focus person. The "circle of friends" group may be comprised of volunteer group members, friends, and other significant people in the individual's life (e.g., parents, siblings). These new and old friends are then empowered through intimate knowledge of the focus person to assist him or her to build friendships and participate in a recreation program. For example, a group leader can prepare a group of nondisabled peers for the inclusion of a person with a severe multiple disability by orchestrating a group discussion of the new member's dreams, goals, nightmares, likes, strengths/gifts/abilities, needs, and potential barriers.

By carefully directing the discussion, the leader could focus the group on the areas that can be capitalized on within the program such as the individual's goals, dreams, strengths/gifts/abilities. The leader could then focus the discussion on the perceived barriers to inclusion and assist the group to create solutions that could promote acceptance into the group. The "circle of friends," the focus person, and the group leader work together to create successful participation for all members.

Networking

It is necessary that persons with severe multiple disabilities have strong support systems if they are to learn and maintain leisure skills throughout their lifetimes. The interdisciplinary approach to programming has been successfully used in our educational system (Rainforth & York, 1987). We cannot afford to provide exemplary services to persons with significant disabilities in school settings, only to have them remain isolated in afterschool environments for a better part of the day. The instructional procedures discussed previously (e.g., careful assessment of needs and preferences, appropriate skill selection, use of behavioral procedures and adaptations during instruction) should be interwoven into the leisure support system network. Only when these practices are implemented carefully and systemwide across home, school, and community settings (Schleien & Meyer, 1988; Schleien & Ray, 1988; Wetherald & Peters, 1986) will it be possible for persons with severe multiple disabilities to experience meaningful, socially connected, and successful lives through expanded leisure and social repertoires and inclusive experiences.

APPLICATIONS OF THE TR PROCESS

Many innovative and effective practices to teach age-appropriate leisure skills to persons with severe multiple disabilities have been developed by therapeutic recreation specialists and special educators in the 1980s and 1990s (Nietupski, Hamre-Nietupski, & Ayres, 1984; Schleien et al., 1995; Schleien & Yermakoff, 1983). Few programs, however, have included individuals with severe multiple disabilities using an environmental perspective (e.g., programs involving family members and care providers in the selection of activities, incorporating programs into community activity). This is unfortunate because an environmental perspective considers skill development within the complete range of environments in which an individual functions (Certo, Schleien, & Hunter, 1983). An environmental analysis enables parents, teachers, and other professionals to develop functional, age-appropriate, leisure skills with instructional content. This approach, coupled with longitudinal planning, could increase opportunities for individuals with severe multiple disabilities to participate successfully in inclusive community leisure settings.

CASE STUDY #1: TEACHING AGE-APPROPRIATE LEISURE SKILLS IN THE SCHOOL AND COMMUNITY

Assessment

Meadowlake School was a K–6 elementary school with five of the classrooms devoted to special education. The school's special education students, ages 4 to 11 years, had disabilities ranging from mild mental retardation to severe mental retardation with multiple disabilities. Participants were two children with severe multiple disabilities and two same-age peers without disabilities.

Amy, a 5-year-old whose diagnosis was congenital cytomegalic virus inclusion (CMV) disease with microcephaly, was nonambulatory with very limited use of her left side. Amy used a wheelchair and could also roll on the floor for mobility purposes. Her score of 118 on the Bayley Scale of Infant Development (a ratio I.Q. score of 32) placed her in the severe to profound range of mental retardation. She showed high rates of inappropriate crying during activity transitions, particularly when events did not go her way (e.g., termination of free play to begin instruction on activities of daily living). Crying rarely occurred during highly motivating activities or when she received one-on-one attention by her teacher or mother. She communicated using informal methods such as pointing, touching, and moving her hands. Bobby, an 8-year-old whose diagnosis was a hypotonic form of cerebral palsy, crawled or scooted for mobility and was beginning to walk with assistance. He also functioned in the severe to profound range of retardation, which was determined through criterion-referenced behavioral observations (a standardized test score was not available for him). Bobby recognized people he had met and communicated with simple gestures such as pointing his finger or hand flailing. When this program began, Amy and Bobby were not participating in any age-appropriate leisure activities. Their nondisabled companions were selected from a second-grade class from the same school.

Program Goals

The goals of the program were to increase positive social interactions between students with severe multiple disabilities and their peers who were not disabled, and to allow students to acquire the skills needed to participate in age-appropriate recreational activities in their homes and community recreation centers. Three games including Toss Across; Flash, The Electronic Arcade Game; and Simon were selected for leisure skill instruction. The rationale for the selection of these games included the following concerns: (a) age appropriate—played by nondisabled peers of the same chronological age; (b) functional—can be played in homes, schools, parks, and other environments; (c) social—encouraged social interaction by allowing two or more players to participate in the activity simultaneously; (d) motor—required motor skills that were written into the students' Individual Education Plans (IEPs) (e.g., use of the upper extremities for grasping and releasing, gross motor movements of throwing, tossing, and reaching); (e) reactive—responded to players' manipulations with sensory reinforcement (e.g., visual and auditory stimulation); and, (f) family "friendly"—family members expressed interest in their children's participating in the selected activities.

Intervention

The leisure educators received training in the use of instructional techniques and contingent reinforcement strategies and provided each dyad with instruction during a one-hour time period, two days per week. The companions participated in leisure skills instruction alongside their peers with severe multiple disabilities during only one of these sessions each week. Each leisure skill was task analyzed, and instruction was provided using an assistance hierarchy (i.e., least-to-most intrusive) or error correction procedure as follows: The task was presented with the initial cue (i.e., "Let's play Toss Across."). A correct response was rewarded with behavior-specific positive feedback (BSPF). An error response or no response within five seconds was followed by a verbal cue from the instructor (e.g., "Amy, pick up the bean bag."). If a correct response occurred, it was rewarded with BSPF. An error response or no response within five seconds was followed by the instructor's repeating of the verbal cue and modeling the correct response (i.e., picking up the bean bag). If the modeling did not evoke the correct response, the instructor repeated the verbal cue while physically guiding the learner through the activity and providing BSPF.

Home Training. The children with severe multiple disabilities received additional training on the leisure skills by their parents, at home, once each week to facilitate generalization to the natural environment and skill maintenance. Initially, parents were familiarized with the three leisure activities. During the first home session, the instructors demonstrated the use of the task analysis and the error correction procedure, and also trained the parents in the use of BSPF. For the remaining five home sessions, parents provided instruction to their children with the instructors present but not interactive.

Community Recreation/Generalization. One generalization probe on all three leisure activities was conducted at a neighborhood recreation center for each participant. To accomplish this, the instructors met the parents and participants at the recreation center. The nondisabled companions attended the session and participated in all activities. At these sessions, a parent was instructed to give a general verbal cue to the participants and a maintenance probe was conducted.

Evaluation

Ongoing evaluation revealed low and stable baseline performances on each leisure skill with the exception of Amy's performance on Flash, The Electronic Arcade Game, which showed a slight increase in performance. In the baseline session immediately preceding the intervention phase of the program, Bobby demonstrated independent performance in 2 (10 percent) of the task-analytic steps of Toss Across, 2 (7 percent) of the steps of Flash, The Electronic Arcade Game, and 0 (0 percent) of the steps of Simon. His overall mean baseline performance on the three leisure skills were 17 percent, 9 percent, and 0 percent, respectively. Amy performed independently in 4 (20 percent) of the task-analytic steps of Toss Across, 5 (18.5 percent) of the steps of Flash, The Electronic Arcade Game, and 0 (0 percent) of the steps of Simon during the final baseline session. Her overall mean baseline performance on the same three leisure skills were 15 percent, 14 percent, and 0 percent, respectively.

During nonreinforced baseline probes, generalization from one leisure setting to another was apparent but minimal (i.e., school, to home, to recreation center). The ability to transfer instruction minimally to other environments was especially noticeable when the leisure skills were introduced into the neighborhood center. Bobby returned to baseline levels of performance following the introduction of the activity to a new environment except for Flash, The Electronic Arcade Game, where he improved slightly. Amy's rate of independent leisure skill performance also decreased in the new environments, with the exception of Flash, The Electronic Arcade Game. Both learners increased in their levels of independent performance following instruction on the activities in the new leisure environments. Both Bobby and Amy displayed minimal improvement in the third leisure skill, Simon, due possibly to the fact that the students received only five to six instructional sessions on how to play Simon in school because of the extended baseline and the termination of the school year. Moreover, it is possible that Simon was a more complex task relative to the other activities, necessitating more sophisticated motor and cognitive skills.

Prior to the implementation of the companions training program, Bobby received at least one social initiation from his companion, on the average, during 20 percent of the recording intervals. He did not respond to any of his companion's initiations. Following the companions training program, Bobby's companion initiated at least one social interaction on the average of 67 percent of the intervals observed on a daily basis. During intervention, Bobby responded to his companion's initiations on the average of 26 percent of the intervals. Amy received at least one social interaction from her companion, on the average, during 30 percent of the intervals, prior to the implementation of the companions training program. She responded to her companion's initiations 67 percent of the time. Following companions training, Amy's companion initiated social interactions toward her during an average of 80 percent of the intervals. Amy responded to the initiated social interactions on the average of 76 percent of the time.

Both children with severe multiple disabilities gained enough skill to participate "independently" in two of the three targeted leisure skills. The use of task analysis and other behavioral methods, including BSFP, contingent reinforcement for positive social interactions, and parent/home training within an inclusive leisure setting, were effective in developing their play repertoires and, to some extent, their social skills. The participants' minimal abilities to generalize the newly acquired leisure skills to the home and neighborhood recreation center support the findings of existing generalization research that has identified lack of transfer of training to nontrained environments as a problem (Crawford, 1986; Horner, Albin, & Ralph, 1986; Horner, Williams, & Knobbe, 1985; Stokes & Baer, 1977). Only after systematic instruction was provided by parents in the home setting (which Stokes and Baer refer to as "Train Sufficient Exemplars") did Bobby and Amy perform in the leisure activities at acceptable rates (i.e., 75 percent proficiency). In fact, following every training session at home on Toss Across and Flash, The Electronic Arcade Game, Bobby and Amy improved their leisure skill performance in school. These data support Horner, Williams, and Knobbe's (1985) findings concerning the "opportunity to perform," implying that newly acquired skills will be maintained in natural performance settings only if there are additional opportunities to practice the skills following acquisition. Thus, the willingness of parents and other care providers to follow through on school-based leisure education programs appears to be critical. The care provider/leisure skill instructor partnership is vital to the maintenance of leisure activity repertoires in persons with severe multiple disabilities.

The social interaction and appropriate play results support the inclusion of children with severe multiple disabilities and same-age peers without disabilities. Both participants demonstrated improvements in these behaviors from baseline to intervention. A fairly steady increase in the receiving of social interactions by the participants with disabilities from their companions and their subsequent responding to these initiations was found. These increases in social contacts may have been due to several factors, including increased level of mastery of the play skills, BSPF provided for their socializing appropriately, companions training, increases in cooperative play exhibited by the children with severe multiple disabilities, and familiarity between participants.

CASE STUDY #2: SOCIAL INCLUSION AT SUMMER CAMP

Assessment

Jamie was an 11-year-old student in a self-contained, segregated classroom serving children with severe multiple disabilities. He was profoundly mentally retarded, and was diagnosed with cerebral palsy, microcephaly, and low-vision impairment. Jamie's mother was engaged in preparations to integrate him into his neighborhood middle school. His mother's greatest fear was that Jamie did not know any of the other children who attended the local school. She believed that social isolation and rejection by the regular education students would become Jamie's reality. She believed that the path to success in his inclusion at school was to help him build relationships before the school year began. To assess Jamie's current relationships and friendships, his mother and the CTRS constructed a "Circle of Friends" diagram (see Figure 9.6).

In this figure, each circle represents a different type of relationship. The first circle around Jamie represents his very best friends (i.e., the people with whom he shares his most intimate secrets and with whom he spends the most time). The second circle represents his best friends (i.e., the people who he really likes and with whom he spends a significant amount of time, but not as much as those in his inner-most circle). The third circle represents Jamie's recreational friends and extended family who live out of town (i.e., the people with whom he does things periodically). The outer circle represents the professionals who are paid to be in Jamie's life, such as doctors, teachers, integration facilitator (CTRS), and others who have a defined role to perform on behalf of Jamie (O'Brien et al., 1989).

Program Goals

Only two same-age peers appear on Jamie's initial "June" diagram. One peer, on his third circle, is a girl who lives three blocks away and visits Jamie periodically. Jamie does not see her outside of these visits. The second peer represents the rotating "special friends" children who help and teach in the special education classroom. These peers have a transient and defined role within Jamie's life, and thus, have been placed in his fourth circle. This diagramming procedure documented Jamie's need to build friendships and other relationships with his peers. This became the focus of Jamie's therapeutic recreation program during the summer months.

Intervention

To offer Jamie and his neighborhood peers an opportunity to get to know one another, two long-term

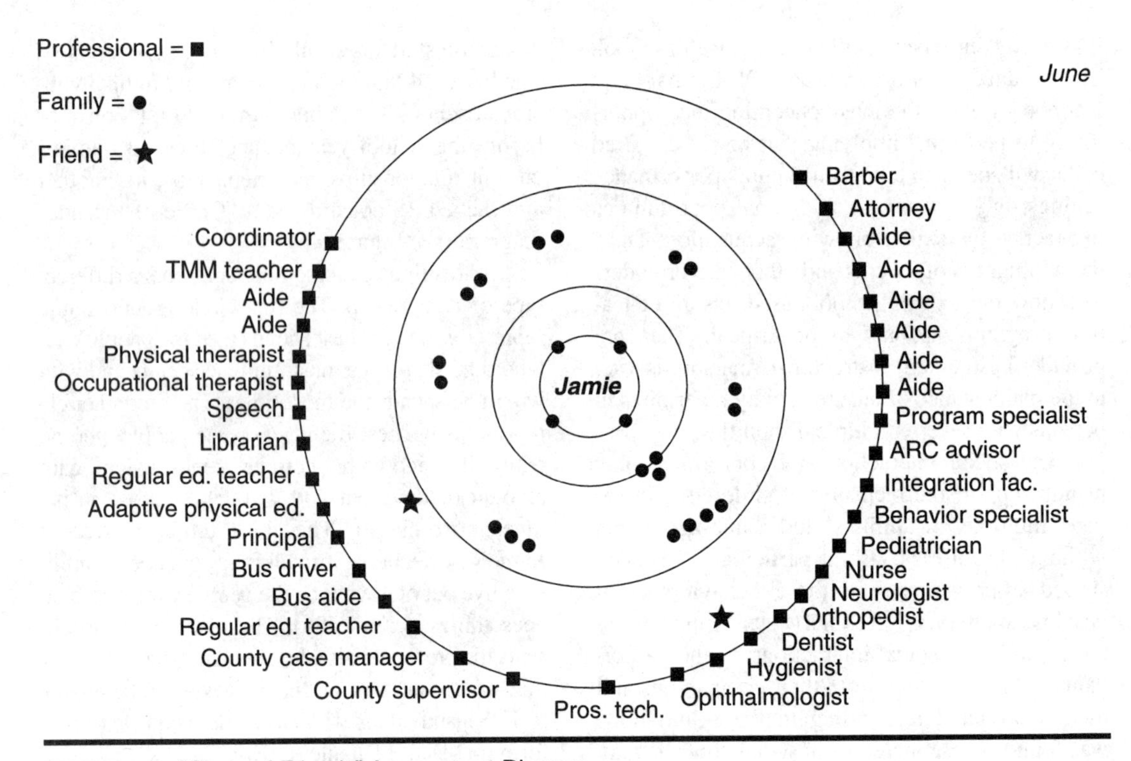

FIGURE 9.6 "Circle of Friends" Assessment Diagram

social/recreational programs were selected for Jamie's inclusive participation. The two programs included a supervised eight-week playground program at a neighborhood park and a two-week day camp program. Careful planning, communication, and support building were undertaken by Jamie's parents, the Integration Facilitator (CTRS), aides, park and recreation supervisors, and site personnel prior to the program's commencement. Formal and informal environmental assessments, preference assessments, and leisure skill inventories (Schleien & Ray, 1988) were completed and staff training was performed.

The second phase of the "Circle of Friends" process was to involve the playground participants in the process of integrating Jamie into the program. Jamie was introduced by the CTRS as an 11-year-old boy who lived in the neighborhood and would be attending fifth grade at the local middle school in the fall, and who wished to participate in the program. A photo album was shared to give the children an opportunity to see the activities that Jamie and his family enjoy.

The CTRS and the recreation staff were apprehensive that the summer program might not be a success for everyone. The nondisabled participants were asked why they thought that the adults were uneasy about Jamie joining the program. The children responded with, "We may tease or ignore Jamie." Then, they were asked, "What are the things we want you to do to make this program a success?" and the children responded, "We can say hello, invite Jamie to play, talk with him, and show him how to play the games." The CTRS followed this introduction with question and discussion areas (i.e., Jamie's dreams, nightmares, likes, strengths, needs) that the "Circle of Friends" process identifies. The responses that Jamie's parents and siblings provided previously were shared with the other children at this time. This discussion empowered the participants to contribute to Jamie's success.

Within the program, the aide that assisted Jamie was identified as being responsible for his personal needs (i.e., toileting, feeding, mobility) and for attempting to facilitate interactions between Jamie and his peers. The CTRS sharpened the general friendship skills (e.g., "friends take turns, smile at each other, stay close when playing together") of the peers without disabilities, and presented a short social skills program. For example, the peers learned when and how to model and/or physically guide a response when Jamie indicated that he did not know what to do. They also learned basic sign language that Jamie often used (e.g., play, friend).

Throughout the summer, program leaders encouraged and empowered the children to make suggestions and adaptations, and to create new games or ways that Jamie could participate successfully. By the end of the summer, it was the consensus of the staff and Jamie's aide that his peers had invented many creative ways to include Jamie and make it fun for everyone. The children outperformed the adult leaders in identifying solutions to potential program barriers.

Evaluation

To evaluate Jamie's goals of inclusion and friendship development, another "Circle of Friends" diagram was constructed with the help of playground staff, Jamie's aide, and the other children. The children were asked, "If you feel that you are a friend of Jamie's, please place your name on the chart as close to him as you feel." This second diagram, appearing in Figure 9.7, suggests that the summer program was a huge success for everyone, including Jamie.

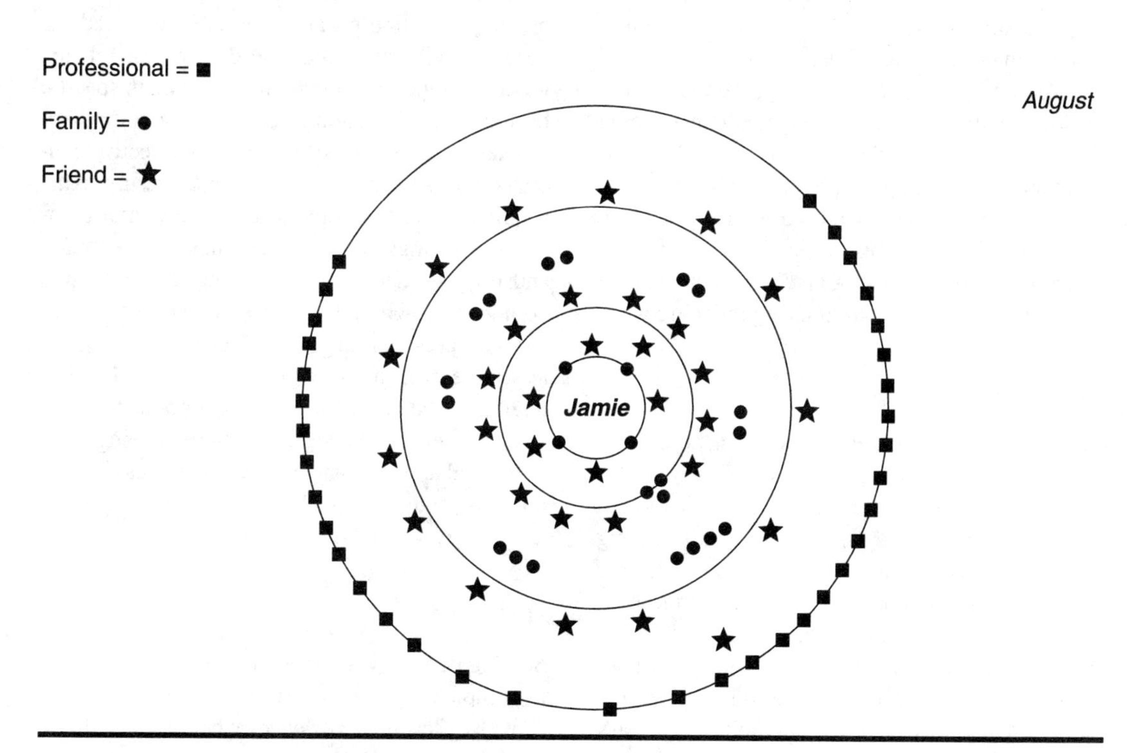

FIGURE 9.7 "Circle of Friends" Evaluation Diagram

Stories of social inclusion continued for Jamie. In the fall, he was welcomed by his playground friends at his neighborhood school where another "Circle of Friends" was developed to assist in his school inclusion. The following summer, he played daily with a friend who lived down the street. Jamie was often invited to her home for snacks and play time. Jamie enrolled in the day camp program for a second consecutive summer. When the CTRS introduced Jamie on the first day of day camp, ten of the eighteen campers listed Jamie on their "Circle of Friends" diagrams, before the program commenced.

Sociometry and "Circle of Friends" techniques are examples of environmental strategies that can be used in leisure environments. The intent of these techniques is to affect the targeted individual's environment in order to make it more inclusive, accessible, and conducive to socialization and friendship development. For Jamie, his peers were prepared to meet, play, and socialize with him, and the program was structured to promote maximum positive interactions and friendships.

As Jamie's parents can verify, the facilitation of social networks and friendships can become the most significant roles of the CTRS. The combination of program goals, including learning appropriate leisure and social skills and preparing nondisabled participants for inclusive activities, made it possible for Jamie and his peers to share leisure experiences in a mutually gratifying way.

TRENDS AND ISSUES

The current trends in the provision of therapeutic recreation services for persons with severe multiple disabilities reflect a growing sophistication in both philosophy and approach. Chief among these trends is the provision of specific leisure skill instruction in home, school, and community environments on an individualized basis. Related to this programming approach is the use of increasingly sophisticated behavioral engineering strategies and instructional methods (e.g., task analysis, shaping and chaining, cue hierarchy and prompting systems) to facilitate leisure skill acquisition. Additionally, the use of the recreational experience to help facilitate collateral skills development (particularly in the areas of communication and language) and social inclusion signals a new interdisciplinary era of cooperation and accommodative services.

Along with these trends, however, remain several issues that pose significant challenges to therapeutic recreation service delivery. Clearly, a coordinated interdisciplinary effort is needed to resolve the use of multiple definitions in identifying and describing these individuals. The current conceptual hodgepodge of definitions (some based on type of service received and some on functional characteristics of the person) is too unwieldy and confusing to be useful in planning interdisciplinary interventions and in networking services across agencies. Community resource issues are also a consideration. Therapeutic recreation specialists must particularly deal with the substantial gap that exists between what is available in inclusive community recreation programs and the real needs of persons with severe multiple disabilities. Finally, within therapeutic recreation there remain specific leisure skill instruction issues. Chief among these problem areas is the development of effective generalization strategies for transfer of leisure skills acquired in instructional settings to natural community settings. Perhaps the most conceptually and programmatically challenging, however, will be how to teach and then accommodate the concept of personal preference and choice in the leisure experiences of these individuals. The dilemma faced in identifying and/or honoring personal preference in leisure versus allowing nonfunctional and age-inappropriate activities to occur presents both technical and philosophical challenges that will not be resolved easily.

SUMMARY

Serving persons with severe multiple disabilities is a complex, intense, and often extensive task. Providing leisure experiences where these individuals are active and participating members is a challenge directly related to the therapeutic recreation specialist's ability to provide leisure knowledge to the participant, prepare "user-friendly" environments, and establish inclusive leisure opportunities.

To be an active participant capable of choosing age-appropriate leisure activities, persons with severe multiple disabilities must be provided with a knowledge base that enables them to establish leisure repertoires. Systematic behavioral methods must be implemented to facilitate independent leisure behavior that includes skills that are both functional and age appropriate. These skills should also promote participation in lifelong leisure activities, and of most importance, generalization to and social inclusion in the larger community of citizens.

An individual with severe multiple disabilities—knowledgeable and capable of making his or her own leisure choices—must have access to environments that encourage participation. To establish such user-friendly environments requires preparation of physical and human components. This preparation requires the creation or modification of sites with access to all citizens. Materials designed to assist with the adaptation of activities must be created and field-tested. Therapeutic recreation specialists must be provided with usable curricular materials designed specifically for this population. Leaders prepared to service persons with severe multiple disabilities must be educated to their needs and characteristics. These needs include participation in already existing programs and ongoing interaction with nondisabled peers. Peers without disabilities, too, should be educated so that they can appreciate and understand the nature of a person's disabilities and eliminate the barriers that ignorance often creates.

When the person with a severe multiple disability is capable of making personal leisure choices and is provided with environments in which to exercise personal choice, an effective social inclusion process can commence. Through inclusive community programs, the individual can exercise his or her basic human right for meaningful participation in recreation activities. It is then that we all can begin to realize the goals of the recreation experience, including socialization, friendship, play, and fun.

READING COMPREHENSION QUESTIONS

1. Briefly explain the definition problem in regard to individuals with severe multiple disabilities.
2. Describe the idea of skill deficit as it pertains to persons with severe multiple disabilities. Why is this an important issue to the therapeutic recreation specialist?
3. Describe why choice making and self-initiation skills are important components of an individual's leisure repertoire to both individuals with and without disabilities. Why are these skills of critical concern in programming for persons with severe multiple disabilities?
4. Identify at least five goals of a therapeutic recreation program for persons with severe multiple disabilities.
5. Why is a needs assessment important, and what types of information should be solicited during the assessment?
6. What are the factors that should be considered when a therapeutic recreation specialist selects skills to be taught to a person with a severe multiple disability?
7. Describe the concept of task analysis and the benefits for using it.
8. What are the collateral skills (i.e., leisure-related support skills) necessary for playing a typical board game?
9. Why is networking a vital component to the maintenance and generalization of leisure skills for the individual with a severe multiple disability?
10. Identify and describe what are, in your opinion, the three most important issues facing the therapeutic recreation specialist in regard to programming for persons with severe multiple disabilities.
11. Identify and describe your own personal definition of social inclusion. How do you know when you are socially included or excluded from a group?
12. Identify and describe two social inclusion intervention methods. What are the differences between them, and how do you choose which one to use?

SUGGESTED LEARNING ACTIVITIES

1. As the therapeutic recreation specialist for a child who is severely mentally retarded and severely visually impaired, generate a list of possible ways to modify materials and environments to promote independent leisure participation.
2. As a therapeutic recreation specialist, you want to include a child with autism and severe behavioral problems into a community recreation program. You arrange a meeting with the center director. The director listens carefully to your suggestion but finally rejects your idea, arguing that the center's programs are not designed to serve children with autism. The director suggests that you take your idea to a recreation center designed specifically for this special population. Outline and justify the steps you would take to gain access to this program for this child.
3. Select a board game and develop a task analysis that could be used for a leisure skills program with an individual who is severely multiply disabled.
4. In a group, role-play the people involved and types of interventions that should transpire in assuring the generalization and maintenance of horseshoes as a leisure activity for an adult with cerebral palsy and severe mental retardation.
5. A major manufacturer of toys and games contacts you for ideas on developing play materials designed specifically for individuals with severe multiple disabilities. Give reasons for supporting or rejecting this company's endeavor. Write a letter to the company stating your position and rationale.
6. Make your own "Circle of Friends" diagram. Ask yourself the following questions: Would I like to have more friends on my first, second, third circles? Are there friends on my list with whom I have lost track? Do I want to reconnect with them? Are there people on my list with whom I would like to strengthen my friendships, and how would I go about doing that?

REFERENCES

Abery, B. H., et al. (1989, December). *A descriptive study of the social networks of youth and young adults with developmental disabilities.* Paper presented at the annual meeting of The Association for Persons with Severe Handicaps, San Francisco, CA.

Abery, B. H., et al. (1990, May). *The social networks of adults with developmental disabilities residing in community settings.* Paper presented at the annual meeting of the American Association on Mental Retardation, Washington, DC.

Adkins, J., & Matson, L. (1980). Teaching institutionalized mentally retarded adults socially appropriate leisure skills. *Mental Retardation, 18,* 249–252.

Alajajian, L. (1981). Jogging program for deaf-blind students improves condition and reduces self-stimulation. *News . . . about Deaf-Blind Students, Programmed Services in New England, 6*(1), 3–4.

Bambara, L., et al. (1984). A comparison of reactive and non-reactive toys on severely handicapped children's manipulative play. *Journal of the Association for Persons with Severe Handicaps, 9*(2), 142–149.

Banks, R., & Aveno, A. (1986). Adapted miniature golf: A community leisure program for students with severe physical disabilities. *Journal of the Association for Persons with Severe Handicaps, 11,* 209–215.

Barrett, S. (1987). Trends and issues in developing community living programs for young adults who are deaf-blind and profoundly handicapped. In A. Covert & H. Fredericks (Eds.), *Transition for persons with deaf-blindness and other profound handicaps: State of the art* (pp. 39–49). Monmouth, OR: Teaching Research.

Bates, P., & Renzaglia, A. (1982). Language instruction with a profoundly retarded adolescent: The use of a table game in the acquisition of verbal labeling skills. *Education and Treatment of Children, 5*(1), 13–22.

Baumgart, D., et al. (1982). Principle of partial participation and individualized adaptations in educational programs for severely handicapped students. *Journal of the Association for the Severely Handicapped, 7,* 17–27.

Bellamy, T. (1985). Severe disability in adulthood. *The Association for Persons with Severe Handicaps Newsletter, 1,* 6.

Belmore, K., & Brown, L. (1976). A job skill inventory strategy for use in a public school vocational training program for severely handicapped potential workers. In L. Brown, N. Certo, K. Belmore, & T. Crowner (Eds.), *Papers and programs related to public school services for secondary age severely handicapped students. Vol. VI, Part 1.* Madison, WI: Madison Metro School District. (Revised and republished: N. Haring, & D. Bricker (Eds.). (1977). *Teaching the severely handicapped Vol. III,* Columbus, OH: Special Press.)

Bercovici, S. M. (1981). Qualitative methods in cultural perspectives in the study of deinstitutionalization. In R. H. Bruininks et al. (Eds.), *Deinstitutionalization and community adjustment of mentally retarded people* (Monograph #4, pp. 133–144). Washington, DC: American Association on Mental Deficiency.

Bercovici, S. M. (1983). *Barriers to normalization: The restrictive management of retarded persons.* Baltimore: University Park Press.

Birenbaum, A., & Re, M. (1979). Resettling mentally retarded adults in the community—almost four years later. *American Journal of Mental Deficiency, 83,* 323–329.

Bogdan, R., & Taylor, S. J. (1987). The next wave. In S. J. Taylor, D. Biklen, and J. Knoll (Eds.). *Community integration for people with severe disabilities.* New York: Teachers College Press.

Brown, L., et al. (1979). A strategy for developing chronological age appropriate and functional curricular content for severely handicapped adolescents and young adults. *Journal of Special Education, 13*(1), 81–90.

Bruininks, R. H., Thurlow, M. L., & Lange, C. (1987). *Outcomes for students with moderate–severe handicaps in an urban school district.* Minneapolis: University of Minnesota, University Affiliated Program.

Bruininks, R. H., Thurlow, M., & Steffans, K. (1988). *Follow-up of students after schooling and suburban special education district: Outcomes for people with moderate to severe handicaps.* Minneapolis: University of Minnesota, Institute on Community Integration.

Certo, N., Schleien, S., & Hunter, D. (1983). An ecological assessment inventory to facilitate community recreation participation by severely disabled individuals. *Therapeutic Recreation Journal, 17*(3), 29–38.

Cheseldine, S., & Jeffree, D. (1981). Mentally handicapped adolescents: Their use of leisure. *Journal of Mental Deficiency Research, 25,* 49–59.

Covert, A. (1987). Summary, conclusions, recommendations and implications of the conference: Purpose and format. In A. Covert and H. Fredericks (Eds.), *Transition for persons with deaf-blindness and other profound handicaps: State of the art* (pp. 147–157). Monmouth, OR: Teaching Research.

Crapps, J. M., & Stoneman, Z. (1989). Friendship patterns and community integration of family care residents. *Research in Development Disabilities, 10,* 153–169.

Crapps, J., Langione, J., & Swaim, S. (1985). Quantity and quality of participation in community environments by mentally retarded adults. *Education and Training of the Mentally Retarded, 20,* 123–129.

Crawford, M. (1986). Development and generalization of lifetime leisure skills for multi-handicapped participants. *Therapeutic Recreation Journal, 20*(4), 48–60.

Crawford, M., Griffen, N., & Mendell R. (1978). The assessment process in recreation with severely and profoundly retarded populations. *Practical Pointers, 2*(1), 1–9.

Dattilo, J., & Barnett, L. (1985). Therapeutic recreation for individuals with severe handicaps: An analysis of the relationship between choice and pleasure. *Therapeutic Recreation Journal, 19*(3), 79–91.

Dattilo, J., & Mirenda, P. (1987). An application of a leisure preference assessment protocol for persons with severe handicaps. *Journal of the Association for Persons with Severe Handicaps, 12,* 306–311.

Dattilo, J., & O'Keefe, B. M. (1992). Setting the stage for leisure: Encouraging adults with mental retardation who use augmentative and alternative communication systems to share conversations. *Therapeutic Recreation Journal, 26*(1), 27–37.

Dattilo, J., & Rusch, F. (1985). Effects of choice on leisure participation for persons with severe handicaps. *Journal of the Association for Persons with Severe Handicaps, 10,* 194–199.

Day, H. (1987). Comparison of two prompting procedures to facilitate skill acquisition among severely mentally retarded adolescents. *American Journal of Mental Deficiency, 91,* 366–372.

Dixon, J. (1981). *Adapting activities for therapeutic recreation services: Concepts and applications.* San Diego: Campanile.

Donegan, C. & Potts, M. (1988). People with mental handicap living alone in the community: A pilot study of their quality of life. *British Journal of Mental Subnormality, 34,* 10–22.

Fardig, D. (1986). Informal assessment for the severely mentally handicapped, Sec. II: Special issues. *Pointer, 30*(2), 47–49.

Favell, J. (1973). Reduction of stereotypes by reinforcement of toy play. *Mental Retardation, 11*(4), 21–23.

Ford, A., et al. (1984). Strategies for developing individualized recreation and leisure programs for severely handicapped students. In N. Certo, N. Haring, and R. York (Eds.), *Public school integration of severely handicapped students: Rational issues and progressive alternatives* (pp. 245–275). Baltimore: Paul H. Brookes.

Fredericks, H. (1987). Those with profound handicaps: Who are they? How can they be served? In A. Covert & H. Fredericks (Eds.), *Transition for persons with deaf-blindness and other profound handicaps: State of the art* (pp. 3–9). Monmouth, OR: Teaching Research.

Fredericks, H., & Baldwin, V. (1987). Individuals with sensory impairments. In L. Goetz, D. Guess, and K. Stremel-Campbell (Eds.), *Innovative program design for individuals with dual sensory impairments* (pp. 3–12). Baltimore: Paul H. Brookes.

Garner, J., & Campbell, P. (1987). Technology for persons with severe disabilities: Practical and ethical considerations. *The Journal of Special Education, 21*(3), 122–132.

Goetz, L. (1987). Recreation and leisure: Practices in educational programs which hold promise for adult service models. In A. Covert and H. Fredericks (Eds.), *Transition for persons with deaf-blindness and other profound handicaps: State of the art* (pp. 119–130). Monmouth, OR: Teaching Research.

Gollay, E. (1981). Some conceptual and methodological issues in studying community adjustment of deinstitutionalized retarded people. In R. Bruininks, et al. (Eds.), *Deinstitutionalization and community adjustment of mentally retarded people* (pp. 89–106). Washington, DC: American Association on Mental Deficiency.

Green, F., & Schleien, S. (1991). Understanding friendship and recreation: A theoretical sampling. *Therapeutic Recreation Journal, 25*(4), 29–40.

Hare, A. (1976). *Handbook of small group research* (2nd ed.). New York: The Free Press/Macmillan.

Hart, J. W. (1976). Identifying ways of distinguishing "choice activity" from "closure movements" when administering pictorial sociometric techniques to the mentally retarded. *Group Psychotherapy, Psychodrama, and Sociometry, 29,* 121–126.

Hauber, F., et al. (1984). National census of residential facilities: A 1982 profile of facilities and residents. *American Journal of Mental Deficiency, 89,* 236–245.

Hayden, M., et al. (1992). Social and leisure integration of people with mental retardation in foster homes and small group homes. *Education and Training in Mental Retardation, 27,* 187–199.

Hill, B., Lakin, K., & Bruininks, R. (1984). Trends in residential services for people who are mentally retarded: 1972–1982. *Journal of the Association for Persons with Severe Handicaps, 9,* 243–250.

Hill, B. K., et al. (1989). *Living in the community: A comparative study of foster homes and small group homes for people with mental retardation (Report No. 29).* Minneapolis: University of Minnesota, Center for Residential and Community Services.

Hill, B., Rotegard, L. L., & Bruininks, R. (1984). The quality of life of mentally retarded people in residential care. *Social Work, 29*(3), 275–281.

Hill, J., Wehman, P., & Horst, G. (1982). Toward generalization of appropriate leisure and social behavior in severely handicapped youth: Pinball machine use. *Journal of the Association for the Severely Handicapped, 6*(4), 38–44.

Horner, R., Albin, R., & Ralph, G. (1986). Generalization with precision: The role of negative teaching examples in the instruction of generalized grocery item selection. *Journal of the Association for Persons with Severe Handicaps, 11,* 300–308.

Horner, R., Williams, J., & Knobbe, C. (1985). The effect of "opportunity to perform" on the maintenance of skills learned by high school students with severe handicaps. *Journal of the Association for Persons with Severe Handicaps, 10,* 172–175.

Horst, G., et al. (1980). Developing chronologically age-appropriate leisure skills in severely multihandicapped adolescents: Three case studies. In P. Wehman and J. Hill (Eds.), *Instructional programming for severely handicapped youth: A community integration approach* (pp. 84–100). Richmond, VA: School of Education, Virginia Commonwealth University.

Intagliata, J., Willer, B., & Wicks, G. (1981). Factors related to the quality of community adjustment in family care homes. In R. Bruininks et al.,

(Eds.), *Deinstitutionalized and community adjustment of mentally retarded people* (pp. 217–230). Washington, DC: American Association on Mental Deficiency.

James, S., & Egel, A. (1986). A direct prompting strategy for increasing reciprocal interactions between handicapped and nonhandicapped siblings. *Journal of Applied Behavior Analysis, 19,* 173–186.

Kennedy, C. H., Horner, R. H., & Newton, C. (1989). Social contacts of adults with severe disabilities living in the community: A descriptive analysis of relationship patterns. *Journal of the Association for Persons with Severe Handicaps, 14*(3), 190–196.

Kibler, C. (1986). Board games for multihandicapped players. *Perspectives for Teachers of the Hearing Impaired, 4*(4), 21–23.

Lagomarcino, A., et al. (1984). Leisure-dance instruction for severely and profoundly retarded persons: Teaching an intermediate community-living skill. *Journal of Applied Behavior Analysis, 17,* 71–84.

Lakin, K. C., et al. (1992). *An independent assessment of Minnesota's home and community based services waiver program.* (Project Report #37). Minneapolis, MN: Center for Residential Services and Community Living.

Matthews, P. (1982). Why the mentally retarded do not participate in certain types of recreational activities. *Therapeutic Recreation Journal, 14*(1), 44–50.

McDonnell, J. (1987). The effects of time delay and increasing prompt hierarchy strategies on the acquisition of purchasing skills by students with severe handicaps. *Journal of the Association for Persons with Severe Handicaps, 12,* 227–236.

Meehan, D., Mineo, B., & Lyon, S. (1985). Use of systematic prompting and prompt withdrawal to establish and maintain switch activation in a severely handicapped student. *Journal of Special Education Technology, 7*(1), 5–11.

Meyer, L. H., et al. (1985). Monitoring the collateral effects of leisure skill instruction: A case study in multiple-baseline methodology. *Behavior Research and Therapy, 23,* 127–138.

Meyer, L., McQuarter, R., & Kishi, G. (1984). Assessing and teaching social interaction skills. In W. Stainback & S. Stainback (Eds.), *Integration of severely handicapped students with their nondisabled peers: A handbook for teachers.* Reston, VA: Council for Exceptional Children.

Moreno, J. L. (1984). *Who shall survive?* Washington, DC: Nervous and Mental Disease.

Nietupski, J., Hamre-Nietupski, S., & Ayres, B. (1984). Review of task analytic leisure skill training efforts: Practitioner implications and future research needs. *Journal of the Association for Persons with Severe Handicaps, 9,* 88–97.

O'Brien, I., et al. (1989). *Action for inclusion: How to improve schools by welcoming children with special needs into regular classrooms.* Toronto, Ontario: Frontier College.

Orelove, F., & Sobsey, D. (1987). *Educating children with multiple disabilities: A transdisciplinary approach.* Baltimore: Paul H. Brookes.

Powers, J., & Ball, T. (1983). Video games to augment leisure programming in a state hospital residence for developmentally disabled clients. *Journal of Special Education Technology, 6*(1), 48–57.

Putnam, J., Werder, J., & Schleien, S. (1985). Leisure and recreation services for handicapped persons. In K. Lakin & R. Bruininks (Eds.), *Strategies for achieving community integration of developmentally disabled citizens* (pp. 253–274). Baltimore: Paul H. Brookes.

Rainforth, B., & York, J. (1987). Integrating related services in community instruction. *Journal of the Association for Persons with Severe Handicaps, 12,* 190–198.

Ray, M., et al. (1986). Integrating persons with disabilities into community leisure environments. *Journal of Expanding Horizons in Therapeutic Recreation, 1*(1), 49–55.

Rogow, S. (1981). Developing play skills and communicative competence in multiply handicapped young people. *Visual Impairment and Blindness, 5,* 197–202.

Rosen, J. W., & Burchard, S. N. (1990). Community activities and social support networks: A social comparison of adults with and without mental retardation. *Education and Training in Mental Retardation, 25,* 193–204.

Rynders, J., et al. (1980). Producing positive integration among Down syndrome and nonhandicapped teenagers through cooperative goal structuring. *American Journal of Mental Deficiency, 85,* 268–273.

Rynders, J., & Schleien, S. (1991). *Together successfully: Creating recreational and educational programs that integrate people with and without disabilities.* Arlington, TX: The Arc-United States;

National 4-H; and the Institute on Community Integration, University of Minnesota.

Rynders, J. E., et al. (1993). Improving integration outcomes for children with and without severe disabilities through cooperative structured recreation activities: A synthesis of research. *The Journal of Special Education, 26*(4), 386–407.

Salzberg, C., & Langford, C. (1981). Community integration of mentally retarded adults through leisure activity. *Mental Retardation, 19*(3), 127–131.

Sandler, A., & McLain, S. (1987). Sensory reinforcement: Effects of response-contingent vestibular stimulation on multiply handicapped children. *American Journal of Mental Deficiency, 91,* 373–378.

Schalock, R. L., & Lilley, M. A. (1986). Placement from community-based mental retardation programs: How well do clients do after 8 to 10 years? *American Journal of Mental Deficiency, 90,* 669-676.

Schleien, S., et al. (1981). Developing independent cooking skills in a profoundly retarded woman. *Journal of the Association for the Severely Handicapped, 6*(2), 23–29.

Schleien, S., et al. (1988). Acquisition and generalization of leisure skills from school to the home and community by learners with severe multihandicaps. *Therapeutic Recreation Journal, 22*(3), 53–71.

Schleien, S., Certo, N., & Muccino, A. (1984). Acquisition of leisure skills by a severely handicapped adolescent: A data-based leisure skill instructional program. *Education and Training of the Mentally Retarded, 19,* 297–305.

Schleien, S. J., et al. (1990). Building positive social networks through environmental interventions in integrated recreation programs. *Therapeutic Recreation Journal, 24*(4), 42–52.

Schleien, S., Heyne, L., & Dattilo, J. (1995). Teaching severely handicapped children: Social skills development through leisure skills programming. In G. Cartledge & J. Milburn (Eds.), *Teaching social skills to children and youth: Innovative approaches* (3rd ed.) (pp. 262–290). Needham Heights, MA: Allyn and Bacon.

Schleien, S., Kiernan, J., & Wehman, P. (1981). Evaluation of an age-appropriate leisure skills program for moderately retarded adults. *Education and Training of the Mentally Retarded, 16,* 13–19.

Schleien, S., & Larson, A. (1986). Adult leisure education for the independent use of a community recreation center. *Journal of the Association for Persons with Severe Handicaps, 11*(1), 39–44.

Schleien, S. J., et al. (1993). *Integrated outdoor education and adventure programs.* Champaign, IL: Sagamore.

Schleien, S., & Meyer, L. (1988). Community-based recreation programs for persons with severe developmental disabilities. In M. Powers (Ed.), *Expanding systems of service delivery for persons with developmental disabilities* (pp. 93–112). Baltimore: Paul H. Brookes.

Schleien, S., et al. (1995). *Lifelong leisure skills and lifestyles for persons with developmental disabilities.* Baltimore: Paul H. Brookes.

Schleien, S., & Ray, M. (1988). *Community recreation and persons with disabilities: Strategies for integration.* Baltimore: Paul H. Brookes.

Schleien, S., Wehman, P., & Kiernan, J. (1981). Teaching leisure skills to severely handicapped adults: An age-appropriate darts game. *Journal of Applied Behavior Analysis, 14,* 513–519.

Schleien, S., & Werder, J. (1985). Perceived responsibilities of special recreation services in Minnesota. *Therapeutic Recreation Journal, 19*(3), 51–62.

Schleien, S., & Yermakoff, N. (1983). Data-based research in therapeutic recreation: State of the art. *Therapeutic Recreation Journal, 17*(4), 17–26.

Sedlak, R., Doyle, M., & Schloss, P. (1982). Video games: A training and generalization demonstration with severely retarded adolescents. *Education and Training of the Mentally Retarded, 17,* 332–336.

Seligman, M. (1975). *Helplessness: On depression, development, and death.* San Francisco: W.H. Freeman.

Sherrill, C. (1986). *Adapted physical education and recreation: A multi-disciplinary approach* (3rd ed.). Dubuque, IA: William C. Brown.

Singh, N., & Millichamp, C. (1987). Independent and social play among profoundly mentally retarded adults: Training, maintenance, generalization, and long-term follow-up. *Journal of Applied Behavior Analysis, 20,* 23–34.

Stokes, T., & Baer, D. (1977). An implicit technology of generalization. *Journal of Applied Behavior Analysis, 10,* 349–367.

Storey, K., Bates, P., & Hanson, H. (1984). Acquisition and generalization of coffee purchase skills by adults with severe disabilities. *Journal of the Association for Persons with Severe Handicaps, 9*(3), 178–185.

Todd, S., Evans, G., & Beyer, S. (1990). More recognized than known: The social visibility and attachment of people with developmental disabilities. *Australian and New Zealand Journal of Developmental Disabilities, 16*(3), 207–218.

Vandercook, T. (1991). Leisure instruction outcomes: Criterion performance, positive interactions, and acceptance by typical high school peers. *Journal of Special Education, 25,* 320–339.

Verhoven, P., Schleien, S., & Bender, M. (1982). *Leisure education and the handicapped individual: An ecological perspective.* Washington, DC: Institute for Career and Leisure Development.

Voeltz, L., & Wuerch, B. (1981). Monitoring multiple behavioral effects of leisure activities training upon severely handicapped adolescents. In L. Voeltz, J. Apffel, & B. Wuerch (Eds.), *Leisure activities training for severely handicapped students: Instructional and evaluational strategies.* Honolulu: University of Hawaii, Department of Special Education.

Voeltz, L., Wuerch, B., & Wilcox, B. (1982). Leisure and recreation: Preparation for independence, integration, and self-fulfillment. In B. Wilcox & G. Bellamy (Eds.), *Design of high school programs for severely handicapped students* (pp. 175–209). Baltimore: Paul H. Brookes.

Wehman, P. (1979). *Recreation programming for developmentally disabled persons.* Austin, TX: Pro-Ed.

Wehman, P., & Schleien, S. (1980). Assessment and selection of leisure skills for severely handicapped individuals. *Education and Training of the Mentally Retarded, 15,* 50–57.

Wehman, P., & Schleien, S. (1981). *Leisure programs for handicapped persons: Adaptations, techniques, and curriculum.* Austin, TX: Pro-Ed.

Wehman, P., Schleien, S., & Kiernan, J. (1980). Age appropriate recreation programs for severely handicapped youth and adults. *Journal of the Association for the Severely Handicapped, 5,* 395–407.

West, P. (1981). Vestiges of a cage: Social barriers to participation in outdoor recreation by the mentally retarded and physically handicapped, (Monograph No. 1). Ann Arbor: University of Michigan, Natural Resources Sociology Research Lab.

Wetherald, L., & Peters, J. (1986). *Mainstreaming: A total perspective.* Silver Spring, MD: Montgomery County Department of Recreation, Therapeutics Section.

York, J., Nietupski, J., & Hamre-Nietupski, S. (1985). A decision-making process for using microswitches. *Journal of the Association for Persons with Severe Handicaps, 10*(4), 214–223.

York, J., & Rainforth, B. (1995). Enhancing leisure participation by individuals with significant intellectual and physical disabilities. In S. Schleien, et al. (Eds.), *Lifelong leisure skills and lifestyles for persons with developmental disabilities.* Baltimore: Paul H. Brookes.

Zetlin, A. G., & Murtaugh, M. (1988). Friendship patterns of mildly learning handicapped and nonhandicapped high school students. *American Journal of Mental Retardation, 92*(5), 447–454.

CHAPTER 10

NEUROMUSCULAR DISORDERS

GAIL R. LEVINE

OBJECTIVES

- Understand the functioning of the central nervous system, voluntary muscles, and their interrelationship.
- Identify the characteristic symptoms of cerebral palsy, muscular dystrophy, multiple sclerosis, spina bifida, spinal cord injury, and Parkinson's disease.
- Understand the purpose and application of the therapeutic recreation process (therapy, leisure education, and recreation participation) in the interdisciplinary treatment process of persons with neuromuscular disorders.
- Identify and apply appropriate interventions at each stage of the treatment process and in a variety of settings in which treatment may be carried out.
- Understand the importance of maximizing independent functioning and current best practices for these disorders.
- Recognize the implications of current issues and trends.

DEFINITION OF NEUROMUSCULAR DISORDERS

The central nervous system (CNS) consists of the brain and its various parts (i.e., cerebral cortex, medulla, cerebellum, pons, hypothalamus, thalamus), and the spine (consisting of the spinal cord, vertebrae, and axial nerves radiating from the spinal cord to various parts of the body). The voluntary muscles of the body are linked to the CNS through the network of afferent and efferent nerve fibers which transmit impulses between the CNS and voluntary muscle groups. The proper working of the voluntary muscles and the CNS enables us to achieve mobility, to maintain erect posture, and to grasp objects. Voluntary muscles of the trunk (i.e., the intercostal muscles of the rib-cage and the diaphragm) and of the mouth and throat (tongue, jaws, and esophageal muscles) are needed for respiration and for swallowing which are functions of the autonomic nervous system. These functions can become disturbed and, in some cases, disrupted entirely in persons with certain types of neuromuscular disorders. *Neuromuscular disorders* refers to any impairment in the structure or functioning of the voluntary muscles themselves and to any impairment of the structures and functioning of the CNS which transmits nerve impulses to and from the voluntary muscles. Damage to any part of this highly integrated system due to malformation of structure, injury, or degeneration results in impairment in mobility, affects posture, balance and the ability to grasp objects. The degree of impairment of the affected functions will vary according to the location of the damage and its extent. Muscular dystrophy is sometimes classified as a musculoskeletal impairment (Carter, Van Andel, & Robb, 1995), since the movement disorder does not result from a defect or injury to the CNS. In keeping with the classification system used by Lockette and Keyes (1994), it will be included with other neuromuscular disorders in this chapter because both the musculo-skeletal and the central nervous systems are integrally involved in producing movement. Impairment in function of one system renders the other ineffective or less effective. As we shall learn, muscular dystrophy is actually caused by a defect in protein metabolism (Fidzianska et al., 1982) which leads to the progressive degeneration and atrophy of muscle tissue and its replacement by fatty tissue. The wasting of muscle tissue affects not only voluntary movement but static posture and respiratory function as well. In the case of muscular dystrophy, nerve impulses transmitted over efferent nerve fibers to the voluntary muscles do not produce an effect because the muscle tissue has atrophied and is not capable of responding.

Some of the conditions to be discussed in this chapter appear at birth and are related to problems occurring during the prenatal, perinatal, or congenital (birth to 2 years) phases of developments. Some conditions do not become manifest until later childhood, adolescence, or early to middle adulthood. Of the neuromuscular disorders, Parkinson's disease alone, rarely occurs before 50 years and is primarily associated with the onset of old age at about 70 years. Some neuromuscular disorders like muscular dystrophy follow a progressive course which leads inexorably to further degeneration of muscle function and premature death. Cerebral palsy, on the other hand, has a nonprogressive course and with regular physical activity and physical therapy, some of the problems associated with disuse and aging, muscle atrophy, and tightening tendons need never occur (*Aging and Cerebral Palsy,* 1990). With progressive neuromuscular disorders such as muscular dystrophy and Parkinson's disease, there is a deterioration in the individual's ability to carry out the basic life functions of respiration, chewing, and swallowing food, and this ultimately shortens the individual's lifespan. Progression of the disorder may be gradual over the course of many decades as in Parkinson's, or it may be rapid as in some types of muscular dystrophy, such as amyotrophic lateral sclerosis (ALS). This chapter will familiarize the reader with the basic characteristics of each type of neuromuscular disorder, the typical limitations of function especially as they apply to recreation participation, and the application of the therapeutic recreation process to treatment.

CLASSIFICATION OF DISORDERS AND DESCRIPTION OF LIMITATIONS

Cerebral Palsy

Cerebral palsy (CP) is a nonprogressive neuromuscular disorder originating during the developmental period (birth through 22 years) which is characterized by the individual's difficulty in controlling voluntary movement. The primary etiological factor in CP is injury to the motor cortex of the brain due to anoxia during the birth process or following birth. Premature birth and low birth weight are also highly correlated with the incidence of cerebral palsy (*Aging and Cerebral Palsy,* 1990; Blacklow, 1983; Gilroy, 1990). The brain lesion occurs early in the pregnancy during the perinatal phase (at the time of labor and delivery) or during the infant's first month. Other factors that can cause cerebral palsy are infections of the brain and its linings (i.e., meningitis and encephalitis), exposure to toxic substances such as lead, the absorption by the fetus of alcohol or drugs that the mother ingested during her pregnancy, and severe malnutrition. The majority of individuals with cerebral palsy have a congenital form, but cerebral palsy can be acquired at any point during the developmental period due to head trauma resulting from auto accidents, falls, and physical abuse. The extent and location of the lesion in the brain will determine the type and severity of symptoms the individual will exhibit. Seizures as well as visual and, in some cases, hearing impairments may be features of the disorder in any given individual. Mental retardation is often, but not always, concomitant with CP. Of the 5,334 adults with cerebral palsy who were surveyed by New York State's OMRDD, 90 percent were found to have a diagnosis of mental retardation, half at the severe/profound level (Brown, Bontempo, & Turk, 1991). Difficulties in communication due to dysarthria or to limitations in processing and using language (aphasia) are common features of cerebral palsy. Cerebral palsy is not inherited. At one time, incompatibility between the mother's Rh blood factor and her fetus' could result in cerebral palsy, but with premarital blood testing and the vaccine Roggam, this cause is virtually nonexistent in the United States. Cerebral palsy is a lifelong condition, but with early intervention and therapeutic management geared to habilitation and rehabilitation, individuals may be able to maximize their ability to perform daily life skills independently.

Classifications of Cerebral Palsy. Classification of cerebral palsy into types is based on the quality of the movement produced and the parts of the body affected. No two individuals with cerebral palsy will manifest exactly the same characteristics (Blacklow, 1983; Gilroy, 1990). The following are the basic categories that have been identified:

Spastic type: This type is characterized by hypertonus of the muscles and is the most common form of cerebral palsy.

Athetoid type: This type is characterized by wave-like, uncoordinated movements. Muscles may also exhibit hypotonus.

Ataxic type: This type of cerebral palsy primarily affects the individual's balance. Gait may be unsteady and poorly coordinated.

Rigidity: This quality can also be found with other types of CP and may be intermittent.

Tremor: Intention tremor, an involuntary motion with a regular rhythm, may occur when the individual is making a directed movement. Resting tremor can occur at any time. Tremor may occur in combination with other types of CP.

Cerebral palsy is also further classified according to the part of the body and number of limbs affected:

monoplegia—one arm or leg
paraplegia—both legs
hemiplegia—one side of the body, both limbs
triplegia—three limbs
quadriplegia—all four limbs

The degree of severity of muscle control is also used to classify individuals with CP:

mild impairment—usually ambulatory; speech is understandable;

moderate—some impairment of mobility; may require assistive devices for ambulation; speech is impaired;

severe—uses a wheelchair for mobility; unable to use speech.

Description of Limitations. Young children with cerebral palsy may have their movements restricted by having to wear braces or by being confined to a wheelchair and may not move spontaneously to explore their environment. This leads to sensory deprivation and to passivity. "Purposeless, irregular movements beyond the child's control, disturbances in balance and clumsy coordination all prevent his taking in experience through action. The ensuing monotony, boredom, and environmental deprivation induce either lethargy or violent acting out" (Michelman, 1974). Children with cerebral palsy should be stimulated and encouraged to move in order to develop gross motor skills, eye-hand coordination, to develop and improve spatial/motor concepts, and to improve their sense of vestibular balance. Young children with cerebral palsy need to be involved in early intervention programs which provide adapted physical education and adapted aquatics sessions. Children with cerebral palsy have difficulty using conventional toys and playground equipment, and these need to be adapted to their individual abilities. Muscle atrophy and reduced range of motion can result from prolonged inactivity and disuse.

Adolescents and adults with cerebral palsy should be encouraged to participate in physical activities in order to prevent these outcomes. Spasticity and hypertonus are exacerbated by cold. Swimming in warm water (95°F) relaxes and lengthens the muscle fibers and will increase range of motion (ROM). Adaptation of equipment used in sports and art activities will be required in many cases. Individuals with CP experience difficulty organizing and coordinating their movements, and activities which call for adherence to a pattern of movement, or to a fixed rhythm, as in aerobic dancing, can be overly frustrating for them. Most persons with cerebral palsy have difficulty using speech and language for communication due to dysarthria or aphasia. Expressive modalities such as art, music, photography, and writing, using assistive technology, can expand the range of communication and the social network for the individual with CP. Intellectual functioning of the individual needs to be taken into account in recommending specific activities and in modifying some aspects of an activity. Some individuals with cerebral palsy have seizures, and this may limit an individual's participation in certain types of activities. Factors relevant to an individual's seizure threshold, such as temperature and degree of emotional stimulation, will have to be taken into account. Sensory impairments such as visual and auditory difficulties also have to be taken into account in selecting modalities to work with and in adapting communication and instruction to individual needs.

Muscular Dystrophy

Muscular dystrophy is a group of progressive, neuromuscular conditions caused by a genetic defect in protein metabolism which affects the production of muscle tissue on the cellular level (Fidzianska et al., 1982). The primary symptom is weakness in the movements of the affected muscles. Muscle tissue wastes away and is replaced by connective tissue or by fat. Some of the early symptoms are difficulty in climbing stairs and in rising from a recumbent posture. Usually there is a sway-back posture and a waddling gait caused by weak gluteal muscles. Most of the varieties of MD have an early onset with a slow progression (Adams & Victor, 1989; Blacklow, 1983). There are other varieties of MD which occur in the second to third decades and which may affect facial muscles, shoulder girdles, or both limb girdles. The diagnosis of muscular dystrophy is confirmed by analysis of the cerebrospinal fluid (CSF) and by serum proteins, by muscle biopsies, tests of muscle strength, and by respiratory tests.

Classifications of Muscular Dystrophy. The various types of muscular dystrophies are classified according to age of onset of symptoms and the location of the muscle groups affected.

Early Onset Varieties. *Duchennes dystrophy, Spinal Muscular Atrophy (SMA)* and *Friedrich's Ataxia (FA)* are the types of muscular dystrophy that manifest themselves during childhood and adolescence. *Duchennes dystrophy* is usually manifested by the age of six. Its progression is rapid and by the age of ten, most children with Duchennes are in wheelchairs. *Spinal Muscular Atrophy (SMA)* and *Friedrich's Ataxia (FA)* are the other types of childhood muscular dystrophy. Duchennes and SMA affect the deltoid muscles of the shoulders, impairing the child's ability to raise and lower his arms and restricting range of motion (ROM) and the spine itself, causing frequent falling and poor balance. In the Duchennes and SMA types, the diaphragm and the intercostal muscles of the rib-cage become weakened and this affects respiration. Shallow breathing leads to frequent pulmonary infections and greater fatigue. *Friedrich's ataxia* manifests itself in early adolescence and is inherited as an autosomal recessive trait. There is atrophy with demyelinization involving the posterior columns and spinocerebellar and corticospinal tracts of the spinal cord (Blacklow, 1983). In an attempt to compensate for poor balance, the person with FA walks with a wide-based gait. The life-span of those with early onset forms of MD is shortened. Most will usually live only until their second decade.

Adult Onset Varieties. These are *Limb Girdle Dystrophy (LGD), Fascio-scauplar-humeral dystrophy (FSH),* and *Amyotrophic Lateral Sclerosis* (ALS,) also known as "Lou Gehrig's Disease"). ALS progresses the most rapidly of all the late-onset dystrophies and is always fatal. In LGD, the muscles of the pelvic girdle are primarily affected. The degree of muscle weakness ranges from mild to severe. In ALS and FSH, the muscles of the tongue, lips, and jaw are ultimately affected making verbal communication difficult and, in some cases, impossible. FSH also affects the deltoid muscles of the upper shoulder and the scapula. The progression in FSH tends to be more gradual than in other adult-onset types. Advances in computerized technology can facilitate communication for some individuals with advanced cases of ALS and FSH but there is an increase in social isolation. There is no loss of intellectual ability with any of the dystrophies and pincer grasp is usually retained until the final stages.

Description of Limitations. Due to the progressive nature of both early and adult onset types, there will be a steady reduction in the individual's range of motion (ROM) and muscle strength. The rate of progression varies for each individual and will necessitate ongoing, periodic assessment of ROM, muscle strength, and evaluation and grading of functional abilities. The psychosocial and psychosexual development of children with these early onset varieties of muscular dystrophy is delayed due to their reduced ability to participate with age peers which leads to isolation and marked restriction of their experiences. Eventually, they are unable to perform many self-care skills independently such as dressing, washing, feeding, and toileting themselves. Dependency, in turn, lowers their self-esteem and self-confidence which further inhibits socialization. Individuals should be encouraged to do as much for themselves as possible. The adaptation of household tools, including the telephone and television, can make it possible for the person with MD to feel more independent. Moderate physical activity should be encouraged within the capabilities of the individual. Usually, fine motor control and pincer grasp are retained until the final stage making writing, artistic expression, and many craft projects possible. Loss of self-esteem and depression are psychological effects of the progressive diminution of personal abilities. They can be countered by creating opportunities for the individual to experience success and social validation through volunteer work, exhibiting art work, involvement in advocacy work, and participation in support and social groups. Leisure counseling throughout the course of the disease process can help the individual focus on utilizing the intellectual and creative capacities which do not diminish. Intellectual and expressive activities such as poetry writing, current events discussion, reading, journalism, and calligraphy could be a source of continuing gratification and pride for the person with MD.

There is a tendency to withdraw into social isolation. The individual with MD should be encouraged to maintain contact with friends by telephone and letter writing. For all adults who develop any of the types of muscular dystrophy, there are major changes in work and social activities that are necessitated as the condition progresses and abilities diminish. The individual who is part of a couple will become more dependent upon his partner for caretaking with dressing, feeding, toileting, and personal care. This may make the individual feel more like a dependent child than an adult. There is an impact on the couple's sexual relationship due to the limitations that restrict movement, as well as from the feelings of inadequacy, loss of self-esteem, and general feelings of unattractiveness which negatively affect sexual expression. Support groups in addition to individual counseling can be extremely helpful for adults as well as adolescents with MD by helping individuals deal with the "mourning" of lost abilities and by cultivating new sources of self-esteem. The individual with MD needs to be included in family gatherings and activities to the fullest extent possible. Participation in a support group or in structured leisure activities provided by a local chapter of the MD Association is desirable to optimize socialization and active participation throughout the course of the disease. Loss of respiratory function and shallow breathing are the causes of most secondary infections among those with MD and exacerbate fatigue. Proper positioning in the wheelchair and the importance of deep breathing need to be promoted. Yoga breathing (diaphragmmatic breathing) should be taught as a tool for maximizing lung volume and maintaining good lung function.

Multiple Sclerosis

Multiple sclerosis is a disease affecting approximately 500,000 people in the United States today (Gopalan, 1994). Its cause is unknown but it has been strongly suggested that it may result from the individuals' exposure to a virus which causes them to produce antibodies that then attack the myelin sheathing protecting their nerves and spine (Rosner & Ross, 1992; Scheinberg, 1983). Myelin is a fatty substance that coats and insulates the nerve cells in the spinal cord and brain. The destruction of the myelin, a process called demyelination, causes scar tissue (sclera) to form in place of the myelin, a process called gliosis. The symptoms of MS result from the demyelination of the spinal cord, peripheral nerves, midbrain, and cerebrum. The lesions, or sclera, interfere with the transmission of nerve impulses to various parts of the body and produce the characteristic symptoms of numbness, blurred or double vision, impaired coordination, dragging of the feet, intention tremor of the hand, and partial or complete paralysis of parts of the body, among others. The location and the extent of the scarring will determine the specific symptoms and the functional impairments the individual experiences. Multiple sclerosis is acquired and is more prevalent in the temperate zones (i.e., the United States, Canada, and Europe) than in tropical regions. The lowest frequency for it is found in Africa and Asia. It is noncontagious and usually is manifested between the ages of 20 and 40; however, in women the age of onset is closely associated with puberty. The risk of developing MS decreases by the time of menopause (Scheinberg, 1983). It is a lifelong condition and there is no known cure. The treatments are focused upon symptom reduction and management. The goal is to maximize the individual's independent functioning and to maintain as much of his/her pre-illness lifestyle as possible.

Classification of Multiple Sclerosis. Each individual case of MS presents a unique pattern of symptoms. Since the course of the disease waxes and wanes with episodes of exacerbations followed by periods of remission, MS is classified mainly by the major parts of the body affected and by the symptoms. For instance, if the demyelination affects the optic nerve, the individual could experience blurred vision or a "blind spot in the middle of the field of vision." This symptom will usually disappear in a day or so and may never recur, or it may return sporadically. Gopalan (1994), citing a study by the United States Department of Health and Human Services, reports that, "Some doctors feel that the MS pattern established during the first 3 to 5 years may be indicative of the long-range course." Symptoms may be classified as sensory (vision, numbness, and tingling sensations), muscular (including intention tremor, spasticity, muscle weakness, lack of coordination, and poor control of bowel and bladder), vestibular (dizziness and loss of balance), and emotional (depression, secondary to impairment and loss of functioning). There is no loss of intellectual functioning throughout the course of the disease. Although return to normal functioning is possible during a period of remission from symptoms, it is not uncommon for individuals to lose functional abilities, never to regain them. Increased dependency upon others for personal care may occur over time.

Diagnosis of MS is difficult because the symptoms are so variable and the initial presentation may look like other disorders. Analysis of spinal cord fluid has shown that in 75 percent of the people with MS, the level of protein immunoglobulin G (IgG) is higher than within an individual without MS (Gopalan, 1994). Other methods to confirm the diagnosis of MS involve the use of computerized axial tomography (CAT scans), and myelograms or angiograms to detect and localize areas of demyelination and scarring. Once the diagnosis is confirmed, MS may be classified as following a pattern of exacerbation-remission or a chronic progressive pattern without recovery. "Exacerbating-remitting MS tends to eventually manifest itself into the chronic progressive form" (Gopalan, 1994).

Description of Limitations. MS is a dynamic disorder and the patient's condition will vary, necessitating frequent assessment of functioning and modification of activities. The stresses of adapting to lifestyle changes and the discomfort of symptoms may create a depressed mood and irritability. Stress and fatigue can, in turn, exacerbate symptoms. The symptoms of MS become worse upon exposure to heat and persons with MS should remain in air conditioned rooms in hot weather. Swimming in cool water (71–75° Fahrenheit) can be very beneficial for reduction of symptoms since cold increases the transmission of nerve impulses and the range of motion. Leisure counseling is helpful to guide the patients in selecting and modifying activities as the individual's condition changes and in maintaining as much of his or her previous leisure lifestyle as possible. Support groups have also been found to be helpful in helping individuals with MS to maintain morale and to exchange information about new types of treatments. Medications such as valium, which are used to relax rigid muscles, produce symptomatic improvement but may also create the undesirable side-effects of drowsiness. Inderal may be used to reduce hand tremor. Corticosteroids (prednisone, prednisolone, adrenocorticotropic hormone, and others) are used to reduce inflammation of joints which causes pain and restricts movement. These drugs also produce the unpleasant side-effects of fluid retention and weight gain, gastrointestinal irritation, and headache. Relaxation training, meditation, and modified yoga exercises have also been found to promote relaxation of muscles and produce a general sense of well-being. Seventy-five percent of all persons with MS remain ambulatory and never need a wheelchair so moderate physical activity should be encouraged (Scheinberg, 1983). A walking stick can help those whose balance is affected. Individuals with MS should be integrated into family and other social activities so that the individuals retain as much of their pre-illness lifestyle as possible. Support groups and special activity groups provided by the local MS chapter can be helpful.

Parkinson's Disease

Parkinson's disease, named in 1817 by James Parkinson, a London surgeon, is a progressive neuromuscular disorder that results from the destruction of the substantia nigral cells in the brain. These darkly pigmented cells produce the neurohormone dopamine, which is essential for the transmission of impulses from neuron to neuron across the synapses. In the brain of a person with Parkinson's, these cells become depigmented and die. Scientists do not know what causes the initial destruction of nigral cells. The reduction in the level of dopamine deprives the striatum of a sufficient supply of this neurohormone. The striatum is a center of brain activity, transmitting nerve impulses to the muscles. Lacking an adequate supply of dopamine, the striatum is unable to create smooth, continuous voluntary movements or to maintain normal muscle tone and posture. Parkinson's disease results in a relative lack of tone (or pull) in the extensor muscles which produces the flexed arms and legs and the stooped posture characteristic of this disease. The lack of pull by the extensors further weakens them, leading to their progressive atrophy (McGoon, 1990). Parkinson's does not directly injure the muscles or joints. The improper functioning of the muscles and joints is what leads to the impairments of gait, posture, and the rigidity.

Parkinson's is characterized by symptoms affecting movement and muscle control, balance, speech, and cognitive functioning. The movement impairments typical of this disease are bradykinesia (slowness and paucity of movement), rigidity of the limbs, and resting tremor primarily of the hands and feet. In addition, it may appear in the face, lips, tongue, or jaw as freezing, in which the individual is unable to move for varying lengths of time and must remain in a fixed position; joint aches and pain which stem from the rigid position in which the muscles are held, and the stooped posture. Impairment of balance causes falling which can produce serious injury and safety risks. Some of the cognitive impairments that gradually occur are loss of short-term memory, aphasia, concrete thinking, and an inability to reason logically. The course of the disease may progress rapidly or slowly, but it is chronic and will inevitably lead to decreased functioning. Generally, some aspect of the four cardinal signs of Parkinson's will be present in a patient: resting tremor, rigidity, bradykinesia, and postural instability.

The age of onset for Parkinson's is usually in the fifth and sixth decades of life, but it has been known to appear in individuals in their forties (Lieberman & Williams, 1993).

Classification of Parkinson's Disease. Patients are classified by the stage of the disease they are in according to the Hahn-Yahr Scale (Lieberman & Williams, 1993):

Hahn-Yahr Scale

Stage 0—no visible disease.
Stage 1—involves one side of the body.
Stage 2—involves both sides of the body but no impairment of balance.
Stage 3—impaired balance or walking.
Stage 4—markedly impaired balance or walking.
Stage 5—complete immobility.

A variety of medications is used in varying combinations to minimize the effects of the impaired nerve transmission of impulses to the muscles. Some of the medications used to treat the symptoms of Parkinson's are:

Sinemet—a combination of Levodopa and Carbidopa to increase the level of dopamine in the brain.
Parlodel and Permax—used in combination with Sinemet to smooth out the "on-off" effect seen in long-term Levodopa treatment.
Symmetrel (Amantadine)—relieves tremors, rigidity, and bradykinesia.
Eldepryl (Selegeline)—an MAO B inhibitor. Increases the amount of dopamine in the brain by blocking enzyme MAO B that breaks down dopamine.
Inderal—decreases tremors.
Artane and Cogentin—anticholinergics; used to decrease tremors and rigidity.

Description of Limitations. Sinemet eventually loses some of its effectiveness. After three to five years, 50 percent of all Parkinson's patients find the effects of Sinemet to have decreased (Lieberman & Williams, 1993). The powerful medications used to treat the symptoms of Parkinson's produce many negative side effects. Dystonia, abnormal muscle tone, can occur as a side-effect of levodopa therapy. Dyskinesia, involuntary or abnormal movement, is the most common and the most disruptive side effect of long-term anti-Parkinson's medication. Orthostatic hypotension, a sudden drop in blood pressure causing dizziness, can be caused by Sinemet and other anti-Parkinson drugs. Mobility exercises, stretching exercises including Yoga postures, and daily walking can minimize and reduce some of the atrophy and rigidity that are made worse when the individual becomes too sedentary (McGoon, 1990). Instability of mood is common in Parkinson's. The symptoms of depression probably result from the decreased levels of norepinephrine and serotonin (neurotransmitters), which are also characteristic of the brain levels found in clinically depressed persons without Parkinson's. McGoon (1990) states that 25 percent of the Parkinsonian population who have taken levodopa for more than three years experience visual hallucinations, which can be quite frightening for the patient. A readjustment of the Sinemet dosage usually diminishes this disturbing side effect. Dysphagia, a disturbance of the swallowing function, does not occur until the late stages of the disease. Instability of balance and a shuffling gait characteristic of Parkinson's may necessitate use of a cane or walker to increase stability. Persons with Parkinson's need to carefully select areas for walking, considering such factors as amount of traffic, gradient, and paving materials. Confusion and disorientation, which may be side effects of medication, make walking alone risky for the individual with Parkinson's. It is a good idea to have someone accompany the individual.

Spina Bifida

Spina Bifida is a congenital birth defect affecting the spinal column and/or cord. It occurs early in prenatal development as the neural tube is forming. There is defective fusion of one or more posterior vertebral arches which is sometimes accompanied by protrusion of the meninges, spinal cord, or nerve roots beyond the normal limits of the spinal canal (Stark, 1977). The area of the defect is usually the lumbar area of the spine. There is displacement of the covering of the spinal cord and a sac-like protrusion is formed which may be externally exposed. This causes a defective fusion of one or more vertebrae. The effects of spina bifida vary widely, ranging from mild with little impairment of function to severe, characterized by hydrocephalus with mental retardation or paraplegia. If there is damage in the sacral area of the spine (S2–4), there may be impaired bladder function as well (Stark, 1977). There may be some loss of sensation and movement in the area of the body connected by nerves to the defective portion of the spine.

Classification of Spina Bifida. There are two main varieties: spina bifida cystica and spina bifida occulta.

Spina bifida cystica encompasses two very different types of lesions: myelomeningocele and meningocele.

Myelomeningocele is the most serious form of spina bifida. It is a pronounced protrusion at the lumbar (L) level. Actual segments of the vertebrae and portions of the spinal cord are contained within the protruding sac. The areas of exposed neural plate, membrane, and skin vary in extent from individual case to case. The degree of neurological impairment will depend upon the vertebral level of the cord lesion. Hydrocephalus is a common secondary problem of this type of spina bifida, occurring when spinal fluid "leaks" from the unclosed areas of the spinal cord into the cranial cavity, causing the head to enlarge and putting pressure on the cerebral lobes. This can result in seizures and brain damage unless shunting is performed. In shunting, a small tube is inserted into the spinal tube at the base of the head and excess spinal fluid is drained.

Meningocele is a sac-like protrusion from the vertebrae, but it contains only spinal fluid. Immediate closure is required to prevent infection (meningitis). This type of spina bifida usually produces minimal impairment.

Spina Bifida Occulats. Spina bifida occulats affects only a single vertebrae. It consists of a minor defect and it can go unnoticed because the skin and spinal cord are unaffected. No treatment is required for this type.

Description of Limitations. Individuals with spina bifida, which affects the S2–4 portion of the spine, will probably have poor bowel and bladder control due to loss of sensation and lack of control of voluntary muscles in this area. This will necessitate a bathrooming schedule and regulation of meals and the taking of a laxative. Swimming can be recommended once bowel function is regulated. Loss of sensation in the limbs and poor circulation predispose the individual with spina bifida to the formation of decubitus ulcers. Frequent monitoring will be required to ensure that this does not occur. Individuals should be encouraged to participate fully in all activities and to expand their leisure skills. Temperature and activity level should be monitored if the individual has seizures.

Spinal Injury

The spine consists of thirty vertebrae arranged in a column surrounding the spinal cord. Neural messages to and from the brain are transported by the cord. Any damage to the cord itself will result in impairment of this function. The nature and degree of the impairment depend upon the location and the extent of the injury.

Injuries to the spinal cord itself are not reversible. A complete injury to the cord results in total loss of sensation and movement below the site of the injury. A partial injury to the cord results in some loss of sensation and diminution of mobility, depending upon the location and extensiveness of the injury. Fractures of the thoracic and lumbar vertebrae can be repaired in some cases through surgery to realign them in the hope that they will fuse. With a cervical fracture, a metal device known as a "halo" is worn by the patient in an effort to achieve realignment externally.

Spinal cord injury (SCI) is usually the result of a traumatic injury and happens suddenly. Sixty-two percent of all spinal cord injuries occur to young people under 18 years of age and 80 percent are male. The most frequent causes are automobile accidents and accidents resulting from participation in high-risk sports like diving, motorcycle riding, and surfing. Recently, there has been a growing percentage of SCI cases that result from gunshot wounds, particularly among inner-city youths. Over 200,000 persons in the U.S. have spinal cord injuries.

Classification of Spinal Injuries. Injury can be to the vertebrae (fractures or compression) or to the spinal cord itself. Vertebrae are arranged by area of the body in which they are located: Cervical (region of the neck and shoulders), Thoracic (chest and trunk to the top of the pelvis), Lumbar region (lower back, top, and posterior of the pelvis), and Sacral area. Each vertebra is numbered and preceded by the alphabetical letter corresponding to its region of the body. Injuries are classified by referring to the letter of the area of the body in which the injury is located (C, T, L, S) and by the number of the vertebra affected. For instance, vertebrae in the neck region are numbered C1–C8. Damage to the fourth cervical vertebra is referred to as C–4. There are twelve vertebrae in the thoracic region, numbered T1–T12. Vertebrae of the lumbar region are numbered L1–L5 and vertebrae of the sacral area are numbered S1–S5. Since any injury to the spine results in loss of sensation and movement (complete or partial) to areas below the site of injury, injury to the cord at the C–2 level (referred to as a "high cord" injury) will affect everything from the upper neck down to the toes. Injury to the cord at the L–5 level will cause a loss of sensation and movement in the legs and may cause incontinence of bowel and bladder due to loss of sensation in this area. Classification of spinal injuries is also made according to the degree of voluntary function and sensation: partial or complete and according to the number of body parts affected, paraplegia (both limbs are affected), and quadriplegia (all four limbs are affected). With a complete injury there will be no motor function and no sensation below the level of injury. With an incomplete injury, there will be some motor function and some sensation will be present below the level of the injury.

The higher the location of the site of the injury, the more severe the impairment of movement will be since nerve transmission to muscles located below the level of the injury will be interrupted.

Cervical. Vertebrae in the neck region are numbered C1–C8. Damage at the level of the fourth cervical vertebra is referred to as "a C–4 injury." Since any injury to the spine results in loss of sensation and movement (complete or partial) to areas below the site of injury, injury to the cord at the C–2 level (referred to as a "high cord" injury) will affect everything from the upper neck down to the toes. Persons with high level cervical injuries (C–1 to C–3) will usually need to rely upon respirators for breathing and will need to use motorized wheelchairs equipped with sip and puff switches as their movements will be very limited.

Thoracic. There are twelve vertebrae in the thoracic region, numbered T1–T12. Injury at this level will affect muscles of back and chest. Trunk stability will be poor, requiring support and stabilization. The patient will be able to use a manual wheelchair independently. Injury at this level may cause incontinence of bowel and bladder due to loss of sensation and voluntary control of the muscles involved.

Lumbar. Vertebrae of the lumbar region are numbered L1–L5. Any injury at this level will affect flexion of the hips and movement of the legs. A person with an injury at this level may be able to ambulate independently using assistive devices.

Sacral. Vertebrae of the sacral area are numbered S1–S5. Persons may have control of bowel and bladder functions. Sexual functioning may be normal.

Classification of spinal injuries is also made according to the degree of voluntary function and sensation: *partial* or *complete* and according to the *number of body parts affected:*

Paraplegia (both limbs are affected);
Quadriplegia (all four limbs are affected).

With a *complete injury* there will be no motor function and no sensation below the level of injury. With an *incomplete injury,* there will be some motor function and some sensation will be present below the level of the injury.

Types of Spinal Injuries. Injuries may involve the vertebrae with or without damage to the spinal cord. These injuries are classified as:

1. fracture dislocation,
2. compression fracture,
3. hyperextension injury.

Damage to the cord itself can be detected through the use of x-rays, myelograms, and tomograms.

Generally, the greatest readjustment to the disability will occur during the first six months following the injury. Long-term treatment involving an interdisciplinary rehabilitation team will focus on helping the individual to: redevelop self-esteem and a sense of self-worth, develop coping skills, develop a support system, develop an appropriate leisure lifestyle that maximizes independent functioning, reenter vocational training or develop an educational plan, and engage in rehabilitation for mobility, work, and sexual functioning.

Description of Limitations. The individual with a spinal cord injury suffers greatly from the psychological ramifications of this disorder as well as from the actual physical changes in functioning brought about by the damage to the spinal cord or vertebrae. Unlike the person with spina bifida or cerebral palsy who was born with the disability and has a constant self-image, the self-image of this individual changes from that of an active and independent person to one dependent upon others for personal care, and one who may not even be in control of basic bodily needs and functions. These effects, combined with the effects of the injury on independent functioning, may have a devastating impact on the individual's leisure lifestyle in the absence of interventions such as leisure counseling. Depression, denial, and anger are commonly experienced as the individual struggles to adapt to the limitations and losses brought about by the injury.

The individual's sexual and social functioning undergo dramatic changes as a result of spinal cord injury, as many aspects of self-image, body image, and sexuality are interrelated. The ability to achieve erection and orgasm will depend upon the level of injury to the cord. A sex therapist can assist the individual in examining the values upon which his or her ideals of sexual functioning and identity are based, facilitate in the development of a more positive self-image, and help the partner in the relationship develop creative and loving ways of relating.

The individual with SCI experiences several types of pain:

Pain above the level of the lesion, which may affect muscles, joints, and tendons;
Pain at the level of the lesion (hypesthesia); and
Pain below the level of the lesion (phantom pain or paresthesia).

Pain may decrease or limit interest in participation in leisure activity and may increase depression.

The use of self-hypnosis, meditation, and relaxation techniques may reduce perceived pain.

Respiratory problems, including difficulty in coughing, are common in instances of high cervical or thoracic damage. These individuals require careful respiratory management. Deep breathing exercises and frequent changes of position help prevent the formation of a pulmonary embolism. Those with severely compromised respiration may require a respirator.

Changes in blood pressure and circulation, which result from the injury, necessitate insuring that the person is properly dressed and insulated. Phlebitis, hypotension, and cardiac arrhythmias can also develop, and those with these conditions need to have their physical activity level monitored closely. Physical activity performed at high intensity or for long durations would be contraindicated.

Generally, SCI results in disturbed bowel and bladder functions. This needs to be taken into account in planning for outings or swimming activities. Urinary infections are common and symptoms need to be monitored by the individual and the therapist.

PURPOSE OF THERAPEUTIC RECREATION

The goal of treatment with persons who have neuromuscular disorders is to maximize independent leisure functioning in the least restrictive setting and to facilitate the individual's development of an appropriate, satisfying leisure lifestyle. The specific objectives and treatment plans should reflect these goals. The principle of normalization should guide every decision made by the therapist and client regarding leisure experiences. More specific treatment objectives are the following:

1. To promote overall physical growth and development by providing opportunities for varied movement experiences using necessary adaptations of equipment, instruction, and movements. To encourage the individual to be as physically active as possible within the range of his or her abilities and to maximize independent movement.
2. To facilitate the individual's development of an appropriate social support network both for friendship, information, and emotional support as well as for recreation.
3. To provide leisure education in order to facilitate the learning of lifetime leisure skills and to help the individual increase his or her knowledge of available leisure resources.
4. To facilitate the individual's use of community recreation resources by helping him or her transfer leisure skills acquired to the more inclusive setting.

Many interventions are incorporated into treatment plans. Discussion of five therapeutic recreation interventions follows.

Aquatics

Swimming and water exercise are the most widely used methods of treatment for the person with a neuromuscular disorder. Indoor and outdoor pools are available in public community centers, schools (public and private), "YMCAs", and other nonprofit organizations that offer physical fitness and recreational activities. Many of these are accessible to individuals with disabilities through the use of a hoyer lift, ramps, or steps into the pool. Individuals of all ages and degrees of disability are able to benefit from the experience of moving in the water. Water temperature must be considered for the individual with spasticity and those who have multiple sclerosis. With the aid of flotation devices, even severely impaired individuals can achieve mobility and pleasure in the water. The general therapeutic benefits of aquatic activities are:

1. Possible increased range of motion;
2. Relaxed muscles; this is particularly beneficial for those with spasticity;
3. Sensory stimulation and improved circulation;
4. Maintenance or improvement of strength and endurance;
5. Greater independence;
6. Increased sense of accomplishment.

A therapeutic swim session might include a combination of swimming skill lessons and practice, water games with a small group, exercises to promote improved balance and coordination, and a relaxation cool-down.

Wheelchair Sports

Prior to World War II, wheelchair sports were virtually nonexistent. With the return to civilian life of significant numbers of young soldiers who had suffered amputations and spinal cord injuries in the line of duty, there was a demand for more active and competitive sports activities at the VA hospitals. Many of these young soldiers had been athletes prior to their injury and they wanted to continue these activities. From its beginning in 1948, the National Wheelchair Basketball Association (NWBA), founded by Professor Timothy Nugent, has grown to 100 teams in the U.S. In 1957, Ben Lipton, of the Bulova School of Watchmaking, founded the National Wheelchair Athletic Association (NWAA) which broadened the scope of wheelchair athletics to include more than one sport and to open the door for more severely disabled athletes to participate competitively. NWBA teams have been open to women since 1974. There are several all-women teams and there is a National Women's Wheelchair Basketball Tournament. There is also a youth division. The rules of the National Collegiate Athletic Association govern wheelchair basketball with only a few modifications. Baskets remain at the 10 ft level and the game is played on either a full or half court. There is a classification system for players, grouping them according to the severity of injury. There must be a high cord injury (Class 1) player on every team for widest participation. This game requires a great deal of upper body strength, balance, and coordination, so it primarily appeals to athletes with lower SCI or with disabilities that affect only their legs but have good upper body strength. The NWAA includes a broader range of events such as: track, field events (shotput, javelin throw, discus), swimming, weight lifting, archery, and slalom. The classification system used in the NWAA includes more categories than does the one used by the NWBA. The NWAA has five classification categories for athletes (six for swimmers). Since the format is individual competition within medical classification, this organization's events afford greater opportunities for participation to quadriplegics. Participation is also wider because team membership is not necessary. United Cerebral Palsy Athletic Association (USCPAA) sponsors the National CP Games. They use their own classification system which includes categories for those who ambulate with crutches, canes, and walkers, as well as categories for those who are nonambulatory. The events in which athletes can participate in the USCPAA games are: weightlifting, horseback riding, soccer, bowling, table tennis, track and field, rifle shooting, and swimming. The Paralympics movement has been successful in scheduling wheelchair competitions parallel with competitions in the same events performed by nondisabled athletes. The U.S. Olympic Committee includes a Committee on Disability and Sports which has advocated parallel competition. Research studies indicate that the benefits of wheelchair competitive sports are both physical and psychological. Self-image and self-esteem are enhanced and the goals of normalization and integration are advanced (Hedrick, 1986; Patrick, 1986). Public attitudes and negative stereotypes about people with disabilities are changed through the example of competitive athletes with disabilities.

Creative Arts

Human beings have always found ways to express complex emotions and ideas through the various modalities of music, painting, sculpture, poetry, theatre, literature, and dance. In spite of, or perhaps even because of, the difficulties of communicating orally and limitations in the avenues for social intercourse available to them, individuals with disabilities have found their voice, so to speak, through these various mediums. Christy Brown, who has cerebral palsy, wrote the novel *My Left Foot,* which later became a movie. Toulouse Lautrec achieved worldwide fame for his prints and paintings despite his orthopedic disability. Individuals with neuromuscular disorders can achieve a great deal of satisfaction using creative expression through the arts. Intellectual functioning may not be impaired in many cases, and fine motor skills may not be affected until the very advanced stages of conditions like MD. Technological advances in computer typewriters make creative writing possible for quadriplegics, and adaptive devices can make painting and sculpting possible, even for those who have severe disabilities. The therapeutic benefits of creative arts/expressive activities are the following:

1. Reduce social isolation as the individual finds ways to communicate feelings and ideas;
2. Enhance self-esteem and feelings of accomplishment that come from creating something that is socially valued;
3. Improve and maintain physical, intellectual, and social skills which the individual utilizes in creating and presenting his work;
4. Dispel stereotypes about disabled individuals by highlighting the emotions and thoughts we all have in common and foster empathy and understanding;
5. Provide an avenue for economic self-sufficiency through exhibition and sale of artistic work.

Groups like the National Theatre of the Deaf are internationally acclaimed and afford individuals with disabilities opportunities for artistic expression equal to artists who are nondisabled.

Arts and Crafts

The therapeutic arts and crafts program can incorporate specific individual treatment goals for the patient and broaden the scope of the patient's leisure skills. Personal self-esteem and feelings of accomplishment are enhanced through the creation of socially valued objects. The individual's sense of achievement is strengthened by mastering the use of art materials or specific techniques.

Individuals with neuromuscular disorders such as muscular dystrophy and paraplegia are able to maintain a high degree of fine motor control and finger dexterity, enabling them to paint, do calligraphy, and drawing with pencil, pen and ink, and work in mosaic tiles. Those with cerebral palsy, Parkinson's disease, and multiple sclerosis may experience hand tremor and incoordination, making fine work difficult. If head and neck control is good, a paintbrush or pencil may be attached to a velcro headband. Other adaptations of equipment include the following:

1. Small pieces of sponge held by clothespins can be used to create interesting textures and designs;
2. Pieces of foam attached to the handles of brushes and implements make gripping easier;
3. Toothbrushes and men's shaving brushes can be used instead of conventional paintbrushes and create interesting textures;
4. Ink rollers used for printmaking make interesting, colorful designs when rolled in printing inks of different colors.

Sculpting in clay or sculpey, which can be baked, offers little resistance for those with weak finger pressure and the results are most pleasing. Collage is another medium which docs not require hand strength or a high degree of fine motor control, but which affords endless opportunities for creativity and personal expression. Music may be used as a background to facilitate rhythmic arm movements while painting and drawing or to create a mood and to stimulate visualization.

Social Games

Card playing and board games of all types are the mainstays of a therapeutic social recreation program. They facilitate social interaction which reduces the isolation and helplessness felt by many individuals who have neuromuscular disorders. Knowledge of social games enables individuals with neuromuscular disorders to experience greater independence as they can initiate activity on their own and develop confidence in approaching others to request them to play. In most cases, the fine motor skills needed to participate are retained sufficiently to allow most individuals to continue playing until the most advanced stage of the progressive conditions. The intellectual abilities required for playing most card and board games are maintained in all of the neuromuscular disorders with the exception of the later stages of Parkinson's disease and in some cases of cerebral palsy in which severe or profound mental retardation is present. The recreation therapist will get an idea of the social game skills the individual possessed before the onset of illness from the administration of the leisure assessment. Those individuals whose disability had a later onset (teens, young adulthood, or adulthood) will usually have acquired some social game skills to a greater or lesser degree as compared with those whose disorder had an early onset. The individual's preferences, in addition to his or her skills, must always be taken into account.

Individuals may wish to expand their repertoire of social game skills by participating in a class for beginners of Bridge or Chess, for example. These classes are often offered in Adult Education programs at community centers or the local high school or college. Participation in more inclusive community settings should be encouraged if the facility is accessible and the individual feels comfortable. This will help the individual feel less cut off from the mainstream. More debilitated individuals, or those who are not psychologically ready for community settings, may feel comfortable learning social games as part of a special interest activity group that is organized for members of a therapeutic program or for residents in a residential treatment setting. Some popular social games are the following:

Card games: Bridge, Poker, Canasta, Rummy and Gin Rummy, Blackjack
Board games: Chess, Checkers, Scrabble, Backgammon, Parcheesi, Trivial Pursuit, Monopoly, Chinese Checkers.

Adapted equipment for card playing includes a card holder and an automatic shuffler. Several companies offer board games that are specially designed for persons who have visual impairments as well as fine motor impairments.

COMMON SERVICE SETTINGS

Therapeutic recreation services for individuals with neuromuscular disorders are most commonly delivered in institutional settings like hospitals (general and specialized), long-term care facilities like nursing homes or rehabilitation facilities (privately owned and operated or publicly funded), and in community-based settings such as small group residences, social and recreational groups, and day programs sponsored by nonprofit organizations located in the community or provided to individuals who live at home on a consultative basis.

Hospitals

Patients with neuromuscular disorders may be treated on an acute-care, short-term unit if they have been admitted for surgical or diagnostic procedures or because of a relapse. The therapeutic recreation specialist (TRS) would offer diversionary activities in keeping with the patient's interests and abilities. On a longer-term rehab unit, the TRS functions as an integral member of the interdisciplinary treatment team and helps to formulate treatment goals and short-term objectives for the patient based on a careful assessment. The leisure skills and recreation activities included in the individual treatment plan are designed to further the patient's recovery and to maximize independent functioning and reintegration. Some specialized hospitals focus on the rehabilitation of patients with spinal cord injuries or strokes. In these hospitals, some patients are being prepared for eventual return to the community while others are at the later stages of progressive disorders. Therapeutic recreation specialists working in long-term rehab facilities gear their program to the goals of the patient and the patient's current level of functioning.

Long-Term Care Facilities

These may be government operated or privately owned and operated facilities for individuals who are severely impaired. Generally, individuals are placed in long-term care when family or guardians are unable to care for them. Sometimes there are no alternatives for the individual. The majority of patients in long-term care facilities are adults.

In government funded (i.e., federal, state, county, or municipal) long-term care facilities, a recreation therapist will be a member of the interdisciplinary team. Individual treatment plans based on an assessment of each patient will state both long-term goals as well as short-term objectives for each patient; however, because of the large numbers of patients in public long-term care institutions, most of the recreation programming is geared to groups and the emphasis is on the acquisition of basic leisure and socialization skills. Group outings to community places of interest and for entertainment are an effort to preserve the overall goals of normalization and reintegration, even though most of the recreation programming takes place in the restrictive and exclusive setting of the long-term care facility.

Rehabilitation Center

The rehabilitation center may be privately owned or operated by a nonprofit organization like United Cerebral Palsy or the Muscular Dystrophy Association. Transportation may be provided by the organization. Clients (they are not referred to as "patients") usually live in their own homes with family or independently, or they live in group residences and come to the rehabilitation center for daytime or evening programs which include leisure skills and recreation activity groups. This reflects the philosophy that recreation is a basic human need and is an integral part of the rehabilitation process. Various age groups may have separate programs at the center. The recreation therapist may be assigned to work exclusively with children, teens, or adults. In large rehabilitation centers, each program has its own interdisciplinary team which may contain one or more therapeutic recreation specialists. The focus of all programming at the rehabilitation center is to maximize the independent functioning of each client. The therapeutic recreation specialist, working as part of an interdisciplinary team, assesses each client on her team and develops treatment goals and objectives with the client's participation. The TR treatment goals become part of the client's overall Individual Treatment Plan (ITP) and progress is evaluated regularly. Many rehabilitation centers offer weekend recreational programming to clients and some operate summer programs.

Residential Care Settings

These are small group homes, housing six to eight residents, under the auspices of a governmental authority (state, county, or city) or a nonprofit organization such as United Cerebral Palsy, Inc. Residents are provided with a homelike situation in which they have an individual bedroom and share common cooking and living room facilities. Staffing is provided on a 24-hour basis including recreation therapy staff. Each resident has an individual program which provides for attendance at school (if under the age of 21) or a day program or sheltered workshop during the day and specifies a number of hours in the evening and on weekends for structured leisure activity. This may be directly implemented by the recreation therapist or planned by the recreation therapist and carried out by house staff who are trained by the recreation therapist. Residents in the small group home have frequent contact with community neighbors on local shopping trips, visits to local restaurants and coffee shops, and mini-excursions to local parks and places of interest. The recreation therapist makes maximum use of community resources. The overall goals of normalization and community reintegration are emphasized in this type of treatment setting.

Social and Recreational Groups: Day Programs in Community Settings

These are usually small groups funded and operated by nonprofit organizations like the Muscular Dystrophy Society or the Multiple Sclerosis Society. The nonprofit group may be a local chapter of a much larger national organization. The types of programs offered may focus on evening and weekend social recreation groups or specific recreation activities like swimming groups.

Clients register for the specific groups in which they are interested. Recreation therapists may be responsible for the planning of activities, organizational arrangements, recruitment, and registration of clients, and for the actual implementation of the activity groups. The approach is not treatment-oriented. The goal is to expand leisure opportunities for individuals with particular neuromuscular disorders in the community setting and to promote normalization.

Community Recreation Programs and Centers

> *Most persons with disabilities who live in the community do not require the therapy normally associated with therapeutic recreation, nor do they wish to be stigmatized as being recipients of therapeutic recreation services. Like other citizens, the vast majority of people with disabilities and their families simply want the opportunity to take part in recreation experiences (Kennedy, Smith, & Austin, 1991).*

Many individuals with nonprogressive or mild cases of neuromuscular disorders who live in the community, either independently or in small group residences, are able to participate in the regular recreation activities offered by the local public recreation agency or by the local "Y" or adult education agency if the physical facilities are accessible and if reasonable accommodations can be made. Normalization and community integration are furthered when recreation services are provided in the least restrictive, most inclusive setting possible. Some public recreation agencies are providing special classes for individuals with a particular type of disability. Such "special recreation" programs offered in community settings may serve the needs of those disabled individuals who are unable to benefit from participation in the regular program offered. The "special recreation" program is usually headed by a recreation therapist or by a staff member trained in adapted physical education or in adapted aquatics. It is becoming more common to see a few children with neuromuscular disorders "mainstreamed into" regular recreation activity classes and groups for activities like swimming, where volunteers or field work students in TR may work with them individually. Community recreation personnel must have some basic knowledge about working with individuals who have disabilities under the Americans with Disabilities Act, so that reasonable accommodations can be made when the disabled individual wishes to participate in the regular, ongoing program.

Private Care

Some individuals with neuromuscular disorders are able to pay for individual, personal services provided by a therapeutic recreation specialist acting on a consultant, fee-for-service basis. This is not common as most insurance plans will not pay for this service rendered apart from an institutional setting, and most individuals cannot afford to bear this cost on their own. A TR consultant would develop a personal treatment program with the individual based on a leisure needs assessment and would implement the program.

CURRENT BEST PRACTICES AND PROCEDURES

Assessment

The gathering of accurate information about an individual client's past and present functioning provides the basis for appropriate treatment planning. The methods used for assessment, both formal and informal, must yield accurate information. Information can be gathered from the client's medical charts, school records, and by interviews with family members, close friends, therapists, and teachers who have worked with the client. Formal, standardized instruments for assessing the client's leisure skills, interests, and attitudes such as the Leisure Activities Blank (LAB) are available but, depending upon the requirements of the setting and Department policy, informal, homemade assessment inventories and questionnaires may be equally useful. The assessment process for a given individual may take several weeks. Some of the methods used could be:

1. direct observation of the client engaging in structured and unstructured activities, alone and with others;
2. an interest inventory;
3. a structured questionnaire; or
4. performance tasks such as assembling puzzles of varying complexity.

Each agency or department usually has preferred methods and tools for client assessment and the supervisor or Department Chief should be consulted before any assessment is undertaken.

A comprehensive assessment for individuals with neuromuscular disorders would include items from all of the following domains: cognitive abilities; gross motor skills; fine motor skills; perceptual motor skills; balance (static and dynamic); speech and language skills; interpersonal communication skills; social awareness; social skills; affective (self-esteem; mood; body-image) (Peterson & Gunn, 1984).

Information about skill levels and abilities in each domain area could be obtained from any of the following sources: school records; IQ test scores; medical test findings; clinical reports; projective test findings; interviews with counselors, teachers, or other professionals who have worked with the client; family members and close friends. Leisure interests, attitudes, and skills can be assessed through formal instruments like the LAB or interest inventories or in a depth interview with the recreation therapist.

The comprehensive assessment is written up following the format used by each department. In many hospitals, the therapeutic recreation assessment is placed in the individual patient's chart under the section for rehabilitation. Time-frames for completing individual assessments vary with the treatment setting. Hospitals generally require that it be started within 24 to 48 hours of admission. The time-frame is longer in residential and in community settings.

Planning

The design of the individual's treatment plan is based on the comprehensive assessment and should involve the active participation of the patient. Both long-term and short-term goals and objectives need to be identified by the patient with input from the recreation therapist and other members of the interdisciplinary team. In the rehabilitation process, the patient must identify with the goals as worthwhile aims that are personally meaningful. There can be no valid rehabilitation process if the patient feels the goals are being imposed upon him or that the goals reflect the therapists' wishes rather than his own. Goals are generally long-term aims that address the need areas or deficits identified in the individual's assessment. Objectives are the specific steps the patient needs to take in order to accomplish the goal. Objectives are stated in behavioral terms and are usually observable and measurable (Kennedy, Smith, & Austin, 1991; Peterson & Gunn, 1984). They are usually stated as the desired outcome of the behavior: "Client X will be able to throw the four-inch ball using either an underarm or overhand throw," or the objective statement will describe the circumstances under which the desired outcome will occur: "When asked to choose between two games to play with a partner during leisure time, Client Y will be able to make a decision." Objectives are usually stated in one of three domains: cognitive, affective, and psychomotor (Kennedy, Smith, & Austin, 1991).

Wilhite and Keller (1992) state that objectives may be written as outcomes to be achieved in any of the three therapeutic recreation service areas: treatment, leisure education, and recreation participation. "Rehabilitation or treatment should address functional deficiencies that could limit leisure involvement. Leisure education should focus on the knowledge required for successful leisure participation and recreation participation should provide opportunities for utilizing leisure-related skills while participating in activities of choice" (p. 45). For example, let us assume that Mr. Jones has just been diagnosed with Parkinson's disease and is starting to take medication to alleviate some of the stiffness and tremor he is experiencing. Prior to discharge to his home, he was referred to the local chapter of the Parkinson's Society which sponsors weekly social and recreational activities. The therapeutic recreation specialist who conducts the group has read Mr. Jones's medical chart and meets with him for an initial assessment. Based on the assessment, the TRS and Mr. Jones identify the following major need as a treatment goal and the short-term objectives which follow:

Goal: to maintain maximum range of motion and flexibility of movement.
Objective 1: to work out an individualized exercise program with the therapeutic recreation specialist to be followed daily;
Objective 2: to designate an area of his home for indoor exercise and to inform his wife of his plan;
Objective 3: to identify several physical activities he enjoys doing outside the home either by himself or with others and to include at least one of these activities in his weekly exercise program.

Additional goals for Mr. Jones from other service areas of the TR continuum will be developed based on his assessed needs. He might need to become better informed about various types of stretching and exercise approaches that have been developed for people with Parkinson's (Leisure Education), or he might need to try to continue maintaining his current leisure lifestyle (Participation). Obviously, as Mr. Jones's condition changes over time, goals may need to be revised and new goals added with objectives specific to each goal. He may require more emphasis on goals in the Rehabilitation and Treatment services portion of the continuum as his physical and cognitive functioning declines. Treatment plans need to be reviewed periodically and should be revised as needed. Various treatment settings mandate specific time-periods for review of each patient's treatment plan. In Day Treatment settings, it may be required every three months. Progress, or the lack of it, is indicated for each specified objective with the date on which it was achieved. The treatment plan reviews are discussed with the entire interdisciplinary treatment team (depending upon the setting).

In hospitals (short- and long-term) and rehabilitation centers, discharge planning and transition planning are the final phases of treatment planning. Discharge planning is an ongoing process that begins with the patient's identification of long-term goals and the progressive clarification and evaluation of these goals in terms of the patient's present level of functioning during the rehabilitation process. Transition planning usually begins several weeks before the patient leaves the treatment setting and includes activities from the Leisure Education service area (i.e., familiarizing oneself with the leisure resources available in the community to which the patient will return) and Participation (i.e., beginning to participate in some community recreation activity of choice prior to actual discharge). The patient and therapeutic recreation specialist can discuss any difficulties that arise for the patient during this transitional period and additional support can be provided for the patient's efforts to develop or resume a leisure lifestyle that is independent.

Implementation

The carrying out of the treatment plan takes place within the context of the treatment setting and, thus, will be influenced by all of the components of the treatment setting: (1) agency or institutional affiliation, (2) legal mandate of the agency and department of program, (3) program philosophy and goals, (4) patient/client population, (5) funding source, (6) staffing, and (7) facilities.

Agency of Institutional Affiliation. If the agency is a public (government) funded and operated institution, it may have clear legal mandates to provide specific services to all who meet certain criteria. For example, psychiatric hospitals operated under the Veterans Administration (Federal government) are required to provide outpatient as well as inpatient psychiatric and substance abuse treatment services to all servicemen (women), and those services are to be provided free of charge, regardless of income. Voluntary, nonprofit agencies such as university-affiliated teaching hospitals, and private, for-profit institutions may offer a limited range of services to a select population such as those who have private insurance or who meet certain criteria for admission established by the institution. Each type of agency or institution operates under a legal charter and must maintain a minimum level of acceptable treatment standards as set forth by government regulations and by professional accrediting organizations like JCAHO.

Program Philosophy and Goals. The mission of the program will determine the type of services offered and the manner in which they are delivered. Partial hospitalization and transitional programs, for example, focus on community reintegration and will offer time-limited, short-term services. The therapeutic recreation program in this setting would make maximum use of community facilities and would emphasize leisure education in individual plans. The agency's philosophy of rehabilitation will determine and shape which specific rehabilitation services will be provided. The inclusion of sexuality education by United Cerebral Palsy of New York City in all of its day treatment programs for teens and adults stems from the agency's philosophy that sexuality is an integral part of normal human functioning and that individuals with cerebral palsy need to learn and to develop attitudes and skills that will enable them to express their sexuality.

Patient/Client Population. The interests and skill level of the patient or client direct the selection of the type of leisure and recreation activities presented. The initial assessment will provide a baseline for determining the client's past leisure experiences and acquired skills as well as for identifying areas needing development and strengthening. Individual planning should always include the active participation of the client.

Funding Source. To some extent, the budget available to the recreation therapist through the Recreation Therapy Department of the agency will limit the scope of activities offered. Recreation therapists need to make use of free resources and may improvise materials in lieu of purchasing costlier pieces of equipment. However, certain pieces of equipment will be imperative in order to conduct an adapted aquatics program with a population that has neuromuscular disorders. Flotation devices of several kinds will need to be purchased as these cannot be improvised. Lightweight bats and wiffle balls made of light weight plastic must be substituted for standard bats and balls if baseball is played. Bowling ramps and basketball return chutes are necessary items in a sports program for individuals with neuromuscular disorders. The budget of the department must be adequate to support a range of activities that are beneficial to this population.

Staffing. The recreation therapy staff working with individuals with neuromuscular disorders should have prior experience with the specific population with which they are working. Since each individual with a neuromuscular disorder will present certain unique combinations of symptoms and will vary in terms of the severity of symptoms, staff should ideally have had prior exposure to a broad range of individuals with these disorders. Knowledge and understanding of the neurobiological basis of movement (i.e., kinesiology, perceptual/motor functioning) and the working of the central nervous system are important for the ability to structure physical activities and fine motor tasks that are within the ability of the patient and that will correct or improve some aspect of motor or fine motor functioning, or which will enable the person to participate in a specific leisure activity. An adequate level of staffing will be needed for adapted aquatics activities and for outings, depending upon the ambulatory status of patients. Recreation therapists working with individuals with neuromuscular disorders should be familiar with lifting and transferring techniques and may be requested to be involved with feeding and self-care activities of clients as the agency requires. Knowledge of the operation of wheelchairs as well as familiarity with other adaptive devices (i.e., Canadian crutches, walkers, orthopedic braces, canes) is important for staff to possess. Familiarity with assistive communication technology is helpful as many individuals with neuromuscular disorders use various devices to facilitate communication if the oral production of speech is not possible. Regular in-service training sessions to update and review these skills will be beneficial.

Facilities/Equipment. Under the provisions of Section 504 of the Rehabilitation Act of 1973 and the Americans with Disabilities Act of 1990, many public indoor and outdoor swimming facilities are accessible to the extent that there may be a hoyer lift or platform enabling individuals with impaired mobility to enter the water. Water temperature in most public pools tends to be about 71 to 75°, which would increase spasticity for individuals with cerebral palsy. Fully adapted pools and gyms are usually found only in large rehabilitation centers specializing in the comprehensive rehabilitation of individuals with neuromuscular disorders like the United Cerebral Palsy Rehabilitation Campuses in Brooklyn and the Bronx, New York, and the Kessler Institute in New Jersey. Smaller agencies try to share or rent facilities owned by other community institutions. Asphalt Green, a nonprofit community recreation and cultural arts center on the upper East Side of Manhattan, has developed an exemplary aquatics and fitness program that meets the needs of individuals with neuromuscular disorders by offering special classes and sessions in addition to a multitude of classes and sessions open to all of its members. The facility is fully accessible and is well utilized by individuals with neuromuscular disorders who come with school classes or on their own. Given the legal mandates to include those with disabilities in community recreation facilities and programs and the cost-effectiveness of designing facilities that can be used by all, we may witness more community centers following the Asphalt Green model of inclusion. There is no accurate way of estimating how many individuals with neuromuscular disorders who are living in the community would avail themselves of community recreation facilities if reasonable accommodations were made and if transportation were available.

Programs differ with respect to emphasis on specific services, setting, population served, and agency requirements, but the basic components of structured, purposeful recreation/leisure programs for individuals with neuromuscular disorders will remain constant. The following daily schedules will provide some idea of the type of therapeutic recreation services that might be provided in two very different settings: an early intervention preschool program for children with cerebral palsy conducted at the local UCP Rehabilitation Center, and a rehab unit for individuals with spinal cord injuries at a VA Hospital.

The early intervention preschool program accepts children ages 2 to 5 years of age who have been diagnosed with cerebral palsy. Children attend for half a day. Transportation and lunch are provided by the agency.

10–10:45 A.M. Gym program—each child in the group has an individualized mobility program which they work on in the gym with the TRS, PT, and OT. Mobility exercises (creeping and crawling on mats and wedges), vestibular stimulation (swings, balance rocker), eye-hand coordination (tether ball).

Aquatics exercise session is conducted twice a week in the fully adapted therapeutic swimming pool in lieu of the gym program. The TRS, OT, and PT work with individual children on ROM and flexibility for arms and legs: standing balance and eye-hand coordination (reaching for colorful plastic shapes floating on the water).

11–11:45 A.M. Individual assessment—TRS assesses one or two children for sensorimotor abilities in a variety of toys equipped with battery-operated switches and musical instruments.

Noon–1:00 P.M. Lunch—work on feeding skills (eating from a spoon, chewing and swallowing).

1–1:30 P.M. Story Time—work on developing receptive speech and listening skills.

APPLICATION OF THE TR PROCESS

CASE STUDY

Sylvia, a 55-year-old wife and mother of two sons, ages 14 and 17 years old, has recently been diagnosed as having Parkinson's disease. For the past year and a half, she noticed that she experienced fatigue when performing routine household chores. Both she and her husband, Morris, had observed a slight hand tremor even when her hands were at rest. While the family was on vacation the previous summer, she found that she had difficulty keeping up when they went for hikes. Her left foot dragged and her gait was becoming unsteady. The diagnosis of Parkinson's was confirmed after extensive neurological testing was done at an institute that specializes in neurological and neuromuscular disorders. At this point in time, Sylvia is considered to be at the Stage 3 level of the disease according to her rating on the Hahn-Yahr scale, a widely used scale to rate the progression of Parkinson's. At this level, both sides of the body are affected (tremor in both hands), and balance and gait are affected. The family has been told that Parkinson's can progress rapidly or slowly; there is no way to predict how rapidly Sylvia's condition will decline. This is a very close-knit family that maintained a leisure lifestyle emphasizing family togetherness activities like travel vacations to places of scenic and historic interest, entertaining relatives and friends frequently, and barbecues in the family's backyard. The social worker at the Neurological Institute where Sylvia is receiving outpatient treatment (i.e., medication) recommends that she contact the local chapter of the Parkinson's Foundation to learn about the services they can provide. The Foundation sponsors a chapter located near the family's home. They have a day program which individuals can attend on a part-time basis. The program is designed for persons in the early stages of Parkinson's and offers a range of services, including therapeutic recreation. Sylvia and Morris decide it would be beneficial for Sylvia to attend the day program two days a week. Their sons, ages 14 and 17 years, are in high school all day. Morris could drive her to the program in the morning on his way to work and the social worker says they can arrange for a car service to take Sylvia home at the end of the day.

Assessment

Sylvia meets with the TRS (therapeutic recreation specialist) on her first day attending the program. The TRS has Sylvia fill out a Leisure Interest Inventory to assess her past and present knowledge, interest, and participation in a wide variety of leisure experiences and recreation activities. They meet for an hour-long interview to find out in more depth about Sylvia's leisure lifestyle, family, and social network, and for the TRS to assess her mood. The TRS will review the neurological findings which the Institute forwarded to the program and will ask Sylvia about her walking gait, balance, hand grasp (i.e., tremor), and general mobility. The TRS will make note of any restrictions of mobility, balance, resting tremor, and coordination at this point.

Planning

The TRS and Sylvia agree that a major goal will be trying to help Sylvia participate in the family's social and leisure experiences to as great an extent as possible. This should include entertaining relatives and friends for meals, holiday celebrations and other special occasions, cookouts in the backyard, and summer travel vacations. Another major goal decided upon was the need for Sylvia to follow an exercise and walking program that would help her increase or maintain flexibility, muscle strength, balance, and erect posture. Sylvia will require leisure counseling to help her plan her activities for times of the day when her medication is most effective and she will need to learn to cope with the side effects of her medications. Leisure counseling will also help her adapt her activities and self-expectations as her status changes over the years.

Sylvia and the TRS list her major long-term goals as:

1. Improving and maintaining optimum physical mobility, balance, and posture through a prescriptive exercise program;
2. Maintaining an independent leisure lifestyle as long as possible which encompasses family

activities, socialization with friends and relatives, and participation in community activities;
3. Individual leisure counseling sessions with the TRS to facilitate Sylvia's adjustment to her limitations and to changes in her physical abilities over time and to strengthen her coping skills to enable her to deal effectively with her medication regimen, physical discomfort, and mood changes.

With these long-term goals defined, Sylvia and the TRS identify the short-term objectives in each of the TR service domains:

Objective 1. Sylvia will participate in the prescriptive exercise group at the chapter on the two days she attends the program. The exercises follow the program developed by the United Parkinson Foundation (McGoon, 1990, pp. 85–92). She will purchase the cassette tapes of the program so she can carry it out at home on the days she is not in program. These exercises are designed to maintain and improve flexibility by putting the joints through full range-of-motion movements, minimize stooped posture through stretching and strengthening the extensor muscles of the arms and back, improve balance and coordination through exercises, walking, and dancing activities which emphasize foot placement, static and dynamic balance, and change of direction. Equipment Sylvia will need to purchase in addition to the program cassettes are one- and two-pound dumbbells and a folding, lightweight exercise mat (therapy service area).

Objective 2. With her family's cooperation and active involvement, Sylvia, Morris, and both sons will take walks on the weekends in an effort to increase Sylvia's stamina and to maintain and improve her gait and coordination (therapy and participation service areas).

Objective 3. Sylvia will check out the indoor swimming pool at the local YWCA and will resume swimming twice weekly on the days she is not attending program. Swimming will help to maintain flexibility by putting the arm, shoulder, knee, and hip joints through full range-of-motion (therapy and participation service areas).

Objective 4. Sylvia will meet with the TRS on a weekly basis for an individual leisure counseling session that will focus on any difficulties she is experiencing in maintaining her social and community relationships. These sessions will also help Sylvia monitor and manage any mood fluctuations she experiences as a result of her medication regimen and as the disease progresses (therapy and leisure education service areas).

Objective 5. Sylvia will participate in the day program's meal preparation activity both days she attends in an effort to enable her to maintain her ability to handle cooking utensils and to prepare light meals. It is important to Sylvia that she feels she is fulfilling her role as housewife and mother. Cooking was also an important part of her social life (i.e., entertaining relatives and friends and dinners and holidays) (leisure education and participation service areas).

Objective 6. Work with the TRS in leisure counseling to plan and manage activities at times her medication is at peak effectiveness. Learn to adjust her activity levels and their timing to her medication schedule and learn to cope with side effects (therapy and leisure education service areas).

Objective 7. Continue to plan family travel vacations that will take into account Sylvia's physical limitations (leisure education and participation service areas).

All of these short-term objectives can be carried out in the outpatient (i.e., day program) and community setting. It is increasingly common to see hospitals and Long-Term Care Facilities conducting day programs in outpatient settings in an effort to maintain people in the community and in independent living situations for as long a time as possible. Many of the short-term objectives fall into the therapy service area of therapeutic recreation. Others are in the leisure education and participation service areas where the emphasis is on learning skills and gaining proficiency in skills for the purpose of using them for intrinsic reward or to promote the values of socialization and family togetherness. Some objectives partake of aspects of two service areas. The TRS would meet with family members to engage them in supporting Sylvia in carrying out her exercise and walking program at home.

Implementation

The TRS met with Sylvia, her husband Morris, and their two sons to present Sylvia's long-term goals and short-term objectives. The TRS emphasized that Sylvia needed their support and encouragement in carrying out her exercise routine at home. Space considerations for this were discussed and the family decided that part of the finished basement could be used for this purpose. The exercise mat and dumbbells will be kept there. The TRS encouraged Morris and their sons to join Sylvia for walking on the weekend, to make it a "family walk," perhaps culminating with brunch at a local diner. This is a way to promote the goals of family togetherness and improved physical functioning. Sylvia purchased the cassette tapes for the exercise program developed by the United Parkinson Foundation (McGoon, 1990) and used them at home when she did not attend the program. On both days that she attends the program she participates in the exercise and conditioning group which also uses the United Parkinson Foundation Program. This makes transfer of training possible and strengthens learning. Sylvia will continue to prepare meals for her husband and sons as she feels that this is an important part of her role as wife and mother. She finds that participating in the group meal preparation activity at the day program has been helpful. The group is supervised by the recreation therapist who has introduced individual participants to adapted utensils and electric can openers which compensate for weak hand grip. Sylvia has decided to purchase some of these devices to make cooking easier for her at home. At subsequent leisure counseling sessions, the TRS suggested that Sylvia invite some friends over to her house for afternoon tea. This was very successful and gave Sylvia the confidence to invite some family members over for dinner. Sylvia and the TRS worked out the timing of meal preparation so it coincided with the time when Sylvia's anticholinergic medication (Cogentin) was at its peak so that her hand tremor did not interfere. They decided that Sylvia will continue to invite friends and family members over for tea, lunch, or dinner at least twice a month in order to maintain her social network and to feel more independent.

Sylvia checked out the swimming pool at the local YWCA. She had been fearful that because her balance was unsteady and maneuvering her feet was difficult and awkward, she would not be able to use the ladder to enter the pool. She found that the pool had a chair lift, making entry into the water possible and safe for her. On days she does not attend program, Sylvia has been swimming at the "Y" twice a week for thirty minutes each session. She has met some new people in her age group who use the pool regularly. One woman has arthritis and another recently underwent a hip replacement operation. Swimming was prescribed for them, also. Sylvia feels that they constitute a little "self-help support group" because they all try to encourage and help each other. Sylvia has been using a local car service to transport her to and from the "Y." Arranging her own transportation makes her feel more independent.

The TRS began working with Sylvia and her family in March to make plans for their two-week travel vacation in July. They will need assistance in locating hotels and motels that afford such accessible features as grip bars in the toilet and shower/bath; rooms located a short distance from the parking area; level, smoothly paved paths; and close proximity to eating facilities. The TRS had directories of accessible lodging places which Sylvia began to check out. The TRS will help Sylvia plan activities she can do by herself when the boys and Morris go off hiking or engage in more strenuous physical activities. As the itinerary is planned, consideration will have to be given to her endurance level and stamina. The TRS will encourage Morris and Sylvia to include a sufficient mix of sedentary activities like boat rides, movies, attending outdoor concerts, outdoor cookouts and picnics, fishing off a dock or boat, and reading a good book while seated on a lawn chair. Sylvia doesn't want to feel she's holding back her sons and husband from participating in more active pursuits requiring greater stamina, endurance, and balance than she possesses. She wants to feel that she has enjoyable things to do on her own at times when they are off doing other thins.

The TRS will continue to work with Sylvia on an ongoing basis in individual leisure counseling sessions. The focus is on problem solving to deal with increasing difficulties she will experience over time in performing everyday living activities and maintaining a satisfying leisure life. The TRS can help Sylvia develop better coping mechanisms that will enable her to handle frustration and depression.

Long-term planning for a patient with Parkinson's must respond to the abilities of the patient and the family's needs, making evaluation at regular and fairly frequent intervals important. As Sylvia experiences greater difficulty being at home, the TRS may recommend that her attendance at the day program be increased to full time. Family members may need to take over some of the meal preparation as needed. Sylvia will be encouraged to maintain contact with friends and family members by telephone and writing and to continue inviting them over on weekends when the entire family can assist in entertaining. In this manner, Sylvia's social network can be maintained and family togetherness activities can be continued. Should Sylvia eventually require a wheelchair, the family's weekend walks to the diner should continue on a regular basis.

Evaluation

The physical and cognitive decline in the person who has Parkinson's can progress very gradually over the course of several decades. Evaluation at regular and frequent intervals is important in guiding the TRS and other therapists working with the patient with Parkinson's and their family in making modifications to current plans and in formulating long-range plans.

Sylvia's regular attendance twice a week in the day program and her active participation in the prescriptive exercise group, the meal preparation activity, and other activities of her choice will provide the TRS and other staff of the program with observational data to indicate whether Sylvia is becoming depressed, irritable, or experiencing mood swings (sometimes a side effect of the mixture of medications that parkinsonian patients are prescribed). They will be able to observe and evaluate any changes in her physical status such as range of motion, increasing bradykinesia, or "freezing", which might indicate that her medication requires adjustment.

Feedback from family members will be important. They will be able to provide feedback to the TRS as to how they see Sylvia functioning at home in her roles as housewife, mother, and wife. During individual leisure counseling sessions with the TRS, Sylvia will discuss her ability to do the prescriptive exercise program at home and any problems she is having with her social activities and swimming.

With early stage Parkinson's, there is often some difficulty with normal sexual activity. If Sylvia or Morris report that they experience this and want to improve the situation, the TRS may refer them to a sex therapist or counselor who specializes in sexual rehabilitation with people who have disabilities.

When Sylvia revisits the neurological institute where she was diagnosed, the Hahn-Yahr test should be readministered every three to six months to determine whether the disease has progressed. These results should be sent to the day program and will guide the TRS in planning how to modify Sylvia's activities.

Sylvia should be seen for pharmacological consultation every month to determine whether her medication levels need to be readjusted. The TRS should be informed of any changes in her medication and may wish to inform the prescribing physician of any changes observed in Sylvia's physical functioning or moods.

There will be a time when Sylvia's thinking may become confused as a side effect of her medications. At these times, information from others about her physical, social, and emotional status will be more reliable. The TRS will make detailed observational notes each time Sylvia attends program and will use these observations in making treatment decisions and modifying plans.

TRENDS AND ISSUES

Section 504 of the Rehabilitation Act of 1973 mandated that all facilities and programs receiving federal funding provide access to disabled persons. The recreation facilities of public high schools and colleges fall under this law but implementation still varies. In some universities, for example, the swimming pool and locker rooms may be wheelchair accessible but the weight-training machines may not. Public swimming pools in municipal and state parks may have chair lifts, hoyer lifts, or ramps, but may lack staff who are knowledgeable about teaching persons with neuromuscular disabilities how to swim.

More recently, the Americans with Disabilities Act of 1990 has mandated that privately owned facilities used by the general public provide "reasonable accommodations" for people with physical, sensory, and mental disabilities. Clearly, the utilization of movie theaters, hotels, health clubs, and other facilities by people with neuromuscular disorders will increase. However, constraints arising from the specific requirements of individuals with certain types of neuromuscular disorders may prevent them from being able to use a particular facility. For example, individuals with spastic type cerebral palsy find that swimming in water that is 75° exacerbates their spasticity; yet this is the usual temperature of most community swimming pools. A community having only one public pool may not be able to accommodate all of the different water temperature preferences of residents. A noteworthy example of a community center that has provided for differing aquatic temperature requirements is Asphalt Green, Inc., a nonprofit community recreation and cultural arts center on the upper East Side of Manhattan. This center has provided a smaller pool heated to 90°F for aqua-exercise classes for adults with arthritis and other conditions that benefit from warm water.

Hopefully, the programming model at Asphalt Green indicates a trend toward greater integration of people with neuromuscular and other disabilities in recreation facilities in the community. Information about the sports and fitness programs for people with disabilities at Asphalt Green can be obtained by writing to: Asphalt Green, Inc., Judy Goldberg, Coordinator, Fitness Program for Persons with Disabilities, 1750 York Avenue, New York.

The trend in health care in the country is pointing away from hospitals and long-term care facilities for the delivery of rehabilitation services and toward community day programs. Efforts will be made to maintain people with neuromuscular disorders in their own homes for as long as possible (Fein, 1994). With advances in pharmacological treatments of Parkinson's and increased awareness of the importance of exercise in maintaining flexibility and joint mobility, persons who develop Parkinson's can expect to maintain most of their pre-illness leisure lifestyle for many years. The role of leisure counseling and leisure education in day programs will expand as individuals with progressive and dynamic neuromuscular disorders (Parkinson's, muscular dystrophy, and multiple sclerosis) will need to learn to adapt, physically and psychologically, to changes in their abilities while trying to maintain as independent a leisure lifestyle as possible. The trend toward greater emphasis on community-based, day centers focusing on restorative and rehabilitation services will continue to increase due to changes in the policies of the major insurance companies. This trend will have an impact on families and caregivers and will increase the need for homemaker services to assist with the custodial and maintenance duties involved in caring for a disabled family member (Fein, 1994).

An additional trend is the expanded use of therapeutic aquatic activities for persons with neuromuscular disorders. Aquatic exercises have been found to promote and to maintain flexibility and range of motion. This is extremely beneficial for individuals with cerebral palsy (spastic type), Parkinson's disease, and multiple sclerosis. The National Therapeutic Recreation Society (NTRS) has recently formed an Aquatic Therapy Network. The American Therapeutic Recreation Association (ATRA) has established an Aquatic Therapy Committee. Both organizations are developing standardized training for recreation therapists who wish to learn how to apply aquatics with persons who have neuromuscular and other disabilities.

Research continues in the development of more effective medications to treat the symptoms of Parkinson's disease and to increase our understanding of the biochemistry and genetics involved in muscular dystrophy. It is possible that with advances in genetic engineering, the defect in protein metabolism at the cellular level which lays at the root of MD may one day be preventable.

The new medical specialty of psychoneuroimmunology has documented the interrelationships between mind and body and the deleterious effects that stress can have upon the tissues and systems of the body (Cousins, 1989). Interventions such as relaxation training, meditation, and breathing exercises have been used with individuals who have multiple sclerosis, a condition in which stress can exacerbate pain and inflammation. Recreational activities and leisure experiences rather than clinical relaxation techniques taught by therapists have been found to provide some patients with a preferred means of relaxing (Levine, 1993). Further research is needed on the benefits of the application of formal relaxation techniques as well as the exploration and reinforcement of activities the patient finds both enjoyable and relaxing. Practitioners need to familiarize themselves with these techniques and become more skilled at applying them with this population.

We will continue to witness growth in the field of rehabilitation engineering. Persons with neuromuscular disorders are benefitting from advances made in the development and application of electrical and computer-based technology for use in assistive devices and faculties such as speech and writing (Adam, 1994). The technology enables persons with limited mobility and arm and hand control to function more independently in all areas of their lives, as well as expanding their opportunities to participate in leisure experiences. Progress will continue to be made in the use of electrical stimulation to extend the range of mobility of persons who are nonambulatory (Kobetic, 1994). Developments in robotic technology as well as research on repairing nerve tissue damaged as a result of spinal-cord injury affords many nonambulatory persons and those who have difficulty controlling arm and hand movements a greater sense of freedom and independence in their daily lives. Functional Electrical Systems (FES) have been used in an effort to restore hand grasp to quadriplegic persons and research continues to be done on using FES to enable paraplegics to walk (Kobetic, 1994).

SUMMARY

This chapter familiarized the reader with the basic characteristics (etiological, symptomatic, psychological, and biological) of the major neuromuscular disorders: Parkinson's disease, cerebral palsy, muscular dystrophy, multiple sclerosis, spina bifida, and spinal cord injury. The role of the therapeutic recreation process (i.e., treatment, leisure education, and participation) and its application during the acute phase of neuromuscular disorders, and during the phases of the rehabilitation process and recovery was described. Appropriate interventions at each stage of the treatment process and the variety of settings in which interventions may be carried out with persons who have neuromuscular disorders were identified. Promoting and maximizing independent functioning of the client through every intervention was emphasized as an overall goal. Current best practices for therapeutic recreation specialists working with persons with neuromuscular disorders were identified and discussed. Leisure counseling plays an important role in assisting individuals with neurological disorders to adapt and adjust to the dynamically changing circumstances of their conditions while trying to maintain a qualitatively satisfying lifestyle that reflects their values and interests. This chapter explored the implications of some of the trends and issues involving attitudes toward disabled persons by society as a whole: scientific and legal developments and innovative therapeutic recreation interventions with this diverse population.

READING COMPREHENSION QUESTIONS

1. What is the value of early intervention programs for young children (less than five years of age) with cerebral palsy? What kinds of therapeutic recreation interventions with young children who have cerebral palsy could stimulate and facilitate development? What are some design considerations that would need to be taken into account in selecting toys and playground apparatus for children with neuromuscular disorders?
2. Describe the importance of leisure counseling and frequent assessment of leisure abilities with individuals who have a progressive neuromuscular disorder such as muscular dystrophy or Parkinson's disease.
3. Recommend different types of sports activities and modifications which might be appropriate for teens and young adults at these various levels of spinal cord injury: C6–C8, T1–T5, T6–T9.
4. What are some of the psychological and social ramifications for teenagers and young adults who have neuromuscular disorders? What kinds of needs and demands must all adolescents deal with? What additional demands does an adolescent with a neuromuscular disease have to deal with? What kinds of therapeutic recreation interventions could be helpful during this stage of development?
5. Why is frequent assessment of the individual with multiple sclerosis important? What kinds of abilities and skills should a therapeutic recreation specialist working with this population possess?
6. Mention and discuss the ways in which aquatic activities can be used with persons who have neuromuscular disorders at each phase along the continuum of services in therapeutic recreation.

SUGGESTED LEARNING ACTIVITIES

1. Visit recreation activities or programs sponsored by non-profit organizations that provide services to persons with neuromuscular disorders. Such organizations include United Cerebral Palsy, the Multiple Sclerosis Society, the Muscular Dystrophy Association, and Eastern Paralyzed Veterans Organization. These organizations have local chapters which sponsor recreation activities, such as wheelchair basketball, as well as vacation and camp programs. Compare the recreation services offered by each organization. Find out how activities are selected. Do participants have input into the selection process? Are the people conducting the activities and programs paid professionals or volunteers? What training do they possess? In what settings are the programs and activities conducted? Is there a relationship between the severity of the disorder that participants manifest and the type of setting in which the activities are conducted?
2. Interview adolescents and adults who have various neuromuscular disorders. Find out what kinds of difficulties they have experienced in trying to develop an independent leisure lifestyle. What kinds of leisure services would they find most valuable that are not currently being provided?
3. Survey some of the public recreation/leisure facilities in your community to identify whether there are architectural barriers that could be impediments to persons with neuromuscular disorders. What kinds of activities that are offered could be appropriate for individuals with neuromuscular disorders? What level of function or ability would be needed to participate? Find out whether individuals with disabilities currently participate in activity programs and/or use the facilities?
4. Become familiar with some mind/body interventions, such as diaphragmatic breathing techniques, yoga, Progressive Muscle Training, and

"Respiratory-One Meditation." How can these interventions be used with persons who have neuromuscular disorders to treat symptoms?

5. Spend approximately six hours in a wheelchair at a time when you would normally have leisure. Determine what constraints you experience in your usual and preferred activities. Relate these constraints to environmental versus psychological and social factors.

6. Attend a wheelchair basketball game or tennis tournament and note any modifications of the rules or the court. Talk with coaches from UCP Sports Association or the Wheelchair Athletics Association and learn about their training, how players are selected and trained, and how facilities are prepared.

REFERENCES

Adam, J. A. (1994, October). Advancing step by step. *IEEE Spectrum,* 24–26.

Adams, R. D., & Victor, M. (1989). *Principles of neurology* (4th ed.). New York: McGraw-Hill.

Aging and Cerebral Palsy (InfoFacts, No. 91–02). (1990). Albany, NY: State OMRDD, Bureau of Aging Services and Special Populations.

Aaseng, N. (1991). *Cerebral Palsy.* Venture Book, Franklin Watts.

Blacklow, R. S. (1983). *MacBryde's signs and symptoms* (6th ed.). London: J. P. Lippincott.

Brown, M. C., Bontempo, A., & Turk, M. (1991). *Adults with Cerebral Palsy* (InfoFacts 92–06). Albany, NY: New York State OMRDD, Bureau of Program Research.

Carter, M. J., Van Andel, G. E., & Robb, G. M. (1995). *Therapeutic recreation: A practical approach* (2nd ed.). Prospect Heights, IL: Waveland Press.

Cousins, N. (1989). *Head First: The biology of hope and the healing power of the human spirit.* New York: Penguin Books.

Fein, E. B. (1994, December 19). Caring for mom, and burning out. *New York Times,* B1.

Fidzianska, A., Goegel, H. H., Lenard, H. G., & Heckmann, C. J. (1982). Congenital Muscular Dystrophy: A collagen formative disease? *Neurological Science, 55*(1), 79–80.

Gilroy, J. (1990). *Basic neurology* (2nd ed.). New York: Pergamon Press.

Gopalan, N. (1994, Summer). Multiple Sclerosis. *Ability Magazine,* 44–46.

Hedrick, B. N. (1986, Fourth Quarter). Wheelchair sport as a mechanism for altering the perceptions of the nondisabled regarding their disabled peer's competence. *Therapeutic Recreation Journal, 20*(4), 72–84.

Kennedy, D. W., Smith, R. W., & Austin, D. R. (1991). *Special recreation* (2nd ed.). Dubuque, IA: Wm. C. Brown.

Kobetic, R. (1994, October). Advancing step by step. *IEEE Spectrum,* 27–31.

Levine, G. R. (1993). *An investigation of the phenomenon of relaxation training among adult psychiatric patients: An interview study.* Ann Arbor, MI: UMI.

Lieberman, A. N., & Williams, F. L. (1993). *Parkinson's disease: The complete guide for patients and caregivers.* New York: The Philip Lief Group, Inc.

Lockette, K. F., & Keyes, A. M. (1994). *Conditioning with physical disabilities.* Champaign, IL: Human Kinetics.

McGoon, D. C. (1990). *The Parkinson's handbook.* New York: W. W. Norton & Company, Inc.

Michelman, S. S. (1974). Play and the deficit child. In M. Reilly (Ed.), *Play as exploratory learning.* Beverly Hills: Sage Publications.

Patrick, G. D. (1986, Fourth Quarter). The effects of wheelchair competition of self-concept and acceptance of disability in novice athletes. *Therapeutic Recreation Journal, 20*(4), 61–71.

Peterson, C. A., & Gunn, S. L. (1984). *Therapeutic recreation program design* (2nd ed.). Englewood Cliffs, NJ: Prentice Hall.

Rosner, L. J., & Ross, S. (1992). *Multiple Sclerosis.* New York: Fireside, Simon & Schuster.

Rusk, H. (1972). *Rehabilitation medicine: A textbook on rehabilitation medicine.* St. Louis: Mosby.

Scheinberg, L. D. (1983). *Multiple Sclerosis: A guide for patients and their families.* New York: Raven Press.

Stark, G. D. D. (1977). *Spina bifida: Problems and management.* Oxford: Blackwell Scientific Publications.

Wilhite, B. C., & Keller, M. J. (1992). *Therapeutic recreation: Cases and exercises.* State College, PA: Venture Publishing, Inc.

CHAPTER 11

COGNITIVE REHABILITATION

MIRIAM LAHEY

OBJECTIVES

- Identify a minimum of three specific cognitive impairments.
- Distinguish among three treatment models for cognitive rehabilitation.
- Describe the three major types of recreation programming planned for the cognitively impaired: therapeutic, leisure experience, and leisure education.
- Explain the relationship between cognitive impairment and social and affective functioning.
- Discuss four current issues in cognitive rehabilitation.

DEFINITION OF COGNITIVE REHABILITATION

Cognitive rehabilitation aims at maximum restoration of lost cognitive skills, including the following: perception, attention, memory, judgment, thinking, decision-making, language (both speaking and comprehension), nonverbal communication, problem solving, rote learning, and generalization of learning. Designating these skills as "lost" implies that the person who has lost them once possessed them, and indeed the focus of this chapter is on those adults who have previously enjoyed full cognitive functioning and then lost it to some degree.

Such loss can come from many sources: depression, infectious diseases, improper medication, excessive use of alcohol or drugs, a brain tumor, vitamin or mineral deficiency, or a spinal cord injury (discussed in Chapter 10). This chapter will limit discussion to rehabilitation of cognitive impairments resulting from head injuries and cardiovascular accidents (strokes), the two largest diagnostic categories seen in rehabilitation settings. The object of the chapter is not so much to provide detailed differential descriptions of cognitive impairments, but rather to familiarize the reader with behavioral and attitudinal patterns commonly observed among patients recovering from head injuries and strokes, and with therapeutic recreation's role in treating these patients.

Both head trauma, resulting from exterior accident, and stroke, resulting from internal accident, may result in a variety of limitations—physical, emotional, behavioral, social, and cognitive. A comprehensive rehabilitation program addresses all these limitations.

CLASSIFICATION OF COGNITIVE THERAPIES

Treatment of stroke and head trauma patients has undergone revision over the years of its relatively brief history, and a number of different approaches can be identified (Toglia, 1992; Thomas &Trexler, 1982; Diller & Gordon, 1981). In the first, or classical approach, taxonomies of cognitive dysfunction attempted to identify the location, severity, and extent of brain damage. For, traditionally, cognition was viewed as a higher-level cortical function with treatment protocols based on the location and structural changes of neuropathology (Stumbo & Bloom, 1990). This approach to cognitive therapy, which has been called reductionist, biologist, or syndrome-specific, associated specific cognitive skills with particular areas of the brain. It basically sought to break down complex skills into their component parts for which the therapist would construct specific remedial tasks. A major problem with this approach is that neuropathology is an inexact science, in spite of advances in technological medicine, so the extent and area of brain damage are very difficult to assess.

A second approach, which might be called psychometric or deficit-specific, views cognitive functioning as divided into separate subskills such as attention, memory, organization, reasoning, and problem solving. It is based on testing designed to identify specific cognitive deficits derived from analyses of performance on the tests. Examples of such tests are the Purdue Pegboard Test, MacQuarrie Test for Mechanical Abilities, Developmental Test of Visual Motor Integration, Rey Osterriech Complex Figure Test, Hooper Visual Organization Test, Wechsler Adult Intelligence Scale, and Woodcock Johnson Test of Achievement. A poor performance on a particular test (designed to measure e.g., attention) is assumed to indicate a deficit in the skill (e.g., attending) which the test was designed to measure (Toglia, 1992). Most of the literature on cognitive rehabilitation emphasizes the deficit specific approach (Trexler, 1987). Based on a hierarchy of skills acquisition, treatment in this approach focuses on the repetition of activities designed for remediation of the specific deficit identified in testing. Limitations to this approach are its failure to acknowledge overlap in cognitive problems, and its implication that cognitive deficits occur in isolation.

Yet a further approach, and one which perhaps lends itself best to the practice of therapeutic recreation, might be termed dynamic, or holistic. Cognition in this approach is defined as the individual's capacity to acquire and use information in order to adapt to environmental demands (Lidz, 1987), and rehabilitation is related more directly to real world tasks. Cognition (information processing and learning) is seen as an ongoing product of the dynamic interaction among individual, task, and environment (social, physical, cultural). It is a multicontext treatment approach which involves practicing the same processing strategy with a variety of tasks, movement patterns, and environments (Toglia, 1992). Part of the move away from a deficit model of treatment occurring across the rehabilitation spectrum, this approach, sometimes called the recovery model, is still rather new. Acknowledged limitations are its reliance on verbal communication and, because of its newness, lack of supporting empirical research.

DESCRIPTION OF LIMITATIONS

The specific approach used to assess and treat a patient who manifests difficulties in cognitive functioning will determine the way in which limitations are perceived. Those who follow the syndrome-specific model will view patients' limits in terms of specific areas and extent of brain damage. Performance scores on tests will indicate to those of the deficit-specific school precisely what cognitive impairments need remediation. The holistic approach, or recovery model, will attempt to help the patient navigate more efficiently through unknown environments. Whichever model is used, it is recognized that the patient is experiencing functional limitations beyond those which are expected in ordinary life.

The following are some of the cognitive limits which may result from stroke or head trauma: problems in attention, memory, organizational skills, simultaneous thinking, and problem solving (Rourke, 1989), rigidity and overdependence on rules and regulations (Semrud-Clikeman &

Hynd, 1990), deficiency in visual-spatial skills (Abramson & Katz, 1989), poor sense of direction (Tranel et al., 1987). Language disorders include: difficulty maintaining conversation and conveying information (Rourke, 1989), tangential speech, tendency to overuse jargon, talkative tendencies (Semrud-Clikeman & Hynd, 1990), difficulties with the rhythm of speech, eye contact and accompanying gestures (Tranel et al., 1987), and problems with interpreting the speech and the nonverbal cues of others (Murray, 1991). There may be motor impairment, even paralysis. There may be bowel or bladder incontinence.

Cognitive losses experienced by persons recovering from strokes and head trauma may affect their social and emotional functioning. The patient may be irritable because he or she cannot focus sufficient attention on a task to complete it; or, may be frustrated because of problems with memory. Perhaps the patient is depressed at the sense of having no control over his or her life. There may be distraction because of inability to process stimuli. Some react with guilt, interpreting the accident as punishment for some real or imagined transgression. Others associate it with death. In all of these examples, it is clear that cognitive impairment does not occur in a vacuum. It affects the lives of all those who experience it; not only the patient, but the family and caregivers as well.

Both strokes and head trauma occur without warning, bringing sudden, dramatic changes in lifestyle. In addition to the limitations directly imposed by the extent and severity of the accident, reactive distress can generate further limitations. Especially when the victim is a young adult, and the principal breadwinner of a family, the shock of moving from full vigor to a greatly restricted lifestyle can be overwhelming. Both stroke and head trauma require radical adjustment. Patients' responses reflect not only the severity of the disorders, but also inherent personality patterns, coping skills, emotional conflicts existing at the time of the accident, environmental factors, and interpersonal relations. In some cases the patients' coping mechanisms may be denial; in others, there may be depression.

Interpersonal relations can be particularly affected when the impact of the accident is felt in identity. For example, when physical prowess or attractiveness has been central to identity, not only might the injured person suffer a crisis of identity, but there may also be resulting confusion in relation to others. A further impact on interpersonal relations comes when the accident necessitates radical role shifts; for instance, when the wage earner in a family becomes dependent on others to take over tasks associated with that role.

The acknowledgement of cognitive losses may evoke a sense of shame, depression, or fear. Such responses may shape the client's whole outlook on life. While there may be emotional reactions to the accident, cognitive impairments are not to be equated with disturbances of affective functioning. The immense affective resources of the client with diminished cognitive capacity can be an important factor in his or her rehabilitation.

Cognitive limits require clarification. Both stroke and head trauma patients experience problems with attention. The attention span may be drastically shortened, or the focus of attention may be vague. With shifting of attention often comes impulsiveness of behavior, a limitation of particular significance in determining and pursuing goals.

Diminished capacity to focus attention may contribute to or accompany memory problems. Short-term, long-term, or rote memory may be affected, or some combination of these, with very different presenting problems in each case. Some people are skillful at compensating for their memory losses; for others, the resulting insecurity is a major limitation to social interaction and to structuring and organizing behavior. Perhaps more than any other limitation, memory loss can create enormous dependency on others.

A further cognitive limitation can occur in the area of abstract thinking. In these cases clients will be more comfortable with concrete tasks. Rigidity of thought characterizes others. A general slowing of mental processes may also limit client abilities. Even more, it may limit others' perceptions of those abilities.

Particularly for those patients who suffer motor impairment as a result of their accidents, a number of secondary health problems may be anticipated (e.g., urinary tract complications, pressure sores, spasms. Where these are protracted, depression rates will be raised, and other secondary psychosocial disabilities are often observed (Graitcer & Maynard, 1990).

Finally, it is important to realize that not all client limitations can be attributed to the client. Some come from the institutional environment, some from family, and some from the therapist. Those who entertain reduced quality of life expectations for patients can indeed strictly limit rehabilitation. For, whatever the extent of cognitive loss, client limitations in these cases are not nearly so global and unremitting as staff and family sometimes imagine. Even the very severely impaired, whose potential for cognitive rehabilitation is perceived as minimal, will have occasions when they are able to focus their attention and even make decisions.

PURPOSE OF THERAPEUTIC RECREATION

As with any other special population, the purposes of therapeutic recreation with the cognitively impaired may be broadly divided as follows: (1) therapeutic/clinical, in which the therapeutic outcome is paramount; (2) leisure/recreational, in which quality of life and subjective experience are paramount; and (3) educational, in which the development of leisure awareness, skills, and resources is paramount. The first of these frequently is perceived as primary in rehabilitation settings.

For clients with cognitive impairments, therapeutic outcome centers around the acquiring or reacquiring of specific physical, affective, cognitive, or social skills. Because of the radical changes in lifestyle occasioned by the accident, vocational goals are seen as very important in the treatment of those recovering from stroke and head trauma. While these goals have a very important place for staff in the third, or educational, phase of rehabilitation, for many clients the overwhelming imperative is to return to work; thus, for them, goals related to work function may be paramount through all stages of rehabilitation. When cognitive impairment is concurrent with physical disabilities, the primary therapeutic outcome sought may be the maximizing of physical functioning. Generally, the physical/medical aspects are emphasized in rehabilitation in the United States (Coyle et al., 1993).

Where the client's affective response to his or her loss represents the greatest obstacle to functioning, it will, ideally, be the central focus of intervention. Therapeutic recreation purposes in the affective domain may seek to reduce excessive/inappropriate affect or may attempt to facilitate release through expression. Affective goals will depend on the nature and extent of the affective disorder, which will reflect many variables, such as personality, coping styles, support systems, and role reversals.

Cognitive retraining as an explicit purpose of therapeutic recreation has been the scope of much recent investigation (Fazio & Fralish, 1988). Indeed, recreation, because it can be more familiar and less threatening than many other interventions, may be a most effective vehicle for cognitive retraining. The word retraining implies a potential for restoration of functioning, but such restoration does not come about automatically. It is a process, at times a very slow process. Cognitive training requires all the effort, patience, and commitment required for physical training. These qualities are not generally associated with leisure experience values, such as fun, freedom, and enjoyment, but they are paramount for success in the clinical phase of rehabilitation.

More than anything else, perhaps, cognitive retraining requires full collaboration between client and professional. Through this collaboration, skill can be strengthened in such a way as to touch many areas of a client's life. A recreational activity can be chosen to build a particular skill, such as attention. Strengthening attending skills can bring about reduction of impulsive behaviors, irritability, and frustration arising from the inability to focus attention. Reducing these unpleasant emotional responses will allow the client to participate in social situations with greater confidence. In this way, the circle of gain can expand so that therapeutic outcome is extended to many dimensions of the client's life.

If, at the same time, the chosen recreational activity is one that brings joy and delight and a sense of fun and freedom, then not only is the client's life enriched, but the leisure experience serves as a refreshing break from the stress and demands of rehabilitation. Moreover, not only is the leisure experience refreshing, freeing, and healing—in the holistic sense of that word—but for clients whose lifestyle has been thoroughly changed, it provides a continuity with life before the accident. Recapturing the enjoyment of former leisure pursuits is a way of rejoining one's own past. For these clients, that means being reconnected with a life that in many other respects is lost to them. In order to make this experience possible, it is important for therapeutic recreation professionals who are strongly committed to the clinical aspects of the profession to recognize that there is a time for the client to move into a leisure experience mode.

Therapeutic recreation purposes in cognitive rehabilitation look beyond the rehabilitation setting to the transitional phase of treatment and join the purpose of all interventions—to prepare clients for independent community living as far as possible. Social skills, adjustments to the disability, confidence, and other facets of reintegration are all part of the therapeutic recreation professional's goals for the client (Hackel et al., 1986). Towards that end, therapeutic recreation staff work to develop leisure awareness, leisure skills, and a leisure resource file for each client and his or her family. The leisure education program can mean, for the cognitively impaired client, the difference between successful community reintegration and a sense of loneliness and boredom that leads to further regression. Research indicates that leisure education is especially important for those clients who will not be able to return to work, as they are at great risk of boredom (Coyle et al., 1993).

COMMON SERVICE SETTINGS

The accidents that result in head trauma or stroke are very different. Strokes are internal, and the precise moment of occurence may not be known; head trauma is external and usually accompanied by violence. In spite of these differences, they have many factors in common. Because both result in brain damage, the injured person is brought initially to an acute care hospital for emergency treatment. After emergency measures are completed, intensive care and surveillance follow. There is then a period in a rehabilitation unit until discharge to a transitional living facility or the patient's home. Each of these four treatment phases takes place in a different service setting. During the emergency treatment and intensive care, of course, patients are too seriously ill for recreation. In the rehabilitation and transitional phases of treatment, however, recreation has a very important contribution to make to a client's recovery, well-being, and future quality of life.

Within these two settings, therapeutic recreation specialists are an integral part of the rehabilitaion team, working together with pychiatrists, psychologists, nurses, social workers, speech therapists, occupational therapists, physical therapists, and neurologists. The team approach is considered the most effective way to provide holistic treatment (Adamovich, Henderson, & Auerbach, 1985). The therapeutic recreation specialist, working within the team, is concerned not only with appropriate leisure functioning, but also with recreation activities to promote general treatment goals; for instance, strengthening social skills, cognitive skills, and other skills needed to live and work in the community.

At interdisciplinary team meetings, priorities are determined for intervention with stroke and head trauma patients. In many rehabilitation centers, a separate team is assigned to each disability;

for example, there may be a stroke team, a head trauma team, and a spinal cord injury team. The teams become familiar with precise patterns within their areas of specialization. The therapeutic recreation specialist on the stroke team, for instance, would learn to see activity analysis in reference to the recurring needs of stroke patients. Team sharing can be very enriching for the professional as well as the client, but it can be very time-consuming. Furthermore, it requires close communication among team members and a capacity to move beyond traditional interpretation of professional roles (Howe-Murphy & Charboneau, 1987). A danger with the team approach is that professionals may become so caught up in their own interaction that they leave out the most important member of the team—the patient.

In some rehabilitation and transitional settings, the educational model predominates. Particularly for young adult accident victims, vocational training is seen as a priority, for the primary goal is to enable them to rejoin society as productive, self-sustaining members of the work force. The schedule in such settings resembles a school or work situation, with a highly structured series of classes or training sessions. Units with this type of focus may allocate the evening or weekend hours to recreation programs. Such an approach is not inappropriate for the patients, because even though seemingly displaced by work and school, leisure remains a central factor in the overall treatment program, and the real-life situation is mirrored in such an arrangement (Barthe, Chandron, & Fichter, 1985).

CURRENT BEST PRACTICES AND PROCEDURES

The dramatic increase in survivors of head injury and stroke has necessitated the expansion of services to clients suffering from these injuries. Postacute rehabilitation services in particular are now more carefully differentiated to reflect levels of client need (Zahara & Cuvo, 1984). At-home care promises to become an important area of future service development for both these client groups, particularly in the light of persistent secondary, chronic conditions (Seaton, 1988). Family involvement is increasingly recognized as an important factor in rehabilitation (DeJong, Batavia, & Williams, 1991), although differences among families must also be acknowledged. Above all, the move away from deficit-specific intervention models implies more involvement of the client in goal setting and evaluation, and relies increasingly on self-monitoring to expedite cognitive rehabilitation. Research in cognitive rehabilitation of stroke and head trauma clients has benefitted from recent expansion of single case and small group studies (Giles & Clarke-Wilson, 1988). The best therapeutic recreation practice will reflect these recent developments in the traditional four phases of intervention.

Assessment

As remarked above, the treatment approach will govern all phases of intervention. This is true especially for assessment. The biological, or syndrome-specific, approach will assess the patient in terms of area and extent of brain injury; the psychometric approach will base assessment on tests to determine cognitive deficit; the holistic approach will look to the patient to assess his or her situation and specify treatment goals. There are, of course, patients who may not be capable of deciding on their own goals. They may be represented by a surrogate decision-maker, or by the therapist, depending on the procedure of the facility.

In any case, the assessment of cognitively impaired clients is similar to that of other clients treated by therapeutic recreation professionals with the addition of particular input related to cognitive functioning. Since reactions to cognitive impairment play an important part in these cases, it is important to have information about the patient's pre-morbid condition, including such items as outlook, strengths, coping skills, interaction patterns, roles, and motivation.

An important focus of the assessment process is on enabling the patient to return to previous roles. As with any other special population, assessment procedures with the cognitively impaired rely on observation, interviews with client, family, and staff, and review of the case history, inluding medical charts. Because these patients cannot always speak for themselves, careful observation is central to their assessment. In working with cognitive loss, it is important not to label clients as incompetent. Because their response is slow, their attention flits, and they find it hard to focus, it is easy to perceive stroke and head trauma patients as incapable of thinking, learning, or deciding. The staff's inner labeling can be a confirmation of the patients' own dark fears, so special care must be taken to entertain the maximum realistic expectations for their recovery.

Planning (Task Analysis/Activity Analysis)

Following assessment and prioritizing among treatment goals with the client, program planning in therapeutic recreation takes the same course with this population as with any other group, except that activities will be planned with special emphasis on accepting, compensating for, or retraining around cognitive losses and concurrent emotional and physical losses. Cognitive retraining is a special part of preparing for life at home, including social and leisure dimensions as well as the work role.

Leisure activities for the development of cognitive skills can begin very simply. Games of strategy and chance are appropriate for guiding clients from step to step in the process of organizing information, making decisions, and planning a course of action. For those with very low tolerance for interference or competition, the first steps may have to be made in the company of the therapist alone or with a single partner. For example, Depoy and Burke (1992) describe the use of a radio with ear phones for a client troubled by auditory distraction. Also, for those whose social skills have been reduced secondary to stroke or brain trauma, there are a number of computer games which make no social demands but do call for selecting a strategy in order to win points. Once a client is comfortable in strategizing, he or she can try a more competitive or interactive game, perhaps requiring eye contact and other nonverbal forms of communication.

Caldwell and Weissinger (1994) suggest that skill level is a very important factor for cognitively impaired clients. Their research, which focused on persons with spinal cord injuries, found that lack of perceived skill or competence made boredom more likely for these clients than did lack of perceived choice or control. In light of this finding, computer games have a distinct advantage in their skill-level adaptability (Lynch, 1982). For the therapeutic recreation specialist who is interested in becoming an entrepreneur, developing software applications for the cognitively impaired client would no doubt yield double gains. Above all, software pertaining to activity analysis (task analysis) is greatly needed.

Writing is especially valuable as an activity for stroke and head trauma patients. The physical act itself is beneficial, but even more important is the opportunity to get in touch with one's thinking through seeing it in writing. Educators for some time have recognized the importance of writing for learning—not just for learning to write, but for tracking one's process of thinking (Fulwiler, 1987; Parker & Goodkin, 1987). Keeping personal logs, free writing (very informal) or focused free writing (informal but directed), double-entry notebooks in which actions and reflections are recorded in separate columns, imaginary dialogues with favorite authors or heroes—all of these writing activities will enable clients to develop their powers of expression and at the same time will help them analyze their thinking process. If the client chooses to share these writings with the therapist, such sharing is received with utmost respect. The writings are in no way intended to be diagnostic indicators or the subject of team discussions. They are very private and personal. Freedom and not being judged are an important part of their therapeutic value.

Clients who choose to do so may collaborate with a group in creating a poem, essay, or story. A vignette can be presented and the group can develop a story from it. A beginning group may design a rather rudimentary story, while a more sophisticated group may devise something more complex, such as a mystery to be solved.

The creative arts, too, can be used as a source for writing. Listening to music, contemplating a piece of fine art, watching a dance or a play, in addition to being enjoyable experiences, can serve to provoke reflection, and the reflection can be written up, either for an increased sense of control of one's thoughts, for self-knowledge, or for sharing with the therapist, a friend, or even a group—all at the discretion of the client.

Implementation

The therapeutic recreation specialist learns from working with clients who are cognitively impaired that even apparently simple recreation activities require the capacity to organize information, to make decisions, and to engage in complex cognitive planning that is taken for granted in normal life. When these skills are lost, they require careful rebuilding. The most successful rebuilding takes place when all the agents are working together; this means that the client must have an integral part in planning the program. Because discharged clients plan their own programs, it is necessary that they begin to address this task within the rehabilitation setting. In a group, for example, clients can plan outings, listing the possibilities with their advantages and disadvantages, and working through to a shared decision. Such a task could be as simple as selecting a movie from a list of those available, or as complex as planning a dinner outing which involves making reservations and travel arrangements. At a more sophisticated level, the group might work through to a compromise on decisions.

As clients are assisted through problems and difficulties, the process moves from being staff responsible to being client responsible. All of this, although part of a normal recreation program, involves the clients at a much more decisive level of participation than in the therapeutic recreation program for some other special populations. It is important to constantly press clients to greater levels of self-determination (Gaudet & Dattilo, 1994). Through making mistakes, clients learn to correct their errors and prepare for a future when there will be no staff around to solve their problems.

Evaluation

The therapeutic recreation professional constantly observes, analyzes, and records patient progress. In cognitive rehabilitation, precise documentation of functional change is imperative, for the whole team needs to be aware of gains or regressions, and these may make themselves manifest in the recreation hour as in any other. Checklists are prepared by some therapeutic recreation professionals to facilitate the gathering of client Dattilorecise data are especially important for working with these clients who are often not able to describe their experience.

The whole team is depending on the precise progress notes of all team members. As the time for discharge draws near, the patient is carefully evaluated for reentry into the community. Evaluation of leisure awareness, leisure skills, and a leisure resource file is critical. Trips to the community are part of the development of leisure resources. Evaluation of the family support group and of the capacity to return to the world of work is also part of predischarge planning. It happens, not infrequently, that upon discharge the client goes from being the center of therapeutic attention to being left to his or her own devices. Thus, in addition to the other rehabilitation tasks which must be met, is the added burden of dealing with apparent abandonment by the rehabilitation team.

Among the goals for leisure education programs for head injured adults in rehabilitation, the following were reported by Fazio & Fralish (1988) as rated the most important by clients:

development of social skills, decreasing isolation and withdrawal, community integration, and independent leisure involvement. To the extent that these goals are met, a therapeutic recreation program with the cognitively impaired might be evaluated as successful.

APPLICATION OF THE TR PROCESS

CASE STUDY

George is a 24-year-old white male who sustained multiple injuries, including head injuries, in an automobile accident. The left side of his brain was injured, with resulting right side limited mobility and expressive aphasia. George has a wife, aged 20, and a 2-year-old daughter. Prior to his accident, he was employed as a shoe salesman in a retail store. He is greatly concerned about the welfare of his wife and child, for whom he is the sole means of support. His anxiety is exacerbated by his inability to express himself. Physical therapy and speech therapy are his main interests. He is especially eager to return to his work.

Assessment

Before meeting George, the therapeutic recreation professional will have reviewed the pertinent medical records, discussed the case with other members of the treatment team, and interviewed George's wife and other members of his family. An important fact is gathered in this process, namely, that George is left-handed, so his right hemiplegia is not as disruptive to his functioning as it would be if he were right-handed. He is able to write, although he cannot speak. George has a number of cognitive disorders—difficulty concentrating, attending, and communicating—however, the most serious obstacle to his functioning is affective. This is readily apparent at the initial assessment interview. His anxiety escalates as he attempts to communicate to the therapeutic recreation specialist that he is not interested in recreation. He sputters and stammers in his attempt to speak, and finally bursts into tears. The therapeutic recreation professional sits with him in silence for a few moments; then, in a brief empathic (not pitying) response, lets him know that she will return and that together they will work on his goal of returning to his home and work.

As is often the case, the first interview with George occurs when the client is at a very low point. He has just been discharged from acute care but is still unaccustomed to the radical life change brought about by the accident, and is unable to cope with the idea of his limitations, both real and imaginary. A major task in this first interview is to establish a relationship of mutual trust and respect, to deal honestly with the client, and to communicate a willingness to collaborate with him in the pursuit of his goals. Even though little seems to be accomplished in the initial interview with George, the assessment process has begun. It will continue, but sufficient information has been gathered to start the program planning.

Planning

Together with the interdisciplinary team, the therapeutic recreation professional focuses on the need to reduce anxiety as the immediate treatment goal for George, since his anxiety is a major obstacle to his ability to determine his own goals. Beyond that, therapeutic recreation goals are to strengthen attending skills through participation in adapted bowling. (George's wife has indicated that prior to the accident he had been enthusiastic about bowling.) A long-term goal is to help George identify activities that he might enjoy when he returns to the community, and to help him find community settings where he might participate in the selected activities. Appropriate behavioral objectives for George might be stated as follows:

- He will daily undertake to write about his feelings in a personal journal.
- He will engage in the bowling activity at least once weekly.

- He will identify a minimum of three activities in which he would like to participate in the community.
- He will make at least three trips to the community to visit recreation facilities near his home.

Implementation

From the outset, it is important that the therapeutic recreation professional recognize her own feelings about George's impairments. In this case, George was an innocent victim of an automobile accident, but it often happens in head trauma cases that the patient has been responsible for the accident in which he (and perhaps others) was injured. Professionals must develop self-awareness so that their feelings and attitudes do not cloud the therapeutic procedure. Furthermore, dealing with George's reaction to his impairments calls for much patience and insight. In this case, for example, George pressed forward towards independent functioning. At times, however, clients, particularly stroke patients, may regress into dependency and make what seem like unwarranted requests. Furthermore, given the relatively high incidence of depression among disabled persons, reduced motivation can be expected. It is important that therapists understand the origins of such apparent lack of motivation.

Following upon the first visit, the therapist can invite George to attend a movie or other entertainment program, either with his wife or in the company of a staff person. He can be encouraged to write down a reaction to the experience, for through writing down his thoughts and feelings, he can get some sense of control over them, especially important since he has little control of his speaking. He may choose to share his journal with his wife or the therapist; when he gains some emotional control, he may wish to share his writings in a discussion group.

If possible, one of the patients who belongs to the bowling group could escort George for his first bowling session, ideally a patient who had been impaired as George has, but who shows improvement. Later, in his wife's company, George can be escorted to a few community recreation facilities in order to see which offer the activities he is interested in, which are most accessible, in short, which will be most suited to his needs.

Because George will be in the rehabilitation unit about six weeks, he has time to pursue his objectives at the same time that he works to regain his speech and ambulation. Usually he would be allowed a home pass two weeks prior to discharge in order to help him adjust to his living situation.

Evaluation

The therapeutic recreation professional keeps accurate and detailed notes of George's progress. Because he is highly motivated to get better, each gain spurs him on to new aspirations. It is important to keep these aspirations realistic and not to let him try to do everything at once, or he will set himself up for disappointment. If bowling, at which he once excelled, proves to be a source of disappointment to him because he cannot reproduce his former high level of proficiency, then another activity may have to be substituted.

Essentially, the evaluation process asks if the goals set at the beginning of the therapeutic recreation process have been met. In responding to this question, concrete examples are provided as evidence. In the ideal situation, a follow-up program would be drawn up in which, after discharge, George could return to the rehabilitation facility once a month for leisure counseling with the therapist. Since this is rarely possible, the therapeutic recreation professional might ask George and his wife if she could call from time to time to see how he is progressing. Providing for some follow-up contact at the time of closure signals to the client and family that the therapist indeed does care, that the trust that has been built is genuine, founded on a professional relationship.

TRENDS AND ISSUES

Improvements in medical technology have recently brought higher levels of sophistication to the rehabilitation of stroke and head trauma patients. New interventions are costly, however, and recent attempts to contain medical costs have sharply limited the length of stay in rehabilitation facilities. Therapeutic recreation professionals will be drawn into this process, principally by being asked to document precisely the evaluation of their interventions. It means more paperwork and also a more stringent environment in which to pursue rehabilitation goals. Precisely what must be avoided with head trauma and stroke patients is a sense of hurry, yet there will be much pressure to hurry when time constraints are brought to bear. It will mean a higher level of stress for the treatment team.

Increasingly important in rehabilitation are such ethical issues as the right to refuse treatment, the right to be informed precisely of the procedures and objectives of treatment, and the right to surrogate decision-makers for those who are incompetent. Such considerations add to the time and costs of service. They are very important parts of service delivery, but they place additional burdens of responsibility on rehabilitation professionals.

As noted above, newer treatment approaches tend to focus on the acquisition of real world skills perceived by the client as important rather than remediation of deficits indicated by neuropathology or psychometric testing. This new approach, which stresses client empowerment, will almost certainly shape rehabilitation services in the future; however, serious research is needed about its application, client progress, long-term benefits, cost-benefit analysis, and experiences of therapists. Therapeutic recreation, as a profession, is in a unique position to enter into the empowerment model, and can lead the way in research for the application of this model.

While not a new issue, the sexuality of clients with cognitive impairments has recently begun to be discussed more openly. The treatment team will be expected to respond intelligently and sensitively to this issue, something which may be difficult even when dealing with nondisabled clients. Cognitively impaired persons may experience judgment problems which makes it difficult for them to recognize boundaries between self and others. They may lack insight into the appropriateness of their behavior. Indeed, a host of difficulties may surface around their sexual needs and behaviors. Dealing in a professional manner with this issue is expected of therapeutic recreation staff as well as the other team members. Often, the recreation activity is the occasion when clients have the opportunity to make social/sexual contact with others (Schover & Jensen, 1988).

Home care promises to assume greater importance in health service delivery in the future. Not only is it perceived to be less costly than acute care, but it avoids some of the disadvantages of institutional settings. The lengthy rehabilitation required for both stroke and head trauma patients makes home care vital for them. Unfortunately, therapeutic recreation has tended to follow the acute care, highly clinical model, to the neglect of home care. Particularly for those nonworking clients continuing their cognitive rehabilitation at home, leisure counseling can be a pivotal factor in progress.

Development of software for task and activity analysis will be critical as advances in medical technology permit more and more patients with extensive brain damage to survive. Working towards the rehabilitation of these patients is a lengthy, costly, labor-intensive process. Activity analysis software would expedite program planning and tracking of patient progress.

SUMMARY

Cognitive impairment may be attributed to a number of causes. This chapter focused on two of them—head trauma and cardiovascular accident (stroke). Both result in brain damage that may impair not only cognitive but also physical, affective, and social functioning. Complications may be occasioned by the accident victim's reactions.

A number of treatment approaches have been identified. The earliest model was based on neuropathology; then followed a psychometric, deficit-specific model; recently, an empowerment model is gaining recognition. Advantages of the empowerment model for therapeutic recreation professionals include its relationship to real-world skills, its stress on client self-determination, and its positive attitude towards client as whole person.

Whatever treatment approach is utilized, the therapeutic recreation professional plays a vital role in the rehabilitation of persons with cognitive impairments. As part of the treatment team, he or she shares the primary goal of assisting the client to reach his or her highest possible level of functioning.

Three different types of recreation programming are planned for the cognitively impaired: (1) a clinical program, in which activities are chosen to achieve rehabilitation goals; (2) a leisure experience program, in which quality of life is enhanced, and connection is made with past leisure enjoyment; and (3) a leisure education program, which prepares clients for a full leisure lifestyle in the community.

Working with cognitively impaired persons is highly rewarding for professionals who can believe in the rehabilitation potential of this client group, and who can work patiently with them in the challenge of rebuilding their lives.

READING COMPREHENSION QUESTIONS

1. In what ways may the impact of stroke or head trauma affect the patient's sense of identity?
2. Describe three different approaches to the treatment of stroke and head trauma patients.
3. In addition to cognitive impairment, what other losses may accompany stroke or head trauma?
4. Why are precise observation records of special importance for working with the cognitively impaired?
5. Discuss three new trends in cognitive rehabilitation and their implications for therapeutic recreation.

SUGGESTED LEARNING ACTIVITIES

1. Visit a nearby rehabilitation facility and observe a therapeutic recreation activity designed for cognitive retraining.
2. Survey community recreational resources within a one-mile radius of your home or school. Note accessibility.
3. Role-play the following dialogue with a classmate. One person plays a therapeutic recreation professional; the other plays a client in a rehabilitation setting who is suffering damage to the right side of the brain from a motor accident. The client explains to the therapist how it feels suddenly to be unable to ambulate or to move one's left arm. The therapist responds.
4. Interview a therapeutic recreation director in a rehabilitation facility. Ask about length-of-stay restrictions in the facility and about the impact of such restrictions on service delivery.
5. Interview three cognitively impaired clients in a rehabilitation setting. Ask them what they see as most important in a therapeutic recreation program.
6. Discuss the ethical implications of labeling clients "cognitively impaired."
7. Prepare a very thorough task analysis of an activity which would lend itself to use in cognitive retraining.

REFERENCES

Abramson, R., & Katz, D. (1989). A case of developmental right-hemisphere dysfunction: Implications for psychiatric diagnosis and management. *Journal of Clinical Psychiatry, 50*(2), 70–71.

Adamovich, B., Henderson, J., & Auerbach, S. (1985). *Cognitive rehabilitation of closed head injured patients: A dynamic approach.* San Diego: College Hill Press.

Barthe, B., et al. (1991). Rehabilitation and clinical neuropsychology. In S. Fiscov & T. Boll (Eds.), *Handbook of clinical neuropsychology*. New York: John Wiley & Sons.

Caldwell, L., & Weissinger, E. (1994). Factors influencing free time boredom in a sample of persons with spinal cord injuries. *Therapeutic Recreation Journal, 28*(1), 18–25.

Coyle, C., et al. (1993). Psychosocial functioning and changes in leisure lifestyle among individuals with chronic secondary health problems related to spinal cord injury. *Therapeutic Recreation Journal, 27*(4), 239–253.

DeJong, G., Batavia, A., & Williams, J. (1991). Who is responsible for the lifelong well-being of a person with a head injury? In R. Marinelli & A. Dell Orto (Eds.), *The psychological and social impact of disability*. New York: Springer Publishing Co.

Depoy, E., & Burke, J. (1992). Viewing cognition through the lens of the model of human occupation. In N. Katz (Ed.), *Cognitive rehabilitation: Models for intervention in occupational therapy*. Stoneham, MA: Andover Medical Publishers.

Diller, L., & Gordon, W. (1981). Rehabilitation and clinical neuropsychology. In S. Fiscov & T. Boll (Eds.), *Handbook of clinical neuropsychology*. New York: John Wiley & Sons.

Fazio, S., & Fralish, K. (1988). A survey of leisure and recreation offered by agencies serving traumatic head injured adults. *Therapeutic Recreation Journal, 22*(1), 46–54.

Fulwiler, T. (Ed.). (1987). *The journal book*. Upper Montclair, NJ: Boynton Press.

Gaudet, G., & Dattilo, J. (1994). Re-acquisition of a recreation skill by adults with cognitive impairments: Implications to self-determination. *Therapeutic Recreation Journal, 28*(3), 118–133.

Giles, G., & Clark-Wilson, J. (1988). The use of behavioral techniques in functional skills training after severe brain injury. *American Journal of Occupational Therapy. 42*, 658–665.

Graitcer, P., & Maynard, F. (Eds.). (1990). *Proceedings: First colloquium on preventing secondary disabilities among people with spinal cord injuries*. Atlanta: U.S. Department of Health and Human Services, Centers for Disease Control.

Hackel, J., Berger, A., & Putz, G. (1986). How much reintegration can be achieved in patients after severe head and brain trauma? *Anaesthetist, 35*(3), 171–176.

Howe-Murphy, R., & Charbonneau, B. (1987). *Therapeutic recreation: An ecological perspective*. Englewood Cliffs, NJ: Prentice-Hall.

Lidz, C. (1987). Cognitive deficiencies revisited. In C. Lidz (Ed.), *Dynamic assessment*. New York: Guilford Press.

Lynch, W. (1982). The use of electronic games in cognitive rehabilitation. In L. Trexler (Ed.), *Cognitive rehabilitation: Conceptualization and intervention*. New York: Plenum Press.

Murray, E. (1991). Hemispheric specialization. In A. Fisher, E. Murray, & A. Bundy (Eds.), *Sensory integration: Theory and practice*. Philadelphia: F. A. Davis.

Parker, R., & Goodkin, V. (1987). *The consequences of writing: Enhancing learning in the disciplines*. Upper Montclair, NJ: Boynton Press.

Rourke, B. (1989). *Nonverbal learning disabilities: The syndrome and the model*. New York: Guilford Press.

Schover, L., & Jensen, S. (1988). *Sexuality and chronic illness: A comprehensive approach*. New York: Guilford Press.

Seaton, D. (1988, January/February). Independent living: The need to recognize long term support. *Cognitive Rehabilitation*, 32.

Semrud-Clikeman M., & Hynd, G. (1990). Right hemispheric dysfunction in nonverbal learning: Social, academic, and adaptive functioning in adults and children. *Psychological Bulletin, 107*(2), 196–209.

Stumbo, N., & Bloom, C. (1990). The implications of traumatic brain injury for therapeutic recreation services in rehabilitation settings. *Therapeutic Recreation Journal, 24*(3), 64–80.

Thomas, J., & Trexler, L. (1982). Behavioral and cognitive deficits in cerebrovascular accidents and closed head injury: Implications for cognitive rehabilitation. In L. Trexler (Ed.), *Cognitive rehabilitation: Conceptualization and intervention*. New York: Plenum Press.

Toglia, J. (1992). A dynamic interactional approach to cognitive rehabilitation. In N. Katz (Ed.),

Cognitive rehabilitation: Models for intervention in occupational therapy. Stoneham, MA: Andover Medical Publishers.

Tranel, D., Hall, L., Olson S., & Tranel, N. (1987). Evidence for a right hemisphere developmental learning disability. *Developmental Neuropsychology, 3*(2), 113–127.

Trexler, L. (1987). Neuropsychological rehabilitation in the United States. In M. Meier, A. Benton, & L. Diller (Eds.), *Neuropsychological rehabilitation.* New York: Guilford Press.

Zahara, D., & Cuvo, A. (1984). Behavioral applications to the rehabilitation of traumatically head injured persons. *Clinical Psychology, 4,* 477–491.

CHAPTER 12

GERIATRIC PRACTICE

MICHAEL L. TEAGUE
WITH VALERIE L. MCGHEE
BARBARA A. HAWKINS

OBJECTIVES

- Identify the classification of mental disorders for the elderly by emotional, functional, and developmental categories.
- Discuss the purpose of rehabilitation of the elderly as a unique process.
- Discuss the role of therapeutic recreation in psycho-social rehabilitation of the elderly.
- Critique reality orientation, stimulation programs, behavior therapy, and psychotherapy as psychosocial treatment models for the elderly.
- Identify the most common types of programs and settings in which the elderly population may receive therapeutic recreation services.
- Identify appropriate assessment, planning, implementation, and evaluation information for elderly clients.
- Describe the best practices in program implementation and evaluation.

DEFINITION OF AGING

Aging involves a myriad of aging processes that consist of lifelong changes beginning shortly after birth. The dictionary definition of aging is simply "becoming old" or "becoming aged." However, three views of aging—biological (senescence), sociological (eldering), and psychological (geronting)—are commonly recognized.

Biological aging is defined as the individual's present position with respect to potential life span. Measurement of biological aging encompasses the assessment of functional capacities of life organ systems. Social aging refers to roles and norms with respect to other societal members. Measurement of social aging is the assessment of the dynamic process or eldering, that is, the individual's course of life through the social institutions of which one is a member. Psychological aging refers to the behavioral capacities of individuals to adapt to changing environmental demands. Thus, psychological aging addresses the adaptive capacities of memory, learning, intelligence, skills, feelings, motivations, and emotions for exercising behavioral control or self-regulation.

CLASSIFICATION OF MENTAL IMPAIRMENTS

Older adults with mental impairments constitute a small but significant subgroup of the aged population. Approximately 7.8 percent of all community-residing older adults have a need for professional psychiatric services. But, only 2.5 percent of elderly needing professional help for mental health receive such services and only 2.4 percent receive help from primary care physicians (Burns & Taub, 1990). The primary care physician is still the most likely professional to identify, treat and refer older adults for mental health services. Classification of mental impairments can be divided into three categories: (1) emotional, (2) mental disorders, and (3) developmental disabilities.

Emotional Problems

Adaptation implies a continual interaction between the person and his or her environment, each making demands on the other. Positive adaptation may be viewed as the person's ability to meet biological, social, and psychological needs satisfactorily in light of changing environmental conditions. Negative adaptation is the person's failure to meet basic needs, or the ability of the person to meet these needs only at the cost of suffering, pain, and/or disorder. Thus, negative adaptation to the changes—both social and personal—that characterize later life may lead to emotional problems (e.g., grief, loneliness, guilt, depression, anxiety, sense of impotence, helplessness, rage).

Although adaptation is a necessary process common to individuals of all ages, some sources of adaptive changes are more common in later life. Figure 12.1 identifies three major sources of change in later life and potential issues related to each source. The reader will note that there are some sources of adaptive change that are unique to the elderly; for example, retirement, age segregation, grandparenthood. Pfeiffer (1977) has suggested that most age-specific adaptation issues are variations of three adaptive problems: (1) adaptation to loss, (2) identity review, and (3) remaining active. Adaptation to loss (e.g., loss of spouse, loss of work relations) is one's ability to replace some of those losses with new relationships and roles, or learn to make do with less. Identity review is an evaluative backward glance at one's life in which the person weighs such elements as accomplishments versus failures and satisfaction versus disappointments. Failure to delineate a self-identity that is reasonably positive is likely to result in emotional problems. Remaining active implies that a positive correlation exists between participation in satisfying activities and the maintenance of healthy physical, social, and psychological functioning (Teague & MacNeil, 1992).

The salient issue is not that old age carries with it unique adaptive changes. Instead, the critical issue is the extent to which older adults are capable of adapting to the challenges of later life. A principal by-product of negative adaptation to environmental challenges is stress. Coping with stressful events requires the mentally healthy individual to assess the situation, choose a way to respond, act upon the choice, and evaluate the success or failure of the chosen action. However, a stressor perceived as too overwhelming to be handled by the usual coping mechanisms may lead even the mentally healthy adult to resort to alternative damaging strategies. Substance abuse and suicide, a well-documented response of the inability of many older adults to cope with insurmountable stress, are among such strategies. For example, older adults account for approximately 17 percent of reported suicides, despite representing only 12 percent of the population. Depression and failing health are the most common reasons cited for suicide in later life (Koenig & Blazer, 1992). When we consider social and cultural correlates of mental health and illness, we find that depressed elderly persons are most likely to be women, unmarried or widowed, lower socioeconomic status, experienced stressful events, lack of supportive social network, and have co-existing physical conditions (NIH, 1991).

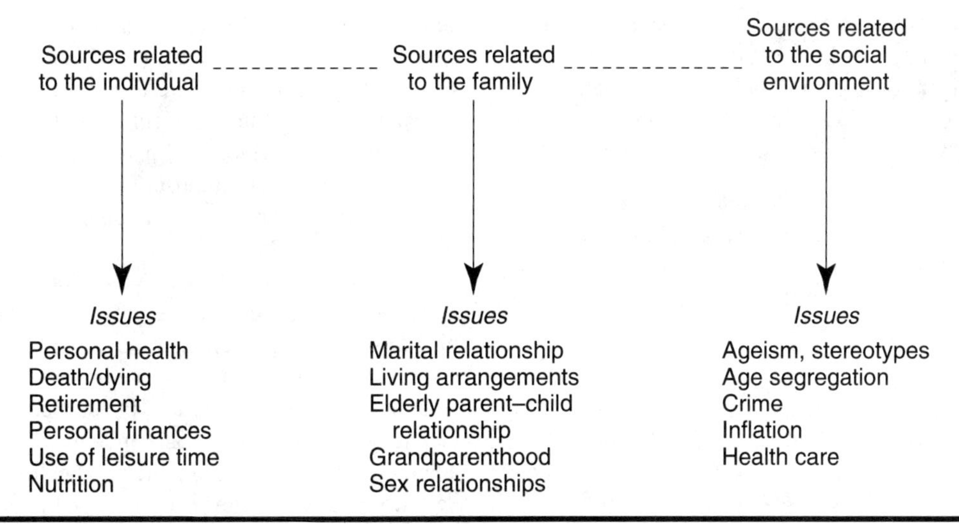

FIGURE 12.1 Common Sources of Major Adaptive Change in Later Life
Source: From D.M. Rosenthal & N. Colangelo, "Counseling the Elderly: Individual, Family, and Social Perspectives," in M.L. Teague, R. D. MacNeil, & G. Hitzhusen (Eds.), *Perspectives on Leisure and Aging in a Changing Society* (Columbia, MO: Department of Recreation & Park Administration, 1982). Reprinted by permission of the University of Missouri Board of Curators.

It was once believed that depression was prevalent in over 25 percent of the elderly. New studies, however, suggest that depression occurs more frequently with younger adults. Still, the most common reason for admission to psychiatric hospitals for the elderly is depression. Depression is also reported in frequencies of 25 to 50 percent of persons suffering from strokes, Parkinson's disease, or multiple sclerosis. The incidence of minor depression among nursing home residents is estimated between 15 to 25 percent (Gatz & Smyer, 1992).

Mental Disorders

Mental disorders including the dementias are a biopsychosocial phenomena and their understanding requires the integration of biological, psychological, social, and environmental perspectives and factors. To compound the diagnostic process, age related developments influence the outcomes. Unlike many physical illnesses, most mental disorders lack clear, objective markers. Instead, mental illnesses are diagnosed on the basis of symptoms reported by patients and observed by mental health professionals. The official diagnostic classification of psychiatric disorders is the American Psychiatric Association's Diagnostic and Statistical Manual of Mental Disorders (DSM-IV). The Fourth Edition is entitled the DSM-IV. According to DSM-IV, each of the mental disorders is conceptualized as a clinically significant behavioral or psychological syndrome or pattern that occurs in a person, and that is associated with present distress (a painful symptom) or disability (impairment in one or more important areas of functioning) or with a significantly increased risk of suffering death, pain, disability or an important loss of freedom. Whatever its original cause, a mental disorder must currently be considered a manifestation of a behavioral, psychological, or biological dysfunction in the person. (APA, 1994).

Today, mental disorders in late life refer to the timing of their occurrence and not to any particular form or content. Jablensky (1990) notes that mental disorders occurring in the elderly are no longer considered to belong in a separate category of morbidity. Some of the common classifications that we see with the elderly include:

> *Psychoses—mental disorders in which impairment of mental function has developed to a degree that interferes grossly with insight, ability to meet ordinary demands of life or to maintain adequate contact with reality.*
>
> *Neurotic disorders, personality disorders and other nonpsychotic mental disorders have no demonstrable organic basis in which the patient may have considerable insight. The patient has unimpaired reality testing, in that he usually does not confuse his morbid subjective experiences and fantasies with external reality. Behavior may be greatly affected, although it usually remains within socially acceptable limits. The principle manifestations include anxiety, hysterical symptoms, phobias, obsessional and compulsive symptoms, and depression.*
>
> *Organic mental syndromes and disorders—organic mental syndrome refers to psychological or behavioral signs and symptoms without reference to etiology (e.g., organic anxiety syndrome, dementia). In such syndromes, there is a clear deterioration of intellectual functioning in clear consciousness, which sets this syndrome apart from other disorders of cognition such as mental retardation and intoxication. Organic mental disorder is used when the etiology is known or presumed such as alcohol withdrawal delirium or multi-infarct dementia (APA, 1994).*

Cognitive impairment increases with age. According to the Epidemiological Catchment Area Study, those aged 65 to 74 have about a 2.9 percent likelihood of impairment. As one ages to 75 to 84, the chances are 6.8 percent, and over 85, 15.8 percent. For men aged 65 to 74, they will experience cognitive impairment of 4.2 percent as compared with 1.9 percent for women (Regier et al., 1988). Kohlmeyer reports that the neurobiologic changes identified by Alzheimer's disease are said to account for over 50 to 60 percent of dementias after the age of 60 and, possibly, as much as 20 percent more in accompaniment with vascular disease. Folstein et al., (1985) did a major survey with older adults and discovered that the prevalence for definite dementia syndrome was 6.1 percent; subdivided as 2 percent Alzheimer's dementia, 2.8 percent multi-infarct (vascular) dementia and 1.3 percent for other dementias (Folstein et al., 1985).

Instead of thinking about old age primarily in terms of compensating for deficits, we are beginning to view aging in terms of maximizing human resources. Mental health is a phenomenon to consider not just in times of crisis, but as a process to be engaged in on a daily basis and an entity to be acquired. By focusing on mental health every day, we may have better coping skills to adapt to old age. We now realize that as we age we have increasing diversity and heterogeneity. We can no longer look at mental health/mental disorders in isolation, but as a process throughout life.

Kivnick (1993) emphasized that those in the field of gerontology may need to ask some basic questions and have a better understanding of an older adult's unique profile of thematic life strengths and weaknesses. Birren, Sloane, and Cohern (1992) describe mental health in much broader terms. Mental health is a function of many aspects of modern society, such as family life, caregivers, community and institutional care, ethnic and sociocultural differences, and urbanization. It is important to specify the effects of the aforementioned influences as the numbers of older adults continue to increase. Mental health is not merely the absence of a mental disorder, but is a subjective sense of well-being which can be described as overall happiness or satisfaction with life. Positive mental health has been described in a number of ways but some of the most common themes tend to be a positive self-image, mastery of self-actualization, and autonomy. Also, it is important to note that the individual's state of physical health and other biological factors generally have a greater impact on a person's mental health than one's chronological age (Birren et al., 1992).

Developmental Disabilities

Definitions of aging developmentally disabled adults have been generally based upon clinical assumptions rather than empirical data. Janicki and colleagues (1985) note that most of these definitions imply that the beginning of aging for developmentally disabled persons occurs around the mid- to late 40s or early to mid-50s, depending on the nature of the disability. In other words, most definitions associate entry into an aging status with chronological age. Janicki and colleagues argue, however, that three other factors in addition to chronological age should be used to classify a developmentally disabled person as aging. They are "(a) greater physical disability and lessening of physical reserve attributable to chronological age (rather than trauma or illness); (b) diminishing levels of functional skills, particularly in areas of self-care, personal hygiene, and toileting; and (c) for less mentally impaired individuals, the self-perception of aging and desire to seek age-appropriate or normative roles and activities" (p. 291).

MEDICAL LIMITATIONS

Drug treatment used for mental disorders raises many issues for the elderly population. Some considerations that need to be addressed before a treatment regime is put into place are: older adults tend to have multiple physical illnesses/chronic health problems; they rely on polypharmacy or the use of multiple drugs, either prescription or over the counter; there is an increased sensitivity of the aging central nervous system to psychotropic drugs; and there are alterations in the aging body's ability to bind, distribute, and dispose of psychotropic drugs (Birren et al., 1992). Also, older adults may have more difficulty with their medication regime, either from overuse, underuse, inappropriate use, or nonuse.

A discussion of pharmacodynamic changes associated with aging and the impact of individual drugs on physical activity (e.g., individuals with diabetes must carefully balance physical activity intensity and duration because of insulin injections that may lead to insulin shock) are beyond the scope of this chapter. The reader is encouraged to consult Graedon and Graedon (1988) for a thorough discussion of drug implications for physical activity programs. It should be noted, however, that the elderly are particularly sensitive to central nervous system depressant drugs because of changes in brain tissue caused by aging. Thus, it is imperative that the therapeutic recreation professional have a working knowledge of how drugs work and their effects on body function in order to avoid an interaction between a drug and the intended recreation program.

PURPOSE OF THERAPEUTIC RECREATION

The purpose of rehabilitation, "to restore an individual to his/her former functional and environmental status, or alternatively, to maintain or maximize remaining function, needs to be at the heart of all care provided to the aged to help them live as full a life as possible" (Jette, 1986, p. 2). Thus functional independence, not disease eradication, has become the principal goal of care for the aged. However, it is very important to note that rehabilitation of the elderly is quite different from rehabilitation of the young. The impact a disability has on an individual's life is not only a function of the nature of the disability. The stage of life in which it occurs, the number of alterations in lifestyle that it demands, the way it is perceived by the individual, and how the individual and significant others respond influence the elderly as well.

The nature of a psychosocial view of geriatric rehabilitation has to do with the issues of the mind and the relationship of the elderly individual with society. These issues are imperative because therapists interact with (treat) whole persons whose minds (psycho) and relationships with society (social) are intensely relevant to the quality of life of the elderly (Davis, 1986). The elderly are marked already by fewer resources and a decrease in status, roles, and authority. Elderly persons who add an afflicted disability need timely and effective psychosocial intervention to regain their maximum independence or to maintain their present independence. The following three approaches to treatment are reviewed: (1) stimulation programs, (2) behavior therapy, and (3) psychotherapy. The review includes a discussion of their purpose, methods, and effectiveness.

Stimulation Programs

Stimulation programs employ a highly structured group approach directed at improving overall functioning or such aspects of functioning as environmental awareness, physical movement, perceptual integration, attention span, daily living skills, and level of interaction with the environment. Regressed elderly patients who exhibit varying degrees of lethargic, apathetic, and withdrawal behaviors are the targets of stimulation programs. Many patients in these programs are noncommunicative and display limited environmental awareness (Gugel & Eisdorfer, 1986).

Each program session consists of a variety of components that include activities that emphasize bodily response, perceptual integration, cognitive stimulation, and function. Concrete activities with specific stimuli for each program aspect are the foundation of stimulation programs. Familiar activities that promote security and a sense of mastery are used, with at least one novel activity in each program component to stimulate and promote higher-level functioning. Stimulation programs require a highly skilled group leader who has the professional ability to properly engage elderly regressed patients. Recreation therapists and occupational therapists are generally charged with such leadership responsibility.

Weiner, Brok, and Snadowsky (1978) have reported success in using stimulation programs with regressed elderly patients. However, most studies on stimulation intervention have been subjective evaluations. Despite the lack of strong empirical evidence, stimulation programs are promising for improving the function of regressed elderly persons in areas of environmental awareness and overall responsiveness, and for increasing sociability and appropriate behavior. But it is not clear whether the effects of stimulation programs can be generalized to other settings or whether such effects are sustained after program termination (Gugel & Eisdorfer, 1986).

Behavior Therapy

Behavior therapy is used to change nonfunctional behavior to functional behavior. Focus areas for change include self-care, verbal behavior, walking behavior, food consumption, incontinence, purposeful activities, appropriate behavior, and sociability (Krasner, 1971). Positive reinforcement is the specific technique employed in behavior therapy programs; for example, praise, refreshments, prizes, special privileges, and tokens. This intervention technique requires a thorough understanding of the basic steps of behavioral therapy. They include analysis of the nonfunctional behavior, definition of the specific behavior to be treated, and establishment of a baseline frequency of the behavior. Once behavior has been established, therapy requires formulation of concrete goals, identification and training of staff who will provide the treatment, an outline of specific treatment procedures, and accurate documentation (Gugel & Eisdorfer, 1986).

Empirical evidence does suggest that behavior therapy is an effective intervention technique for altering specific behaviors in elderly patients. Particular success has been reported in the areas of sociability, self-care, and purposeful activity. Changing cognitive and emotional functioning levels has generally not been successfully attained through this psychosocial technique. Moreover, behavior therapy success tends to become extinct when the program is terminated. Despite evidence supporting the value of behavior therapy, few clinicians use this technique.

Psychotherapy

Interest in psychotherapy with older adults and credible research about the impact are fairly new discoveries in the mental health field. The challenges are many. It is well documented that older adults do not access mental health services readily and that financial barriers exist. However, once elders are in place, the establishment of the therapeutic relationship is still necessary for optimal therapy. As with other age cohorts, several interventions can be used; the individual psychotherapy psychodynamic approach, or behavioral approach, or the group setting. Other methods may include: (1) Validation—The Feil Method, and (2) Reminiscence Therapy.

Validation therapy in some instances has replaced reality orientation. This type of therapy has been used quite successfully with disoriented older adults, or those aged 80 to 100, with the rationale that each human being is different and valuable, regardless of the impairment caused by some form of dementia that causes disorientation. Feil (1982) writes that early learned emotional memories replace intellectual thinking in the disoriented older adult and when emotional memories are certified or "validated with" this form of therapy, a person regains dignity. The goals of the program are to restore self-worth, reduce stress, justify living, resolve unfinished conflicts from the past and to feel happier, even though the person may have significant cognitive deficits. With validation therapy, the use of genuine touch, eye-contact and an overall caring attitude is essential to the success of the program. In the past, those who were labeled as "demented" or "disoriented" or "senile" were grouped all together as if their personalities became identical, regardless of their background and cumulative life experiences.

Reminiscence is a narrative therapy. Stories emerge that have a beginning, middle, and an ending and include the following four parts: the selection of a past experience to reminisce; immersion into the experience remembered; distancing from that memory; and closure (Schafer, 1994). Many questions have arisen about the method of life review and the frequency by which elders participate in this practice, either independently or at the prompting of a healthcare professional. Because reminiscence may evoke strong emotional feelings, there are many researchers who believe that this type of therapy must be dealt with carefully and only with trained professionals in the field of mental health.

COMMON SERVICE SETTINGS

Therapeutic recreation services for the elderly have traditionally been more fully developed and entrenched in long-term care settings such as nursing homes. However, an increasing share of public funds is now beginning to be directed toward community settings. This shift in public funding demands that therapeutic recreation professionals be creative in adapting programs to fit the diverse needs of the elderly in both institutional and community settings.

Long-Term Care Setting

With the growing numbers of elderly who want to continue to live on their own, a growing number of community-based services and housing options are available. These services and housing options fall under the category of long-term care and include the following:

Service options

Chore services may include such tasks as minor home repairs, cleaning, and yard work.

Personal services include nonmedical services to assist persons in their home with bathing, dressing, cooking, cleaning, laundry, and errands.

Meals programs can be provided in the home for those medically in need or in congregate meal sites in local communities.

Friendly visitation or companions are often volunteers who regularly visit personally with individuals or call them on the telephone. Some businesses have become an integral part of the long-term care services (e.g., utility company employees may check on homebound residents during their normal business hours and refer those in need to appropriate agencies).

Housing options

Continuing Care Retirement Communities (CCRC) provide a full range of housing from independent apartments to skilled nursing home care within a given location.

Accessory Apartments are self-contained apartment units within a house that allows the resident to live independently without having to live alone.

Elder Cottage Housing Opportunities (ECHO) are small, self-contained units that can be placed in the back or side yard of a single-family house.

Assisted Living Facilities are between independent living and nursing home care and the bundle of services will vary from one facility to another based on the needs of the residents. The services may include meals, personal care, emergency call buttons, light housekeeping, transportation, and recreational activities.

Homesharing is becoming increasingly popular and refers to shared housing between two or more unrelated people living together in a house or apartment.

Congregate Housing is a group-living situation in which some meals are shared in a central dining room and staff is available to provide social and recreational activities.

Nursing Home Care is a long-term care facility with varying degrees of nursing care available and rehabilitative services (AARP, 1992).

Older adults or family members historically have found information gathering about eldercare services to be a difficult process. With that in mind, the "Eldercare Locator" was designed as a toll-free number that connects someone to information and referral services on a local level. This service is an initiative of the Administration of State Units on Aging.

A relatively new profession for service and housing location is called "Care Managers." Care management services, or case management, can help families and individuals in funding, arranging, and monitoring long-term care services. Care managers can coordinate the necessary services and save families a great deal of time and effort (AARP, 1992).

Community Settings

Community-based programs and services are increasing rapidly all across the nation. Senior centers, adult day care, in-home services, retirement communities, senior volunteer programs, and senior educational programs are a small sampling of such programs. Senior centers and adult day care are discussed.

Senior Centers provide a place for older adults to come together for socialization, leisure activity, and other services. The growth of popularity in senior centers was enhanced by the 1965 Older Americans Act. A national survey completed by the National Institute of Senior Centers in 1974 indicated that most of the senior centers were located in urban and suburban programs. Today, however, it is not uncommon to find an increasing number of senior centers and programs in small rural areas.

Some senior centers are highly organized, with full-time and part-time staffing and a well-developed program of activities. Other centers are loosely organized, managed by a small professional staff and/or volunteers, and primarily focused on community involvement by seniors. In either case, the primary concept behind senior centers is to promote senior citizen involvement in the community.

Typical services found in senior centers include leisure services, education, information, counseling and referral, health programs, employment assistance, financial aid and counseling, legal aid, nutrition, transportation services, in-home services, and day care (Teaff, 1985). Centers deliver these services either by providing center-based programs and outreach services, or by making the needed linkages with community service agencies.

Adult Day Care programs are also developing rapidly in communities. Adult day care is a general term. Behren (1986), however, provides a more specific definition:

> *(An adult day care program is) a community-based group program designed to meet the needs of functionally impaired adults through an*

individual plan of care. It is a structured, comprehensive program that provides a variety of health, social and related support services in a protective setting during any part of the day but less than 24-hour care (p. iii).

The term *adult day health care* is used when the program focus becomes medically oriented; the term *adult day care* is used when the program focus is essentially social.

Adult day care centers are a relatively new community-based resource for older adults who have a level of impairment that necessitates supervision and care. In a national survey of such centers (Behren, 1986), more than half the respondents cited four service priorities: (1) alternatives to premature or inappropriate institutionalization, (2) maximizing functional capacity, (3) respite for care giver, and (4) psychosocial supportive services.

The range of services commonly provided in adult day care programs, either by contract or by direct care staff, includes medical and health-related care (e.g., podiatry, dentistry); social services; physical, occupational, speech, recreational, art, music, and reality therapy; dietary counseling and meals; transportation; and personal grooming and care (AARP, 1992). Typical funding sources for adult day care are Medicaid, participant fees, Social Services Block Grant, Title III of the Older Americans Act, local government funds, and donations and fund raisers. Services are provided by full-time and part-time administrative and professional staff, and a significant contribution is made by volunteers (AARP, 1992).

CURRENT BEST PRACTICES AND PROCEDURES

The understanding of late adulthood is a very complex task that requires one to appreciate the image of later maturity as a function of both past and present status. One must view the life course as a series of changes marked by the "succession of age-related roles prescribed by the culture, by the biological and cognitive development of the individual, and by the particular historical events . . . that define the context in which the individual lives" (McCrae & Costa, 1984, p. 298). Therapeutic recreation practices and procedures are grounded in this life review process and include four principal phases: assessment, planning, implementation, and evaluation.

Assessment

Standardized instruments and procedures for assessing the leisure skills and interests specific to the elderly have not been fully developed or validated. There are, however, acceptable applications that may provide useful information for guiding therapeutic recreation interventions. These applications for a psychosocial assessment of the older adult should minimally include the following:

A mental status examination to assess major cognitive and emotional difficulties and help define the proper psychological treatment, based upon standard methods and procedures.

A social and vocational history focusing on previous roles, marriages, and sexual history, sources of life satisfaction, achievements, and values.

A personality assessment focused on the individual's self-perception, character, method of dealing with crises in the past, interpersonal relations, responses to stress, and nature of previous losses.

The person's own perception of the rehabilitation process and motivation for improvement.

An assessment of the current family situation, including relations with family members, sources of support, quality of housing, and the presence of other sick or disabled persons.

An assessment of the current family situation, including relations with family members, sources of support, quality of housing, and the presence of other sick or disabled persons.

An interview of the patient's family (if agreeable with the patient) to determine their view of the patient, concerns, and resources (Kemp, 1985, p. 659).

Psychosocial or behavioral aging can be assessed by building a social history of the patterns of behavior and lifestyle for the individual client. Interviews with individual clients, as well as family members or other care givers, can be useful in understanding psychosocial aspects of later maturity, such as changes in personality, role, and activity, social and health attitudes, self-concept, and socioeconomic status (Davis, 1986). Understanding and documenting major life events that may influence adjustment (e.g., loss of a loved one, illness) and/or needs for socialization (e.g., recent relocation to a new residence) will be important to understanding the life course and the need for therapeutic intervention.

Leisure skills and interests, both past and present, will be the key information in the assessment record. Leisure interest surveys can be used or developed to gather information regarding the older client's past behavior patterns as well as current activities and interests (Herrera, 1983; McKechnie, 1975). Using a variety of approaches, information should be sought regarding the older person's repertoire of activities, preferences, interests, and expectations, as well as capacity for independence (such as activities of daily living, use of public transportation, capacity for self-protection, and the like). Howe (1984) noted that leisure assessment instrumentation can be organized by those measuring leisure attitudes, leisure states, leisure behavior, leisure satisfaction, and leisure interests. For a more complete listing of instruments in these categories, consult Howe (1984, p. 17).

For clients with verbal skills and higher cognitive functioning, interviews and pencil/paper surveys are useful approaches (Davis, 1986). For lower functioning individuals, constructing leisure behavior patterns from client records and observations may be the applied data collection technique. Few assessment instruments exist for application with older developmentally disabled clients. However, Joswiak (1975), Herrera (1983), and Cousins and Brown (1979) provide sample assessment instruments to use with these clients. Gallo, Reichel and Andersen (1988) provide an especially valuable source book for geriatric assessment.

Functional assessments of the elderly's independent living skills should also be assessed for the following reasons in geriatric practice: (1) establish a diagnosis; (2) determine the personal, social, and environmental dynamics that maintain, control, and influence behavior; (3) establish a baseline measure to assess the effects of treatment programs or natural changes in the disorder; and (4) assess the person's self-care ability. Activities of Daily Living Skills (ADL) and Instrumental Activities of Daily Living Skills (IADL) instruments are used for this purpose. Elderly who cannot perform IADLs may still be able to live at home if they can perform ADLs, but often they will still need outside assistance or supervision. Patterns of dysfunction on ADLs and IADLs often relate to underlying disorders. For example, elderly with dementia may lose the ability to perform IADLs before they lose the ability to perform ADLs. IADLs require more cognitive skills while ADLs focus primarily on physical skills. Elderly with severe depression may lose the desire to perform either ADLs or IADLs.

Frequently used instruments are the Katz Index (Katz et al., 1963) and the Direct Assessment of Functional Status (Loewenstein, et al., 1989). ADLs measure such activities as eating, dressing, grooming, toileting, bathing, transferring, and mobility. IADLs measure money management, household chores, use of transportation, shopping, health maintenance, communication, and safety preparedness. The use of ADLs and IADLs is an essential part of any psychiatric diagnosis. The Diagnostic and Statistical Manual (DSM-IV) stresses the need to determine how the functional abilities of the older person are affected before making a psychiatric diagnosis. Diagnosis alone does not predict the outcome or ability of an older adult to live independently. Assessment of functional skills is also important to educate others as to the older adults performance capacities and support needs (Birren, Sloane, & Cohen, 1992).

Planning

The objectives for psychosocial intervention include (1) assessment of the client's cognitive, affective, and functional status; (2) resolving the crisis of disability, depression, and grieving; (3) helping clients maintain independence; (4) promoting self-esteem; (5) improving family relations; and (6) identifying suspected organic ailments that may impair optimal functioning (Kemp, 1985). Therapeutic recreation professionals play a key role in meeting these objectives through a variety of programs and services. Programs briefly discussed here include physical fitness, reminiscence, nutrition, and activities of daily living.

Physical Fitness is a program area that has received considerable attention in recent years. The intent of physical fitness programs includes cardiovascular endurance, flexibility, strength and endurance, body composition, balance, and motor coordination. Psychological benefits from exercise have also been derived for stress relief and anxiety reduction. For a complete review of fitness programs for older adults, consult Teague and McGhee (1992), Piscopo (1985), and Evans and Rosenberg (1991).

Reminiscence draws attention to the importance of and use of life review both as a recreation experience and as a strategy for identifying potential recreation activities for the client. This technique is important not only for emotional development in the later years but as a device for bridging the gap between the young and the old through recapitulation of past and present significant events. Recapitulation can be very important for emotional and social adjustment (e.g., reduced feelings of isolation) and for reducing cognitive dissonance about who we are, particularly for those elderly persons who are newly institutionalized and are experiencing an exacerbated sense of loss of control. Thus, reminiscence can be viewed as both a recreative tool and as a process for re-experiencing past leisure activities and interests. Consult Wolfe (1985) for an excellent presentation on how reminiscence can be used with older adults.

Nutritional Programming extends beyond meeting nutritional health needs by including opportunities for social interaction. For many older adults, meals may be one of the very few opportunities for experiencing interpersonal relationships beyond immediate family members. Meal sites, as well as homebound meal programs, are excellent vehicles for the expression of cultural heritage (e.g., holidays and other celebrations), for developing and maintaining social relationships, and for enhancing general health. The reader can consult Teague and McGhee (1992) for a review of nutrition as a health promotion and social adjustment program for older adults.

Activities for Daily Living (ADL) serve two principal purposes: (1) development or maintenance of self-help skills (e.g., eating, dressing, personal grooming, financial management, shopping, personal safety), and (2) development of and participation in recreational activities. The ADL program is a major area for promoting involvement, productivity, social interaction, the expression of personal interests and skills, and reinforcing fine motor and communication skills. ADL programs are also an excellent way of promoting an older person's sense of belonging to the larger community.

Other types of common programs for older adults include senior creative arts programs, volunteer activities, educational programming (preretirement, adult education), travel and touring, horticulture, and outdoor recreation. Each of these programs provides opportunities for therapeutic intervention and diversion. Consult Teaff (1985), and Teague & MacNeil (1992) for an excellent review of these programs.

Implementation

Typically, older adults want to be treated with dignity. Developing programs that enhance dignity requires the structuring of program autonomy, independence, and meaningful involvement.

Obviously, leadership skills employed by the therapeutic recreation professional are essential for implementing programs that meet these criteria. Jones (1987) provides the following leadership considerations that apply especially for working with older adults. Staff should do the following:

> Demonstrate respect for mature adults.
> Cultivate understanding and empathy through the demonstration of interest and genuine concern for the individual.
> Show enthusiasm by projecting excitement and/or enjoyment of being with the older client.
> Be flexible and adaptable by developing and expanding activities as situations occur, thus cultivating spontaneity.
> Recognize planning and creativity as important cornerstones to successful programs and services (pp. 4–8).

Other considerations in program implementation should include environmental design and modification to accommodate physical changes commonly associated with aging. Older adults benefit from environments that support easy access to rest rooms, have flexible climate control, do not pose undue obstacles to movement around the facility, and support diminished vision and hearing with appropriate lighting and acoustical design features. Teague and MacNeils (1992) discussion of developing "open" environments may be especially helpful in designing appropriate program settings.

Evaluation

The aim of rehabilitation, "to restore (the elderly client) to his/her former functional and environmental status, or alternatively, to maintain or maximize remaining function" (Jette, 1986, p. 2), lies at the heart of the evaluation process. As cited earlier in this chapter, the goal of rehabilitation is functional independence, not disease eradication. Thus, health professionals need to evaluate their programs in reference to impairments, functional disabilities, and handicapped conditions. Kiresuk, Lund, and Schultz's (1981) quality assurance model and Austin's (1982) stepwise program evaluation model are valuable evaluation tools. However, the rehabilitation therapist may improve these evaluation models by incorporating them within the functional assessment/evaluation process described in Figure 12.2.

The salient point of Figure 12.2 is that the processes of assessment, planning, implementation, and evaluation are interconnected. However, the bottom line is the impact that program interventions have on functional disabilities that are represented by basic living skills (walking, performing bed-to-chair transfer, dressing) and instrumental living skills (climbing stairs, preparing meals, washing dishes, shopping, taking medication). Pertinent instruments used in the assessment of basic and instrumental living skills include the Functional Status Index (Harris et al., 1986), Functional Independence Measure (Granger et al., 1986) and the Older Americans

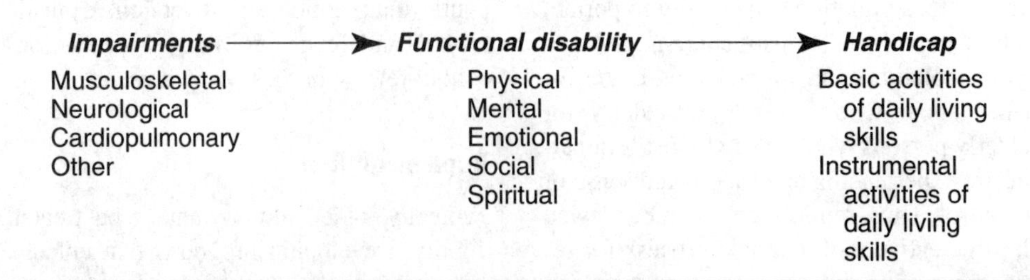

FIGURE 12.2 A Conceptual Framework for Functional Assessment

Resource Service Multidimensional Functional Assessment Questionnaire (Fillenbaum, 1985).

APPLICATION OF THE TR PROCESS

The elderly segment of the general population is a unique group in terms of the general needs associated with this life stage. It also is a diverse group in that there is broad variety among older citizens in terms of individual experience, interests, and needs. The following case example provides a unique and diverse view of an older man with mental retardation who lives in a group home for older adults.

CASE STUDY

Joe is a 61-year-old man with Down's syndrome. Joe recently moved into the group home because of the failing health of his then-living father (since deceased) and mother. His surviving aged mother lives in a nearby rural community of under 10,000 people, where Joe also lived prior to his move to the group home. Joe has a younger sister who lives out of state with her husband and two children.

Assessment

History. Joe spent most of his adult life working in a sheltered work activity center in a nearby community. During his mid to late fifties, Joe showed changes in his behavior that were characterized as withdrawn and uncooperative. He was easily distracted from his work. This situation regressed until he was unmotivated to participate in his work activities. His mother requested that he be moved out of vocational activities and be given greater opportunities to explore other day activities that focused on his recreational interests. Because Joe has had fairly good health except for occasional arthritis inflammations, he was successfully transitioned out of the workshop and into adult day activities that focused on maintaining his physical and social involvement. Before moving to the group home in a larger community, Joe was being prepared to enter a senior day activity program.

Present Behaviors. Joe is interested in bowling, swimming, watching game shows, cooking (which he did a lot of with his mother), talking about his family, taking long rides in the car, eating, and mealtimes. Many of these pursuits are activities that he has done with his parents and their friends for most of his life. He did belong to a bowling team from the work activity center where he was previously employed.

Joe frequently has periods of withdrawal and depression, and needs to be careful about his diet and weight. Joe has needs for assistance with his adjustment to the group home. He also needs help dealing with the loss of his father and the separation from his mother. Building upon his strengths, it is possible to use many reinforcers to get Joe to talk about his feelings and become involved in home activities.

Planning

Because Joe is easy to draw out, his individual habilitation plan is based upon maintaining his repertoire of skills and involvements, in addition to expanding opportunities for developing new interests and friendships through accessing community-based senior programs.

Long-Term Goal. To minimize periods of loneliness, withdrawal, and depression.

Short-Term Goals. (1) To assist Joe in developing ways to cope with feelings. (2) To develop new opportunities for Joe to participate in his favorite leisure activities.

Objectives. Joe will be given opportunities to prepare meals and lead mealtime socialization in order to (1) build his relationships with housemates, (2) reinforce his interests in cooking, (3) learn about diet and nutrition, (4) help him deal with troublesome feelings, and (5) maintain connection with his past through reminiscencc. Joe will prepare at least two meals per week for the next three months, and assist with the preparation of other meals.

Joe also will be taken to the local senior citizen center at least twice per week for the next four weeks to visit its programs and enroll in at least one program.

Joe will call his mother two to three times per week and visit with her at least once in every two weeks.

Content. Joe will discuss and plan meals, talk about his family and his interests, and increase his awareness of recreation activities available in his new community, specifically at the senior center. Joe will maintain contact with his mother and other family members.

Process. Senior center staff will (1) encourage Joe to attend the programs, provide background understanding of Joe and his abilities and needs, and identify a peer model at the senior center for Joe; (2) assess Joe for identifying additional leisure interests; (3) hold sessions with Joe to develop reminiscence skills; and (4) make provisions using the transportation program for the elderly to visit Joe's mother.

At this stage of programming, the therapeutic recreation specialist will be implementing both an individual plan with the client as well as developing the capacity of both the home environment and the community environment to accept Joe.

Implementation

The client will participate in the home routine, with a special emphasis on the use of meals as a social and daily skills building program. New leisure activities will be sought as the client gains access to the community senior program. Anecdotal and frequency records will be maintained for the client's moods and behaviors.

Evaluation

The Individual Habilitation Plan (IHP) for the client will serve as the documentation of client goals and objectives, as well as progress in meeting them. Periodic review of progress notes and changes/additions to the client IHP provide evaluative feedback to the primary care givers and therapeutic recreation professional. Other significant persons should be consulted for their review of the client's progress and program design. (In Joe's case, staff and other participants at the community-based senior program could be consulted for information useful in the evaluation of his program and progress.) Comprehensive review of the IHP on an annual basis should also include a conference with Joe, his mother, and other family members.

TRENDS AND ISSUES

It is the contention of the authors that the practice of psychosocial rehabilitation has much to offer the disabled elderly for attaining more normal and useful lives. The graying of the American population and the concurrent increase in chronic illness and disease will require a more equitable distribution of psychosocial rehabilitation services for the elderly. The trend will not be the invention of new systems of care for the elderly, but a more effective and efficient use of the health systems we presently have. Inherent within this trend is the rehabilitation focus for treating functional deficits of the elderly in order to promote greater independence.

Functional areas of concern include mobility, sensory abilities, communication, emotional stability, hand dexterity, activities of daily living, and health maintenance. These areas are not the usual domain of traditional medical and nursing practice. Thus, allied health professions will continue to develop to meet these functional needs. Medical and allied health professionals can be expected to be organized into an interdisciplinary rehabilitation team, because the elderly are likely to have multiple chronic conditions, periodic acute medical problems, and psychosocial complications (e.g., less family support, less societal visibility). Members of the interdisciplinary teams will include physicians, psychiatrists, nurses, physical therapists, social workers, occupational therapists, speech therapists, nutritionists, and recreation therapists.

SUMMARY

Professionals who work to rehabilitate the elderly often experience frustration. The frustration rarely stems from not knowing how to treat psychosocial or physical disabilities alone. Rather, the professional is challenged by the multiple, concurrent problems of the elderly, each influencing the others and affecting the quality of the clients' lives. For example, when arthritis leads to severe depression, confusion, and despair, the therapist is tempted to treat only the physical symptoms associated with the disease rather than such potential concurrent factors as death of a spouse or a financial crisis.

The underlying theme throughout the authors' discussion of psychosocial rehabilitation programs for the elderly is that recreation therapists interact with more than just bodies. Charm and fascination of work with the elderly are a byproduct of their unique personalities. As Davis (1986) states: "They are (for the most part) interesting people who have led long lives characterized by day-to-day decisions that have brought them unique characters" (p. vi). Thus, the nature of the psychosocial views of rehabilitation has to do with the issues of the mind and the relationships of the individual with society. The more the recreation therapist knows about psychosocial aspects of rehabilitation, the better prepared he or she is to effect meaningful change.

READING COMPREHENSION QUESTIONS

1. Debate this statement: "Therapeutic recreation programs are primarily diversionary rather than treatment interventions used in psychosocial rehabilitation of the elderly."
2. Adaptation is a process common to all ages of life, but some sources of adaptation appear to be unique in older life. List the adaptive changes you view as unique, and compare this list with your classmates.
3. Your authors stated that rehabilitation of the elderly is quite different from rehabilitation of the young. Do you agree with this statement? Why or why not?
4. Assume that you are interviewing for a job as a recreation therapist in a geriatric rehabilitation facility. One of the interviewers asks that you explain the role that therapeutic recreation can play in reality orientation, stimulation, behavior therapy, and psychotherapy programs. What is your response?
5. Compare and contrast the following three types of institutional facilities: (1) skilled nursing facilities, (2) intermediate care facilities, and (3) congregate care facilities.
6. Compare and contrast the following three types of community settings: (1) senior centers, (2) adult day care, and (3) in-home services.

SUGGESTED LEARNING ACTIVITIES

1. Assume that you have been invited to teach a unit on cognitive disorders associated with aging to a group of college students. Provide a list of exam questions you could use to test the students' knowledge of the following:
   a. Chronic Brain Syndrome
   b. Acute Brain Syndrome
   c. Senile dementia
   d. Pre-senile dementia
2. Arrange an interview with staff and volunteers at a state institution. Ask the staff and volunteers about the major rewards, problems, and frustrations they experience when working with elderly clients.

3. Survey your local senior centers to determine the types of services and programs they provide to meet the biological, sociological, psychological, and spiritual needs of senior residents.
4. Inventory the long-term care facilities in your community. Determine the number of facilities and the types of services rendered, costs, patient characteristics, and so on.
5. Make a list of a number of elderly individuals who you think are living proof that mental abilities can remain strong throughout life. Compare your list with other classmates. What principal characteristics do these elderly individuals have that contribute to their mental strength in later life?
6. Assume that you are asked to give an in-service workshop to a nursing home's nonrecreation personnel. Your assigned topic is "The Role of Therapeutic Recreation in Psychosocial Rehabilitation of Institutionalized Elderly." Outline the major ideas you would stress in your presentation. Compare your ideas with those of your classmates.

REFERENCES

American Association of Retired Persons (AARP). (1992). *Staying at home.* Washington, DC: American Association of Retired Persons.

American Psychiatric Association. (1994). *Diagnostic and statistical manual of mental disorders* (4th ed.). Washington, DC: American Psychiatric Association.

Austin, D. R. (1982). *Therapeutic recreation processes and techniques.* New York: John Wiley & Sons.

Behren, R. V. (1986). *Adult day care in America: Summary of a national survey.* Washington, DC: The National Council on Aging and National Institute on Adult Daycare.

Berg, R. L., & Cassells, J. S. (Eds.). (1992). *The second fifty years.* Washington, DC: National Academy Press.

Birren, J. E., Sloane, R. B., & Cohen, G. D. (Eds.). (1992). *Handbook of mental health and aging* (2nd ed.). San Diego, CA: Academic Press, Inc.

Brody, E. M. (1981). The formal support network: Congregate treatment settings for residents with senescent brain dysfunction. In N. E. Miller & G. D. Cohen (Eds.), *Clinical aspects of Alzheimer's disease and senile dementia aging* (Vol. 15, pp. 301–333). New York: Raven Press.

Burns, B., & Taub, C. (1990). Mental health services in general medical care and in nursing homes. In B. Fogel, A. Furino, & G. Gottlieb (Eds.), *Mental health policy for older Americans: Protecting minds at risk.* Washington, DC: Psychiatric Press.

Butler, R. N., & Lewis, M. I. (1983). *Aging and mental health.* New York: Mosby.

Clements, W. M. (1982). Therapeutic functions of recreation in reminiscence with aging persons. In M. L. Teague, R. D. MacNeil, & G. Hitzhusen (Eds.), *Perspectives on leisure and aging in a changing society* (pp. 339–351). Columbia, MO: Department of Recreation and Park Administration.

Cousins, B., & Brown, E. (1979). *Recreation therapy assessment.* Jacksonville, FL: Amelia Island ICFMR.

Davis, C. M. (1986). Introduction. *Topics in Geriatric Rehabilitation, 1*(2), vi–ix.

Evans, W., & Rosenberg, I. H. (1991). *Biomarkers: The 10 determinants of aging you can control.* New York: Simon & Schuster.

Feil, N. (1982). *VF validation.* Cleveland, OH: Edward Feil Productions.

Fillenbaum, G. G. (1985). Screening the elderly. *Journal of the American Geriatrics Society, 33*(10), 698–706.

Finkel, S. I. (1993). Mental health and aging: A decade of progress. *Generations: Journal of the American Society on Aging, 17*(1), 13–20.

Fisher, M. (Ed.). (1989). *Guide to clinical preventive services.* Baltimore, MD: Williams and Wilkins.

Folstein, M. F., et al. (1985). The meaning of cognitive impairment in the elderly. *Journal of the American Geriatrics Society, 33,* 228–235.

Gallo, J., Reichel, W., & Andersen, L. (1988). *Handbook of geriatric assessment.* Rockville, MD: Aspen Publishers, Inc.

Gatz, M., & Smyer, M. (1992). The mental health system and older adults in the 1990s. *American Psychologist, 47*(6), 741–51.

Graedon, J., & Graedon, T. (1988). *50+: The Graedon's people's pharmacy for older adults.* New York: Bantam Books.

Granger, C. L., et al. (1986). Advance in functional assessment for rehabilitation. *Topics in Geriatric Rehabilitation, 1*(3), 59–74.

Gugel, R. N., & Eisdorfer, S. E. (1986). Psychosocial intervention. *Topics in Geriatric Rehabilitation, 1*(2), 27–34.

Harris, B. A., et al. (1986). Validity of self-report measures of functional disability. *Topics in Geriatric Rehabilitation, 1*(3), 31–42.

Henig, M. R. (1988). *The myth of senility.* Washington, DC: American Association of Retired Persons.

Henney, R. L. (1983). *Persons who are developmentally disabled in nursing homes in the state of Indiana.* Valparaiso, IN: Institute for Comprehensive Planning.

Herrera, P. M. (1983). *Innovative programming for the aging and aged mentally retarded/developmentally disabled adult.* Akron, OH: Exploration Series Press.

Howe, C. Z. (1984). Leisure assessment instrumentation in therapeutic recreation. *Therapeutic Recreation Journal, 13*(2), 14–24.

Jablensky, A. (1990). Diagnosis and classification of dementias in the elderly with special reference to the tenth revision of the international classification of diseases (ICD–10). In R.L. Kane, J.G. Evans, & D. Macfadyen (Eds.), *Improving the health of older people: A world view* (pp. 683–693). Oxford: WHO/Oxford University Press.

Janicki, M. P., et al. (1985). Service needs among older developmentally disabled persons. In M. P. Janicki & H. M. Wisniewski (Eds.), *Aging and developmental disabilities* (pp. 289–304). Baltimore, MD: Paul H. Brookes.

Jette, A. M. (1986, April). Functional disability and rehabilitation of the aged. *Topics in Geriatric Rehabilitation, 1*(3), 1–8.

Jones, L. (1987). *Activities for the older mentally retarded/developmentally disabled.* Akron, OH: Exploration Series Press.

Joswiak, K. F. (1975). *Leisure counseling program materials for the developmentally disabled.* Washington, DC: Hawkins & Associates.

Katz, S., et al. (1963). Studies of illness in the aged. The Index of ADL: A standardized measure of biological and psychological function. *Journal of the American Medical Association, 185,* 914–919.

Kemp, B. (1985). Rehabilitation and the older adult. In J. E. Birren & K. W. Schaie (Eds.), *Handbook of the psychology of aging* (pp. 647–663). New York: Van Nostrand Reinhold.

Kiresuk, T. J., Lund, S. H., & Schultz, S. K. (1981). Service delivery and evaluation from the consumer's point of view. *New Directions for Program Evaluation: Assessing and Interpreting Outcomes, 9,* 57–70.

Kivnick, H. Q. (1993). Everyday mental health: A guide to assessing life strengths. *Generations: Journal of the American Society on Aging, 17*(1), 13–20.

Koenig, H., & Blazer, D. (1992). Mood disorders and suicide. In J.E. Birren, R.B. Sloan, & G. Cohen (Eds.), *Handbook of mental health and aging* (pp. 379–407). San Diego, CA: Academic Press.

Krasner, L. (1971). Behavior therapy. *American Review of Psychology, 22,* 483–532.

Loewenstein, D., et al. (1989). A new scale for the assessment of functional status in Alzheimer's disease and related disorders. *Journal of Gerontology, 44*(4), 114–121.

McCrae, R. R., & Costa, P. T. (1984). Aging, the life course, and models of personality. In N. W. Shock et al. (Eds.), *Normal human aging: The Baltimore longitudinal study of aging* (DHHS-NIH Publication No. 84–2450, pp. 292–303). Washington, DC: U.S. Government Printing Office. (Reprinted from *Review of Human Development,* 1982. New York: John Wiley & Sons.)

McKechnie, G. E. (1975). *Manual for the leisure activities blank (LAB).* Palo Alto, CA: Consulting Psychology Press.

National Institutes of Health. (1991). *Diagnosis and treatment of depression in late life.* (Reprinted from NIH Consensus Development Conference Statement, 1991, Nov. 4–6, Washington, D.C.)

Pfeiffer, E. (1977). Psychopathology and social pathology. In J. E. Birren & K. W. Schaie (Eds.), *Handbook of the psychology of aging* (pp. 640–671). New York: Van Nostrand Reinhold.

Piscopo, J. (1985). *Physical activity and aging.* New York: John Wiley & Sons.

Regier, D., et al. (1988). One-month prevalence of mental disorders in the United States. *Archives of General Psychiatry, 45,* 977–86.

Schafer, D. E. (1994). *Reminiscence and nursing home life.* New York: Garland Publishing, Inc.

Severns, S. R. (1986). *Answers to commonly asked questions about the home care campaign.* Unpublished manuscript.

Sirrocco, A. (1987). *The 1986 inventory of long-term care places: An overview of facilities for the mentally retarded. Advance data from vital and health statistics* (No. 143). (National Center for Health Statistics, DHHS Publication No. PHS 87–1250). Washington, DC: U.S. Government Printing Office.

Teaff, J. D. (1985). *Leisure services with the elderly.* St. Louis, MO: Times Mirror/Mosby.

Teague, M. L., & MacNeil, R. D. (1992). *Aging and leisure: Vitality in later life.* Dubuque, IA: Wm. C. Brown Communications, Inc.

Teague, M. L., & McGhee. V. L. (1992). *Health promotion: Achieving high-level wellness in the later years.* Dubuque, IA: Wm. C. Brown Communications, Inc.

Wantz, M. S., & Gay, J. E. (1981). *The aging process: A health perspective.* Cambridge, MA: Winthrop Publishers.

Weiner, M. B., Brok, A. J., & Snadowsky, A. M. (1978). *Working with the aged: Practical approaches in the institution and community.* Englewood Cliffs, NJ: Prentice Hall.

Wolfe, M. (1985). The meaning of education in late life: An exploration of life review. *Gerontological Geriatric Education, 5*(3), 51.

Wykle, M. L., & Musil, C. M. (1993). Mental health of older persons: Social and cultural factors. *Generations: Journal of the American Society on Aging, 17*(1), 7–11.

CHAPTER 13

PEDIATRIC PLAY

JERRY G. DICKASON
*ANDREW CHASINOFF**

OBJECTIVES

- Understand the purpose of therapeutic recreation in a pediatric setting.
- Distinguish between pediatric play and therapeutic recreation.
- Understand the hazards of pediatric classification systems.
- Identify appropriate recreation intervention techniques.
- Comprehend the application of the therapeutic recreation process.
- Review current trends and issues in recreation services for exceptional children.

DEFINITION OF PEDIATRIC PLAY

Children play. Play manifests a child's developmental process. All play theories have one thing in common: people engage in play because it contains that undefinable experience—fun. When a child's play is hampered, all other aspects of the child's life are adversely affected.

Pediatric play is a structured program, in a health care setting for children, that encourages normal patterns of play behavior and minimizes disability and psychological trauma. The play program is designed to encourage cognitive, psychological, sensorimotor, and social functions so that children can develop skills to meet their personal leisure needs and adapt to the demands of their environment. Through play, children explore the *I am* (identity factors such as self-esteem) and the *I can* (identity factors such as self-competency and control) attributes of growth and development (Carmichael, 1993). Pediatric play encourages children to discover, explore, and develop personal abilities in relation to their situation and/or condition. The program is conducted by qualified personnel and encourages the participation of all staff, volunteers, and family members.

CLASSIFICATION OF CONDITIONS

Former Secretary of the U.S. Office of Health, Education, and Welfare (HEW) Elliott L. Richardson, called for a systematic review of the classification and labeling techniques used in the treatment of children. In response to his call and

*The authors wish to thank Teresa L. Boeger, Ms, CSRS/CCLS, Child Life Manger of Phoenix Children's Hospital, for her professional contributions to this chapter.

the existing national concern, ten federal agencies joined together to sponsor the Project on the Classification of Exceptional Children. The project was to increase public understanding of problems associated with the classification and labeling of children who were disabled, disadvantaged, or delinquent. An objective of the project also was to improve the professional practice of educators, psychologists, physicians, lawyers, social workers, and others responsible for the well-being of exceptional children.

On completion, the project would provide a rationale for public policy. It would identify practical suggestions for legislation and for administrative regulations and guidelines bearing on classification and its consequences. The two volume *Issues in the Classification of Children: A Source Book on Categories, Labels and Their Consequences* (Hobbs, 1976) describes the results of the project's research on the current practice and thinking of classifying of exceptional children.

The project found that classification systems generally fall under three different theoretical perspectives: (1) as a science (biologically based); (2) as pyschometric procedures (that measure mental states); and (3) as sociological/social control consequences (environmentally induced factors). The project also concluded that all three of these perspectives and their subsystems are inadequate in relation to what current understandings permit. It established that classification systems cause serious problems because of: lack of sophistication in taxomony; presence of strong-running professional biases; preoccupation with dominant symptoms to the neglect of important determinants of behavior; transposition of adult-appropriate schemes to children; use of classification to legitimize social control of the individual.

Consequently, to classify children's (infant to twelve years) and adolescents' (thirteen to twenty) performances sensitively and accurately as possible, personnel must address three fundamental conditions:

1. The child's current status (health/developmental/medical picture);
2. The genesis of the child's condition (etiology) in relation to a social/medical history of the developmental stages, family experiences, and other factors; and
3. The implications of intervention, in regard to choice of treatment, method, and prognosis, with possible and/or desirable integration among all these factors.

DESCRIPTION OF LIMITATIONS

It is clear that personnel working with exceptional children must maintain an open position in regard to a child's ability for anything. Children are not accustomed to functioning with preconceived behavior limitations. Their world of play allows them to transcend to a level of satisfaction. Thus, they naturally function in the realm of abilities, not disabilities. Child development is sequential only within each individual, and the progression of developmental stages takes the form of adjustments to changes in the child's physical, emotional, and cognitve experiences. Some changes enhance abilities and some evoke limits. Children's adjustments to these changes (very often through play) show that they are making sense of, or rather assigning some sort of order to, their experiences. Thus, the adults in a child's life should not arbitrarily assign limits but rather try to understand the self-imposed limits, if any, that are in place.

Personnel must be aware of the effect of drug medications. Children and adolescents are much more unpredictable in regard to reaction time and length of effect. Certain settings, by their nature of treatment, imply limitations, particularly in play programs. For example, in psychiatric programs, sharp implements (scissors and knives) must be used under strict supervision. Isolation orders can severely limit play activity and require a great deal of ingenuity.

PURPOSE OF THERAPEUTIC RECREATION

The purpose of therapeutic recreation, regardless of age or of setting, is to use recreation/play/leisure activity as a treatment modality for some predetermined health/developmental/medical concern.

The aim or overall goal of therapeutic recreation is to enable individuals to function in any leisure pursuit of their choice at the maximum of their potential. Proper therapeutic recreation programming will move each child along a planned path of steadily decreasing therapist involvement. The therapist encourages the child to become increasingly inner-directed or intrinsically motivated.

Pediatric play programs vary according to setting. Not all pediatric play is therapeutic nor is all therapeutic recreation play. Pediatric play is exactly what it says—children with health/developmental/medical conditions, requiring intervention services, voluntarily at play. Therapeutic recreation is a predetermined plan of recreation/play/leisure activities designed, for an individual or a group, in response to a specific diagnostic condition. Medically-oriented play modalities fall into the latter catagories. Medical play is an intervention technique that is "therapeutic when the medical props stimulate role play, experimentation and exploration of objects and events that are likely to be distressing to childen" (Azarnoff, 1986). Medically-oriented play is generally conducted by Child Life specialists. Child Life is a newly organized discipline within pediatric settings. Child Life programs ". . . strive to promote optimum development of children, adolescents and families, to maintain normal living patterns and to minimize psychological trauma. As integral members of the health care team in both ambulatory care and in-patient settings, Child Life staff provide opportunities for gaining a sense of mastery, for play, for learning, for self-expression, for family involvement and for peer interaction" (Child Life Position Statement revised and approved by the Child Life Council, Spring 1983, Association for the Care of Children's Health (ACCH), 3615 Wisconsin Avenue, Washington, D.C. 20016). The goals of Child Life programs are the following:

1. To minimize stress and anxiety for the child and adolescent.
2. To provide essential life experiences.
3. To provide opportunities to retain self-esteem and appropriate independence.
4. To educate persons interested in becoming child life specialists.

Whether it is pediatric play, medically-oriented play, or therapeutic recreation, the commonality is usually so strong that the therapeutic recreation department offers all of these services. To illustrate the duality of this purpose, note the six objectives for the Therapeutic Recreation Department of Children's Specialized Hospital of Mountainside, New Jersey. The first three objectives are designed to allow for both pediatric play and therapeutic recreation. The last three objectives are not treatment goals but rather they are designed to advocate play opportunities for disabled children as well as promote therapeutic recreation as a service.

1. Provide recreational opportunities to best maintain existing abilities and facilitate interests of the child in as meaningful and purposeful a manner as possible.
2. Introduce leisure activities to promote independence, allow self-direction, and encourage development of self-discipline in the adjustment to irreducible and progressive disablity.
3. Heighten the child's awareness of the recreational opportunities available through organized private and community programs and commercial leisure services.
4. Enhance the overall effectiveness of the rehabilitation process by sharing information, training, and skills with all other team members so that the child may derive maximum benefit from therapy.
5. Heighten community awareness of the "Role of the Recreation Therapist and Therapeutic Recreation" in a rehabilitative children's hospital.
6. Offer a comprehensive training experience for therapeutic recreation students, aiding them in their clinical preparation to best serve children in a therapeutic activities program. Exposure to program planning and "team oriented" treatment is emphasized.

COMMON SERVICE SETTINGS

Children play everywhere; play is not confined to or dependent upon a location. Children can play alone or with others, with or without toys or any props. Pediatric play refers to play that goes on in those settings that offer health/developmental/ medical care to children.

Pediatric care services usually fall into three categories based on length of stay: long term (over thirty days), short term or acute (less than thirty days), and day care (one day only). Long-term and acute services are residential by their very nature of services in order to provide a continuity of care in treating the diagnosis. Examples of long-term and acute care settings are developmental centers for the mentally retarded and multiply handicapped, physical rehabilitation centers for the physically disabled, juvenile delinquency residences for the socially maladjusted or disenfranchised, psychiatric centers for the emotionally and mentally ill, hospitals and hospices for the terminally ill, residences for the blind or the deaf, and general hospitals for the unexpected accidents and illnesses. Many of these settings offer day care services as well as local recreation and parks departments, human service agencies, and disability-specific agencies. Educational institutions such as public and specialized schools are now offering recreation and play programs as part of an Individual's Education Program (IEP).

CURRENT BEST PRACTICES AND PROCEDURES

Practice is based on some theoretical notion of what is an effective intervention in a given situation. Best practices are not generic but rather depend on the type of service setting, the mission of therapeutic recreation in that setting, the conditions of the child, and the talents of the professional staff. Attributes of best therapeutic recreation practices in pediatric play include a theoretical framework for the intervention programs, interdisciplinary information gathering and sharing, and family support and involvement in the child's medical/developmental/ health care. In developing a theoretical framework, it is important to keep in mind that play has many meanings. Common to all theory is that play provides a "window into the operations of the child's mental functioning and self representations" (Solnit et al., 1993, p. 2). (This quote is italized in the original text.) Best practices are built on programs that foster "windows" to see into the child's world.

An interdisciplinary focus on the whole child integrates the efforts of all care givers to affect the most efficient rendering of therapuetic services. Cooperation among the service team members provides a more effective approach to achieving the child's goals and objectives.

The family is the child's primary support system. "Family members may need assistance in determining their appropriate responsibility, level of concern, and involvement in the child's developmental and health care" (Carmichael, 1993, p. 170).

Unlike practice which is dependent on differentiating variables, therapeutic recreation procedures are based on a four-phase cyclical process. It begins with the therapist assessing (evaluates/ tests) the child's needs, followed by the therapist et al. planning goals and objectives to address the assessed needs. Implementing programs in response to those goals and objectives is the third phase. This is followed by applying a systematic evaluation procedure that allows the therapist to determine the effectiveness of the implemented program.

Assessment

Assessments, evaluations, and/or tests are terms often used interchangably; yet, they are three distinct functions. Assessments are inventories of the child's current state. Evaluations are estimates about behavior judged against a standard behavior, for consideration of change. And, testing is a quantitative measurement of the child's ability. However, assessment, evaluation, and testing are considered as one procedure under this term assessment.

Most settings have their own established procedure for doing assessments. These assessments gather information in one of three ways—

observations, interviews, and/or testing. The information received is generally recorded on predetermined forms, which are referred to as instruments or tools for collecting the information. Most therapeutic recreation instruments are patterned after well known instruments such as the Gesell Chart on Childhood Development, Erik Erikson's Stages of Development, Central Wisconsin Center for the Developmentally Disabled, and the Adaptive Behavior Scale of the American Association on Mental Deficiency.

The following instruments are available to specifically assess performance abilities for therapeutic recreation purposes:

Burlingame Software Scale (Burlingame)
Bus Utilization Skills assessment Manuel (BUS, Burlingame)
Communication Device Evaluation (Burlingame)
Comprehensive Evaluation in Recreational Therapy: CERT-Physical Disabilities (CERT-PD, Burlingame)
Comprehensive Evaluation in Recreational Therapy: CERT-Psych/Behavioral (CERT-PB, Burlingame)
Freetime Boredom Measure (Burlingame)
Functional Assessment of Characteristics for Therapeutic Recreation (FACTR, Burlingame)
FOX-Activity Therapy Social Skills Baseline (FOX, Burlingame)
General Recreation Screening Tool (GRST, Burlingame)
"I Can" (Wessel)
Idyll Arbor Leisure Battery (Burlingame)
Leisure Diagnostic Battery (LDB, Compton and Witt)
Maladapted Social Functioning Scale (Burlingame)
McCree Leisure, Play and Therapy (Psychological Corp.)
Measure of Social Empowerment and Trust (Burlingame)
Ohio Functional Assessment Battery (Psychological Corp.)
Play Observation Scale (POS; Rubin, Fein, and Vandenberg)
Recreation Behavior Inventory (RBI; Berryman et al.)
Recreation Early Development Screening Tool (REDS, Burlingame)
School Social Behavior Scales (Burlingame)
Structured Observation of Academic and Play Settings (SOAPS; Roberts, Milich, and Looney)

Assessments in an educational setting are based on the requirements given in the Individuals with Disabilities Education Act (IDEA), Public Law 101-476. There are thirteen categories of disabilities under which a child may be eligible for special services. The National Information Center for Children and Youth with Disabilities (NICHCY) is a clearinghouse of information that addresses effective means for stimulating growth, reducing poverty, and promoting democratic and humanitarian ideals regarding children and youth. NICHCY publishes a *News Digest* on "Assessing Children for the Presence of a Disability" (Waterman) that includes a bibliography for families as well as for schools assessing children for the presence of a disability.

Planning

Therapeutic recreation is one of many services that exist for the sole purpose of the betterment of the child. Most settings encourage all service programs to meet jointly and prepare, in an interdisciplinary effort, the best program possible for each child.

In an educational setting this program is referred to as an Individual Education Plan (IEP). In a clinical setting the program is referred to by any number of acronyms: Individual Treatment Plan (ITP), an Individual Program Plan (IPP), and/or a Team Treatment Report (TTR).

Regardless of setting, all plans are formulated to meet the individual need of each child. They address the needs of the whole child through their interdisciplinary design. Plans are goal oriented with objectives to achieve specific behaviors. Goals are those identified functional skills to achieve in the duration of the plan, and objectives are those steps designed to achieve the functional skills. They are implemented through sequential procedures; and are continually evaluated to determine future direction of improvement.

Implementation

A full array of program ideas and activities are possible tools for implementation. Such ideas and activities should express the general interest of the child. The activities should be specific and within the capacity of the individual or group to provide an opportunity for immediate satisfaction and evident progress. An activity should be a stimulation for further related activity. However, for treatment purposes, it is important to remember that activities are only tools to achieve therapeutic recreation goals.

For example, puppetry as an activity provides an opportunity to indulge in fantasy and unadulterated play. As a therapeutic tool, puppetry allows the child to express feelings directly through another character. And through such expression, a child can relay concerns about confinement, abandonment, body image, and medical uncertainties. At the same time, verbalizing through the other character allows the child to control the concerns by promoting the transfer of thoughts to his or her own situation (Linn, 1986).

To accomplish therapeutic ends through activities, the therapist must:

1. Plan actions for each child based on listening, analyzing, and acting in accordance with the evaluated data;
2. Increase his/her knowledge through observations of the child and discussions with other therapists;
3. Use all existing facilities to enrich the program;
4. Teach and lead activities in order that the child learn skills as well as have fun;
5. Help the child lead activities and gain his or her own skills in sharing learned activities;
6. Use other specialists to add breadth and variety to the program;
7. Plan for future actions using foresight and hindsight facilitated by recording and evaluating past meetings and experiences.

Evaluation

Keeping in mind that evaluations are estimates about behavior judged against a standard behavior, the therapist first must identify the expected standard of behavior. The therapist then can determine how far the behavior deviates from the standard.

The therapist's judgment of this deviation is the evaluation and can be recorded in several different ways. The common recording methods are progress notes, evaluation instruments, and team meeting summaries. Progress notes, the therapist's written comments on the progress and/or performance of the child, are kept in the child's chart. They are to be recorded after each therapy session. Evaluation instruments provide a list of predetermined standards, against which the therapist rates the child's present level of performance. The same instrument is used periodically to document change in the child's performance. Team meetings summaries are recorded summary statements declaring the child's current performance. These summary statements result from interdisciplinary staff discussions of the child's performance.

Each evaluation is a benchmark for determining further action and becomes the new starting point with new or renewed long- and short-term goals for treatment of the child. Thus the cycle is complete and initiates its own beginning.

APPLICATION OF THE TR PROCESS

In order to better understand the therapeutic application of recreation, Joey is presented to illustrate the TR process. Information regarding Joey's case is given in each of the four phases.

CASE STUDY

Joey is a 12-year-old boy who was involved in a motor vehicle accident and sustained a spinal cord injury. He was transferred to Children's Special Hospital for rehabilitative services. Shortly after his admission, he was referred by the attending physician for therapeutic recreation.

Assessment

The therapist gathered information in the following catagories before the initial contact with Joey:

1. Specific etiology of the impairment. Joey has a spinal cord lesion at the T-12 level. T-12 is the thoracic vertebra just above the first lumbar vertebra. A traumatic disruption of the spinal cord is often associated with extensive musculoskeletal involvement; such trauma may cause varying degrees of paraplegia and quadriplegia.

2. Functional limitations. Joey is a non-ambulatory, paraplegic. He must use a wheelchair and back brace, and perform self-catheterization every four hours.

3. Family social history. Joey is the third child of five children with two brothers older (16 and 14 yrs.) and two sisters younger (11 and 7 yrs.). His father is an electrician and his mom is a school teacher (second grade). The family is very active in their church and community affairs. Additional information is most often available through the social service department's intake report which is placed in the child's medical chart.

4. School standing/school report. Joey is in the seventh grade. He is an average (B–, C+) student and played first string on the soccer team.

After collecting the above information, the recreation therapist makes contact with Joey and conducts an initial assessment within 48 hours from the admission date. During this initial contact the therapist carries out the following tasks:

1. Develop rapport by informally introducing self to Joey and his family before beginning any questions. This is followed by explaining the purpose and functions of the TR department, and the role of the recreation therapist(s) as well as the various programs, activities, and their locations. To put Joey at ease the therapist can ask Joey general information questions (i.e., age, school, siblings, interests).

2. Determine Joey's past recreation and leisure experiences and current leisure/prevocational interests. This is accomplished by first having informal conversations with him regarding his interests, hobbies, music, or sports activities. Are there any strong interests or dislikes? Family members often provide unsolicited descriptions of the child's interests. The therapist then conducts a leisure interest survey, reviews social service assessment, and gathers information from other team members to augment the informal discussions.

3. Assess Joey's behaviors. What are his gross motor and fine motor abilities? What is his cognitive ability as well as his sensory abilities?

4. Record assessment of Joey's interests, abilities, behavior characteristics, orientation, affect, and self-image. The therapist must observe Joey's relationships with other children and staff; is he friendly, withdrawn, manipulative, cooperative? What is his emotional state? Does he laugh or smile; is he depressed, immature, shy, or impatient? What are Joey's conversation patterns? Can he initiate conversation or only respond when spoken to? Does he need help in staying on the topic? Does he need frequent cueing to recollect words? Is he able to express wants and needs? During discussions about recreation interests and the leisure interest survey, the therapist should document whenever Joey shows interests to recreation activities.

5. Assess Joey's gross and fine motor skills. Do the lower extremities (LE) function? What is the body's posture? Is there balance and coordinated movement? Do the upper extremities (UE) function (i.e., dominant hand, grasp/release of objects, tremors, manipulation of objects, writing skills, left UE and/or right UE weakness/paralysis, use of nondominant UE as gross motor assistance during activities)? Are there coordinated movement and bi-lateral skills (i.e., use of both arms, cross mid-line)?

6. Assess Joey's cognitive skills. Record his level of orientation. For example, is he oriented to person, place, and time? Is he aware of the environment and those around him? Determine his memory ability. Does he display past (before the injury), recent (within a month), or immediate (within two hours) memory? Observe attention span; comprehension of auditory and visual information; problem solving skills; ability to organize and present sequential information, and level of safety awareness.

7. This information becomes a part of Joey's therapy treatment report (TTR). When the first note is written, a copy of the initial TTR is sent to medical records to be coordinated with the notes of other disciplines of the interdisciplinary team working with Joey.

Planning

When planning therapeutic recreation goals and objectives, the therapist must take into account the overall goals of the rehabilitative team and the data collected from the initial assessment.

Joey's overall rehabilitative goals are to acquire independent mobility, develop upper extremity strength, and have command of his activities of daily living.

The therapist now reviews the observations noted from other discipline's initial TTR. Joey in general demonstrates a positive affect. He easily engages in conversation with staff, openly expresses his opinions, is friendly and outgoing, initiates interactions with roommates, and has become familar with other staff in the hospital in a short amount of time.

He appears to function at age-appropriate levels. He displays good attention span as well as carry-over, follow through, and organization and strategy formulation abilities.

He is able to talk sensibly about his life before the accident, and demonstrates memory for past, present, and immediate events. He talks about his participation in school sports and is oriented to person, place, and time. He seems extremely close to father; appears to have a good relationship with both parents. He is beginning to show an awareness of the implications of his impairment.

Before determining the therapeutic recreation goals and objectives, the therapist should consider the following factors:

At what age did the accident occur ?

What factors were relevant to the patient's life at that time, such as family relationships, network of friends, and social events?

What were the previous interests and level of participation?

What is the psychological impact of the transition from being ambulatory to nonambulatory?

How easy is it for the patient to communicate with staff and peers? What are the possible cognitive deficits?

How involved will the family be in the rehabilitative process?

After considering all of the information gathered above, the recreation therapist can determine both long- and short-term TR goals. In Joey's case the goals are:

Long-term goals

1. initiate voluntary participation in out-trips
2. participate in wheelchair sports in the community
3. participate in commerical travel programs

Short-term goals

1. improve upper extremity strength
2. improve wheelchair mobility
3. increase peer interaction/socialization
4. increase involvement in various recreation groups—adaptive cooking, teen group, evening programs
5. increase awareness of wheelchair sports
6. increase awareness of the opportunities for trips and travel

Within one month from his initial involvement in therapeutic recreation, the previously set goals for Joey are reviewed and new treatment plans are formulated which involve the following participation requirements. Joey will:

1. Participate in a minimum of three gross motor activities a week to strengthen UE to adjust to wheelchair mobility.
2. Interact with peers in a small group setting three times a week for thirty minutes each.
3. Participate in one evening out-trip.
4. Be introduced to a racing chair used in wheelchair sports.

Implementation

During this phase of the treatment process, the therapist works toward addressing the emotional, physical, and social needs of the patient. Initial sessions help the patient become familar with the therapists, staff, and hospital setting. This contributes to establishing a rapport of concern and trust with the patient. The recreation therapist needs to be creative in planning, adapting, and carrying out activities that are challenging to the patient and that encourage him to achieve his potential.

In Joey's case, the recreation therapist first schedules him for individual recreation, 1/2 hour daily. During these sessions the therapist introduces him to gross motor activities (wheelchair basketball and hand soccer), and cognitive games. On a one-to-one basis Joey is able to express feelings and talk about his injury and the impact it is having on his life. Such sessions prepare Joey for the transition from individual to small group activity. The small group environment of patients about the same age and cognitive ability enables Joey to generalize his condition and realize that others are similarly handicapped. This allows Joey to socialize with his peers in a relaxed atmosphere and share experiences with them.

Throughout both individual and group sessions, the therapist gradually introduces Joey to wheelchair sports, which allow him to remain physically active and provide healthy opportunities to compete against himself as well as others. Simultanieously, Joey participates in several community trips to local and regional softball games, movie theaters, and concert auditoriums. During trips to nonstructured settings, the therapist observes Joey's ability to negotiate physical barriers, such as curbs and rough terrain, and social barriers, such as having people stare or make an issue of his condition. From these observations the therapist is able to "coach" Joey on some technical maneuverability skills and make him feel comfortable with his own responses to the environment. Consequently, Joey begins to feel comfortable enough to reestablish contacts with his commmuity and to establish new contacts, especially among wheelchair sports enthusiasts.

Evaluation

During this final phase, the therapist compares observations of the patient from the time of admission until the patient's discharge. The therapist's evaluation report should include statements about:

1. Affect, behavior, social skills.
2. Physical, mental, and social level at the time of discharge.
3. Recreation skill levels at time of discharge.
4. Gains made in recreational therapy.
5. Areas that still need improvement.
6. Suggestions for future involvement in recreational/leisure activities.

On the basis of such information, the therapist determines the effectiveness of the activities/programs selected for the patient's treatment as they relate to the pre-established goals and objectives.

In regard to Joey's case, the recreational therapist continues to assess his behavior and performance weekly. Directly following his treatment sessions, the therapist notes observations for future documentation in monthly progress reports.

Throughout his hospitalization, Joey was included in a variety of recreational therapy programs. Joey's behavior remained fairly consistent over the four months that he was seen. He was a friendly, cooperative, and outgoing participant in most programs. He most often displayed a positive affect, had a good sense of humor, and interacted well with both peers and staff.

During both individual and group sessions, Joey was introduced to a variety of higher-level cognitive games which he was able to play independently. At the time of discharge, he was able to select appropriate activities for these sessions as well as teach them to peers and staff.

In terms of his gross motor abilities, Joey was able to participate actively in such sports as wheelchair basketball. He learned to maneuver his wheelchair fairly accurately and was able to negotiate rough/smooth terrain such as grass and pavement. During one hospital leave to his home, Joey participated in a practice basketball game with a local adult wheelchair team.

Through the various trips, Joey became aware of several barriers/obstacles that he would have to consider in his own community/environment before going out with family and friends. While participating in such trips, Joey displayed appropriate social skills and good safety judgment.

At the time of discharge, the staff recommended that Joey pursue his interest in active sports through a wheelchair sports program and/or established wheelchair basketball team.

Through a series of leisure counseling sessions, the recreation therapist provided him and his family with the necessary resources in their community that would promote his involvement in wheelchair sports in his area. In summation, therapeutic interventions led to the accomplishment of the short-term rehabilitation goals. At the time of discharge, Joey's coordination and strength were greatly improved through his participation in gross motor activities such as wheelchair basketball and hand soccer. He was able to maneuver his wheelchair independently over various types of terrain. Participation in active games and trips strengthened his wheelchair mobility. The involvement in such trips with small groups also increased his spontaneity in initiating interactions with peers. Teen group and adaptive cooking activities had increased his involvement in various groups. At the time of discharge, Joey had successfully made the transition to group sessions. He no longer required individual treatment to manage his feelings about his disability.

TRENDS AND ISSUES

The hospitalization of children has declined considerably over the past several years. This decrease is caused by several factors: an increase in the number of physicians with knowledge about health care who treat the problem before it becomes serious; an expansion of community health care services that focus specifically on children's services; and lowered birthrate.

Because the pediatric in-patient occupancy rates are declining nationally, hospitals feel a need for new programs to generate income. Such programs use existing pediatric facilities and staff resources without adding to the hospital budget. An exemplary new program is a children's sick room where parents can bring sick children on a day-to-day basis. This concept meets several community needs.

Most schools and day care programs do not provide medical attention or even the supervision of medical treatment. There is a growing number of families where both parents have careers and such health care is necessary so parents are not required to use sick days or vacation days. Also, there is a growing number of working single parents who need such services to maintain their children's health as well as the family's source of income (Harrison et al., 1987).

Sickness usually restricts play behavior, but boredom remains. Quiet play activities and caring attention are needed to enhance the recuperating process. For such reasons, the pediatric home care programs are an emerging trend for children with special needs of a longer duration, but who do not require constant specialized services. Play and recreation opportunities are extremely important to these children during convalescence. Community follow-up programs are in greater demand than is currently being met. Many new programs such as Opportunity Project for brain injured young people are founded by parents with the support of local and state advocate associations of particular disabilities.

In Radlett, England, the Save the Children Fund cosponsored Playtrac, a unique mobile play resources center that travels from setting to setting including community homes and institutions. Playtrac's aim is to give advice on creative play and support to workers and relatives of mentally handicapped people. Playtrac also offers training to staff on play methods and helps them be aware of the role of play (Landford, 1987).

Pediatric programs are beginning to conduct parent orientation programs that encourage parents to be an active part of their child's treatment program. Some settings offer planning sessions with parents to establish individual guidelines as to how the parents can participate in the care of their child. In such settings the recreation staff invite family members to participate with their children in on site and off-ground programs (Koch-Critchfield, 1987).

Technological advances in alternate breathing procedures, mechanical ventilation, and specialized respiratory equipment have evolved into the subspecialty of neonatology. Consequently, there is an ever-growing number of survivors who are dependent on these life-support devices and sophisticated care. It was noted during the 1982 Surgeon General's Workshop on Children with Handicaps and Their Families that this new technology has created the ventilator-dependent patient (VDP), and that ventilator-dependent children particularly need additional technology as well as staff-family training and communication to relieve the state of dependency. Posch and Edwards (1988) point out that in New Jersey's Children's Specialized Hospital "an increasing number of admission inquiries regarding ventilator-dependent children has been received, prompting the hospital administration to explore the feasibility of and need for a special program." A program was initiated. The therapeutic recreation staff's assessment of the needs of these children determined that play and developmental activities would be conducted bedside. They would be performed on an individual basis until the patient was able to participate physically, emotionally, and technologically with others.

Adventure challenge programs are becoming part of the therapeutic recreation protocol of services, especially with mental health care populations. It is a program of experiential learning through challenge by choice that fosters immediate self-realization and/or immediate feedback from peers and/or facilitators on behavior and performance. Skills areas readily addressed in adventure challenge programs through a progression of activities are communication, cooperation, decision making, leadership, self-esteem, team work, and trust. Adventure challege programs require specialized equipment and facilities as well as trained facilitators who can assist participants in negotiating goals and achieving desired outcomes. Jeff Whitman of Philhaven Hospital, Mt. Gretna, PA, has developed assessment instruments derived from the adventure challenge experience that measure (1) cooperation and trust, and (2) social empowerment and trust. These instruments are available through Idyll Arbor, Inc.

Video games have been used as a treatment tool. Burlingame offers a software scale to aid therapists in their selection of computer games. Caution is prudent in using video games. "Since the first description of 'space invader epilepsy' in 1981, more than 20 cases of video game induced seizures have been reported" (Ferrie et al., 1994).

Charles E. Schaefer has edited a book of *Innovative Interventions in Child and Adolescent Therapy* (1988). He offers therapy techniques in four broad categories that cut across diagnostic groupings and theoretical constructs: (1) creative arts techniques, (2) relaxed state techniques, (3) altered view of reality techinques, and (4) miscellaneous techniques that include animal, life story, photography and video techniques. Some of these techniques require qualified training, yet many can be adapted to the therapeutic recreation modality.

Because of the increasingly diverse and growing fields of recreation and therapy techniques, recreation therapists are finding it necessary to gain competencies in specific therapy modalities and for specific diagnostic groups. This trend is observed in the numbers of therapists seeking adventure challenge course certification, therapists seeking special education courses to qualify working with the school systems, therapists acquiring certification to work as substance abuse counselors, and child life specialists.

SUMMARY

This chapter provides an overview of pediatric play services in a variety of settings that specialize in health/medical care for children. Pediatric play is a structured program in a health care setting for children that encourages normal patterns of play behavior and minimizes disability and psychological trauma.

Pediatric diagnostic classification systems generally fall into three different theoretical perspectives: (1) as a biologically based science; (2) as pyschometric procedures that measure mental states; and (3) as sociological/social control consequences (environmentally induced factors). Regardless of the classification system, all systems must address (1) the child's current health/medical status; (2) genesis of the child's condition (etiology) in relation to a social/medical history of the developmental stages, family experiences, and other factors; and (3) implication of intervention in regard to choice of treatment, method, and prognosis, with possible and/or desirable integration among all these factors.

Pediatric play programs vary according to setting. Not all pediatric play is therapeutic recreation, nor is all therapeutic recreation play.

In spite of the increase of specialized medical services for children, the hospitalization of children has declined considerably over the past several years.

READING COMPREHENSION QUESTIONS

1. Why are classification systems inadequate?
2. Cite some examples of how a classification becomes a labeling device.
3. What is the difference between pediatric play and therapeutic recreation?
4. How do therapeutic recreation objectives vary depending upon the setting?
5. Identify the difference between assessment, evaluation, and testing.
6. What is an IEP and an ITP or TTR? What do they have in common?

SUGGESTED LEARNING ACTIVITIES

1. Visit two different pediatric play programs.
2. Discuss with the recreation therapists in each setting the focus of recreation for their program.
3. Compare the two settings and justify their different approaches to providing recreation services.
4. After visiting a pediatric setting, discuss with your classmates the classification system used in that setting.
5. Identify the therapeutic recreation objectives that are unique for a particular setting.
6. Review the assessment, evaluation, and/or testing instruments of a pediatric play program. What kind of questions are asked? What is done with the information received?
7. Identify community-based programs serving youths with special recreation needs. Visit several of these programs and identify the transition procedures between the hospital setting the the community.

REFERENCES

Azarnoff, P. (1986). *Medically-oriented play for children in health care: The issues.* (Monograph No. 3). Santa Monica, CA: Pediatric Projects Inc.

Batshaw, M. L., & Perret, Y. M. (1986). *Children with handicaps: A medical primer.* Baltimore: Paul H. Brookes Publishing Co.

Berryman, D. L., & Lefebvre, C. B. (1981). *Recreation behavior inventory.* Denton, TX: Leisure Learning Systems.

Burlingame, J., & Blaschiko, T. M. (1990). *Assessment tools for recreational therapy.* Seattle, WA: Idyll Arbor, Inc.

Carmichael, K. D. (1993). Play therapy and children with disabilities. *Issues in Comprehensive Pediatric Nursing, 16*(3), 165–173.

Cella, D. F., & Cherin, E. A. (1990). Measuring quality of life today: Methodological aspects. *Oncology, 4*(5), 29–38.

Child Life Position Statement. (1983). Association for the Care of Children's Health, 3615 Wisconsin Avenue, Washington, D.C. 20016.

Erikson, E. D. (1950). *Childhood and society.* New York: Norton.

Ferrie, C. D., et al. (1994). Video game induced seizures. *Journal of Neurology, Neurosurgery and Psychiatry, 57*(8), 925–31.

Gottfried, A., & Brown, C. C. (Eds.). (1986). *Play interactions.* Lexington, MA: Lexington Books.

Greenspan, S., & Greenspan, N. T. (1985). *First feelings.* New York: Viking.

Harrison, L., et al. (1987). Establishing and evaluating a children's sick room program. *American Journal of Maternal Child Nursing, 12*(3), 204–206.

Hart, R., et al. (1992). *Therapeutic play activities for hospitalized children.* St. Louis: Mosby.

Hobbs, N. (Ed.). (1976). *Issues in the classification of children: A source book on categories, labels and their consequences* (2 vol.). San Francisco: Jossey-Bass, 1976.

Koch-Critchfield, M. (1987). When a child needs his parents most: Caring for a dying child. *RN, 50*(7), 7–8.

Landford, R. (1987). Time to play. *Nursing Times, 83*(7), 40–41.

Linn, S., et al. (1986). Puppet therapy with pediatric bone marrow transplant patients. *Journal of Pediatric Psychology, 11*(1), 37–46.

Opportunity Project, Inc. 225 Millburn Avenue, Suite 202A, Millburn, NJ 07041. 201-376-8290.

Philhaven. 283 South Butler Road, P.O. Box 550, Mount Gretna, PA 17064. 717-273-8871.

Posch, C. M., & Edwards, P. A. (1988). The ventilator-dependent child: Challenge and opportunity, *Rehabilitation Nursing, 13*(1), 15–18.

Psychological Corporation. P.O. Box 839554, San Antonio, TX 78283–3954.

Roberts, M. A., Milich. R., & Looney, J. (1985). *Structured observation of academic and play settings (SOAPS): Manual.* (Available from Mary Ann Roberts, Ph.D., Hospital School, University of Iowa, Iowa City, IA 52242.)

Rubin, K. H. (1986). Play, peer interactions, and social development. In A. Gottfried & C. C. Brown (Eds.), *Play interactions* (pp. 163–174). Lexington, MA: Lexington Books.

Schaefer, C. E. (1988). *Innovative interventions in child and adolescent therapy.* New York: John Wiley & Sons.

Solnit, A. J., et al. (1993). *The many meanings of play: A psychoanalytic perspective.* New Haven: Yale University Press.

Waterman, B. B. (1994). Assessing children for the presence of a disability. *News digest: National Information Center for Children and Youth with Disabilities, (4):*1. (Available from NICHCY, P.O. Box 1492, Washington, D.C. 20013. (800-695-0285 (Voice/TT) and 202-884-8200 (Voice/TT).)

Wessel, J. (1977). *Planning individualized education programs in special education, with examples from "I can" physical education.* Northbrook, Illinois: Hubbard.

Witt, P. A. (1982). *The leisure diagnostic battery user's guide.* Denton, TX: Division of Recreation and Leisure Studies, North Texas State University.

CHAPTER 14

CARDIAC REHABILITATION

FRANCIS A. McGUIRE
JANE YOUNG
LODENE GOODWIN

OBJECTIVES

- Know types of cardiac conditions.
- Comprehend the phases of cardiac rehabilitation programs.
- Appreciate the role of therapeutic recreation in cardiac rehabilitation.
- Demonstrate knowledge of the settings where cardiac rehabilitation takes place.

DEFINITION OF CARDIAC DISEASES

In the first edition of this book, we discussed the absence of therapeutic recreation specialists in cardiac rehabilitation programs. This situation continues, but changing trends in rehabilitation suggest a greater possibility of therapeutic recreation involvement. The current emphasis on lifestyle changes and quality of life opens the door for therapeutic recreation specialists to provide expertise in helping cardiac patients adopt and maintain improved health behaviors.

According to Ford (1986), mortality from cardiovascular disease (CVD) has changed to the point where more people are living longer with CVD than ever before. Monteiro (1979) estimates that 85 percent of the individuals experiencing an acute myocardial infarction (heart attack) will survive and return to previous activity. The decreasing mortality rate from myocardial infarction and the subsequent greater population with cardiovascular disease also will increase the likelihood that therapeutic recreation professionals will work with clients with cardiac conditions. In some cases this may occur in cardiac rehabilitation programs. In other cases this may occur in other settings since cardiac diseases are pervasive in our society.

According to Montoye and colleagues (1988), cardiovascular disease is "a term for any of the many diseases that can negatively affect the health of the heart and/or blood vessels" (p. 220). Ford (1986) provided the following facts about CVD:

- CVD is the leading cause of death in the United States.
- Approximately 42 million Americans suffer from CVD, more than any other disorder.
- More deaths result from CVD than from cancer and accidents combined.
- The most common types of CVD are hypertensive heart disease (37 million patients), coronary heart disease (4.5 million), rheumatic heart disease (2 million), and cerebrovascular accident (stroke) (1.8 million).

CLASSIFICATION OF CARDIAC DISEASES

The largest categories of cardiovascular diseases are heart attacks and strokes. Because strokes are discussed in Chapter 11, this chapter will focus on heart attacks and other cardiac conditions.

Most heart diseases are actually vascular diseases that constrict or block normal flow of blood either in or out of the heart. Other diseases, such as rheumatic fever, syphilis, and infections, also cause heart damage.

Congenital heart disease results from some defect in the development of the heart before birth. The heart begins to develop toward the end of the first month of fetal life and looks like an adult heart toward the end of the second fetal month. Congenital heart disease is a condition originating from failure of the necessary twisting, joining, and division of two primitive arteries to take place in proper sequence, as the heart is forming its four chambers, valves, and arteries. Congenital defects of the heart and residuals from rheumatic fever are two common causes of heart disease, and in both areas, cardiac surgery has had remarkable results (DeBakey & Gotto, 1977).

In hypertensive heart disease, the heart is forced to pump harder because of the constriction of the arteries caused by increased blood pressure. This disease strikes all ages and both sexes, although African Americans are more commonly affected than whites.

Heart failure is described as the failure of the heart to pump sufficient blood to maintain normal circulation. It can result from high blood pressure, heart attack, birth defects, or rheumatic heart disease. Congestive heart failure occurs when heart failure results in congestion in the body's tissues. Fluid gathers in the legs, lungs, and abdomen. Rheumatic heart disease results from damage done to the heart as a result of rheumatic fever. The heart valves are typically damaged in rheumatic heart disease (American Heart Association, 1980).

Coronary heart disease results from the narrowing of coronary arteries and a resulting decrease in blood supply to the heart. Coronary heart disease is also called ischemic heart disease and coronary artery disease (American Heart Association, 1980).

Arteriosclerosis, the most common form of heart disease, is actually a group of diseases that are characterized by a thickening and loss of elasticity of the artery walls. Atherosclerosis is a type of arteriosclerosis in which deposits of a fatty substance, called plaque, make the inner layer of the artery wall thick and irregular (American Heart Association, 1980).

Any abnormality of the heart rate or rhythm is called cardiac arrhythmia. An arrhythmia may decrease the amount of blood the heart pumps each minute, which in turn decreases blood supply to the body organs.

Cardiac arrest, or cessation of the heartbeat, results in a drop in blood pressure and curtailment of circulation of the blood. There are often no warning signs prior to cardiac arrest, and the first symptom of cardiovascular disease may be sudden death (Kaplan, Sallis, & Patterson, 1993).

A myocardial infarction, commonly called a heart attack, is the death or damaging of an area of the heart muscle as a result of an interruption in the blood reaching that area (American Heart Association, 1980).

Angina pectoris is severe pain in the chest caused by a restricted flow of blood in the coronary arteries. The pain may radiate to the left shoulder. Angina pectoris is not fatal in itself, but it may signal the onset of a myocardial infarction, which may become fatal (Kaplan, Sallis, & Patterson, 1993).

PURPOSE OF THERAPEUTIC RECREATION

A greater number of people survive open heart surgery and myocardial infarctions today than twenty years ago. Indications are that even greater numbers will survive in the future as a result of better medical care, advanced technology, and emphasis on prevention. Increasing emphasis is being placed on postinfarction care and postoperative care of patients. Rehabilitation is designed to assist the patient in achieving the greatest physical, social, and economic usefulness possible.

Generally, the physical aspects of recovery are less trying on the cardiac patient than are the emotional and social recovery. The individual who has experienced a cardiac event faces emotional adaptation during recovery (Mayou, 1990; Scherck, 1992). The patient responds psychologically to a loss and may experience functional problems such as fatigue, shortness of breath, sleeplessness, loss of appetite, nervousness, and impotence. The functional problems are symptomatic of the grieving process. Denial may be one strategy used by some; others may be very knowledgeable of their illness, thus attaining a feeling of greater control. Prescribed exercise of a physical nature may produce a feeling of control as the pain decreases and the heart develops greater efficiency (Gentry & Williams, 1975; Roviaro, Holmes, & Holsten, 1984).

Individuals who do not develop effective coping strategies experience a higher mortality rate due to prolonged physiological stress. Psychological intervention should be accomplished to assist the cardiac patient in developing more effective and appropriate coping skills (Faller, 1990; Kaufman et al., 1985-1986).

Although the role of exercise in the cardiac rehabilitation process has been well established, leisure's role is less clearly identified. Hoeft (1982) stated that there are few references made concerning the enhancement of cardiac patients' leisure attitudes, interests, satisfaction, and leisure skills concept. She indicated, however, that there is limited evidence that a lack of leisure satisfaction correlates with stress in postmyocardial patients.

Activities that assist patients in reducing stress and other factors (such as obesity, smoking, lack of exercise, and poor nutrition) are a necessary component of the rehabilitation process. Efforts designed to assist patients in developing lifestyle changes that reduce the likelihood of further cardiac problems are often included in patient education programs (Hayes & Antozzi, 1982; Anderson, 1992).

According to Cornett and Watson (1984), a cardiac rehabilitation program has three goals: (1) assisting the patient in returning to work and previous activities, (2) educating the patient about heart disease, its management and prevention, and (3) maintaining psychological and social well being. The therapeutic recreation specialist can be instrumental in meeting these goals. Programs such as stress reduction, use of leisure activities to incorporate more physical activity gradually into the patient's life, and lifestyle education all aim at identifying and removing risk factors such as poor nutrition, smoking, and lack of physical activity.

Rehabilitation begins almost immediately upon hospitalization and must extend beyond this period of recovery. Cornett and Watson (1984) report that cardiac patients who receive expert care during the acute phase of their illness but are discharged with no further treatment often require readmission to the hospital. Therefore, rehabilitation is a lifelong process focusing on disability adaptation, health maintenance, and illness prevention (Cornett and Watson, 1984). The four-phase rehabilitation program that has received wide acceptance is designed to accomplish those goals.

The focus during the rehabilitation process shifts as the patient progresses. Phase I is an inpatient program lasting approximately seven to fourteen days. Phase II is an outpatient program lasting approximately two to three months. Phase III is a supervised community-based program lasting six to twelve months, and Phase IV is an unsupervised or maintenance program which is indefinite in duration (Wilson, Edgett, & Porter, 1986).

The primary foci during cardiac rehabilitation are exercises to return the patient to as high a level of physical functioning possible and education to reduce the likelihood of a further cardiac event. The relative importance of these two purposes shifts as the patient passes through the four phases, but they are present at all times.

COMMON SERVICE SETTINGS

There are primarily four settings where cardiac rehabilitation services occur: hospital inpatient, hospital outpatient, the community, and the home. Rehabilitation begins almost immediately upon admission to the hospital and continues through discharge. While in the hospital, rehabilitation moves from the patient's room to a cardiac rehabilitation facility within the hospital. After discharge from the hospital, patients continue rehabilitation through regular outpatient programs at the rehabilitation center as well as at home. Upon completion of the rehabilitation program at the hospital, patients typically continue to participate in community based programs in facilities such as YMCAs.

According to Wenger (1986), rehabilitation of cardiac patients should be designed to limit the impact of the illness while seeking to maintain and restore an optimum level of functioning in all areas of behavior. This process begins during the first days of hospitalization (Phase I). Initial rehabilitation efforts, done within the first days, are aimed at early ambulation and education. Helping the patient develop a positive attitude is also part of this early inpatient rehabilitation. Early ambulation programs are appropriate for individuals with uncomplicated myocardial infarction. Physical activities during this initial rehabilitation phase are limited to activities that are low in intensity. These include activities such as eating, simple self care, simple passive and active arm and leg movements, and sitting in a chair. These occur while the patient is still in the intensive care or coronary care unit.

Upon leaving this unit, the focus is on increasing cardiovascular functioning to a level sufficient for personal care and independent living upon discharge from the hospital. Typical activities include simple leg and arm movements, simple calisthenics, and walking.

The outpatient phase (Phase II) of the rehabilitation program has several objectives (Fardy, 1986). These include a restoration of physical functioning, restoration of confidence, reduction of anxiety and depression, enhancement of lifestyle habits, development of a commitment to physical activity, and management of myocardial arrhythmias (p. 424). A program of exercise and education is followed to meet these objectives.

Fardy suggests that Phase II exercise programs focus on rhythmic movements of large muscle groups. These would include upper as well as lower extremities. Anaerobic activities, heavy resistance activities, and isometric exercises are contraindicated during this phase of rehabilitation. Patient education during this time should focus on providing information that will provide physical and emotional support during rehabilitation (Fardy, 1986).

Miller and colleagues (1986) state that many individuals can enter community-based rehabilitation programs sooner than ever before after their heart attack. As a result, Phase II rehabilitation may not be necessary for all individuals. In that case, the patient would enter a community program. This traditionally has been considered Phase III in the rehabilitation process.

The community program focuses on the development of a healthy lifestyle. Patients are provided education on risk factors, and they improve functional capacity during this phase (Miller et al., 1986). This period, ranging from six to twelve months, is a time when the patient works to replace destructive habits with constructive ones. Locations available for community-based cardiac rehabilitation programs include university medical schools, community colleges, public schools; YM and YWCAs, community centers, hospitals, and independent cardiac rehabilitation facilities. Heart clubs, often sponsored by the heart association, are primary community support organizations for heart disease patients.

The traditional phase-based structuring of cardiac rehabilitation programs is undergoing some alterations reflective of the current focus on risk factors and lifestyle changes. HeartLife, a program of the Heart Institute of the Greenville Hospital System in Greenville, South Carolina, exemplifies a program with a comprehensive, progressive approach to rehabilitation. In the HeartLife program, "risk stratification," a way of classifying the severity of the patient's illness, determines the stage of rehabilitation most appropriate for the patient. The program has three major emphases: diet, exercise, and stress management.

Phase I of the Greenville Hospital cardiac rehabilitation process begins at the patient's bedside. It will occur in the patient's room or on the nursing floor. Once a patient has progressed sufficiently, Phase I rehabilitation shifts to an inpatient exercise center within the hospital. Equipment such as stationary bicycles, treadmills, and stairs are used in the rehabilitation program. In addition, patients and their spouses or other family members receive education on the risk factors associated with heart disease.

Phase II participants are those discharged from the hospital. They enter a twelve-week program located at the Life Center, a Greenville Hospital System facility that accommodates the HeartLife and other rehabilitation and prevention programs. In addition to their prescribed exercise protocols, patients in Phase II participate in nutrition education including cooking classes, and weekly stress management classes. Each stress management class provides an hour of education about stress and an hour of practicing relaxation techniques. Patients are provided with taped cassettes to guide their relaxation exercises and are expected to use them at home.

In the HeartLife program, Phase III is considered a one-month transition phase leading into the Heart Disease Reversal Program as conceived by Ornish (1990). During this time, patients are encouraged to adopt gradually the Ornish program which stresses a vegetarian, low-fat diet (fat intake limited to 10 to 20 percent of daily calories from fat sources), exercise, relaxation practices, and participation in a patient support group. These are the emphases of the HeartLife Phase IV.

An additional Phase V may be unique to the Greenville Hospital System's HeartLife Program. Established in 1990, Phase V is aimed at prevention of cardiac disease. Participants request membership in the program and undergo screening according to their risk factor status. If minimal risk factors are present, these individuals may use the Life Center facilities without medical supervision. HeartLife staff monitor attendance and other pertinent data through computer entries made by the participant. Phase V applicants who do not pass minimal risk factors and screening must enter the Reversal Program.

Participants in Phases II–V of the HeartLife Program are offered various educational and training programs related to the three major aspects of rehabilitation. A sample schedule of events in a two-week period includes the following listings: Supermarket Tour, Yoga, Mended Hearts Support Group, Techniques to Calm the Mind, Individual Nutrition Consults, Fat Counts, Heart-to-Heart Support Group, and Diabetes Education Class (Greenville Hospital System, 1994).

The treatment team at HeartLife includes nurses, exercise physiologists, nutritionists, a vocational rehabilitation counselor, and a physical therapist on a consulting basis. Similar progressive programs in other states may have a psychologist on the treatment team, but this appears to be influenced by policies of third-party reimbursement in the particular state. The HeartLife program does make referrals as appropriate, based on psychological assessment.

CURRENT BEST PRACTICES AND PROCEDURES

Assessment

Assessment of cardiac patients is designed to gather data in two main areas: medical and lifestyle. The medical information is used primarily to develop an appropriate exercise regimen for the patient. The lifestyle assessment is done to identify risk factors, such as poor nutrition or inactive leisure, that will become the focus of a behavioral modification program. Although the recreation therapist must be aware of the medical assessment and any activity contraindications resulting from it, he or she will be more directly involved in the lifestyle assessment unless he or she is trained in exercise physiology.

Comoss and colleagues (1979) define assessment with cardiac clients as "the collection and analysis of information about the patient's health status." The precise nature of the assessment process they describe varies across the four phases of the rehabilitation process. During Phase I, data related to early educational needs of the patient, as well as physiological factors such as heart rate and blood pressure, are crucial. The focus during Phase II shifts to assessing activity readiness as well as determining the educational needs of the client in areas such as stress reduction, nutrition, smoking, medical procedures, or activity management.

Assessment during Phase III focuses on gathering subjective information related to demographics, cardiac history, general health, and a psychosocial history dealing with the client's lifestyle. In addition, exercise testing is done to measure work capacity.

Phase IV assessment revolves around a nursing history, cardiovascular examination, and an exercise stress test. Part of the nursing history assessment is designed to identify factors, such as chronic congestive heart failure, that limit exercise participation. In addition, signs to be aware of during exercise, such as angina, will be identified during the Phase IV assessment. Information is needed also about medications and their side effects.

Cornett and Watson (1984) identify specific areas to be included in an activity assessment. These include a description of daily and weekly activities, frequency and type of exercise, living arrangements, sexual activity, and sleep patterns. They also acknowledge that all aspects of the rehabilitation process, including assessments, should be carried out by a team of professionals.

The therapeutic recreation specialist will be most heavily involved in assessing the patient's social history. According to Wilson, Fardy, and Froelicher (1981), the social history will include information related to occupational physical activity; job satisfaction; family and work responsibilities; physical activity in leisure time; family medical and socioeconomic history; smoking, drinking, and eating habits; sexual activity; and geographic history (p. 235).

Planning

A basic term therapeutic recreation specialists should understand prior to planning programs for cardiac rehabilitation clients is *Metabolic Units* (MET). One MET is the equivalent of the energy the body consumes when it is at rest. METs provide a way of evaluating activities to determine their energy cost (Cohn, Duke, and Madrid, 1979; Anderson, 1992).

As patients move through the four phases of cardiac rehabilitation, they are capable of increasing the METs at which they can function. Cornett and Watson (1984) indicate that activities in the 1–2 MET range are appropriate as the Phase I program begins; they call this the "acute" phase. In Phase II, the "convalescent" phase, patients progress to activities requiring 3–4 Mets. This includes activities such as gardening, bowling, horseshoes, and slow bicycling.

The therapeutic recreation specialist should work with the exercise physiologist or physician who has developed an exercise prescription for the patient in order to incorporate recreation activities into that prescription. Consultation will also help the therapist identify the maximum physical load to place on clients.

In addition to planning activities that provide appropriate levels of activity, TR specialists must also participate in educational activities that will foster the client's long-term lifestyle changes. This includes planning programs aimed at stress reduction, use of leisure in productive ways, and appropriate levels of leisure involvement within the patient's level of physical fitness (Wendland, 1981).

Limitations

The primary limitations on cardiac rehabilitation patients are in the area of physical activity. The use of the MET requirement of activities is useful in identifying upper levels of exertion. In addition, individuals working with cardiac patients must be aware of danger signals that indicate excessive exercise. According to Cornett and Watson (1984), an activity is excessive if it results in a variety of symptoms including diaphoresis (copious perspiration), pallor, cyanosis (bluish discoloration of the skin), nausea, and dyspnea (difficulty breathing). A significant increase in blood pressure, as well as marked increases in heart rate, also indicate excessive activity. Concerns after exercise include insomnia, excessive excitement, exhilaration, weakness, fatigue, muscular cramping, skeletal muscular pain, gastrointestinal disturbances, nausea, and vomiting (Wilson, Fardy, and Froelicher, 1981, p. 371).

A variety of drugs are used in cardiac programs (Ford, 1986; Lowenthal and Stein, 1986; Cornett and Watson, 1984), and a variety of classification systems are used. Any individual working in a cardiac rehabilitation program should learn the names of prescribed medications and their purposes. Any activity contraindications linked to a specific drug must be followed.

The American Heart Association (1980) has identified several drugs used by cardiac patients. Among these are digitalis, which increases the strength of the heart's contractions; diuretics, which increase the output of salt and water from the body; vasodilators to relax blood vessels; beta blocking agents, which reduce heart rate and the strength of contractions; anticoagulants to prevent clotting; drugs to lower cholesterol; and calcium channel blockers to help control high blood pressure, coronary spasms, and angina.

Wilson and colleagues (1981) provide specific activity guidelines based on medication being used by patients. For example, they suggest that beta blocking agents reduce heart rate and as a result, the maximal heart rate clients should reach is reduced to 100 to 125 beats per minute. Nitrates, including nitroglycerin, can result in headaches or fainting. Any recreational therapist working with cardiac clients must have an in-depth understanding of medications and their effects.

APPLICATION OF THE TR PROCESS

CASE STUDY

Fred is a 43-year-old male who has been admitted to the hospital after experiencing a myocardial infarction. He is married and has two children aged ten and twelve. He owns and manages a clothing store.

Assessment

The assessment will vary as Fred moves through the phases of rehabilitation. Based on the traditional four phases, Fred's assessment involves examination of his current health status and risk factors. It also includes a lifestyle inventory and history. According to Comoss and colleagues (1979), Phase I assessment will include a description of the illness that brought the patient to the coronary care unit and his past and family medical history. It will include an assessment of physiological stability, including measurements such as heart rate, blood pressure, and findings from the cardiovascular examination. In addition, it is necessary to assess his educational needs relative to understanding the heart problem and how to manage it during this early stage.

Phase II assessment includes gathering data on the patient's physical state, his psychological state, and his educational needs related to both lifestyle and the cardiac condition. In addition, the patient's physical readiness to participate in activities must be determined. This would be a time to assess leisure interests and to relate preferred activities to recommended MET levels.

Phase III assessment includes an examination of previous hospital records, family history, exercise test results, and medications. Psychosocial assessments, including activity preferences and involvement, also must be completed.

Prior to the initiation of Phase IV, a cardiovascular examination should be completed and reviewed to ensure the patient's safety during activity involvement. An exercise stress test should be done to determine exercise capacity. Assessments should be completed to determine educational needs in areas such as stress management and activity selection.

It is likely the transition from the hospital-based program in Phases I and II to the community-based Phase III will result in a change in personnel. In that case, the TR specialist working with the client in the hospital will need to communicate assessment information to the therapist assuming responsibility during Phase III.

Planning

The assessment indicated Fred was extremely work oriented, which resulted in a great deal of stress in his life. In addition, he participated in few noncompetitive leisure activities.

After gathering information from Fred, the therapist involved in his Phase II rehabilitation identified the following actions:

- Assist Fred in gradually increasing his activity level as his physical functioning improves.
- Assist Fred in developing an activity agenda that he will use as he moves through the rehabilitation process. The activities will be selected within the appropriate MET levels at each point in rehabilitation.
- Help Fred identify lifestyle changes that will reduce the risk of further cardiac problems. Specifically, assist Fred in developing stress reduction strategies.
- Enhance Fred's motivation to actively participate in the Phase I rehabilitation and continue with Phase II upon discharge.
- Help Fred explore current leisure preferences and develop a plan for incorporating leisure into post-discharge life.

Implementation

The recreation therapist will use a variety of approaches to reach the objectives outlined for Fred. Because several of the changes in his life will involve the entire family, the family members should be involved in his therapy. Specifically, Fred should become involved in a leisure counseling program to identify leisure activities suitable for his preferences and a more active lifestyle. Once those activities have been identified, methods of adapting them to the appropriate cardiac requirements must be employed. The MET requirements of a variety of leisure activities must be determined, and their role in Fred's exercise program should be established. Fred should participate in a stress reduction class with other cardiac rehabilitation clients.

Evaluation

Prior to release from the hospital and completion of the Phase I program, a discharge summary will be completed for Fred. Evaluation will include a predischarge exercise test to determine if he is able to participate in activities at the expected 3 MET level. These activities would include bicycling, bowling, billiards, fishing, dancing, hiking, and playing musical instruments (Comoss et al., 1979). Evaluation of psychosocial and educational outcomes, including knowledge of heart disease and risk factors related to heart disease, should be conducted. Knowledge of pulse taking, prescribed medications, and exercise requirements should also be evaluated at this time.

TRENDS AND ISSUES

A major issue for therapeutic recreation specialists is their absence from treatment teams associated with cardiac patients (Hayes & Antozzi, 1982). There are few settings where they are included. In fact, while researching materials for this chapter, little mention of therapeutic recreation specialists was found in any of the general literature. The role of a variety of professionals, including physical educators, exercise physiologists, occupational therapists, and physical therapists, was discussed. However, the field of therapeutic recreation was conspicuous by its absence. Clearly, therapeutic recreation specialists need to educate physicians responsible for cardiac rehabilitation programs. In addition, this outreach effort must be accompanied by increased competency in the area of exercise physiology if TR specialists are to establish themselves as contributing therapists with this population.

Increased public awareness of risk factors associated with cardiovascular diseases, as well as the use of drugs to prevent heart disease, will reduce the number of individuals suffering heart disease. Already this is resulting in an increased focus on prevention programs, similar to Phase IV, designed to bring about lifetime cardiac fitness. Improved medical care and technology may also result in increased life expectancy in those individuals who experience a cardiac problem. Therefore, it is likely that while the number of individuals with cardiac conditions will decrease, the number of individuals who survive cardiac disease will increase and participate in rehabilitation programs.

SUMMARY

This chapter has examined cardiac conditions and the role of the therapeutic recreation specialist in the rehabilitation process. Cardiac rehabilitation programs are long-term efforts that progress from the coronary care unit in the hospital to at-home rehabilitation that lasts for life. During the rehabilitation process, the focus is on physiology as well as lifestyle. Patients must learn to deal with the cardiac event as well as develop strategies that optimize recovery and reduce the likelihood of further problems. These efforts revolve around exercise, diet, and behavior modification.

Many cardiac rehabilitation programs occur in four phases that begin with hospitalization and continue to community-based programs. Throughout the process, the therapeutic recreation specialist must assist the client in developing new lifestyle patterns that will contribute to cardiac wellness.

If recreation therapists want to become part of the growing field of cardiac rehabilitation, they will need a background that includes study in exercise physiology. Other skills that will be useful in a cardiac rehabilitation program include leisure counseling, activity analysis and adaptation, and stress reduction techniques.

READING COMPREHENSION QUESTIONS

1. Define cardiovascular disease and identify at least five types.
2. What are the four phases of cardiac rehabilitation?
3. List the two major purposes of cardiac rehabilitation programs.
4. What risk factors increase the likelihood of a heart attack? What role can the therapeutic recreation specialist have in reducing these risk factors?
5. What are METs, and how do they relate to the selection of recreation activities for patients in cardiac rehabilitation?
6. Explain the relationship of therapeutic recreation specialists to other members of the treatment team in cardiac rehabilitation programs.
7. Identify the major categories of drugs used by cardiac patients. What are some activity contraindications of each?

SUGGESTED LEARNING ACTIVITIES

1. Develop a list of all the recreation activities you do in a typical 24 hour period. Use a MET table to determine the MET level of each.
2. Visit a cardiac rehabilitation program. Discuss the role of therapeutic recreation in cardiac programs with the physician in charge.
3. Discuss why therapeutic recreation specialists traditionally have not been included on treatment teams for cardiac patients. How might the profession change this state of affairs?
4. Take a stress test, and discuss the role of such a test in the cardiac rehabilitation process.
5. Examine your lifestyle, and identify risk factors that may increase the likelihood of your having a heart attack. What can you do to reduce these risk factors? How might you help clients reduce risk factors in their lives?

REFERENCES

American Heart Association. (1980). *The American Heart Association heartbook.* New York: E. P. Dutton.

Anderson, U. (1992). The person participating in inpatient and outpatient cardiac rehabilitation. In D. Guzzetta & B. Dossey (Eds.), *Cardiovascular nursing: Holistic practice.* St. Louis: Mosby-Year Book, Inc.

Cohn, K., Duke, D., & Madrid, J. (1979). *Coming back: A guide to recovering from heart attack and living confidently with coronary disease.* Reading, MA: Addison-Wesley.

Comoss, P., et al. (1979). *Cardiac rehabilitation: A comprehensive nursing approach.* Philadelphia: J. B. Lippincott.

Cornett, S., & Watson, J. E. (1984). *Cardiac rehabilitation: An interdisciplinary team approach.* New York: John Wiley & Sons.

Debakey, M., & Gotto, A. (1977). *The living heart.* New York: David MacKay.

Ewy, G. A., & Bressler, R. (Eds.). (1982). *Cardiovascular drugs and the management of heart disease.* New York: Raven Press.

Faller, H. (1990). Coping with myocardial infarction: A cognitive-emotional perspective. *Psychotherapy and Psychosomatics, 54,* 8–17.

Fardy, P. S. (1986). Cardiac rehabilitation for the outpatient: A hospital-based program. In M. Pollock, D. Schmidt, & D. Mason (Eds.), *Heart disease and rehabilitation* (2nd ed.). New York: John Wiley & Sons.

Ford, R. D. (Ed.). (1986). *Cardiovascular care handbook.* Springhouse, PA: Springhouse Corporation.

Gentry, W. D., & Williams, R. B. (Eds.). (1975). *Psychological aspects of myocardial infarction and coronary care.* St. Louis: C. V. Mosby.

Greenville Hospital System. (n. d.). *Cardiac rehabilitation center.* Greenville, SC: Greenville Hospital System.

Greenville Hospital System. (1994). *Heartlife calendar of events.* Greenville, SC: Greenville Hospital System.

Hayes, G. A., & Antozzi, R. K. (1982). Philosophical basis for therapeutic recreation and leisure lifestyle adjustment in cardiac rehabilitation. In L. L. Neal & C. R. Edginton (Eds.), *Extra perspectives: Concepts in therapeutic recreation.* Eugene, OR: Center for Leisure Studies.

Hoeft, T. M. (1982). Leisure counseling: A component of cardiac rehabilitation and heart disease intervention programs. In L. L. Neal & C. R. Edginton (Eds.), *Extra perspectives: Concepts in therapeutic recreation.* Eugene, OR: Center for Leisure Studies.

Kaplan, R. M., Sallis, J. F., & Patterson, T. L. (1993). *Health psychology.* New York: McGraw Hill.

Kaufmann, M. W., et al. (1986–1989). Psychosomatic aspects of myocardial infarction and implications for treatment. *International Journal of Psychiatry in Medicine, 15*(4). 371–380.

Lowenthal, D. T., & Stein, D. T. (1986). Drug effects: Exercise testing and training. In M. Pollock, D. Schmidt, & D. Mason (Eds.), *Heart disease and rehabilitation* (2nd ed.). New York: John Wiley & Sons.

Mayou, R. (1990). Quality of life in cardiovascular disease. *Psychotherapy and Psychosomatics, 54,* 99-109.

Miller, H. S., et al. (1986). Community programs of cardiac rehabilitation. In M. Pollock, D. Schmidt, & D. Mason (Eds.), *Heart disease and rehabilitation* (2nd ed.). New York: John Wiley & Sons.

Monteiro, L. A. (1979). *Cardiac patient rehabilitation: Social aspects of recovery.* New York: Springer Publishing.

Montoye, H. J., et al. (1988). *Living fit.* Menlo Park, CA: Benjamin/Cummings Publishing.

Ornish, D. (1990). *Dr. Dean Ornish's program for reversing heart disease.* New York: Ballantine Books.

Roviaro, S., Holmes, D., & Holsten, R. (1984). Influence of a cardiac rehabilitation program on the cardiovascular, psychological, and social functioning of cardiac patients. *Journal of Behavioral Medicine, 7,* 61–81.

Scherck, K. A. (1992). Coping with acute myocardial infarction. *Heart and Lung, 21*(4), 327–324.

Wendland, L. V. (1981). The psychodynamics of coronary heart rehabilitation: Some basic understandings for allied health professionals. *Journal of Allied Health, 10,* 41–48.

Wenger, N. (1986). Rehabilitation of the patient with acute myocardial infarction during hospitalization:

Early ambulation and patient education. In M. Pollock, D. Schmidt, & D. Mason (Eds.), *Heart disease and rehabilitation* (2nd ed.). New York: John Wiley & Sons.

Wilson, P. K., Edgett, J. W., & Porter, G. H. (1986). Rehabilitation of the cardiac patient: Program organization. In M. Pollock, D. Schmidt, & D. Mason (Eds.), *Heart disease and rehabilitation* (2nd ed.). New York: John Wiley & Sons.

Wilson, P. K., Fardy, P. S., & Froelicher, V. F. (1981). *Cardiac rehabilitation, adult fitness, and exercise testing*. Philadelphia: Lea & Febiger.

CHAPTER 15

CONVULSIVE DISORDERS

MARK R. JAMES
MICHAEL E. CRAWFORD

OBJECTIVES

- State a concise definition of the term *seizure.*
- Understand the classification of seizures.
- Understand the relationship between seizures, convulsive disorders, and epilepsy.
- Recognize the side effects from anticonvulsant medications.
- Realize that most individuals with epilepsy are able to stabilize their seizures with medications and life-style adaptations.
- Recognize the key areas where therapeutic recreation services are appropriate.
- Understand the possible activity limitations for clients with epilepsy.

DEFINITION OF CONVULSIVE DISORDERS/EPILEPSY

The term *convulsion,* or *seizure,* refers to an involuntary spasm or contraction of muscles resulting from chemical imbalances in the body. The causes of these chemical imbalances may come from a variety of sources, such as insufficient amounts of sugar or calcium in the blood, toxic poisoning, and disease or injury to the brain or central nervous system (Bleck, 1987).

The diagnostic category of epilepsy refers to a heterogeneous group of syndromes unified by their tendency to produce repeated convulsions, or seizures. Epileptic convulsions result from temporary chemical imbalances in the brain (as opposed to other chemical imbalances) that cause a rapid discharge of intercellular electrical activity. This electrical "overload" in turn produces a motoric seizure (and in some cases CNS blackout). Epilepsy itself is not a disease, but is a symptom of disturbed brain functioning. Although epilepsy represents the largest subgroup of convulsive disorders, it should be noted that not all clients who have convulsions are epileptic.

Prevalence estimates for epilepsy have consistently ranged from 0.5 to 1.5 percent of the general population (Hauser, 1978; Juul-Jensen & Foldspang, 1983; Epilepsy Foundation of America,1995). The most recent estimate stands at 2.2 million individuals in the United States. In addition to epilepsy, there are over 100 other neurological syndromes that may cause convulsions. Thus, the total number of individuals impacted by convulsion disorders is estimated at 3.6 million

(Anderson, Hauser, & Rich, 1986; Epilepsy Foundation of America, 1995).

Age of onset varies widely; approximately 20 percent of all adult cases had their first seizure before age ten. Another 30 percent do not experience seizures until the second decade of life. Twenty percent have their first seizure activity in their thirties and the remainder have relatively late onset at forty and beyond.

There are a variety of negative cultural/social stereotypes about seizure disorders still in existance among the lay public. Despite the fact that many famous personages have had seizure disorders such as Alexander the Great, Julius Caesar, Vincent Van Gogh, and Alfred Nobel (Howie, 1994), the overall history of social acceptance is far from positive. Throughout early European and early North American history many persons with epilepsy were thought to be "possessed," (their seizures viewed as evidence of demonic possession) and many were summarily "burned at the stake." At the turn of the century through to present day the dominant negative sterotype has been the notion that epilepsy occurs in concert with mental illness and/or mental retardation. Thus, epileptics have been individuals to be feared and/or shunned. During the "eugenic scare" of the late 1800s and through the 1920s, many were institutionalzed and sterilized over fear of transmission. In addition, many states passed constitutional amendments declaring it illegal to marry a person with epilepsy (Wolfensburger, 1972).* Most of these marriage laws were not removed until the 1960s (Alabama's was not repealed until 1984). Even in relatively modern times it was not uncommon for individuals with epilepsy to be misdiagnosed as learning disabled by psychologists and educators (as was so often the case in the early 1970s for persons with petit mal or so called "absence seizures" in which awareness is only briefly and episodically lost) or for physicians to label them as sleepwalkers (as was the case for many persons whose form of epilepsy manifested itself as a psychomotor seizure where a specific motor memory "loop" such as the sequence for walking, or chewing, or even undressing, etc., is triggered during the seizure activity). There are also various anecdotal accounts of police officers and similar authorities detaining and arresting individuals with epilepsy when seizures have been mistaken as signs of psychosis or public intoxication (Siegler and Osmond, 1974). Many Hollywood science fiction and horror "B" movies of the 1950s and '60s frequently displayed individuals with epilepsy in horrific charicatures; as villainous despoilers of young girls and similar "innocents," who were best kept locked in the attic or basement (preferably in chains) lest another uncontrollable epileptic "fit" send them into another psychotic "rage" (during which they were visually depicted as frothing and foaming at the mouth). The effect of the dark history of care and various negative cultural influences has been to leave many individuals with epilepsy intimidated (or even ashamed) (Epilepsy Foundation of America, 1995). Public opinion regarding epilepsy has taken a long time to change, and there are still pockets of bigotry and resistance. Despite the implementation of the Americans with Disabilities Act in the early 1990s and its many guarantees for personal and civil rights, many individuals with epilepsy continue to be discriminated against vocationally and socially and remain reluctant to disclose their condition.

CLASSIFICATION OF SEIZURE DISORDERS

In 70 percent of all cases the cause of epilepsy is idiopathic or "unknown." Despite this relatively mysterious nature, parental concerns for "passing" the disorder onto their children may be somewhat comforted by the fact that only a 6 per-

*The reader is encouraged to consult Wolfensburger for a full historical accounting of the national eugenic scare of the late 1800s. Mass roundups, brutal institutionalization, and the loss of personal and civil rights depicted care for persons with developmental disabilities, epilepsy, and other socially "deviant" subgroups during this time.

cent chance for inheritance exists, even when both parents have the disorder. In the 30 percent of cases where etiology or cause/effect transmission is clear, some ten factors have been identified as contributory (Bleck, 1987). Seven are clearly implicated in epilepsy, or repeated seizure syndromes, whereas three are related to episodic, or single seizure occurrences. Table 15.1 displays these ten factors.

For epilepsy, or repeated seizure syndromes, the seven most prominent causes are (1) genetic influences, (2) birth trauma, (3) various central nervous system infections, (4) head injuries, (5) brain tumors, (6) cerebrovascular diseases or strokes, and (7) immunological disorders. Episodic, or single seizure, occurrences are caused by (1) drug/alcohol withdrawal, (2) acute drug intoxication, and (3) metabolic disorders.

It is important for therapeutic recreation specialists to be able to recognize and describe the various seizure types. This knowledge is necessary for proper documentation of seizures that occur during clinical sessions, and to give feedback to the appropriate medical personnel who work with the client who had the seizure. Although accurate clinical observations are vital to diagnosis,

TABLE 15.1 Etiological Factors of Seizure Disorders

Epilepsy
1. Genetic influences
2. Birth trauma
3. Central nervous system infections
4. Head trauma
5. Tumors
6. Cerebrovascular diseases or strokes
7. Immunological disorders
Single Seizures
1. Drug/alcohol withdrawal
2. Acute drug intoxication
3. Metabolic disorders

Source: Bleck (1987).

they do not always give a clear indication of the specific disorder; a variety of seizure types may be observed for individual disorders.

The classification of seizure types remains somewhat confused in the United States today because multiple systems remain in use. Many physicians prefer the traditional or clinical classification system with its emphasis on terminology like Grand Mal, Petit Mal, Jacksonian, Jackknife, and Psychomotor seizures. In fact many contemporary medical and educational textbooks continue to publish the clinical classification system (Sherrill, 1993). Advocates for change feel that such terms have become emotionally and negatively charged over time and now connote negative stereotypes. Their argument is similar to the changeover in classification terminology that has occurred for persons with mental retardation (i.e., we no longer use terms like imbecile or moron for the severely or profoundly retarded even though these were once legitimate psychological IQ classifications). An International Classification System was adopted by the World Health Organization as early as 1970 (CTILE,1981) and is now the preferred system of the Epilepsy Foundation of America (1995). The current classification of seizure types has evolved historically from the distinction between convulsive, or so called "grand mal" seizures; and absence, or "petit mal" seizures—clinical labels that are now used less frequently. The two basic divisions of seizures used in the international classification system are: (1) partial seizures, and (2) generalized seizures. Table 15.2 presents an outline of the current seizure types according to the preferred international system.

Partial seizures are those that begin in one specific body site and may or may not involve the loss of consciousness. If consciousness is not impaired, the term *simple partial* is used. If consciousness is impaired, the seizure is referred to as *complex partial.* A complex partial seizure is the most common type in adults with epilepsy. Under the old clinical classification system, simple partial seizures were referred to as "Jacksonian" seizures, and complex partial

TABLE 15.2 Classification of Seizure Types

A. Partial Seizures (begin in one specific body site)
   1. Simple partial seizures (consciousness is not impaired)
   2. Complex partial seizures (consciousness is impaired)
   3. Partial seizure evolving into a generalized seizure
B. Generalized Seizures (not confined to one body site)
   1. Absence seizures
   2. Myoclonic seizures
   3. Clonic seizures
   4. Tonic seizures
   5. Tonic-clonic seizures
   6. Atonic seizures
   7. Akinetic
   8. Infantile spasms
C. Unilateral seizures
D. Unclassified seizures

Source: Adapted from Commission on Classification and Terminology of the International League Against Epilepsy (1981) and amended according to Sherrill (1993).

seizures as "Psychomotor" or temporal lobe epilepsy. Simple partial seizures tend to be one-sided (involving just one hemisphere of the CNS) and frequently involve simple tremoring of the fingers, hand, and arm. By contrast, it is the complex partial seizures that can produce the specific motor loop behaviors discussed earlier in this chapter in which auomatic activity (which is not remembered due to CNS blackout) is carried out (e.g., sleepwalking, talking, striking, chewing, throwing behaviors, etc.). Some partial seizures begin in one body site and progress to a more global type known as a *generalized seizure.*

Generalized seizures do not start in one isolated body site, but rather involve several sites or entire body areas such as the trunk or the extremities. Absence seizures are typified by an abrupt interruption of awareness and behavior, without any loss of muscle tone. It is frequently noted that clients with these seizures display slight eye blinking, mouth twitching, and hand movements. These seizures generally last five to thrity seconds. Under the old clinical classification system, these seizures were referred to as Petit Mal. It is this form of epilepsy that frequently caused individuals to be misdiagnosed as learning disabled. Since these seizures can occur hundreds of times per day in some individuals, it is easy to see how many of them had difficulty keeping up academically.

The five other subgroups of generalized seizures are differentiated by the display of various tonic and clonic movements (tension and relaxation of the muscles). Tonic only and clonic only seizures do occur but are relatively rare. Somewhat more common are myoclonic seizures (extreme contraction and flexion of muscles). The muscle activity during the seizure is generally quite brief or episodic in nature and can be quite violent (often manifested as a sudden head jerk and/or strong dramatic contraction of arm and leg muscles). Atonic siezures affect postural control of the trunk and head and are characterized by a sudden partial collapse or sagging of the affected body part—like absence seizures there is an accompanying momentary CNS black out. Akinetic seizures used to be referred to as "drop seizures" or "drop attacks" among the lay public. The expression, "He's got a case of the drops!" was born from this somewhat rare form of epilepsy (Siegler and Osmond,1974). The manifestation of akinetic seizures is literally a drop to the ground (or down the stairs depending upon where the person happens to be) and is caused by a sudden and complete loss of muscle tone throughout the major antigravity muscle systems. Many cerebral palsied and profoundly retarded individuals have akinetic seizures as an accompanying disorder. These individuals are frequently helmeted when ambulatory to prevent injuries to the face and skull because of the high likelihood for injury that manifestation of this disorder brings. Infantile spasms (which were called "Jackknife" siezures under the old clinical classification system) tend to occur in young children (before the first birthday), and in the classic form look like a jack-knife dive off a springboard—a sudden doubling of the trunk (though more typically a lesser form involving arm and leg flexion and/or head flexion occurs).

Tonic-clonic seizures are referred to as grand mal under the old clinical classification system. It is the tonic-clonic seizure that drives the majority of the lay public's perceptions and stereotypes of seizures in contemporary society. Tonic-clonic seizures in fact are the majority form of the disorder and represent some 30 percent of all cases (the second most frequent is the absence form which accounts for 8 to 11 percent). It is this version of epilepsy that has definite stages to the course of the seizure and which much of common safety publications focus on regarding seizure management (American National Red Cross, 1994; Epilepsy Foundation of America, 1995).

One of the most misunderstood elements of the tonic-clonic seizure is the first stage or the so-called experience of "Aura." Only about half of those individuals who have this form of epilepsy are fortunate enough to experience aura—fortunate in the sense that aura is a form of an early warning mechanism regarding seizure activity. It is most frequently experienced as a sensory perception (e.g., the person might smell an acrid smell like burning leaves, others report tasting a sickly sweet sensation on the tips of their toungues, or tingling sensations in their fingers and toes), although anecdotal accounts include other manifestations including feelings/cognitions of euphoria. For those who experience aura it represents a brief window of time to find a relatively comfortable position and safe place to experience the rest of the seizure cycle. In the continuous contraction or tonic phase of the seizure (remember for some this is the first phase), the CNS blackout occurs and various affected muscle systems are flooded with neurological overflow; arms and legs will stiffen, and as a result, if the persons are standing they will lose their balance and frequently fall (this should not be confused with akinetic seizures where the individuals also fall but the fall itself is caused by loss of muscle tone). Some individuals will vocalize; the "shout of rapture" described in the early 1920s was no doubt a clinician's attempt to describe/integrate the phenomenon of emotional aura and the tonic vocalization phenomenon of some patients (Gastaut, 1970). Occasionally individuals will also become cyanotic (turn blue due to restriction of respiratory muscles in the chest cavity), particularly if the tonic phase lasts more than its typical short course of approximately thrity to forty-five seconds (in some it can last several minutes). It was in response to occasional cyanosis within the tonic phase that first-aid courses circa the 1950s urged persons monitoring seizures to place an oral block in the person's mouth. This practice was built upon the mistaken notion that the person was turning blue because they had "swallowed their tongue" something that is impossible to do (just check your mouth, your tongue is attached to the bottom by muscle and thus impossible to swallow).

The next phase, the clonic phase, is characterized by arhythmical contraction and flexion of the voluntary muscle sets. This phase can last for several minutes and is the longer or "working" phase of the seizure. During the clonic phase, some individuals injure themselves by biting through their tongues or lower lips as the jaw muscles work up and down. It is also during this phase that many would be "rescuers" who were inserting oral blocks (e.g., their wallets, or combs, whatever was handy) lost parts of their fingers. Occasionally, the oral block itself would cause injury, if wood or plastic items splintered under the force of jaw contractions. The individual would frequently regain consciousness from the seizure with a bloody mouth and imbedded particles. Some individuals will lose control of their bowel and bladder sphincters during the clonic phase and soil themselves as a result. For most, the active tonic-clonic phase of the seizure cycle lasts only one to five minutes, stopping spontaneously. Infrequently, seizures will continue beyond five minutes. Should this occur, the client is considered to be in a state of "status epilepticus." This is a very serious condition, and prompt medical attention is needed to prevent residual brain damage or possible death. Recent evidence suggests that permanent neuronal damage can occur after about twenty minutes of status epilepticus (Bleck, 1983). Additionally, for some individuals the active tonic-clonic cycle is so strenuous that the adrenal gland may be triggered and heart rates may accelerate to dangerous levels (over 200 bpm) where the likelihood of a heart attack is considerable. Due to the dual risks of permanent neurological damage and/or potentially fatal heart arrest that "status epilepticus" poses, it is critical that observers of a tonic-clonic seizure begin timing the seizure and call for medical assistance if the active part of the cycle exceeds five minutes. The final phase of the tonic-clonic seizure is the sleep or coma phase. Most regain consciousness quickly and may only need your assistance in finding a restroom to collect themselves and, if need be, attend to personal hygiene matters. For others the seizure is much more draining; they may be only semiconscious and need several hours of sleep to fully recover. In either case, it is important to remember that no memory of events during the working phase of the seizure will be available to the person due to the CNS black-out that always accompanies tonic-clonic seizures.

Dual Diagnosis: Seizure Disorders and Other Pervasive Conditions

In addition to the direct consequences of suffering from a seizure disorder, individuals with epilepsy are commonly considered to be at high risk for other psychological/psychiatric problems (Fenton, 1981). These dual-diagnosed clients present difficulties to their interdisciplinary treatment teams in respect to establishing treatment priorities.

Psychopathology as related to epilepsy generally refers to psychosis, aggression, sexual dysfunction, affective disorders, significant personality and behavioral changes, and other problems. Research into the correlations between epilepsy and psychopathology notes three specific etiological influences: (1) the seizures themselves, (2) social and environmental stressors, and (3) side effects from anticonvulsive medications (Finchan, 1986). It is generally felt that either singly or in combination, these three influences foster the greater incidence of psychopathology in clients with epilepsy.

It is not uncommon for a therapeutic recreation specialist who works in a long-term residential treatment center to encounter clients who have mental retardation and epilepsy (approximately one-third of all severely retarded persons have some form of epilepsy (Sherrill, 1993), or cerebral palsy and epilepsy (estimates range from 25 to 50 percent of the adult cerebral palsied population) (Sherrill, 1993). In some cases, there may be a single underlying disorder (e.g., Lennon-Bastaut syndrome, tuberous sclerosis) or two separate conditions. Many metabolic disorders that induce seizures respond poorly to medication and thus over time will result in residual brain damage. These cases are rare in comparison with the entire population of individuals with convulsive disorders, but they are commonly seen in certain long-term treatment settings (e.g., state schools or developmental centers for the mentally retarded/developmentally disabled, chronic psychiatric and state forensic hospitals for the mentally ill and, to a lesser extent, what remains of the old state sytems of residential care for the deaf and/or blind).

DESCRIPTION OF LIMITATIONS

Two key areas present long-term difficulties and challenges to clients with epilepsy: (1) chronic side effects from anticonvulsant medications, and (2) lifestyle modifications. Not surprisingly, how clients handle these two areas significantly affects the stabilization of their seizures. With careful, ongoing monitoring, most individuals achieve satisfactory freedom from seizures.

Clients who have recurrent epileptic seizures should be treated with anticonvulsant medications. There are a variety of appropriate drugs that can be used individually or in combination

(Fincham, 1986; PDR, 1994). Although general guidelines are available for determining which drug works best for specific types of seizures, working out an effective anticonvulsant treatment regimen is a complex task. Table 15.3 outlines some of the seizure types and common medications that may be the drugs of first choice. It should be emphasized that these are guidelines only.

Clients must understand the anticonvulsant medications do not cure or correct epilepsy, but rather offer a method of prevention of future seizures. The effectiveness of these medications depends upon the maintenance of a stable level of the drug in the client's bloodstream at all times; hence the need for ongoing monitoring. All anticonvulsant medications have the potential to cause a variety of side effects. Therapeutic recreation specialists need to be aware of these in order to conduct valid assessments and outline appropriate treatment strategies. Refer to Table 15.4 for some of the more common side effects.

Several factors have been identified that are thought to aggravate or spontaneously induce seizures (Bleck, 1987; Sherrill, 1993; Burlingame & Blaschko, 1990). Each of these is somehow related to a chemical change in the client's bloodstream. Because each of these factors is partially under the control of the client, they often can be monitored and stabilized by lifestyle modifications. These factors are the following:

1. *Sleep deprivation.* It is commonly believed that rapid changes in sleep habits will hinder the stabilization of seizures.

TABLE 15.3 Anticonvulsant Medications

Trade Name	Generic Name	Seizure Type
Dilantin	Phenytoin	Simple partial
		Complex partial
		Partial with secondary generalization
		Generalized
Luminal	Phenobarbital	Simple partial
Mysoline	Primidone	Complex partial
		Partial with secondary generalization
		Generalized
Tegretol	Carbamazepine	Simple partial
		Complex partial
		Partial with secondary generalization
		Generalized
Clonopin	Clonazepam	Absence
		Myoclonic
Zarontin	Ethosuximide	Absence
Depakene	Valproic Acid	Partial with secondary generalization
		Generalized
		Absence
		Myoclonic

Source: Bleck (1987); Fincham (1986); PDR (1994).

TABLE 15.4 Possible Anticonvulsant Medication Side Effects

Sedation	Nausea
Slowed mental processing	Vomiting
Uncoordinated muscle movements (ataxia)	Unsteady gait
Anemia	Gastric irritability
Slurred speech	Headache
Drowsiness	Tremors
Fatigue	Emotional irritability
Vitamin deficiencies	Water retention
Blurred vision or nystagmus	Cardiac arhythmias
Depression	Psychosis
Dizziness	Hair loss
	Weight gain

Source: Fincham (1986); PDR (1994).

2. *Changes in alkalinity in the blood.* It is preferable for seizure-prone individuals to maintain a slightly acidic diet, usually accomplished by adhering to a ketogenic diet. Foods that are suggested include high-fat milk, butter, eggs, and meat.
3. *Changes in sodium in the blood.* For example, at specific times in the menstrual cycle, women tend to retain sodium, which reduces their seizure threshold.
4 *Excessive drinking of alcoholic beverages.* This does not refer to seizures induced by alcohol withdrawal, but the tendency for individuals' natural seizure thresholds to be reduced by drinking too much alcohol.
5. *Avoidance of physical environment with rapidly oscillating visual effects.* Such arenas as laser light shows, disco-dance floors, and rock concerts with strobe light effects should be avoided as they have been known to have a so-called "trigger" effect. These visual displays can overstimulate and bring CNS seizure potential to threshold. (Note: this last caution is particularly important for those individuals whose etiology is idiopathic and where seizures remain uncontrolled by medication.)

Lifestyle modifications also refer to a variety of activities that are contraindicated for seizure-prone individuals. Contraindicated activities are those that would present a health threat to the client with epilepsy and other participants if a seizure were to occur during the activity. Activities in this category would include scuba diving, sky diving, hang gliding, rock climbing, and unsupervised swimming activities.

Some physicians take a more conservative stance and restrict involvement in sports that may result in head injuries. Examples of these activities include boxing, tackle football, ice hockey, soccer, gymnastics, rugby, lacrosse, and wrestling. Yet other physicians advocate a more liberal position that allows clients to participate in most activities as long as a nonseizure-prone partner is present. These latter physicians still recommend careful consideration for activities where the partner would be unable to offer immediate help, such as scuba diving and hang gliding.

Individuals with epilepsy need to be seizure free for a period of time prior to obtaining a driver's license. This time period is different from state to state. In respect to all potentially restricted activities, it is important to remember that when the seizures are well controlled, those individuals are no different than anybody else (Sherrill, 1993); they need the opportunity to experience risks and challenges just as their peers do.

Seizure Management

General first aid precautions that the therapeutic recreation specialist should be aware of when a client has a seizure during a session are discussed by Austin (1991) and Crawford (1984) and are also available from a variety of sources including the American National Red Cross (1994) and the Epilepsy Foundation of America (1995). The clinician should not be concerned with trying to stop the seizure, but rather with ensuring the client's safety during the seizure, and assisting in his or her comfort and dignity following the seizure. It is important for the CTRS to remain alert in observing the duration and observable nature of the seizure as this will assist the medical staff and enable accurate documentation on the client's medical chart. Important steps to follow, particularly for the tonic-clonic form are as follows:

1. Assist the client to a comfortable position, usually a side-lying or prone position is preferred. Place something soft under his or her head—a rolled up jacket, blanket, beach towel, etc.

2. Check that the mouth and nose are clear and that breathing is unimpaired.

3. Manage the physcial environment. Remove any furniture or object from around the client to lessen the likelihood of injury or abrasion from coming in contact with such. If practical, gently move or drag the client so that he or she is free from contact with walls, corners, handrails, etc.

4. Begin timing the seizure as soon as you are sure the client is relatively safe and comfortable.

5. Manage the social environment. Do not allow a crowd to gather around the client. The last thing a person coming out of a seizure wants is to be greeted by a crowd of faces staring down at him or her. Remain calm and professional and ask someone to take responsibility for crowd control, assure concerned onlookers that everything is under control.

6. After several minutes, if seizure activity remains unabated, check for cyanosis (bluing around the corners of the mouth, nose, or in the fingers. If you observe such evidence or hear labored respiration, adjust the person's head and/or trunk position. Recall that while it is physically impossible to "swallow" your tongue, it is possible for the tongue to flip backwards inside the oral cavity and block the airway. Usually adjusting the head to a side lying position or slightly elevating the head through a shrugging motion (grasp under the armpits and elevate briefly several times in succession) will free the airway.

7. Check for bleeding in or around the oral cavity. If any is observed, call for a first aid kit or medical assistance.

8. If the active phase of the tonic-clonic seizure lasts longer than five minutes, call immediatly for emergency medical assistance; the individual has entered a state of "status epilepticus" and is in danger.

9. If the seizure ends uneventfully (no bleeding, no status epilepticus), then it is most helpful for you to (a) tell the person what has happened ("you have had a brief seizure"), and (b) offer to assist him or her in finding either a restroom (if they have lost bowel or bladder control) or a place to lie down and rest (many will need to sleep, or may be in the semiconscious coma phase and need your active assistance to find a place to recuperate for several hours).

Special Environments

There is one important additional addendum regarding seizure management for aquatic environments. Since many CTRS's utilize adapted aquatics and various forms of aquatic therapy within their programming, and since many special recreation settings also employ aquatic environments (e.g., camps, special olympics programs, municipal swimming pools, etc.), there is a distinct likelihood that seizure activity could occur in these areas. Many individuals are unnecessarily injured during episodes of aquatic seizures due to poor seizure management. They are injured by the recreation staff as they are pulled onto pool decks or lifted into boats or onto docks (frequently dropped in the process because they are slippery and hard to hold and unable to cooperate due to seizure activity). So long as the CTRS is well organized and has sufficient swimming competence, one of the safer places for a seizure to occur is in the water, so long as one important condition can be maintained: an airway. Because the water is by nature a nonabrasive environment, many of the associated injuries that accompany strong tonic-clonic seizures are automatically eliminated. A water seizure team should be assembled and trained ahead of time (Crawford, 1984). A distinct audible signal should be selected to notify all members of the seizure team that a seizure is occuring (e.g., three sharp blasts on a whistle, or simply shouting the phrase "seizure team now"). Seizure team members then hand their clients/swimmers off to other volunteers/staff, or assist their clients to the deck or shallows and then assist with maintaining an airway in the water. The only piece of equipment that is required is a seizure mat or towel (kept by the guard stand or near other rescue epuipment). A standard gym exercise or wrestling mat works well for adults, large beach towels can be doubled and used for children. All that is neccessary is for the mat or towel to be positioned under the client experiencing the seizure, and then using a simple four-corner formation, each member of the team grabs a corner of the mat or towel and the client is elevated to the top of the water so that an airway can be effectively and safely maintained. The team members at the head corners need to monitor breathing and mouth position. It may be neccessary for a fifth team member to provide a head cradle (hands under shoulder blades, head cradled bewteen forearms) to prevent severe rotation of the head and inhalation of water. If the seizure occurs in a swimming pool, the seizure team can manage the seizure very effectively by swimming to the shallows and standing in the four-corner formation. If the seizure occurs in open water (e.g., boat dock area of a lake), and sufficient numbers of competent swimmers are not available so that a four-corner formation can be maintained by treading water, then transferring the client out of the water, even while seizure activity is occuring, is sometimes the most prudent course of action (better to risk injury from dropping than water inhalation and potential drowning).

PURPOSE OF THERAPEUTIC RECREATION

Therapeutic recreation specialists who work with clients with convulsive disorders typically are focusing on either a secondary diagnosis (e.g., mental retardation, mental illness, physical handicaps), psychopathology associated with epilepsy (e.g., learned helplessness, anger, depression), or specific needs related to lifestyle modifications that would benefit from leisure counseling. Table 15.5 outlines these areas.

In focusing on a second diagnosis, the clinician needs to remain aware of certain activity limitations, medication side effects, and appropriate procedures for handling seizures that may occur during sessions. The therapist should then follow appropriate strategies outlined for the specific second diagnosis. The latter two areas of concern (psychopathology and lifestyle modifications) are more directly related to clients' seizures, and thus can be viewed as specific intervention domains of therapeutic recreation services for convulsive disorders.

TABLE 15.5 Therapeutic Recreation Intervention Areas for Clients with Epilepsy

A. Secondary diagnoses (e.g., mental retardation, mental illness, physical handicaps)
B. Concomitant psychopathology (e.g., depression, anger, learned helplessness)
C. Lifestyle adaptations (e.g., restricted leisure activities)

As noted earlier, clients with epilepsy are at risk for other psychological or psychiatric conditions. Therapeutic recreation specialists should take an active role in addressing some of the psychosocial needs of this population. Three topics will be discussed to highlight this area: (1) stress reduction, (2) leisure lifestyle, and (3) locus of control.

Mittan and Locke (1982) noted that most individuals with epilepsy live with pervasive fears about having seizures, with approximately 70 percent believing that they might die during their next seizure. In some instances these fears may be realistic (e.g., persons with a history of strong tonic-clonic seizures or seizures ending in status epilepticus), emphasizing the need for a comprehensive assessment. These individuals should be assessed for their knowledge and use of stress reduction and relaxation skills to counteract the effects of chronic stress. Therapeutic recreation has a documented research base for promoting healthy, effective stress reduction activities, and thus can take a leadership role in providing therapeutic intervention in this area.

Considerable evidence supports the theory that clients with epilepsy are stigmatized by the disorder, even when the seizures are well controlled (Arangio, 1980; Betts, 1982; Sherrill, 1993). This stigmatization is both real and perceived, indicating that both society and the clients need to overcome their stereotypes about seizures. In reaction to perceiving this stigmatization, clients commonly reflect affective disorders such as anxiety and depression. When social withdrawal and self-enforced social isolation are common parameters, an activities program focusing on strong experiential work in social settings is the most effective prescription. By strengthening a client's leisure skill repertoire and developing a rewarding leisure lifestyle with others, therapeutic recreation services can assist individuals to remain active participants in social activities, dispelling some of the disorder's stigmatization.

Clients with epilepsy have also been shown to reflect higher external locus of control scores than nonepileptic individuals (DeVellis et al., 1980). These findings indicate that these clients do not believe they have the ability to control their lives. While this may be a realistic consequence of having a chronic health problem, it is nonetheless psychologically debilitating when the feeling of uncontrollability becomes generalized to other aspects of individuals' lives and can result in depression and lowered self-esteem. Locus of control and perceived control in respect to leisure activities have been discussed by other authors (Iso-Ahola, 1980; Ellis & Witt, 1984), and a comprehensive assessment (the Leisure Diagnostic Battery) has been developed for use by therapeutic recreation specialists (Ellis & Witt, 1990). In the case of external locus and low-esteem parameters, the activity therapy approach should be toward the development of mastery experiences. Only through feelings of personal competence and higher levels of skill can individuals be convinced to change their perceptions of locus of control.

The various adaptations that relate to clients' leisure lifestyles are appropriate topics for therapeutic recreation. Although certain physical activities may be contraindicated (or need modifications), it should be remembered that clients with epilepsy still need a well-rounded leisure lifestyle. This would include social recreational activities, individual and team sports, and solitary hobbies and interests. It should not be assumed that all clients with epilepsy need leisure counseling, but for some individuals these services are appropriate.

By conducting a comprehensive leisure assessment, the clinician can develop recommendations based on clients' strengths. In this manner, clients can focus on the vast activities allowed, rather than dwelling on the few activity limitations.

COMMON SERVICE SETTINGS

Therapeutic recreation specialists will encounter clients with convulsive disorders in all service delivery areas. This is because epilepsy is spread throughout the general population and will be noted randomly in any clinical setting. The majority of clients with convulsive disorders who are in need of therapeutic recreation services will reside in long-term residential treatment centers. These clients include those who are developmentally delayed, have a primary psychiatric diagnosis, or have a variety of multihandicaps in addition to their convulsive disorder.

Clients who are not dual diagnosed will usually be able to stabilize their seizures with medications and, therefore, will likely reside in the community. These individuals may be intermittently referred for therapeutic recreation services to assist with concomitant psychopathology or lifestyle adaptations as they move through lifespan developmental stages. Common service settings for these clients would include community mental health centers, outpatient clinics in general hospitals, university or medical center clinics, or private practices.

Therapists who work in drug and alcohol detoxification units will witness seizures with chronic alcoholics on a regular basis. These seizures are episodic (unless the client also has a convulsive disorder) and are one of the possible features of the alcohol withdrawal syndrome. In these cases immediate medical attention is the standard protocol, and therapeutic recreation services would resume only after the client has passed through this stage of detoxification.

CURRENT BEST PRACTICES AND PROCEDURES

In discussing appropriate services, special attention will be directed toward individuals with concomitant psychopathology or difficulty with lifestyle adaptations. Readers are referred to other chapters in this text for practices and procedures related to secondary diagnoses such as mental retardation and mental illness.

Assessment

Four global areas should be considered when assessing clients with convulsive disorders: (1) stress reduction and relaxation training, (2) locus of control, (3) social skills, and (4) leisure lifestyle. Each of these areas can provide useful information to document the need for therapeutic recreation services. The four topics noted here, as well as suggestions regarding the origins of psychopathology peculiar to individuals with convulsive disorders, are derived from common practice. Additional areas will become evident on an individual basis.

A wide variety of standardized assessment tools are available for locus of control (Rohsenow & O'Leary, 1978; Ellis and Witt, 1990) and leisure lifestyle concerns (Howe, 1984; Neulinger, 1990). Checklists, questionnaires, surveys, and therapist observations are more commonly used for identifying stress reduction skills and social skills (e.g., communication, cooperation, and leadership skills) (Navar, 1990).

Few assessment formats have originated specifically for individuals with convulsive disorders, so the clinician will need to be familiar with contraindicated activities when conducting assessments. In most cases no adaptations will be necessary, but the therapist should review clients' medical records and speak with appropriate medical staff prior to beginning an assessment.

Planning

Following the completion of a comprehensive interdisciplinary assessment, the therapy needs must be prioritized and corresponding goals and objectives identified. For most clients the seizures themselves will be stabilized and monitored by the medical staff. Other needs will then be prioritized in consideration of their relationship to each client. Lifestyle adaptations that are necessary to help stabilize the occurrence of seizures will be given a high priority. An example of this would be the establishment of a healthy balance between proper diet and exercise. If either of these two areas is severely neglected, it may be more difficult to maintain the proper anticonvulsant medication level in a client's bloodstream. If seizure onset has been late in life, the therapist may have to utilize continuity/discontinuity theory (Sessoms, 1980) in attempting to re-establish previous activity interests, if a more recent area (e.g., mountain biking, rock climbing, etc.) is now contraindicated because of seizure potential.

Relaxation training sessions and physical activities to reduce stress can be presented through core therapy sessions (developing prerequisite or preleisure skills) (Sylvester, 1992) or counseling sessions (assisting the client to utilize fully the skills already present) (Austin, 1991). Experiential group cooperation activities are useful both for promoting an internal locus of control and for developing appropriate social skills. The topic of leisure counseling encompasses a broad spectrum of services that basically seek to assist the individual in developing a rewarding leisure lifestyle.

Implementation

The general interaction style of the therapist will vary widely in consideration of the clients' needs. Individuals with severe mental retardation and sporadically-controlled seizures needing to develop communication skills will probably do better with a more structured therapy setting than with an adult executive who is avoiding all physical activities out of fear of having a seizure.

All clinical strategies should be continuously monitored to ensure their relevance to the clients' identified needs. The therapist should always remain aware of certain activity limitations, medication side effects, and appropriate procedures for handling seizures if they do occur. Specifically, the therapeutic recreation specialist should watch for signs of extreme fatigue during and after physical activities, excessive breathing, skipping meals, as well as other idiosyncrasies identified on an individual basis. Additionally, noting motor patterns of seizure activity, intensity, duration and post-seizure state of mind if seizures occur, are all important priorities in observing and charting.

Evaluation

In those instances where standardized assessments are used (e.g., locus of control), a post-therapy assessment is appropriate. Check sheets and questionnaires should also be monitored to ensure that the progress stated in the goals and objectives was achieved. One question that is important for this particular clinical population is whether the actual activities exacerbated the clients' conditions. This could have been addressed immediately by the therapist, but it should be highlighted in the clients' evaluation summaries and medical records as well.

APPLICATION OF THE TR PROCESS

CASE STUDY

Edward is a 34-year-old single, college-educated client who was referred for outpatient counseling for depression. Edward works as an accounts receivable clerk at an industrial manufacturing company. Edward's epilepsy was initially diagnosed at age seven and has been stabilized since that time, with the last seizure occurring at age 23 and the one previous to that at age 17. In conjunction with helping a co-worker who had a seizure at work, Edward disclosed to his employer that he also has epilepsy. This occurred six years ago, and Edward attributes this to his being overlooked for job promotions since that time. Feelings of depression, helplessness, and extreme frustration led Edward's physician to recommend outpatient counseling.

Assessment

Edward's physician referred him to a local community mental health center that provided outpatient counseling services. Following an initial screening interview, Edward was advised to attend an outpatient leisure counseling group that met twice weekly. The group used a 12-week program format which was conducted by a certified therapeutic recreation specialist. As part of the therapeutic recreation assessment, Edward completed a nonstandardized leisure interest survey, a questionnaire that identified his current leisure lifestyle—the Perceived Freedom in Leisure-Short Form (PFL-SF) (Ellis & Witt, 1984)—and the Adult Nowicki-Strickland Internal-External Locus of Control Scale (ANSIE) (Nowicki & Duke, 1974).

The results of the questionnaires indicated that Edward has a diverse, well-rounded repertoire of leisure skills and interests, but had stopped participating in social activities over the past several years. The PFL-SF noted that Edward felt that he was not able to choose his leisure activities freely, that social and environmental constraints dictated his choices. The ANSIE identified that Edward had a global belief that he did not control his actions and reinforced in general the results from the PFL-SF.

Planning

Based on the results of the therapeutic recreation assessment battery, Edward's physician's comments, the initial screening information, and Edward's own observations, Edward contracted to attend the 12-week outpatient leisure counseling group. Edward and the therapeutic recreation specialist also considered referrals to a clinical psychologist for individual counseling, and classes in biofeedback training (services offered at the same agency). It was decided that these referrals might be appropriate following the 12-week leisure counseling sessions.

Implementation

The 12-week leisure counseling protocol consisted of a structured education/lecture group on each Tuesday. These groups identified specific interests, skills, and strategies that the individual clients could use immediately. On Fridays, individual clients presented specific problem areas for discussion and feedback. It was the responsibility of the clients to follow up on the suggestions made in groups, relating their experiences in the following sessions. Clients who had difficulty being self-motivated were seen individually by the therapeutic recreation specialist to provide more structure. Specific topics that were presented during the Tuesday sessions included the following: the relationship between leisure and work; time management; matching interests with available options; identifying local and regional resources; solitary versus social recreation; self-responsibility; and others. The Friday sessions were more open-ended, typically following up on how individuals were able to generalize the suggestions discussed on Tuesdays into their leisure lifestyle.

The therapeutic recreation specialist served as the group leader and resource person, offering considerable options and suggestions for the clients to select. It was of prime importance that each client take control of his or her leisure activities, a concept that was repeatedly emphasized throughout the sessions. As long as the group stayed focused and progressed in a productive manner, the clinician retained the role of a resource person during the Friday sessions.

Evaluation

Edward attended all 24 sessions during the 12-week program without demonstrating the need for individual sessions. Edward actively participated in each group and seemed to begin using the suggestions and feedback roughly around the fifth week. During the course of the program, Edward was confronted with his repeated rationalizations and excuses for making positive changes in his life. Edward appeared to accept this positive criticism, albeit reluctantly.

Post-therapy evaluations included the PFL-SF, the ANSIE, and a questionnaire covering the main points of the twelve Tuesday lectures. Edward reflected a more internal locus of control score, was taking more responsibility for his leisure activities, and understood the key concepts of the lectures. Edward noted that he was less depressed and preoccupied about his employment situation, and in fact had spoken to his supervisor about a possible promotion. Edward did not receive the promotion, but received a minor pay raise and seemed satisfied with his supervisor's comments. Apparently, Edward was not only taking a more self-responsible, assertive role in his leisure lifestyle, but had successfully generalized this concept to other aspects of his life. At a follow-up contact made three months later, Edward reported no recurrence of his symptoms of depression. Edward had continued to make progress by attending a local biofeedback seminar sponsored by the local community library, and he began a moderate exercise regimen twice weekly with several co-workers.

TRENDS AND ISSUES

The stigma associated with epilepsy is undoubtedly the greatest issue with which persons with epilepsy must deal. While the ancient notions regarding "possession" have dissappeared from contemporary society, the lay public continues to associate seizure disorders with other severe psychological and medical problems, including psychopathology and mental retardation, at a disproportionate rate. As discussed earlier in the chapter, even those individuals whose seizures are well controlled face stigma. Both persons with epilepsy and society in general need to overcome stereotypes held about seizure disorders. A related issue is the lack of understanding on the part of some helping professionals regarding lifestyle modifications for persons who have seizures. Although common sense dictates prudence in the selection of recreational activities, excessive limitations are often imposed on individuals with epilepsy. Fortunately, there is a growing trend toward awareness on the part of both lay persons and helping professionals that most individuals with epilepsy can achieve freedom from seizures by taking anticonvulsant medication, permitting them to have few lifestyle restrictions.

SUMMARY

Convulsions are caused by abnormal amounts of electrical discharge between cells in the brain. As a result of this, the body sites that are controlled by those brain cells will display spasms or muscle contractions. Epilepsy refers to a group of syndromes that produce recurrent seizures. Although between 2.2 and 3.6 million individuals in the United States have epilepsy (or some other form of seizure disorder), most are able to stabilize their seizures through medications and lifestyle modifications alone.

Therapeutic recreation services are typically sought for assistance with a secondary diagnosis, concomitant psychopathology, or specific lifestyle modifications. Certain activity limitations may be recommended on an individual basis because of the individual's seizure history and the nature of the activity. Other activity precautions can be instituted to allow individuals with epilepsy to participate in most activities.

READING COMPREHENSION QUESTIONS

1. What is a convulsion? A seizure? Epilepsy?
2. What are the ten factors that are believed to cause most convulsive disorders?
3. What are the differences between the two global seizure classifications?
4. What should a therapeutic recreation specialist do if a client has a seizure during a session?
5. What are the three areas for which therapeutic recreation specialists usually receive referrals?
6. Are medications usually given to individuals with epilepsy? What are some of the possible side effects?
7. Should clients with epilepsy be allowed to scuba dive? Play volleyball? Tackle football?
8. When would leisure counseling be a recommended approach for clients with epilepsy?

SUGGESTED LEARNING ACTIVITIES

1. Prepare a 3- to 5-page paper that summarizes the history of seizure classification, discuss the pros and cons of the two different classification systems in use. Which do you prefer?
2. In class, organize two debate teams. One team will take the stance that individuals with epilepsy should not participate in high-risk activities; the other team will advocate for their inclusion.
3. In a small discussion group, identify some of the psychosocial difficulties that individuals with epilepsy may develop. Discuss how therapeutic recreation services may impact on these needs.
4. Prepare a 2- to 4-page paper that discusses one of the three key areas of therapeutic recreation services for this population.
5. Research the local regulations that individuals with epilepsy must satisfy before obtaining a driver's license.
6. Prepare a 3- to 5-page paper that speculates how your lifestyle would need to be adapted if you had epilepsy.

REFERENCES

Anderson, V. E., Hauser, W. A., & Rich, S. S. (1986). Genetic heterogeneity in the epilepsies. *Advances in Neurology, 44,* 59–75.

American National Red Cross. (1994). *Instructor's manual for emergency first aid instruction.* Washington D.C. (Stock #421208).

Arangio, A. (1980). The social worker and epilepsy: A description of assessment and treatment variables. In B. P. Hermann (Ed.), *A multidisciplinary handbook of epilepsy.* Springfield, IL: Charles C. Thomas.

Austin, D. R. (1991). *Therapeutic recreation processes*

and techniques (2nd ed.). Champaign, IL: Sagamore Publishing, Inc.

Betts, T. A. (1982). Psychiatry and epilepsy. In J. Laidlaw & A. Richens (Eds.), *A textbook of epilepsy* (2nd ed.). Edinburgh: Churchill-Livingstone.

Bleck, T. P. (1983). Therapy for status epilepticus. *Clinical Neuropharmacology, 6,* 255–269.

Bleck, T. P. (1987). Epilepsy. *Disease-a-Month, 33,* 601–679.

Burlingame, J., & Blaschko, T. M. (1990) *Assessment tools for recreation therapy: Redbook #1.* Ravensdale WA: Idyll Arbor Inc.

Commission on Classification and Terminology of the International League Against Epilepsy. (1981). Proposal for revised clinical and electroencephalographic classification of epileptic seizures. *Epilepsia, 22,* 489–501.

Crawford, M. E. (1984, May). Instructional techniques and progressions in water adjustment for the severely disabled. *Nebraska adapted physical education resource manual* (pp. 225–42). Kearney, NE: Kearney Sate College Publications.

DeVellis, R. G., et al. (1980). Epilepsy and learned helplessness. *Basic and Applied Social Psychology, 1,* 241–253.

Ellis, G. D., & Witt, P. A. (1984). The measurement of perceived freedom in leisure. *Journal of Leisure Research, 16,* 110–123.

Ellis, G. D., & Witt, P. A. (1990). *The leisure diagnostic battery.* State College, PA: Venture Publishing Co.

Epilepsy Foundation of America. (1995). Personal communication with author via consumer information toll number (800) 332-1000 Feb. 7, Washington D.C.

Fenton, G. W. (1981). Personality and behavioral disorders in adults with epilepsy. In E. H. Reynolds & M. R. Trimble (Eds.), *Epilepsy and psychiatry.* Edinburgh: Churchill-Livingstone.

Fincham, R. W. (1986). Epilepsy in adolescents and adults. In C. Cann (Ed.), *Current therapy.* Philadelphia: W. B. Saunders.

Gastaut, H. (1970). Clinical and electroencephalographic classification of epileptic seizures. *Epilepsia, 11*(3), 102–103.

Hauser, W. A. (1978). Epidemiology of epilepsy. In B. S. Schoenberg (Ed.), *Advances in neurology: Neurological epidemiology.* New York: Raven Press.

Howe, C. E. (1984). Leisure assessment instrumentation in therapeutic recreation. *Therapeutic Recreation Journal, 18*(2), 14–24.

Howie, L. (1994, Nov. 14). Society prejudices lull change. *The Missourian,* p. 10a.

Iso-Ahola, S. E. (1980). *The social psychology of leisure and recreation.* Dubuque, IA: William C. Brown.

Juul-Jensen, P., & Foldspang, A. (1983). Natural history of epileptic seizures. *Epilepsia, 24,* 297–312.

Mittan, R., & Locke, G. E. (1982, January/February). Fear of seizures: Epilepsy's forgotten problem. *Urban Health,* 40–41.

Navar, N. (1990). *State technical institute leisure assessment process.* Ravensdale, WA: Idyll Arbor Press.

Neulinger, J. (1990). *What am I doing scale.* Dolgerville, NY: The Leisure Instititute Press.

Nowicki, S., & Duke., M. P. (1974). A locus of control scale for college as well as non-college adults. *Journal of Personality Assessment, 38*(2), 136–137.

Physician's Desk Reference. (1994). Oradel, NJ: Jack Angle Publishing Co.

Rohsenow, D. J., & O'Leary, M. R. (1978). Locus of control research on alcoholic populations: A review of development, scales, and treatment. *International Journal of the Addictions, 13*(1), 55–78.

Sessoms, D. (1980). Lifestyles and life cycles; a recreation programming approach. In T. Goodale and P. Witt (Eds.), *Recreation and leisure: Issues in an era of change.* State College, PA: Venture Publishing Co.

Sherrill, C. (1993). *Adapted physical activity, recreation, and sport* (4th ed.). Dubuque, IA: W.C. Brown, Co.

Siegler, M., & Osmond, H. (1974). *Models of madness, models of medicine.* New York: Macmillian Publishing Co.

Sylvester, C. (1992, 2nd Quarter). Therapeutic recreation and the right to leisure. *Therapeutic Recreation Journal,* 9–20.

Wolfensburger, W. (1972). *Normalization: The principal of normalization in human services.* Toronto: National Institue on Mental Retardation.

CHAPTER 16

ACQUIRED IMMUNODEFICIENCY SYNDROME (AIDS)

ARNOLD H. GROSSMAN
ORAZIO (ORI) CAROLEO

OBJECTIVES

- Distinguish between HIV infection and AIDS.
- Describe how HIV is and is not transmitted.
- Comprehend the extent of the HIV/AIDS pandemic and the limitations of current treatments.
- Appreciate the purposes and benefits of therapeutic recreation for people with HIV/AIDS.
- Identify the psychosocial issues of working with people with HIV/AIDS.
- Demonstrate the application of the therapeutic recreation process to facilitate the development of an appropriate leisure lifestyle for a person with HIV/AIDS.
- Discuss the trends and issues related to HIV disease and their implications for therapeutic recreation practice.

DEFINITION OF AIDS

AIDS stands for *acquired immunodeficiency syndrome* and is caused by the human immunodeficiency virus (HIV). At this writing, more than 400,000 cumulative cases of AIDS have been documented in the United States since it was first reported on June 5, 1981. During these thirteen years, the number of AIDS deaths has increased each year, from 135 deaths in 1981 to more than 240,000 cumulative confirmed AIDS-related deaths in 1994 (Centers for Disease Control and Prevention, 1994). According to projections by the Centers for Disease Control and Prevention (CDC) (1993a), the cumulative number of deaths related to AIDS will likely exceed 300,000 by the end of 1994.

Being infected with HIV is not the same as being diagnosed with AIDS. HIV infection ranges from asymptomatic infection to the full-blown clinical disease labeled AIDS. Today, the CDC estimates that one million Americans (i.e., one in every 250) are infected with HIV. It takes an average of ten years before a person with HIV infection develops AIDS. For infants and some adults, this time may be much shorter (Surgeon General's Report, 1993).

In this second decade of the AIDS epidemic in the United States, "men who have sex with men," (i.e., gay and bisexual men) and injecting drug users continue to account for the majority of AIDS cases reported each year. However, AIDS is becoming a more prominent disease among adolescents and heterosexual men and women. It is now one of the three main causes of death for women and men twenty five to forty four years of age, and it is among the top ten causes of death for children one to four years old (Surgeon General's Report, 1993).

The World Health Organization reports 4 million cumulative, full-blown AIDS cases worldwide, and it estimates that about 17 million people have been infected with HIV (Pollack, 1994). It further estimates that 30 to 40 million people will have been infected with HIV by the end of the century (Full-Blown AIDS Cases, 1994). Despite the facts that throughout the world 75 percent of those infected with HIV are heterosexual, and well over 90 percent of the newly infected adults acquire their HIV infections from heterosexual intercourse, many uninformed people continue to associate HIV and AIDS with homosexuality (WHO Press, 1992). This has two unfortunate outcomes: first, it enhances the myths about homosexuality, and second, it provides a false sense of security among heterosexuals regarding their susceptibility to HIV infection.

CLASSIFICATION OF HIV DISEASE

The body's health is defended by its immune system. When HIV causes the immune system to fail, a person may develop a variety of life-threatening illnesses. When HIV enters the body, it infects certain white blood cells called T-lymphocyte cells (CD4+) where the virus grows. The virus slowly kills these cells, and as more and more of the T cells die, the body's ability to fight infection weakens. Therefore, HIV disease is a progressive disorder, with a long period when the infected person has no symptoms, eventually resulting in AIDS. About half of the people infected with HIV develop AIDS within ten years, but the time between HIV infection and the onset of AIDS may vary greatly.

People are classified as having AIDS when they have laboratory-confirmed HIV infection and certain indicator diseases (e.g., pneumocystis carinii pneumonia (PCP), Kaposi's sarcoma (KS), or invasive cancer of the cervix). In addition, the 1993 expanded AIDS case definition for adults and adolescents included HIV-infected persons with CD4+ lymphocyte counts of less than 200 cells per cubic millimeter of blood (Centers for Disease Control, 1993b). No vaccine or cure currently exists for HIV/AIDS, but medical treatments can prevent or postpone many illnesses associated with AIDS. Consequently, many individuals with the disease are able to continue working and being active for increasingly longer periods of time. Furthermore, the Americans with Disabilities Act, which prohibits discrimination against workers with disabilities, includes people disabled by AIDS. It requires employers with more than fifteen workers to make "reasonable accommodations" for them (Navarro, 1992).

HIV is transmitted by sexual contact with an infected person (i.e., vaginal, anal, and oral intercourse), by needle-sharing with an injecting drug user who is infected, or through transfusions of blood or blood-clotting factors (which is very rare in countries like the United States, where all blood donations are screened for HIV antibodies). HIV is not transmitted through casual contact such as touching, hugging, sharing cans of soda, using swimming pools or toilet seats, or sharing sports equipment and facilities.

Babies born to HIV-infected women may become infected before or during birth, or through breast feeding after birth. Some of the babies found to be HIV-positive at birth later experience a sero-conversion to HIV negative, indicating that their mothers' HIV antibodies are no longer present in their blood. Two recent studies from scientists in New York State indicated that the likelihood of infecting offspring rises with the amount of virus in a pregnant woman's blood (Altman, 1994). Another recent medical finding indicates that ZDV (zidovudine, an antiretroviral drug) can sharply reduce the chances that HIV-infected women will pass the virus to their babies ("Zidovudine cuts," 1994).

Although AIDS was first detected and diagnosed in gay men in the United States, it is now known that everybody is at risk for HIV infection and AIDS. Therapeutic recreation specialists providing services to such populations as the mentally ill, mentally retarded and developmentally disabled, alcohol and other substance abusers, and mentally ill chemical abusers (MICA) will more than likely find people with HIV infection or AIDS among their clients. In addition, specialists providing services to individuals with cognitive impairments, neurological disorders, psychiatric disabilities, or to pediatric clients will discover that some of them are directly affected by HIV's impact on the central nervous system. Consequently, people with HIV/AIDS often have multiple diagnoses, representing more than one special population.

DESCRIPTION OF LIMITATIONS

At this writing, four antiretroviral drugs have been approved by the Federal Food and Drug Administration for treatment of HIV. The most widely used drug is AZT (now called ZDV for zidovudine). In many people, ZDV causes side effects such as sleep problems, leg cramps, headaches, nausea, diarrhea, anemia, and confusion. When adult and pediatric patients are not adequately responding to, are intolerant of, or have a contraindication to ZDV, physicians prescribe didanosine (ddI) or dideoxycytidine (ddC). Adverse effects from ddI include pancreatitis, numbness in hands and feet, nausea, diarrhea, confusion, and seizures; adverse effects from ddC include ulcers, peripheral neuropathy, stomatitis, and cutaneous eruptions (Agency for Health Care Policy and Research, 1994).

The fourth virus-fighting drug is d4T (otherwise known as stavudine or Zerit). It is similar in chemistry and activity to AZT. Switching from AZT to d4T reduced the drug-related side effects among individuals enrolled in one clinical trial. People who started on d4T saw their red and total white blood cell counts improve as the bone marrow suppression that is a common side effect of AZT disappeared. But the rate of serious neuropathy (numbing or painful nerve damage), about fifteen percent after one year, was higher than for the group kept on AZT (Link & Gilden, 1994).

HIV infection in infants, children, and adults results in a high incidence of a wide spectrum of neurologic diseases. HIV may cause neurologic dysfunction through the direct or indirect effects of a primary infection of the brain with HIV. Neurodevelopmental delays or regression and neuropsychological deficits are common in HIV-infected infants and children, while HIV-associated neuropathies and myopathies are common in adults (Agency for Health Care Policy and Research, 1994).

As indicated above, HIV attacks an individual's immune system. As the number of HIV-infected cells grows, the immune system's ability to fight opportunistic infections (OIs) decreases. (OIs are illnesses caused by organisms that do not usually cause disease in a person with a healthy immune system.) Medications administered for prophylaxis and treatment of opportunistic infections produce numerous and varied side effects from rashes, fevers, vision changes, hearing loss, vomiting, diarrhea, and itchy dry skin to malabsorption, liver toxicity, low blood pressure, low blood counts, abnormal heartbeat, colitis, and pancreatitis. Therapeutic recreation specialists should check with patients and/or their primary care providers for the possible side effects and drug interactions (with alcohol, massage oils which contain alcohol, antacids, foods, as well as with other drugs) of their medical regimens.

While there are a number of ocular complications associated with HIV disease, they generally occur at a late stage of the disease. Cytomegalovirus retinitis (CMV retinitis) is the most common opportunistic infection associated with visual loss in HIV infection (Agency for Health Care Policy and Research, 1994). Therapeutic recreation specialists should be aware that the gradual loss of vision and blindness commonly lead to periods of despair and depression in clients.

Additionally, therapeutic recreation specialists must be aware that certain materials (e.g., clay), foods (e.g., soft cheeses, raw mushrooms, and inadequately cleaned and cooked chicken) and substances (e.g., dust, mildew), normally associated with various recreation activities, may be contraindicated for people with compromised immune systems. Specialists must also monitor their health as well as the health of volunteers who work with clients with AIDS. Persons with AIDS are particularly susceptible to colds, flus, tuberculosis, and other transmittable diseases.

PURPOSE OF THERAPEUTIC RECREATION

The increasing presence of HIV in every United States community necessitates that therapeutic recreation specialists become involved in and knowledgeable about providing services for individuals with HIV/AIDS. Whether one or more of its members are HIV infected, HIV affects the whole family. Crises occur on an ongoing basis, including hospitalizations, deaths, expenditure of energy and time in being a caregiver, or becoming an orphaned child.

The purpose of therapeutic recreation is to facilitate the development of an appropriate leisure lifestyle for the person who is diagnosed with HIV infection or AIDS. AIDS is known to have a progressive course, no curative treatment, and an extremely poor prognosis, and it frequently occurs among members of socially stigmatized groups (Flaskerud & Ungvarski, 1992). Consequently, specialists should provide therapeutic recreation services that enhance coping with the diagnosis of a communicable, sexually-transmitted, fatal disease; focus on knowledge, attitudes and skills that facilitate a day-to-day behavioral expression in the face of increasing opportunistic infections and physical and cognitive limitations; and maintain functional independence as the disease progresses with its accompanying neurological complications and physical debilitation.

Goals of a Therapeutic Recreation (TR) Program

TR programs designed to provide services for persons with HIV/AIDS should include the following treatment objectives:

1. To decrease cognitive and emotional stressors associated with HIV/AIDS diagnoses;
2. To provide opportunities for day-to-day behavioral expression that lead to increased self-esteem;
3. To provide recreational activities and experiences designed to reduce feelings of stigmatization, discrimination, isolation, alienation and learned helplessness;
4. To assist patients in maintaining and enhancing personally satisfying leisure experiences as the disease progresses;
5. To empower patients to take an active role in their treatment and recreational choices;
6. To provide ongoing recreational opportunities for verbal and nonverbal expressions of positive feelings and emotions through diverse forms and mediums; and
7. To provide meaningful social and interpersonal experiences in a safe environment.

Additional goals and treatment objectives are necessary when the TR program is designed for individuals who are members of a specific population of those diagnosed with HIV/AIDS (e.g., children, adolescents, injecting drug users).

To achieve the TR goals, a variety of intervention strategies should be developed into the program designs and treatment plans. Interventions should be selected to improve the overall functioning of the patient (e.g., boost the immune system, decrease fatigue, improve stamina, prevent weight loss, promote relaxation). Among the interventions that appear to be effective in promoting appropriate leisure lifestyles and improving the well-being of people with HIV infection and AIDS are the following.

Stress Reduction Programs

Stress reduction programs are probably the most utilized intervention methods for working with people with HIV/AIDS. They range from simple visualization activities to complex education workshops and training sessions. Stress reduction programs can easily be incorporated into a TR program regardless of the setting. As indicated earlier, people with HIV/AIDS are confronted with many new stressors (e.g., HIV diagnosis, diagnosis of first opportunistic infection, diagnosis with AIDS, and deciding whom to tell about these diagnoses). Helping patients learn to identify and reduce these stressors assists them in dealing and coping with living with HIV/AIDS.

Stress reduction programs may include visualization activities, breathing exercises, yoga, massage, Tai Chi, time management strategies, meditation, and aerobic and nonaerobic exercise. Stress reduction workshops provide patients with opportunities to learn about the nature of stress, to assess its impact on the immune system, to identify stressors in one's life, and to develop approaches for reducing and managing stress, including strategies for seeking and asking for help. Workshops should also provide opportunities for patients to experience and develop a variety of stress reduction techniques and skills.

Exercise Programs

Studies have indicated that exercise programs actually increase one's T4 cell count, decrease levels of depression, and improve psychosocial well-being (Goleman, 1992; Schlenzig et al., 1989). Some exercise regimens, such as aerobic exercises, may involve risks to patients. Although one of the benefits of an aerobic exercise is increased metabolic rate, this outcome may problematic for a person with AIDS. Therefore, special considerations are needed before involving patients in aerobic exercise programs (e.g., educational sessions specifying the necessity and techniques to increase caloric consumption should be conducted). This might include a triage with a nutritionist to provide information about high caloric drinks, and the distribution of high caloric snacks before, during, and after exercise. Regardless of the specific exercise activities selected (e.g., aerobic, free weights, cycling, jogging, hydrafitness machines), patients should receive clearance from their physicians prior to participation. The TR specialist's initial assessment should include the following: (a) the types of physical pain the patient may be experiencing, (b) current medications and their side effects, and (c) patients' exercise participation before and since HIV and AIDS diagnoses.

After the initial assessment and physician's permission, ongoing progress notes should be maintained by the patient. The notes should include: the amount of time engaged in various exercises, the number of repetitions (if appropriate), the amount of weight utilized for weight-training exercises (if appropriate), and the patient's weight. An update of the patient's medications should be routinely recorded. The patient should be encouraged to take a copy of these progress notes to his or her physician(s) at periodic intervals, or at a time of crisis.

Verbal and Nonverbal Activities

It is necessary to provide opportunities for patients to express their feelings about living with HIV/AIDS. For some, support groups work well; for others, support groups are culturally unacceptable or not a viable option. Drama therapy, art therapy, poetry writing, painting, and drawing may be more appropriate interventions to facilitate communication and expressions of feelings. It is, however, recommended that the word "therapy" be dropped from drama and art therapy groups. Patients who have difficulty becoming members of support or counseling groups may also have difficulty entering activities labeled "therapy."

Drama groups may range from producing plays about living with HIV/AIDS to simple role-play situations that empower patients. Art groups may focus on painting, free expression through sculpting, or finger painting, while poetry workshops allow patients to write their feelings, which may be shared with others in the group or kept private. For those who choose not to write, reading books of poetry may have the benefits.

Social Activities

Social activities and interactions are common forms of recreation for most individuals. Having an HIV or AIDS diagnosis, with its accompanying stigmatization, discrimination, and increasing physical limitations, frequently leads individuals to withdraw from such activities and to become isolated. Peterson and Gunn (1984) indicate that social isolation is often a defense or form of self-protection. This is particularly true for individuals with HIV/AIDS who often believe that people can detect their diagnosis even if there are no physical manifestations of the disease.

Regardless of the cause(s) of social isolation, the TR specialist can assist patients in combatting it by including social activities (e.g., picnics, parties, dinners, day trips) into the program design. Such activities enable people with HIV disease to experience their therapeutic benefits while providing opportunities to develop new social support networks, share information regarding treatments, experience a variety of cultural traditions, and discuss the challenges of living with HIV/AIDS. These activities also provide opportunities for patients to invite family members, children, friends, and significant others, where they can see, meet, and learn about other people living with HIV disease. Experiences such as these often lead others to reduce their own stressors related to HIV disease and thereby increase their capacities to provide more support to the persons living with HIV disease.

Social activities are also favorable times to assist persons with AIDS in increasing their caloric intake. Many individuals with HIV/AIDS disease suffer from wasting syndrome, nausea, fat intolerance, diarrhea, and a decreased sense of taste. These physiological problems, combined with psychosocial problems (e.g., isolation, depression, loneliness) may cause some individuals to decrease their food intake, compounding the severity of the disease. Social events that offer high caloric snacks and meals in a leisure environment often result in increased food consumption.

Volunteer Activities

A large percentage of individuals are diagnosed with HIV/AIDS during their thirties, at a time when people are generally focusing on their careers and most often define themselves by their occupation. An HIV or AIDS diagnosis often derails personal career goals. Medical regimens, physical limitations, or discrimination may force people into early departure from the work environment. For these individuals, volunteer opportunities are often necessary to improve self-esteem and self-worth.

Lack of employment is not the only reason to suggest volunteer activities to patients. For some individuals, the concept of a daily routine and a need to contribute to society may be motivational catalysts to engage in volunteer activities. Additionally, some cultures view engaging in play activities as frivolous and contrary to work and cultural ethics; therefore, volunteering may provide needed meaningful activity.

Leisure Education and Counseling

Leisure education and counseling are program components that should be incorporated into all recreation programs. Leisure education should focus on assisting individuals to obtain awareness about the role of leisure in their lives and enhancing leisure skill development. Leisure counseling may be necessary to assist individuals in shifting their self-identity from occupational to leisure lifestyles. This eventually becomes necessary for individuals with HIV/AIDS when they lose their jobs or have to go on disability. The TR specialist should not only assist individuals with understanding the value leisure may or is playing in their lives, but describe other activities that may provide similar experience and benefits. It is equally important to assist individuals in locating resources and developing techniques to plan leisure and select activities appropriate to their changing physical limitations and mental health status.

COMMON SERVICE SETTINGS

The first part of this section describes various service settings where people with AIDS receive treatments. The second part is devoted to exploring the psychosocial issues of working with people with HIV/AIDS, regardless of the setting.

Service Settings

In the early years of the AIDS epidemic, the most severe complications of HIV disease received the most attention in hospitals. The focus has since evolved to emphasizing health maintenance, outpatient care, prevention of hospitalization, and integration of the patient and loved ones into a system providing supportive home care services. Frequently, persons with AIDS participate in supportive and leisure activities or therapeutic recreation programs provided by various community-based organizations, such as Gay Men's Health Crisis (GMHC), Senior Action in a Gay Environment (SAGE), and the Hispanic AIDS Forum in New York City.

Hospitalization often becomes necessary to detect possible causes of various symptoms (e.g., opportunistic infections), for special treatments (e.g., blood transfusions, bone marrow infusions), and for specialized procedures (e.g., insertion of a catheter). Persons who have a number of opportunistic infections as well as various manifestations of HIV disease (e.g., central nervous system complications) may require longer stays in a hospital's AIDS-designated medical unit. Mentally ill chemically abusing individuals with AIDS are likely to be placed on the hospital's psychiatric unit.

When the patient's condition becomes stabilized in the hospital setting, but he or she is homeless or there is no possibility of adequate home care, residential facilities (including cluster apartments) and long-term care facilities are increasingly becoming settings of choice. Transitional housing and single room occupancy dwellings are sometimes necessary stop-gap residences. As the disease progresses, some people choose a hospice setting when they come to the terminal stage of AIDS, while others prefer to die at home, if this is at all possible.

A service setting that has become increasingly concerned about persons with AIDS is prisons. Many prisoners are individuals who are either injecting drug users (who became HIV infected through sharing infected needles and works), alcohol and other substance users (who contracted HIV through engaging in unsafe sexual practices while intoxicated), or individuals who sold (unsafe) sex for drugs or engaged in prostitution. Additionally, some individuals engage in unsafe sexual practices in prisons.

PSYCHOSOCIAL ISSUES OF WORKING WITH PEOPLE WITH HIV/AIDS*

Many therapeutic recreation specialists and other health care providers succumb, consciously or unconsciously, to victim-blaming and applying old-fashioned conservative ideologies to specific populations (Ryan, 1986). The result is that they tend to blame persons who have contracted HIV infection or are diagnosed with AIDS instead of blaming the virus. Consequently, this thinking becomes the primary basis of the psychosocial issues that they have to confront in working with persons with HIV disease. These and other issues are examined within the conceptual framework of counter-transference. "Countertransference refers to those conscious, preconscious, and unconscious responses and feelings of the therapist that can be both a problem and a valuable therapeutic and diagnostic tool" (Dunkel & Hatfield, 1986, p. 115).

*This section is based on a previously written article: A.H. Grossman. (1993). Psychosocial issues confronting health care professionals working with people with AIDS. In M.P. Lahey, R. Kunstler, A.H. Grossman, F. Daly, S. Waldman, & F. Schwartz (Eds.). *Recreation, leisure and chronic illness: therapeutic rehabilitation as intervention in health care* (pp. 39–49). New York: The Haworth Press. Reprinted with permission.

Stigmatization of Gay People and IDUs. American society has stigmatized gay people and injecting drug users (IDUs) as second-class citizens. In doing so, it has created myths and stereotypes to support bigotry, discrimination, and oppression. In relation to gay people, this is clearly stated by Delaney and Goldblum (1987):

> *Homophobia, the irrational fear (and often hatred) of gay people, is deeply imbedded in our culture. Although some consider it a normal and moral state of mind, many psychologists now recognize homophobia, not homosexuality, as a mental disorder. When we as gay people show symptoms of this ugly disease, we call it "internalized homophobia." It is widespread in our community, although it is a more subtle form than that demonstrated by obvious bigots (p. 269).*

Education about gay people and IDUs helps one to learn about the unjustified negative statements and to stop "blaming the victims." It is important to remember that HIV is incapable of discriminating among homosexual, bisexual, and heterosexual people, or injecting drug users.

Fear of Death and Dying. Confronting one's own mortality is a common phenomenon among health care providers who work with individuals having terminal diseases. This is particularly true among providers who place a high priority on "beating death" (Dunkel & Hatfield, 1986). The fear of death is exacerbated in relation to AIDS by seeing the untimely deaths of children and people who are in the prime of their lives. Having experiences with death and learning not to deny the personhood of the individual dying from complications related to AIDS can help mitigate this fear.

Powerlessness and Helplessness. These feelings result from the inability to change the course of the disease, successfully treat multiple opportunistic infections, and save lives. They also appear among therapeutic recreation specialists who have a knowledge deficit regarding the reality of HIV/AIDS and its related complications. Obtaining up-to-date knowledge and being available, reliable, and empathetic with persons who have HIV/AIDS are necessary for effective care.

Anger and Hostility. Fellow health care providers become targets of anger and hostility because of their prejudices, discriminatory behaviors, insensitivity, or failure to provide treatment. Family members and significant others may arouse the same feelings for their acts of condemnation, recrimination, or abandonment. Members of the religious right and other groups arouse these feelings with views that AIDS is God's punishment for immoral behavior. Therapeutic recreation specialists and other providers need to acknowledge these feelings and give themselves permission to express them appropriately (e.g., through advocacy activities) both individually and within professional associations. The specialist must be vigilant in not using the person with AIDS as the "poster person" to express the provider's anger at members of the various constituencies.

Frustration. Feelings of frustration arise in relation to the reluctance of politicians and other bureaucrats to provide explicit HIV/AIDS prevention education programs (to prevent partner infection or reinfection of the person with HIV) and drug treatment and rehabilitation facilities. In many localities, there are also insufficient HIV/AIDS treatment facilities, skilled nursing facilities and hospices willing to provide services for people with HIV disease. In addition, poor case management and working without sufficient resources can be time-consuming and extremely frustrating. It is important that therapeutic recreation specialists and other providers identify the sources of the frustration and resulting anger, and that they have support groups in which they express these feelings. They must also make certain that their frustration and anger are not misdirected to persons with HIV/AIDS.

Overidentification with Clients. veridentifying with clients, whether they be children, women, or members of minority groups and gay people, causes therapeutic recreation specialists and other providers to lose their ability to be objective. As a result, they tend to fuse their personal and professional needs and responsibilities, investing unrealistic amounts of time and energy in specific clients and/or the clients' significant others. Therapeutic recreation specialists who are most vulnerable are those who either have the same lifestyle, are the same age or ethnic background, have children of their own, or have lost a family member or significant other to complications from AIDS.

Guilt. This feeling usually emerges in therapeutic recreation and other specialists who are not infected, although they participated in behaviors that put them at high risk for HIV infection. It is exacerbated among those providers who are suffering from "survivor's syndrome" or are experiencing the continuing loss of many people to the disease. Guilt also emerges among providers who are not able to face their professional responsibilities in the face of the HIV/AIDS epidemic. Individual and group counseling may assist providers in dealing with their feelings of guilt.

Fear of the Unknown and Fear of Contagion. Even in the thirteenth year of the HIV/AIDS epidemic, there are therapeutic recreation specialists and other providers who believe that all of the routes of HIV transmission may not be known or that the current infection control procedures are inadequate to protect them from becoming HIV infected in the workplace. Many times these irrational fears are a result of pressure from families, friends, and significant others to not accept or to discontinue assignments related to treating people with HIV disease. One has to recognize, however, the rational fear of occupational transmission (e.g., needle-sticks and mucosal splashes) although the rate of such transmission is infinitesimal. Following infection control procedures (i.e., universal precautions and blood and body substance isolation promulgated by the CDC) can realistically protect any provider and minimize these fears.

Working with Difficult Clients. Sometimes labeled noncompliant or obnoxious clients, these are HIV-infected individuals who either continue to have unsafe sex and refuse to tell their sexual partners or are IDUs who are manipulative and continue to use drugs overtly or covertly. They can also be individuals such as those with neuropsychiatric complications, people who attempt suicide, or individuals who continue to share hypodermic needles. These individuals incite feelings of helplessness, fear, and guilt that may result in anger and blaming the victim. Therapeutic recreation and other specialists have to become conscious of their anger and make certain it does not distance them from, and thereby block empathy with and emotional availability to, these types of clients. Support groups for providers working with difficult clients with HIV/AIDS are a must.

The psychosocial issues just explored are but some of the most common faced by therapeutic recreation and other specialists working with people who have HIV/AIDS. Each specialist will bring his or her own issues to the task. Accepting the human challenge of working effectively with people with HIV disease will not only fulfill professional and legal mandates, but also provide many opportunities to enhance one's professional growth and development.

CURRENT BEST PRACTICES AND PROCEDURES

HIV/AIDS disease is a complex series of symptoms, opportunistic infections, psychosocial, and physiological problems affecting no two people in the same manner. Frequently, the severity of the disease is compounded by another diagnosis (e.g., mental illness or substance use). The complexities of the disease require the TR specialist to use a variety of assessment, planning, implementation, and evaluation strategies to facilitate outcomes of a satisfying leisure lifestyle appropriate to a patient's level of health and well being.

Assessment

TR assessments for people with HIV and AIDS must incorporate the many complexities of the disease to ensure that activity selections will meet the needs of individual patients. Some facilities may be mandated to complete a TR assessment within 72 hours of admission, others allow an ongoing assessment that permits TR specialists to observe, interview, and discuss their findings with colleagues. The latter approach gives the TR specialist opportunities to develop a rapport with patients while assisting them in identifying leisure interests, problems, and challenges during the assessment process.

The TR specialist should focus on the following categories in developing a treatment plan based on patients' needs: psychosocial status, stage in disease process, cognitive/perceptual status, sensorimotor status, cultural background, and leisure interests.

1. Psychosocial status should include:
   - **a.** Established life role—questions regarding employment, spouse, lover, significant other, child(ren), extended family members.
   - **b.** Social support system—questions regarding support system (e.g., who comprises it, places where people in it are engaged, degree of accessibility of the people, and who does and who does not know about HIV/AIDS diagnosis) and behaviors that may have led to HIV infection (e.g., homosexual/bisexual, injecting drug use).
   - **c.** Coping mechanisms—questions related to the patient's ability to meet the challenges of living with HIV/AIDS, patient's capability of organizing time, and managing stressors associated with living with HIV disease.
   - **d.** Interpersonal style and skills—patient's pattern of interacting with others (e.g., out of anger, denial, fear), questions about how the patient responds to inquiries regarding his/her health, ability to acknowledge an HIV/AIDS diagnosis, or membership in a stigmatized group.
2. Stage in disease process should include:
   - **a.** Medical status of the patient—opportunistic infections the patient has experienced, current symptoms and illnesses, difficulties (e.g., tires easily, fatigue, forgetful, insomnia).
   - **b.** Medications—current medications, including prophylaxis and treatment medications, and their side effects. As side effects differ from one person to another and as HIV/AIDS patients frequently take medications prescribed by different physicians, the TR specialist needs to assess the variety of reactions each patient may be experiencing.
3. Cognitive/perceptual status should include:
   - **a.** Reality orientation—questions about the patient's awareness of what is occurring in his/her life, including day, date, year and current events. Are there signs of AIDS dementia complex?
   - **b.** Memory capacity—patient-demonstrated ability to recall recent events as well as a medication regimen. Are there signs of cognitive and memory impairment?
   - **c.** Organization skills—questions relating to the patient's ability to demonstrate organized and logical thought processes and to respond appropriately to questions.
   - **d.** Sensory acuity—has the patient experienced any impairments with taste, hearing, seeing?
   - **e.** Safety awareness—questions about the patient's knowledge and understanding of issues regarding transmission, universal precautions, high-risk sexual or injecting behaviors.
4. Sensorimotor status should include: an assessment of balance, gait, muscle tone, coordination, sensation, pain, and strength.
5. Cultural background should include:
   - **a.** Ethnic traditions—specific activities that may conflict with any cultural or traditional belief systems the patient may have.
   - **b.** Religion—religious beliefs, traditions, or practices, that may limit the patient's participation in any activities. Such limitations may include dancing, eating certain foods, or touching others.
6. Leisure interest assessment should include a full understanding of the patient's pattern of participation in leisure activities, pre- and post-diagnosis with HIV disease. For many individuals pre-diagnosis activities included family, friends, and employment. After diagnosis, psychosocial factors cause many individuals to withdraw from recreation and other activities. Standardized leisure assessments may be used, or TR specialists may customize or develop one specific to a particular type of patient group.

Planning

Once initial assessments are completed, TR specialists and patients can jointly begin to develop activity plans that focus on the needs, strengths, and interests of individual patients. The term initial assessment is used since ongoing assessment is necessary for persons with HIV/AIDS. The disease is cyclical in nature (i.e., periods of good health followed by periods of ill health). This necessitates constant changes of the TR plan. An activity that may be contraindicated today may be beneficial in three weeks. Also, patients may not be consciously aware of gradual visual and auditory degeneration. Only by observing patients over a period of time can the TR specialist assist them in recognizing acquired limitations.

The key element in developing a TR plan for persons with HIV/AIDS is flexibility. The plan should permit patients to select and engage in activities that include adaptations for periods of good health and illness. Although the plan should be flexible, it must include specific goals and strategies to achieve them. A TR plan for a patient with HIV disease may include activities that are either treatment oriented, educational, or social, depending on the specific needs of the patient.

Treatment-oriented activities are those that assist the patient in improving physical and emotional health. These include stress reduction activities, exercise programs, drama and art groups, and volunteering. Educationally-focused activities are those that assist patients in developing new strategies and skills to cope with HIV/AIDS disease, empower them to take an active role in selecting appropriate recreational activities, and help them to develop and engage a positive leisure lifestyle. These include stress-reduction workshops, leisure education and counseling programs, art groups, and other recreational skill development groups. Social activities are those that provide patients with opportunities to develop new or strengthen current social skills and support networks. Many activities offered by a TR department are viewed by patients as being socially oriented as they enable high levels of interaction among individuals. Although these activities may have a social component (e.g., crafts groups or bowling), they are offered to provide outcomes (e.g., motor-skill development and eye-hand coordination). Social activities, however, focus on leisure-oriented experiences in safe and nonthreatening environments, where persons with HIV disease can behave authentically versus hiding the disease because of fear of rejection and discrimination.

TR specialists working in facilities such as day treatment programs and community centers should assist clients in identifying community leisure resources during times the facility may be closed (e.g., evenings and weekends). Hospitals should develop discharge plans with patients that identify community leisure resources, which enable patients to continue participating in recreation and leisure activities that provide leisure satisfaction. TR specialists should develop working relationships with these community groups and resources. Providing patients with contact names at community centers eases the anxiety associated with joining a new group.

Implementation

Implementing the TR plan requires the development of strategies that will foster patients' involvement in the chosen activities. Implementation should consider the patients' current levels of health, strength and motivation to participate in various activities. For some patients, implementation strategies may require a gradual process that eases the patient from one-on-one activities to small-group activities to socials.

A variety of motivational techniques may also be utilized to stimulate the patient to participate in the activities. The TR specialist should know what and who motivates the patient. A spouse or lover may be able to assist the TR specialist in motivating a patient, or a particular individual may require a challenge, a competitive situation, or some type of risk-taking to stimulate motivation. The TR specialist may also engage members of the interdisciplinary team in the implementation process, including: (a) the case manager, to assist the patient in dealing with the complexities of living with HIV/AIDS; (b) the physical therapist, to assist in the enhancement of physical functioning; (c) the occupational therapist, to assist with activities of daily living; (d) the art, music and dance therapists, to assist in facilitating expressions of feelings; and (e) the activity leaders.

During the implementation stage it is important for the TR specialist to develop a trusting relationship with patients. Persons with HIV/AIDS disease are particularly sensitive to biases, discrimination, and condemnation. The TR specialist must confront feelings within him- or herself related to these issues in order to demonstrate the leadership qualities necessary to motivate patients with HIV/AIDS. The TR specialist working with this population must be knowledgeable about HIV and AIDS and deliver the service in a nondiscriminatory, nonmoralizing, nonblaming, and nonpatronizing manner. Behaviors related to these issues are frequently subtle; however, they are frequently detected by patients. The TR specialist must relate to patients in an honest and respectful manner if she or he expects to develop a trustful and meaningful working relationship.

TR specialists and other health professionals in the United States have access to HIV/AIDS training and educational opportunities provided through federally-funded programs. These programs provide continuing education about such topics as the continuum of HIV disease, HIV/AIDS confidentiality laws, neuropsychiatry of HIV, psychosocial issues of working with persons with HIV/AIDS, and cultural competency in the HIV epidemic. Some programs also provide opportunities for providers to participate in support groups in which they can express their feelings about ongoing work with persons with HIV/AIDS and the continuing loss of patients through death.

Evaluation

The challenge of evaluating the planned intervention with a patient having HIV/AIDS in the TR program is the constant evaluation of the patient's health status and its impact on the level of participation in various activities. An individual may progress from a modified low-impact aerobic activity to a high-impact aerobic one; however, medical complications may require a return to a modified low-impact aerobic activity. If the TR specialist's counseling and support enables the patient to make and adapt to these changes with minimal psychological distress, this is progress. The TR specialist must record what appears to be a setback as progress. The act of lower-level participation must not be viewed as the most critical issue at this point. The major issue is the patient's continued participation.

The evaluation must include ongoing observation notes that include both patient progress and problems that may be symptoms of serious health complications. The evaluation process should also include feedback from patient. What has the experience been for him or her? Is he or she enjoying the activity? Are new skills being developed? Are new activities being sought? Are benefits, frustrations, and challenges being verbalized? Overall, the TR specialist must use the various information to judge whether or not the TR program is effective in achieving the desired outcomes with a particular patient with HIV/AIDS. If not, the program needs to be modified, reimplemented, and reevaluated.

APPLICATION OF THE TR PROCESS

Jose is a 29-year-old gay man who was diagnosed with AIDS three years ago. His opportunistic infection at time of diagnosis was PCP. He is now hospitalized for cytomegalovirus (CMV). Jose recently lost his job at a gay bar and lives alone in an urban area. His family, with whom he regularly communicates, resides in Puerto Rico.

Assessment

During the assessment it was learned that Jose's lover of seven years recently died from AIDS complications. Jose stated that the bar, where he was employed for four years, fired him because he began drinking heavily after his lover died. He believed the bar fired him because he has AIDS and was afraid they would lose business if an employee looked ill. Jose admitted that during this "drinking spell" he did not necessarily keep himself well groomed, but stated adamantly that drinking is not a problem.

Jose indicated that he does not have many friends who are particularly close. Most of his acquaintances were people at the bar or his lover's friends. Many are now dead. Jose's family does not know about his HIV/AIDS diagnosis, as he does not want them to know he is gay. When the time comes that he must inform them of his illness, he plans to blame the disease on drug use. He stated that his family's strong religious and cultural ties lead them to believe that homosexuality is a sin. Jose said his father believes that homosexuals are men who want to be women, which means they are mentally ill. He would never want to embarrass his family by admitting his sexual orientation.

Jose believes he is coping well with his illness. However, since he lost his job, he has begun to isolate himself from everyone and seldom leaves his apartment. He has substituted alcohol for many meals. He stated that he is not going to worry about getting a new job until his savings are depleted. Since he worked off the books, he is not eligible for unemployment insurance, and he has no medical coverage. He anticipates that his funds will be exhausted in three months. Jose has never met with a social worker to discuss disability benefits, but he realizes that he may have to do so in the future.

Jose is relatively shy, personable, and friendly. He is clean shaven with neatly trimmed hair and nails, which conflict with his statement about not maintaining a well-groomed appearance. At the bar he was employed as a disk jockey. He loves music and dancing. When asked what he specifically likes about music and dancing, Jose stated that the words of many songs represent how he feels, and dancing permits him to feel the music and use his body. His body is well toned and defined.

Jose said that he never participated in many recreation activities; however, when growing up he loved to swim in the ocean. Even today, he goes to the beach as often as possible to swim and play volleyball.

Jose indicates that he is currently taking some preventative medications for PCP, and he started to take AZT after his lover died to delay his death and dying. Jose did not know much either about CMV or what type of medication he would likely be given to treat it. He hoped that whatever the medication, it would not have side effects.

Planning

After the initial assessment the TR specialist developed and reviewed the TR plan with Jose. The plan included participation in: (a) a writing group to help Jose address the loss of his lover and his feelings about being diagnosed with AIDS; (b) a stress management workshop to assist Jose in identifying techniques to relieve his stress and anxiety without the use of alcohol; (c) a drama group to assist Jose in disclosing his illness to his parents and addressing his multiple losses to AIDS; (d) an HIV/AIDS education group to enhance his understanding of opportunistic infections and treatments; (e) an aerobic class to provide Jose with an opportunity to maintain muscle tone while moving to music; and (f) a social planning group so that Jose can utilize his knowledge of music and dancing in the planning of social events and to develop new relationships with individuals who have similar interests.

The TR specialist developed long-range plans that included engaging Jose in volunteering at socials as a disk jockey, and identifying community resources that Jose could utilize when discharged, such as community pools, fitness facilities, and Alcoholics Anonymous groups for persons with HIV/AIDS. The TR specialist also contacted the case management department to notify them about Jose's financial situation, the nutrition counselor to assess his dietary condition, a substance use counselor to assess his alcohol use, and a priest to help Jose discuss his family's religious beliefs in the context of his illness. Another note was made to inquire about the CMV diagnosis and prescribed medications in relation to their specific impact on Jose's health status and functioning.

Implementation

Utilizing a team approach, the TR specialist met with the aerobic instructor, the case manager, the nutritionist, the priest and activity leaders. The TR specialist discussed the plan that was developed with Jose. To implement the TR plan the TR specialist began by introducing Jose to small-group activities and aerobics, as he is shy and communicates better on a one-to-one basis. During the implementation phase, the TR specialist continued to develop a rapport with Jose, so as to continue assessing his needs. As Jose began to feel comfortable with small-group activities, the TR specialist accompanied him to larger-group activities, such as drama and social planning groups, to introduce him to the participants.

During the implementation phase, the TR specialist continued to meet on a regular basis with the treatment team to discuss Jose's progress. Based on the information provided by members of the treatment team, the plan required modifications (i.e., Jose is ready to begin large-group activities before the date initially outlined in the plan).

Jose was placed on infusion medication that required him to have an operation for the purpose of placing a catheter in his chest. It was also learned that the CMV has affected his optical nerve, which has resulted in some visual impairment.

The TR specialist discussed with Jose the possibility of his participation in larger-group activities and supported Jose as he learned about his prognosis related to his vision. The TR specialist realized that new questions had to be addressed with Jose when he was ready to discuss them, such as the effect of the infusion therapy on Jose's future working and dancing activities, and his wanting to swim at a public pool with the catheter attached to his chest. To assist Jose with the news about his prognosis the TR specialist introduced him to other patients in the larger groups who were on infusion therapy, hoping Jose would receive the needed support.

EVALUATION

Jose's evaluation indicated that he had enjoyed participating in the recreation activities and that his drinking had been a result of losing so many friends to AIDS. His work in the social support group had led to the best parties the TR department had organized, with great music and with the patients stating that they had enjoyed themselves. It was clear by the expression on Jose's face that he had enjoyed the compliments from other patients when they discussed how great the parties had been. His participation in the stress management workshop had led him to join the Tai Chi group. Jose reported that Tai Chi allowed him the benefits of breathing exercises and visualization with the ability to move his body, just like "dancing real slow."

With the support of the case manager, Jose applied for public assistance, with no plans to return to the work force. He felt that the friendships developed during his hospital stay would continue once he was discharged. He told the TR specialist that he and a few other men had exchanged telephone numbers and were planning to go to a meals program for persons with AIDS, join the local YMCA together, and attend a community recreation program.

TRENDS AND ISSUES

There is no HIV protective vaccine or curative drug. Although the outlook for HIV vaccines appears to be considerably brighter, there remain major obstacles and considerable gaps in knowledge, as well as major ethical issues and enormous financial obstacles to their development (Schoub, 1994). Either a vaccine that protects against HIV infection or one that prevents individuals who are asymptomatically HIV infected from converting to AIDS would have a dramatic effect on controlling the AIDS pandemic. At the present time, any type of vaccine appears to be years away.

With no curative drug, there is no way of eliminating HIV or preventing the onset of disease and death once it enters a person's body. According to Schoub (1994):

> *At present, one would need to be content with the conception of an idealized situation where infected patients could be maintained symptom-free*

by life-long treatment with drugs which are relatively non-toxic, and where problems of resistance could be overcome, for example by alternating with different drugs, and where costs could be kept to reasonable levels (p. 181).

Scientists at the Tenth International Conference on AIDS in Yokohama, Japan, indicated hope for a new class of experimental antiviral drugs called protease inhibitors, which can be used in combination with existing AIDS drugs. Early data have been encouraging but they are too scanty to be conclusive (Pollack, 1994).

In the meantime, fear, rejection, stigmatization, and discrimination continue to follow HIV and AIDS in every country. "These vexatious measures arise from minds obsessed with impurity and sin, crime and punishment. They bear witness to the persistence of magical thinking in the world, and, despite appearances, have no medical justification" (Grmek, 1990, p. 188).

People infected with HIV who seek and receive medical attention are living longer because many conditions that afflict those with AIDS are treatable and preventable (Stoddard, 1994). Many people with HIV, however, do not know there is any hope. Stoddard attributes the "very term AIDS [as] part of the problem. It connotes imminent death and despair; people with AIDS are simply written off" (p. A19). He suggests that "AIDS" has outlived its usefulness and the condition should be relabeled "HIV disease" by the Centers for Disease Control and Prevention.

As people with AIDS continue to live longer, therapeutic recreation specialists are developing growing and expanding roles in enhancing the daily behavioral expressions of these clients in dignified settings within supportive environments. These are places where therapeutic recreation specialists have eliminated condemnation, ostracism and stigmatization of people with HIV/AIDS and have instituted HIV prevention education programs that eliminate risky behaviors which lead to reinfection of clients or the infection of their sexual partners.

The increasing spread of HIV disease in pockets of poverty, crime, prostitution, and drug abuse in the United States as well as in many Third World countries calls for conceptualizing new solutions. Therapeutic recreation specialists and other health providers must find innovative ways to reach people about one of their most basic pleasures in order to foster safer-sex practices, reduction of the number of sexual partners, consistent use of condoms, or abstinence until one finds a non-HIV-infected, monogamous partner.

SUMMARY

AIDS is a lethal disease for which there is no cure or preventative vaccine. It is caused by the human immunodeficiency virus (HIV), and there is no way of eliminating HIV or preventing the onset of disease and death once the virus has entered a person's body. The disease is relatively simple to prevent; however, prevention approaches—including sex education, condom distribution, and protecting the blood supply—have been inadequate in stemming the course of the pandemic. Lack of knowledge concerning people's sexual attitudes and societal factors such as discrimination, poverty, and lack of education have been strong impediments to effective prevention strategies.

The field of therapeutic recreation has not been prominent among the health professions that have been on the front line of the HIV/AIDS epidemic, such as nurses and social workers. However, the increasing presence of HIV in every United States community necessitates that therapeutic recreation specialists become involved in and knowledgeable about providing services for individuals with HIV/AIDS.

The purpose of therapeutic recreation is to facilitate the development of an appropriate leisure lifestyle for the person who is diagnosed with HIV infection or AIDS. Consequently, specialists should provide therapeutic recreation services that enhance coping with the diagnosis of a communicable, sexually-transmitted, fatal disease; focus on knowledge, attitudes, and skills that facilitate a day-to-day behavioral expression in the face of increasing opportunistic infections and physical and cognitive limitations; and help the person to maintain functional independence as the disease progresses with its accompanying neurological complications and physical debilitation.

Therapeutic recreation interventions that have appeared to be effective in enhancing appropriate leisure lifestyles of people with HIV infection and AIDS include: stress reduction programs, exercise programs, verbal and nonverbal activities, social activities, volunteer activities, and leisure education and counseling. The application of the components of the therapeutic recreation processes to working with people with HIV/AIDS were described, and a case study of a gay man with AIDS was developed to illustrate the phases of assessment, planning, implementation, and evaluation.

A brief overview of trends and issues included the following points: there are many obstacles to the development of an HIV protective vaccine or curative drug; the pandemic is continuing to grow; fear, rejection, stigmatization, and discrimination follow HIV and AIDS in every country; people with AIDS are and will continue to live longer; and there is an increasing role for therapeutic recreation specialists in enhancing daily behavioral expressions of people with HIV/AIDS as well as in fostering safer-sex practices to prevent primary and secondary infections.

A recent study of 100 men who were tracked for a three-month period found that a pleasant event can boost the immune system for as long as two days, while negative effects of a stressful encounter mainly take their toll for only one day (Goleman, 1994). Dr. Stone, the principal investigator, "found that stresses like being criticized at work weakened immune function on the day they occurred. But events like a pleasant family celebration or having friends over enhanced the immune system for the next two days" (p. C11). Although the study has yet to be replicated with people in various stages of HIV disease, the current findings point to the importance of providing recreation activities to enhance immune functioning—a definite mandate for therapeutic recreation for persons with HIV disease.

READING COMPREHENSION QUESTIONS

1. What are the differences between HIV infection and AIDS?
2. What are the ways in which HIV is transmitted? Is not transmitted?
3. What are the types of treatments for HIV infection and opportunistic infections? What are their limitations?
4. What are the purposes and benefits of therapeutic recreation for people with HIV/AIDS?
5. Which therapeutic recreation interventions appear to be effective in enhancing appropriate leisure lifestyles for people with HIV/AIDS?
6. What are the common service settings in which therapeutic recreation specialists work with people with HIV/AIDS and what are the challenges in working in each of them?
7. With which psychosocial issues do therapeutic recreation specialists have to cope in working with people with HIV/AIDS?
8. What are some of the major categories under each phase of the therapeutic recreation process in its application to facilitating the development of an appropriate leisure lifestyle for a person with HIV/AIDS?
9. What is the importance of trends and issues in HIV disease to the provision of therapeutic recreation services?

SUGGESTED LEARNING ACTIVITIES

1. Set up two debate teams: one in favor of and one opposed to stigmatizing, discriminating, and rejecting people with HIV/AIDS.
2. Interview a person with AIDS and write a two- to five-page paper that describes how the person has adapted or changed his or her leisure participation patterns.

3. In a small discussion group, identify and discuss some of the psychosocial issues that a therapeutic recreation specialist in your community might face in working with people with HIV/AIDS.
4. Research local and state laws relating to confidentiality and disability nondiscrimination related to people with HIV/AIDS.
   a. Write a three- to five-page paper on how these laws relate to the American Disabilities Act and Section 504 of the Vocational Rehabilitation Act regarding protection of people with HIV/AIDS.
   b. Write a three- to five-page paper describing these laws and how they may impact on the provision of therapeutic recreation services in your state and community.
5. In role play situations, assume that you are a therapeutic recreation specialist conducting an initial assessment interview with a person with AIDS in a hospital setting who is either (a) a gay man, (2) an injecting drug user, (3) a person with schizophrenia, (4) a pregnant woman who is a single parent with two previous children, or (5) a person with cognitive impairments, including recent memory loss.

REFERENCES

Agency for Health Care Policy and Research. (1994). *Evaluation and management of early HIV infection.* (AHCPR Publication No. 94–0572). Washington, DC: U.S. Department of Health and Human Services.

Altman, L.K. (1994, August 17). High H.I.V. levels raise risk to newborns, 2 studies show. *The New York Times,* p. C8.

Centers for Disease Control and Prevention. (1993a). *Facts about the scope of the HIV/AIDS epidemic in the United States.* Atlanta, GA: Author.

Centers for Disease Control and Prevention. (1993b). *HIV/AIDS surveillance report, 5*(3), 18–19.

Centers for Disease Control and Prevention. (1994). *AIDS information: Cumulative cases,* p. 1.

Delaney, M., & Goldblum, P. (1987). *Strategies for survival: A gay men's health manual for the age of AIDS.* New York: St. Martin's Press.

Dunkel, J., & Hatfield, S. (1986). Countertransference issues in working with persons with AIDS. *Social Work, 31*(2), 114–117.

Flaskerud, J.H., & Ungvarski, P.J. (1992). *HIV/AIDS: A guide to nursing care* (2nd ed.). Philadelphia, PA: W.B. Saunders.

Full-blown AIDS cases estimated at 4 million. (1994, July 2). *The New York Times,* p. 8.

Goleman, D. (1992, February 12). Relaxation and exercise plan may slow pace of AIDS virus. *The New York Times,* p. C12.

Goleman, D. (1994, May 11). Seeking out small pleasures keeps immune system strong. *The New York Times,* p. C11.

Grmek, M.D. (1990). *History of AIDS: Emergence and origin of a modern pandemic.* Princeton, NJ: Princeton University Press.

Link, D., & Gilden, D. (1994). d4T gets a nod from FDA panel. *GMHC Treatment Issues, 8*(5), 3.

Navarro, M. (1992, November 23). As H.I.V. patients stay at work, problems, and solutions, emerge. *The New York Times,* pp. A1, B8.

Peterson, C.A., & Gunn, S. L. (1984). *Therapeutic recreation program design: Principles and procedures* (2nd ed.). Englewood Cliffs, NJ: Prentice Hall.

Pollack, A. (1994, August 12). Meeting lays bare the abyss between AIDS and its cure. *The New York Times,* pp. A1, A9.

Ryan, W. (1986). *Blaming the victim.* New York: Vintage Press.

Schlenzig, C., et al. (1989). Supervised physical exercise leads to psychological and immunological involvement in pre-AIDS patients. *Proceedings of the V International Conference on AIDS.* Montreal, Canada.

Schoub, B. D. (1994). *AIDS & HIV in perspective: A guide to understanding the virus and its consequences.* Great Britain: Cambridge University Press.

Stoddard, T. (1994, August 17). Don't call it AIDS. *The New York Times,* p. A19.

Surgeon General's Report to the American Public on HIV Infection and AIDS. (1993). Washington, DC: National Institutes of Health.

WHO Press. (1992, February 12). World Health Organization, Global Programme on AIDS, United Nations.

Zidovudine cuts mother-infant infections. (1994, No. 1). *Global AIDS News,* p. 10.

CHAPTER 17

MANAGEMENT, CONSULTATION, AND RESEARCH

JUDITH E. VOELKL

OBJECTIVES

- Describe how the management of a department or facility may influence the professional growth of a therapeutic recreation specialist.
- Explain the difference between general supervision and clinical supervision.
- Define consultation.
- Explain the differences among the four types of consultation.
- Describe the roles that the consultant may take in the consultation process.
- Identify the six areas of research that have been identified as very important to the therapeutic recreation profession.
- Describe one research method that is frequently used in therapeutic recreation.
- Know resources that provide therapeutic recreation specialists with information on current research studies.

MANAGEMENT, CONSULTATION, AND RESEARCH

Throughout this book a great deal of information has been presented on the use of the therapeutic recreation process with individuals who have a variety of disabilities. As a result of these readings or previous experiences, many readers may have identified a specific group of individuals with whom they would like to work. Future course work and practical experiences may be planned to allow the student to gain specialized skills in the provision of services for a particular group of individuals. What many students may not have considered, however, are the avenues an entry-level therapeutic recreation specialist must have for continuing the attainment and enhancement of his or her clinical knowledge and skills. The continued attainment of high-level knowledge and skills, and the refinement of previously learned skills, will aid the therapeutic recreation specialist in providing quality services for clients.

The responsibility that each therapeutic recreation specialist has for improving his or her clinical knowledge and skills is evident in the

National Therapeutic Recreation Society's Code of Ethics. The Code of Ethics states that the therapeutic recreation professional "is committed to the continuous task of learning and self-improvement to increase his/her competency and effectiveness as a professional . . . [and] is guided by the accepted responsibility of encouraging and providing quality services to the client/consumer" (Code of Ethics, 1985). Individuals studying therapeutic recreation may consider what processes inherent in the workplace will continue to support and enhance their professional growth following the completion of their formal education.

The purpose of this chapter is to consider several processes within the workplace and the profession that support the professional growth of therapeutic recreation specialists. In the first section we will reflect upon how management and the supervision process may enhance the further development of clinical skills; in the second section the focus will be on the consultation process; and in the third section the role research plays in enhancing our professional knowledge will be addressed.

Management

Management involves the planning, organizing, staffing, directing, and controlling of human and nonhuman resources (Culkin & Kirsch, 1986; McConnell, 1993). In therapeutic recreation management, a manager considers a therapeutic recreation staff member to be a human resource and assigns staff members specific job responsibilities that are in line with departmental and organizational goals. Managers of therapeutic recreation departments oversee not only human resources, such as a therapeutic recreation specialist, but they also deal with nonhuman resources, such as equipment, supplies, and space or work areas available to staff members (Keller, 1985). In this section we will explore how management influences the job responsibilities, availability of resources, professional participation, and supervision that a staff member receives. Furthermore, we will briefly examine how these areas influence a therapeutic recreation specialist's opportunities for professional growth in an agency.

Most entry-level therapeutic recreation specialists report to or are directly responsible to a supervisor who is in a management position. The manager/supervisor may be the director of therapeutic recreation services, the director of activities, or a director or chief of a unit within a hospital or agency. The manager/supervisor is an important person to consider when an entry-level therapeutic recreation specialist is interviewing for a position at an agency. The entry-level therapeutic recreation specialist may ask the following questions to discover the viewpoint of management and how this viewpoint may influence his or her job responsibilities and opportunities for professional growth:

- What are the goals of the manager/supervisor in relation to the department or unit?
- How does the manager/supervisor interpret the supervisee's job description and role within the department/unit/agency?
- How does the manager/supervisor influence the supervisee's access to equipment, supplies, or moneys for new items?
- What types of supervision are provided for the staff?
- Does the department or agency support the staff's participation in professional organizations?

The way in which the manager/supervisor interprets an employee's job description and the goals the manager/supervisor has for the department may directly influence a staff member's job responsibilities. For instance, a therapeutic recreation specialist interested in developing a leisure education program within a program for adults with a chemical dependency may not feel professionally challenged or fulfilled while working under a manager who believes that the job responsibility of the staff member is to provide general recreation programs. This type of work situation would, most likely, prevent the therapeutic recreation specialist from further developing his or her skills as a leisure educator. When considering a therapeutic recreation position, an individual needs to "interview" the manager/supervisor carefully by asking questions regarding the purpose of the therapeutic recreation service and the associated job responsibilities.

Another area that may influence a therapeutic recreation specialist's task of providing services is the availability of resources such as equipment, supplies, space for running activities, and moneys for the purchase of new equipment and supplies. A therapeutic recreation specialist without the proper location or equipment may need to cancel an activity, for it may be unsafe to implement an activity under those conditions. It is important for a therapeutic recreation specialist considering a potential job to ask the manager/supervisor about the availability and allocation of nonhuman resources.

The types of supervision provided by a department or agency are another area for a potential employee to consider when applying for a professional position. Most therapeutic recreation specialists receive general supervision, which entails a supervisor directing and evaluating employees' work, and informing employees of policies, procedures, standards, or legislation that affect the provision of services (Austin, 1986; 1991; McConnell, 1993). In recent years an increased amount of attention has been paid to the provision of clinical supervision for therapeutic recreation specialists (Austin, 1986).

Clinical Supervision. Clinical supervision is a dynamic process in which the supervisor, often a person different from the individual providing general supervision, works with a therapeutic recreation specialist in order to identify his or her strengths and weaknesses in regard to clinical practice (Munson, 1993). The supervisor possesses extensive experience, skills, and knowledge in the area of therapeutic recreation services. The supervisor and the therapeutic recreation specialist share in the task of identifying clinical skills that the therapeutic recreation specialist would like to improve. The clinical skills that are addressed in the clinical supervision process may include charting, development of individualized treatment plans, or selection and application of a counseling approach (e.g., behavioral, client-centered, cognitive-behavioral) for a therapeutic recreation group. As part of the process, the supervisor and the therapeutic recreation specialist decide how they will work together and how to evaluate progress. Throughout the clinical supervision process, the supervisor and supervisee discuss the difficulties of learning new skills and acknowledging areas of weaknesses. Supervisors seek to support and acknowledge a supervisee's progress and feelings about clinical supervision.

Therapeutic recreation specialists participating in clinical supervision may be involved in individual or group sessions. Individual sessions are held on either a weekly or biweekly basis, and the content addresses the identified needs of the supervisee. Group sessions may occur biweekly or monthly, and the content may address preidentified needs of the group or a discussion of specific problems germane to the provision of therapeutic recreation services (Austin, 1986; 1991).

The benefits of participating in clinical supervision are evident in the fact that it has been found to influence employees' work satisfaction positively (Cherniss & Egnatios, 1977; Munson, 1993). Furthermore, the positive outcomes of clinical supervision include an improved level of services for clients, which enhances the achievement of organizational goals and the provision of professional growth for supervisees (Austin, 1986). It appears that the process of clinical supervision will support the therapeutic recreation specialist who is attempting to "increase his/her competency and effectiveness as a professional" as is stated in the Code of Ethics of the National Therapeutic Recreation Society (1985, p. 71).

Professional Organizations. Participation in professional organizations is another avenue therapeutic recreation specialists have for enhancing their professional growth. Several national-level organizations exist (e.g., American Therapeutic Recreation Association, National Therapeutic Recreation Society), and numerous organizations exist on the state level for therapeutic recreation specialists. Professional organizations are instrumental in the dissemination of information regarding new developments and issues in the field (Keller, 1989). For example, members of professional organizations in therapeutic recreation may receive information regarding how standards, legislation, and research influence professional practice. Many professional organizations sponsor yearly conferences with sessions on such topics as innovative programs, tips for devising effective treatment plans, or practical approaches for working with specific groups of individuals. Information received from professional organizations may directly influence and enhance the therapeutic recreation specialist's delivery of service in the workplace. The entry-level therapeutic recreation specialist considering a position needs to discover how the management of a department and agency views professional involvement. More specifically, therapeutic recreation specialists need to clarify whether management will provide time and possibly the financial support for membership in professional organizations and attendance at professional meetings.

Conclusion. The management of a department, including departmental goals, design of job descriptions, availability of equipment and facilities, the types of supervision offered, and support for participation in professional organizations, all interact to influence the opportunities a staff person has for developing clinical knowledge and skills. Therefore, these areas directly influence a therapeutic recreation specialist's opportunities for professional growth in the workplace. Therapeutic recreation specialists seeking positions need to consider how the management of a specific department or agency will enhance or hinder their professional growth and development.

Consultation

Consultation involves a process in which a consultant, an individual with specialized knowledge, works with a consultee. The consultee may be a therapeutic recreation specialist, a therapeutic recreation department, or an agency that includes therapeutic recreation personnel. Consultees usually enter into the consultation process on a voluntary basis. The purpose of consultation is for the consultant to help consultees become more effective and efficient in their work (Kurpius, 1978; Rieman, 1992).

In this section we will explore the conditions under which an entry-level therapeutic recreation specialist may work with a consultant. Furthermore, information on the types of consultation, the consultation process, and several roles that the consultant may use during the process will be presented. We will begin by presenting several case examples in order to exemplify when a consultant may assist a consultee in addressing problems that occur in the workplace (see Table 17.1).

The case examples exemplify various situations in which a consultee may benefit from a consultant's specialized knowledge and skills. Different types of consultation may be used to address the problems in these various situations. Caplan (1970; Erchul & Schulte, 1993) outlined four types of consultation: **Client-centered case consultation** involves a consultant helping a consultee plan an effective treatment plan for working with a specific client. **Consultee-centered consultation** focuses on providing staff with the necessary skills for working with clients for whom they were previously unable to provide services effectively. For instance, it may involve a consultant working with staff regarding common problems or issues in working with a group of clients, as was described in Case Example 1. Two other types of consultation are focused at the agency or management level. **Program-centered administrative consultation** involves program development. Program-centered administrative consultation would be the type of consultation used in Case Examples 2 and 4. **Consultee-centered administrative consultation** assists the consultee in examining problems and issues in administration. Consultee-centered administrative consultation would be the approach taken in Case Example 3.

The Roles of the Consultant. Within each consultation situation, a consultant may take on several

TABLE 17.1 Case Examples

Case Example 1: A group home for individuals with emotional disturbances has decided to begin accepting individuals with mental retardation. Most of the staff members have had little experience working with individuals with mental retardation. A consultant with expertise in working with individuals with mental retardation is hired to help staff provide services to meet the needs of the new clients.

Case Example 2: A new psychiatric facility hired a number of occupational therapists and a number of therapeutic recreation specialists. While developing the program, tension arose between the OTRs and the TRSs regarding the differences between the programs provided by each group. A consultant is hired to help mediate the process of how staff identify the boundaries between the OTRs and the TRSs.

Case Example 3: A 160-bed nursing home was recently reviewed by the state. The therapeutic recreation department was cited for failing to comply with several standards. When talking with the administrator, the director of therapeutic recreation states that her department is doing the best it can with limited resources, and she feels unsure of how to meet all the standards. The administrator suggests that a consultant be hired to help the director evaluate current services and consider alternatives that would ensure the meeting of all standards.

Case Example 4: The director of the therapeutic recreation department at a free-standing rehabilitation hospital is interested in designing an applied research project. The focus of the study will be an evaluation of their community sports reintegration program. None of the staff members in the department have extensive education or experience in conducting research. The administrator of the facility suggests that the therapeutic recreation department hire a consultant to guide them in the development of a research project designed to evaluate the community sports reintegration program.

roles in order to assist a consultee in addressing the issue or problem at hand. For example, the consultant hired in Case Example 1 may take on the roles of technical specialist and trainer/educator in order to provide staff with the knowledge and skills necessary for successfully working with individuals with mental retardation (Lippitt & Lippitt, 1986). In contrast, the consultant hired in Case Example 2 may serve as a mediator for the two groups and would focus on finding out the facts, reflecting the feelings and beliefs of the consultees, and processing the interactions among staff. Lippitt and Lippitt suggest that the roles used by a consultant may include being an advocate for a specific method or intervention. Other roles include functioning as a problem solver, information specialist, trainer/educator, collaborator or joint problem solver, identifier of alternatives, fact finder, process specialist, or objective observer. A consultant may also take on the role of a mediator or collaborator in the consultation process.

Another role frequently used by consultants is being a catalyst of change. Thinking back on the case examples, it seems that change would need to occur in order to begin addressing any of the issues. For instance, in Case Example 3, staff may need to alter the manner in which they provide services in order to ensure that they meet state standards. Change is an essential part of most consultation processes. In many instances, however, change is difficult for people. There are times in the consultation process when it is upsetting for a consultee to consider the changes that will occur, and he or she may feel that the changes being suggested are an indication of professional weakness or a form of criticism. One of the skills possessed by consultants is the ability to help people adjust to the process of change. In the consultation process, time is provided for consultees to discuss how they feel about change, including the drawbacks and benefits of the change process. Frequently, the benefits of change are observed in the increased quality of care and the opportunities for personal and professional growth on the part of the consultees.

It appears that the consultant who can address the needs of all the consultees listed in the case examples would need to be a miracle worker! In reality, it may be that four different consultants, each possessing different strengths and specialized knowledge, need to be found for the case examples.

The Consultation Process. Undertaking work with a consultant typically involves a five stage process, including entry, data gathering and diagnosis, intervention, evaluation, and termination. The first stage in the consultation process allows a consultee to find the best consultant for a specific job. This occurs during the **entry stage** of the consultation process. The consultee would spend time talking with several different consultants to make sure that the consultant who is chosen has the necessary knowledge and skills, understands how staff feel about change, and exhibits an approach to working with people that would fit in well in the agency (Snow & Corse, 1986). The entry stage allows the consultant and consultee to size each other up! If both parties agree that they could work well together, a contract is drawn up. Most entry-level therapeutic recreation specialists would be involved in meeting potential consultants, even though supervisory level personnel usually draw up the contract.

After an agreement is worked out between the consultant and the consultee, they enter the **data gathering and diagnosis** stage. They work together to identify the facts surrounding the problem or issue that has brought them together. They want to discover the reasons for the problem. The consultant will ask questions, observe, ask consultees to keep records surrounding the problem issues, and interview individuals and groups of employees (Snow & Corse, 1986). The results of the data gathering will be presented to all the consultees, and a diagnosis will be made by the consultant and consultees.

After correctly identifying the problem, the consultees and consultant must decide on an **intervention.** An intervention is a plan of action that outlines the changes that will occur, the tasks related to each area of change, and the parties responsible for each task. How actively involved the consultant is in this decision will depend on the role he or she has taken. If a consultant is serving as a mediator or collaborator, he or she will support the consultees in making decisions. However, if the consultant is serving as a provider of specialized information, he or she will take a more active role in identifying the appropriate intervention. When deciding on an intervention, decisions need to be made regarding each individual's role, a time line, and how the intervention will be evaluated (Snow & Corse, 1986).

Evaluation will be an ongoing process that starts with the beginning of the intervention. If the evaluations indicate that the outcome of the intervention is not satisfactory, changes need to be made. In instances where the outcomes are positive, the intervention is seen as working as anticipated.

When positive outcomes are found from an intervention, the consultant and consultees must decide how long the consultant will stay working in the system. Plans for **termination** of the consultant's services need to be made. Plans will include the identification of tasks that need to be attended to by the consultee rather than the consultant. It may also be decided that the consultant will conduct periodic checkup visits with the consultee in order to make sure all is running smoothly.

We have reviewed a great deal of information regarding the types of consultation, roles of a consultant, and the stages of the consultation process. Many entry-level therapeutic recreation specialists may find that they take part in a consultation process. In order to clarify how the various aspects of consultation may be experienced by an entry-level therapeutic recreation specialist, let's take Case Example 2 and work through the process (see Table 17.2).

In the case of the Golden Acres Nursing Facility discussed in Table 17.2, Connie, the consultant, spent approximately nine months in the facility. This is an example of a short-term consultation process. Some consultation processes may span several years and are considered long-term consultation.

As we have discussed in this section, consultation is a process that involves a consultant assisting a consultee in making changes. The consultation

TABLE 17.2 Consultation Process and Roles: Golden Acres Nursing Facility

Sarah—the Director of Therapeutic Recreation
Connie—the Consultant

Current Situation: A 160-bed nursing home, the Golden Acres Nursing Facility, was recently reviewed by the state. The therapeutic recreation department was cited for failing to comply with several standards. While talking with the administrator, Sarah states that her department is doing the best it can with limited resources, and she feels unsure of how to meet all the standards. The administrator suggests that a consultant be hired to help Sarah evaluate current services and consider alternatives that would ensure the meeting of all standards.

Entry Phase: Sarah and Connie will meet to discuss problems with meeting standards. Connie will talk about her approach to working with a consultee. Connie tells Sarah that she considers this type of consultation a consultee-centered administrative consultation, and she will act as a collaborator, identifier of alternatives, and catalyst of change. Following the meeting with Connie, Sarah recommends that the administrator of the nursing home hire Connie as the consultant.

Data Gathering and Diagnosis: Sarah and Connie review the report filed by the state inspector and the job description/responsibilities of each employee in the therapeutic recreation department. Connie interviews the employees and asks them to keep a diary of how they spend their time. Connie and Sarah meet to discuss findings and alternatives. Connie and Sarah meet with the department to discuss findings.

Intervention: The department decides on an intervention that alters each person's job responsibilities to ensure that state standards are met. As part of the intervention, Connie provides an in-service training session on treatment plans and progress notes.

Evaluation: While planning the intervention, the department decides that Connie will conduct monthly reviews on the employees' progress and will meet with them after three months and then after six months. Improvement is noted at the three-month and six-month reviews.

Termination: At the six-month review, it is decided that Sarah will take over monthly reviews. Connie no longer is an official consultant with the nursing home. However, she periodically talks with Sarah to check on how the therapeutic recreation department is getting along. The therapeutic recreation department receives an excellent report during the next state inspection.

process allows the consultee to learn new skills and approaches to problem solving that will assist him or her in functioning more competently as a therapeutic recreation specialist.

Research

Research is defined as a systematic and well-planned process that allows the researcher to gather information about a phenomenon (Babbie, 1992; Kerlinger, 1973). Research in therapeutic recreation typically enhances our knowledge or understanding of some aspect of the leisure functioning of individuals with disabilities. For example, a research study may be designed to examine the effect of participation in a recreation activity upon individuals' perceived competence in leisure. A study designed to examine the influence of various leadership styles on client outcomes in therapeutic recreation groups is another example.

The importance of designing research studies in therapeutic recreation has been discussed by numerous leaders in the field (Austin, 1982; Compton, 1984; Coyle et al., 1991; Iso-Ahola, 1988; Malkin, 1993; Witt, 1988). Entry-level practitioners and students of therapeutic recreation may have a number of questions regarding research in therapeutic recreation. For instance, what are the research questions most frequently asked by therapeutic recreation specialists? What methods are typically employed by researchers in therapeutic recreation? What role may an entry-level therapeutic recreation specialist take in relation to therapeutic recreation research? How do therapeutic recreation specialists stay informed of research being conducted in the field? Each of these questions will be addressed in the following sections.

Research Questions Most Frequently Asked by Therapeutic Recreation Specialists. Over the past decade, numerous leaders and scholars in therapeutic recreation have called for research designed to assist the profession in documenting the efficacy of our services (Compton, 1984; 1989; Coyle et al., 1991; Iso-Ahola, 1988; Witt, 1988). Although the call for research has been heard by the profession, many individuals have questioned the specific focus that research in TR should address. Due to the work of several faculty members at Temple University, in addition to that undertaken by our professional organizations (i.e., American Therapeutic Recreation Association and National Therapeutic Recreation Society), the field has begun to identify several areas in need of research.

In 1988 Temple University's Program in Therapeutic Recreation was awarded a grant from the National Institute on Disability and Rehabilitation Research, U.S. Department of Education. One aspect of this grant called for a national conference designed to identify (a) treatment outcomes associated with therapeutic recreation, and (b) research priorities (Riley, 1991). The conference was structured to discuss the benefits of therapeutic recreation pertaining to the following population groups: developmental disabilities, geriatrics, mental health, pediatrics, physical disabilities, and substance abuse. The proceedings of this conference have been extremely important in the development of a research agenda for the profession of therapeutic recreation. Students are encouraged to review the published proceedings entitled "Benefits of Therapeutic Recreation: A Consensus View" that was edited by Drs. Coyle, Kinney, Riley, and Shank and published in 1991 by Temple University.

As an outcome of the Temple conference, six global outcomes or benefits of therapeutic recreation were identified. These outcomes include (a) physical health and health maintenance, (b) cognitive functioning, (c) psychosocial health, (d) growth and personal development, (e) personal and life satisfaction, and (f) societal and health care system outcomes (Coyle, Kinney, & Shank, 1991). Shank, Kinney, and Coyle (1993) indicate that future research undertaken in therapeutic recreation should be designed to substantiate the conditions under which clients experience these six positive outcomes. Examples of research questions for each topical area are listed in Table 17.3.

Research Methods and Process. It is necessary for entry-level practitioners to possess a basic understanding of various research methods in order to benefit from research conducted in therapeutic recreation. Knowledge of research methods and current research conducted in therapeutic recreation allows practitioners to discuss the benefits of interventions with clients and health care providers representing other disciplines (e.g., medicine, social work, psychology, occupational therapy). Knowledge of research findings may also impact on the interventions designed by therapeutic recreation specialists. Readers are, therefore, encouraged to take courses to further their understanding of research methods and the paradigms underlying these methods (Bullock, 1993; Dattilo, McCormick, & Scott, 1991; McCormick, Dattilo, & Scott, 1991). In this section the reader will be introduced to several research methods, along with examples of select studies utilizing these methods.

To date, a majority of research studies in therapeutic recreation have used experimental methods and survey methods (Bedini & Wu, 1994; Voelkl, Austin, & Morris, 1992). Recently, many therapeutic recreation practitioners have begun to report on the efficacy of their interventions using the case history method. Therefore, we will review basic definitions of these three

TABLE 17.3 Questions Exemplifying the Research Priorities in Therapeutic Recreation*

Physical Health and Health Maintenance

Does participation in a strength training program increase the upper body strength and independent use of leisure time of adults with physical disabilities?

Does participation in a walking/exercise program increase the length of ambulation, range of motion, and frequency of self-initiated social interactions of older adults residing in a nursing home?

Cognitive Functioning

Does participation in a group writing program increase the general cognitive abilities and frequency of self-initiated social interactions of older adults?

Does participation in a recreation based cognitive retraining program increase the number of steps an adult with a traumatic brain injury can complete independently in a preferred leisure activity?

Psychosocial Health

Does participation in a recreation based self-esteem program increase the self-esteem of adolescents with depression?

Does a leisure education program focused on social skills development increase the social skills and frequency of participation in independent leisure activities of adults with schizophrenia?

Growth and Personal Development

Does participation in a leisure education program increase the independent leisure functioning of children with mental retardation? Does it increase the number of peers with whom they interact on a weekly basis?

Does participation in a family leisure education program increase the frequency in which a family participates in joint leisure pursuits? Does it decrease the number of aggressive statements made among family members over the course of a week?

Personal and Life Satisfaction

Does participation in a community reintegration program increase the life satisfaction of adults with chronic mental illnesses?

Does an increase in the number of daily high-challenge and high-skill experiences increase the level of daily affect of older adults residing in retirement apartments?

Societal and Health Care System Outcomes

Does participation in a high adventure outdoor recreation program decrease the frequency of drug use among a group of adolescents with drug addictions?

Does participation in a sensory stimulation program decrease the number of times an older adult with dementia is restrained over the course of a month?

* The research priorities listed in this table were reported by Coyle, Kinney, and Shank (1991).

methods (i.e., experimental, survey, case history) and provide examples of their use by TR researchers and practitioners.

Experimental designs involve a researcher manipulating or changing something in the environment, which is considered the independent variable, and measuring its effect on the dependent variable (Babbie, 1992). **Survey methods** typically involve a researcher asking subjects a large number of questions at one point in time (Babbie, 1992). This may be done by sending a questionnaire through the mail or during an interview conducted face-to-face or over the telephone. **Case studies** examine phenomenon within the real life situation (Yin, 1994). Therapeutic recreation specialists frequently use case studies to document a client's behavior as he or she is involved in each phase of the TR process. In order to better understand the usefulness of these methods in therapeutic recreation, let's review several research studies that have used these methods.

Experimental Design. Several studies utilizing an experimental design have been conducted to examine whether efficacy information provided to depressed adolescents during participation in video games enhances their perceived efficacy and performance (Ellis, Maughan-Pritchett, & Ruddell, 1993; Maughan & Ellis, 1991). These studies were designed to test the use of Bandura's Self-Efficacy theory in therapeutic recreation interventions. Self-efficacy theory indicates that individuals assess a situation by considering the abilities needed to successfully execute a task and an assessment of whether they possess the abilities needed. Individuals draw information from four areas, including performance accomplishments, vicarious experiences, emotional arousal, and physiological arousal (Bandura, 1986).

Maughan and Ellis (1991) hypothesized that adolescents with diagnoses of major depression who received the four sources of efficacy information would have higher efficacy expectations for playing a video game than adolescents who did not receive the efficacy information. They tested this hypothesis with a group of thirty-two adolescents hospitalized on an in-patient psychiatric hospital. Using an experimental design, half of the subjects received the efficacy information while playing a video game (i.e., the treatment group) and half received no efficacy information while playing the video game (i.e., the control group).

You may be wondering what a therapeutic recreation specialist could do to provide efficacy information to the participants in the treatment group. Well, keep in mind that the four sources of information include vicarious experiences, emotional arousal, performance accomplishments, and verbal persuasion. As each subject entered the room to play the video game, Maughan and Ellis (1991) arranged the situation so that the subject would observe a "confederate" who was presumed to be a peer playing the game successfully. This provided a vicarious experience! The therapeutic recreation specialist would then offer the choice of opening windows or dimming the lights (i.e., controlling emotional arousal). The verbal persuasion and performance accomplishments were provided during the ten minutes of playing video games. The specialist was able to use any of ten preselected phrases to persuade the subject to continuing playing and to attribute success to the subject. These phrases included: "you are very good at this game" and "great move" (Maughan & Ellis, 1991). The subjects in the control group were invited to play the video game for ten minutes; although, they received none of the four sources of efficacy information. Following the intervention (i.e., participation in video games) all subjects were asked to complete a questionnaire that measured their perceived efficacy in playing video games.

Did these sources of information effect subjects' perceived efficacy in video games? Maughan and Ellis (1991) reported that the subjects who participated in the treatment group and received the efficacy information had scores on an Efficacy Questionnaire that were significantly higher than those subjects in the control group who received no efficacy information. The findings of this study substantiate the role of the therapist in structuring leisure experiences that foster positive outcomes for clients. Ellis, Maughan-Pritchett, and Ruddell (1993) have continued this line of research in order to identify the effect of each specific source of information on clients' perceived efficacy.

Survey Methods. Studies may utilize survey methods to examine how leisure attitudes, motivations, levels of perceived freedom are related to demographic and disability variables (e.g., Blakely & Dattilo, 1993; Caldwell, Adolph, & Gilbert, 1989; Coyle et al., 1993; Smith & Yoshioka, 1992). For example, Blakely and Dattilo examined the relationship between demographic characteristics of individuals with alcohol and drug addictions and levels of leisure motivation associated with the intellectual, social, competence-mastery, and stimulus-avoidance subscales of the Leisure Motivation Scale (Beard & Ragheb, 1983). Thirty-one adults participating in treatment programs were asked to complete a questionnaire pertaining to demographic variables (e.g., age, gender, education, choice of drug) and the Leisure Motivation Scale.

When examining how the participants' scores on the four subscales of the leisure motivation scale differed in relation to demographic variables, the researchers reported that individuals who were thirty-five or younger reported a higher level of motivation for competence-mastery pursuits than those over the age of thirty-five. Levels of leisure motivation were not found to vary by education. However, men were found to report higher levels of leisure motivation for intellectual, social, and competence-mastery pursuits than women. Lastly, the researchers reported that individuals who identified alcohol as their drug of use reported a significantly higher level of motivation for intellectual pursuits than individuals who chose cocaine or crack.

You may be wondering how these findings may be useful to a therapeutic recreation specialist. As we consider the findings, it is important to remember that Blakely and Dattilo (1993) indicated that the sample is very small and cannot be generalized to all individuals with addictions. However, they suggest that it is important for therapeutic recreation specialists to realize that our clients differ in level and type of motivation for leisure. Perhaps, therapeutic recreation specialists designing interventions with and for clients with addictions may find it beneficial to identify a client's area of motivation and build on the client's leisure motivation when initially involving him or her in treatment. Further work is needed to identify the "whys" of motivation. For instance, are individuals showing a low level of motivation in certain areas because they do not possess skills in that area? If that is the case, interventions may be designed to increase skill level and outcome measures could assess whether as skills increase, motivation for participation increases.

Case Study Methods. Case studies may be developed to report on the therapeutic recreation process as carried out with a specific client. Negley (1994) developed such a case history based on her work with a 25-year-old woman who had a diagnosis of major depression. The therapeutic recreation intervention was implemented on an outpatient basis and designed to increase the client's ability to express feelings, experience feelings of self-worth, and engage in leisure and social experiences. Sessions were held twice a week for approximately two years. Negley reported using a variety of recreation activities, including art, music, journaling, and physical activities. Over the course of treatment, Negley documented the client's change in self-expression and leisure and social behavior. Therapeutic recreation specialists reading this published case history may benefit from examining the rationale for the use of certain activities and how the client responded to these interventions. This information may influence the treatment plans they develop with clients displaying characteristics similar to those of the client in Negley's case history.

Green and DeCoux (1994) presented a case history in which the effectiveness of a community recreation integration program with an 8-year-old boy with spina bifida was evaluated. The client, Nic, attended a regular second grade, participated in an integrated t-ball league at the local YMCA, and was interested in being integrated into the City Recreation Department's Youth Basketball Program. The City Recreation Department did not have a therapeutic recreation specialist employed on staff. Therefore, the authors served on a committee with Nic's parents and the community recreation director. The committee developed adaptations for basketball that would ". . . promote a positive, active leisure experience for Nic and his teammates, and their opponents" (Green & DeCoux, 1994, p. 43). Adaptations included having a member of the opposing team use a wheelchair whenever Nic was playing in the game. The committee also developed means of evaluating the integrated league for both Nic and other players. The evaluation data indicated that Nic had approximately the same number of opportunities to pass the ball during each game; however, he had significantly fewer opportunities to catch the ball. Social acceptance was evaluated by asking all members of the team to identify whom they would invite to a hypothetical birthday party. Nic was selected by his peers in equal proportion to other teammates. Therapeutic recreation specialists reading this case history may benefit from considering the adaptations that allowed Nic to be integrated successfully into a community-based program. This information may influence the reader's current and future approaches to integrating clients into community recreation programs.

As an entry-level practitioner you may have the opportunity to observe a researcher conduct a research project using an experimental, survey, or case history method. It is also possible that you may assist with some aspect of a research study. Given either of these opportunities you will notice that the research process follows a number of steps. The research process may be broken down into six general steps:

1. The researcher begins by identifying the problem, which often begins by asking questions.
2. The researcher then investigates what is currently known about the research problem. A review of literature is undertaken.
3. At this point the researcher is ready to begin designing the study. The researcher decides what methods to use for collecting data and identifies subjects/clients for inclusion in the study.
4. Data are collected.
5. Data are analyzed.
6. Findings are reported. The researcher will usually report the findings to the agencies involved in the study. Furthermore, findings are reported at professional conferences and in professional journals.

The research studies that we reviewed by Maughan and Ellis (1991) and Blakely and Dattilo (1993) followed these general steps. The works by Negley (1994) and Green and DeCoux (1994) followed a modified application of these steps, as is appropriate for case histories (Yin, 1994). All of the reviewed studies were published in the *Therapeutic Recreation Journal*.

Research and the Entry-Level Practitioner. Over the course of the past decade there has been much discussion as to the roles a therapeutic recreation practitioner may take in regard to research. Based on a survey of members of the National Therapeutic Recreation Society in the southeastern region of the United States, Bullock, McGuire, and Barch (1984) reported that practitioners indicated that their two most important roles in relation to research were to (a) keep up to date on research in the field, and (b) incorporate research findings into their jobs.

More recently, there has been much discussion as to how educators, researchers, and practitioners may work together to generate research in therapeutic recreation (Savell, Huston, & Malkin, 1993). Savell, Huston, and Malkin have proposed a collaborative research relationship that is initiated by practitioners in therapeutic recreation. This approach fosters the development of research studies that address issues encountered by practitioners on a daily basis. Following the practitioner's identification of a research question, an educator or researcher is invited to collaborate in the development and implementation of the applied research project.

Entry-level practitioners may be employed in a setting in which collaborative research is being conducted. Further, as entry-level practitioners enhance their clinical knowledge and skills, they may choose to develop a collaborative relationship with researchers in order to address clinical issues in therapeutic recreation.

Staying Informed on Current Research in Therapeutic Recreation. Striving to stay informed of current research allows therapeutic recreation specialists to be aware of innovative and unique approaches to carrying out the therapeutic recreation process. Furthermore, research findings allow therapeutic recreation specialists to begin to understand under what conditions therapeutic recreation interventions are effective.

A number of journals are available for therapeutic recreation students and professionals who are interested in keeping themselves informed of the research findings in the field. The *Therapeutic Recreation Journal* and the *Annual in Therapeutic Recreation* are publications that include research reports. Therapeutic recreation specialists may also stay informed of current research in the field by attending national and regional conferences where research is presented. The Leisure Research Symposium, which is part of the National Recreation and Park Association Congress, the American Therapeutic Recreation Association Annual Conference, and the Midwest Symposium on Therapeutic Recreation are several of the conferences that sponsor presentations of therapeutic recreation research.

As mentioned earlier, further study of research methods and processes will assist students and entry-level therapeutic recreation specialists in fully understanding research reports and articles. Many students are able to take classes designed to focus solely on the research process. Being able to understand research reports and staying informed of the research being conducted in the field is one way for therapeutic recreation specialists to broaden their understanding of the effectiveness of the therapeutic recreation process. Research is another avenue therapeutic recreation specialists have for enhancing their knowledge and seeking professional growth.

SUMMARY

Therapeutic recreation professionals are continually committed to gaining new knowledge and refining previously learned clinical skills. Upon entering the workplace, there are a number of avenues available to therapeutic recreation specialists seeking professional growth. The management of the department or agency in which one works will influence staff members' job descriptions, resources, and supervision. A therapeutic recreation specialist who finds himself or herself in a position with a job description that matches his or her professional interests, indicates adequate resources, and offers general and clinical supervision may be in an optimal environment for professional growth. The consultation process is another arena in which a staff member may have the opportunity to develop further his or her professional skills. Lastly, research in therapeutic recreation is an exciting means by which therapeutic recreation specialists may continually question current practice and broaden their understanding of the effectiveness of the therapeutic recreation process.

READING COMPREHENSION QUESTIONS

1. What is meant by human and nonhuman resources?
2. What types of questions would a job applicant want to ask a manager/supervisor in order to obtain information on opportunities for professional growth?
3. What is the difference between general and clinical supervision?
4. Name several clinical skills that may be evaluated during the clinical supervision process.
5. In what contexts does clinical supervision occur?
6. Outline a situation that calls for a consultant. What type of consultation would you need in this situation?
7. What are the different types of consultation?
8. What types of roles does a consultant use during the consultation process?
9. Why is it important for a consultant to act as a catalyst of change?
10. Describe the stages in the consultation process. How do they differ from one another?
11. Define research.
12. What are the research topics that are currently identified as very important by therapeutic recreation specialists?
13. How do therapeutic recreation specialists stay informed of research being conducted in the field?
14. Describe two types of research.
15. Outline the steps in the research process.

SUGGESTED LEARNING ACTIVITIES

1. Invite several therapeutic recreation supervisors to class to discuss opportunities that entry-level therapeutic recreation specialists have for professional growth.
2. Contact the professional organization for therapeutic recreation in your state. Request information on the cost and benefits of membership. Also ask for information on the organization's committees, including the titles and tasks of the committees and how the committees disseminate information to the members.
3. Work on the following problem in a small group. You are a therapeutic recreation specialist working in a rehabilitation facility. Plans for a geriatric wing have been announced. Your department has the opportunity to hire a consultant who is knowledgeable in the area of gerontology to help plan a new program. Discuss the type of consultation, consultant roles, and the process that you would most likely experience in this situation.
4. Interview a therapeutic recreation consultant and determine the types of consultation and roles most frequently used by the consultant.
5. Working with a small group of students, identify one research question for each of the six areas of research identified in Temple University's *Benefits of therapeutic recreation: A consensus view* (Coyle et al., 1991).
6. Review a research study that has been reported in *Therapeutic Recreation Journal, Journal of Expanding Horizons in Therapeutic Recreation,* or *Annual in Therapeutic Recreation.*

REFERENCES

Austin, D.R. (1982). Therapeutic recreation research: An overview. *Abstracts from the 1982 Symposium on Leisure Research.* Washington, DC: National Recreation and Park Association.

Austin, D.R. (1986). Clinical supervision in therapeutic recreation. *Journal of Expanding Horizons in Therapeutic Recreation, 1,* 7–13.

Austin, D.R. (1991). *Therapeutic recreation: Processes and techniques.* Champaign, IL: Sagamore Publishing.

Babbie, E. (1992). *The practice of social research.* Belmont, CA: Wadsworth Publishing Company.

Bandura, A. (1986). *Social learning theory.* Englewood Cliffs, NJ: Prentice Hall.

Beard, J., & Ragheb, M. (1983). Measuring leisure motivation. *Journal of Leisure Research, 15,* 219–228.

Bedini, L.A., & Wu, Y. (1994). A methodological review of research in *Therapeutic Recreation Journal* from 1986 to 1990. *Therapeutic Recreation Journal, 28*(2), 87–98.

Blakely, T.L., & Dattilo, J. (1993). An exploratory study of leisure motivation patterns of adults with alcohol and drug addictions. *Therapeutic Recreation Journal, 27*(4), 230–238.

Bullock, C.C. (1993). Ways of knowing: The naturalistic and positivistic perspectives on research. In M. Malkin & C.Z. Howe (Eds.), *Research in therapeutic recreation: Concepts and methods* (pp. 25–42). State College, PA: Venture Publishing.

Bullock, C., McGuire, F., & Barch, E. (1984). Perceived research needs of therapeutic recreators. *Therapeutic Recreation Journal, 18*(3), 17–24.

Caldwell, L.L., Adolph, S., & Gilbert, A. (1989). Caution! Leisure counselors at work: Long term effects of leisure counseling. *Therapeutic Recreation Journal, 23*(3), 41–49.

Caplan, G. (1970). *The theory and practice of mental health consultation.* New York: Basic Books.

Cherniss, C., & Egnatios, E. (1977). Styles of clinical supervision in community mental health programs. *Journal of Consulting and Clinical Psychology, 45*(6), 1195–1196.

Code of Ethics of the National Therapeutic Recreation Society. (1985). *Therapeutic Recreation Journal, 19*(1), 71–72.

Compton, D.M. (1984). Research priorities in recreation for special populations. *Therapeutic Recreation Journal, 18*(1), 9–17.

Compton, D.M. (1989). Research initiatives in therapeutic recreation. In D.M. Compton (Ed.), *Issues in therapeutic recreation: A profession in transition* (pp. 427–444). Champaign, IL: Sagamore Publishing.

Coyle C. P. et al. (1991). *Benefits of therapeutic recreation: A consensus view.* Philadelphia, PA: Temple University.

Coyle, C.P., Kinney, W.B., & Shank, J.W. (1991). A summary of benefits common to therapeutic recreation. In C.P. Coyle et al. (Eds.), *Benefits of therapeutic recreation: A consensus view.* Philadelphia, PA: Temple University.

Coyle, C.P., et al. (1993). Psychosocial functioning and changes in leisure lifestyle among individuals with chronic secondary health problems related to spinal cord injury. *Therapeutic Recreation Journal, 27*(4), 239–252.

Culkin, D.F., & Kirsh, S.L. (1986). *Managing human resources in recreation, parks, and leisure services.* New York: Macmillan.

Dattilo, J., McCormick, B., & Scott, D. (1991). Answering questions about therapeutic recreation Part II: Choosing research methods. *Annual in Therapeutic Recreation, 2,* 85–95.

Ellis, G.D., Maughan-Pritchett, M., & Ruddell, E. (1993). Effects of attribution-based verbal persuasion and imagery on self-efficacy of adolescents diagnosed with major depression. *Therapeutic Recreation Journal, 27*(2), 83–97.

Erchul, W.P., & Schulte, A.C. (1993). Gerald Caplan's contributions to professional psychology: Conceptual underpinnings. In W. P. Erchul (Ed.), *Consultation in community, school, and organizational practice: Gerald Caplan's contributions to professionals psychology* (pp. 3–40). Washington, DC: Taylor & Francis.

Green, F.P., & DeCoux, V. (1994). A procedure for evaluating the effectiveness of a community recreation integration program. *Therapeutic Recreation Journal, 28*(1), 41–47.

Iso-Ahola, S. (1988). Research in therapeutic recreation. *Therapeutic Recreation Journal, 22*(1), 7–13.

Keller, M.J. (1985). Creating a positive work environment for therapeutic recreation personnel. *Therapeutic Recreation Journal, 19*(1), 36–43.

Keller, M.J. (1989). Professional leadership: Honor or responsibility? In D.M. Compton (Ed.), *Issues in therapeutic recreation: A profession in transition* (pp. 35–48). Champaign, IL: Sagamore Publishing.

Kerlinger, F.N. (1973). *Foundations of Behavioral Research.* New York: Holt, Rinehart & Winston.

Kurpius, D. (1978). Consultation theory and process: An integrated model. *Personnel and Guidance Journal, 56,* 335–338.

Lippitt, G., & Lippitt, R. (1986). *The consulting process in action.* San Diego, CA: University Associates.

Malkin, M.J. (1993). Issues and needs in therapeutic recreation research. In M.J. Malkin & C.Z. Howe (Eds.), *Research in therapeutic recreation: Concepts and methods* (pp. 3–23). State College, PA: Venture Publishing.

Maughan, M., & Ellis, G.D. (1991). Effect of efficacy information during recreation participation on efficacy judgments of depressed adolescents. *Therapeutic Recreation Journal, 25*(1), 50–59.

McConnell, C.R. (1993). *The effective health care supervisor.* Gaithersburg, MD: Aspen Publishers, Inc.

McCormick, B., Dattilo, J., & Scott, D. (1991). Answering questions about therapeutic recreation research Part I: Formulating research questions. *Annual in Therapeutic Recreation, 2,* 78–84.

Munson, C.E. (1993). *Clinical social work supervision.* Binghamton, NY: Haworth Press.

Negley, S.K. (1994). Recreation therapy as an outpatient intervention. *Therapeutic Recreation Journal, 28*(1), 35–40.

Rieman, D.W. (1992). *Strategies in social work consultation.* White Plains, NY: Longman.

Riley, B. (1991). Introduction. In C.P. Coyle et al. (Eds.), *Benefits of therapeutic recreation: A consensus view.* Philadelphia, PA: Temple University.

Savell, K., Huston, A., & Malkin, M. (1993). Collaborative research: Bridging the gap between practitioners and researchers/educators. In M. Malkin & C. Z. Howe (Eds.), *Research in therapeutic recreation: Concepts and methods* (pp. 77–96). State College, PA: Venture Publishing.

Shank, J.W., Kinney, W.B., & Coyle, C.P. (1993). Efficacy studies in therapeutic recreation research: The need, the state of the art, and future implications. In M. Malkin & C. Z. Howe (Eds.), *Research in therapeutic recreation: Concepts and methods* (pp. 301–335). State College, PA: Venture Publishing.

Smith, S.A., & Yoshioka, C.F. (1992). Recreation functioning and depression in people with arthritis. *Therapeutic Recreation Journal, 26*(4), 21–30.

Snow, D.L., & Corse, S.J. (1986). The process of consultation: Critical issues. In F.V. Mannino et al. (Eds.), *Handbook of mental health consultation* (pp. 393–431). Washington, DC: Department of Health and Human Services.

Voelkl, J.E., Austin, D.R., & Morris, C. (1992). An analysis of articles published in the *Therapeutic Recreation Journal* during the 1980s. *Therapeutic Recreation Journal, 26*(2), 46–50.

Witt, P. (1988). Therapeutic recreation research: Past, present, and future. *Therapeutic Recreation Journal, 22*(1), 14–23.

Yin, R. K. (1994). *Case study research: Design and methods.* Thousand Oaks, CA: Sage Publications.

CHAPTER 18

ISSUES AND TRENDS

MICHAEL E. CRAWFORD

OBJECTIVES

- Describe the relationship between economic forces present in American society and community special recreation services.
- Identify populations at risk in American society and the contributory social force responsible for this status.
- Understand what effect political forces exerted on the TR service ethic in the last ten years.
- Identify critical issues for special recreation in the area of service motive.
- Realize the relationship between applied and action research priorities and specific client treatment issues.
- Understand the issues surrounding uniformity of TR university curricula on a national basis.
- Describe the relationship between licensure of personnel and extended preparation of practitioners.
- Know the issues surrounding the concept of clinical specialization in TR university curricula.
- Identify specific problems with TR internship guidelines for students.
- Differentiate between certification and licensure of personnel.
- Understand the issues surrounding multinational organizations for TR.
- Describe the relationship between TR and other national activity therapy groups.
- Realize the issues involved in creating a mechanism whereby a code of ethics can be monitored and enforced.

In Chapter 2, six different characteristics of a profession were presented to organize a discussion of the chronology of therapeutic recreation as it has occurred in this country. In this chapter we will continue to organize the internal trends and issues affecting therapeutic recreation along these six criteria. Additionally, certain economic, social, and political trends in society at large will be alluded to. These larger macrotrends of American society will be discussed briefly as external forces shaping human services philosophy and delivery in general, and professional therapeutic recreation services specifically.

EXTERNAL FORCES SHAPING THERAPEUTIC RECREATION

Issue: Economic Forces. The so-called "taxpayer revolution" began in California in the late

1970s with the passage of Proposition 13, the now famous tax lid bill. The impact of Proposition 13, which effectively set limits on the amount of money a legislature could spend, was a reprioritization of public spending (Murphy, 1980, p. 207). Unfortunately for recreation professionals, most taxpayers agreed that fire, police, and sanitation services were more important than recreation centers, parks, and golf courses. As copycat bills of Proposition 13 spread across the country, traditional recreation services suffered greatly in the "budget wars" that followed. Because of this mandated reduction, recreation budgets were reprioritized, and within this process, programs for special populations were either substantially reduced, eliminated, or as was more often the case, never established. The recreation profession thus was placed at a great disadvantage in attempting to respond to the normalization and mainstreaming ethics of the time. Just as legal and social trends were placing emphasis on provision of community services for formerly institutionalized citizens, the recreation profession's ability to respond in kind with greater diversity of programming was severely limited budgetarily. As a result, there are still many communities today (particularly in small town settings, populations of 100,000 or less) where no formal municipal special recreation programs exist or only a few token efforts, such as participation in special olympics or senior centers, are provided as a very unsatisfactory partial solution.

Things have not improved a great deal in the 1990s. In a recent national survey of public parks and recreation departments (Havitz & Spigner, 1992) it was concluded that the unemployed (whether retired or homeless) were the most at risk of being denied access to basic recreational services. In fact, in communities with the greatest need, 31 percent offered no discounts or free admission for low income groups, and 16 percent offered nothing to senior citizens. In addition, the full impact of the American with Disabilities Act (ADA) has yet to be felt. The retrofit of existing playgrounds, swimming pools, and other facilities to satisfy both the accessibility and usability requirements of the ADA has added additional pressure to already tight operations budgets. Though a financial exigency option is available under the law (particularly needed for small/rural operations without significant numbers of physically challenged consumers residing in their area), the majority of municipal, county, state, and public recreation providers are required to respond to ADA mandates. Some have chosen to close or dismantle facilities such as playgrounds rather than engage in expensive retrofits. In these cases it could be argued that the ADA impact actually has been to limit access for everyone (e.g., where once stood a playground, now stands a bare field). The cost of opening new facilities has also climbed dramatically because of ADA requirements, and as a result, both the number and rate of new public facilities have slowed (Crawford, 1995). One of the most pressing challenges for therapeutic recreation practitioners in the 1990s and beyond will be to reintroduce the service ethic of the TR profession to public recreation services by pushing for increased budget and programming resources in order to respond to the legislative mandates of the laws such as the ADA, as well as respond to our moral service imperative to provide services for the socially disadvantaged.

Issue: Social Forces. Many sociologists and social psychologists have discussed the 1980s as the end of the era of social activism (Raab & Lipset, 1980, p. 138). The eighties were the decade when the "me" generation came to the forefront. Suddenly social issues that had been so central to American thought in the 1960s and '70s (e.g., environmental quality, racial desegregation, normalization of institutionalized special populations, etc.) took a back seat to more myopic causes. The so-called neoradical movements of the eighties, women's rights, gay rights, and the unionization of traditionally professional groups resulting in teacher and nursing strikes, etc., were symptomatic of a society that had become self-concerned. As the "I've got mine, you get yours" approach to lifestyle became more entrenched, many important social programs and movements which had flourished and gained momentum in the 1970s were cut back (Lasch, 1984).

Today, the result of this backsliding of social concern can be seen in part in the large number of homeless and street people that has hit epidemic proportions in our country. Current estimates now top three million individuals, including entire family networks with small children (Samuelson, 1991). Over one million of these individuals are thought to suffer from some serious mental health problems such as post traumatic stress disorder or schizophrenia (Marine, 1993) and over 750 die on the streets each year due to lack of medical care (Mercer, 1993). Perhaps equally as troubling is the growing "compassion fatigue" so many of our civic leaders and general population seem to have adopted toward this population (Mercer, 1993).

Similarly shocking social statistics include the number of children living below the poverty line. In 1993 the number of children living in poverty hit a thirty year high mark with 15.7 million (nearly one in four) being raised under conditions of economic duress (Usdansky, 1994). Coupled with this are the shocking statistics that between three and five children are killed by their parents or caregivers daily in this country (Mones, 1994). In the area of child abuse, official reported incidents have risen nearly four-fold since the 1970s. In 1993 one million cases of abuse and neglect were confirmed (over three million were reported). Over 1,300 of these cases ended with a child's death. We also now know that disabled children are likely to be abused at twice the rate of "normal" children (AP Wire Services, 1993). Overburdened and underfunded state run child protective services (caseworker loads of up to one per 250 families) simply cannot keep pace (Edmonds, 1995).

We see further evidence of social disdain and decay in the rise in violent crimes as once again (for the third year in a row) the FBI Uniform Crime Bureau reported that murder, aggravated assaults, rape, and robbery rose over 10 percent nationwide from the previous year (Rowley, 1994). We also have convincing evidence of disenfranchised youth that should sober us regarding our lack of concern—the dramatic rise in suicide rates among gay and lesbian youth is now three times that of heterosexual teenagers (Farrow & Delsher, 1991). Obviously lingering prejudice and stigmatization continue to contribute to feelings of despair and social isolation (Grossman, 1992).

In addition to these tremendous social problems, we have increasing recidivism in our institutional mental health systems (*Time,* 1987; Martinsen, 1990), overcrowded prisons (Hull, 1987; Grant & Johnstone, 1991) and deplorable conditions in many of the nation's nursing homes (Teaff, 1985, p. 5; Bergman, 1991). All of this evidence speaks to a society that has effectively turned a deaf ear to the cries for social reform necessary to build the "kinder and gentler society" that President Bush called for in his 1988 campaign.

In the 1990s there is some evidence that a turn in public perceptions may be slowly emerging. The Roper Center (1990) reported that people identified leisure as "more important" than work for the first time in fifteen years of national survey work. Similarly, a 1992 Gallup Poll showed that volunteerism was growing fastest among those eighteen to twenty-four (at least one day per year per person), and second fastest among people sixty or older. A report from the National Volunteer Center in 1993 concluded that the total worth of American volunteerism reached $182 billion, and that some 40 percent of the total population contributed. Perhaps the "me" generation does feel a new sense of social responsibility. High profile programs like former president Jimmy Carter's "Habitat for Humanity" undoubtedly make a role model contribution to the new "feel good about giving back" movement.

Along with these optimistic facts and figures, however, come some disturbing trends as well. There is evidence that Americans are feeling more stressed and stretched than ever before. As Juliet Schor, Harvard economist and author of *The Overworked American; The Unexpected Decline of Leisure* notes; ingredients for national fatigue have been slowly accumulating for a long time. Contributing factors include the explosion of single-parent families, the trend for both parents to work outside the home, the substitution of part-time and second jobs in place of leisure and family time. There are also the psychological hazards of corporate downsizing that many people face daily (fear of losing their jobs for not working hard enough), and for others the growing emotional duress caused from the increasing gap between society's problems and the inability of our social institutions to provide meaningful solutions (e.g., teachers, social workers, police) (Hancock et al., 1995).

The invasiveness of technology also seems to contribute to modern "leisure-lack," as more and more Americans work from home or in their cars or commuter trains. Increasing numbers of us are literally not able to really get away from the work-self identity. The high technology revolution as of 1995 has put 25 million beepers in use. Cellular phones are used by 11 percent of the population, 6 percent of all households now have fax machines and 37 percent have some form of personal computer (Hancock et al., 1995). It can be argued that high technology has not led to more efficient work so much as it has added/extended the reach of work behaviors to our cars, homes, walks with the dog, picnics with the family, etc. The results can be measured in the increasing cases of fatigue and depression (Martinsen, 1990) as well as unfit population (seven out of ten adults are now overweight according to the U.S government height and weight tables) (Hancock et al., 1995).

Therapeutic recreation services can and should have an impact in the repair of the social welfare network and the improvement of our human services systems. We also have a place within the wellness movement and have the potential to make a difference with the quality-of-life problems so many Americans are now facing. To do so, however, requires greater assertiveness with policy makers at the national level as well as effective local educational and political strategies. One of the greatest "survival" issues for the TR profession as we proceed through the 1990s will be whether the TR profession is sufficiently mature enough to launch new service initiatives. If the profession is to continue it's role as an important social advocate for our populations that are in crises, an expanded and aggressive social agenda is required.

Issue: Political Trends. The majority of the legislative efforts of the seventies and early eighties were aimed at prohibiting exclusion of persons with disabilities from facilities and programs. To this end, a number of laws (the most important of which were reviewed in Chapter 2) were enacted to guarantee equal opportunity. In the main, however, these laws were limited to rights of physical access, thus while you could not build a building with federal monies that a wheelchair patron could not physically get in and out of, there were no forceful companion programming provisions which insisted or encouraged you to provide anything inside the building. The wave of fiscal conservatism for social programming that flourished during the eight years of the Reagan presidency resulted in shrinking federal dollars for human and social services. The rationale for such cuts were that new social factors, namely increased volunteerism, corporate giving, and cooperation between advocate associations and recreation and park departments would take place and, in effect, take up the fiscal slack. As noted above, however, the "me" generation wasn't particularly interested in such social advocacy, and corporation giving either didn't keep pace, or was mistargeted. For example, offering public symphony concerts in the park as a one-shot charitable programming event does a lot for the corporate image of giving but doesn't exactly meet the daily recreation needs of inner-city youth and the problems they face with so much unchallenged discretionary time. Thus, in the 1980s, the budget dollars to support the programming needs that had been established by the important legislative inroads in the areas of equal access and educational and vocational equality didn't materialize.

As the political agendas for the 1990s develop, it remains to be seen if the recreation profession can reestablish itself as a key ingredient in master social planning. The Reagan era essentially promoted deprofessionalizing the public image of recreation services and to a degree was successful (why fund it when you can do it with volunteers and corporate advocacy). The reprofessionalization of service delivery will depend in large measure on mounting a counter public campaign that will arrest the steady erosion of financing therapeutic recreation in the public sector.

However, as the political agenda for the 1990s has developed thus far, an increasing and ever divergent set of economic, political, and social forces are pulling macrosocial policy planning in simultaneously incompatible directions. Chief among these forces are the debates over unfunded mandates and the so-called "new federalism," problems with social security and SSI programs, and the national debate on health care reform. Each of these forces may have tremendous effects (either positively or negatively) on the delivery of the TR service mission.

The ADA may well be the last of the great federal mandates. Following in the tradition of the Equal Education Act of the 1970s (P.L. 94-142) the ADA's sweeping requirement for accessibility and usability across public services represents a true landmark accomplishment in the civil rights movement for persons with disabilities. However, it comes with an equally impressive price tag. The estimates for fully implementing the ADA across public transportation systems alone is staggering (over $25 billion by the year 2020) (West, 1991). On the heels of this legislation has come an increasingly heated national debate on the now complex and cumbersome relationship between federal, state, and local governments (Webber, 1995). The cry to curtail and/or even reverse or eliminate unfunded federal mandates (like the ADA) is growing stronger. The key objection is that state and local governments should not be required by the federal government to provide specific programs or services without receiving corresponding funding. The raw politics of unfunded mandates are rather simple. The nation's governors and state and local leaders have made it clear that elimination of unfunded mandates is the prerequisite to a debate on a constitutional amendment to balance the federal budget. They are afraid that Washington officials will simply pass the burden onto them.

As the debate on mandates intensifies, instances of defiance and/or lack of compliance with previous federal mandates is mounting. Regarding the ADA, the June, 1994, report of the Government Accounting Office (GAO) presented to the U.S. Congress a disturbing picture of foot-dragging. Nearly half of the businesses and government facilities visited by GAO auditors had yet to remove a single barrier, and half of these had no specific plans to do so in the future (TADAR, 1994). Whether due to technical uncertainty or linked to attitudes of defiance or cries of financial exigency, ADA compliance remains weak and the resources of the federal government to ensure such have clearly been exceeded.

Without improved accountability and responsibility for federal mandates already on the book, the likelihood of revisiting or even rescinding current laws like the ADA becomes more plausible with the passage of time. Negative press coverage of the ADA has also begun to appear. A recent national AP wire story spotlighted a Dade County, Florida expenditure of $18,500 to provide wheel chair ramp access so that a single complaint regarding access to the county's only nude beach could be resolved (AP, 1995). The cumulative effects of such negative reporting, while difficult to measure, clearly serve to reinforce opponents not only of the ADA, but those critics of big federal government who continue to assert that matters relating to social programs, education, job training, and the like are best left to local and state governments. Ultimately some form of unfunded mandate legislation will emerge from Congress. Whether it will assist or injure the case for the ADA (and similar health/human service programs that impact the TR service mission) remains to be seen.

Social Security's surplus will come to an end by about 2010 when demands for benefits will outstrip revenues. Without serious adjustment, the deficit for that program alone may well topple one trillion dollars (Welch, 1995). At the heart of the debate over social security spending is the "smoke and mirrors" budget practice of the U.S. Congress in raiding the social security trust fund on an annual basis in order to reduce the overall size of the federal deficit. In 1994 social security represented 22 percent of the federal budget and became the largest federal social program. In the same year, some 70 billion dollars were "raided" and replaced with federal I.O.U.'s that may become worthless in time.

The problems of the social security program, though, are not solely driven by the inevitable explosion of retirees due to arrive in the next century, or by Congress's current mismanagement of the fund. In 1990 a U.S. Supreme Court decision made it easier for poor disabled children to qualify for federal aid under the Supplemental Security Income (SSI) program. Since this 1990 court decision, the number of disabled children supported by SSI (which is administered by the social security administration) has risen from 340,000 (1974) to 771,000 (1994). The cost of the program has also more than doubled. These trends and figures make SSI the most expensive and fastest growing federal welfare program. The number of recipients has risen sharply due to broadened eligibility, as well as a sharp rise in the number of low birth-weight infants, crack babies, and HIV infected children nationwide. Oddly, the cost of providing services has also been sharply and adversely affected by improved technology and devicing to assist the disabled. Motorized and adapted wheelchairs for instance can range from $3,800 to $24,000 or more and may last no longer than three to five years (McKee, 1995). Unfortunately, anecdotal cases of fraud have recently also hurt the legitimacy of SSI service. A recent investigation discovered instances where parents/caregivers had coached children to "flunk" I.Q. tests in order that the family might qualify for more aid (McKee, 1995).

As Congress struggles to put forward a balanced budget amendment, the ability to protect social security's "sacred cow" status will be increasingly difficult. Reductions in benefits and/or draconian measures like the elimination of SSI and aid to families with dependent children programs will surely be proposed and, if adopted, will lead to serious quality of life declines for the disabled and large numbers of retirees. Both of these populations are important constituencies of the TR service mission and depend upon our political lobby to help preserve their well being and favorable status as social claimants.

The health care crises in America has reached disturbing proportions (*Time,* 1991). Over 30 million Americans are without medical insurance, many small towns and rural areas cannot attract physicians, rising malpractice insurance rates have impacted quality pediatric care by forcing many physicians out of business (leading to a renewal of midwifery), and instances of profiteering among the leading pharmaceutical companies, medical fraud and poor care by physicians, and duplicitive and costly service among hospitals have all combined to create a quagmire of health care problems. The structure of relationships between doctors, health care agencies, and insurance companies are changing in very fundamental ways. As Congress continues to debate health care reform, the system itself is moving and the dominant forces have become pharmaceutical corporations, organized delivery systems and managed care programs. In fact, we are moving from cost-based reimbursement systems, where the incentive was to provide health care, to one of capitation and managed care, where the incentive is not to provide care (Benson, 1995). We are creating large and impersonal bureaucratic systems of health care with coverage and services based upon homogonized diagnostic related groups (DRGs) which frequently fail to provide needed care. The individual's right for regress under these systems is always "after the fact." One can appeal, or sue, or change coverage (if practical).

This march to lower health care costs comes with increased risk for all consumers but disporportionately for those who are traditionally vulnerable (e.g., the poor, the elderly, and persons with mental illness or developmental disabilities). Wolfensburger (1992) feels the coming complexity of national health care reform will take a particularly insidious turn toward socially devalued persons. As evidence, he cites a recent nursing study in which nurse responses were slower and more negative to patients with terminal illnesses than to those who were expected to recover.

Indeed, today a blend of defensive assertiveness and intelligence regarding technical procedures and cost coverage seems a requirement for all health care consumers. Those who cannot advocate for themselves are often at the total mercy of "the system."

As policy makers struggle to develop new mechanisms to curtail costs, health care consumers must insist on not being treated as statistical aggregates. The level of government oversight (some might say intrusion) to assure consumer protection has yet to be determined. However, the national trend to limit and/or restrict the number of days of in-patient treatment and the move toward increased treatment precision and accountability will ultimately force TR practitioners to move more swiftly in the areas of program delivery and justification.

For all of the rhetoric and furious debate about crime and drugs in this country, the federal response (as well as most state courthouses) has revolved around two main thrusts: hire more police officers, and build more prison cells. Crime and punishment is perhaps the one area in which Americans seem to completely lack the "generative spirit" that Eric Erikson (1968) links to maturity; the willingness to make short-term sacrifice that will produce long-term benefits for the next generation. Instead of responding to increased deviancy with treatment, we have used the more childlike knee-jerk reaction to punish. The result of dual national wars on drugs and crime are a clogged criminal justice system coupled with overflowing prison facilities about to collapse under their own weight. From 1990 to 1995, drug related arrests have increased ten-fold nationally to over one million court cases (Ortbals, 1995). Needless to say, the numbers of prosecutors, judges, public defenders, and probation officers have not similarly increased. Added to the war on drug arrests figures are the new "get tough" crime standards, the 1994 Federal Crime Act and an increasing number of sister state provisions (the so-called three strikes you're out laws) are now serving to clog already overcrowded state and federal prison systems. Many of the new inmates have been convicted for life on nonviolent drug possession offenses. This new generation of lifetime offender not only pose no significant threat to life or property, they also represent classes of individuals in which treatment and aftercare programs have been substantially validated. In fact, by incarcerating drug offenders in the poorly controlled prison environment (where gangs and illegal drug trafficking are the dominant social forces), one can argue that the convicted user has simply been sent to a life of use and addiction. In fact under our current set of laws, people who suffer from substance abuse are put into two classes—those who are not jailed and given treatment (alcoholics) and those who are, or will be, jailed and given no treatment (all other forms of drug dependent personalities). Public policy planners must decide whether limited prison space is to be reserved for violent offenders and those who pose a great risk to others, or whether we will continue to build more and more cells. The decriminalization of drug addicts and the reform/revision of the three-strike laws would be one step in reducing the financial burden to society. The Federal Office of Management and Budget predicted in 1995 (Ortbals, 1995, p. 12) that if current rates of federal spending held unabated, U.S. taxpayers would owe 82 percent of their income to government programs by the year 2010. Obviously many of the quick-fix "feel good" laws of the eighties and early nineties regarding crime and drugs will need to be revisited as the bills now coming due for enforcement and incarceration rise higher and higher. The painful truth is that dealing with complex issues with unsophisticated thinking often leads to expensive oversight or shortcomings. The overcrowding of our prisons and courts as a result of our approaches, our declaration of social war, is beginning to have a tremendous financial impact. Whatever the outcome, the TR profession must be prepared to respond to the needs of an aging and overcrowded prison population as well as contribute to treatment and aftercare programs as alternative models to incarceration and punishment.

Macrosocial, political, and economic issues may well determine ceilings under which therapeutic recreation services can operate in the upcoming years. However, the direction and development of the profession is still in large measure in our own hands. With this in mind there are a number of internal issues and trends, some positive and some negative, which bear identification and elaboration. Using the six characteristics of a profession previously identified in Chapter 2 as an organizational scheme, some of the more prevalent issues and trends will be briefly discussed.

Service Motive

In some ways the most pressing agenda for the TR profession in bringing its service motive forward is a more aggressive posture in ensuring that what limited practice standards exist are enforced. While it is encouraging that NTRS has finally asserted practice guidelines for clinical, residential, and community settings and that ATRA has followed suit with standards of their own (see Chapter 2), the compliance aspect of these documents is still purely voluntary. Even so, these standards have undoubtedly affected service in a positive way. Simply having the force of a national association behind you in attempting to convince an administrator or treatment team that a certain approach or resource is essential can go a long way in helping you to achieve that resource. However, most authorities acknowledge that the current standards do represent rather minimal attempts in defining a service mandate (Mobily, 1983; Carter, 1991).

A critical issue for both associations is to what extent monitoring and enforcement mechanisms can be designed and implemented. One of the earliest publications on quality assurance by ATRA (Riley, 1987) and a follow up sister publication on quality management (Riley, 1991) represent tangible first steps in detailing specific standards of TR practice which monitoring and compliance mechanisms might be based on. In the 1990s the main agenda for the ATRA leadership has clearly been to seek close political and programmatic affiliation with the allied health professions lobby. The collective accomplishments of having TR credentials and standards endorsed by the Joint Commission, CARF and HCFA (Health Care Finance Administration for Medicare and Medicaid) organizations, have dramatically and effectively extended, and to some extent solidified, the TR service motive. The failure of NTRS to address these key issues is in part one of the principle reasons ATRA's membership eclipsed NTRS's in such a short period of time in the 1990s.

While one could argue that one of the side issues facing clinical standards is perhaps one too many organizational advocates (NTRS, NCTRC, and ATRA combined), thus creating the potential for disagreement and confusion, an equally problematic issue for community practice standards is the lack of organized advocacy from an organizational standpoint. The "special recreation movement" (Kennedy, Smith, & Austin, 1991) within the TR profession has attempted to raise the visibility of special populations programming within communities by asserting it as the responsibility more or less of all recreation and park personnel. While such sentiments are understandably supportive of the overall goals of mainstreaming, they do little in the way of defining specific roles for the TR specialist. Are TR personnel with the special recreation settings to be consultants? Active program leaders? Evaluators? How are special recreators to interface with CTRS's and clinical services? Sylvester (1992) has asserted that TR should not simply accommodate itself into the health care system (as the ATRA and NCTRC leadership have so stridently pursued), but rather should challenge the status quo and insist that leisure for the purpose of well being become a focal point for reform of health care providers. Despite an eloquent, well-grounded moral and philosophical discourse, however, he provides no tangible first steps or operational plan for this "right to leisure" position. If the special recreation movement is to continue to be a dynamic force within TR, a strong organizational advocate must emerge and further the proposed service mission by providing programmatic details and support. Some have suggested this as the logical mission of NTRS over the coming decade, yet a definitive action plan to facilitate such has yet to be articulated.

Perhaps more disappointing than the lack of specific practice standards which clearly define role and mission of either clinical TR or special recreation is the lack of integration of the existing research base within service. By way of example, consider the current research base for community programming with the mentally retarded. This particular literature is more advanced and conclusive than any other aspect of our science to date. We have validated that the use of precision teaching techniques combined with small group instruction conducted in natural environments will result in increased leisure functioning for even the severely and multihandicapped individual (Crawford, 1986). The meta-analysis of research completed through the Temple University grant project (Coyle et al., 1991) validated the science of community integration, friendship role theory, and lifetime leisure skill development for the developmentally disabled. This review of scientific literature included over 300 citations. This process of programming should, therefore, be our practice standard. Yet as Schleien and his associates have so clearly articulated, we continue to accept massed, segregated programming within community centers in what has been described as a paramilitaristic takeover of the facility (Schleien et al., 1985) as an acceptable and all too often dominant form of program delivery. In addition, special camps dedicated to single disability groups, as well as Special Olympics programs and special centers continue to dominate the community special recreation scene. It is simply unacceptable, with the knowledge we have, to allow "yellow bus" programming of special participants to continue to dominate service provision within our communities. It should rapidly become an historical footnote for us (just as physicians tell their students of the days they used to give insulin shock therapy to the mentally ill instead of treatment through psychotropic medication, we too should eventually have to whisper about the days that we had to conduct massed segregated programming within communities). A critical issue for TR remains the failure of practitioners to incorporate the TR research base into contemporary practice.

One final side issue related to service motive deals more with the effective stagnation of our service delivery reach. Our inability to respond quickly to rapid societal needs in service settings remains a symptom of our relative youth. The 1991 National research conference at Temple (Coyle et al., 1991) was restricted (as driven by the state of the literature) to six key areas: Developmental Disabilities, Chemical Dependency, Gerontology, Pediatrics, Physical Medicine, and Psychiatry. The extension of service motive beyond this model to nontraditional areas and so-called minority conditions is relatively weak. Only in the 1990s has rhetoric for the staggering homelessness problem begun to emerge in the professional literature (Kunstler, 1991; Lahey, 1991) or has research documentation begun in earnest regarding low-incidence sub-specialties in mental health such as childhood sexual abuse survivors (Leitschuh & Brotons, 1991; Meister & Pedlar, 1992) or post-traumatic stress disorder (Attarian & Gault, 1992), or the role of leisure in alcoholism and drug addiction recovery (Carruthers & Hood, 1992; Blakely & Dattilo, 1993).

Perhaps most troubling of all has been our slow response to the AIDS crisis. Though declared a national epidemic by the Centers for Disease Control as early as 1986, the sum total of our response has been to collate and report on the progress of other disciplines in developing technique and process for working with these clients (Keller & Turner, 1990; Keller, 1992). The incorporation of a chapter on AIDS in this text is the first such TR curriculum incorporation among major publishing houses. As more and more of the population at large require medical care in skilled nursing, hospice, and death and dying centers over the next few decades, the question must be raised how will TR respond? Have we assembled a national task force to study the issue and recommend policy? What place does our therapy have within the treatment cycle for the AIDS patient? Other members of the Allied Health professions team are scrambling to lobby the public and private sectors for support and funding so they may more effectively respond to the crisis at hand. Unfortunately, TR has barely begun a response. We have a prime opportunity to extend, promote, and define clearly our service motive and abilities to the public. Our failure to organize and contribute in a meaningful way will not serve us well as future crises befall society. By contrast, during the polio scare of the 1950s (the last national health scare analogous to the hysteria surrounding the current AIDS crisis) activity therapists among polio wards were very much in demand and very central to hospital adjustment, care, and treatment of polio patients. This may have happened in part because the polio disease was so endemic to children (more than any other age group) and somehow the public, as well as our own professional perception, saw the importance of recreation as magnified. By contrast, AIDS, which is largely a disease of adults who are for the most part members of deviant or "devalued" groups (i.e., drug addicts and homosexuals), has not roused within us a clamor for action. This response displays at best indifference, and at worst social bigotry, on our part as professionals. Whether or not the national leadership of NTRS or ATRA can organize and respond in this current hour of need may write a great deal of the profession's future history in medical care settings.

Scientific Basis

Our body of knowledge has a very uneven base overall. The landmark review of research published through the efforts of the Temple University faculty (Coyle et al., 1991) covered only six client populations. Within this review, some populations had a wealth of research documentation (e.g., developmental disabilities and some psychiatric populations). Yet for other low-incidence groups (so-called minority disabilities) the review of research in TR ranged from scarce to nonexistent (e.g., HIV/AIDS, Cystic fibrosis, etc.). The summary typology from the Temple meta-analysis set forth a validated (in the sense that it was grounded in research across a variety of disorders/diseases/conditions) list of TR treatment benefits. These included (1) physical and health maintenance, (2) cognitive functioning, (3) psychosocial health, (4) growth and development, (5) personal life satisfaction and (6) prevention of secondary disability. An ATRA publication, Therapeutic Recreation Services (1992), provided complimentary (though poorly documented) support for the Temple typology. This document attempted to match treatment outcomes to a disability driven "menu" of common clinical disorders. It provided one interesting extension to the Temple review by identifying pain disorders as a clinical focus for TR. Its ultimate contribution however is from its organizational format and its marriage of disorder symtomology to treatment outcomes of TR. These two publications in the early 1990s represent the first true steps toward the formulation of standardized clinical treatment protocols which are grounded in research as opposed to philosophical position (e.g., the leisurability model) or historical programming practice (e.g., the monthly calendar model of diversionary service).

The lack of applied and action research studies which validate the effectiveness of the TR process as a client change agent in residential, clinical, and community setting remains the number one research priority of the field. Near the top of the list in this regard is the need for specific documentation of the long-term effectiveness of leisure counselling and education interventions and how these techniques might relate to reduced recidivism among institutional populations.

In a related vein, there are service- or client-specific side-issues which urgently need to be addressed. Perhaps most pressing is the growth of high-technology innovation within the medical rehabilitation field and what these rapid and exciting advancements might mean for increased leisure functioning. New sophisticated orthotic and prosthetic devising needs to be evaluated for recreational applicability. Adaptations like the "Chicago hand" (an adaptation of space age robotics driven by miniature servo-mechanisms controlled by the amputee's own residual nerve endings at the stump site) now can replace in some cases the old claw utility hook (Social Issues and Health Care Review, 1988). Similarly, extero-nervous and skeletal systems using the latest in microcomputer technology and aluminum and plastic robotics are making it possible for para- and quadrapelegics to ride bikes and walk again (Frank, 1988; Sherrill, 1993). Experimental work is also occurring with personal radar units and artificial optical systems for the blind (National Federation for the Blind, 1985; Sherrill, 1993), as well as increasingly sophisticated interactive computer technology for the multihandicapped (Dattilo & Barnett, 1985; Dattilo & Camarata, 1991). TR professionals should have a role in the development, testing, and refinement of these systems. Our own researchers and social scientists should be in the forefront of setting goals, prioritizing and defining development issues for the engineers, biomechanists, and computer scientists to solve. Yet all too often we are in a reactive mode when it comes to such innovation. Positioning ourselves as a profession to move to a proactive versus a reactive status regarding the cutting edge of medical technology should become a high priority for the field as the turn of the century approaches.

Regarding scientific professional issues, still unresolved is empirical grounding of the "leisure versus therapy" debate within therapeutic recreation service. The NTRS Code of Ethics and mission statements both assert the "right to leisure" as the purpose for TR services. Yet as Sylvester (1992, p. 10) reminds us, "Simply asserting a right, does not make it valid. It must also be justified." The Peterson and Gunn (1984) "Leisure Ability Model" remains an unvalidated service philosophy (some would say process) across most service settings and for many disability groups. If NTRS is to provide more than philosophical and moral arguments regarding the "rights" individuals with disabilities have for leisure, play, and recreation (Reynolds & O'Morrow, 1985, p. 226), then scientific evidence that leisure is a real social need (the absence of which is detrimental) and that the Leisurability Model is the vehicle whereby it is best afforded, must be forthcoming.

Extended Preparation

In 1983 Mobily wrote: "the current uniformity of national TR educational curricula is a mess." Unfortunately this criticism remains valid for the 1990s and probably will through the turn of the century. Despite two decades of life, the NRPA/AALR curriculum accreditation guidelines have not realized their desired effect. In 1994, 177 colleges and universities sent TR graduates through the NCTRC examination process (Connolly, 1995) yet only thirty-nine of these curricula have been formally reviewed and accredited by NRPA/AALR. Further, only eighty-eight programs had at least ten or more alumni sit for the exam (the minimum criterion for establishing a school's mean performance on the exam). The conclusion drawn from these figures is obvious. There are a lot of small recreation/leisure studies programs (perhaps only one or two faculty total) teaching a lot of unregulated curricula. To make matters worse, even among the accredited curricula the approach to standards is amazingly disparate. In general, the body of knowledge is still debated, not well organized, and elective course patterns designed to support it are across curricula widely divergent. Also, even though many standards are clearly articulated, the relative importance or weight of such is unclear. In one curriculum, leisure counselling skills are an entire course; in another, not more than a two-week unit within an advanced tools class, etc. Part of the current confusion over skill is based in part on how to divide the three basic areas of knowledge, skills, and abilities into a fair and representative position within the curricula. Personal competency in all three areas are needed for effective TR practice: (l) Knowledge, or the knowing of reality, (2) Skills, technical expertise with activities, evaluation instruments, etc., and (3) Abilities often referred to as the "art of therapy" (centrally these are the attitudes, values, and ethics that each practitioner brings to the therapeutic relationship). Probably this last area of personal abilities is the most under-researched and under-represented area within current curricular approaches in higher education (Reynolds & O'Morrow, 1985, p. 136). Only curriculum models in special education and counselling and guidance have really developed effective methods of developing and delivering feedback to students in the area of personal abilities. TR educators would do well to attempt to emulate these efforts as curriculum enrichment achieves more stature within our educational endeavors.

It was inevitable that some standardization of the curricula across all colleges and universities take place beyond the voluntary NRPA/AALR accreditation standards. It was essential to professional survival. Thus in 1988 with the publication of "Course Content Guidelines" the NCTRC leadership (concerned with the slow growth of accredited curricula) began to assert their own set of curriculum standards on the practice of therapeutic recreation (see Chapter 2 of this text). Many smaller programs have long argued that the expense of bringing an accreditation team to their campus was prohibitive. Thus for many, the NCTRC educational standards provided a guide that would ensure their graduates entry into the profession regardless of their participation in the NRPA/AALR accreditation program. However, with the upgrade in support coursework requirements for the graduating class of 1996, NCTRC's standards may well prove to be just as exclusionary for small schools as the accreditation process. The requirement for specific courses outside of the recreation/leisure studies program (specifically, anatomy, abnormal psychology and human development) will cause problems for many smaller programs whose host institution's course catalogs lack the breadth or quality to deliver.

In addition to NRPA/AALR accreditation standards and the NCTRC course requirements, ATRA has also entered the educational arena as yet another national association concerned with the preparation of personnel. By establishing formal committees and using national conference forums to establish its position and priorities for internships, curriculum and support courses, ATRA is further clouding an already confused and at times conflicting set of standards for higher education. The "true" national standardization of curriculum content and process cannot occur until considerable exchange and debate among all the principle players (e.g., NRPA/AALR, NCTRC, and ATRA) takes place. Unfortunately, there is no formal forum or mechanism for such an exchange.

The Society for Park and Recreation Educators (SPRE) does produce an annual journal with a focus on pedagogical concerns; however, a more direct organization of TR educational knowledge is probably needed in order for work on such reform across curricula to begin in earnest. Despite the difficulties in achieving standardization, we should not be dissuaded from pursuit of it, nor underestimate the importance of it. We commonly accept, in fact insist, that medical surgeons, regardless of what medical school they attended, employ standard diagnostic procedures, standard and accepted surgery procedures, etc. Why then is it unreasonable to expect that the delivery of leisure education curricula, the employment of a leisure history inventory, the procedure used to evaluate post-hospital leisure functioning, not be standardized at a minimum level across the country? Surely any profession which considers itself worthy of licensure of its personnel should "have it together" well enough to ensure a more or less standard core education for its work force.

The trend toward licensure of personnel as the central goal of formal higher education brings us to another problem with therapeutic recreation education. The issue is the bachelor's degree as our entry-level degree. Currently, the CTRS is often the most undercredentialed member of the treatment team. Almost every other discipline requires at least a master's degree in order that a person "qualify" for hire (this is true in social work, psychology, educational therapy), or that they come from a professional school of training with a rigorous and highly specialized curricula (as is the case for occupational and physical therapists). Because of our historical ties to traditional parks and recreation degree programs, TR students inherit requirements for core classes (ranging from twelve to twenty-seven hours nationally) that only indirectly support their training as clinicians. Further, and perhaps less helpful still, is the traditional notion among parks and recreation professionals that the bachelor's degree is sufficient training for entry-level professional responsibilities. Faced with a rapidly expanding knowledge base, increasingly specialized job functions, and a rigid traditional curriculum with little room for negotiation or reform, TR educators simply are not able to fit everything into as few as three courses and a supervised internship. In the next decade of degree development, something will have to give. Either bachelor's degree programs will have to add additional hours as more and more TR courses must be developed to keep up with the knowledge base (forcing TR majors to graduate with more hours than other types of recreation majors), or serious and radical reform of core requirements within recreation and parks for TR majors will have to occur (meaning that the old adage that you are a parks and recreation professional first and a TR major second will have to be reversed in order of importance), or the field must push for expansion to a fifth year program for the master's degree to become the entry level degree (as have the fields of clinical audiology, speech therapy, psychology, etc.).

Related to the topic of curriculum expansion and reform previously noted is the issue of content specialization within curricula. Proponents of the need for clinical specializations basically assert that the TR educational model should emulate the course of development within special education curricula. Thus, students would be expected to take a minimal TR core (in addition, one assumes, to a minimal general parks and recreation core) and then select one or more areas of clinical specialization, a decision driven for the most part by what population and service a student was most interested in. By way of example then, just as there are special education teachers who have certificates which limit their employment to deaf/blind, or mentally retarded, or learning disabled, etc., there would be CTRS's who would be certified only in clinical areas, like geriatrics, mental retardation, psychiatric service, etc. Conceivably of course one could elect as few or as many clinical specializations as desired. The criticisms of this approach are many. Some argue that decisions about how much coursework should constitute an area of specialization would at this time be arbitrary (Carter, 1984; Mobily, 1983), that we are too young a field in terms of research base to worry about specialization and have too few university programs large enough to support all of the coursework patterns that would be necessary to support such a model. Others argue that such diversity would considerably complicate such personnel issues as certification and licensure. Different exams and procedures would be needed for different clinical specializations, for example. However, one should note that the current approach to internship within the field does have the effect of "forcing" specialization upon the student. Despite a more or less generic pattern of TR coursework the student must pick a specific service and clientele to complete their training. This requisite of a single experience is much different from our sister therapies of P.T. and O.T. where students do multiple affiliations across a variety of client and service settings. It seems clear that we need to decide where we will diversify within the curriculum. If we want to produce a generic entry-level specialist that can work across settings, then the current approach to internship works directly against such a goal. If, on the other hand, we wish to move to specializations within entry-level positions, then inevitably we must begin curricula expansion and face an equally tough set of decisions regarding degree alignment and requirements. To do nothing in the face of these two dilemmas is to ignore the rapidly approaching obsolescence of the bachelor's degree within the allied health field.

Macrochanges in the design and structure of curriculum aside, simply trying to work with upgrading and timely revision of the current competencies already in place is in and of itself a very unpredictable and uneven process. The "minimal" competencies by which curricula are currently evaluated and accredited will need continued assessment and upgrading as the knowledge base of the field continues to grow. By way of example, fifteen years ago concepts such as quality assurance, third party reimbursement, and interagency cooperation were simply not considered, or were at the very periphery of the curriculum. Today, these are the hottest topics at national and regional training symposia, yet their place within a national curricula is unclear. Formal alliance between traditional education curricula standards and continued education efforts might be an effective means of prioritizing student needs. If something like 10 percent of formal curricula is set aside for revision and reallocation every three years for example, each college or university program could establish a trends and issues course that every three years, on the basis of regional and national practice issues, could be subject to formal expansion or shrinkage. A national curriculum council might be invoked to provide leadership and serve as a broker for materials to be shared. Not to plan for curriculum expansion of basic competencies at a national level assures eventual obsolescence.

Within many TR curriculums there are also facilitation skills being taught that are practiced on an interdisciplinary basis and are increasingly the subject of bitter debate regarding ownership in practice act disputes between O.T.'s, P.T.'s, rehabilitation counselors, nurse practitioners, and CTRSs. Perhaps the best examples are stress management techniques. The traditional Jacobsonian deep-breathing muscle relaxation techniques can be practiced in some way by all of the above, as well as by psychologists, nurses, and M.D.'s and are represented in some measure in the professional preparation of each. Yet some practice acts have narrowly defined services in such a way as to preclude one professional from delivering something as simple as relaxation techniques because only the "licensed" therapy can do so. Thus you have techniques developed originally by a physical educator that have now become the sole province of physical therapy in one state, an O.T. in another, or can be delivered only by physician prescription and direction in another. You could also get a situation where in one midtown hospital the psychologists are the only ones to deliver these techniques, and in another hospital across town only nurse therapists may do so, etc. The educational dilemma facing curricula designers is what to keep in and what to leave out as skills and techniques are territorialized. If we reach a point where a majority of states do not allow TR specialists to conduct relaxation sessions, then we should by default eliminate it from all of our curricula. On the other hand, to do so may give away our position to lobby for preservation for interdisciplinary practice. No national statistics are kept at present related to some of the more intimate details of skills and techniques that are being territorialized that have traditionally been interdisciplinary in nature. A watchdog posture is important over the next few years so that we do not find ourselves in the position of preparing clinicians to deliver techniques which are no longer our province.

One final word on curriculum regarding standards for internships. There are currently two different sets of internship standards. The certification requirement for NCTRC is ten continuous weeks for a total of 360 hours. By contrast NTRS calls for 600 clock hours at fifteen weeks. On top of this disparity are varied university requirements with some schools who operate on quarters using eight week internships and others who have traditionally required ten, twelve, or fourteen weeks. The confusion and pragmatic complexities this situation has caused within and across universities must be resolved. The University of Missouri provides an interesting case study of this problem. Missouri has required a twelve week internship for all recreation majors for the last fifteen years. Yet graduate students argue that ten weeks to meet certification standards of NCTRC is all they should have to take, particularly since they have already completed a bachelor's degree, and so they are allowed to do so. Thus the twelve-week internship manual is reduced to ten. At the same time several undergraduates are accepted by clinical facilities whose directors insist on following the more stringent NTRS standards for fifteen weeks. Now the twelve-week manual is expanded to fifteen. Still other undergraduates are accepted by facilities who agree to accept the university twelve-week requirement. Therefore at Missouri during any given semester there are now TR interns receiving ten, twelve, and fifteen weeks of internship experience. The disparities across facilities and experiences can be remarkable. A related issue is whether or not the current requirement of continuity of experience within a single setting doesn't force specialization of interest. By contrast, OT students do three separate clinical internships (known as affiliations) across a variety of client and service setting. If the B.A. is to remain the entry-level degree for TR specialists, then shouldn't it be a more generic degree (using a multiple internship approach) instead of providing a student field experience in only a single setting?

In closing the discussion on extended preparation of personnel, it is important to note some disturbing trends in higher education in general, and for recreation/leisure studies programs in particular in the 1990s. The financial crises for higher education in the nineties and beyond is quite real (Elmer De-Witt, 1993). Facing declining enrollments driven by a fading baby boom generation, rising costs, flat state budgets and shrinking federal grant money, many institutions have begun serious overhaul of their education structure and course catalogs. Within this process reallocation of positions and budget through program elimination has emerged as a central theme. The principle criteria used in the reallocation game has been "centrality to mission" and many recreation/leisure studies programs on the so-called "flagship" research campuses have been eliminated or seriously reduced as a result (the list in the 1990s now includes such nationally reputed programs as University of Illinois, University of Oregon, University of Maryland, and University of Missouri). The critical loss of TR doctoral programs (Maryland, Oregon, and Illinois) is most telling in recent national statistics. A report by the U.S. Department of Education (Department Chair, 1994) indicated that the five-year trend for Ph.D. production in recreation and leisure studies evidenced a 31 percent decline. The total number of Ph.D.'s granted in 1990–91 was only twenty-seven (just six of these were in the subspecialty of therapeutic recreation). By contrast, the field of psychology graduated 3,422 doctorates in this same time period. The obvious question from these statistics is who will write curriculum for the next generation of therapists? A profession can rise no higher than its leadership, and without a vibrant national "brain trust" to lead serious inquiry, the ability of TR to reach its full potential as a profession will be severely compromised if not stunted altogether. Without a sharp reversal in the downward trend of national Ph.D. production, much of the content of this chapter, perhaps of this entire text, may in time prove to be moot.

Autonomy of Judgment

In some ways, one of the most potentially derisive issues in the field of TR today revolves around the certification versus licensure debate. Simply put, this controversy has served to divide the field into two rival camps, which unfortunately more often than not have been academics against practitioners. It is not difficult to understand how this division has occurred. Each group is motivated by a different agenda for the profession. The academic camp argues that essentially those professionals urging licensure of the work force are way ahead of the knowledge base of the profession. To make individual practitioners legally "liable" for their actions or inactions (one aspect of licensure acts) is premature. They argue the subjectivity inherent within activity prescription and leisure counselling techniques currently practiced supports the basic premise of the antilicensure lobby. Those practitioners in the front line counter that the future of the profession is now, and if we wait too long to assert ourselves, we will find our professional "turf" already accounted for by our sister therapies. In support of this position are the licensure laws already on the books in some states in which OTs have successfully won definition of their services to include such things as leisure counselling, development of play skills, and delivery of recreational services. The licensure "wars" for skills directly related to our service delivery model, as well as for the more generic traditionally interdisciplinary skills discussed in the previous section related to curriculum are not minor issues. Additionally, a concurrent movement among hospital administrators to provide resources only to those services which can generate third party reimbursement (usually limited to "licensed" personnel) makes the crisis more acute.

There are no easy answers to this dilemma. It is difficult to argue against the very compelling political realities of service that pro-licensure advocates point to. Increasingly, hospital administrators, when faced with the decision of hiring a CTRS (whose salary comes out of the fixed bed rate of the facility) or hiring an OTR (whose salary can be paid largely through insurance company reimbursements that can be directly billed for) will hire and support the more independent and income generating activity therapist. There are instances where entire recreation therapy programs have been eliminated and where RT and OTR departments have been merged under a single activity therapy department with RTs being placed under the "supervision" of OTRs so that costs of services could be recouped (Cook, 1987). Yet, on the other hand, to "sell the public" on a service ethic that we cannot fully validate or account for is too similar to the carnival "snake oil salesman" approach (e.g., come to TR and we will fix your self-esteem, increase your leisure repertoire, positively impact your value system, etc.) for many researchers to accept. Currently, with the exception of the two states that have licensure, the field has accepted a kind of holding pattern. Many CTRSs continue to lobby against licensure acts of sister therapies in an attempt to postpone or prevent our own interests as well as interdisciplinary skills from being "gobbled up," while at the same time holding off on moving very aggressively or proactively on a TR act. Nebraska serves as an interesting case study of this division. In 1988 a group of practitioners did circulate and attempt to introduce a practice act for TR, and a group of university faculty felt obliged on the basis of ethical and scientific grounds to write a formal letter of protest to the president of the state association indicating their lack of support. The result for Nebraska was that the bill was withdrawn for further "study." Interestingly enough just the year before, a powerful interdisciplinary lobby comprised of individuals from both of these TR groups blocked an overly aggressive OT practice act within the state. Whether or not TR can continue successfully to hang on to its identity in the face of current political and fiscal pressures while the knowledge base catches up remains to be seen.

Regardless of the eventual outcome of the national certification versus licensure debate there are more immediate problems with which we should be concerned. The field now finds itself operating under multiple systems of autonomy of judgment (national certification exam, independent state certification standards in some areas, as well as licensure requirements in Utah and North Carolina). Thus, there is also a personal practice issue related to the unevenness in state-to-state standards now in existence. For the first time, CTRS's must consider personal geographic and career mobility restriction (Carter, 1984). Practitioners now face, at best, impediments in moving from state to state and, at worst, could find themselves relocating into a state where they could not pass the licensure examination and not be able to work. Given how rapidly the curriculum in higher education for TR has expanded and how uneven undergraduate preparation is (based on minimal standards), it is remarkable that an examination of licensure could be put in place so early (Utah, 1975, and Georgia, 1981) and not face a legal test by those not passing it. The alternate argument of course would be that current exams are so easy or watered down (so as to be all-inclusive by design) that they truly do not meet the intent of licensure (a term that by definition is put forward as a governmental action to "protect" the consumer from poor services). In a related light, if more and more states pass licensure acts (recall that North Carolina added a protection act in 1992, see Chapter 2) then eventually reciprocity between states has the potential to become even further diluted, and more and more of the work force may find themselves in uncomfortable and untenable positions in negotiating across state boundary moves.

If we consider what has happened to our sister therapy OT as they have developed licensure, we find a further unenviable dilemma. Despite the fact that the national OT leadership produced and distributed a model practice act for OT in some states, this practice act had been considerably expanded, and in others considerably compromised, depending upon the nature of the political lobby for or against it. Thus, in some states OTs are allowed to develop play skills and conduct leisure counselling and to actually supervise recreational therapists, and in other states they may not. The point being that what an OT may have been trained to do, and what they are allowed to do may not always match up well, depending upon the specifics of the state's practice act. Conceivably, we could reach this same point in TR. Thus, in the future, a TRS may make the decision not to move to take a job in another state, not only out of fear of not being able to pass the state's licensing examination, but also because the restrictions of the practice act are such that the day-to-day job of being a CTRS may be considerably different from the way they want to practice (either restricted or expanded from their current duties).

Before the TR profession becomes too caught up in the licensure debate, a more useful focus regarding autonomy of judgment would be to deal with the large numbers of uncredentialed practitioners and their refusal to embrace the CTRS standards. On the one hand, the 1995 U.S. Department of Labor statistics which estimate our national work force in excess of 32,000 is good news. However, the fact that only 13,000 (a scant 40 percent of those practicing) have bothered to credential themselves after five years of national testing is simply abysmal. Remember that the heart of this issue is our ability to assure the public that each individual practicing the TR process is responsible and is following acceptable standards. Our ability to mount effective political lobby, conduct meaningful physician education, and extend our service mission to other sectors all hinge upon our ability to be accountable. It may be that the greatest danger to the profession's vitality and growth is not from external forces (e.g., health care, reform, sister therapy encroachment, etc.), but from our own lack of cohesiveness and enthusiasm for our profession. So long as participation in client services without professional credentialing is tolerated by hospital/health care administrators and physicians, the TR profession will not reach autonomy of judgment maturity. If the 60 percent of the current work force who are not credentialed were going to do so out of intrinsic motivation and professional pride, then most have had ample time to act. It is time for the national leadership and fully credentialed CTRSs to deal with the issue of recalcitrant incumbents decisively, for they now represent a heavy burden on the continued growth of the profession.

Professional Organizations

The reader will recall from Chapter 2 that the early days of TR were dominated by different organizational forces and philosophies that in the main could not relate to one another. One of the two principle majority perspectives was the position of the Hospital Recreation Section of the American Recreation Society which essentially held the "recreation for all" (sometimes referred to as the recreation for recreation's sake) perspective. These professionals felt that the inherently beneficial aspects of recreation should be available to every one, especially those confined to institutions as a result of illness or disability. The second and principally rival philosophy held by the National Association of Recreation Therapists (NART) has over time been referred to as the "recreation as therapy" viewpoint. The major premise is that recreation could serve as an intervention, a specific tool of treatment or rehabilitation effective in combatting primary disability (Austin, 1986). The merger of these two groups into a single NTRS membership in 1966 can now be viewed as an uneasy coalition. With the formation of ATRA in 1984 the old NART philosophy, or recreation as therapy position, once again separated, and a separate organizational advocate emerged. It would be inaccurate to infer that all of the remaining NTRS membership necessarily hold to the recreation for all ethic of the old Hospital Recreation Section of ARS (it should be noted that some professionals do hold dual memberships across ATRA and NTRS). However, the key aspects of this position are present in the modern-day definition of the leisure ability model that NTRS has adapted as its national philosophy position. So while it is true that the old hospital recreation ethic is alive only in part within NTRS, the creation of ATRA in the main represents a renewal of an old philosophical struggle of recreation versus therapy and remains a nagging undercurrent within the professionalization priorities of the field. You simply can't develop what you can't define, and the philosophical divisiness of professionals has resulted in an organizational circle game. This leaves us in some ways no better off organizationally than we were in the 1950s. Every other aspect of the field's professionalization could be affected by a duality of missions across organizations. Issues ranging from curriculum development up to and including the overall political effectiveness of our national lobby effort could be seriously compromised. Some argue that a new organization simply reflects a metamorphosis of thought which will help the profession grow more swiftly. The underlying premise to this more optimistic view is that once the effective growth work is done (work that supposedly could not take place within the NTRS structure), the main body of new ideas and concepts will be reassimilated into a majority position within the field.

The membership and work force numbers, however, do not support either association as particularly vital at this time. While ATRA members are particularly proud that in just ten years their numbers have climbed from a founding fifty to over 3,600, and while NTRS members may be somewhat dismayed that their numbers have fallen to 2,400, neither group has room to boast about representation for a national work force of over 32,000. Even among individuals who are professionally active and fully credentialed as CTRS's (over 13,000) the majority refuse to participate in either organization. Why are so few participating? Is the work force confused, tired, or just plain angry over the age-old pull between rival philosophies and competing national organizations?

At the very eve of ATRA's formation, Nesbitt (1984), while asking the question "Heroic or Foolish?" wrote: "The ATRA may be a vain, ill-timed, in some ways self-serving, futile effort that will serve to dissipate limited resources, widen professional schisms . . . and do irreparable damage to the future of recreation therapy" (p. 15). As Nesbitt predicted, the future of ATRA has been the response of the younger professionals, and based on most recent membership numbers and demographics, the short-term philosophical victory in the 1990s clearly goes to ATRA. Is merely winning an internal debate by slight numerical advantage really a "victory" with so much of the incumbent work force nonparticipatory? Either in cooperation or competition, until a clear organization advocate speaks for the majority of the work force the accomplishments of either group ring somewhat hollow. Perhaps Nesbitt's original concerns regarding ATRA's potential for negative impact can be seen in the large numbers of professionals still sitting on the organizational sidelines. Perhaps the answer to the philosophical debate between the two organizational missions need not be exclusive; perhaps an entirely new structure is needed.

While there may be some logic to the more optimistic view of what dual national organizations may afford in terms of creative growth, there are few precedents for such actions across our sister therapies. Neither occupational nor physical therapists have to be asked the question, "So which organization do you belong to and why?" If the TR profession cannot come to agreement regarding philosophical mission, then rather than persisting along the path of separate organizations (what will be next—a new national organization for community recreation and TR?), it would be far more effective to follow the subspecialization model that the American Psychological Association (APA) has perfected. Within the APA there are twelve different branches of subspecialization, each with its own journal, mission, and constituency, yet there is one APA political lobby, one APA unified membership, one APA code of ethics, etc. Why isn't it possible for a single national TR organization to offer a clinical branch, a community branch, etc.? At a time when TR's political effectiveness is most needed to offer resistance to hostile practice acts from other therapies and to lobby proactively for increased federal, state, and local support for services, the very public fractionalization of the membership that having two national organizations provides for sends a very disjointed and potentially problematic message to outside groups.

A related issue to organizational effectiveness and range is the situation created by outlier activity therapy groups: the so-called singular medium therapies like dance therapy, music therapy, horticulture, and art therapy. Here again we have professionals who use some form of activity medium in a therapeutic sense yet define themselves as separate from TR and have created their own national organizations, curriculum, political lobby, etc. Another outlier group, the largest group, and in some ways a group that represents the greatest failure of TR to develop a truly encompassing or more global service ethic, is the national Activities Director Association (ADA). In recent years the ADA national plan has become a near carbon copy of the NCTRC certification plan. Their approach to continuing education, political lobby efforts, etc., has resulted from a careful study of NTRS efforts. Why does the public need two different activity therapy organizations concerned with the delivery of services within nursing homes? As in the scenario above regarding ATRA and NTRS, an umbrella organization, representing a powerful combined membership and political lobby built along the lines of the APA branch model, could bring all of the singular medium therapies as well as incorporate the service concerns of ADA, NTRS, and ATRA under a single activity therapy banner. Such a coalition, could it ever be achieved, would represent a significant advancement in the overall professionalization of activity therapy as a public service ethic. As Sylvester (1992, p. 18) has recently noted, "After all, TR does not own a patent on recreation activity anymore than art therapy has domain over finger painting . . . multiple activity therapies, therefore, may result in excessive specialization and unnecessary duplication." The old adage, "united we stand, divided we fall," may prove particularly relevant in the years ahead as increasingly high health costs, changing insurance standards, licensure bills, and mandates from federal regulatory bodies continue to assault and demand swift change and accountability across all of the activity therapies.

Code of Ethics

This aspect of professionalism is still in its infancy for the TR profession, although the existence of multiple codes of ethics (NTRS, ATRA and NCTRS—see Chapter 2) is at least a start in the right direction. Until organizational enforcement mechanisms are put into place, however, the code of ethics is largely window dressing. The reader will recall from Chapter 2 that only NCTRC has enforcement for its code of conduct, and this relates in the main to the credentialling process and not to the act of practice (with the important exception of felony conviction related to patient service delivery). Furthermore, with approximately 19,000 individuals currently practicing as recreational therapists and not credentialled by NCTRC, the vast majority of our profession is not bound by any code of ethics.

The inability to develop enforcement is directly tied to the subjectivity of current practice and the underdeveloped research base under which we are currently operating. Theoretically, if a CTRS is programming against current practice standards, you enforce those standards. But how do you translate general standards of practice into specific procedures and practices? For example, if a physician delivered an outdated treatment to a patient (say treating an aggressive psychiatric patient with insulin shock therapy), then the consumer can point to a clear violation of current best practice standards and force revocation of license to practice. What is the parallel example for a CTRS? If a CTRS practices in such a way as to inhibit or prevent the social development or personal development of their client (e.g., offering only segregated services to mentally retarded clients instead of normalized ones), then should they be found guilty of professional misconduct and face being stripped of their certification privileges? These are difficult distinctions to draw made more difficult by the lack of a definitive research base against which to reference outcomes and practices.

How does the debate over certification of personnel versus licensure impact a code of ethics and enforcement of such? If a CTRS in a state with licensure (meaning a professional is personally culpable for their treatment decisions) recommends a suicidal youth for an off-campus outing and during the course of said outing, the patient suicides, shouldn't this decision to prescribe such an activity be subject to professional review and possible revocation of license to practice? Is the CTRS guilty of poor diagnosis and activity prescription, perhaps forcing a level of social stimulation that was excessive? Or is the CTRS simply guilty of providing poor supervision, in effect using poor judgment while conducting the activity? Or is the CTRS culpable at all? Therapy does occasionally fail—we do lose people to depression and suicide—often unpredictably. Certainly if a physician prescribed a drug that had a lethal or ill effect on a patient the family would seek recourse. If a fully licensed CTRS prescribes an activity program that results in similar consequences, then shouldn't we be as culpable as the physician? The world of activity therapy has more gray than the black/white world of physical medicine. The development of clear clinical protocols (designed to reduce the area of gray) clearly must precede code of ethics practice review boards. If eventually we can agree on more precise clinical protocols, how will we monitor transgressions? Will we have a state, regional, or national board of ethics? Do we need all three with a built-in appeals system or should each state be responsible for enforcement? If professionals are stripped of certification in one state, should they be allowed to practice in others? If not, how will the profession inform service providers nationally of individuals "banned" from the profession?

The first legal tests of our professional code of ethics have not occurred because, as a profession, we have not developed the report, review, appeal, and enforcement aspects that physicians, psychologists, and social workers all have in place. Consider that from 1986 to 1995 over 10,000 physicians were disciplined or censured nationally by state and/or federal ethics boards (CNN, 1995). Are we to assume that during this same period of time not a single recreational therapist should have been censured? At present we even lack a "public" accounting of the NCTRC reviews related to credentialling. Clearly we have a long way to go in this regard. Licensed professionals lay their careers and personal credibility on the line daily in making clinical decisions about treatment efficacy and effectiveness. If the day comes that our own research base will support similar precision in our practice standards, then the time will come to fully operationalize our code of ethics and to hold our membership accountable personally for their actions or inactions. Until that time our code of ethics remains a philosophical position that we can say we believe in, and even are committed to, yet are still striving toward.

SUMMARY

In this chapter external economic, social, and political forces affecting the growth of the TR profession were discussed. Events like the taxpayer revolution, shifting social consciousness, political agendas for health care reform, federal mandates such as the ADA, and failed strategies such as corporate giving have all effectively combined to limit the programmatic vitality of TR (primarily because of their effect on budgets and resources). More aggressive promotion of our service ethic within the public sector is needed to reverse these effects.

The six characteristics of a profession reviewed originally in Chapter 2 provided a forum to discuss trends and issues internal to the profession.

Among the most prevalent are: more clearly defining our practice standards, validating the leisure ability process across clients and settings, improving curriculum uniformity and dealing with issues of providing for clinical specializations and more sophisticated internships, resolving the certification versus licensure dilemma for personnel, dealing with the philosophic complexities of multi-TR and rival activity therapy organizations, and, finally, developing enforcement mechanisms for our professional code of ethics.

In some ways the work ahead, challenging us on so many simultaneous fronts, seems overwhelming. Yet when we consider how far we have come, from such humble and disconnected beginnings, it is easier to accept the burden of the future by taking the long view and being patient enough to measure change across generations and not years. It is possible to see a future where the full professionalization of TR will take place. For now, those of us in the front lines must continue to push ahead where we can and accept what we cannot immediately change as the challenge for the next generation.

READING COMPREHENSION QUESTIONS

1. What was the result of the so-called "taxpayer revolution" for community recreation services?
2. The general backsliding of social concern that occurred during the "me" generation has left what special populations at "crisis" in this country?
3. What social factors did politicians offer as solutions (in lieu of funding) for recreational programming in the 1980s?
4. If you were to establish a programming standard for community special recreation services for the mentally retarded, what would that standard incorporate?
5. Do you agree with the parallel drawn between the AIDs and polio epidemics, and further with the suggestion as to why TR hasn't been more involved?
6. Can you identify some of the high-technology advancements under research and development which TR may have to interface with at the turn of the century?
7. Do you agree that national standardization of TR curricula is an important issue for the field?
8. Can you articulate the criticisms of why the bachelor's degree in TR is considered obsolete by some as the national entry-level degree?
9. Do you agree that clinical specializations for CTRSs is the model our curricula reform effort should adopt?
10. Which skills are the subject of debate among TR and other interdisciplinary groups regarding practice acts?
11. What do you think about the differences in the TR internship requirements and OT clinical affiliations? Should TR students have to do more than one internship?
12. What activity therapies are classified as "single medium" therapies?
13. Do you agree that the APA model of professional specialization makes sense for TR? For the inclusion of other activity therapies as well?
14. Do you favor individual states having separate licensure laws or is a national certification plan the best way to proceed in developing our demonstration of autonomy of judgment?
15. Can you identify clear violations of conduct you feel should result in an individual's national certification being rescinded? Should that person ever be allowed back into the profession? Under what conditions?

REFERENCES

Associated Press Wire Service. (1993, October 17). Disabled kids face abuse more often. *Missourian,* p. 8a.

Associated Press Wire Service. (1995, March 5). Disabled nudists tickled pink by wheelchair ramp. *Missourian,* p. 3a.

ATRA. (1992). *Therapeutic recreation services.* Hattiesburg, MS: ATRA Publications Monograph.

Attarian, A., & Gault, L. (1992, April). Treatment of Vietnam veterans with post traumatic stress disorder; a model program. *JOPERD,* 56–69.

Austin, D.R. (1986). The helping profession: You do make a difference. In A. James & F. McGuire (Eds.), *Selected papers from the 1985 Southeast therapeutic recreation symposium.* Clemson University Extension Services.

Benson, P. (1995, February 8). Empower health care providers. *Lincoln Journal and Star,* p. 11b.

Bergman, G. (1991). Why build more nursing homes? *Aging Today, 12*(2), 6–8.

Blakely, T.L., & Dattilo, J. (1993, 4th Quarter). An exploratory study of leisure motivation patterns of adults with alcohol and drug addictions *Therapeutic Recreation Journal*, 231–238.

Carruthers, C.P., & Hood, C. D. (1992, April). Alcoholics and children of alcoholics: The role of leisure in recovery. *JOPERD,* 48–51.

Carter, M. J. (1984). Issues in continuing professional competence of therapeutic recreation. *Therapeutic Recreation Journal, 18*(3), 7–10.

Carter, M. (1991, May/June). Leisure in the year 2000: An emerging or true profession? *JOPERD,* 26.

CNN. (1995, February 6). Health in review electronic broadcast.

Connolly, P. (1995). Educators link: Newsletter for TR educators. Thiels, NY: NCTRC Press.

Cook, G. (1987). Personal communication with author. Ms. Cook is former director of therapeutic recreation at St. Joseph's Hospital, Omaha, Nebraska.

Coyle, C., et al. (1991). *Benefits of TR: A consensus view.* Philadelphia, PA: Temple University Press.

Crawford, M.E. (1986). Development and generalization of lifetime leisure skills for multi-handicapped participants. *Therapeutic Recreation Journal, 20*(4), 48–60.

Crawford, M.E. (1995). A review of playground conversion/retrofit as a result of the ADA. [A private publication.]

Dail, P.W. (1992, April). Recreation as socialization for the homeless: An argument for inclusion. *JOPERD,* 37–40.

Dattilo, J., & Barnett, L.A. (1985). Therapeutic recreation for individuals with severe handicaps: An analysis of the relationship between choice and pleasure. *Therapeutic Recreation Journal, 19*(3), 79–91.

Dattilo, J., & Camarato, S. (1991). Facilitating leisure involvement through self-initiated augmentative communication training. *Journal of Applied Behavior Analysis, (23),* 249–59.

Edmonds, P. (1995, March 2). Agencies ask, is this parent fit or not? *USA Today,* p. 1a.

Elmer De-Witt, E. (1993, February 18). Higher education: At the crossroads. *Time,* pp. 45–48.

Erikson, E.H. (1968). *Identity, youth and crisis.* New York: Norton.

A Family Down and Out. (1987, January 12). *Newsweek,* p. 44.

Farrow, R., & Delsher, R. (1991, June). Risk factors for attempted suicide in gay and bisexual youth. *Pediatrics, 87*(6), 27–34.

Frank, K. (1988, Spring). Beyond stigma: Visibility and self improvements of persons with congenital limb deficiencies. *Journal of Social Issues, 44,* 95–116.

Grant, M., & Johnstone, B.M. (1991). Research priorities for drug and alcohol studies; The next 25 years. *The International Journal of Addictions, 25*(24), 201–219.

Grossman, A.H. (1992, April). Inclusion not exclusion: recreation service delivery to lesbian, gay and bisexual youth. *JOPERD,* 45–7.

Hancock, L., Rosenberg, D., Sprinen, K., Rogers, P., Brant, M., Kalb, C., & Gegax, T. (1995, March 6). Breaking Point. *Newsweek,* pp. 56–61.

Havitz, M., & Spigner, C. (1992, April). Access to public leisure services: A comparison of the unemployed with traditional target groups (41–45). *Leisure Today.* Reston VA: AAHPERD Publications.

Health care crises. (1991, November 25). *Time,* pp. 5–11.

Hull, J.D. (1987, February 2). Slow descent into hell. *Time,* p. 26.

A job but no place to live. (1987, December 28). *Time,* p. 27.

Keller, M.J., & Turner, N.H. (1990–91). Children with AIDS and related illnesses: The role of TR with this terminal illness. *Leisure Information Quarterly, 16*(4) 7–9.

Keller, M.J. (1992, April). Children and HIV/AIDS: A role for physical educators and recreation professionals. *JOPERD,* 34–36.

Kennedy, D.W. , Smith, R.W., & Austin, D.R. (1991). *Special recreation: Opportunities for persons with disabilities.* Dubuque IA: W.C. Brown Co.

Kunstler, R. (1991, 2nd Quarter). There but for fortune: A TR perspective on the homeless in America. *Therapeutic Recreation Journal,* 31–40.

Lahey, M.P. (1991, 2nd Quarter). Serving the new poor: TR values in hard times. *Therapeutic Recreation Journal,* 9–19.

Lasch, C. (1984). *The culture of narcissism: American life in an age of diminishing expectations.* New York: W.W. Norton and Company Inc.

Leitschuh, C.A., & Brotons, M. (1991, April). Recreation and music therapy for adolescent victims of sexual abuse. *JOPERD,* 52–54.

Making life more livable. (1988, February). *USA Today, 18,* p. 4.

Marine, J.C. (1993, October 16). Stress disorder plagues homeless. *San Francisco Examiner,* 5a.

Martinsen, E.W. (1990). Benefits of exercise in the treatment of depression. *Sports Medicine, 9*(6), 380–389.

McKee, T. (1995, February 16). Chair costs price some from market. *Missourian,* p. 8b.

Meister, T., & Pedlar, A. (1992, April). Leisure patterns and needs of adult survivors of childhood sexual abuse. *JOPERD,* 52–55.

Mercer, M. (1993, November 10). Sympathy for the homeless diminishing. *Media General Newspapers,* Wire service #12a.

Mobily, K.J. (1983). Quality Analysis in Therapeutic Recreation Curricula. *Therapeutic Recreation Journal, 17*(l), 18–25.

Mones, P. (1994, Novemer 22). Parents killing kids shocking but not rare. *Los Angeles Times,* p. 4a.

Murphy, J.F. (1980). An enabling approach to leisure service delivery. In T. L. Goddale & P. A. Witt (Eds.), *Recreation and leisure: Issues in an era of change* (p. 197–210). State College, PA: Venture Publishing Co.

National Federation of the Blind. (1985). *Rising expectations on the part of the blind.* Status Report, Washington DC.

Nesbitt, J.A. (1984). The new/old American TR Association Inc.: Heroic or foolish. *Journal of Iowa Park and Recreation, 10*(4), 14–15.

New Products and Technology. (1988, Spring). *Social Issues and Healthcare Review,* 3(2), 18–20.

Ortbals, G. (1995, February 15). Political quick fixes don't satisfy voters. *St. Louis Post Dispatch,* p. 3c.

Peterson, C.A., & Gunn, S.L. (1984). *Therapeutic recreation program design* (2nd ed.). Englewood Cliffs, NJ: Prentice Hall, Inc.

Raab, E., & Lipset, S.M. (1980). The prejudiced society. In M. Wertheimer (Ed.), *Confrontation: Psychology and the problems of today* (p. 135–45). Glenview, IL: Scott Foresman and Company.

Reynolds, R., & O'Morrow, G. (1985). *Problems, issues and concepts in TR.* Englewood Cliffs, NJ: Prentice Hall, Inc.

Riley, B. (1987). *Evaluation of therapeutic recreation through quality assurance.* State College, PA: Venture Publishing Co.

Riley, B. (1991). *Quality management: Applications for TR.* State College, PA: Venture Publishing.

Roper Center. (1990, May/June). *The public perspective: A Roper Center review of public opinion polling* (No. 1).

Rowley, J. (1994, October 22). Violent crime rises across the US. *Missourian,* p. 2a.

Samuelson, S. (1991, November 19). Study: Homeless children worry about basic needs. *San Francisco Examiner,* p. 3a.

Schleien, S., Olson, K., Roger, N., & McLafferty, M. (1985). Integrating children with severe handicaps into recreation and physical education programs. *Journal of Park and Recreation Administration, 3*(l), 50–66.

Sherrill, C. (1993). *Adapted physical activity, recreation and sport* (4th ed.). Dubuque, IA: W.C. Brown Co.

Sylvester, C. (1992). Therapeutic recreation and the right to leisure. *Therapeutic Recreation Journal, 2,* 9–20.

Szasz, T. (1988, March). Homelessness is not a disease. *USA Today, 116,* p. 28.

TADAR (The ADA Report). (1994, Fall). GAO report on accessibility (pp. 8–9). Columbia, MO: University of Missouri Press.

Teaff, J.D. (1985). *Leisure services with the elderly.* St. Louis, MO: C.V. Mosby Co.

Usdansky, M.L. (1994, November 14). In 1993 child poverty level hit 30 year high. *USA Today,* p. 2a.

Webber, D. (1995, February 2). Unfunded mandates and federalism. *Missourian,* p. 1b.

Welch, W. (1995, March 2). Social security on double time. *USA Today,* p. 4a.

West, J. (1991). *The ADA: From policy to practice.* New York: Milbank Publications.

Wolfensburger, W. (1992). *A guideline on protecting the health and lives of patients in hospitals, especially if the patient is a member of a socially devalued class.* Syracuse, NY: Syracuse University Press.

Author Index

Subject Index